BETTER REGULATION

The discourse of 'Better Regulation' is a hot topic, intimately associated with the drive for cost savings and a more efficient economy. In the UK and in the EU, rule-makers have lately endeavoured to achieve a more satisfactory balance between the demands of proper protection from market failure and inequity on the one hand, and commercial freedom and the potential for innovation on the other. But who is the regulator listening to, and what effect does this have on the regulatory pattern governing the integrating EU market? What is best practice in the matter of regulatory assessment? The essays in this collection explore these and other questions and will foster greater understanding of UK and EU regulation, the accountability issues involved, and problems of enforcement. It is no coincidence that since efforts to construct a Constitution for Europe have stalled, the attention of policy-makers, politicians and the business community has turned instead to the quest for Better Regulation—or perhaps, it might be said, a 'Better European Union'.

Volume 6: Studies of the Oxford Institute of European and Comparative Law

Studies of the Oxford Institute of European and Comparative Law

Volume 1: The Harmonisation of European Contract Law: Implications for European Private Laws, Business and Legal Practice
Edited by Stefan Vogenauer and Stephen Weatherill

Volume 2: The Public Law/Private Law Divide
Edited by Mark Freedland and Jean-Bernard Auby

Volume 3: Constitutionalism and the Role of Parliaments
Edited by Katja S Ziegler, Denis Baranger and A W Bradley

Volume 4: The Regulation of Unfair Commercial Practices under EC Directive 2005/29: New Rules and Techniques
Edited by Stephen Weatherill and Ulf Bernitz

Volume 5: Human Rights and Private Law: Privacy as Autonomy
Edited by Katja S Ziegler

Better Regulation

Edited by
Stephen Weatherill

·HART·
PUBLISHING

OXFORD AND PORTLAND, OREGON
2007

Published in North America (US and Canada) by
Hart Publishing
c/o International Specialized Book Services
920 NE 58th Avenue, Suite 300
Portland, OR 97213-3786
USA
Tel: +1 503 287 3093 or toll-free: (1) 800 944 6190
Fax: +1 503 280 8832
E-mail: orders@isbs.com
Website: www.isbs.com

Hart Publishing, 16C Worcester Place, OX1 2JW
Telephone: +44 (0)1865 517530 Fax: +44 (0)1865 510710
E-mail: mail@hartpub.co.uk
Website: http://www.hartpub.co.uk

British Library Cataloguing in Publication Data
Data Available

ISBN-13: 978-1-84113-715-5 (hardback)

Typeset by Compuscript Ltd, Shannon
Printed and bound in Great Britain by
TJ International Ltd, Padstow, Cornwall

Preface

This book represents the fruit of a conference entitled 'Regulating the European Market' presented jointly by Global Law Firm Clifford Chance and the Institute of European and Comparative Law in the University of Oxford. The Conference was held at St Anne's College, Oxford, in March 2006. Both conference and book reflect the successful collaboration developed between the Institute and Clifford Chance over the last decade, which involves not only financial support of the Institute's activities but also the exchange of ideas at an annual joint event.

The chosen topic of *Better Regulation* invites appreciation from academic (and not simply legal) perspectives and also from the standpoint of legal practice and commerce, as well as that of the regulators themselves. It invites domestic and European insights. It is, in short, a perfect topic for bringing together a range of approaches and drawing out a deeper insight into the current struggle to balance the demands for proper protection from harm and the fear of damaging over-regulation. That is the aim of this book. And the 2006 conference's exploration of these issues was informed by an empirical survey of business attitudes conducted under the guidance of Clifford Chance, and included as an Appendix to this book.

At the conference we were grateful for the support of the following speakers: Stephen Weatherill, Joe McCahery, Anand Menon, Dan Keleman, Denis MacShane, Stuart Popham, Mads Andenas, Daniela Weber-Rey, Philip Wood, Niamh Moloney, Jenny Payne, Jane Welch, Rick Haythornthwaite, Jeffrey Kenner, Hans Schulte Nölke, Francis Chittenden and Elisabetta Olivi. Happily most have also been able to convert their thoughts into written form, while this book also includes several chapters by other contributors who have much to add but could not be fitted into the conference programme. At the conference Sir David Edward helped greatly by acting as Chair, and our thanks are also due to him.

Jenny Dix helped a great deal in the organisation of the conference and we would like to thank her. Dorota Leczykiewicz and Vanessa Mak also helped to ensure the conference ran smoothly and we are also grateful to them. Paul Adams undertook the task of editing the chapters under severe time pressure, and did a splendid job for which we are very grateful. Hart Publishing sustained a splendid tradition by offering peerless support and guidance along the way.

Stephen Weatherill and Stefan Vogenauer
Oxford, November 2006

Contents

List of Contributors

Tim Ambler is a Senior Fellow at London Business School.

Peter Andrews is Head of Economics of Financial Regulation at the Financial Services Authority, London.

Robert Baldwin is a Professor of Law at the London School of Economics and Political Science where he teaches Criminal Law and Regulation at undergraduate and graduate levels.

Michael Bohlander is a Professor of Law at Durham University. He was a member of the German judiciary from 1991 to 2004, and the senior legal officer of a Trial Chamber at the International Criminal Tribunal for the Former Yugoslavia from 1999 to 2001.

Seamus Burns is a senior lecturer in law, and has lectured at Sheffield Hallam University for the past 15 years.

Francis Chittenden is ACCA Professor of Small Business Finance, Manchester Business School.

Rick Haythornthwaite is Chairman of the Better Regulation Commission. Rick is also Managing Director at Star Capital Partners Limited and Non Executive Chairman of Mastercard. He is non-executive director of ICI plc.

Gérard Hertig is Professor of Law at ETH Zurich, where he is the professor responsible for the post-graduate 'Intellectual Property' programme. He was previously Professor of Administrative Law and director of the Centre d'Etudes Juridiques Européennes at the University of Geneva Law School. He has also been a visiting professor at leading law schools in Europe, Japan and the US and practised law as a member of the Geneva bar.

R Daniel Kelemen (PhD, Stanford University) is Associate Professor of Political Science at Rutgers University. Prior to this, Kelemen was Fellow in Politics, Lincoln College, University of Oxford.

Jeff Kenner is Professor of European Law at the University of Nottingham.

John Kitching is a Senior Researcher in the Small Business Research Centre, Kingston University.

Joseph A McCahery is Professor of Corporate Governance and Business Innovation at the University of Amsterdam Faculty of Economics and Econometrics and Professor of Financial Market Regulation at Tilburg University Faculty of Law. He is also Goldschmidt Visiting Professor of Corporate Governance at the Solvay Business School (Brussels).

Anand Menon is Professor of European Politics and Director of the European Research Institute, University of Birmingham.

Anne Meuwese is a research fellow in Politics at the Centre for Regulatory Governance, University of Exeter. She is currently completing her PhD in Law at Leiden University, where she is a visiting fellow at the Department of Constitutional and Administrative Law.

Niamh Moloney is Professor of Capital Markets Law, School of Law, University of Nottingham.

Anthony Ogus is Professor of Law at the University of Manchester and Research Professor at the University of Maastricht.

Elisabetta Olivi is a European civil servant with many years experience within the Commission. She is currently Senior Policy Adviser at the institution's Representation in London. In the past she has worked in the internal market and competition fields.

Jennifer Payne is the Travers Smith University Lecturer in Corporate Finance in the Faculty of Law, University of Oxford, and a Fellow and Tutor of Merton College, Oxford.

Jacopo Torriti is a research fellow at the King's Centre for Risk Management, King's College London.

Frank Vibert has been Director of the European Policy Forum since co-founding it in 1992. He was previously Deputy Director at the Institute of Economic Affairs and has held senior positions at the World Institute for Development Economics Research at the UN University Helsinki, and at the World Bank.

Stephen Weatherill is the Jacques Delors Professor of European Law in the University of Oxford, a Fellow of Somerville College and Deputy Director for European Law in the Institute of European and Comparative Law.

Daniela Weber-Rey is Partner at Clifford Chance in Frankfurt and Head of the German Financial Institutions Group. She is a Member of the Advisory Group on Corporate Governance and Company Law and the Expert Group on removing obstacles for cross-border investments at the EU Commission.

Jane Welch is Director of the European Financial and Corporate Law Centre at the British Institute of International and Comparative Law in London. She has spent a large part of her career dealing with EU financial services legislation, first at the UK Securities and Investments Board and later as the first Head of European Law at the FSA. She has just been appointed by the European Parliament as one of four EU experts on EU financial services law to advise the Economic and Monetary Affairs Committee of the Parliament.

Deming Xiao is an MBA Course Participant, Manchester Business School.

Table of Cases

EUROPEAN COURT AND COMMISSION OF HUMAN RIGHTS

EUROPEAN COURT OF JUSTICE AND COURT OF FIRST OF INSTANCE

Alphabetical

Numerical

UNITED KINGDOM

Table of Legislation

EUROPEAN UNION

Decisions

Directives

Recommendations

Regulations

GERMANY

INTERNATIONAL

ITALY

NETHERLANDS

UNITED KINGDOM

Statutory Instruments

UNITED STATES OF AMERICA

1

The Challenge of Better Regulation

STEPHEN WEATHERILL*

A. THE PATTERN OF THE POLITICAL DEBATE ABOUT BETTER REGULATION

'REGULATION' OCCUPIES A vast rolling terrain in modern political, economic and legal life. To offer a precise definition is to risk arguments at the margin, but the broad notion of 'regulation' embraces practices that serve to constrain or influence the behaviour of individuals or firms. It may accordingly catch not only binding rules, but also measures designed to influence conduct and, more broadly still, any kind of social control or influence, irrespective of its precise legal form or even its intent. Regulation understood in this sense is today evidently ubiquitous.

For at least 20 years its role and impact have been under intensely critical scrutiny. Two governmental White Papers published in the United Kingdom in the mid-1980s took as their titles slogans that vividly captured the nature of the then-perceived problem associated with patterns of regulation: in 1985—'Lifting the Burden';[1] in 1986—'Building Businesses Not Barriers'.[2] The Thatcher administration which had gained power in 1979 was in many areas of activity characterised by a vigorous rhetoric favourably disposed to its versions of freedom and choice and deeply hostile to perceived state interference. So, in the field of regulation, the White Papers could scarcely have been more uncompromisingly styled—state regulation was a *burden*, a *barrier*, and its withdrawal would set enterprise free. The rhetoric of deregulation dominated the day.

The rhetoric changed in 1997. The incoming Labour Administration selected a new slogan, that of 'better regulation'. The intent was doubtless to signal a more balanced, less ideological stance. 'Regulation' would not

* Jacques Delors Professor of European Law at the University of Oxford and Fellow of Somerville College, Oxford.

[1] DTI, 'Lifting the Burden' (Cmnd 9571, London, HMSO, 1985).

[2] DTI, 'Building Businesses Not Barriers' (Cmnd 9794, London, HMSO, 1986).

be treated as such with suspicion but nor would regulation be embraced as an inevitable good. Instead regulation would be 'better'—it would, in the tones of the time, undergo 'modernisation'. In 1997 the Better Regulation Task Force (today named the Better Regulation Commission) was duly established as an advisory body, devising a set of principles of better regulation, while Regulatory Impact Assessment was promoted with vigour. The Regulatory Reform Act entered into force in 2001.

But the rhythm of reform has an uncanny bias. In 2005 the Better Regulation Task Force released its report, *Regulation—Less is More*.[3] That year also saw the publication of the Hampton Review on *Reducing Administrative Burdens*.[4] If the shift in 1997 from an emphasis on 'deregulation' to 'better regulation' was rhetorically significant but not conspicuously novel in its impact on policy choices or regulatory output, much the same could be said of the *volte-face* performed in 2005. Nonetheless, rhetoric counts for much, and it was remarkable to see the resuscitation of a more sceptical agenda which once again aggressively advertised a link between regulation and *burdens*.

The lawmaking institutions of the European Union have also engaged in the process of regulatory reform. They have launched that process rather later than the UK and, moreover, neither their methods nor their expectations are necessarily directly comparable. Concern for 'Better' Regulation and for impact assessment, exemplified by the Commission's impact assessment guidelines and the Inter-Institutional Common Approach to Impact Assessment agreed by the EU's three main political institutions in 2005, has to be infused by appreciation of the EU's unique institutional architecture. That allocates to the Commission the strategically important position of holding an exclusive right of legislative initiative for most purposes under the EC Treaty, while reserving ultimate decision-making power to the Council and the Parliament acting for most purposes under the EC Treaty according to the Article 249 'co-decision' procedure. The interplay does not resemble a state's internal institutional balance. Moreover, better regulation in the EU has also become inextricably linked with the question of vertical distribution of powers—which level of governance should do what and, if there is to be centralisation, at what level of intensity and/or exclusivity. Thus 'subsidiarity' has become entwined with the Better Regulation agenda.[5] But even so, taking due account of the peculiarities of the EU context, including also its heavy dependence on national-level rule enforcement, there are certain key themes which are capable of connecting, and in practice do connect, regulatory reform in the EU and in the UK. Transparency,

[3] Better Regulation Task Force, *Regulation—Less is More* (London, Cabinet Office, 2005).

[4] P Hampton, *Reducing Administrative Burdens* (London, HM Treasury, 2005).

[5] Eg recently, Commission Report, 'Better Lawmaking 2005', COM(2006)289, 13 June 2006. Cf D Halberstam, 'Of Power and Responsibility: the Political Morality of Federal States' (2004) 90 *Virginia Law Review* 731.

consultation, clarification, simplification, impact assessment—these are common concerns, even if they raise distinct problems at the level of detail. And in the EU, as in the UK, a spirit of concern to regulate *less* has regularly infused the programme of commitment to regulate *better*. In 2006, for example, a raft of legislative proposals was noisily withdrawn.[6]

One readily acquires the impression of a general malaise in regulatory culture. One would be all too easily persuaded that things are not right. There should, the discourse insists, be as a minimum 'better' regulation and, more radically, 'less' regulation. Several factors have fuelled the introspection. The debate is in part driven by claims that failure to 'deregulate', or at least failure to regulate 'better', will generate corporate flight to jurisdictions with more hospitable regimes. Whether or not this migration is plausible or backed by empirical evidence, it is likely that such perceptions are of themselves enough to generate significant deregulatory pressures.[7] More generally—in the UK, and so too in the EU—the expectation is that 'better regulation' promises economic growth. The 2000 Lisbon European Council hitched the EU's concern to promote better regulation to the ambitious, not to say vainglorious, mission to project the EU to the top of the world's economies, as judged by competitive and dynamic knowledge-based qualities. The intensified attention to the nature and purpose of regulation is also attributable to changing political fashions. Political insistence on avoiding tax increases, a feature of recent British practice, has lured governments to find other less visibly financially onerous instruments for expressing their policy preferences. The 'regulatory state', which commands but does not increase taxation, is a manifestation of this pressure. But it too, as much as the 'taxing state' in the past, stands under suspicion. The EU itself is a creature with a relatively small budget but a very broad rule-making power—it too is predominantly regulatory in nature.[8] And it too is asked to justify its model of regulation.

Regulation is ubiquitous. So too is eagerness to make it better.

B. 'BETTER REGULATION'

As a slogan 'Better Regulation' invites neither contradiction nor even debate. Who would promote 'Worse Regulation'? Accordingly the 'Better Regulation' mantra has gathered prolific support in the political debate about the shaping of a regulatory environment that is apt to meet the

[6] 'Withdrawal of Commission Proposals Following Screening for their General Relevance, their Impact on Competitiveness and other Aspects' [2006] OJ C64/3.

[7] See eg C Hay and B Rosamond, 'Globalization, European Integration and the Discursive Construction of Economic Imperatives' (2002) 9 *Journal of European Public Policy* 147.

[8] Cf A Moravcsik, 'The European Constitutional Compromise and the Neofunctionalist Legacy' (2005) 12 *Journal of European Public Policy* 349.

challenges of modern governance. All over Europe, it seems, public and private actors are competing to be the most devout in the pilgrimage towards the holy shrine of 'Better Regulation'.

But what does 'Better Regulation' really mean? One may readily suppose that it connotes a drive for judiciously chosen rule-making, cost savings and the promotion of a more efficient economy. Again: who would argue with that? And yet nothing is so simple. In the UK and in the EU rule-makers have endeavoured to achieve a more satisfactory balance between the demands of proper protection from market failure and inequity, on the one hand, and commercial freedom and the potential for innovation on the other. Here already lies the problem—and the challenge. 'Better Regulation' in this sense is far from value-free. Notions such as 'satisfactory balance', 'proper protection' and the shape of commercial freedom involve measurement and value judgement which is both complex and controversial. 'Better Regulation', then, rubs shoulders with some immensely sensitive choices about the trajectory of the mixed economy in the modern state and in the developing transnational European market.

C. 'BETTER REGULATION' AS A BRANCH OF THE STUDY OF 'REGULATION'

To an extent the inquiry into 'Better Regulation' stands on the shoulders of the existing literature on 'Regulation'. Some highly sophisticated and intellectually ambitious scholarship has in recent times transformed our understanding of the phenomenon of Regulation—its shape, its intent, its successes and its failures.[9] In a political climate which has lately tended to offer a noticeably cool treatment of 'Regulation', an important starting-point is the simple perception that regulatory intervention can be readily supported on the basis that, without it, markets are left to malfunction. So, for example, legal intervention to ensure disclosure of information may be appropriate to improve the operation of the market. Famously and influentially, George Akerlof explained how in a market where goods of different quality are available at varying prices, but where the consumer is completely unable to distinguish between goods on the basis of quality, the result will be consumer unwillingness to pay at the higher end of the price scale. As a result, sellers will simply withdraw better quality goods from that market. The process will continue; bad will drive out good. 'Lemons' predominate. Legal intervention is justified as a means of

[9] It is invidious to provide a list which is not comprehensive: but without suggesting that other work does not deserve such recommendation see A Ogus, *Regulation* (Oxford, Hart Publishing, 2004); R Baldwin and M Cave, *Understanding Regulation: Theory, Strategy and Practice* (Oxford, OUP, 1999); R Baldwin, C Scott and C Hood, *A Reader on Regulation* (Oxford, OUP, 1998); C Hood, H Rothstein and R Baldwin, *The Government of Risk: Understanding Risk Regulation Régimes* (Oxford, OUP, 2004).

correcting market failure problems caused by such intransparency.[10] Moreover there are easily discerned rationales for intervening in the market where the costs of particular types of behaviour can be 'externalised'. Where A and B conclude a contract that will make both better off, but will prejudice a third party X, then the simple assumption that the deal is desirable and deserves non-interventionist legal respect requires more careful inquiry. Perhaps A and B can compensate X—but why should they? Perhaps they are legally obliged to do so as a matter of, for example, tort law. But the legal rights of X will frequently be difficult to identify with clarity (the suffering of economic harm caused by the conduct of others is not of itself a cause of action under English law) and moreover even where X has a legal right, its effective vindication through legal proceedings or the threat thereof will not be cost-free. The pattern becomes all the more complex and all the more prone to shelter A and B (or A alone, if the initial action is unilateral) from accounting for the full costs of their actions where there are many Xs, each suffering only a small amount of harm and each accordingly unlikely to have an incentive to pursue legal redress. Laws controlling pollution (inter alia) provide examples of regulation introduced under an assumption that the market underpinned by private law fails to provide an adequate basis for ensuring that the costs of particular forms of conduct fall on those pursuing them, and that accordingly the unregulated market allocates resources inefficiently. Consider, too, laws controlling firms which exercise monopoly power in the market. One might chose to generate structural change in the market in order to promote competition—but commonly the preference is to acquiesce in the absence of competitive restraint on the monopolist's conduct but to regulate in order to force the monopolist to behave *as if* sensitive to competition.

These are orthodox insights, yet in a climate of popular and political concern to 'deregulate' and/or to 'regulate better' within a broader discourse about the need to release business from regulatory inhibitions it is salutary to keep in mind that in some circumstances regulation is introduced not as an alternative to market freedom but rather as an antidote to market failure. A theme which connects several of the contributions to this book is an assumption that regulation may have identifiable and tangible benefits for the public interest, but that these are commonly overlooked in the popular and the political discourse.

However, as an empirical observation 'Regulation' is not simply a matter of curing market failure. A wide range of interventions in the market have been employed because of perceptions that the market does not function *fairly*. So regulation is devoted to dealing with the consequences of the operation of markets—and, in particular, to curtailing what may be seen as excessive successes accruing to some participants. It concerns wealth

[10] G Akerlof, 'The Market for Lemons: Qualitative Uncertainty and the Market Mechanism' (1970) 84 *Quarterly Journal of Economics* 488.

(re-)distribution and the promotion of social justice. This type of regulation is perfectly familiar—it embraces, for example, choices about the structure of a taxation system, approaches to inequality and the growth (and modernisation) of the welfare state. One commonly encounters the label 'action in the public interest' in such circumstances, but that conceals some hotly debated issues about the disincentives to growth and innovation which may be created by such regulation, as well as whether the intended or stated aims of such intervention are achieved or achievable. Furthermore one may readily make connections here to a much broader debate over fundamental questions about fairness in society.

Scholarship too has promoted a clearer understanding of the choice between particular *techniques* of regulation. An emphasis on outright prohibitions and models of 'command and control' has gradually given way to a much more nuanced understanding of the types of regulatory instrument from which a regulator may choose. Within this area of inquiry one may expect to find exploration of shifts towards prescribing performance targets as a means to allow greater scope for those subject to regulation to choose how to comply than is typically possible under orthodox 'command and control' regimes. This inquiry also encompasses the place of schemes which are not predominantly coercive, but rather aim to offer financial incentives—charges or taxes (to deter) or subsidies (to encourage). The rise of standards-setting, codes of practice and guidance is at stake—so too yet softer strategies of mutual learning and fashionable 'benchmarking'.

Some of the most significant insights in the modern literature involve greater elucidation of regulatory *failure*. It is plainly irrational to identify something that is perceived to be 'wrong' with an unregulated market and then simply to introduce a regulatory response without considering whether it is fit for purpose. It is perfectly conceivable that the cure is worse than the malady. An illuminating starting point is offered by Lord Diplock's comments in *Tesco Supermarkets Ltd v Nattrass*[11] about the scope of the defence that reasonable precautions have been taken, available to a trader accused of a criminal offence under the Trade Descriptions Act 1968:

> If considerations of cost and business practicability did not play a part in determining what employers carrying on such businesses could reasonably be expected to do to prevent the commission of an offence under the Act, the price to the public of the protection afforded to a minority of consumers might well be an increase in the cost of goods and services to consumers generally.

High standards may cost money; high standards may exclude competition and choice. The dictum represents an unusually clear judicial statement of the key theme that regulation may produce winners and losers. In short, regulation is not cost-free. But there is a great deal more to the potential

[11] [1971] 2 All ER 127, at 151h.

for regulatory failure. Regulators may be 'captured' and deliver decisions reflective of the interests being regulated rather than the broader public interest they are designed to serve. Beyond the more limited notion of capture, 'public choice' analysis is devoted to the idea that impartial and efficient decision-making cannot be delivered by public agencies. The state is a corporate enterprise, 'selling' laws to powerful interest groups which are for these purposes 'buyers'.[12] Such approaches are sceptical, even ultimately contemptuous, of the notion that the 'public interest' is neutrally served by the actors that drive the regulatory process. And, broader still, regulators answerable to electorates, who typically misperceive risk, rationally produce responses to high-profile scares which are driven by popular misperception and not by any objective risk assessment—in the UK citation of the Dangerous Dogs Act triggers a despairing whiff of poorly judged regulation. The nuanced task of risk assessment and risk management is too often conveniently crushed into the implausible but politically tempting language of risk elimination.

The general lesson of such insights is that one must look carefully at proposed and actual initiatives to identify possible gulfs between the stated purposes of regulation and its actual impacts. If one is persuaded that the orthodoxy of political wrangling is unsuitable for such appraisal, one may readily advocate the assignment of tasks to independent agencies as a means to insulate decision-making from short-term horizons. This happens in national systems. The EC itself, especially in the shape of the supranational institutions, is in part an exercise in shifting control out of the hands of individual Member States in order to embed structures apt to deliver credible long-term planning and commitments to act in common. And not only in the EC but also in looser patterns of international organisation agency-creation is gaining increasing attention.[13] But even here questions of institutional design pertaining to accountability and ensuring fidelity to the delegated task loom large and troubling. Why should agencies be trustworthily objective? In sum, the risk of regulatory failure should be taken every bit as seriously as market failure. This argues for a degree of regulatory humility.

D. 'BETTER REGULATION'—THE SCOPE AND SHAPE OF THIS BOOK

Where, then, does Better Regulation lie on this map? It plainly suggests a desire to examine more closely the capacity of regulation to achieve its stated aims. Can a particular policy goal be achieved more cost-effectively

[12] A major influence is J Buchanan: see, eg, *Liberty, Markets and State* (Brighton, Wheatsheaf, 1986).

[13] Cf eg A-M Slaughter 'Global Government Networks, Global Information Agencies, and Disaggregated Democracy' (2002–3) 24 *Michigan Journal of International Law* 1041.

by a different regulatory technique? If so—change: do it better! Within that process of appraisal it is plainly necessary to clarify just what the stated aims of regulation may be. So 'Better Regulation' typically involves an emphasis on transparency and, more generally, more elaborate policy articulation. Also at stake is an emphasis on the need for thorough assessment of the impacts of regulation, in order to ensure that the decision whether it can be done 'better' is informed by the proper broad context. So transparency and thoroughness in consultation are likely features of a 'Better Regulation' agenda, and so too are *ex post* calculation and review of the actual performance of a regulatory tool. So what is at stake is vetting new laws and also looking hard at old laws.

In this vein *Rick Haythornthwaite*, chairman of the UK's Better Regulation Commission, takes the opportunity in this book to describe the contours of 'Better Regulation' from the perspective of the UK itself and the UK in co-operation in with the European Commission. Insisting on the virtues of simplification, consultation and awareness of alternative routes to chosen goals, he depicts well-judged 'Better Regulation' as a 'win-win agenda'.

This immensely appealing vision suggests a separation between 'Better Regulation' as a policy programme and the wider terrain of 'Regulation'. The former is an objective exploration of how best to go about achieving defined ends—the latter engages more controversial assessment of what the ends really should comprise. And certainly some aspects of the 'Better Regulation' agenda are driven by the quest for a *process* of regulation which will deliver a better informed and more transparent range of choices, exposing the relevant costs and benefits and serving up freshly cooked impact assessment, from which the political process can then select, though without presuming to interfere with the exercise of political judgement.

There is evident appeal in the quest to deliver superior cost-benefit analysis as a basis for guiding regulatory choices. And the aspiration to offer a more enlightened basis for selecting between diverse available forms of intervention is similarly attractive. Making public regulation fit for purpose is an exercise in efficient allocation of scarce resources. The rougher and more challenging edges of the 'Better Regulation' agenda ask where the weightings in these cost-benefit analyses and 'impact assessments' are calculated and how they are measured; and they question how far the 'Better Regulation' agenda itself shades into the wider politics of regulation. Is there something of tangible didactic value at the core of the promise to deliver 'Better Regulation', or has the whole programme instead become merely a vacuous exercise in re-branding the grubby business of everyday rule-making? Worse—does the 'Better Regulation' agenda threaten to throw an apparently respectable cloak of objective appraisal over what is in truth politics-as-usual and accordingly deserving of the most demanding critical scrutiny? Is it a device for confirming preconceptions and for dressing them up with the veneer of rational inevitability?[14] It is a matter of fierce controversy whether one can consistently separate out the achievement of a better *quality* of regulatory process from the intensely contested debate about the content of regulation itself.

E. BETTER REGULATION, DEREGULATION AND LESS REGULATION—THE UK DEBATE

Several papers in this collection inquire into the measurements that are involved in regulatory impact assessment. They reveal that the current agenda is contested and fascinating. In his contribution *Robert Baldwin* expresses the anxiety that the role of Regulatory Impact Assessment in 'Better Regulation' has a tendency to induce reliance on more traditional command-and-control mechanisms, at the expense of softer and potentially 'smarter' techniques of regulation, which are less predictable and so more resistant to the concrete calculations that drive Regulatory Impact Assessment (RIA). Moreover RIA may neglect cumulative wider effects of regulation and play down the practical questions of enforcement. To this accusation that RIA may induce regulatory narrow-mindedness one may juxtapose the views of *Peter Andrews*, who champions the worth of RIA as a means to reveal likely consequences of proposed measures. He is bullish about regulators' preparedness to take on the challenge of devising smart—not simple—options. The two papers are, however, united by anxiety to see successful prosecution of a strategy of impact assessment—Baldwin insists on incrementalist strategies and rejects pretensions to comprehensive rationality, arguing for the location of RIA within a broader iterative process of review, and Andrews seeks to set out the conditions under which market failure analysis and RIA can be structured in order to deliver their most useful results.

In similar vein *Jacopo Torriti* examines the 'standard cost model', which serves as a method for measuring the administrative burdens imposed on business by regulation. Quantification is centrally important, and *Torriti* considers practices in the UK and in the EU—which are not identical.

'Better Regulation' should also accommodate concern for 'better enforcement', a point made with vigour by *Anthony Ogus*. Using insights from the economic analysis of law he shows that improvements can be found in designing enforcement techniques that make best use of available resources. He argues, for example, that a higher priority should be given to the supplementary role of private enforcement and, in the sphere of public

[14] For assembly of American inter-disciplinary perspectives see MD Adler and EA Posner, *Cost-Benefit Analysis: Legal, Economic and Philosophical Perspectives* (Chicago, Ill, University of Chicago Press, 2001).

enforcement, that there should be an increase in the use of administrative financial penalties, against a strong background assumption that current patterns of reliance on the criminal justice system are cumbersome and frequently unhelpful.

Several contributors lament the poor quality of Regulatory Impact Assessment undertaken so far in the UK and in the EU, but none dismisses its potential worth. 'Better Regulation' deserves to transcend its status as cliché and instead to lead to an intellectually exciting excavation of its multiple impacts and intents. But successful prosecution of that mission is conditional on achieving a clear understanding of what is being promoted in the name of 'Better Regulation'. A line of criticism that holds that chosen forms of regulation are poorly designed and will not achieve their ends—or at least that those ends can be better achieved by more sophisticated regulatory choices—is distinct from a claim that the end itself is ill-chosen. Better Regulation is much more obviously a strategy aimed at addressing the first of these issues. And yet the debate has been broadened—and made disturbingly less precise—by a political culture which has, first, frequently failed to make much of the virtues of regulation and, secondly, been prepared to use a broad brush when painting its vices. It is moreover common to encounter a commercial discourse which is headlined by an emphasis on the need for less intrusion—'Business leaders urge Brown to ease City's burdens',[15] 'Business bears the burden of drilling through red tape',[16] 'Red tape burden as heavy as ever in spite of reform promises',[17] for example. Appeals from business to be subjected to 'better' or 'less' regulation are commonly little concerned by the desirability of intellectual precision, and frequently conflate anxiety about 'better regulation' narrowly understood with claims to be regulated for different reasons and typically with a lighter touch. Is the plea for a lighter touch really reflective of a modest desire for more sensitive regulation—or is it instead in fact an attempt to promote the view that the intended benefits of the regulation should be seen as inadequate to compensate for their costs (on business)? Advancing the latter point of view is, of course, eminently defensible—but it shows the strain that may be placed on attempts to portray 'Better Regulation' as a neutral process. And, one may ruefully reflect, how often does one discover commercial pressure for deregulation as a generally desirable outcome qualified by a nagging preference to retain particular sector-specific rules unaltered as a means to avoid the costs of short-term adaptation? Regulation can be a safe harbour, a reassuring 'old teddy bear'[18]—a welcome barrier to market entry by competitors which firms and professionals secretly cherish and will not lightly surrender.

[15] *Guardian*, 16 Oct 2006, at 28.

[16] *Financial Times*, 5 July 2006, at 3.

[17] *Financial Times*, 13 Apr 2006, at 2.

[18] R Haythornthwaite, 'Britain's secret shame: we just love red tape', *Financial Times*, 9 Feb 2006, at 15.

The argument that there is a major difference between a debate about 'Better Regulation' and one about 'Different Regulation' has a distinct constitutional resonance. At its margins the 'Better Regulation' agenda is close to matters which *should* engage vibrant political debate and should not be sheltered by a cloak of spuriously woven value-neutrality. The concern that the UK government's Legislative and Regulatory Reform Bill 2006 tends to present a case for 'Better Regulation' while in fact putting in place a mechanism for achieving significant politically contested regulatory reform without direct Parliamentary scrutiny lies at the heart of the chapter by *Seamus Burns*. He shows how the political debate has exposed the constitutional sensitivity to enhancing executive power in the name of regulatory reform and flexibility. Here, very clearly, one may see how 'Better Regulation' can be used as a vehicle for much more than attention to improved regulatory *process*. *Michael Bohlander* is similarly exercised by the deceptively simple case frequently made in favour of flexible rule-making as a reason for permitting the circumvention of relatively slow-moving procedures of Parliamentary oversight. He finds the government's 2006 Bill strikingly weak in the safeguards presented against undue concentration of power in the hands of the executive, and he touches on dark German memories to remind us where giving too little weight to the value of Parliamentary control over the law-making processes might lead.

Identifying the proper limits of 'Better Regulation' as a concern with process and the beginning of a properly contested terrain of regulatory reform is not confined to the constitutional sphere. It is directly relevant to the core of the examination of the purpose of regulation. One can readily gain the impression that the discourse about 'regulation' is contaminated by misperception, and perhaps even strategic obfuscation, of the discrete elements of this complex phenomenon. *John Kitching*, drawing on experience from the small-business sector in the UK, pursues an explanatory framework which attributes three distinct features to regulation—*enabling* actors to pursue particular courses of action, *motivating* actors by providing an incentive to choose particular options over others, and *constraining* by limiting the available scope for action. He asserts that much previous research has prioritised the constraining tendencies of regulation, including the imposition of potentially costly obligations on (small) business, while being relatively neglectful of enabling and motivating tendencies which do much to improve the potential for successful commercial activity. In particular in popular discourse the focus on *constraining* regulation causes a negative tone to permeate the debate. And, as his case studies demonstrate, the tendency of small businesses subject to regulation is to focus on the constraining feature of the regulatory environment within which they operate, and to acknowledge the beneficial effects of regulation only under prompting. If one wished to promote restructuring of the discourse, a good question, therefore, might be to ask what happens if a particular instrument of regulation is taken away?

What kind of 'freedom' is there in being exposed to, for example, unscrupulous competitors who exploit the elimination of quality standards by selling goods and services of poor quality but which cannot be identified as such by consumers—Akerlof's lemons![19] This may give pause for thought about the virtues of regulation as well as potential vices. But there is at present, Kitching suggests, an 'anti-regulation' discourse prevalent in society which is neglectful of the full picture.

This is not at all to suggest that the debate should always be sunny in tone. Of course regulation may be ill-suited to its task. Of course the choice of task may itself be controversial. And business may rationally oppose regulation in so far as it is fully intended that, although the costs will be exceeded by the benefits, the costs for individual businesses will not be exceeded by benefits for them because the intended beneficiaries comprise a more diffuse class (consumer, environmental interests, for example). But a debate that takes as its starting point that regulation diminished is regulation improved is a debate that makes wholly unrealistic assumptions about the operation of 'free markets'.

F. THE EU'S COMMITMENT TO REGULATORY RENOVATION

There are ready echoes elsewhere. At EU level, most of all, it is dispiritingly common to read of yet another survey in which commercial interests complain about the weight of EU regulation. 'Business chiefs say EU rules outweigh benefits'[20] was recently literally front-page news. Connecting EU rules with their perceived over-enthusiastic implementation at national level, one learns of 'Small business hit by overuse of EU rules'.[21] Yet it is counter-intuitive to suppose that the business interests are opposed to the EC's market-making rules (unless they are fearful of cross-border competition and eager for a quiet protected life on national territory). Indeed it is a well-noted feature of EU rule-making that it is commonly driven by demand from commercial operators for a reliable set of common rules apt to provide the foundation for an integrated EU-wide business strategy.[22] At EU level firms need a new teddy bear.[23] As *Daniel Kelemen and Anand Menon* emphasise, the EU *depends* on a rather aggressive pattern of common regulation as a means to break down the fragmenting effect of diverse and, in some cases, centuries-old regulatory traditions in the Member

[19] Above n 10.

[20] *Financial Times*, 16 Oct 2006, at 1.

[21] *Financial Times*, 7 Sept 2006, at 3.

[22] See eg W Sandholtz and A Stone Sweet, *European Integration and Supranational Governance* (Oxford, OUP, 1998); J Greenwood, *Interest Representation in the European Union* (Basingstoke, Palgrave, 2003).

[23] Cf the text above at n18.

States: without such a framework of legal rules, states, their firms and their citizens are exposed to damage caused by the undesirable impact of regulation (or its lack) in their neighbours. Once one appreciates that starting-point it is no paradox that the EU's quest for market deregulation is closely tied to strong institutions and legally powerful rules.[24] Again, an illuminating question is: what happens if this regulation is taken away? Take away the EU's rules on the free movement of goods and services, for example, and what is revealed is Europe's shattered, inefficient and deeply business-unfriendly past. This contextual appreciation of the scale and nature of the current 'problems' of EU regulation informs *Elisabetta Olivi*'s discussion of the approach of the Commission. Of course, this is not to suppose that *all* the EU's rules are capable of justification with such unconditional comfort. *Kelemen and Menon* depict the internal market as a dynamic regulatory project, within which the Commission may be tempted to take on new tasks and the Member States, lured by the appealing prospect of discarding the risk of blame should policies fail, may be keen to approve such a transfer. Siting the delivery of regulation in Europe is an intensely political process, and it may often be driven by shrewd political opportunism flavoured by exploitation of the EC political process by well-funded private interests. *Jacopo Torriti* shows how commercial attitudes to the scope and intensity of EU regulation cannot be treated as homogenous.

Appreciation of this complex landscape helps to move the focus closer to the type of commercial complaint about the EU's regulatory environment which, properly understood, frequently lies at the heart of expressed irritation. In general, if one were to pin down with more precision the nature of the typical commercial objection to EU regulation it is unlikely to take the form of distaste for the whole package, given that successful market-making is in the business interest. It is typically likely to involve an objection to the scope or the particular *content* of the EU's rules, and typically reflects an understandable preference that the EU's rules should resemble as closely as possible the pre-existing national regime and/or that the EU's rules should be as light as possible. So once again the message is that a critical approach to 'Regulation' in general and 'Better Regulation' in particular demands nuanced appreciation of its multiple functions and of the different opportunities and incentives for public and private actors to gain access to the regulatory process.

So the *Business Survey* commissioned by Clifford Chance, reproduced as an Annex to this book, shows that it is to the EU that business looks for solutions to problems that hamper their opportunities to operate on a transnational scale. In short, businesses need the EU. And there is a

[24] On how a programme presented as an exercise in securing market freedom inevitably involves a sustained commitment to rule-making see M Egan, *Constructing a European Market* (Oxford, OUP, 2001).

considerable level of satisfaction with its performance—61 per cent of our sample rates the EU as meeting commercial aspirations to make good use of the single market either *very well* or *quite well*. On the other hand, there is a clear disquiet with the number of opportunities allowed for consultation and input into the regulatory process. There is also a perception that national implementation of EU rules is patchy, which tends to subtract from the envisaged benefits. The focus on problems of national implementation reminds us that the EU's character as a relatively lean bureaucracy, denied direct means of enforcing its rules (other than in the field of competition law), has benefits in the shape of budgetary restraint but must absorb costs consequent on frequently uneven and fragile national fidelity in enforcing the agreed rules.[25] The broad message from business is *not* one that is supportive of aggressive deregulation, but there is evident general sympathy for the tone of the 'Better Regulation' agenda which has become a thematic priority for the Barroso Commission as a key element in its drive to improve the quality of EU governance within a wider quest to enhance the EU's legitimacy.[26]

Social policy and labour market regulation have been areas of long-standing controversy. Should the EC be directly involved in regulating these spheres? How? Why? In fact it has always been involved in the area to some degree, for the original Treaty of Rome stipulated a rule of equal pay for equal work by men and women, achieving both social protection and equalisation of competitive conditions between the Member States. But how far should the EC reach in determining rules in these areas? The notorious but illuminating saga of the regulation of working time is tracked by *Jeff Kenner*. Tension between the aim of protecting workers and that of preserving a degree of flexibility in the organisation of working time has led to a troublingly complicated structure of regulation, examined in detail in the chapter.

In its elucidation of the possibilities for flexibility and diversity in the content and application of EU rules *Kenner*'s chapter displays thematic connection with that of *Hertig and McCahery*. Examining company law regulation they suggest that the EU may be wise to admit tolerance of regulatory models that do not assume that one size can and should fit all. They ask whether the EC has been too heavy-handed in mandating common rules, which burden firms and deny them choice. They prefer a model of 'legal options' coupled to a limited range of default rules. This anxiety to emphasise the costs of centralised rule-making readily conforms to a

[25] Eg E Mastenbroek, 'EU Compliance: Still a Black Hole?' (2005) 12 *Journal of European Public Policy* 1103.

[26] White Paper on Governance, COM(2001)428. See H Hofmann and A Türk, *EU Administrative Governance* (Cheltenham, Edward Elgar, 2006); C Harlow, *Accountability in the European Union* (Oxford, OUP, 2002); A Arnull and D Wincott (eds), *Accountability and Legitimacy in the European Union* (Oxford, OUP, 2002).

broader agenda that presses the case for the EU to develop more openly as a site of managed diversity.[27]

Daniela Weber-Rey covers developments in the field of corporate governance which have been illuminatingly infused by the aspirations contained in the Better Regulation agenda. A readiness to withdraw or modify legislative proposals is visible; there are several instances of measures designed to simplify the pattern of EU regulation in this sector; and impact assessment and consultation play their part too. A pressing concern to achieve a degree of flexibility in regulation is prominent in the current debate.

As a general observation 'impact assessment' at EU level does not mirror UK practice, but it is driven by motivations which largely align with those visible in the UK. The promotion of transparency and accountability in rule-making is planned as a strategy to limit the scope for arbitrary, or at least concealed, choices by regulators who are vulnerable to diversion away from their stipulated mission. *Ex ante* statements of applicable criteria are designed to structure the exercise of discretion. But—how apolitical can such criteria really be? Do they tend to intrude on matters that really should be open to political judgement? And do we really imagine that bureaucrats whose job is to turn the wheels of power are much constrained in practice by appealingly written paperwork? No one imagines that such questions are easily answered yet (if ever), but they are central to exposing the depth of the challenge presented by the 'Better Regulation' agenda at transnational level.[28]

The practice of formal impact assessment began in the Commission in 2003, and its importance now and into the future is emphasised from the perspective of the Commission by *Elisabetta Olivi*. *Francis Chittenden, Tim Ambler* and *Deming Xiao* offer an account of the first three years of Impact Assessment in the EU. It is irresistibly amusing to discover that the Commission's guidance notes have already grown longer, suggesting that regulation has its own expansionist dynamic, even when embedded in a framework dedicated in part to simplification and clarification. However, the authors construct a carefully presented narrative of serious commitment by the Commission to a thorough process of impact assessment *on paper*, combined with some optimistic findings about the practical dimension of the process, including *inter alia* readiness to take account not only of benefits envisaged and intended in one area but also of costs inevitably

[27] Cf F Scharpf, 'Legitimate Diversity: the New Challenge of European Integration' in T Börzel and R Cichowski (eds), *The State of the European Union* (Oxford, OUP, 2003), ch 4; B De Witte, D Hanf and E Vos (eds), *The Many Faces of Differentiation in EU Law* (Antwerp, Intersentia, 2001).

[28] Cf C Radaelli and F De Francesco, *Regulatory Quality in Europe: Concepts, Measures and Policy Processes* (Manchester, Manchester University Press, 2006); JB Wiener, 'Better Regulation in Europe', [2006] *Current Legal Problems*, available at SSRN: http://ssrn.com/abstract=937927.

incurred in another. Admittedly quality of impact assessment is not likely to be uniform across all Directorates General—a criticism made directly by *Rick Haythornthwaite,* who also injects the important point that it is not only the Commission but also—perhaps especially—the Parliament and Council as the EC's law-makers that must digest best practice in the field. Our *Business Survey* also detects concern that it is not the Commission alone in the EU's institutional architecture that could profitably pay greater attention to commercial aspirations, and the chapter by *Jane Welch* makes a similar point in connection with financial services. *Anne Meuwese* also demonstrates that Impact Assessment requires respect from all the EU's institutions, and she develops our understanding of the institutional richness that should characterise successful impact assessment. Her chapter explores the ambiguity of impact assessment by taking the Commission's statement that it should serve as 'an aid to decision-making, not a substitute for political judgement'[29] and considers what is embedded in these notions. How really to define a separation between aiding decision-making and the exercise of political judgement? In this ambiguously shaped space different public and private actors can seek to exploit the process of impact assessment for their own—different, potentially conflicting—ends.

The EU's Financial Services Action Plan offers an especially rich case study in regulatory reform in the transnational context. *Jane Welch* examines the obstacles to better quality drafting and successful impact assessment which are caused by the complexity of the institutional processes that generate EC secondary legislation. As *Niamh Moloney* puts it, what is at stake in this sector is rule-making in 'an institutionally complex, multi-actor, multi-dimensional law-making and policy formation process'. An influential role is attributed to the Committee of European Securities Regulators (CESR), but whereas allowing this body autonomy seems crucial to ensuring its effective functioning, that in turn raises deeply sensitive questions about how to hold it accountable. Is Europe's evolving system of regulation in this sector durable? *Moloney* highlights a remarkable degree of uncertainty about whether the legislative package will truly transform the market, but the acceptance of the EU as the site of governance ensures that for the time being that is where the expression and promotion of commercial concerns will occur. And CESR itself is (rather belatedy) joining the club of regulators that accept the discipline of impact assessment. *Jennifer Payne* also devotes attention to CESR, depicting it as a site for supervisory convergence in Europe—less than a 'European securities regulator' as yet, but operating in an environment of dynamic change which may feasibly ultimately deliver such a single dominant institutional actor. Her analysis shows how the EU is pursuing a complex combination of regulatory competition (legally

[29] European Commission, 'Communication from the Commission on Impact Assessment', COM(2002)276 final, at 3.

underpinned by the Treaty's free movement rules) increasingly studded by mandatory common regulation.

Frank Vibert's chapter ranges more broadly over the phenomenon of agency creation at EU level as an instrument for achieving better regulation. He finds scope for supposing that the agencies can find opportunities to move beyond the limits placed on their activities by their founding instruments and makes a normative case in favour of embedding them more deeply into the policy-making and (especially) the policy-implementation process in order to exploit their expertise as a source of improved regulatory performance. He acknowledges, but is not deterred by, the need to select legitimate systems ensuring appropriate forms of accountability.

G. CONCLUDING REMARKS

The interrogation of the phenomenon of 'Better Regulation' demands input from the perspectives of law, politics, economics and management. It requires trans-frontier expertise, not least because of the intimate relationship between the UK's and the EU's insistence on the virtues of 'Better Regulation'. It is enriched by attention to how closely the rhetoric of regulatory reform is matched by the practice. The chapters collected in this book aim to provide in aggregate an appreciation of what is at stake in current discourse about 'Better Regulation', while also pointing the way forward. The composition of the book has been concocted with a deliberate plan to ensure that the full mix of disciplinary and jurisdictional perspectives is respected and accommodated. If it convinces the reader to accept its message that the 'Better Regulation' agenda offers a platform for deeper understanding of how and why regulation can improve markets and societies then it has realised a worthwhile aim.

2

Better Regulation in Europe

RICK HAYTHORNTHWAITE*

BETTER REGULATION HAS been high on the political agenda in the UK for some time and is now a hot topic in the EU, and rightly so. Badly designed and badly implemented regulation damages our economy as well as suffocating innovation and curbing our growth. The challenge to deliver a proportionate and effective regulatory framework is perhaps greater at EU level, but not insurmountable.

I am chairman of the Better Regulation Commission, an independent body which advises on and monitors the UK government's regulatory activity. All of our members are unpaid volunteers, with the business world, the public sector, the voluntary sector and trade unions all represented, to ensure a balanced view is heard. We provide an independent, expert reality check and challenge government and regulators by asking the question 'Is this the best way to achieve the desired outcomes?'. As an independent voice we can and do say what we want, even if key individuals and institutions may disagree.

For us, better regulation is a win-win agenda. It is a means of securing protections for citizens without imposing unnecessary or excessive regulatory cost; it is a means of enhancing competitiveness, growth and employment, and also promotes a better quality of life. Better regulation is not about eroding essential regulatory protection; it is about achieving agreed policy goals in the most effective and efficient way possible.

The cost of regulation to advanced economies is estimated to be 10 to 12 per cent of GDP, and that compares to the 10.9 per cent of GDP that we in the UK collect as income tax. But think how carefully tax spending is monitored compared to how readily the government has waved in new regulations in the past, often in a knee-jerk fashion. Much of this 10 to 12 per cent is of course good regulation that society values, with outcomes such as clean air, clean water, safe products and the removal of barriers

* Chairman of the Better Regulation Commission. This is a written version of a speech given at the Clifford Chance/Institute of European and Comparative Law conference on 'Regulating the European Market' on 17 Mar 2006.

to trade. But about a third of it could be in the bad regulation category, delivering unwanted bureaucracy, unnecessary administration and needless form-filling. It is this bad regulation that we must address and eradicate in the UK and in the EU if we want our business people, voluntary organisations and public sector workers to thrive.

A. UK ACHIEVEMENTS

There is no doubt that the UK still has a lot to do to improve its regulatory performance. But progress has been made over the last 10 years and there are some things that the UK is doing well that others in the EU can learn from. The Better Regulation Commission's predecessor, the Better Regulation Task Force, put in place a set of hurdles that regulation must overcome before it can become law initially, or remain law thereafter, and we continue to take this work forward.

One of our biggest achievements has been to persuade the UK government to embark on an ambitious programme to measure and reduce the total administrative costs that departments inflict on business and the voluntary sector. This approach, to address the existing stock of bad regulation, has already been successfully adopted in other Member States such as the Netherlands and Denmark, where a target of 25 per cent has been set. This is a very important project for the better regulation agenda; it is estimated that this approach could potentially increase GDP by 1 per cent and make a huge contribution to the economy.[1]

The UK government has endorsed our recommendation of a one-in, one-out approach to law-making, whereby any new regulation must be accompanied by compensatory removal of an existing law or regulation. It is the cumulative burden of regulation that often hinders business and it is vital that we do not keep shovelling new laws onto an ever increasing pile.

There are several measures in place in the UK to stop bad regulation before it is implemented. All new laws are now subject to a 12-week consultation. Regulatory Impact Assessments (RIAs) are now completed as a matter of course. The standard is improving and the government is looking to strengthen the RIA process even further. RIAs must now consider a range of delivery options, including alternatives to regulation. I sit on the Panel for Regulatory Accountability, chaired by the Prime Minister, and Ministers must get our agreement before introducing any major new proposals. To allow stakeholders to prepare for new requirements the government now implements employment and health and safety legislation on common commencement dates, and this initiative is being spread to other sectors.

[1] All of these figures are taken from the Better Regulation Task Force's *Less is More* report (Mar 2005). See http://www.brc.gov.uk/downloads/pdf/lessismore.pdf.

ain Library 2 self issue receipt

ustomer ID: *********4029**

tle: How to protect investors : lessons from
e EC and the UK / Niamh Moloney
): 30110008020480
ue: 11-12-12

tle: Better regulation / edited by Stephen
eatherill
): 30110007488837
ue: 11-12-12

tal items: 2
10 2012
ecked out: 2
erdue: 0
ld requests: 0
ady for pickup: 0

ank you for using
s self issue machine.

B. EU REGULATION

Having established these processes in the UK, it became clear to us that, as approximately half of all new legislation emanates from the EU, we had to look there as well. That is not to say we have better regulation cracked in the UK—far from it. We are only at the beginning of a long journey, but at least we are taking steps in the right direction and have our path clearly marked.

The Better Regulation Commission does not have the same formal clout within the EU that we have in the UK, but, with European regulation playing such a major part in UK law-making, it is important that we engage with the EU institutions and other Member States and influence the agenda. And let us not forget that it is in our interests as members of the EU to ensure that it regulates better. Per capita, GDP growth in Western Europe lags well behind that of the US, and, with the emergence of China, the challenge to our national economies and the collective economy of the EU is set to become even fiercer.

Of course, the regulatory environment is different in the EU from in individual countries. Trade barriers have to be overcome and the diverse cultures of 27 Member States have to be taken into consideration. But this should not be used as an excuse for ignoring better regulation principles. On the contrary, it makes it even more important to get it right, as the consequences of bad regulation are amplified when imposed onto a more varied and complex market. With such a range of views at its disposal the EU needs to act as a platform to share good ideas, as we have seen with the administrative burdens reduction exercise.

With this in mind we identified three core areas as the building blocks of better regulation in the EU and embarked on a trilogy of studies in 2004–5:

- — The simplification of the current statute book;
- — Effective consultation with stakeholders; and,
- — The deployment of less burdensome alternatives to conventional regulation.

We believe that addressing these three areas, combined with an improved Impact Assessment process, is the way forward for the EU, and we are encouraging the Commission, Parliament and Council to implement the improvements we have recommended.

C. SIMPLIFICATION

Our first European report, *Make it Simple, Make it Better*, was published in December 2004, and made recommendations on how to simplify the existing body of EU law.[2] Complex and unclear regulation imposes

[2] Better Regulation Task Force, *Make it Simple, Make it Better* (2004), available at http://www.brc.gov.uk/downloads/pdf/simplebetter.pdf.

excessive administrative burdens. It is hard to enforce, it is often ignored, and in practice it can fail to protect the very people it is intended to help. Further, it seems that the long-term credibility of the EU depends on its ability to review and revise laws that are obsolete, or have been overtaken by technology. It is not enough only to improve the quality of *future* legislation; mistakes that have already been made need to be rectified. There is an enormous body of existing EU regulation, some of which is confusing, contradictory and ripe for reform.

The Commission has launched a rolling programme of simplification since we published our report, but there is still a question about how these proposals for simplification will be delivered. Must we really wait for the tortuous renegotiation of complete legal instruments? There is a longstanding public commitment in the form of the Inter-Institutional Agreement on Better Law-Making[3] to establish an ad hoc structure to expedite simplification proposals, but where is it? The institutions must work together to deliver this.

To facilitate further simplification, we believe that each new regulatory proposal should include consideration of how it can be amended in future, should it become obsolete. To ensure consistency we want to see all new proposals include a holistic review of all other relevant legislation and an explanation of how the new proposal will fit with the existing regulatory regime. To reduce administrative burdens we have called for the need to apply for multiple permits and authorisations to be eliminated. To be consistent with the single market, single commercial bodies with operations in different Member States should be allowed to make single applications and notifications.

D. CONSULTATION

Our second European study was launched in September 2005 and looked at how EU consultation procedures could be improved.[4] Consultation is at the heart of better regulation. Policy-makers must engage openly with a full range of stakeholders through the policy-making process—considering their views and acting on the evidence they provide—if the regulations they produce are to meet their objectives at an acceptable cost to the European economy. Good consultation gives business, and other, stakeholders a real stake in the EU's decision-making process. For us, good consultation means consulting the right people at the right time and in the right way.

The European Commission is responsible for preparing proposals and is therefore the leading body for consultation. When examining its practices

[3] [2003] OJ C321/01.

[4] Better Regulation Task Force, *Get Connected* (2005), available at http://www.brc.gov.uk/downloads/pdf/getconnected.pdf.

we found much to applaud—it is clear that the Commission consults better now than ever before. It is open and responsive to stakeholder representations—more so than many Member State administrations—and we support its principles and standards for consultation. We do not believe that the system needs a radical overhaul, but there are still weaknesses in the consultation process that need to be addressed. The Better Regulation Commission is particularly concerned that some existing procedures are not sufficiently transparent. In particular, we would like the European Commission to report annually against key indicators on the compliance of individual Directorates General with its consultation standards.

To improve its performance, we would like the European Commission, on a systematic basis, to identify and consult informally with a range of interested parties before a proposal is released for written public consultation. Stakeholders should have the opportunity to comment on a number of different options for achieving the policy objective, including alternatives to conventional regulation. It should be clear who were consulted and what evidence they provided, and the results of this early consultation should inform the impact assessment that accompanies a published proposal. We want stakeholders to be given more time to respond to public written consultations. The standard period of eight weeks is simply too short. We require 12 weeks in the UK and we would argue that collecting views from 25 Member States needs at least as long. This is not about delaying the legislative process, but about making it better. Time spent on consultation is a sound investment in a proposal's future quality and legitimacy.

It is important to note that consultation is a two-way street. It is not good enough for business to complain about the excesses of EU legislation when it responds to consultation opportunities by sitting on its hands, or by lobbying for competitive advantage.

E. ALTERNATIVES

The third major regulatory area where there is scope for improvement is the EU's use of alternatives. We have urged the EU to give more consideration to using alternatives in our *Routes to Better Regulation* report published in December 2005.[5] The term 'alternative' covers a range of options, such as self-regulation, market-based instruments and, of course, the option of 'no action'. Classic regulation, in the form of prescriptive rules, is the most common response to a policy problem. While it is sometimes the most suitable choice, we need to move away from the position where it is the automatic choice. A more imaginative approach to regulating, with greater

[5] Better Regulation Task Force, *Routes to Better Regulation* (2005), available at http://www.brc.gov.uk/downloads/pdf/routes.pdf.

use of alternatives, can often achieve the desired objectives more successfully, with fewer burdens and at less cost. There are several advantages to using alternatives:

- — They can be quicker and easier to introduce and adapt than classic regulation, as most alternative tools avoid a lengthy legislative process.
- — They can be cheaper to implement and administer. Operators will strive to find the most cost-effective way of achieving objectives if they are given the scope to do so. It is in their interests to meet targets while minimising bureaucracy and costs.
- — Stakeholders are more involved in the implementation and monitoring of alternatives, which taps into their expertise and increases the chances of the proposal achieving its objectives.

Despite these advantages, we have encountered deep-seated prejudices against the use of alternatives which I believe are largely unfounded. We have heard that alternatives are not transparent, and that they create uncertainty and therefore non-compliance. This does not wash, as the same criticisms can apply equally to conventional regulation. It is not the delivery tool that causes these problems—they will arise in any mechanism that is poorly implemented, badly monitored or not in line with our Principles of Good Regulation—proportionality, accountability, consistency, transparency and targeting.

The European Commission, Parliament and Council all signed up to the use of alternative regulatory mechanisms in their Inter-Institutional Agreement on Better Law-Making,[6] but their use is still sporadic at best. More needs to be done to increase awareness and spread best practice found in measures such as the EuroNCAP car safety scheme, the Emissions Trading Scheme and the self-regulation of advertising. The Commission should use its annual report on better law-making and annual work programme to inform stakeholders of where alternatives have been used and where they might be applied. To ensure officials give enough consideration to alternatives during policy-making, the Commission should include regulatory proposals in its annual work programme only where the relevant impact assessment contains an analysis of at least one alternative tool and of the 'no action' option.

This is where the Parliament and Council can play their part. If they take their commitment to the use of impact assessments and alternatives seriously they should review whether alternatives have been considered when assessing Commission proposals, and return proposals for further development if an adequate analysis has not been provided. The Parliament and

[6] Above n3.

Council are wary of the use of alternatives, as they believe it could undermine their legislative roles. However, if they are more involved in the early consideration of alternatives and in monitoring their effectiveness they will safeguard their roles and be in a better position to judge whether each measure is achieving its objectives. For example, Green Papers could be used to foster discussions of the most appropriate means of policy delivery at Council and in Parliamentary Committees. This is not ground-breaking—some committees already examine the implementation of legislation, so why not broaden this to the implementation of non-legislative measures?

F. RISK

Outside the scope of our European studies, the Better Regulation Commission is exploring the concept of risk and regulation in the UK, but the message is equally applicable in the EU. We feel that there is a need for politicians and the general public to recognise that risk is a part of life and cannot be eliminated altogether by regulation—we should not pretend that it can. The usual response to tragic events is to regulate in an attempt to prevent the same thing happening again. Regulation can often be necessary, but can equally be wholly disproportionate to the risk concerned.

While we must do all we can to protect the vulnerable we cannot live our lives in cotton wool—we cannot regulate our way out of risk. I hope that our report on risk,[7] published on 18 October 2006, will spark a productive debate in Brussels.

G. PROGRESS MADE BY THE EU

Since the Better Regulation Commission turned its attention to EU law-making we have seen signs of progress. The concept of better regulation is still comparatively new in Brussels, but the right rhetoric is now being used and some better regulation procedures are being put in place, especially within the European Commission. However, many of these schemes need to be fully ingrained and we still need to see tangible results.

Over the past year or so several worthwhile projects have been introduced. In an attempt to improve the quality of proposals that come into force, the European Commission has published its revised Impact Assessment guidelines, providing officials with a good outline of the factors to consider when preparing policy. However, the quality of completed assessments varies hugely between Directorates General and standards must be raised.

[7] Better Regulation Commission, *Risk, Responsibility and Regulation—Whose Risk is it Anyway?* (2006), available at www.brc.gov.uk/publications/risk_report.asp.

The European Commission must install a stronger clearance procedure to ensure all proposals are accompanied by a robust impact assessment and to reject any that are not.

Last year the European Commission screened all proposals that had been pending for a significant amount of time. Over a third of these proposals have been withdrawn or returned for further Impact Assessment. This is exactly the sort of initiative we want to see installed as common practice. Proposals should be systematically rejected if the Impact Assessment is weak.

The European Commission's rolling programme of simplification is an ambitious project. But, as has already been mentioned, there needs to be a system in place to expedite these proposals. There is no point in creating a list of proposals for simplification without having the means of delivery.

The European Commission has initiated pilot projects to explore administrative burden reduction. I hope that these pilots will lead to the setting of ambitious targets and that the Commission will look to roll these projects out to other sectors.

You will notice that all of these initiatives are guided by the European Commission. It cannot deliver better regulation on its own. And although the Council and Parliament have agreed to several better regulation principles in the Inter-Institutional Agreement on Better Law-Making,[8] we have yet to see this agreement reinforced with the required degree of action. For example, it is alarming that the Council and Parliament can substantially amend proposals put forward by the Commission without revising the Impact Assessment. How can you justify intervention if you do not know what its effect will be? A systematic procedure must be adopted when amendments are made. This may slow down some proposals, but it is better to have legislation that is late but well prepared than legislation rushed through without proper analysis. The Parliament and Council must demonstrate their commitment to the better regulation agenda or it is doomed to fail. The Better Regulation Commission recognises that we need the combined efforts of all three EU institutions to succeed and we are actively engaging all three to get these ideas put into practice.

The EU has a real opportunity to deliver a better regulatory environment. The need for reform is recognised across the board and there is a growing groundswell of support from within the European Commission, amongst some Parliamentarians and from a growing band of Member States. Many worthy words have been written and statements made. But now is the time to deliver real and tangible outcomes and to start turning some of these words into action. We know the objectives—now let's make sure they are achieved.

[8] Above n3.

3

Better Regulation: Tensions aboard the Enterprise

ROBERT BALDWIN*

THE 'BETTER REGULATION' agenda is of central importance to the UK Government, to the OECD and to the European Union. It is, however, a policy thrust that is fraught with tensions and it is one that carries the potential to produce serious counterproductive effects. This chapter focuses on the UK and explores these tensions. It argues that fundamental philosophical difficulties need to be resolved if the better regulation movement is to bring desired outcomes rather than confusions, uncertainties and raised costs. It contends that the EU better regulation movement has to be re-thought in a similar manner.

First, however, it may be helpful to recapitulate on the development of the 'better regulation' movement in the UK.

A. THE RISE OF BETTER REGULATION

Better regulation rose from the ashes of the deregulatory policies of the Thatcher years. In that era there was an emphasis on the need to deregulate by freeing markets and to reduce administrative and legislative burdens.[1] In 1997, however, Tony Blair's Labour Government came into power and made the terminological and philosophical switch from 'deregulation' to 'better regulation'. Dr David Clark, Chancellor of the Duchy of Lancaster, introduced the initiative 'Better Regulation' in July 1997 and argued that good regulation was necessary and that only bad regulation was burdensome.

* London School of Economics and Political Science.

[1] See DTI, 'Lifting the Burden' (Cmnd 9571, London, TSO, 1985); 'Building Businesses Not Barriers' (Cmnd 9794, London, TSO, 1986); 'Releasing Enterprise' (Cm 512, London, TSO, 1988). See also R Baldwin, 'Is Better Regulation Smarter Regulation?' [2005] *Public Law* 485.

The Better Regulation Task Force (BRTF) was set up in 1997 and located at the Cabinet Office. The BRTF was an independent advisory body with a majority of members from the business sector. It was charged with taking the better regulation initiative forward and was given the express task of considering the needs of 'small businesses and ordinary people'. Within a year of its establishment, the BRTF published a set of principles of better regulation[2] (which were subsequently endorsed by the Government) and the Compliance Cost Assessment procedure was replaced by a more developed Regulatory Impact Assessment process. By 1999, the Better Regulation Unit had been renamed the Regulatory Impact Unit at the Cabinet Office, Regulatory Reform Ministers had been appointed in each department and a Ministerial Panel for Regulatory Accountability had been established to scrutinise the implications of regulatory plans and to improve the regulatory system both generally and within departments. Legislative support for improved regulation was provided with the passing of the Regulatory Reform Act 2001, and in the same year the Labour Government's commitment to better regulation was emphasised in its general election business manifesto. (By 2005 the Government had introduced the highly controversial Legislative and Regulatory Reform Bill which was designed 'to make it quicker and easier to tackle unnecessary or over-complicated regulation and to bring about a risk-based approach to regulation'.[3]) In 2004, the Government announced that the Prime Minister would lead the

[2] See now: Better Regulation Task Force, 'Principles of Good Regulation' (London, Cabinet Office, 2003). The principles are: proportionality, accountability, consistency, transparency and targeting. For other definitions of good or better regulation see, eg, Department of the Taoiseach, *Regulating Better* (Dublin, Department of the Taoiseach, 2004), available at www.betterregulation.ie—looking to: necessity; effectiveness; proportionality; transparency; accountability; consistency. See also the Australian Department of Industry, Tourism and Resources, *Regulatory Performance Indicators* (Canberra, DTITR, 1999) which measures whether regulation: confers net benefits; achieves objectives without duly restricting business; is transparent and fair; is accessible to business; creates a predictable regulatory environment; and ensures responsive consultation. The Australian Office of Regulation Review refers to the 7 features: minimum necessary to achieve objectives; not unduly prescriptive; accessible; transparent and accountable; integrated and consistent with other laws; communicated effectively; mindful of compliance burdens; and enforceable. See also S Argy and M Johnson, 'Mechanisms for Improving the Quality of Regulations', Australian Productivity Commission, Staff Working Paper, July 2003. For Canada see Treasury Board of Canada Secretariat, *Federal Regulatory Process Management Standards* (Ottawa, Treasury Board of Canada Secretariat, 1996). The World Bank view is set down in World Bank, *Doing Business in 2004: Understanding Regulation* (Washington, DC, World Bank, and OUP, 2004). See also OECD, *Recommendation on Improving the Quality of Government Regulation* (Paris, OECD, 1995). The OECD has added that good regulatory systems should be set within effective governmental mechanisms for managing, co-ordinating, reforming and updating regulation and ensuring that regulators and regulatory processes are transparent, non-discriminatory and efficiently applied: OECD, *Policy Recommendations on Regulatory Reform* (Paris, OECD, 1995). For other definitions of good or better regulation see Mandelkern, Final Report: Mandelkern Group on Better Regulation (Brussels, European Commission, 13 Nov 2002).

[3] The Bill completed the Committee stage in the House of Lords on 19 July 2006. For condemnation of the Bill see www.saveparliament.org.uk.

effort to reduce the 'red tape burden' by chairing the Panel for Regulatory Accountability; Sir Peter Gershon, Head of the Office of Government Commerce, reported on government efficiency and emphasised the 'desperate' need to rationalise regulation and reduce red tape; and the BRTF launched investigations into unnecessary regulation and 'regulatory creep' (the way regulation grows in unintended ways).

A year later, in March 2005, two important publications signalled a change in direction away from an emphasis on better regulation and towards reducing regulatory burdens. The Better Regulation Task Force (BRTF) released its report, *Regulation—Less is More*[4] and the Hampton Review on Reducing Administrative Burdens[5] was published. The *Less is More* Report recommended the adoption of new steps to reduce administrative burdens on business, and, notably, it urged the introduction of the Dutch approach of applying targets for reducing administrative costs to businesses and the imposition of a 'one in, one out' rule for regulation, whereby new regulations have to be matched by deregulatory measures.

The Hampton Review recommended that regulators as a whole should use comprehensive risk assessments to concentrate resources on the areas that need them most. The Hampton recommendations were endorsed by the Government in the March 2005 budget speech, and government departments have been told to set new targets for reducing (by fixed percentages) the information burdens they impose on businesses.

By 2006 the Better Regulation Commission had taken over the work of the BRTF and the Better Regulation Executive (BRE) had been established in the Cabinet Office with the tasks of reducing regulation and promoting the better regulation agenda in Europe.

Within the European Union, it was in the mid-1990s that the search for better quality regulation became systematic. A protocol attached to the Treaty of Amsterdam (1995) set out the principles of good regulation to be respected at the European level. Further co-ordinated action was stimulated when the 2000 Lisbon European Council emphasised the need to develop better regulation as a part of making the EU the most competitive and dynamic knowledge-based economy in the world. During that year, Ministers of Public Administration from across the EU met and established the high-level Mandelkern group to look at ways of improving regulatory quality. The final report of the Mandelkern group was produced in November 2001 and set down seven core principles of better regulation.[6] It advocated the implementation, to a stipulated timetable, of an Action Plan

[4] Better Regulation Task Force, *Regulation—Less is More* (London, Cabinet Office, 2005).

[5] P Hampton, *Reducing Administrative Burdens* (London, HM Treasury, 2005).

[6] Mandelkern, above n2. The 7 principles of better regulation were: necessity, proportionality, subsidiarity, transparency, accountability, accessibility and simplicity.

for Better Regulation based on core recommendations that included the suggestion that the Commission should produce a set of indicators of better regulation and a new system of impact assessment.

The Mandelkern recommendations were reinforced by the Commission's White Paper on European Governance,[7] which provided the foundations for the Commission's 2002 Action Plan for Better Regulation.[8] Key elements included: the introduction of a two-stage impact assessment process; a commitment to establish minimum standards for consultation; a programme of simplification of existing legislation; and the establishment of an internal better regulation network within the Commission, involving all the Directorates General.

A series of associated initiatives can be seen as part of the same better regulation movement. The Simpler Legislation for the Internal Market (SLIM) initiative was introduced fully in 1998 and was designed to reduce the burden of single market legislation. A European Business Test Panel was also established in 1998 in order to assess business responses to proposed legislative measures. In December 2001 the Commission established the office of the SME Envoy of the Commission in order to feed the concerns of small and medium enterprises more systematically into EU regulatory and other programmes.[9] The Commission committed itself gradually to carrying out impact assessments for all major legislative and policy initiatives.[10] It also committed to removing obsolete legal texts; rewriting legal texts to make them more understandable; developing more user-friendly access to consultations on community law; and to replacing old policy approaches with 'better adapted and proportional regulatory instruments'.[11] Other Communications have dealt with 'Better Lawmaking',[12] 'The Operating Framework for the European Regulatory Agencies',[13] 'Minimum Standards of Consultation'[14] and 'Better Regulation for Growth and Jobs in the European Union'.[15]

[7] COM(2001)428 Final.

[8] European Commission, Action Plan on Simplifying and Improving the Regulatory Environment, COM(2002)278 final.

[9] For arguments that the SME Envoy should play a stronger advocacy role for SMEs within the Commission see L Allio *et al.*, 'Achieving a New Regulatory Culture in the European Union: An Action Plan', European Policy Centre, Working Paper 10, Apr 2004, at 20.

[10] Communication on Impact Assessment, COM(2002)276.

[11] COM(2003)371 Final. See also Commission Staff Working Paper, 'Impact Assessment: Next Steps', SEC(2004)1377 (21 Oct 2004).

[12] COM(2002)275 (5 June 2002).

[13] COM(2002)718 final (11 Dec 2002).

[14] COM(2002)277 final.

[15] COM(2005)97 final: this Communication proposed 3 key action lines—promoting the design and application of better regulation tools at the EU level; working with Member States to ensure consistent application of better regulation principles throughout the EU; and reinforcing dialogue between regulators and stakeholders. In early 2004, the Irish, Dutch, Luxembourg and British Presidencies agreed a joint initiative to prioritise regulatory reform over the course of 2004–5: Irish Presidency, 'Joint Initiative on Regulatory Reform', letter of 26 Jan 2004.

On the broader international stage, the OECD has been the major proponent of better regulation. Over the last 20 years its concerns have moved focus away from deregulation, regulatory reform and 'regulatory management' towards 'better regulation' through 'regulatory policy'—government-wide policy that aims continuously to improve the quality of the regulatory environment.[16] In 1995 the OECD set out the first internationally accepted set of principles on ensuring regulatory quality, which included a 10-point OECD Reference Checklist for Regulatory Decision-making.[17] Since that time the OECD has sought to promote better regulation in member countries by devoting attention to regulatory policies, tools and institutions. Regulatory policies involve the systematic development and implementation of government-wide policies on how governments should use their regulatory powers.[18] Regulatory tools are devices aimed at improving regulatory design and implementation, and the leading tool is the Regulatory Impact Assessment (RIA). Implementation tools focus on improving the accountability and fairness with which regulation is applied and include processes of appeals and reviews. Regulatory institutions are bodies that take forward regulatory policy. They include regulatory oversight bodies within cabinets and the executive governments, and within parliaments. They also include independent regulators and other organisations contributing to better regulation.

The 1997 OECD report on *Regulatory Reform* linked regulatory policy with the broader government policy agenda. In its wake there followed a series of 'country reviews' of regulatory reform,[19] and the OECD has continued to drive forward an emphasis on regulatory policies as a part of broader governmental improvement. At the current time almost all OECD countries have adopted policies on regulatory quality and the OECD has produced a series of leading-edge publications on strategies for improving regulatory policies, tools and institutions.[20]

Back in the UK, it became clear in 2005–6 that a number of competing messages were emerging from the government. The 'better regulation', 'less is more' and 'risk-based' messages offered distinct prescriptions and gave rise to potentially severe tensions. Three such tensions should be noted.

[16] See OECD, *Regulating Policies in OECD Countries* (Paris, OECD, 2002).

[17] OECD, 'Improving the Quality of Government Regulation', OECD/GD(95)95 (Paris, OECD, 1995).

[18] See OECD, above n16, and OECD, *Regulatory Reform* (Paris, OECD, 1997). By late 2000, 24 out of 30 OECD counties had adopted government-wide regulatory policies. The U.K did so in 1985: OECD, above n16, at 40.

[19] The UK Review was carried out in 2001–2: see OECD, *United Kingdom: Challenges at the Cutting Edge* (Paris, OECD, 2002).

[20] Reports have, for instance, dealt with the following: *Choices of Policy Instruments* (1997); *Regulatory Reform* (1995, 1997); *Regulatory Impact Analyses: Best Practices in OECD Countries* (1997); *Voluntary Approaches for Environmental Protection* (1998, 1999); *Information, Consultation and Public Participation* (2000); *Regulatory Compliance* (2000); *Business Views on Red Tape* (2001); *Administrative Simplification in OECD Countries* (2003); *Regulatory Reform in the UK* (2002).

B. TENSIONS WITHIN THE BETTER REGULATION MESSAGE

A first message of the better regulation movement is that regulation can be improved by the application of a series of regulatory improvement tools[21]—tools that are conceived of with some consistency by UK, EU and OECD policy-makers. Within the vocabulary of the OECD there are seven main regulatory improvement tools:

- — Regulatory Impact Assessments (RIAs);
- — Consultations and Transparency;
- — Reducing Burdens and Red Tape: Administrative and Regulatory Simplification;
- — Enforcement Guidelines;
- — Alternatives to Traditional Regulation;
- — Sunset Provisions;
- — Regulatory Policies and Reviews.

It is, however, the RIA that is seen as the centrally important tool of regulatory improvement in the UK, the EU and the OECD.[22] In the UK, the RIA process involves an assessment of the impact of policy options and covers the purposes, risks, benefits and costs of the proposal. It also considers: how compliance will be obtained; expected impacts on small business; the views of affected parties; and the criteria to be used for monitoring and evaluating the regulatory activity at issue. The RIA process precedes a recommendation to ministers and, in carrying out the RIA, the alternatives to regulatory options for achieving policy objectives must be considered.

Since the RIA system was introduced, around 1,000 RIAs have been conducted at a current rate of about 160 to 200 per year.

RIAs are intended to inform decision-making, not to determine decisions or to substitute for political accountability. They are designed to encourage better regulation by the following means:[23]

- — Clarifying regulatory objectives and definitions of problems;
- — Ensuring that regulatory objectives are achieved effectively and at lowest cost by the strategy that maximises benefits over costs;
- — Identifying alternative options for achieving desired objectives;

[21] The roles of regulatory policies and institutions are not to be forgotten but they are not the focus of this chapter—which does see tools as of far greater significance.

[22] For OECD endorsement of the RIA see, eg, OECD, *Report on Regulatory Reform* (Paris, OECD, 1997); *Regulatory Policies in OECD Countries* (Paris, OECD, 2002). See also the Directors of the Better Regulation Group, European Commission Communication on Impact Assessment, COM(2002)276 final. On practice in the EU see *A Comparative Analysis of Regulatory Impact Assessment in Ten EU Countries—A Report Prepared for the EU Directors Better Regulation Group* (Dublin, May 2004).

[23] See Cabinet Office, *Better Policymaking: A Guide to Regulatory Impact Assessment* (London, Cabinet Office, 2003).

— Identifying the informational needs of policy-makers;
— Unpacking assumptions about compliance effects and real world (including business) impacts;
— Facilitating ministerial and parliamentary scrutiny of regulation;
— Increasing regulatory accountability and transparency;
— Furthering the BRTF's five principles for good regulation: transparency, proportionality, targeting, consistency and accountability.

When the BRE published its consultation on 'The Tools to Deliver Better Regulation' in July 2006 the only such tool to be discussed was the RIA—which was described by the Minister for the Cabinet as 'the cornerstone of our approach to better regulation'.[24] Little could have been done to make the primacy of this tool plainer. The problem with the RIA, however, is that the processes that it involves may be in tension with the requirements of 'better' regulation—if better regulation is seen as lighter consistently with 'smarter' regulation.[25]

Here it is necessary to pause in order to outline the requirements of 'smart' regulation.[26] Proponents of 'smart' regulation have argued convincingly that designing good regulatory systems demands a central focus on how best to combine different institutions and techniques.[27] Smart regulation thus moves beyond state controls and looks to mixes of control methods, as applied not merely by public bodies but by other institutions and actors including trade associations, pressure groups, corporations and even individuals. It advocates deploying the combination of instruments that will be most appropriate in a given setting and designing strategies that mix instruments and institutional actors to optimal effect.[28]

The messages of 'better' and 'smart' regulation appear at first glance to be consistent. If, however, we investigate the capacity of the current better

[24] See Hilary Armstrong at 4 of Better Regulation Executive, *The Tools to Deliver Better Regulation* (London, Better Regulation Executive, 2006).

[25] This section draws on R Baldwin, 'Is Better Regulation Smarter Regulation?' [2005] *Public Law* 485.

[26] On 'smart' regulation see N Gunningham and P Grabosky, *Smart Regulation* (Oxford, OUP, 1998). For other discussions of mixed public and private, or 'combined', regimes of regulation see, eg, D Osborne and T Gaebler, *Reinventing Government* (Boston, Mass, Addison-Wesley, 1992); I Ayres and J Braithwaite, *Responsive Regulation* (Oxford, OUP, 1992); C Sunstein, 'Paradoxes of the Regulatory State' (1990) 57 *University of Chicago Law Review* 407; C Sunstein, *After the Rights Revolution* (Cambridge, Mass, Harvard University Press, 1990); C Parker, *The Open Corporation* (Cambridge: Cambridge University Press 2002); G Burchell, C Gordon and P Miller (eds), *The Foucault Effect: Studies in Governmentality* (Chicago, Ill, University of Chicago Press, 1991); J Black, 'Dencentring Regulation: The Role of Regulation in a Post-regulatory World' [2001] *Current Legal Problems* 103; J Black, 'Enrolling Actors in Regulatory Processes' [2003] *Public Law* 62; M Sparrow, *The Regulatory Craft* (Washington, DC, Brookings Institution Press, 2000). On the British regulatory state as a 'smart state' see M Moran, *The British Regulatory State* (Oxford, OUP, 2003), at 21–6.

[27] Gunningham and Grabosky, above n26, ch 6.

[28] *Ibid*, at 91.

regulation movement to deliver smart regulation on the ground, we see that the route to delivery is not unproblematic. Here it is useful to measure the better regulation movement against the five core principles for smart regulatory design.[29] These principles can be summarised as follows:

- — Prefer policy mixes incorporating a broader range of instruments and institutions.
- — Prefer less interventionist measures.
- — Ascend a dynamic instrument pyramid to the extent necessary to achieve policy goals.[30]
- — Empower participants which are in the best position to act as surrogate regulators.
- — Maximise opportunities for win-win outcomes.[31]

Regarding the first principle, the better regulation movement might be expected to perform well since it repeatedly emphasises the need to consider alternative, more imaginative, ways of regulating.[32] In practice, however, a number of factors may militate against its delivery of imaginative regulation. First, the RIA occupies a central place in 'better regulation' but the evidence is that RIA processes are not highly effective in leading policy-makers to consider alternative ways of regulating. RIA processes, moreover, are more attuned to measuring the effects of traditional 'command' systems of control than 'alternative' methods, and this may positively discourage the canvassing of more imaginative regulatory strategies—especially those 'softer' strategies involving voluntary and incentive-driven controls where predicting effects (and hence calculating costs and benefits) is extremely difficult. Secondly, smart regulation is about cumulative regulatory effects and the coordination of regulatory systems with widely varying natures. RIA processes, however, are best suited to looking at the costs and benefits associated with a single, given, regulatory instrument rather than

[29] See *ibid*, at 387–422.

[30] The idea here is that regulation should be responsive and escalate in severity as necessary to achieve compliance: I Ayres and J Braithwaite (in *Responsive Regulation* (Oxford, OUP, 1992)) are concerned with state and business relationships, but Gunningham and Grabosky argue for escalating approaches on 3 planes—not merely one based on state controls but also one founded on commercial and non-commercial quasi-regulation and another on corporate self-regulation. These planes make up the 3 sides of their pyramid: see Gunningham and Grabosky, above n26, at 397–9.

[31] A win-win outcome is where higher levels of socially desirable behaviour produce higher profits: see N Gunningham, 'Beyond Compliance: Management of Environmental Risk' in B Boer *et al* (eds), *Environmental Outlook* (Sydney, ACEL Federation Press, 1994); ME Porter and C Van der Linde, 'Green and Competitive' (1995) 73(5) *Harvard Business Review* 120–33; JC Robinson, 'The Impact of Environmental and Occupational Health Regulation on Productivity Growth in US Manufacturing' (1995) 12 *Yale Journal of Regulation* 388.

[32] See, eg, BRTF, *Imaginative Thinking for Better Regulation* (London, Cabinet Office, 2003); BRTF, *Alternatives to State Regulation* (London, Cabinet Office, 2000). See also OECD, *Regulatory Policies in OECD Countries* (Paris, OECD, 2002), at 51–7.

combinations of approaches. They are most attuned to the 'single strategy.'[33] Those officials who are charged to carry out RIAs would find it very difficult to calculate the costs and benefits of a simultaneously acting combination of very different regulatory strategies and institutions. It would, for instance, be extremely hard for proponents of a combination of, say, state, corporate and trade association laws, codes and guidelines to predict how all the relevant actors will draft, design and apply their different control strategies. This would make calculations of costs and benefits a matter of heroic guesswork and the ensuing uncertainties would undermine the essential value of the RIA. Smart regulation involves too many variables, estimates and judgements to lend itself to the RIA process.

Bureaucratic incentives should also be borne in mind. An official who is contemplating regulating and knows that the RIA process has to be undertaken will experience little impetus to propose complex combinations of regulatory institutions and strategies with all the attendant predictive and calculative difficulties. Rather than aim for a 'smart' form of regulation, he or she will incline towards a simpler regime that can be predicted to pass an RIA. Such bureaucratic incentives may, moreover, militate against the application of a high level of 'regulatory craft' as advocated by Malcolm Sparrow.[34] Such craft calls for the placing of problem-solving at the centre of regulatory design.[35] Problems, when identified, are on this view to be responded to with a variety of strategies in a manner consistent with smart regulation.[36] For an official who faces a potential RIA, however, the incentive to adopt a problem-centred approach may be weak, not merely because this would require the evaluation of costs and benefits regarding a variety of institutions and strategies, but also because it may demand an unpacking of the way that a host of existing regulatory regimes impinges on a problem and an examination, within the RIA process, of potential ways to reshape and re-deploy those regimes in combination with any new regulations.[37] The political and bureaucratic implications would be daunting—the proponent of the RIA would often be questioning the way that numbers of established regulators go about their jobs in order to evaluate their proposed regulation. A far more attractive proposition will be to take any existing controls as givens and consider whether the addition of a new regulation will pass a cost-benefit test.[38] The consideration of alternatives is liable, accordingly,

33 See Gunningham and Grabosky, above n26, at 388.

34 See Sparrow, above n26.

35 *Ibid*, ch 9.

36 See Gunningham and Grabosky, above n26; also Black (2003), above n26 on enrolling a variety of regulatory actors.

37 See Sparrow, above n26, at 310.

38 The Cabinet Office Guide, *Better Policy Making: A Guide to Regulatory Impact Analysis* (London, Cabinet Office, 2003). Ch 2 focuses on the effects of the new regulation at issue and takes existing regulations as givens.

to be straitjacketed by existing regulatory frameworks. Overall, then, if RIA processes are retained at the centre of better regulation, they may not be conducive to smarter regulation as encapsulated by its first principle.

The second principle of smart regulation holds that less interventionist measures should be preferred. Again, it might be anticipated that the 'better regulation' approaches will encourage less prescriptive, less coercive modes of influence. The record of the RIA procedures, however, does not demonstrate that they are well attuned to either the measurement or the consideration of alternative, less interventionist controls. Smart regulation, moreover, demands that attention be paid to enforcement strategy, not merely the formal design of regulatory laws.[39] It is, after all, how a regulatory power is used on the ground that tends to determine its essential character. Here again, however, the RIA process draws attention away from how regulations are applied in practice. First, it is the case (as was noted above) that very many RIAs do not attend to implementation and enforcement issues at all well.[40] Secondly, there are structural reasons why RIAs cannot be expected to come to grips with enforcement strategy in a routinely well-informed manner—RIAs tend to focus *ex ante* on the general design of regulation, and it may be impossible to predict how any regulator or set of regulatory bodies will go about deploying the powers that they are to be given in a proposed regulation.

Smart regulation's third principle urges that 'responsive' strategies of regulation should be adopted and should be employed across mixes of regulatory strategies—as applied by numbers of different institutions and instruments. Smart regulation thus holds out the possibility of escalating degrees of coercion through the interaction of different but complementary instruments and parties.[41] It is difficult, however, to argue that 'better regulation' approaches sit easily alongside this principle. The RIA process, as noted, encounters difficulties in dealing with either questions of enforcement or 'combined' strategies of regulation. These difficulties are likely to be compounded by attempts to evaluate incremental and coordinated escalations up the three sides of a strategic pyramid that reflect the combined use of quasi-regulatory and corporate self-regulatory as well as state controls.[42]

Smart regulation, fourthly, advocates the empowerment of those participants who are in the best position to act as surrogate regulators. This accordingly favours using the influence of quasi-regulators, such as industry associations and pressure groups where appropriate. Here again, the better regulation toolkit might be expected to prompt consideration of alternative regulatory

[39] On the centrality of enforcement and the 'practice of regulation' see Sparrow, above n26, at 3–7.

[40] See National Audit Office, 'Evaluation of Regulatory Impact Assessments', 2005–06 HC 1305 Session 2005–06 (June 2006), at 4.

[41] See Gunningham and Grabosky, above n26, at 400.

[42] On the need to integrate different levels of action from different sides of the pyramid (eg, non-punitive state controls with more severe quasi-regulatory and self-regulatory controls) see Gunningham and Grabosky, above n26, at 398–401.

methods. It may fail, for reasons discussed above, however, to come to grips with 'combined' regulation where quasi-regulatory functions have to be evaluated alongside other regimes. This suggests that it is one thing to develop a set of regulatory improvement tools, but another to use those tools harmoniously. In practice the application of the toolkit may be hindered by tensions between different tools—as between the RIA tool and the consideration of alternatives. The better regulation toolkit, moreover, may fail to empower quasi-regulators optimally for cultural and political reasons—regulators and politicians may produce 'single solution' proposals because, for instance, they see a problem in traditional ways due to their prior commitments to certain styles of control or because important interests distrust non-traditional regulatory methods. It may also be the case that the existence of a toolkit for evaluating regulatory strategies will not necessarily drive the use of surrogate regulators and produce 'smarter' proposals because the messages to be gleaned from, say, RIA processes may be poorly heeded within the political and administrative systems that drive policies—a matter to be returned to below.

Yet another reason why 'better' regulation may be slow to make best use of surrogate regulators and to come to grips with 'combined' sets of controls is that empowering quasi-regulators or making use of corporate self-regulatory controls within combined regimes of control may require an incremental approach to regulatory design in which key actors negotiate and adjust the roles of different controlling institutions and influences over behaviour. This kind of regulation—as is envisaged by smart regulatory theory—involves a reflexive, dynamic approach in which regulatory strategies are constantly revised and 'tuned' to changes in circumstances, preferences and so on. Such ongoing processes are not amenable to evaluations in a 'one-shot' policy-making process. Issues will have to be revisited as different control systems adjust to each other. Those control systems, moreover, will have to deal collectively with changes. This can be portrayed as a process of continuous regulatory coordination and change, rather than the operation of a single fixed design. The better regulation toolkit does envisage the use of a variety of regulatory controls, but it is difficult to see how ongoing regulatory coordination, with all its flexibilities, can be tested in advance by an RIA process as if it is a static single-shot system.

The final principle of smart regulation suggests that opportunities for win-win outcomes should be maximised—so that, for instance, corporations can behave more responsibly and maximise profits at the same time.[43]

[43] On win-win outcomes see ME Porter and C Van Der Linde, 'Towards a New Conception of the Environment-Competitiveness Relationships' (1995) 9 *Journal of Economic Perspectives* 97; J Gobert and M Punch, *Rethinking Corporate Crime* (London, Butterworths, 2003), at 342–5. It is arguable that the main advance on this front is to be made by providing information to firms on how to achieve such outcomes: see Gunningham and Grabosky, above n26, at 416–8. On small business estimates that information is one of the top potential drivers of compliance see R Baldwin, *Better Regulation: Is It Better for Business?* (London, Federation of Small Businesses, 2004).

Win-win outcomes, however, may not always be possible and, in certain circumstances, there are tensions between corporate profit-seeking and some regulatory objectives.[44] In practice, therefore, regulators will need to identify areas and issues that will lend themselves to win-win outcomes if certain stimuli are applied. The targeting of regulatory approaches will, accordingly, be central to success. Regulators of a variety of kinds will have to deploy a wide range of strategies and aim these at different kinds and sizes of enterprise, as well as activities, in order to maximise win-win outcomes. This, again, is exactly the sort of flexible and adaptive regulatory strategy that is extremely difficult to set out and evaluate in advance according to the RIA-centred better regulation toolkit as now encountered.

For the above reasons, it can be contended that better regulation exists at tension with the prescriptions of smarter regulation. A further tension within the notion of 'better' regulation should, however, also be noted. This issue is prompted when asking the question: 'better for whom?'. It is clear from field research that 'better' regulation is conceived of differently by different interests—such as by small and by large businesses.[45] The former, for instance, put an especially high premium on regulatory systems that pay attention to their special sensitivities to certain regulatory effects.[46] Potential dangers of RIA processes are that, as with all cost-benefit analyses, they skew calculations in favour of those parties who benefit from the existing distribution of wealth,[47] and they place emphasis on overall costs and benefits rather than distributional issues—and, accordingly, underplay the question of who bears the costs and who enjoys the benefits. What may be better regulation for large enterprises or urban consumers of services may not be better regulation for small enterprises or rural consumers.

C. TENSIONS BETWEEN 'BETTER', 'LESS IS MORE' AND 'RISK-BASED' APPROACHES

A second set of tensions exists between the messages of the 'better', 'less is more' and 'risk-based' approaches to regulation. The publication of the *Less is More*[48] report in 2005 marked, as noted above, a change in emphasis within UK government—away from the pursuit of better regulation and towards less regulation through the imposition of lower costs on business.

[44] See R Baldwin, 'The New Punitive Regulation' (2004) 67 *MLR* 351.

[45] See Baldwin, above n43. On the meanings of 'good' and 'better' regulation see the references above at n2.

[46] Eg, small businesses find that regulation diverts managerial attention and time away from wealth creation in a far more acute manner than is the case with large enterprises: see Baldwin above n43.

[47] See GR Baldwin and CG Veljanovski, 'Regulation by Cost-Benefit Analysis' (1984) 62 *Public Administration* 51.

[48] Better Regulation Task Force, *Regulation—Less is More* (London, Cabinet Office, 2005).

Regulators were charged to use the Standard Cost Model (SCM) to assess the costs that its regulations place on businesses and to devise ways to meet reduction targets—expressed as percentage decreases in those costs.[49] The SCM estimates the costs of completing activities that are driven by regulation on the basis of a few basic cost parameters—so that the cost per activity (or data requirement) is the product of price (wage costs plus overheads/costs for external services), time (the time taken to complete the activity) and quantity (the population of businesses affected and the frequency of the requirement per year).

The emphasis, it is to be noted, rests on the reduction of administrative costs (ie, information-providing costs) rather than policy costs (ie, the costs of carrying out the required action, such as fitting the guards or filters that control safety or pollution). Such an approach to burdens reduction, argues the SCM Network, brings the advantages of: showing how changes in information requirements will affect costs; identifying parts of legislation that are particularly burdensome for business; and assisting in the calculation of cumulative cost burdens.[50]

An initial difficulty with the SCM approach is that it presupposes that it is possible to separate out policy costs from administrative costs. A second problem is identifying those costs that are imposed by a regulatory requirement and go beyond those costs that will be incurred by competent management in the ordinary course of business. These are issues that involve contentious assumptions and combine to produce the danger that, if industry is asked to assess the cost of administrative burdens (as is the case), they will tend to conflate policy and administrative, as well as regulatory and managerial, costs. The effect will be grossly to exaggerate both the costs of informational burdens and the potential gains to be made by removing a regulation. This is likely to occur in the following way:

> If a business is asked to state what it costs to tell the regulator how often it changes the filters on a ventilation system, it is liable to look to the staff time and other resources spent in keeping records. Such costs are considerably more than those of e-mailing the records to the regulator. Let us suppose the record keeping costs are £5,000 a year and the e-mailing costs £20 per year. The burden-cutting saving is liable to be calculated at £5,020 per year.
>
> In fact the real saving is only £20 because the record keeping needs to be carried out as part of routine management. If, moreover, the obligation to supply the records is removed (in order to achieve the hoped-for £5,020 saving) the regulator will have to undertake investigations to uncover the relevant data. Those investigations will cost considerably more than £20.

[49] By 2006 the Prime Minister had announced 25% administrative burdens reductions targets for the DTI, Defra and HSE and the DTI had published plans to deliver annual business savings of around £200 million a year: Cabinet Office, 'Update on the Implementation of Less is More' (July 2006).

[50] See SCM Network website at www.administrative-burdens.com/.

Not only is the SCM fraught with difficulty but it produces problems for regulators whose activities and proposals stand to be evaluated by means of RIAs. The SCM offers a particular approach to the calculation of costs, but there are dangers. The criteria and assumptions employed in the SCM may not always correspond to those that are used when the actual cost burdens are calculated through the RIA process. A dilemma arises—do regulators use 'notional' costings as demanded by the SCM or do they operate with the costings approaches that they have developed on their particular ground. If they adopt the former approach, the RIA may prove the poorer for it—especially when the SCM criteria are perceived as in need of adjustment. If they take the latter course, there is likely to emerge a divergence between SCM and 'real' costings methods and results.

A further tension between the RIA and the burdens reducing processes may arise out of the Government's desires (a) to reduce quite significantly the burdens of supplying information that regulators impose on it and (b) to ensure that regulators target their enforcement activities more precisely in order to take up less business time.

The problems are, first, that the targeting of enforcement demands that inspections and other actions are based on intelligence and, secondly, that if the obligations of businesses to supply information to regulators are reduced, it is increasingly difficult for regulators to engage in targeting without generating intelligence independently. Such independent generation of data may, of course, prove hugely expensive for regulators—indeed far more expensive for them than for the businesses that they are controlling (which may have the information quite readily to hand).

This is especially likely to prove an issue when, in the wake of the Hampton Review, regulators are expected to target their enforcement actions at those businesses or service providers which pose greatest risks. Risk-based systems are built on risk analyses, which are founded, in turn, on the collection of quantities of good data.

D. TENSIONS BETWEEN BETTER REGULATION AND THE POLICY PROCESS

A third serious tension lies between the prescriptions of the RIA and the realities of normal governmental policy processes. As a result, a key challenge presented to the proponents of RIAs is that of locating the RIAs within the policy process. On this front, a first issue is whether an RIA can be carried out to a high technical standard. The UK holds itself out to be a world leader in carrying out RIAs, but it appears that the current fit between the RIA and policy processes is not conducive to the production of high quality RIAs. A succession of reports from the National Audit Office (NAO) and the British Chambers of Commerce (BCC) have revealed a number of weaknesses. The National Audit Office (NAO) looked at 23 test case RIAs in 2001[51] and reported on 10 further sample RIAs in 2004.[52] The NAO revealed in 2004 that only half the RIAs examined included 'a reasonably clear statement of objectives' and seven out of 10 did not consider any option for regulation other than the one preferred by the department. None of the 10 RIAs considered what would happen in the absence of the regulation. All acknowledged a level of uncertainty about the data that were used for estimates, but such uncertainties were not always reflected in the cost and benefit figures used, which presented single point estimates rather than ranges. Only one out of 10 gave the results of sensitivity tests, and only three out of the 10 contained quantified estimates of benefits (often no market for benefits existed, making quantification difficult). Most RIAs, accordingly, did not offer a quantified comparison of expected costs and benefits. As for considering the likely effects of regulations on the ground, only half of the sample RIAs considered enforcement and sanctioning effects. Most RIAs, moreover, described how the regulation would be monitored, but 'often in a very brief and vague way', and only four stated that there would be a formal review to evaluate the success of the regulation. The NAO's 2005–6 evaluation of RIAs[53] stated that only two out of 12 RIAs analysed levels of compliance well and the same report produced the finding that:

> The purpose of RIAs is not always understood; there is a lack of clarity in the presentation of the analysis; and persistent weaknesses in the assessments.[54]

The NAO's findings were broadly in line with, though perhaps less critical than, the British Chambers of Commerce (BCC) studies of 2003 and 2004 which looked respectively at 499 and 167 RIAs produced by the government in the two periods studied (1998–2002 and 2002–3).[55] The BCC studies noted a series of problems with RIAs and concluded that ministerial statements that benefits justified costs were not in general supported by the evidence in the RIAs. Some departments, indeed, were under-resourced or badly managed for conducting RIAs. On choice of regulatory strategy, the BCC found that the option of not regulating was considered in only a minority of cases (11 per cent in 1998–2002 and 23 per cent in 2002–3) and less than half of RIAs (44 per cent) quantified all the options considered. RIAs are supposed to pay acute attention to business (and especially

[51] See National Audit Office, 'Better Regulation: Making Better Use of Regulatory Impact Assessments', 2001–02 HC 329, Session 2001–02 (Nov 2001).

[52] See National Audit Office, 'Evaluation of Regulatory Impact Assessments Compendium Report', 2003–04 HC 358, Session 2003–04 (Mar 2004).

[53] NAO, above n40.

[54] *Ibid*, at 2.

[55] See T Ambler, F Chittenden and M Shamutkova, *Do Regulators Play By the Rules?* (London, BCC, 2003) and T Ambler, F Chittenden and M Obodovski, *Are Regulators Raising Their Game?* (London, BCC, 2004).

SME) compliance costs, but the BCC reported that costs for business were quantified in only 23 per cent of RIAs and a quarter of RIAs did not consider effects on SMEs at all. A substantial minority of RIAs contained little factual data about consequential costs and benefits and 'scant attention' was given to 'sunset' clauses or to subsequent monitoring or evaluation. Nor was the BCC impressed by new efforts to improve RIAs—it found that the RIA process showed little recent evidence of improvement.[56]

Such criticisms suggest prima facie that the way that RIA processes are accommodated within policy-making procedures is not conducive to technically impressive assessments. Clearly there is room to improve the technical quality of RIAs, and such improvements may be necessary if RIAs are to lead to better regulation. It would be a mistake, however, to assume that technical improvements in RIAs will be sufficient to improve regulation. Those RIAs would still have to be located within legislative and regulatory policy-making processes in a manner that would allow them to influence emergent laws and policies. There are, however, a number of reasons why RIAs tend to prove less influential than might at first be supposed.

Governments, for instance, may be committed to certain regulatory steps and strategies for ideological reasons or because of manifesto commitments or because a political settlement has been made with various interests. They will, accordingly, not be minded to pay too much attention to RIAs that send contradictory signals. Ministers, for example, tend to be predisposed towards legislative solutions and, if they have promised to legislate in order to address a problem, they will not respond enthusiastically to RIAs that propose non-legislative solutions. The costs and benefits of regulation, moreover, tend to be difficult to quantify[57] and the perceived 'softness' of RIAs may reduce their impact on the policy or legislative process. This is liable to be the case especially where costs and benefits can be calculated only on the basis of guesses about the use that various regulatory actors will make of their powers or about the strategies that will be deployed to apply regulatory rules. In 2006 the NAO stated that weaknesses in assessments meant that 'RIAs are only occasionally used to challenge the need for regulation and influence policy decisions'.[58]

[56] The European Commission has, for its part, carried out impact assessments (in qualified form) since the Business Impact Assessment system was introduced in 1986. European impact assessments have, however, possessed many shortcomings. These were analysed between 2000 and 2002 and a new Impact Assessment system was outlined by the Communication on Impact Assessment of 5 June 2002. This formed part of the Better Regulation Action Plan and aimed to analyse the effects of European regulatory proposals on business in order to promote competitiveness, innovation and growth. The first year for carrying out the new Impact Assessment process was 2003, and so it is early to draw conclusions on its performance. A review by the European Policy Centre has, however, suggested that only 30% of proposals have been assessed and that there are a number of general failings, notably: to list alternatives; to comment on or quantify impacts; and to identify data gaps.

[57] The RIA relating to the Employment Act 2002, for instance, noted that 'a great many assumptions' had to be made in its formulation.

[58] NAO, above n40, at 2.

It is also frequently the case that the full nature of the regulatory proposal is unclear from any given item of legislation (eg a framework Act) because the real substance will follow in secondary legislation. The effect will be that regulation escapes a good deal of parliamentary and RIA scrutiny. It might be responded that the secondary legislation will, in all likelihood, be RIA-tested in its own right at a later date, but this may be no complete answer to the point. The framework regulatory strategy within which that secondary legislation is to operate will in most instances be established by the primary legislation that has 'escaped' RIA influence. Many key regulatory issues will already have been decided by the time the 'secondary' RIA is carried out.

Another concern is that even when the secondary legislation is RIA-tested, it may be extremely difficult to assess the substance of a regulatory proposal because its nature will still depend on the use that will be made of the delegated powers involved. Additionally, of course, secondary legislation will not be debated in Parliament in the way that primary legislation is,[59] and any RIA-based messages are, accordingly, all the less likely to influence decisions in the legislature. A further problem that arises in the legislative process is that amendments of laws and rules may be introduced at a late stage in the progression of legislation, and the proposals involved may, for that reason alone, escape RIA attention.

The culture of governmental policy-making may itself prove resistant to the influential use of RIAs. This has been a special concern to the NAO, which found in 2006 that RIAs were often seen by officials as a bureaucratic task rather than being integral to the process of policy-making. The NAO, accordingly, recommended that a number of steps would have to be taken to change that culture—notably:[60]

— It should be made make clear to policy-makers that the RIA is necessary and that the level of effort put in to preparing the RIA reflects its importance.
— Policy-makers should start impact assessment early and use the RIA to project-manage the decision-making process.
— Policy-makers should make greater and earlier use of departmental expertise and, as far as possible, embed expertise into policy teams.

Cultural changes, however, are more easily pleaded for than achieved. The recommendation that RIAs should be used earlier in the policy process than they presently are may, for instance, prove more difficult to implement than might be assumed. A real problem in some areas may arise from tension between the politics of a process and the RIA principles. Within the RIA process policy-makers are supposed to consider and compare the array of regulatory routes to a policy objective, but in the real world a proposal may

[59] See generally R Baldwin, *Rules and Government* (Oxford, OUP, 1995), ch.4.
[60] NAO, above n40, at para 13.

be the product of a process of political negotiation. It arises when compromises and concessions have been made between different interests and, as such, it may be the only feasible option politically.

To compare this proposal with an array of alternatives via the RIA procedure may be to compare a live horse with a number of dead non-runners. (Such a comparison is also likely to be seen by relevant policy-makers as an exercise too far.) This is not to say that RIAs have no value—it is, however, to point out that there may be strict limits to the extent to which RIA processes can be fully embedded within policy processes so that they can influence political decision-making.

E. RE-THINKING THE PHILOSOPHY—TOWARDS REVIEW

The above discussion raises some worrying points, notably that 'better' regulation, as pursued via RIAs, may not produce 'smarter' regulation or lead to lighter touch regimes of control; that it may be at tension with desires for lower information burdens on business and with the Standard Cost Model approach; and that it may impact on policy and legislative processes far less than many of its proponents might imagine.

The way forward is, as indicated, not to focus simply on carrying out RIAs in a technically superior manner. Nor is it to settle for embedding the RIA within the policy-making process more fully. Such steps would not ensure that RIAs would impact on legislative processes in a satisfactory manner or that they would lead to smarter regulation. This is why the Better Regulation Executive's 2006 report, *The Tools to Deliver Better Regulation*, is excessively narrow in its approach to improving RIAs and their impact. The report's 'key' recommendations are staggeringly modest in highlighting the need to: take steps to make RIAs more transparent; shorten the RIA guidance; and have RIAs signed off by Chief Economists as well as Ministers.

What needs to be done is to rethink the better regulation philosophy as a whole. At present, the centrality of the RIA means that better regulation is sought to be achieved by making predictions about the future effects of regulatory regimes, attaching costs and benefit to these, and attempting to convince policy-makers and legislators that they should give weight to what is often perceived of as so much guesswork. (Biases against smarter regulatory methods tend to be omitted from consideration.)

The key change has to involve a shift away from the predictive philosophy and towards one that gives centrality of place to review—a process that involves both evaluation and modification. Assumptions of comprehensive rationality have to give way to incrementalist strategies[61] so that it is

[61] On comprehensive rationality versus incrementalism see, eg, Y Dror, 'Muddling Through: Science or Inertia' (1964) 24 *Public Administration Review* 153; D Braybrooke and C Lindblom, *A Strategy of Decision* (New York, Free Press of Glencoe, 1963).

accepted that regulatory systems cannot be designed *ex ante* (on the basis of ever more sophisticated analyses) and left alone—that steps must be taken, first, to measure whether regulatory systems are working as well as they can (and better than alternatives) and, secondly, to bring about changes in regulatory strategy in order to effect improvements.

It might be argued from within the BRE and OECD that a movement 'from design to review' has already been instituted. It is true that the UK Government, like the OECD, has expressed a commitment to regulatory reviews.[62] The ongoing challenge, however, is to give new emphasis to that review and adjustment process so that, within government, it is seen as more important than design by RIA. Embedding a review philosophy also means that regulatory policy-makers will have to come to grips with the difficulties of post-implementation evaluation and adjustment.

These problems should not be understated. A first difficulty is that reviews and changes may create regulatory uncertainties and trigger adaptation costs. Some regulatory systems may be adjustable at low cost, but others may be difficult to change because high uncertainty and high adjustment costs are involved. All regulators will, accordingly, have to make context-specific judgements about the trade-off between improvements in regulation and the uncertainty costs involved in regime adjustments.

A second problem is that evaluating regulatory performance is extremely difficult technically, not least because formulations of objectives will be contentious, appropriate benchmarks will be difficult to identify and regulatory objectives are liable to change over time.[63] Regulatory statutes tend to allocate large discretions and mandates that are unclear—this means that little legislative guidance on yardsticks can be assumed.

Nor, thirdly, will a move from design to review allow us completely to escape the difficulties of assessing the 'regulatory mixes' that were discussed above in looking at 'smart' regulation. In multi-actor, multi-strategy regimes, attributions of responsibility will be far more difficult to make

[62] Government policy since June 2001 has required departments to review the impact of major pieces of regulation within 3 years of implementation: OECD, *UK Challenges at the Cutting Edge* (Paris, OECD, 2002), at 34. The BRTF recommended post-implementation review in Apr 2000 (BRTF, *Helping Small Firms Cope with Regulation* (London, Cabinet Office, 2000)) but the revised RIA Guidance of 2003 limits systematic reviews to major pieces of legislation and issues only a general prescription: 'say how the policy will be monitored and evaluated/reviewed'. Research for the BCC, as noted, found that this aspect of the guidance was given 'scant' attention in RIAs (BCC (2004), above n55). On the OECD view that *ex post* evaluation of regulatory policies, tools and institutions is of value: see OECD, *UK Challenges at the Cutting Edge* (Paris, OECD, 2002), at 115–6. On the case for revisiting regulatory systems see G Mather and F Vibert, *Reducing the Regulatory Burden* (London, European Policy Forum, 2004).

[63] For a review of benchmarks on regulatory quality see University of Bradford, Centre for European Studies, *Interim Report on Indicators of Regulatory Quality* (Brussels, European Commission, DG Enterprise, 9 May 2004), available at www.bradford.ac.uk/irq; CM Radaelli, Indicators of Regulatory Quality (Brussels, European Commission, 25 Jan 2005).

than in simpler regimes. Other evaluative problems will be severe when mixes are involved. The application of performance measures always produces a danger of counter-productive effects,[64] but in mixed regulatory regimes such effects may be particularly difficult to assess because they will be experienced by a variety of actors in quite different ways. Similarly, the complexity of smart regimes makes it difficult both to evaluate the case for alternative mixes of controls and to bring about adjustments in numbers of institutions and rule systems. What can be said, however, is that evaluations of and adjustments to regulatory mixes, though never simple, will be far easier to carry out in an *ex post* incremental manner than through an *ex ante* design approach.

F. CONCLUSIONS

With these caveats in mind, it can be reasserted that a movement from a philosophy of design to one of regulatory review can be expected to hold out a far more realistic prospect of better regulation than current approaches that give centrality of place to the predictive RIA. Review processes make advancements towards smarter methods of control more realistic. They give greater emphasis to the measurement of results—and improve accountability and transparency. They offer superior ways to evaluate the quality and reliability of regulatory data and they allow policy-making cultures to be reshaped over time rather than presupposing that they can be overridden in a single operation.

At the level of UK regulation, the case for the suggested change in better regulation philosophy seems strong. It should not involve an abandoning of the RIA process or an ending of attempts to improve RIAs and embed them within policy-making practices. A review philosophy would retain such efforts but would not put all eggs in the RIA, or design, basket. The RIA would be seen as the start of the regulatory assessment process rather than the end, and the real locus for shaping regulation would become the review stage.

Do such arguments apply to better regulation at the EU level as much as to domestic government? Arguably they have all the more force since EU regulation usually involves a process of delegation to Member States

[64] On perverse effects see, eg, NAO, *Good Practice in Performance Reporting in Executive Agencies and Non-Departmental Public Bodies* (London, NAO, 2000), para 11; HM Treasury, *Executive Agencies: A Guide to Setting Targets and Measuring Performance* (London, HMSO, 1992); J Sandbach, 'Performance Indicators Could Damage Universities' Health' [1987] *Public Finance and Accountancy* 19; G Bouckaert, 'Improving Performance Measurement' in A Halachmi and G Bouckaert (eds), *The Enduring Challenges of Public Management* (San Francisco, Cal, Jossey-Bass, 1995); C Pollitt, 'Performance Indicators: Root and Branch' in M Cave, M Kogan and R Smith (eds), *Output and Performance Measurement in Government* (London, Jessica Kingsley, 1990).

through the use of directives. This process makes the difficulties of quantifying the anticipated costs and benefits of a regulatory proposal a degree more difficult than is the case in domestic legislation. Even the simplest EU instruction to institute a command and control regime (ie, with no 'mix' of regulatory methods) might demand that those charged to undertake an RIA should make heroic assumptions about the sorts of powers and sub-powers that might be deployed according to some assumed enforcement regime at Member State level.

The better regulation movement involves commendable efforts to reduce the costs of regulation down to absolutely essential levels. It carries within it, however, the potential to place undue emphasis on evaluation mechanisms that are technically difficult, hard to fit into policy and legislative processes, and liable to lead to counter-productive results. A revised philosophy of better regulation is needed if tools such as the RIA are to be used positively.

4

Are Market Failure Analysis and Impact Assessment Useful?

PETER ANDREWS*

MARKET FAILURE ANALYSIS and impact assessment are economic tools that can yield information that is very useful in regulatory policy-making. This applies whether regulation operates mostly through rules or through a combination of rules, principles, guidance, supervision and enforcement. In fact, assessing the impacts—or costs and benefits of regulation—may be easier and more reliable when regulators complement rules with principles and other mechanisms. There are, however, many criticisms, mainly theoretical ones, of the use of market failure analysis and impact assessment. It is suggested here that there are convincing answers to most of these criticisms.

Whether market failure analysis and impact assessment provide useful information in practice depends upon how they are designed and deployed. Design and deployment interact. What needs to be assessed is whether the end result of using these tools is fit for the purpose that they are meant to serve.

Where an important objective of regulation is to increase society's economic welfare, it is suggested that the economic tools used in forming regulatory policy must in practice serve two purposes. The first is to establish whether there is in principle any realistic prospect of regulation improving on the market outcome. This depends on the threat to the regulators' objectives being due to a true market failure—or regulatory failure—rather than to what might be called a fact of life. The second purpose is to establish whether a specific, proposed intervention addresses the relevant market failure or regulatory failure well enough to yield, if it is implemented, a likelihood of net benefits, given its own costs and the circumstances of the relevant economic market. It is strongly suggested that this second purpose should not be pursued at all unless there are sound economic reasons to

* Head of Economics of Financial Regulation at the Financial Services Authority. The views expressed here are the author's, not those of the Financial Services Authority.

suppose that regulation can improve on the market outcome. This is because any resources spent on analysing a measure that has no real prospect of yielding a net improvement in welfare are wasted (when welfare improvement is one's goal). This is also to protect against the risk that, under some organisational arrangements, cost-benefit analysis of a favoured regulatory policy may be unduly optimistic.

It is important to note that the last remark does not detract from the general proposition that cost-benefit analysis typically provides information that is useful in regulatory decisions. It fills some or many of the information gaps that regulators face. If regulators do not undertake cost-benefit analysis, they face greater information problems and have to make more assumptions. A further advantage of cost-benefit analysis is that it can force regulators to be explicit about where assumptions are being made.

Designs of the systems of market failure analysis and impact assessment for use in formulating regulatory policy overlap. To serve the second purpose outlined above, market failure analysis needs to include some high-level cost-benefit analysis, even if this is only to assess whether the benefits of improved market outcomes are likely, given the nature of the improvement and the size of the market, to exceed the sum of the costs of compliance and of any other foreseeable negative consequences of the proposal. Similarly, systems of impact assessment are likely to include a requirement to consider market failures, though they mostly address preparation of a substantial cost-benefit analysis. It is argued here that the details of the design of these systems are important to regulatory outcomes.

Systems of market failure analysis emphasise the initial phases of policy development. They are likely to incentivise regulators to focus on whether it makes sense to intervene at all and, if so, whether a particular intervention is likely to succeed and yield net benefits. Systems of impact assessment may incentivise regulators to pay less attention to the question whether intervention is sensible and more attention to gathering evidence to establish that a particular intervention will yield net benefits. In particular, systems of impact assessment typically do not include a decision by an independent committee at an early stage in policy formation about whether an initiative should proceed. Instead the main decision on whether to proceed is likely to be slated for the very end of the policy-making process. One problem with this is that the information asymmetry between the proponents (developers) of a policy and those who might independently challenge them is then at its greatest. There is also the danger that once substantial resources have been spent on an unhelpful initiative organisations may feel that they have to support it, as not doing so would risk creating reputational damage.

Important aspects of deployment of market failure analysis and impact assessment include resourcing and associated systems and controls. These aspects of deployment may reveal how serious an organisation is about its use of market failure analysis and impact assessment.

Overall, market failure analysis involves less severe technical difficulties than impact assessment because it can often yield sufficient information for regulatory decisions without the need for a full cost-benefit analysis. Also the discussion of the design of systems for market failure analysis and impact assessment outlined above suggests that market failure analysis typically has important advantages in terms of organisational incentives. Market failure analysis may therefore be of more value in practice than impact assessment, provided it includes *high-level* cost-benefit analysis along the lines described above.

A. INTRODUCTION

Over the last 25 years privatisation of utility companies in the UK has given rise to a new breed of economic regulator. The very purpose of these regulators is to combat the malign economic effects of the natural monopolies that the private owners of gas, water and similar companies may enjoy. It is therefore unsurprising that these regulators were given extensive economic powers and made extensive use of economic tools. For example, the Office of Gas and Electricity Markets (Ofgem) has powers such as price setting that originated in the Gas Act 1986 and the Electricity Act 1989 and are necessary to fulfil statutory responsibilities that include:

— The need to ensure that all reasonable demands for electricity and, so far as is economical, gas are met;
— The need to secure that licence holders are able to finance their obligations.[1]

A natural step for economic regulators wishing to set prices was to draw on the techniques of cost-benefit analysis that had been used extensively in the assessment of infrastructure projects since the 1950s. More recently, they have focused on the possibility of intervening to foster competition in markets where natural monopoly might otherwise prevail. To do this, they again deployed economic techniques and analysis. Similarly, the Office of Fair Trading, charged with general oversight of competition in the UK's markets, has deployed a range of economic techniques in fulfilment of its role. This is well illustrated by several of the papers in the list entitled 'OFT reports post 2000', which can be viewed at www.oft.gov.uk. For example, OFT Paper 773 of March 2005, 'Predicting Cartels', is an economic discussion paper that aims to assist in the assessment of cartels through an empirical analysis of how they may be detected and of the economic and structural factors that contribute to their formation.

[1] See Ofgem Proposed Corporate Strategy and Plan 2005–10, available at www.ofgem.gov.uk.

While the case for giving an important role to cost-benefit analysis and competition analysis within utility regulators and competition authorities is obvious, the use of these techniques in other areas of government has a far more chequered history. Baldwin and Cave,[2] for example, speculate that hostility to cost-benefit analysis in the British civil service may be associated with a culture that places a heavy emphasis on administrative judgement about what may be in the public interest. The chequered history is understandable, since the objective function of most of these other areas of government and of regulators other than the economic regulators is not simply to maximise or, at least, to increase welfare in the economic sense.[3] Often it is to pursue an objective that has one or more economic aspects, but also has other important aspects such as fairness or minimum standards. For example, the primary objectives of the Food Standards Agency are to protect and improve public health and to protect consumers' other interests in relation to food and drink. Naturally, the Food Standards Agency is aware that imposing extremely high standards of food safety might affect the availability and prices of food sufficiently to reduce consumption. So it is committed in its decision-making to being proportionate, by taking account not only of risks but also of the costs and benefits of proposals, and to hearing the voices of all interested parties from the earliest stages of policy development.[4]

The UK's Conservative government of the 1980s challenged a number of traditions in the civil service and beyond, and emphasised the role of markets in increasing living standards. Its deregulation initiative may be seen as part of this pattern. Part of this initiative, possibly reflecting the experience of economic tools being used by the new economic regulators of the privatised utility companies, was an obligation on government departments to use market-sensitive economic tools in making policy, in particular by producing compliance cost assessments that set out the costs to business of proposed regulations.[5] While it might be objected that this is a misleading formulation—businesses typically do not bear regulatory costs in the form of lower profits; consumers bear them in the form of higher prices[6]—the initiative was pursued energetically by the government.

[2] R Baldwin and M Cave, *Understanding Regulation* (Oxford, OUP, 1999).

[3] It may be helpful to think of a welfare loss as something that arises when society's resources (labour, materials, etc) are wasted. This is not just a matter of inefficient producers being able to survive in the market, eg because they have market power. The case is more general, arising from the fact that market failures lead to prices differing from the true (marginal) cost of production. Such a difference distorts society's use of resources, inevitably leading to a welfare loss.

[4] This is based on the requirement to consult imposed on the Food Standards Agency by s48 of the Food Safety Act 1990. More generally, see 'The Objectives and Principles of Regulatory Decision-making in the F[ood] S[tandards] A[gency]', available at www.food.gov.uk.

[5] The process began with *Lifting the Burden*, which was produced by the Department of Trade and Industry (Cmnd 9571, London, HMSO, 1985).

[6] This result does not hold invariably. It depends on the state of competition in the relevant market.

A Deregulation Unit with a cross-departmental role was established, as was a Cabinet Committee on regulation. Eventually, in 1994 the Deregulation and Contracting Out Act was passed, with the aim of facilitating deregulation through a reduction in the process required.

The Labour government that took power in 1997 immediately switched the emphasis from deregulation to 'better regulation'. It established the Better Regulation Task Force (BRTF), a group representative of industry, unions, charities and consumers that was given a formal role to advise the government about how to improve regulation. The BRTF later became the Better Regulation Commission (BRC). The Deregulation Unit is now known as the Better Regulation Executive (BRE) and sits in the Cabinet Office. It supports the BRC. It is also responsible for the government's central effort to promote, set standards for and monitor the use of regulatory impact assessment in departments. This form of impact assessment is a major step forward from compliance cost assessment and could be characterised as a comprehensive aid to decision-making that gives an important role to cost-benefit analysis. The BRE's Regulatory Impact Assessment Guidance[7] is required to be used across all departments and the quality of usage is assessed and reported on annually by the National Audit Office.[8]

The UK governments of the 1980s and beyond also encouraged independent regulators to take similar steps. For example, the Financial Services Act 1986 as originally enacted contained no explicit obligation for the designated body, that is, the statutory regulator—in practice, the Securities and Investments Board (SIB)—to take into account the cost implications of their proposed rules.[9] But the legislation was soon amended to include an obligation to have a mechanism to take into account the costs of compliance. Moreover, disquiet about the cost-effectiveness of the regime quickly led to a formal review and report to the Chancellor by Sir Andrew Large. This proposed a shift to more thorough-going cost-benefit analysis. For example, the SIB published cost-benefit analyses of requiring disclosure of prices to purchasers of packaged investment products and of regulating custody services.

Building on this experience and in contrast to the Financial Services Act of 1986, the Financial Services and Markets Act 2000 requires its statutory regulator of financial services, the Financial Services Authority (FSA), to

[7] See: www.cabinetoffice.gov.uk/REGULATION/ria/ria_guidance/index.asp.

[8] See, eg: National Audit Office, *Evaluation of Regulatory Impact Assessments 2005–06—Report by the Comptroller and Auditor General* (London, National Audit Office, 2006), available at http://www.nao.org.uk/publications/nao_reports/05-06/05061305.pdf.

[9] S10 of the Financial Services Act 1986 enabled the designated body to recognise self-regulating organisations that met the criteria set out in the Act. In effect this required self-regulating organisations to have rules and procedures equivalent to those set down by the designated body. Thus, by construction, the self-regulating organisations originally set no formal mechanisms for taking into account the costs of compliance—and the self-regulating organisations undertook most of the regulation that occurred in practice. For a discussion of their role see A Wedgwood, G Pell, L Leigh and C Ryan, *A Guide to the Financial Services Act 1986* (London, Financial Training Publications limited, 1986).

undertake cost-benefit analysis in a wide range of circumstances. Of these, the most important so far has been the obligation in section 155 of the legislation to publish a cost-benefit analysis of proposed rules. The FSA itself has chosen to spell out what this obligation ought to mean in practice by publishing its own guides to cost-benefit analysis and competition analysis.[10]

A number of other European countries have embarked on similar initiatives, although some of these place considerable emphasis on implementation of the Standard Cost Model (SCM), which assesses the costs of businesses reporting to regulators and, in some cases, some of the costs of businesses reporting to consumers. In neither case does the SCM, still less the arbitrary targets for cost-cutting that are typically associated with it, appear *by itself* to provide a complete basis for regulatory decision-making. On the other hand, it may impose a useful discipline over costs where more thorough techniques such as impact assessment are not being deployed.

Other countries, such as Canada, the United States and Australia, have run impact assessment programmes for at least several years. Moreover, the European Commission has recently committed itself to systematic use of impact assessment across its work programme and has published a highly credible guide to impact assessment.[11] For several years prior to 2006 it undertook some impact assessment, but this was on a less thorough-going basis. The Commission also has an ambitious programme of better regulation, including critical assessment of regulatory quality and *ex post* evaluation of legislation and its burden on business.[12]

It is fair to say that many governments and regulators are deploying more resources on impact assessment and similar techniques than at any time in the past. Boyle reports that as long ago as 1996 more than half of OECD countries had adopted programmes of impact assessment.[13] One day, it may be possible to construct a panel data study that controls appropriately for relevant national differences and indicates whether these countries that embraced impact assessment have profited from doing so, relative to countries that did not.[14] Nothing so rigorous is proposed here. Instead, the aim is to consider whether, and under what conditions, two important parts of the economic tool kit—market failure analysis and impact assessment—are likely to benefit their users significantly.

[10] See www.fsa.gov.uk/pubs/other/CBA.pdf on cost-benefit analysis and www.fsa.gov.uk/pubs/other/policy_making.pdf on competition analysis.

[11] See http://ec.europa.eu/enterprise/regulation/better_regulation/impact_assessment/index.htm.

[12] See http://ec.europa.eu/enterprise/regulation/better_regulation/index_en.htm.

[13] R Boyle, *Regulatory Reform: Lessons from International Experience* (Dublin, Committee for Public Management Research, 1999).

[14] A possible reference point for this is the econometric analysis of the value of cost-benefit analysis in the World Bank's project appraisals, which was carried out by Pohl and Mihaljek: G Pohl and D Mihaljek, *Project Evaluation in Practice: Uncertainty at the World Bank* (Washington, DC, World Bank, 1989).

B. MARKET FAILURE ANALYSIS

Market failure analysis is—or ought to be—a vital tool in the armoury of government and regulators because it can indicate whether there is any point in—or any prospect of achieving net economic benefits from—intervening in a market. As will be explained below, it is not necessarily obvious whether net benefits will arise from an intervention. Moreover, one should be sceptical about the possibility of benefits arising since, at any rate in a market economy or a mixed economy, entrepreneurs have strong incentives (an appropriate return on capital) to produce market solutions to many of the 'problems' that affect markets.[15] Thus, those who proceed to intervene in markets without first using rigorous market failure analysis may be doomed to impose net costs on society, no matter how carefully designed their intervention is. Despite that, market failure analysis is rarely given a full treatment in materials on regulation produced by governments or international authorities. It will therefore receive a fuller treatment here than impact assessment, which is much better known.

What is meant by market failure? Bator supplies a conceptual definition:

> Typically, at least in allocation theory, we mean [by market failure] the failure of a more or less idealized system of price-market institutions to sustain 'desirable' activities or to estop undesirable activities. The desirability of an activity, in turn, is evaluated relative to the solution values of some explicit or implied maximum-welfare problem.[16]

Economic text books are not entirely consistent in their categorisation of market failure. The inconsistent lists of types of market failure may reflect the fact that in practice the types of failure within a market are sometimes hard to distinguish from each other. This is because, in a market, it may be the case that only a single type of contract is executed—for example, a contract to purchase a pension—but different failures within the market may interact to produce a sub-optimal set of those contracts. Thus it can be a useful device to consider as a market failure any deviation that an actual market shows from the idealised notion of a perfectly efficient market. Then, defining the perfectly efficient market enables one to identify the main categories of market failure.

Simplifying somewhat, the main characteristics of a 'perfectly efficient market' may be described as follows. It is a market in which, first,

[15] Some economists argue that markets will solve almost any problem that is soluble at an appropriate return on capital, given the level of willingness to pay, in which case one need not consider market failure directly and may instead consider whether the transaction costs are too great for particular contracts to be made. See R Zerbe and H McCurdy, 'The End of Market Failure' (2000) 23(2) *Regulation* 10.

[16] F Bator, 'The Anatomy of Market Failure' (1958) 72 *Quarterly Journal of Economics* 351.

consumers and producers take decisions that reflect all possible relevant information, ie the market failure 'information asymmetry' is absent. Secondly, prices reflect *all* costs, including costs to third parties, ie the market failure 'externality' is absent. Thirdly, firms cannot profitably charge prices in excess of 'marginal' cost (which is the saving in a firm's total cost when output is lowered by a very small unit, and in the long run includes the cost of capital), ie the market failure 'market power' is absent.

In practice, much market failure analysis requires no more than the three categories of market failure listed above. It may, however, also be useful to consider 'public goods'—goods (or services) that it costs nothing for an extra individual to enjoy and from whose enjoyment it is impossible to exclude individuals—and 'missing markets'—goods or services that are not provided even though the cost of provision is less than individuals are willing to pay for them.[17]

Market failure analysis has committed supporters[18] but is not without its critics, and it is important to be clear what the critics are saying and what market failure analysis means. First, market failure analysis is, naturally, of little value when the purpose for intervention is such that it cannot be achieved through making the market work more like a perfectly efficient market. For example, a perfectly efficient market might make society as a whole better off but it would not necessarily reduce inequality. In the extreme, a government might take the Rawlsian view that society should be arranged, subject to the requirements of equal liberty, so that economic inequalities are allowed to exist only where they operate to the benefit of the least advantaged members of society. Under this view, concerns over efficiency and waste, while indirectly relevant as factors affecting the position of the least advantaged members of society, are of rather limited importance. In cases such as this, there seems indeed to be little point in undertaking a market failure analysis.

Secondly, there is the argument summarised by Arthur and Booth as follows:

> The market failure approach to regulation is vacuous—it is literally empty of meaning...It cannot be known what the outcome of a perfectly competitive market process would have been in the absence of the process of competition, since there are undiscovered opportunities for increasing welfare.[19] Therefore, government action cannot correct market failure because government does not know the objective which it is seeking to achieve.[20]

[17] For a much fuller treatment see J Stiglitz, *Economics of the Public Sector* (New York, WW Norton & Company Inc, 2000).

[18] See, eg, R Dodd, *The Economic Rationale for Financial Market Regulation* (Washington, DC, Financial Policy Forum, 2002).

[19] See F Hayek, *Law, Legislation and Liberty* (London, Routledge, 1982).

[20] T Arthur, and P Booth, 'Financial Regulation, the State and the Market: is the Financial Services Authority an Unnecessary Evil?' (2006) 26(2) *Economic Affairs* 22.

It is true that government intervention seems unlikely in general to bring about the outcome of a perfectly competitive market. But this is not because the government does not know what that outcome is. A government may be able to unleash market forces that have been artificially constrained, for example when government action breaks up a complex monopoly. In that case something approaching the outcome of a perfectly competitive market may be achieved, even though the government had no idea what that outcome was when it took its action.

The reason government intervention seems unlikely in general to bring about the outcome of a perfectly competitive (unregulated) market is that the presence of regulation in a market changes the conditions for supply and demand. Due to regulation, different suppliers and different consumers may be present in the market, for example because some entrepreneurs are unwilling to spend time on compliance activities. Moreover, suppliers may face different costs (for example, the costs of dealing with the regulator and the costs of business processes that would not be operated in the absence of regulation). Equally, consumers may face different prices (which could reflect quality increases, such as a safety net, brought about by regulation, or the moral hazard that may arise from regulation). Thus the outcome of a regulated market will very probably be different from the outcome of a perfectly competitive (unregulated) market.

But the argument summarised by Arthur and Booth is not an appealing argument against the use of market failure analysis in regulation. The argument depends upon the idea that the purpose of using market failure analysis is to produce the (unknowable) outcome of a perfectly competitive market. While that may be an ideal objective of regulation, it is not one that is familiar in the statutes that set objectives for regulators.[21] For most regulators, a more realistic objective is to improve on the current state of the market.[22] The value of market failure analysis will then lie in whether it can help them to achieve that objective.

Thirdly, even when it would be useful to the government or regulator to make the market work more like a perfectly efficient market, free market economists sometimes criticise the use of market failure analysis. This is because all markets are likely in practice to depart in some degree from the economists' notion of a perfectly competitive market and, again, because markets have a remarkable capacity to develop solutions to problems.[23]

[21] In the case of the Financial Services Authority see s2 of the Financial Services and Markets Act 2000.

[22] Thoughtful regulators will consider not just the current state of the market but also whether there are signs of dynamic change within the market that will solve the problem concerning them.

[23] For a powerful collection of essays along these lines by neoclassical economists see T Cowen (ed), *The Theory of Market Failure* (Fairfax, Virg, George Mason University Press, 1988). Dodd (above n18) argues that neo-classical assumptions about the economy are very 'strong' in the context of financial markets, that is 'lacking a close and established connection

Therefore, market failure analysis could be used to justify intervention in any market. The answer to this criticism lies in defining market failure—and therefore market failure analysis—in a sensible way. Callum McCarthy, the chairman of the FSA, has made this point as follows:

> In the FSA's work, a principle we have enunciated...is that regulatory action should only be taken when there is market failure. Now this is in fact a weak definition of the circumstances when regulatory action is justified, since all realistic markets—that is all markets which exist in practice—have some elements of market failure...It is an argument too often deployed by those who favour intervention that any market failure justifies intervention. The strong—and to me correct—test goes beyond that: there must be both market failure and the prospect that intervention will provide a net benefit. This involves recognising that regulatory intervention has a cost and...a probability of failure. Identification of a market failure should not lead to the assumption that regulatory failure is less likely, or less costly. It is an open and empirical question, which needs analysis on a case by case basis.[24]

In other words, market failure should be defined as a situation in which the government or the regulator can improve upon the market solution to a problem.

The quotation just given introduces another important concept, that of regulatory failure. Understanding and assessing regulatory failure is important because it may help policy-makers not to intervene or it may show that an adjustment to previous intervention is necessary. It may, for example, arise from technical difficulties in *ex ante* assessment of the impacts of regulation[25] or because regulators' interests are not necessarily aligned with the public interest.[26] Like market failure, the concept of regulatory failure does not receive the coverage it deserves in the material produced by governments and international authorities on regulation. Also like market failure, regulatory failure can be defined in different ways. The two most useful definitions may be the following.

First, when one is considering intervention in a market not yet touched by specific regulations[27] and when one's aim is to make the market work *more* like a perfectly efficient market, regulatory failure may be defined as

to the known facts'. He concludes by showing 'under more realistic assumptions about how markets actually operate that financial markets are more efficient, more stable and less likely to transmit disturbances to the overall economy if they are properly regulated'.

[24] C McCarthy in *Financial Risk Outlook* (London, Financial Services Authority, 2005).

[25] For a broad discussion of the ways in which regulation may go wrong see M Lodge, 'The Wrong Kind of Regulation? Regulatory Failure and the Railways in Britain and Germany' (2002) 22 *Journal of Public Policy* 271.

[26] See, eg, G Stigler, 'The Theory of Economic Regulation' (1971) 2 *Bell Journal of Economics* 3.

[27] Arguably, all markets are affected, if only indirectly, by *general* regulations such as those that define the physical conditions under which employees may be required to work.

a situation in which economic welfare is reduced by regulatory intervention. In plain language, this means that the government or regulator fails to improve on the market's own solution to whatever problem assails it, at least to the extent necessary to offset the costs inevitably associated with regulation: it is important to recognise that even if the regulatory solution is roughly as effective as the market solution, there may still be a *substantial* loss of welfare. This is partly because of the resources that are absorbed in making and complying with regulations. It is also because regulation may have some perverse or unexpected effects even when it addresses the market failure at least as well as the market itself. A well-known example of unexpected costs (at least, if one's measure of welfare is limited to national boundaries) is the decision of regulators in the United States in the 1960s to introduce tough new regulations on foreign exchange trading. One consequence was that much of the business migrated to London and the 'Eurodollar' market was born. These foreign exchange regulations may also be regarded as an example of the danger of regulating without rigorously establishing the presence of a material market failure and designing regulations that do no more than correct the market failure identified—but the argument will not be pursued here.

Secondly, regulatory failure may be defined as any case in which the net benefits of regulation were not as great as they could have been. It may be thought that this definition is hollow because almost any intervention could conceivably be improved upon. But a condition that applies in most practical economic analysis is 'given current technology'. More importantly, the definition is useful for decision-making in the circumstances that regulators typically face: a market in which they have already intervened. The question to be decided is the following: is the regulatory failure, as defined in this paragraph, such that the incremental benefits of alternative or supplemental intervention are likely to be greater than all of the costs that they will bring?

Let us take stock for a moment. Market failure analysis may, when market failure is sensibly defined, enable government and regulators to decide whether certain types of intervention in markets will bring net benefits. In taking those decisions, government and regulators need to be aware of the risk of regulatory failure. Past regulatory failure itself may provide a rationale for fresh intervention in the same market or markets.

The aim of this section is to determine whether market failure analysis is likely in principle to be of significant benefit to its users. If it were obvious whether regulation would improve on the market solution to a market failure, then market failure analysis would provide little value. So, is it obvious whether intervention will yield an increase in welfare? The answer may in extreme cases be 'yes, of course', but in general it is surely 'no'. This is partly because the extent, if any, of any likely improvement over the market solution is hard to assess. It is also because of the uncertain scale of the negative impacts of regulation on markets, such as consumers being driven out of markets by higher prices reflecting any regulatory costs that are passed through to consumers, reduced variety in the products offered and reductions in competition that may be brought about by increases in the minimum efficient scale of operation caused by compliance costs and capital and other requirements. To assess these impacts of regulation, it is necessary to have a clear understanding of what the relevant markets are, how they are working prior to the proposed regulation (ie what is the nature and extent of the market failures) and how they are likely to work after the proposed regulation has been put in place.

Consider, for example, two of the most famous cases of the market failure 'information asymmetry': used cars and insurance. These are described in much-quoted articles by Akerlof and by Rothschild and Stiglitz.[28] In the case of used cars, most countries have decided that regulation cannot improve on the market solution of independent advisers from organisations such as the AA and the RAC, which inspect the individual cars offered by vendors and advise potential purchasers about the condition that those cars are in. On the other hand, in the case of insurance, even where it is not attached to investment products, the member governments of the European Union presumably believe that they can improve on the market solution of advisers who inspect the contracts offered by insurance companies and tell potential purchasers which contract is best suited to their individual needs, circumstances and resources.[29]

What is the crucial difference between these two cases, or is it a combination of factors that leads to little specific regulation of the sale of used cars and much specific regulation of contracts of general insurance? Relevant differences could include: the far greater role of product regulation in the market for cars; differing incentives between car advisers and insurance advisers (reflecting differences in contractual arrangements); the fact that insurance product providers are making promises about the future whereas the car inspected by a car adviser is the finished product; the fact that the insurance adviser needs to make a judgement about the match between each consumer's requirements and the general product on the market but may not have collected all of the information necessary to make a sound judgement; the fact that most consumers may struggle far more to understand what an insurance adviser tells them than what a car adviser tells them; perceived differences in the feasibility of regulating

[28] G Akerlof, 'The Market for Lemons: Qualitative Uncertainty and the Market Mechanism' (1970) 84 *Quarterly Journal of Economics* 488. M Rothschild and J Stiglitz, 'Equilibrium in Competitive Insurance Markets: An Essay on the Economics of Imperfect Information' (1976) 90 *Quarterly Journal of Economics* 629.

[29] Regulation of the activities of agents in the general insurance markets was imposed across the European Union by the Insurance Mediation Directive of 2002 [2003] OJ L9/00, available at http://eur-lex.europa.eu/LexUriServ/LexUriServ.do?uri=CELEX:32002L0092:EN:NOT.

car salesmen and insurance salesmen; and, finally, society may have a greater interest in people buying suitable insurance than it has in people buying high quality cars.

Thus two situations that at first sight appeared broadly analogous in fact seem to have several potentially significant differences when it comes to determining whether they merit regulation. A comparison of other cases of 'information asymmetry' would be likely to reveal a similarly wide range of differences for consideration. Some of these would be the same as and others could be different from those in the list above: whether or not it makes sense to regulate is case-specific and categorising individual cases may be complex. That is why, unless one has a very strong preference for regulation and little regard to its practical effects, it is important to consider markets very carefully before plunging into regulating them. Market failure analysis can provide a structured and disciplined means of giving such consideration to markets. This can be seen if one considers what market failure analysis actually involves.

An example of a thorough approach to market failure analysis is the FSA's website at http:www.fsa.gov.uk/pubs/other/mfa_guide.pdf (at pp 48–50) This approach requires users to answer two sets of questions and present the answers to an independent, internal committee for scrutiny. These two sets of questions serve the purposes set out for tools of economic analysis of regulatory policy at the start of this chapter. Where an important objective of regulation is to increase society's economic welfare, the first purpose of the economic analysis is to establish whether there is in principle any realistic prospect of regulation improving on the market outcome. This depends on the threat to the regulators' objectives being due to a true market failure—or regulatory failure—rather than to what might be called a fact of life. The second purpose is to establish whether a specific, proposed intervention addresses the relevant market failure or regulatory failure well enough to yield, if it is implemented, a likelihood of net benefits, given its own costs and the circumstances of the relevant economic market. The first set of questions in the FSA's approach addresses the first of these two purposes of economic analysis, and is as follows:

A. What is the relevant economic market or markets?

B. What are the material market failures and/or regulatory failures in the relevant market(s) now?

   Step B1: determine which FSA objective is the main motivation for the initiative and then consult the table in this guide on which market failure is likely to be relevant;

   Step B2: determine whether this market failure—and/or another one—is in principle relevant by considering the nature of the relevant economic market; *for this purpose, assume the complete absence of all financial regulation*;

Step B3: determine whether any relevant market failure identified in step B2 has in principle been cured by appropriately targeted regulatory intervention;
Step B4: determine whether a regulatory failure is in principle relevant; this may be in addition to a market failure or, where a risk to the FSA's objectives (RTO) has been identified but steps 2 and 3 suggest that this is unlikely to be due to a market failure, regulatory failure may be the sole cause;
Step B5: check that any relevant market and/or regulatory failure actually is material to the RTO that concerns us.

C. If no intervention or no further intervention takes place, will an improvement in welfare take place? Will the market failures be corrected in the short term?

The FSA's internal processes hold that rule-making initiatives shall not proceed unless the committee mentioned above agrees, on the basis of the analysis set out in the required format, that a credible, relevant and material market failure or regulatory failure is present. Importantly, these processes are underpinned by top management's public commitment to market failure as the basis for intervention. The steps set out above, though, are insufficient to meet the FSA's own definition of market failure which, as already mentioned, requires that the regulatory solution to the problem in the market be superior to the market's own solution, whatever that may be. Thus the committee's decision on whether to instigate a project also depends on the *high-level* answers to a second set of questions that address the second purpose of economic analysis in regulatory decision-making described above. These questions are:

D. What broadly are the regulatory options for the FSA?
E. What are the economic and other costs and benefits of the options, relative to doing nothing?
F. What is the plan for further work on costs and benefits?

Question E is answered by comparing the expected outcome of the broad regulatory options with the status quo, if the market is thought to be relatively static, or with the market as it is shortly expected to be, if the market is expected to change in the short run. It is not a full cost-benefit analysis, subject to all of the difficulties that that would entail. The focus is on assessing whether the benefits of improved market outcomes are likely, given the nature of the improvement that regulation can bring about (ie the nature of the market or regulatory failure that new regulation can correct) and the size of the market, to exceed the sum of the costs of compliance and of any other foreseeable negative consequences of the proposal.

Often, it will be clear even from such high-level analysis whether any of the options is likely to improve on the option of doing nothing. All that needs to be established for a sound decision to be made is whether costs are likely to be materially greater than benefits or vice versa. (Estimates of costs and benefits in cost-benefit analyses are unavoidably subject to a significant degree of approximation, so it will often be sensible to limit the amount of work done on a cost-benefit analysis to that which is necessary to establish where the balance of interests lies.) Sometimes a high-level analysis is insufficient to reveal whether or not intervention will be superior to the market's own solution to a problem. In those cases, the main question is whether the chances of a successful intervention are high enough to justify spending any further resources on investigating the issue.

Finally, in this section, it is notoriously difficult to get direct evidence about the benefits of market failure analysis. Arguably, the main benefit is that regulators and government departments do not pursue initiatives that cannot be justified by market failure or on non-economic grounds, such as social policy. Naturally, regulators and government departments tend not to publish lists of 'bad ideas we had'. Interested parties should consider how many regulatory initiatives in their areas of interest are patently not referable to a market or regulatory failure or, depending on the regulators' objectives, to an avowed social aim. Of course this is very far from saying that all of the initiatives are cost-effective. There may, for example, be errors in policy design such that remedies do not in fact address the market or regulatory failure that is present.

Of course, another main benefit of market failure analysis is that, where an initiative is motivated by a wish to make a market work more like a perfectly efficient market, the market failure analysis, by showing in broad terms what is wrong with the actual market, permits policy remedies to be designed properly. To establish the extent of this benefit one would need to compare the quality of interventions by institutions that do and by otherwise similar institutions that do not use market failure analysis. Such a comparison seems not to be available.

What may be an interesting piece of evidence on the value of market failure analysis has recently been generated by the European Commission. On 17 March 2006 it announced the result of a screening of legislative proposals. This screening was undertaken in accordance with the principles of good regulation, which include market failure analysis. Moreover, the Commission did not undertake a full cost-benefit analysis of the proposals as part of its screening, which indeed seems to have been more of an analysis of principle, along the lines of the market failure analysis and high-level cost-benefit analysis practised by the Financial Services Authority. The result of the screening was that one third of the screened legislative proposals were dropped.[30]

[30] See http://ec.europe.eu/enterprise/regulation/better/better_regulation/index_en.htm.

There are two caveats to note with respect to the Commission's review. First, and by far the more important, the Commission withdrew some of the proposals because they were outdated or not advancing in the legislative process. Secondly, and this is more of a technicality, to the extent that the Commission is seeking to make a reality of the single market in a particular good or service, it is not concerned with market failures as defined here. It is instead concerned with legal or other barriers to the single market. The latter, however, includes regulatory failures and, to that extent, no caveat is needed.

C. IMPACT ASSESSMENT

As already mentioned, impact assessment is widely used by governments and regulators in many different countries. Inspection of the published models used for impact assessment suggests that they share some important characteristics. The analytical core tends to be economic cost-benefit analysis.[31] As far as possible, however, the cost-benefit analysis is presented in a non-technical way, with a view to it being executed by officials from a wide variety of backgrounds.[32] (Here one may recall the warning of Little and Mirrlees: 'we will remark only that simplification and theoretical soundness are not good bedfellows'.[33]) Crucially, the cost-benefit analysis is embedded in a wider structure of decision-making: it is required to be produced at specific times for specific purposes.[34]

By way of example, one of the most thorough approaches to impact assessment is the one set out by the UK Cabinet Office.[35] This has 11 sections:

1. Title of proposal;
2. Purpose and intended effect;
3. Consultation;
4. Options;
5. Costs and benefits—this section is split into four subsections covering a wide range of issues;
6. Small firms impact test;

[31] For a detailed treatment of cost-benefit analysis see E Mishan, *Cost-Benefit Analysis* (London, Unwin Hyman, 1988).

[32] See, eg, (Australian) Office of Regulation Review, *A Guide to Regulation Review* (Belconnen, Office of Regulation Review, 1998).

[33] I Little and J Mirrlees, 'The Costs and Benefits of Analysis: Project Appraisal and Planning Twenty Years On' in R Layard and S Glaister (eds), *Cost-Benefit Analysis* (Cambridge, Cambridge University Press, 1994).

[34] On the importance of embedding cost-benefit analysis in the policy cycle or process see John Howell & Co Ltd, *The Financial Services Authority N2+2 Review of Cost Benefit Analysis Cultural Issues* (London, The Financial Services Authority, 2004). www.fsa.gov.uk/pubs/other/howell_report.pdf.

[35] See www.cabinetoffice.gov.uk/REGULATION/ria/ria_guidance/index.asp.

7. Competition assessment;
8. Enforcement, sanctions and monitoring;
9. Implementation and delivery;
10. Post-implementation review;
11. Summary and recommendation.

From an economic perspective, it seems strange to separate costs and benefits from the assessment of competition. It is precisely the impact of regulation on competition that will determine many of the costs and benefits. Aside from that, taken at face value, such an impact assessment seems obviously to be useful. It provides a discipline over the policy-making process, making it more difficult for groups within an institution to pursue their own interests rather than the objectives of the department or regulator. It provides evidence which ought to improve the quality of decision-making. If it forms part of a consultation process, which typically it seems to, it provides transparency and accountability: stakeholders are shown the basis on which a decision is reached and have the opportunity to challenge the evidence and to provide better evidence of their own.[36]

It is easy to take for granted the benefits of transparency and therefore instructive to consider the position prior to the reforms of government processes mentioned above.[37] In 1974, the position was described as follows:

> Government departments have often been criticized for their disinclination to divulge interesting and useful information to members of the public. The fiction that all departmental decisions were taken by the minister (who is alone politically answerable for them), coupled with a deep-seated belief that any exposure of the processes of departmental decision-making would tend to cause trouble and reduce administrative efficiency, brought about a state of affairs in which secretiveness was sometimes carried to absurd lengths...Criticism of departmental secrecy has recently been concentrated on *nine*[38] main issues...[39]

Nevertheless, the use of impact assessment is not without its critics. There are perhaps two major strands of criticism. One relates to the 'impossibility' of cost-benefit analysis. The other is that impact assessment is mere window-dressing for pre-determined decisions.

On the first, an illustration will be helpful. Suppose one believed that consumers of, say, pensions were suffering detriment as a result of lacking important information. Suppose too that a regulation could be designed that would remove the detriment by perfecting the consumers' information set. In broad terms, the benefit of the regulation would be the value of the detriment being suffered. A cost-benefit analysis of the regulation would

[36] *Ibid.*
[37] See, eg, above n5.
[38] Emphasis added.
[39] S de Smith, *Constitutional and Administrative Law* (Harmondsworth, Penguin Books, 1974).

therefore seek to measure the detriment. Strictly, however, this is impossible. A generalised case of this type was considered by Hunter and others on behalf of the Office of Fair Trading:

> The main problem that is encountered in providing a measure of the consumer detriment that can be estimated with observed data relates to the difficulty of predicting what the level of prices and outputs would be if information were perfect. This is crucial since...the level of consumer detriment depends on the characteristics of the allocation of resources under perfect information. Ideally, one would like to be able to infer the perfect information allocation from the observation of the current set of prices and outputs. This requires making the following steps:
>
> Step 1) To identify how prices and outputs vary with the extent of the consumer information, for any market structure.
> Step 2) To estimate the level of precision in the consumers' information (i.e. how much consumers know about the distribution of prices in the economy or how much consumers overestimate/underestimate quality).
> Step 3) To characterize the market structure.
>
> ...However, we cannot predict what prices and hence the market structure would be if consumers were fully informed, since we are unable to perfectly assess the distribution of search costs in the economy and how much search costs influence consumers' willingness to shop around.[40]

Does this then mean that the cost-benefit analysis element of impact assessment is not useful? The answer to this is 'no', provided that one is prepared to make policy on the basis of approximations of the truth, which practical policy-makers tend to have to do. As already observed, high-level approximations often suffice to show where the balance of interest lies. Thus, for example, Hunter *et al*, in the work quoted above, estimated consumer detriment by assuming that 'under perfect information the market would behave competitively (either perfect competition or monopolistic competition)'. But the approach of making assumptions to abstract from uncertainty is far from uncontroversial amongst economists. Simpson, for example, argues that within the context of neoclassical equilibrium theory the appropriate reaction to uncertainty (the theory of the second best) is to abandon cost-benefit analysis.[41] This produced the following response:

> an analogy was suggested between a person who is unwell and a market that is not working properly. The analogy was as follows. A patient is sick. The general nature of the problem is clear but the doctor cannot establish the exact causes of the illness. The doctor knows a remedy that is generally effective for that type

[40] J Hunter, C Ioannidis, E Iossa and L Skerratt, *Measuring Consumer Detriment under Conditions of Imperfect Information* (London, Office of Fair Trading, 2001).

[41] D Simpson, 'Cost Benefit Analysis and Competition' in D Simpson, G Meeks, P Klumpes and P Andrews (eds), *Some Cost-Benefit Issues in Financial Regulation*, Financial Services Authority Occasional Paper 12 (London, Financial Services Authority, 2000).

> of problem but, given the uncertainty, cannot rule out that the remedy will cause complications. However, if the remedy is not administered, the patient will either die or continue to suffer for a long time (pending self-recovery). The suggestion was that the doctor would administer the remedy rather than agonise about the uncertainty. It was argued that, on the same basis, it is sensible to act on the broad policy implications revealed by cost-benefit analysis, provided that there is robust evidence about the general shape of any new equilibrium likely to result.[42]

A number of other arguments against cost-benefit analysis or impact assessment are closely associated with the 'impossibility' argument outlined above. The most powerful of these are based on data problems and valuation problems.

It is certainly true that all the data that one would like to use in an impact assessment are rarely available. It often turns out that historical data sets have gaps or have not been collected or are no longer accessible. Moreover, data about the future, such as the price of goods or services after proposed regulations have been made, are naturally not available. Whether one despairs at this point or instead uses or develops the best data available probably depends on whether one is a practical regulator or not.

It is important to keep in mind that lack of data is not a problem caused by cost-benefit analysis or impact assessment. It will afflict the decision-maker whether or not the decision-maker uses these techniques. Paradoxically, lack of data strengthens the case for use of these techniques as part of a process involving public consultation because they force the decision-maker to reveal the assumptions that have been made and exactly how important those assumptions are. Also, since regulators are certainly not all-knowing, public consultation on cost-benefit analyses can bring to light fresh information and data that are useful in policy-making. Lack of data does, however, reinforce the point that cost-benefit analysis and impact assessment must not purport to be accurate when accuracy is not achievable. They are necessarily broad-brush estimates, and sensible regulators will present them as such.

The arguments on valuation problems, such as the lack of prices for non-market goods or services, are similar to those on lack of data since valuation problems are really a special case of lack of data. This is not to say that valuation problems in impact assessments or cost-benefit analyses are not severe. On the contrary, there is a very extensive economic literature on issues such as the discount rate to be used when costs or benefits accrue at different times, or even to different generations.[43] Other important issues are valuation of lives, valuation of individuals' time and generation of

[42] Above n34.

[43] See, eg, J Bruce, H Lee and E Haites (eds), *Climate Change 1995: Economic and Social Dimensions of Climate Change* (Cambridge, Cambridge University Press, 1996).

shadow prices when market prices, due to market failure, do not reflect the true marginal social costs or benefits of a product or service.[44]

Valuation problems, just like other data problems, do not disappear if one fails to undertake impact assessment and, again, consultation that features an impact assessment will reveal and open to challenge any assumptions that a regulator is making about values. Thus it seems that we are likely to be better off with impact assessment that focuses the cleansing power of sunlight on decisions whose basis might otherwise be for all practical purposes opaque.

A further reason this is important is that regulators have incentives of their own which will not always coincide with the public interest. Accounting regulators are well-known for not deploying impact assessment or cost-benefit analysis, despite it having been demonstrated that it is in principle possible to do so.[45] Thus Padoa-Schioppa observed that in the United States accounting rules were captured by 'the powerful industrial lobby' and that this hindered transparency, 'preventing early and effective reaction to the problems which materialized in the Enron affair'. The Financial Accounting Standards Board took a 'sluggish and eventually inconclusive stance' on consolidation accounting (and deferred projects on special purpose vehicles and off-balance-sheet abuses).[46] Similarly, in the UK, most businesses were opposed to the replacement of historical cost accounting, which yields erroneous results in times of high inflation, with inflation-reflective accounting. This was because it would have reduced stated profits. The UK's setter of accounting standards delayed action on this important issue for more than a decade. When it did eventually introduce a standard for inflation-reflective accounting, firms could choose to ignore it, with the agreement of their auditors, because inflation was no longer high: the results obtained under historical cost accounting were not materially different.

A related point is that impact assessment, and cost-benefit analysis in particular, is not useful when one's aim is to benefit one group over another. This is because they are concerned with economic efficiency and do not provide tools to determine whether one should be happy to benefit a favoured group by £1 at a cost of, say, £2 or £3 to society as a whole. In substance, this argument has much in common with the Rawlsian argument against using market failure analysis, which was described above. It is worth noting, however, that use of cost-benefit analysis in such a context can

[44] See, eg, S Rosen, 'Safety and the Saving of Life: The Theory of Equalizing Differences' in O Ashenfelter and R Layard (eds), *Handbook of Labour Economics* (Amsterdam, North-Holland, 1986), i.. See also A Sen, 'Shadow Prices and Markets: Feasibility Constraints: Foreign Exchange and Shadow Wages' (1972) 82 *The Economic Journal* 486.

[45] G Meeks and J Meeks, *Towards a Cost-benefit Analysis of Accounting Regulation* (London, ICAEW, 2000).

[46] T Padoa-Schioppa, 'Self Versus Public Discipline in the Financial Field', European Central Bank lecture at the London School of Economics, 2002, available at www.ecb.int/press/key/date/2002/sp020520.en.html.

provide policy-makers with two useful pieces of information. First, it may reveal the size of the societal cost, thereby facilitating the judgement about whether it is appropriate to incur the cost. Secondly, it may show who in reality is likely to meet the cost. (Often, the state of competition means that the price mechanism will operate to ensure that consumers fully fund regulatory costs initially met by suppliers.) Moreover, use of a disciplined approach such as cost-benefit analysis may help the policy-maker to take a similarly disciplined approach to the application of welfare weights, which can be a complex task if undertaken seriously.[47]

Overall, one might say that the first major criticism of impact assessment—that the cost-benefit analysis it involves is impossible to do properly—does not mean that impact assessment should not be undertaken. There are certainly challenges in cost-benefit analysis but, as has been shown above, these do not preclude the production of information that is very useful in regulatory decision-making. Cost-benefit analysis reduces the uncertainty that regulators face and makes explicit the things that regulators do not know. This incentivises regulators to deal properly with those things and allows scrutiny of the choices regulators then make. Without cost-benefit analysis, regulators' information problems would be more, not less, severe and more, potentially erroneous assumptions would have to be made. Regulators inevitably face uncertainty and have varying degrees of risk appetite in decision-making. This leads to varying degrees of certainty being required before decisions are taken. Given this, and since full cost-benefit analysis is resource-intensive, it makes sense to do no more than the high-level cost-benefit analysis described above as a constituent part of a system of market failure analysis, wherever such high-level analysis provides the required degree of certainty.

The other major strand of criticism of impact assessment—that it is mere window-dressing for pre-determined decisions—is difficult to generalise about since it depends on the precise design of the system of impact assessment, the controls over the process, the opportunity for public scrutiny and so on. One way of testing the seriousness and objectivity of any particular system of impact assessment is to measure it against the conditions for successful impact assessment set out by the OECD.[48] These are:

1. Political support at ministerial or parliamentary level;
2. Clear and measurable quality standards (such as cost-benefit tests);
3. Selection of a methodology that is flexible and administratively feasible;

[47] There is a risk that judgements about welfare weights will be influenced by a wish to secure a predetermined result. To counteract this, a thorough approach to using welfare weights is essential. See, eg, the following paper prepared for the Office of Fair Trading: F Cowell and K Gardiner, 'Welfare Weights', Report to the UK Office of Fair Trading (1999), available at www.oft.gov.uk/NR/rdonlyres/.

[48] OECD, *An Overview of RegulatoryImpact Analysis in OECD Countries* (Paris, OECD, 1996).

4. Development of an institutional structure with independent quality control;
5. Testing of assumptions through public consultation;
6. Integration of analysis into administrative and political decision processes;
7. Building of expertise and skills among regulators, including written guidance.

If any of the seven aspects of an impact assessment programme mentioned above are absent, it may be a sign that the institution concerned plans to leave itself a lot of room to make decisions without regard to the outputs of impact assessment. On the other hand, it is possible to envisage a system of impact assessment that in principle worked satisfactorily with just items 4 to 7 in the OECD's list. (Item 4, independent quality control, would need to be rigorous to cover 2 and 3, standards and methodology. Item 6, integration into decision-making, would need to cover 1, political support.)

Another point to note on the criteria is that the main external discipline is testing of assumptions through public consultation (criterion 5). This is certainly important but may be insufficient to ensure that impact assessments are fully objective and well-informed. For that, a formal independent oversight, perhaps along the lines provided by the statutory panels of practitioners and consumer representatives provided for in the Financial Services and Markets Act 2000 or well-resourced involvement by an external stakeholder may be necessary. An interesting example of the latter is the cost-benefit review team run by the Associazione Bancaria Italiana.[49]

An important point against the idea that impact assessment is mere window-dressing is that for most regulators and government departments impact assessment is a repeat game played with its most active stakeholders. Therefore, if a department publishes impact assessments that are biased towards a predetermined outcome and ignores serious representations made to it about the impact assessment and the underlying policy, the department can expect over time to fall into disrepute. Reputation is likely to play a non-trivial role in the objective functions of many departments and their ministers.

On the other hand, Baldwin argues:

> the messages to be gleaned from Regulatory Impact Assessment processes may be poorly heeded within the political and administrative systems that drive policies.[50]

He points out that governments may be committed to certain regulatory steps due to ideological reasons, manifesto commitments or political settlements and therefore be likely to ignore impact assessments that send contrary signals. Far be it from impact assessment to subvert democracy!

[49] See www.abi.it. Details of the work are, however, in the members' section of the site.
[50] R Baldwin, 'Is Better Regulation Smarter Regulation?' [2005] *Public Law* 485.

Again, however, this claim that impact assessment is not useful needs to be assessed carefully. It may be true that governments will sometimes ignore inconvenient impact assessments. On the other hand, if an impact assessment is prepared and shows clearly that the government's original plan is flawed, there will surely be some cases in which the government will change its mind, not least if the impact assessment is made public. The immediate stakeholders in a demand for regulation and even the wider public may change their minds about what they want if they are shown the likely scale of the costs involved or that the original plan is unlikely to yield the required benefits. Moreover, one needs to consider the realistic counterfactual: a world without impact assessment. In the absence of an impact assessment, it seems far *more* likely that a government would refuse to change its mind about a 'bad' proposal because it would not be confronted by the well-ordered and balanced evidence about the proposal's defects that an impact assessment can provide—not, that is, until the proposal had been implemented and imposed net costs on real people.

As already mentioned, the likely effectiveness of impact assessment depends on how it is resourced, fitted into the policy cycle and incorporated within a system of controls. This topic will be revisited below in the comparison of the system of market failure analysis and high-level cost-benefit analysis used by the Financial Services Authority and a typical system of impact assessment. But it is worth pointing out now that much of the criticism of impact assessment concerns the question whether it will always deliver perfect outcomes (of course it will not), rather than the questions that it would be more useful to ask, which are:

— Are we better off with impact assessment than without it or any equivalent technique for bringing order to policy-making?
— If the answer to the question above is 'yes', can impact assessment be improved or profitably replaced by some other technique of ordering?

If one accepts that the approximations necessary for the production of impact assessments do not wholly undermine their information content and that governments and regulators will sometimes be swayed by impact assessments, the answer to the first question would appear to be 'yes'. We could then move to discussing the second question in the final section of this note. But first it is worth considering two more subtle arguments against the use of impact assessment. Again, these are put forward by Baldwin.[51] The arguments seem to boil down to two main propositions:

— Impact assessment may impede 'smarter' regulation in the sense that it will lead to top-down rule setting rather than subtle combinations of tools deployed by different actors in the regulatory game.

[51] *Ibid.*

— Impact assessment may impede strategic regulation in the sense that it will lead to new proposals that are assessed in their own right rather than to strategies based on an overall assessment of existing and new regulations.

If either of these propositions is substantially true, it could lead us to answer 'no' to the first question above: we would be better off without impact assessment or similar techniques. But even that would depend upon whether the costs implied by less smart and less strategic regulation were greater or less than the benefits of having data about the rough size and nature of the market impacts of intervention and of avoiding proceeding with those 'bad' proposals that are identified through impact assessment and consequently rejected. Fundamentally, since in a market or mixed economy regulation must usually in practice work through the market mechanism, it seems highly unlikely that we could be better off without impact assessment or some similar economic tool to reveal the likely consequences of specific proposed interventions.

The core of both of the propositions mentioned above is that the presence of impact assessment will lead administrators to propose only simple solutions to problems—ones that it will be relatively straightforward to subject to impact assessment. This seems to be based on the notion that administrators' dominant motivation is a desire for a quiet life. It seems likely, however, that many administrators have chosen their career precisely because they want to 'make a difference', while others may be only too glad to demonstrate how smart they are.

Turning to the substance, one has to ask again whether, in the absence of impact assessment, administrators would be any more likely to propose smart or strategic initiatives. Certainly, they would be aware that impact assessment of such initiatives would be hard, but at least impact assessment would provide them with a structured route through the unavoidable jungle of complexity. Without impact assessment—in other words, without thinking through such issues as how markets will react to specific stimuli—the analytical task of designing a complex regulatory strategy is daunting indeed. And how, without impact assessment, would administrators explain to those in their chain of command that any particular set of propositions is the right set? It could be argued that the more complex the prescription is, the more it will be dependent on impact assessment to achieve any operational credibility: smart and strategic regulation is too complex for decision-makers to make snap decisions about whether it is 'right'.

Moreover, one should guard against calling impact assessment into question merely because it does not answer all questions that may be of interest to regulators—questions such as how precisely to deploy in a flexible manner certain elements of the 'smart' regulatory toolkit. Impact assessment can form a powerful combination with other ordering techniques to achieve high-quality regulation. For example, government departments in the Netherlands tend to deploy both economic analysis and a 'smart' tool originally known as 'The Table of Eleven', which focuses on how to produce rules that will achieve a high level of compliance.[52] The Financial Services Authority also developed and deployed a wide-ranging, 'smart' regulatory toolkit along the lines proposed by Sparrow.[53] This has resulted in the use of a complex mixture of principles, rules, general guidance about rules, codes, individual guidance, regard to industry codes, surveillance, desk-based monitoring, on-site monitoring, enforcement action and other techniques. But the Financial Services Authority remains committed to its use of market failure analysis and cost-benefit analysis. It recognises that their role is mostly in relation to getting information about the market-wide impacts of certain kinds of intervention and that other ordering techniques are needed to target appropriately other elements of the 'smart' toolkit. But, for example, the market failure analysis supports the detailed toolkit by identifying precisely the behaviour that the regulator wishes to change.

It is worth expanding a little on this important point. The Financial Services Authority uses market failure analysis and cost-benefit analysis to decide whether to use, and to assess the likely impacts of, market-wide tools such as rules, high-level principles and general guidance. Markets will react most strongly to tools of these kinds. From an analytical perspective, it does not make a great deal of difference whether a requirement is framed as a rule or a principle. The empirical questions in the cost-benefit analysis are the same in either case: will the issue of the material cause firms or consumers to change their behaviour and, if so, how? Naturally, one would expect lower costs and fewer changes in the case of principles—because they give firms greater freedom to use existing practices in achieving compliance—but, just as in the case of rules, one needs to understand current practice and to use incentive-based models and surveys to figure out what will happen next. Of course markets respond in some degree to other regulatory stimuli, such as enforcement policy. Again, though, one needs to build an assumption about such policies into one's cost-benefit analysis whether or not the regulatory scheme is a 'smart' one.

In fact, 'smart' regulation, at least in the outcome-focused form that the FSA is implementing, facilitates and improves the reliability of cost-benefit analysis of regulatory proposals. The benefits of regulation are not that firms comply with rules. Rather, the benefits of regulation are changed outcomes in markets. In the case of financial regulation, these include that the level of failure by firms is brought nearer the socially optimal level and that consumers have the confidence to enter financial markets that can meet

[52] For information on this in the Netherlands contact the Ministry of Justice; in the UK contact John Howell & Co Ltd.

[53] M Sparrow, *The Regulatory Craft* (Washington, DC, Brookings Institution, 2000).

their needs, purchase products that are more suited to their circumstances than would otherwise be the case, are offered products with a lower price for a given quality and, even if they buy the same product at the same price as they otherwise would have done, derive greater consumer surplus from it. If these market outcomes are sought solely or mostly through the application of rules, there is a danger of them not being achieved, due to non-compliance and gaming on the part of firms or due to consumers failing to make good use of information supplied by firms under rules (and firms doing nothing about it). These uncertainties complicate cost-benefit analyses and tend to reduce their reliability. The FSA's outcome-focused regulation, however, places more reliance on principles and seeks cost-effectively to achieve changes in market outcomes through three principal mechanisms. These are a much-reduced framework of rules (implementation of which is now starting), providing firms with 'sturdy breakwaters' (against regulatory sanction) by endorsing industry guidance that allows firms freedom to achieve the desired market outcomes in cost-effective ways, and supervision and enforcement based on principles. The last is especially important as it moves regulation away from what can be almost a single shot game from the regulator's perspective (as rules cannot often be changed). Instead, the regulator can respond to any strategic behaviour it observes from firms and, in principle at least, insist on the desired outcome being achieved. Thus the uncertainty needing to be assessed and dealt with in cost-benefit analysis is materially reduced: one can be more confident that the benefits sought will be achieved and one needs to spend less time on trying to identify possible avoidance strategies and their costs. Similarly, there should be less need to try to identify and analyse unexpected perverse effects of regulation as firms are free to achieve outcomes in the manner that best suits their business.

Having deployed its market-wide tools in the manner described above—in effect to provide a framework within which detailed regulation will take place—the Financial Services Authority uses its risk assessment and mitigation tool, 'Arrow', to deal specifically with individual firms or even very large sets of firms. This enables the other elements of the 'smart' toolkit to be used flexibly, case-by-case, as indicated by the size of any identified risks to the objectives and the probability of those risks crystallising. While it is possible in theory that, say, very aggressive use of these other tools could undermine the cost-benefit basis on which the rules were set, this is not typically the case. In any event, were it to happen, it would probably reflect risky developments in the market subsequent to the setting of rules and therefore be entirely justifiable: regulation should not be a one-shot game; rules and principles that do not change regularly provide an element of certainty that enables businesses to price and plan in the presence of regulation; but regulators must react to important changes in the markets.

Thus the argument about 'smart' regulation, though important, seems not to be fatal to the use of impact assessment. ('Smart' regulation in fact seems to facilitate cost-benefit analysis, as explained above.) The same might be said of the argument about strategic regulation. In addition to the points already made on administrators' incentives and the consequences of complexity, one might consider the following.

First, the unit of account of analysis is a choice variable for policy-makers. Policy-makers are unlikely in general to want to spend their time analysing a unit that they know is not meaningful. Secondly, any approach to policy-making that has a sound basis in economics, which impact assessment ought to have, is likely to drive its user to choose a sensible unit of account. It is not possible to think through the market impacts of a proposal without being clear about the definition of the relevant market or markets, how competition in them is operating and what are the regulations and other constraints already affecting them. Thirdly, the cumulative impacts of regulation on markets can usefully be studied through specific *ex post* reviews conducted from time to time.[54]

It is worth reflecting back at this point to the genesis of impact assessment in government and regulatory decision-making. As explained above, it was associated with the realisation in government from the 1980s onwards that markets are crucial to the delivery of improved welfare and that consequently economic tools should be used to understand the interaction between markets and proposed regulations. Neither the fact that it is legally possible to intervene in markets in particular ways nor the will of administrators that a particular outcome shall come about is decisive of the results of regulation. What matters most is how markets will in practice respond to an intervention, and that needs to be assessed by economic tools. The risk arising from not using tools such as impact assessment is huge. There is an increased prospect of policy goals not being achieved or, if they are achieved, of them being achieved only in the presence of substantial perverse effects.

Finally, in this section, what should we make of the empirical evidence about the use of impact assessment? As already mentioned, the National Audit Office has carried out reviews of impact assessments in central government in the UK. The findings are not entirely encouraging. Deficiencies in the process are frequent, as are gaps in the sets of information obtained and in the range of options considered. But, as a matter of common sense, it seems that the situation could only be worse rather than better if officials were not required to carry out an impact assessment: why would those tasked with, and accountable for, an obligation to obtain information obtain more information in the absence of that obligation? Indeed, neither the National Audit Office nor the Cabinet Office, both tasked to make government efficient and effective, has shown the slightest wish to reduce the

[54] See NERA's report on this topic: NERA, The FSA's Methodology for Cost-Benefit Analysis (London, NERA, 2004). This is available at www.fsa.gov.uk/pubs/other/nera_cba_report.pdf.

role of impact assessment. On the contrary, they encourage departments to invest more in impact assessment, in order to secure higher quality outputs and, consequently, higher quality policy. Indeed, the Cabinet Office is in the process of consulting on its standard approach to impact assessment, with a view to improving it. Informally, it is understood that this will involve an increased focus on economic considerations.

Moreover, there have been a number of studies about the practical effects—rather than just the process—of cost-benefit analysis that provide evidence of its considerable value, though they also show that it is not always used well. Boyle surveys international experience of impact assessment and reports that it contributes to a 'cultural shift whereby regulators become more aware of the costs and benefits of their actions' and of the need to take account of costs when regulating.[55] He also reports a 1987 evaluation by the US Environmental Protection Agency of 15 impact assessments. This found that they 'cost $10 million to conduct, but resulted in net benefits of $10 billion arising from revisions to regulations'. He concludes that 'whilst not without challenges in its implementation, Regulatory impact Assessment offers a powerful tool to promote better regulation'.

Similarly, a thorough analysis by Little and Mirrlees concludes:

> Social cost-benefit analysis is not as widely, as well, or as effectively practiced as its expected value might lead one to hope and expect...We went on to consider the bearing of the very considerable uncertainty that has been shown to attend project appraisal upon the value of the appraisal activity itself. We argue that the value is indeed probably diminished by that uncertainty but is nevertheless very large.[56]

D. SYSTEMS OF MARKET FAILURE ANALYSIS AND IMPACT ASSESSMENT COMPARED

Interestingly, there seems to be no distinction between the market failure and high-level cost-benefit analysis approach used by the Financial Services Authority and the government's approach to impact assessment in terms of the OECD's criteria for impact assessment set out above. Both meet all of the criteria:

[55] R Boyle, *Regulatory Reform: Lessons from International Experience* (Dublin, Committee for Public Management Research, 1999).

[56] I Little and J Mirrlees, 'The Costs and Benefits of Analysis: Project Appraisal and Planning Twenty Years On' in R Layard and S Glaister (eds), *Cost-Benefit Analysis* (Cambridge, Cambridge University Press, 1994). See also Pohl and Mihaljek, above n14.

Table 4.1: Approaches to Impact Assessment

OECD	FSA	UK Government
1. Political support at ministerial or parliamentary level.	Board.	Panel for Regulatory Accountability.
2. Clear and measurable quality standards (such as cost-benefit tests).	Published guides on cost-benefit analysis, competition analysis and market failure analysis.	Guide to regulatory impact assessment and Treasury's 'Green Book'
3. Selection of a methodology that is flexible and administratively feasible.	See 2.	See 2.
4. Development of an institutional structure with independent quality control.	Regulatory Policy Committee; sign-off of analysis by central team independent of policy-makers.	Cabinet Committee on Regulation; National Audit Office—although neither of these signs off impact assessments at critical points in their production.
5. Testing of assumptions through public consultation.	Yes.	Yes.
6. Integration of analysis into administrative and political decision processes.	Yes—see 2 and 4.	Yes—see 2 and 4.
7. Building of expertise and skills among regulators, including written guidance.	Yes—see 2; internal training programme.	Yes—see 2; internal training programme.

It may then be that the OECD criteria are better suited to distinguishing between poorly developed and more developed systems of impact assessment than to choosing between two 'more developed' systems.

One reason for quoting the Financial Services Authority's approach to market failure analysis at length above is that most other guides to impact assessment—one could say, most other approaches to disciplining regulators and government departments in terms of the impacts that they may have on markets—skate over market failure analysis in a way that leaves much to the imagination. Although the UK government's approach to impact assessment is one of the most thorough, only one of its 11 sections touches on market failure analysis.[57] This is the section on 'Purpose and intended effect', which has three sub-sections, namely objectives, background and rationale for government intervention. From a market failure perspective, the relevant parts of this are:

> Objectives—define your objective clearly so that it sets out the outcome you are aiming for.
> Background—set out briefly what the current situation is. Describe any current regulations or policies which already deal with the issue.
> Rationale—describe the impact on the current situation if there is no government intervention: this will be your 'do nothing' option. Describe why you think the situation will not be resolved of its own accord. Estimate the likelihood of preventing a particular situation from arising in the future. Explain if the issue is expected to continue at the same rate or get worse, and whether it could cause harm.

On close inspection, there appear to be a number of potentially significant differences between the approach of the Financial Services Authority and the approach of the government. These differences might be said to make the approach of the Financial Services Authority more effective as a means of deciding when—and when not—to intervene in markets, and of making such interventions on balance beneficial. There are, however, two important caveats to this. First, the government is, as already mentioned, updating its approach to impact assessment. Secondly, it might be said that it is unreasonable to compare the government's approach with that of the Financial Services Authority because the government often intervenes in markets for social, environmental or equity reasons, rather than mostly to address economic concerns. Thus its methodology needs to be of wider application.

First, the Financial Services Authority is using market failure analysis as a filter before resources are allocated to carrying out a project. It can lead to a decision not to proceed with any more work beyond the preliminary analysis. The government, on the other hand, is using the material on 'purpose and intended effect' quoted above as part of an explanation of a proposal which has been fully prepared. Thus the material is prepared in a context in which a significant investment has already been made. This seems likely to reduce the objectivity of the material. Those preparing it are likely to be under pressure to justify the resources spent, by gathering evidence that there is a real problem to address, and may be the same people as spent the resources. This is an important issue, as regulators may have agendas of their own, as set out in the 'public choice' literature, or be driven towards inappropriate action by (not always justified) criticism from bodies such as Parliamentary Select Committees.

[57] See www.cabinetoffice.gov.uk/REGULATION/ria/ria_guidance/index.asp.

Secondly, the approach to market failure analysis taken by the Financial Services Authority gives considerable weight to the possibility of past regulatory failure and, as a package, forces policy-makers to consider the relevant parts of the existing regime and the market as a whole. If the government's approach to impact assessment is indeed narrower than this, it would appear to run an increased risk of error. Important lessons may be drawn from the effects of regulations already in place.

Thirdly, the Financial Services Authority is seeking, insofar as is possible, to secure an objective assessment of actual markets. The requirement is to define the market and define precisely the market failure or regulatory failure affecting it, including the reason for supposing that regulation can improve the situation. The government's approach is less precise and mixes aspirational statements with objective facts. It runs the risk of leading to a pursuit of attractive-sounding ideas that markets will in fact not permit to be realised. On the other hand, this flexibility in the government's approach is likely to have important advantages when the prime reasons for intervention are non-economic.

An aspect of the preceding point worth further explanation is use of a proper definition of the relevant market or markets. Economic markets are the unit of account of economic analysis. If more than one economic market is affected by a regulation, they need to be considered separately. How they will react to regulation depends partly on how they are working before the regulation is put in place. Impact assessments not based on realistic definitions of the relevant markets, and how they are working, may be seriously misleading.

A fourth aspect of the Financial Services Authority's approach that is sometimes an advantage is that its *high-level* cost-benefit analysis abstracts from the potentially misleading detail that a full impact assessment may introduce. For the many reasons set out above, a full assessment of costs and benefits is difficult to do and policy-makers need to guard against spurious claims of accuracy. A high-level cost-benefit analysis can sometimes explain, sufficiently and convincingly, precisely why a market, after implementation of the proposal under consideration, will operate so as to deliver material benefits. This can help to guard against providing lots of information about compliance costs—just because they are relatively easy to measure—which may be an unhelpful distraction for decision-makers. (Compliance costs often are a very low proportion of the total costs of production and so, typically, have little impact on markets, beyond an extremely small price increase for consumers.) On the other hand, the detail that the government's approach requires can certainly be useful in difficult cases, and the Financial Services Authority seeks to follow the government's approach in such cases.

It should immediately be pointed out that the Financial Services Authority is independent of politicians and voters, and may therefore have an easier role than government departments. Moreover, the points made above do not mean that the government's impact assessments are not valuable. They are in substance suggestions about how the system, which is already an advanced one, might for some purposes be further improved.

E. CONCLUSION

Sparrow advises regulators to put the problem at the centre of their work[58] and market failure analysis does this very well. When combined with high-level cost-benefit analysis, it can enable regulators to deploy their resources on projects that have a real prospect of yielding net benefits. Likewise, impact assessment can make important contributions to the formation of regulatory policy. Equally, both techniques can be difficult to execute and their limitations must be recognised:

> The central problem of cost-benefit analysis is to identify extremely complex (and to an extent unknowable) interactions within an economy and reduce them to a set of propositions that are simple enough to be readily understood and yet realistic enough to be useful. Thus a cost-benefit analysis might be rather like an impressionist painting—much less detailed than a photograph but much more recognizable than an abstract image would be.[59]

It is strongly contended that an impressionist image is a much better guide than no image at all. Making policy without market failure analysis or impact assessment is, arguably, making policy in the dark. Drawing on the analysis in this chapter, practical experience and the papers published as part of the 'N2+2' Review of the Financial Services and Markets Act,[60] the conditions necessary for successful impact assessment or market failure analysis appear to be:

- — Open consultation with external stakeholders;
- — Effective monitoring from external stakeholders, preferably including ones with some influence;
- — Explicit and active support from the top of the relevant organisation, including a public commitment by top management to the use of market failure analysis and impact assessment ;
- — Decision-making within the organisation that is independent of those who propose policies or prepare impact assessments or market failure analyses;

[58] Sparrow, above n53.

[59] I Alfon and P Andrews, 'Cost-Benefit Analysis in Financial Regulation—How to Do It and How it Adds Value', Financial Services Authority Occasional Paper 3 (London, Financial Services Authority, 1999).

[60] Above n35.

- — Preparation of impact assessments and market failure analyses that is independent of policy-makers—or, if assessments and analyses are prepared by policy-makers, an independent review of them, including the ability to prevent proposals being submitted to decision-makers if the assessments or analyses are unsatisfactory;
- — Embedding of impact assessments and market failure analyses into the policy cycle, for example to ensure that the work is timely and subject to proper control, and has sufficient resources allocated to it at the planning stage;
- — Preparation and use of market failure analyses and high-level cost-benefit analyses (impact assessments) before full policy projects are started, with independent decision-makers able to block proposed projects if the analyses or assessments are unconvincing;
- — Development of a practical and institution-specific methodology for impact assessments and market failure analysis, the methodology to include market definition, regulatory failure and a clear focus on why the regulator thinks it is possible to improve on the market solution to a problem;
- — Training in the use of the methodology and in the specific economics of the relevant markets;
- — Selection of sufficient numbers of staff with the necessary skills and mind set.

5

The Standard Cost Model: When 'Better Regulation' Fights Against Red Tape

JACOPO TORRITI*

THIS CHAPTER INTRODUCES one of the 'better regulation' instruments, the Standard Cost Model (SCM), a method for measuring the administrative burdens imposed by regulation on businesses. It examines the content and purposes of the SCM. It discusses some of the limits of the model and difficulties that public administrations may face in its application and provides recommendations for improving the model. It describes recent applications of the SCM, with a particular focus on the UK and European Commission experiences. It is argued that the introduction of such methodology in the Impact Assessment guidelines may have an effect on the EU 'better regulation' agenda, namely shifting the regulatory pendulum to a more de-regulatory dimension.

A. INTRODUCTION

One of the central aims of 'better regulation' is to ensure that the government refrains from issuing regulation which is not strictly necessary.[1] While Regulatory Impact Assessment is the main instrument in the phase of proposal of new regulation, the Standard Cost Model (SCM) specifically sets out to eliminate either in part or whole legislation which imposes excessive administrative compliance costs on businesses. The reasons for analysing the Standard Cost Model are numerous.

First, no academic research has critically reviewed the SCM methodology. Secondly, the application of the SCM involves resources from public administrations and calls for questions about why public institutions make use of the model. Thirdly, as the empirical use of the SCM is limited to a

* Research Fellow, King's Centre for Risk Management, King's College London.

[1] Better Regulation Task Force, 'Less is More: Reducing Burdens, Improving Outcomes' (Mar 2005), available at www.brtf.gov.uk/docs/pdf/lessismore.pdf.

small number of countries, it is relevant to understand what lessons can be learned from such experiences. Fourthly, even if the model is not designed to be statistically significant, it is worthy of note to stress its limits in order to improve its future application. Fifthly, the applications of the model differ substantially. The EU, for instance, is applying the SCM on the basis of the concept of net administrative costs. This differs substantially from the way in which the Model has been applied within Member States. Is the 'better regulation' agenda destined to change after the introduction of the SCM in the Impact Assessment guidelines?

In order to address these points, this chapter develops as follows. Section B.1 provides a description of the model. As the existing manuals refer to different typologies of costs, section B.2 places the category of administrative compliance costs measured by the SCM in the ordinary scheme of legislative costs. Section C examines the existing literature on business requests for less (or more) regulation. The purpose is to try to define whether businesses constantly require less regulation or the demand for regulation varies. Section D provides a case study of the UK application of the model. Section E provides an analytical critique of the model and some suggestions for improvement. Section F describes the EU application of the model and argues that the SCM has the potential to move the EU 'better regulation' agenda to de-regulatory grounds.

B. THE MAIN FEATURES OF THE SCM

The Standard Cost Model is a method for measuring the administrative burdens for businesses imposed by regulation. Its quantitative methodology is applied by different public administrations to determine the administrative burdens related to existing and new legislation. The SCM can be used to measure a single law, selected areas of legislation or to perform a baseline measurement of all legislation in a country.

The main aim of the model is to ensure that existing regulations and new regulations do not impose excessive administrative burdens on businesses. The focus is not on the policy objectives of each regulation; the measurement focuses only on the administrative activities that must be undertaken in order to comply with regulation, and not whether the regulation itself is reasonable or not. The next section explains the methodology of the SCM and the main formulas.

1. The SCM Methodology for Measuring Administrative Costs: the Concept of Information Obligations

The SCM methodology involves an activity-based measurement of the administrative burdens on businesses, breaking down regulation into a range of manageable components. These are information obligations, and are the units of measurement of the model. They can be defined as the obligations arising from regulation to provide information and data to the public sector. In other words, an information obligation is a duty to procure or prepare information and subsequently make it available to either a public authority or a third party. It is an obligation businesses cannot decline without coming into conflict with the law.[2] An information obligation does not necessarily mean that information has to be transferred to the public authority, but may include a duty to have information available for inspection or supply on request. Typical examples of information obligations are: drawing up and registring annual accounts; applying for permits; general obligations to retain businesses records; provision of information on sick employees to working conditions services, and annual statement of employee insurance to social security body.[3]

For each information obligation price and quantity are calculated as follows:

> Price (Π) consists of a tariff (W), ie wage costs (plus overhead, non-wage costs) for activities done internally or hourly cost for external service providers and time (T), the amount of time required to complete the activity. Wage data are normally taken from statistical sources. For external costs a national average figure is used.
>
> Quantity (Q) comprises of the size of the population (P) of businesses affected and the frequency (Φ) with which the activity must be completed each year.

The following basic SCM formula provides the activity costs related to a single information obligation:

$$\text{Activity Cost}_{(IO)} = \Pi \times Q = (W \times T) \times (P \times \Phi)$$

Activity costs can be defined as the costs of the administrative activities that businesses are required to conduct in order to comply with the information obligations that are imposed through regulation. Each piece of legislation may impose several information obligations, as illustrated in Figure 5.1. Total prices can be expressed as the sum of internal and external prices. The time and money that an entrepreneur spends drawing up and publishing an annual statement with the use of the services of an accountant hired via an accounting firm results in the external price. The time the entrepreneur spends correlating and passing on the information that the accountant needs is the internal price. If no external consultancy of professional accounting

[2] International Working Group on Administrative Burdens, *Standard Cost Model Booklet* (2004), available at http://epp.eurostat.ec.europa.eu/pls/portal/docs/PAGE/PGP_DS_QUALITY/TAB47143266/STANDARD%20COST%20MODEL_DK_SE_NO_BE_UK_NL_2004_EN_1.PDF.

[3] Better Regulation Executive, *UK Standard Cost Model Manual* (London, Cabinet Office, 2005).

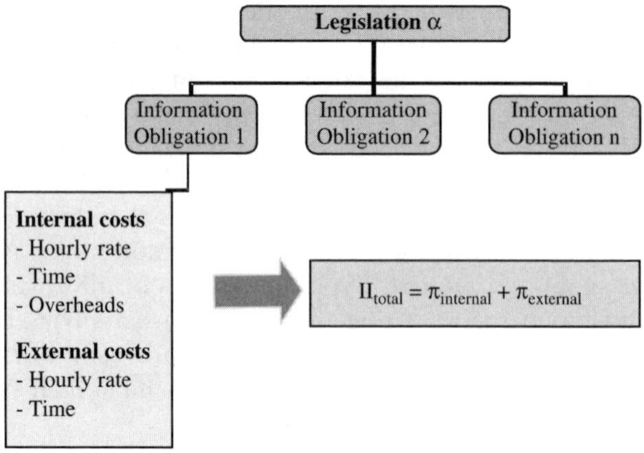

Figure 5.1—Costs related to each information obligation.

advice is needed the external price will be nil ($\pi_{external} = 0$) and the administrative activity will be attributed internally ($\Pi_{total} = \pi_{internal}$).

For example, suppose that an administrative activity takes T = 5 hours to complete and that the hourly cost of the member of staff in the business completing it is W = 15 Euros. The price is therefore $\Pi = 5 \times 15 = 75$ Euros. If this requirement applied to P = 50,000 businesses which each had to comply $\Phi = 2$ times per year, the quantity would be 100,000. Hence the total cost of the activity would be $100{,}000 \times 75 = 7{,}500{,}000$ Euros.

The overall administrative costs related to one regulation are calculated as the sum of all information obligations:

$$\begin{aligned} \text{Activity Cost}_{\text{(Legislation } \alpha)} &= \text{Activity Cost}_{\text{(IO 1)}} + \text{Activity Cost}_{\text{(IO 2)}} + \ldots \\ &\quad + \text{Activity Cost}_{\text{(IO n)}} \\ &= \Sigma\,(\Pi_i \times Q_i) = \Sigma\,(W_i \times T_i) \times (\Pi_i \times \Phi_i) \end{aligned}$$

Note that in the above formula box, $i = (i_1, i_2, \ldots, i_n)$.

The SCM therefore measures the costs related to specific administrative activities. The next section places these costs in the ordinary scheme of the costs imposed by regulation.

2. Regulatory Costs and the Standard Cost Model

Every piece of legislation imposes different costs on businesses, the state, private individuals and private households. The existing SCM manuals mention different categories of costs. This section specifies which costs are measured by the SCM, starting from the distinction between private and social costs.

(a) Private Costs and Social Costs

Private costs for individuals and households are what any one person or one family gives up due to the legislation. Sometimes regulators carry out cost-benefit analyses that seek to assess private cost components only. This happens when the regulation is expected to have effects mainly on single citizens and consequently involves distributional issues. An example is contained in the cost-benefit analysis developed in 2000 during the Italian Presidency of the Council of Ministers for a new regulation introducing mandatory helmets for all moped drivers (Italian Law 472/99). It was estimated that one-off capital costs would amount to 45 Euros per consumer purchasing a new helmet. Normally regulatory impact assessments focus on the cost to society as a whole from an event, action or policy change.[4] Social costs are what society gives up to the legislation. They include negative externalities and do not count costs that are transfers to others, in contrast to private costs.

The equation for net social costs is:

Net social costs = Net private costs + 3rd Party costs – 3rd party gains

When no private third party costs are foreseen, there may nonetheless be an element of public spending. Public spending can derive from developing, administering and enforcing the new regulation. In the case of the mandatory helmets in Italy, the net social costs were expressed as: net private costs (45 Euros x 200,000 new helmets per year) + public spending costs expressed as annual average costs for additional vigilance activity (10.5 Million Euros)—public spending gains expressed as avoided annual direct costs for head-injury hospitalisation (67 million Euros). The resulting net social costs are negative, ie they represent the sum of benefits per year of the new law less the relative costs.[5] Figure 5.2 provides an idea of the division of legislative costs between private households, businesses and the public sector.

(b) The SCM in the Scheme of Costs Imposed by Regulation

The Standard Cost Model focuses on the administrative compliance burdens that legislation imposes on businesses. In particular, it measures those administrative activities that businesses conduct only because regulation requires it. It does not take into account the costs that legislation imposes on private households or the public sector. Similarly, it does not consider: direct financial costs, ie the direct obligation to transfer a sum of money to the government or the competent authority (including administrative

[4] European Commission, Impact Assessment Guidelines, SEC(2005)791.

[5] In this case, by discounting the cash-flow over 5 years using a discount rate of 5%, a Net Present Value of approximately 152 million Euros is obtained.

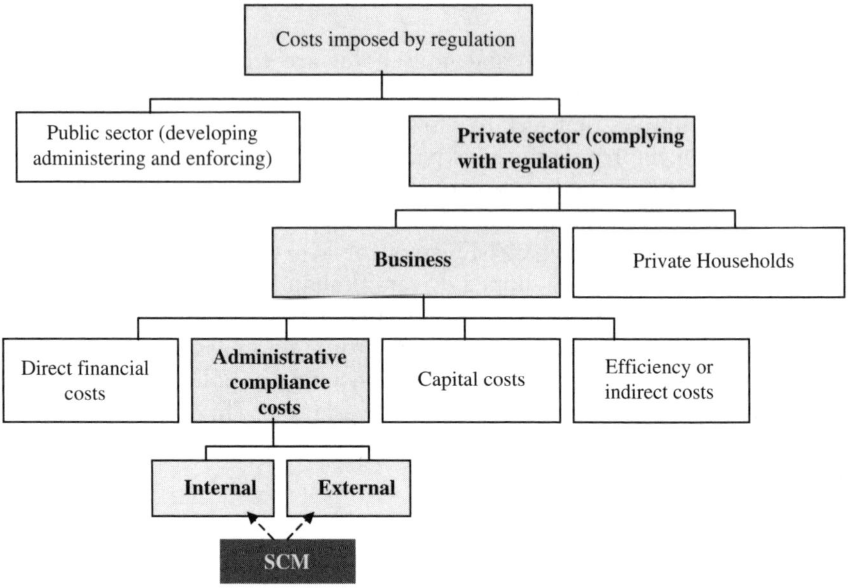

Figure 5.2—Scheme of costs imposed by regulation.

charges, taxes, etc); capital costs, ie the total price spent in purchasing depreciable property (including buildings, equipment, etc); or efficiency or indirect costs, ie lost innovation for time spent in non-productive activities. The UK government simplifies the cost categories represented in Figure 5.2, differentiating between policy costs and administrative costs. Policy costs can be viewed as the essential costs of meeting the policy objectives, while administrative costs usually arise from familiarisation with the requirements, monitoring and enforcement, proving compliance etc. Administrative burdens placed on businesses, charities and the voluntary sector are identified using the SCM.[6]

(c) Recurring Costs and One-off Costs

The SCM measures mainly recurrent administrative costs from regulation. Recurring costs are the administrative costs that businesses constantly incur in complying with the information obligations originating from regulation. They may be costs that arise at regular intervals, eg with VAT returns.

[6] See www.cabinetoffice.gov.uk/regulation/reviewing_regulation/reducing_admin_burdens/what.asp. For the UK implementation of the SCM, 'business' is all organisations defined as being in the private sector by the Office for National Statistics when compiling the National Accounts. This includes charities and the voluntary sector.

They can also be costs that arise at irregular intervals for the individual business, eg if they are to apply for an export subsidy or submit a planning application. They can similarly arise from an administrative task that the individual business experiences on only one occasion, eg in connection with business registration where one applies for a VAT number or applies for authorisation. Recurring costs differ from one-off costs. The latter are incurred only once in connection with the business adapting to a new or amended piece of legislation. This does not include the costs that a business may have in relation to complying with existing regulations for the first time, eg as a consequence of increased turnover or expansion with new areas of activity in the business. Hence, only the introduction of a new or amended regulation can give rise to one-off costs. The one-off costs are not included in the SCM measurement. However they do form part of *ex ante* measurements for inclusion in a regulatory impact assessment. An example is the requirement for firms to read guidance as a result of a once-and-for-all change in a regulation.

C. WHY THE STANDARD COST MODEL?

The application of the SCM is not trouble-free. It requires a significant effort by public administrations in terms of resources. It involves work both internally (co-ordinating units and government departments) and externally (consultants contracted to interview stakeholders and quantify available data). There are two main reasons public administrations make the effort of measuring and then reducing administrative compliance costs: these costs are of a non-productive nature and create frustration across business.

1. Eliminating Non-productive Costs

The SCM is an attempt by the public sector to get rid of the excessive regulatory work produced in past, present and future administrations. In this regard, the SCM, as part of the 'better regulation' agenda, is designed to favour the business community. Money spent in fulfilling administrative tasks does not benefit the economy and cannot be re-invested in profitable activities. At the macroeconomic level, diminishing administrative burdens would cause the GDP to increase in the medium term, because the time and money saved would be redeployed in more productive activities.[7] Albeit reasonable, this statement is just a hypothesis, since it assumes that businesses in the medium term would invest to strengthen their production. This hypothesis cannot be corroborated with empirical evidence because

[7] See BRTF, above n1.

the SCM measures only administrative burdens and does not investigate efficiency costs or opportunity loss (ie how much businesses actually lose due to administrative activities). The model ignores what happens in terms of internal business management, including how productive activities are stimulated as a consequence of the reduction of administrative functions. Section E on criticisms and recommendations for the SCM discusses this issue extensively.

2. Business Complaints about the Administrative Burdens of Regulation

Businesses complain that they spend too much time and money on complying with government requests for information.[8] They claim that such requests are unclear and do not understand why they are made so often or why they need to be repeated. They are irritated by the amount of time and money spent filling in forms and would prefer to spend their time and effort in more productive activities. Previous studies pointed out that industry tends to exaggerate the costs imposed by environmental regulation.[9] The position taken by businesses on the issue of regulation changes according to the advantages and disadvantages that this may bring about.[10] Does more regulation always mean more administrative costs for businesses? Do businesses always require less regulation?

(a) Economic Benefits of ad hoc Regulation

The conventional political economy model of regulation holds that stricter regulatory standards are more likely to be accepted if businesses benefit economically from the particular regulation.[11] Firms considering regulation to be necessary may ask for *ad hoc* regulations, which will improve the industry's profits. In other cases, businesses will oppose any type of regulation which does not bring about economic benefits.

(b) Size of the Business

The request for tighter or more lenient regulation by individual firms or groups of firms within a specific industry may vary according to differences in industrial structure and competitive position. Large firms could apply

[8] M Pollack, 'Public Participation' in H Hotway and M Peltu (eds), *Regulating Industrial Risks* (London, Butterworths, 1985).

[9] A Stirling, 'Limits to the Value of External Costs' (1997) 25(5) *Energy Policy* 517.

[10] A Ogus, 'W(h)ither the Economic Theory of Regulation? What Economic Theory of Regulation?' in J Jacinta and D Levi-Faur (eds), *The Politics of Regulation* (Cheltenham, Edward Elgar, 2004).

[11] G Stigler, 'The Theory of Economic Regulation' (1971) 2 *Bell Journal of Economics and Management Science* 3.

pressure for stricter environmental or consumer regulation that would be too costly for smaller firms to implement, whereas smaller competitors within the same industry could contest such regulation.[12]

(c) EU Level

At the EU level, European firms may require more protection, whereas multinationals may ask for an enhanced deregulation of the market.[13] Much has been written about the proposal on Registration, Evaluation and Authorisation of Chemicals (REACH), and the complaints of the chemical industry about excessively restrictive regulation on chemical products. However, an example of requests for stricter regulation on non-European companies comes from chemical industries. This issue was raised at the Joint European Commission/CEFIC Conference on The Impact of New Regulatory Requirements on the Chemical Industry and its Competitiveness, held in Brussels on 5 October 2000:

> The unfair competitive advantage afforded to companies from non-EU countries, who have full access to the European Single Market without respecting EU legislation on chemicals, is of increasing concern to the European Chemical Industry... While the European Chemical Industry openly welcomes international competition and free-trade, we find it, to say the least, inequitable to allow non-EU country competitors to take advantage of all the benefits of the Single Market without contributing to the accepted costs involved in EU environmental regulation.[14]

(d) Risk Factor and Market Conditions

Businesses tend to complain about excessive regulation especially in periods when markets do not function efficiently.[15] One of the main reasons excessive regulation is not welcome is that it brings about uncertainty and distracts businesses from productive activities. However, in some cases even de-regulative measures provide uncertainty and additional costs, as stakeholders may face one-off costs to fully understand, and get appropriate administrative measures in place to comply with, the new (lighter)

[12] T Bernauer and C Ladina, 'Interest Group Politics and Industrial Competition as Drivers of Environmental and Consumer Regulation' (2004) 24 *Journal of Public Policy* 99.

[13] G Majone, *Deregulation or Re-regulation? Policymaking in the European Community since the Single Act* (Florence, European University Institute, 1993).

[14] D Drohmann, 'Regulatory Compliance and Free-Riders', paper delivered to the joint European Commission/CEFIC Conference on 'The Impact of New Regulatory Requirements on the Chemical Industry and its Competitiveness', 5 Oct 2000, available at http://ec.europa.eu/enterprise/chemicals/conferences/cefic/cefic_2000_en.htm.

[15] P Cecchini, *1992—The European Challenge: the Benefits of a Single Market* (Aldershot: Wildwood House, 1988).

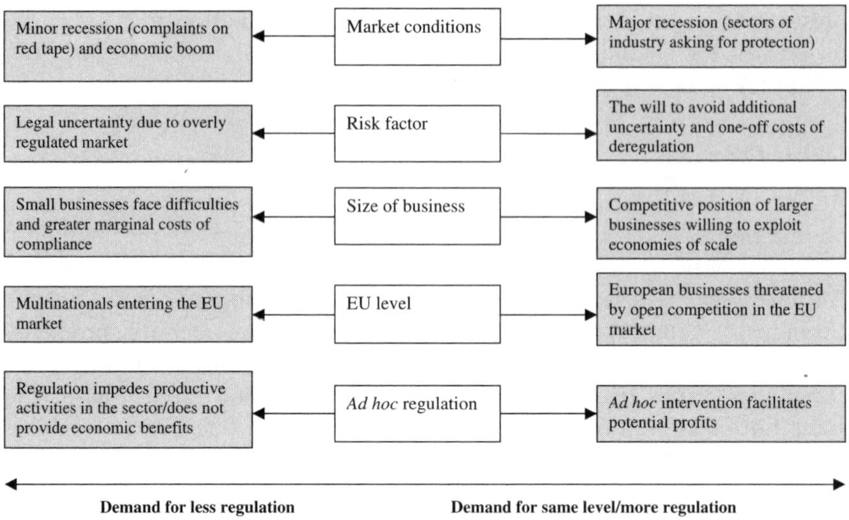

Figure 5.3—Business Demand for Regulation

regulatory regime. Evidence suggests that companies either support or oppose regulation according to their corporate strategies.[16]

Figure 5.3 shows how the demand for more or less regulation by business and industry changes depending on macro-economic and risk factors. The factors affecting demand for regulation analysed in this chapter are far from exhaustive. The reader should interpret them as a possible explanation for changing patterns in the demand for regulation. However, these factors may influence the future profile of the 'better regulation' agenda, which is designed to suit the needs of the business community.

D. APPLICATIONS OF THE SCM

The Standard Cost Model can be applied both *ex ante* and *ex post*. The anticipated administrative consequences of a draft law, draft executive order or other initiative can be contained in the Regulatory Impact Assessment. Similarly, the results from an *ex ante* measurement, for example, may form part of the overall consequence assessment of a bill's economic and administrative effects on the public sector, businesses, citizens, environment, etc. The *ex post* application of the SCM consists of the measurement of the administrative costs that arise after a regulation has come into effect and has been able to have an impact on businesses. In this case the SCM entails the factual administrative consequences for businesses in respect of

[16] S Fisher, 'Growth: The Role of Macroeconomic Factors' in M Baldassari (ed), *International Differences in Growth Rates* (New York: St. Martin's Press, 1994), at 441.

an implemented law, statutory instrument or other initiative. An *ex post* measurement is carried out when a measurement is to be made of the overall administrative costs in an area of regulation, known as a baseline measurement.[17] A baseline measurement, as carried out in the UK, is a statement of the overall administrative costs that businesses have in following a current set of regulations at a given point in time.[18]

The SCM was initially developed in the Netherlands and has also been extensively applied in Denmark among other countries. The international SCM framework is explained in the Administrative Burden declaration,[19] which sets out the SCM approach in summary, and the International Standard Cost Model Manual.[20] The Standard Cost Model is to date the most widely applied methodology for measuring administrative costs.[21] In 2003, a network of European countries was formed consistently to apply the Standard Cost Model. The SCM network currently consists of Austria, Belgium, Flanders (Belgium), Czech Republic, Denmark, Estonia, Finland, France, Germany, Hungary, Italy, Ireland, Latvia, Luxembourg, the Netherlands, Norway, Poland, Sweden and the United Kingdom.

1. The UK Experience

Following on the Dutch and Danish experiences, the Better Regulation Task Force recommended in 2005 that the UK government should measure and reduce the administrative burdens of existing legislation.[22] The measurement of administrative burdens in UK legislation consisted of a one-year intensive exercise. The application of the SCM by the UK government was part of a wider 'better regulation' initiative to reduce regulators and inspectorates from 31 national bodies to seven, introduce new legislation to speed up the process of de-regulation and make EU transposition easier. The Better Regulation Executive within the Cabinet Office had the responsibility for applying the SCM and co-ordinating the *ex post* measurement. It was an unprecedented, ambitious and resolute programme. The measurements were carried out involving 16 government departments. The quantitative measurement was conducted by external consultants who carried out 8,500 interviews with businesses to understand how much time

[17] BRE, above n3.

[18] *Ex post* measurements are also conducted in order to keep the baseline measurement updated with the consequences of new or amended regulations. The BRE (2005) manual suggested that 3 years after implementation is an appropriate time for this to occur. At this time the *ex ante* estimates of the administrative costs produced at the time of implementation can be reviewed and updated if necessary.

[19] Available at www.administratievelasten.nl/default.asp?CMS_TCP=tcpAsset&id=5B09EDCA525141E2866 D881AB2C43157.

[20] International Working Group on Administrative Burdens, above n2.

[21] Organisation for Economic Co-operation and Development (OECD), *The International Standard Cost Model Manual* (Paris, OECD, 2004).

[22] BRTF, above n1.

they spend on administrative activities. Estimates of the time taken for each of the 20,000 information obligations measured were obtained for a 'normally efficient' business.[23] In addition, 200 experts' panels were used to assess areas of regulation that are particularly complex, apply infrequently or affect only a small number of organisations. The UK government effort to measure administrative burdens is unique so far. Indeed, the volume of information produced is appreciable, especially considering the limited amount of time available. This exercise also stressed some of the problems related to the application of the SCM which are explained below.

2. Matters Arising from the UK Experience

The UK measurement is particularly ambitious because it comprises all business-related regulations with information obligations and data requirements. All regulation under the control of the central government is within the scope of this implementation. Also included are EU rules as well as international conventions, to the extent to which they are implemented domestically. Originally, segmentation of UK businesses was foreseen, to reflect differing cost/resource structures in businesses and the incidence of particular regulations. The idea is that firms of different sizes face different resource and cost constraints. A regulatory change may be substantially less significant in its impact on a large business, with resources dedicated to dealing with such changes, when compared with a small business where taking on a change means diverting resources from other activities and incurring unplanned costs. The segmentation took place according to the size of firms[24] and sectors.[25] More problematic was the classification of industry sectors. Different industry sectors face differing levels of regulation. For example, firms handling certain chemicals must comply with additional health and safety rules in addition to other regulations. Analysing the business population and dividing it by industry sector proved extremely difficult due to the high number of typologies of UK firms. Accordingly, many regulations were specific to very small areas of businesses. One les-

[23] The normally efficient business means a business that handles its administrative tasks in a normal manner, ie a business that handles its administrative tasks neither better nor worse than may be reasonably expected.

[24] 4 size bands as far as practicable. The size bands to be used are those defined by the Small Business Service: Micro (0–9 employees); Small (10–49 employees); Medium (50–249 employees); Large (250 or more employees).

[25] The SCM normally-efficient-business-based measurement approach means that in general splitting the measurement by industry sector is not necessary. Sector breakdowns can be derived using statistical population information. For sector-specific regulations the measurement must be segmented to reflect the coverage of the regulation. In general, industry sectors should be recorded using the *Standard Industrial Classification 2003* (SIC 2003) published by the Office for National Statistics. In many cases the SIC was not sufficiently detailed where regulation covered very specific areas of business.

Box 5.1: SCM and Business Population: Two Simple Examples

N: number of businesses
S: number of sectors
R: number of regulations

The SCM does not function properly when businesses are spread over many sectors. The extreme case would be that the number of businesses equalled the number of sectors. Consequently the level of regulation is at least as high as the number of sectors:

$N = S \leq R$

The figure below shows a simple example of a country where there are 5 businesses that operate in 5 different sectors. Each sector is regulated by at least one or more regulations.

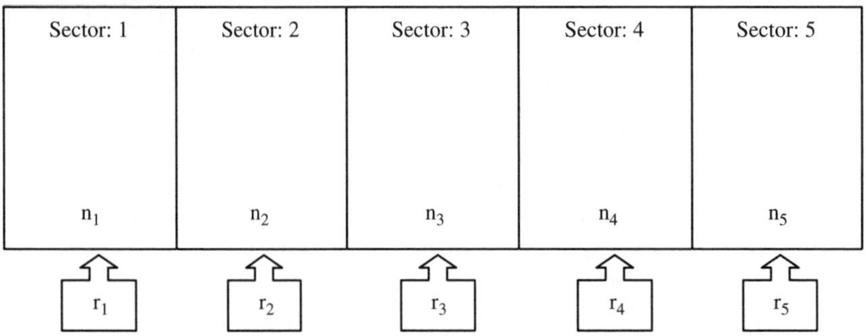

The SCM works better when businesses are concentrated in few sectors. Assuming that each sector requires the same degree of regulation as in the example above, the number of regulations per sector will be less than the number of businesses:

$R \geq S$ and $S < N$

The figure below shows a case of a country where there are 5 businesses that operate in 2 different sectors.

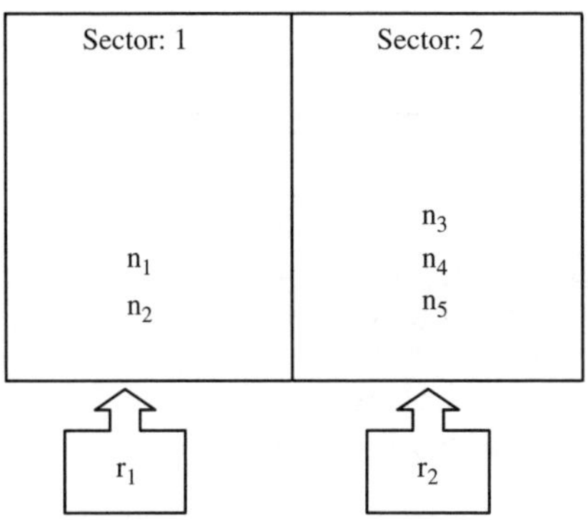

son learnt from the UK application of the SCM is therefore that the model does not work well when the population of businesses (and consequently regulations) is divided into a large number of sectors. Box 5.1 explains how the application of the SCM varies depending upon how the business population is distributed across sectors. It provides an example which simplifies some methodological observations derived mainly from the Dutch and UK experiences.

Besides the problems of segmentation of businesses, the UK measurement exercise proved extremely difficult due to the lack of information and reliable data to employ at the beginning of the exercise: departments did not know how many businesses they regulated or how much regulation they had produced to date. Given this premise, the creation of the baseline for information obligations was far from scientifically exact. An additional drawback was that the measurement was skewed by the inclusion of costs that were not administrative burdens. In other words, the SCM should measure the administrative burdens that businesses face due to compliance with regulation. This excludes administrative activities that businesses might continue if the regulations were removed (see Figure 5.4). Towards the end of the exercise, the Better Regulation Executive identified this problem and named it 'business as usual' costs, ie costs of activities which businesses would be likely to carry out regardless of the regulation in place. For example, most businesses would continue to keep some accounts even without legislation requiring them to do so. As the 'business as usual' costs problem was identified late in the exercise, the data previously collected did not allow such costs to be identified. Hence an *ad hoc*

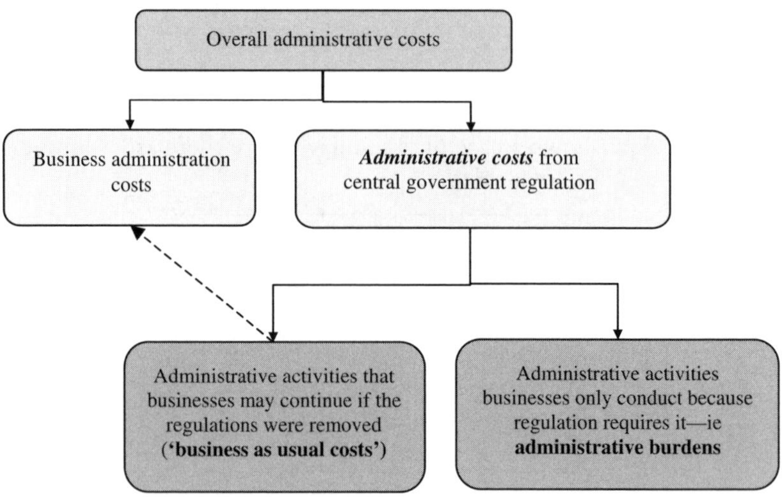

Figure 5.4—Administrative Burdens and 'Business as Usual Costs' (adapted from BRE, 2005).

methodology was introduced to reduce the impact of such costs on the overall measurement.[26]

E. GENERAL CRITICISMS OF THE SCM METHODOLOGY

Besides the matters which arose from the practical application of the SCM in the UK, this section presents some remarks about the overall SCM methodology and making some recommendations for improvement.

The manuals specify that the SCM was developed to provide a simplified method for estimating the administrative costs imposed on businesses.[27] The pragmatic approach to measurement provides estimates which are indicative rather than statistically representative. Moreover, the result of the measurement is only an estimate and, due to the limited sample size and non-random sample design, should not be regarded as necessarily being representative in statistical terms. The UK manual stresses that the method is not static and elements in the method will be constantly developed: 'the manual is not definitive, but will be updated in keeping with the method's continued development'.[28] On this premise, a discussion about certain aspects of the SCM methodology may help improve future versions of the model. By knowing the limits of the methodology, it will be possible to understand to what extent this model can be applied in future measurements.

1. Criticisms of the SCM Methodology

(1) The SCM supposes that the money saved on administrative burdens will be re-invested by industry in productive activities. Making a speculation like this implies a degree of certainty about the change in the management assets within firms, including internal shifts of human resources from administration and accounting offices to internal productive functions. Intuitively, management does not change the structure of a large firm because every year there are two fewer forms to fill in. Arguably, some desk officers will have to deal with less paper, but this does not necessarily imply the elimination of certain administration job categories which remain fundamental in the management of the business.

(2) The effort of calculating and eliminating administrative costs may prove ineffectual if the consequent overall economic improvement cannot be measured. Assuming that companies do benefit from administrative relief, how can this benefit be measured? How can the success of the SCM be measured? GDP is dependent on too many variables to be employed as a direct

[26] The BRE, instead of reviewing the 20,000 information obligations individually, attributed weights to some 300 information obligations.

[27] OECD, above n21.

[28] BRE, above n3.

indicator for the benefits arising from the lightening of administrative burdens. Moreover, the elimination of certain administrative tasks does not imply the opening of new production units, rendering GDP an obsolete indicator.

(3) The SCM assumes full compliance. This means that the measurement is carried out supposing that all businesses comply with the legislation in place. There are studies that have proven that the level of compliance in certain sectors is no more that 50 per cent with regard to existing regulations. Sectoral studies, for instance, state that 41 per cent of businesses do not comply with some part of food safety regulations.[29] Only in 2003–4, UK national regulators issued 357,000 warnings or enforcement notices, and prosecuted or fined almost 11,000 businesses.[30] The assumption of full compliance simplifies the calculations, but takes the measurement far away from reality. The full compliance assumption may also bring about inequalities in the phase of removal of administrative burdens. If the SCM does not take into account that industry sectors have different levels of compliance, businesses within highly compliant sectors may end up disadvantaged due to this generalisation. This may occur because the overall administrative burdens of a less compliant sector will be inflated compared to reality: some costs will be attributed to legislation that businesses do not fully comply with. The risk is in matching real administrative burdens with inflated, fictional administrative burdens and taking decisions based on this unfair matching.

(4) The SCM encompasses a one-size-fits-all approach: administrative burdens are expressed as the cumulative value of how much the 'normally efficient business' spends fulfilling a specific administrative activity multiplied by the number of businesses in the country. The main SCM formula can be read as an arithmetic mean average where dividing the overall activity cost by the number of businesses we can discover how much on average a business spends (Mean = Σ P / Q). Even the concept of 'normal business' is an attempt to identify a discrete frequency the spending of which represents the mode value of the population. This approach presents several problems:

I. No account is taken of distributional issues. It is unrealistic to suppose that all companies spend the same money in fulfilling administrative obligations. The model is not capable of distinguishing between, for instance, company A, which has the capability and willingness to pay €10 per hour to fulfil an information obligation, and company B, which is willing to pay €8 per hour and therefore obtains a less well qualified employee.

[29] Health and Safety Executive, 'Making an Impact on SME Compliance Behaviour: An Evaluation of the Effect of Interventions upon Compliance with Health and Safety Legislation in Small and Medium Sized Enterprises' (Prepared by Kings College London for the HSE), Research Report 366.

[30] HM Treasury, *Reducing Administrative Burdens: Effective Inspections and Enforcement* ('*The Hampton Review*') (London, HM Treasury, 2005).

II. The model does not weigh how much impact administrative burdens have on the wealth of businesses. Even assuming that filling in a form costs every business €10 per hour, the same €10 has a different weight depending on the size of the business. For example, company A has a turnover of €6 million. Spending €600 per year on its information obligation has an effect on 0.01 per cent of the company turnover. Company B has a turnover of €30,000. Spending the same €600 per year on its information obligation has a much more significant effect: over 2 per cent of the company turnover.

III. The manuals say very little about how to identify the 'normally efficient business'.[31] The process of selection is ambiguous in theory and problematic in practice. Even admitting that, per sector, there is a normal area of businesses that operate in normally efficient conditions, this would completely exclude areas of business which face administrative burdens possibly far from the average values.

(5) The SCM takes for granted the constructive cooperation of businesses in the interview phase. The SCM requires wide stakeholder participation (about three businesses per sector). Nevertheless, the UK experience suggests that businesses are not always cooperative. The director of the Better Regulation Commission, Rick Haythornthwaite, deplored businesses' lack of support during the SCM exercise.[32]

2. Recommendations to Improve the SCM Methodology

(1) Research is needed to understand how businesses re-invest once they are relieved of administrative burdens. A full understanding of how individual firms of different sizes react to the reduction of administrative burdens would be useful. The research could address the following questions: do businesses really re-invest? Do they move into more profitable activities? Does the structure of a business change because there are fewer administrative duties to comply with?

(2) How can public administration quantify the benefits of carrying out the SCM? In order to understand how much businesses actually lose due to administrative activities, the SCM model may include the concept of opportunity costs. In this case, opportunity costs will consist of how much each business gives up to fulfil administrative tasks. Opportunity costs

[31] 'One option is to take a random sample and start to contact the businesses to arrange an interview. When it comes to screening the businesses for interview, the businesses can be asked a few questions with a view to gaining an indication as to whether it is typical of the target group': BRE, above n3.

[32] 'The flow of ideas from business to help with the exercise had been lamentable', *Financial Times*, 27 July 2006.

provide an understanding of what the time spent by a single business means in relative terms. Businesses are then asked how they spend their resources in ways alternative to administrative costs. They are subsequently monitored to understand whether alternative investments occur, and if so how. Such investigation could be carried out only on a limited sample of the population. The standardisation and aggregation of opportunity costs gives a rough estimate of the overall benefits of reducing administrative burdens.

(3) Instead of calculating administrative burdens on the basis of full compliance, the government should first investigate the actual level of compliance of businesses and hence estimate administrative costs. Alternatively, if the measurement has already taken place, the total value should be weighted with realistic compliance rates, estimated according to available studies of the sector.

(4) The SCM does not take into account distributional matters because the formulae are based on the principle of statistical mean average. The introduction of the standard deviation would explain the crude SCM figures by providing some understanding of the distribution of costs through the population. Moreover a measure of statistical dispersion would help distinguish firms according to their ability to pay for administrative burdens. Contingent valuation may also help (i) understand how much a business is willing to pay for administrative burdens, and (ii) distinguish the impacts that administrative burdens have on different businesses.

(5) Since businesses do not always cooperate with government, an alternative way of gathering information should be contemplated. The SCM seeks to cover the business population *horizontally*, ie by collecting data from as many types of businesses as possible. This poses questions about the accuracy of the data collected and doubts about at what level (eg junior or senior) employees should be interviewed. An alternative *vertical* technique of data collection may consist of a lower number of businesses interviewed. Interviews carried out with a restricted number of businesses would allow more time for understanding the actual figures provided by businesses. The selection of the sectors on which to focus the measurement could be strategically made on the basis of which businesses require fewer administrative burdens. Ideally, other sectors would volunteer to participate in the measurement once they understood the privileges arising from the relief of administrative burdens from other sectors.

F. THE EU MEASUREMENT OF NET ADMINISTRATIVE COSTS

1. Characteristics

The European Commission developed a common approach for assessing administrative costs associated with existing and proposed Community legislation.[33] The common approach at EU level uses the Net Administrative Cost Model. The main aim of the model is to assess the net costs of administrative obligations imposed on enterprises, the voluntary sector, public authorities and citizens (net costs = costs introduced by legislation minus the costs suppressed by legislation at EU and/or national level). The European Commission specifies that the model is intended for microeconomic purposes,[34] ie to assess the administrative costs imposed by a particular piece of legislation. It should be used in the impact assessment of a proposed measure (*ex ante*) and the simplification of an existing measure (*ex post*). Apparently, the EU methodology has not been designed to suit macroeconomic purposes (eg increasing the overall GDP in EU Member States).

Administrative costs are defined as the costs incurred by enterprises, the voluntary sector, public authorities and citizens in the course of meeting legal obligations to provide information on their activities or production. Information is taken in a broad sense, including costs of labelling, reporting, and monitoring to provide the information, as well as registration. While the calculation will mainly focus on regulatory costs of a recurring nature, one-off costs may also be taken into account (ie costs incurred when (re)designing the way administrative obligations will be met).

2. Differences with UK Approach

With the Net Administrative Cost Model, as with the SCM, an administrative action required by law but corresponding to what an entity would normally do in the absence of any legal obligation is not regarded as an administrative obligation. For example, a large part of accounting and auditing legislation corresponds to normal business practice. Table 5.1 draws a comparison between the UK Standard Cost Model and the EU Net Administrative Cost Model. Noticeably, the EU model differs in its focus on proposals imposing major administrative obligations and particularly burdensome acts. The decision to measure the administrative burdens of the most onerous actions may, on paper, reduce the measurement effort. Directorate General Enterprise, for instance, adopted a pilot case approach where the administrative costs of one sector, the building industry, are assessed through interviews with individual businesses. At the EU level, Member States approximately play the role played by government departments at the national level.

[33] European Commission, 'Better Regulation for Growth and Jobs', COM(2005)97 final.
[34] *Ibid.*

Table 5.1: Comparison between UK Standard Cost Model and EU Net Administrative Cost Model[35]

	UK Standard Cost Model	**EU Net Administrative Cost Model**
Aim	Assesses only the costs of administrative obligations imposed on enterprises, distinguishing between national and non-national origins. Macroeconomic purpose (estimate of administrative burden on the economy as a whole).	Assesses net costs of administrative obligations imposed on enterprises, the voluntary sector, public authorities and citizens, distinguishing between national, EU and international origins. (net costs = new costs – costs suppressed). Microeconomic purpose (*ex ante* impact assessment and *ex post* simplification). No macroeconomic use envisaged.
Definition of administrative costs	The costs of administrative activities that businesses are required to conduct in order to comply with the information obligations that are imposed through central government regulation.	Administrative obligations are defined as the costs incurred by enterprises, the voluntary sector, public authorities and citizens in meeting legal obligations to provide information on their action or production, either to public authorities or to private parties. One-off costs may be taken into account.
Core equation	Σ P × Q (P: Price = Tariff × Time; Q: Quantity = Number of businesses × Frequency). Focus on labour costs and overheads, assumed to be the main input for meeting administrative obligations.	Σ P × Q Where appropriate, types of costs other than wages and overheads will be taken into account.
Scope and frequency	Method applied to all regulatory proposals and all acts in force. 1st Baseline measurement (2005–6). Baseline needs to be updated to reflect	Method applied only to propo-sals imposing major administrative obligations and/or to acts identified as particularly burdensome by end-users. No sector excluded *a priori*, but no sectoral or general baseline measurements envisaged either.

(continued)

[35] Adapted from European Commission, 'Better Regulation for Growth and Jobs', COM(2005)97 final.

Table 5.1: (continued)

	UK Standard Cost Model	EU Net Administrative Cost Model
	progress on simplification and new regulations.	Only applied to the most onerous actions identified in most cases by means of indicative thresholds (based on time required per action and frequency) Review and timeline defined on a case-by-case basis.
Expected level of accuracy & data source(s)	Level of accuracy depends on fieldwork and degree of cooperation by departments.[1]	Expected level of accuracy depends on the degree of Member State cooperation. In exceptional cases, high level of accuracy sought via field work, limited to a sample of Member States and/or to a standard sample of the business community, and simulation. This would apply to required actions likely to be particularly disruptive to the work of the enterprise, and data that are sensitive or costly to produce. In standard cases, rough estimate based on available EU statistics, standard ratios and Member States studies.
Determination of the regulatory origin	Decision tree in three phases and 14 steps.	Decision tree in four steps.
Division of responsibility	Regulatory burdens are costed by departments and consultants, under the guidance and supervision of the Better Regulation Executive (Cabinet Office).	Member States conduct national fieldwork and simulations of typical national firms, while the European Commission defines what is needed to aggregate data.
Report sheet	Standard report template consists of nine points and five annexes.	Standard report sheet including specific columns for EU origin and for transposition 'markers'. Use of a (simplified) typology of administrative obligations only for the *ex post* assessment of transposition measures.

(continued)

[1] Field work: sample of 'typical' businesses are interviewed by telephone. In cases where telephone interviews did not fit the purpose face to face interviews were carried out. Overall 8,500 interviews were carried out.

Table 5.1: (continued)

	UK Standard Cost Model	EU Net Administrative Cost Model
Methodological caveats	Borderline cases are defined. Borderline cases include: treatment of complaints; differentiation between households and businesses; administrative costs of inspections; tribunals, court cases and investigations; and start-ups and first time compliance cases.	List of limitations of the method used (nature of the assumptions and extrapolations made; reminder that the figures are only approximations/estimates; margin of error). Mention whether EU regulation (and the administrative costs arising from it) replaces national regulations and whether EU regulation is in fact reducing costs to operators; etc.

3. Dealing with Data on Costs in the EU

In perspective, the process of gathering and aggregation of the data is even more demanding at EU level than at the national level. The experience coming from Impact Assessment is that EU institutions in the phase of the proposal of new legislation are struggling with insufficient or spurious data. The European Commission is not able to guarantee full knowledge of the costs and benefits of future legislation.[36] To date, cost and benefit rationales have not represented the core foundations for drafting policy proposals.[37] They are supplementary instruments to be used by the European regulator in specific regulatory circumstances, especially when business stakeholders require it. This observation applies also to the employment of any economic and risk analysis techniques. It is difficult to predict whether the introduction of a cost model will change the approach by European institutions to economic analysis. One may argue that an increase in the use of economic analytical instruments may induce the wider use of such instruments.[38] If public servants see the introduction of economic analysis as an imposition, the effect may not be so immediate. Like other public institutions, the European Commission comprises public servants of different backgrounds. The existence of teams of economists is not sufficient to guarantee a systematic economic approach to decision-making. In other words, public servants will not start to base their decisions on costs and benefits just because the Secretariat General produces guidelines that recommend the use of SCM or cost-benefit analysis.[39]

[36] RW Hahn and RE Litan, *Counting Regulatory Benefits and Costs: Lessons for the US and Europe* (Washington, DC, AEI-Brookings Joint Center, 2004).

[37] J Torriti, 'Impact Assessments in the European Union: A Tool for Better Regulation or Less Regulation?', (2007) 10:2 *Journal of Risk Research* 239–276.

[38] R Hahn and R Malik, *Is Regulation Good for You?* (Washington, DC, AEI-Brookings Joint Center, 2004).

[39] Commission, above n4.

4. The Measurement of Administrative Burdens in the 'Better Regulation' Context

The introduction of the common methodology for measuring administrative burdens is coincidental with a time period when institutions focus on the importance of eliminating red tape. In a number of business publications and conferences, the blame for the poor performance of the European economy was laid on the excessive number and rigidity of EU regulations.[40] The climate was one of demand for less regulation, as described in section C.2. The advent of the Barroso Commission in 2004 corresponded with the greatest institutional effort to facilitate the European business community in the 'fight against red tape'.[41] In the name of 'better regulation', Commissioner Verheugen started a campaign of reduction of regulation, calling for a reduction of the *acquis communautaire* by repealing, codifying, recasting or modifying 222 basic items of legislation and over 1,400 related legal acts in the next three years. The inclusion of the model in the Impact Assessment guidelines[42] could be interpreted as a shift in the EU 'better regulation' agenda to more de-regulative grounds. One third of 2006 policy proposals were withdrawn.[43] The focus of 'better regulation' has certainly changed since it was introduced in 2000 by previous European Commission president Romano Prodi as an incentive to improve social and environmental protection in EU regulation. Moreover, as the Net Administrative Cost Model is not about removing pieces of legislation which represent excessive administrative burdens, the European Commission is about to launch a new project in the measurement of administrative burdens having significant financial effects.[44] The rationale of the project is to prove that the amount of regulation originating from Brussels is moderate and to give a strong signal to stakeholders of the Commission's commitment to reducing red tape. The European Commission already knows that the policy areas that will be affected by the measurement and identification of the specific directives, regulations and decisions containing excessive information obligations will be lightened by the existence of the *acquis communautaire*.

When is the 'fight against red tape' due to finish? What is the future of 'better regulation'? It is argued here that the focus on administrative compliance costs will decrease once the hostility to regulation declines. Public institutions take action against administrative burdens because the

[40] W Robinson, *'Bad' EU Regulation: Prevention and Cure* (PLC Global Counsel Dispute Resolution Handbook, 2004), available at www.freshfields.com/practice/comptrade/publications/pdf/externalpub/BadEURegulation.pdf

[41] R Löfstedt, 'The Plateau-ing of the European Better Regulation Agenda: an Analysis of Activities Carried Out by the Barroso Commission' (2006), available at www.aei-brookings.org/admin/authorpdfs/page.php?id=1313.

[42] Commission, above n4.

[43] Withdrawal of Commission Proposals Following Screening for their General Relevance, their Impact on Competitiveness and other Aspects [2006] OJ C64/02.

[44] The overall cost of the project amounts to around €20 million.

business community requires less red tape. Accordingly, the 'better regulation' agenda will change again to meet the needs of businesses. An improvement in the European economy may alter the business community's plea to eliminate regulation. The institutional, mainly legal, difficulties of removing regulation and the private industry costs of adapting to a re-regulated regime may induce both legislators and businesses to refrain from fighting red tape. The shift in the demand for less de-regulation will also depend on the size of business and the sectoral circumstances of demand for *ad hoc* regulation.

F. CONCLUSIONS

This chapter introduced the Standard Cost Model, a 'better regulation' instrument used by public institutions to measure and eliminate the administrative burdens that businesses face due to regulation. The main characteristics and the general mechanism of the model were explained. An overview of the costs generated by regulation was provided in order to clarify which types of costs are measured by the SCM. The chapter explored the reasons why some public institutions are centring their 'better regulation' agenda on administrative compliance costs. It is argued that better regulation is a response of the public sector to the needs of the private sector, above all the business community. Different strands of literature were therefore examined to understand in which cases businesses demand less (or more) regulation. A set of factors that go into business demand for regulation were identified. The main example of national application of the SCM is from the UK. Starting from the UK experience, part of the SCM methodology was critically reviewed because: (i) the model ignores how businesses will re-invest after the easing of the administrative burden; (ii) the benefits of the elimination of administrative burdens cannot be measured; (iii) the full compliance assumption is too distant from reality; (iv) the average mean formula does not take into account distributional issues, does not weigh how much impact administrative burdens have on the wealth of business and is based on the ambiguous concept of 'normally efficient business'; and (v) the model is too dependent on business stakeholder participation. Recommendations were put forward to improve the model or future measurements of administrative compliance costs. Finally the chapter discussed the EU common methodology for assessing net administrative costs, comparing it to the UK SCM. The consequences of introducing such methodology were discussed in the wider context of 'better regulation'.

6

Better Regulation—Better Enforcement

ANTHONY OGUS*

A. THE BACKGROUND

TWENTY YEARS AGO, policy discussion centred on 'deregulation'; now the obsession is for 'better'[1] or 'smarter'[2] regulation. The evolution reflects a movement away from the simplistic notion that there is just too much regulation, some of which could be abolished, and towards a more balanced perspective. This new perspective is characterised by an acceptance that much regulation is necessary but also by a concern that attention must be paid to the choice and design of instrument, so that it may be well targeted to the regulatory objectives. Concerns with this area of the state–industry relationship and efforts to improve it have been widely shared across the industrialised world, notably at the OECD[3] and EU,[4] and of course it has been a constant theme of UK governments since the Thatcher era.[5]

* Professor of Law at the University of Manchester and Research Professor at the University of Maastricht.

1 Reflected in the name given to the key policy-making unit in the Cabinet Office: see OECD, *From Red Tape to Smart Tape: Administrative Simplification in OECD Countries* (Paris, OECD, 2003) 197–8.

2 Perhaps more in vogue in North America than in the UK. See eg US Office of Management and Budget, 'Stimulating Smarter Regulation' (Report to Congress, 2002); Canadian External Advisory Committee on Smarter Regulation, 'Smarter Regulation: A Regulatory Strategy for Canada' (Report to the Government of Canada, 2004). Legal academics may have been more influenced by N Gunningham and P Grabosky, *Smart Regulation: Designing Environmental Policy* (Oxford, OUP, 1998).

3 In addition to 'From Red Tape', above n1, see in particular OECD, *OECD Report on Regulatory Reform* (Paris, OECD, 1997) and OECD, *Regulatory Policies in OECD Countries: From Interventionism to Regulatory Governance* (Paris, OECD, 2002).

4 Eg European Commission, 'Benchmarking the Administration of Business Start-Ups' (Brussels, 2002).

5 See especially White Paper, 'Lifting the Burden', Cmnd 9751 (London, HMSO, 1985); Deregulation Initiative, 'Thinking About Regulating: A Guide to Good Regulation' (London, DTI, 1993); Better Regulation Task Force, 'Alternatives to State Regulation' (London, Cabinet Office, 2000); Regulatory Impact Unit, 'Regulatory Reform: The Government's Action Plan'

The investigations and proposals have covered a wide variety of structural, institutional and procedural topics. While one dimension did indeed involve a retreat from direct state ownership and management of services,[6] another focused on decentralisation, empowering industry to share in regulatory rule-making and relying on financial incentives rather than coercive measures to induce desired outcomes.[7] Then, as regards regulatory policy-making, regulatory impact assessment became the vogue, comprising some form of cost-benefit appraisal and risk assessment.[8]

Investigation of enforcement policy and practices has lagged behind these other developments. Although a favourite topic of the academic literature since the 1970s,[9] governments seem only relatively recently to have been prepared to address the key issues.[10] An explanation for this may, perhaps, be sought in the way in which those key issues are presented in the Hampton Review, the most significant policy document to have emerged on regulatory enforcement.[11] That document is concerned to address what businesses perceive to be the principal problems with current enforcement strategies. What is reported appears to be somewhat ambivalent: on the one hand, the regimes are criticised for involving too much interaction between regulators and industry, including unnecessary inspections and excessive form-filling; on the other hand, the complaint is that enforcement practices are insufficiently effective in punishing offenders and rewarding compliant behaviour.[12]

While this ambivalence may have inhibited pressure for reform, it should not be regarded as precluding careful analysis of enforcement policy and, indeed, both the Hampton Report and the Macrory Review[13] which followed it have thrown up some interesting and important ideas for reform.

(London, Cabinet Office, 2003); Better Regulation Task Force, 'Regulation—Less is More: Reducing Burdens, Improving Outcomes' (London, Cabinet Office, 2005).

[6] Reflecting the highly influential publication D Osborne and T Gaebler, *Reinventing Government: How the Entrepreneurial Spirit Is Transforming the Public Sector* (New York, Plume, 1993).

[7] A Ogus, 'New Techniques for Social Regulation: Decentralisation and Diversity' in H Collins, P Davies and R Rideout (eds), *Legal Regulation of the Employment Relation* (London, Kluwer Law International, 2000) at 83–98.

[8] C Radaelli, 'The Diffusion of Regulatory Impact Analysis—Best Practice or Lesson-Drawing' (2004) 43 *European Journal of Political Research* 723.

[9] Notable monographs include: R Cranston, *Regulating Business* (London, Macmillan, 1979); B Hutter, *The Reasonable Arm of the Law* (Oxford, Clarendon Press, 1988); I Ayres and J Braithwaite, *Responsive Regulation: Transcending the Deregulation Debate* (Oxford, OUP, 1992); K Hawkins, *Law as Last Resort* (Oxford, OUP, 2003).

[10] For a valuable survey see OECD, *Reducing the Risk of Policy Failure: Challenges for Regulatory Compliance* (Paris, OECD, 2000).

[11] P Hampton, *Reducing Administrative Burdens: Effective Regulation and Enforcement* (London, HM Treasury, 2005).

[12] *Ibid*, ch.1.

[13] R Macrory, *Regulatory Justice: Sanctioning in a post-Hampton World* (London, Cabinet Office, 2006).

This chapter reflects on these, and adds to them. It will respond to the apparent dilemma posed by the business community, arguing that it can be resolved by an economic analysis of enforcement options, leading to a more imaginative approach to penalties and enforcement discretion.

B. AN ECONOMIC FRAMEWORK FOR REGULATORY ENFORCEMENT

To address the central issues of regulatory enforcement policy discussed in the Hampton and Macrory Reviews, we need to define what the primary goal of such a policy might be. Let us begin by assuming that it is to maximise regulatory compliance at lowest cost. We might need also to add that the means used to procure this outcome should be consistent with generally accepted notions of fairness.

The next step is to postulate a theory of compliance, and for this purpose we adopt the familiar economic perspective which assumes that traders will be induced to comply with the law if the costs of contravening it exceed the benefits (say U) to them of the contravention.[14] The costs which traders will face as a result of contraventions are principally those arising from legal sanctions (say D), but since not all contraventions will be detected, nor all detected contraventions punished, D must be discounted by the probability (p) of these costs being imposed. The condition of compliance is, then, $U < pD$.

It is, however, important to appreciate that the costs for traders arising from contraventions are significantly broader than the penalties imposed by the law. They include also the 'hassle' and personal inconvenience arising from encounters with the victims of regulatory contraventions and with public officials, legal and other defence expenditures, as well as any loss of market reputation resulting from the contravention being detected. It follows that some of the costs to the trader will be incurred even if there is no formal condemnation by a tribunal or other authorised institution. Because not all cases reach the ultimate stage of condemnation, involving the imposition of the formal sanction, it is helpful to rewrite the *ex ante* additional cost arising from the contravention as $qE + pD$ where qE represents the probability and the associated costs of the relevant act being detected, and pD the probability of a formal condemnation and its associated costs,

[14] For the basic model see GS Becker, 'Crime and Punishment: An Economic Approach' (1968) 76 *Journal of Political Economy* 169. For overviews of the large literature to which the model has given rise see: E Eide, 'Economics of Criminal Behavior' in G De Geest and B Bouckaert, *Encyclopedia of Law and Economics* (Cheltenham, Edward Elgar, 2000) at 345–89; A M Polinsky and S Shavell, 'The Economic Theory of Public Enforcement of Law' (2000) 38 *Journal of Economic Literature* 45.

including notably the prescribed sanction.[15] The condition of compliance thus becomes $U < qE + pD$.

Although the value of U, whether for individual cases or in aggregate, will not be known to policy-makers, reasonable conjectures can be made. Maximising compliance will then entail organising the institutional framework for enforcement such that $qE + pD$ exceeds that estimate. There are three principal variables which policy measures can influence. The value of q can be raised by increased monitoring, the better targeting of monitoring (ie focusing on those more likely to contravene), and facilitating third-party reporting. That of p can be raised by reducing or eliminating procedural and other obstacles to establishing liability for the formal penalties. And there are of course a wide variety of sanctions which can be imposed on those found to have committed contraventions, thus raising the value of D.

Nevertheless, as is indicated above, the policy choice must be driven also by cost-minimisation considerations. Three categories of cost are particularly important. First, and most obviously, there are the administrative costs (say C_a) associated with the different processes, notably those associated with monitoring and dealing with traders, preparing and adjudicating formal procedures, and imposing sanctions. The second set of costs arises from the fact that procedures and institutions are not perfect and some decisions will erroneously impose sanctions or other losses on those who have not contravened the law. Given that some institutions and procedures (for example those in the criminal law process) may be designed specifically to reduce such errors, we need to take account of the propensity of the various policy options to generate these losses, what we can call 'error costs' (C_e).[16] Thirdly, we should not ignore costs to the wrongdoing traders themselves (C_t). This may seem paradoxical since the deterrence theory assumes that costs have to be imposed, or threatened, to induce traders to comply. However, there is still an economic argument that the costs imposed on lawbreakers should be no greater than those which are necessary for deterrence purposes—lawbreakers should not be given a perverse incentive to increase the amount of unlawful activity ('better to be hung for a sheep than for a lamb...').[17] In any event, excessive penalties may conflict with principles of fairness, particularly where they are disproportionate to the offence which has been committed.[18]

[15] A Ogus, *Costs and Cautionary Tales: Economic Insights for the Law* (Oxford, Hart Publishing, 2006) at 102–5.

[16] DL Rubinfeld and DEM Sappington, 'Efficient Awards and Standards of Proof in Judicial Proceedings' (1987) 18 *Rand Journal of Economics* 308; N Garoupa and F Gomez-Pomar, 'Punish Once or Punish Twice: A Theory of the Use of Criminal Sanctions in Addition to Regulatory Penalties' (2004) 6 *American Law and Economics Review* 410.

[17] D Friedman and W Sjostrom, 'Hanged for a Sheep: The Economics of Marginal Deterrence' (1993) 22 *Journal of Legal Studies* 345.

[18] A Ashworth, *Sentencing and Criminal Justice* 3rd edn) (Cambridge CUP, 2000) at 72–4.

C. DETERRENCE AND THE CRIMINAL JUSTICE SYSTEM

In the light of the economic framework outlined in the last section, we can now revisit the problems with regulatory enforcement identified in the Hampton and Macrory Reviews. Perhaps the most important were the perceptions that:

> Penalties handed down by courts are not seen as an adequate deterrent to regulatory non-compliance as the level of financial penalty can often fail to reflect the economic benefit of non-compliance with regulatory obligations. The range of enforcement tools available to many regulators is limited, giving rise to disproportionate use of criminal sanctions which can be a costly, time-consuming and slow process.[19]

The background to these observations is that British regulatory regimes, unlike those in many other jurisdictions,[20] tend to rely almost exclusively on the criminal justice system for the imposition of financial penalties. Criminal prosecutions for regulatory contraventions are relatively rare, accounting for, at the most, some 0.05 per cent of reported contraventions[21] (and therefore the percentage prosecuted of all contraventions must be much smaller). We also know that, although the legislation typically confers powers on the courts to impose large fines on offenders, the amounts in fact imposed tend to be quite modest for most regulatory contraventions. For example, in 2005, the average fine imposed for prosecutions brought by the Environment Agency was just over £5,000.[22]

If, for the purposes of the economic framework, we can thus (optimistically) assume that $p = 0.05$ and $D = £5,000$, it follows that the average cost to traders of breaking the law is $(0.05 \times £5,000) + qE = £250 + qE$, where qE is the informal cost of being apprehended. Then, unless the value of qE is significant, the profit that traders make by the illegal act need be only relatively small for them to benefit overall from the contravention. If this is the case then the enforcement system provides inadequate deterrence.

Why is the prosecution rate so small? There used to be a suspicion that this was a consequence of 'regulatory capture', or at least of a pusillanimous approach by enforcement agencies.[23] A much more convincing explanation

[19] Macrory, above n13, para 2.2, summarising Hampton.

[20] European Commission, 'The System of Administrative and Penal Sanctions in the Member States of the European Communities' (Brussels, Office for Official Publications of the European Communities, 1994); Australian Law Reform Commission, 'Civil and Administrative Penalties', Consultation Paper (Sydney, Australian Law Reform Commission, 2000).

[21] See the empirical evidence cited in A Ogus and C Abbot, 'Pollution and Penalties' (2002) 20 *Research in Law and Economics* 493, 497–8.

[22] Macrory, above n13, Table 2.1.

[23] See J Rowan-Robinson, P Watchman and C Barker, *Crime and Regulation: A Study of the Enforcement of Regulatory Codes* (Edinburgh, T&T Clark, 1990), 8, and the references there cited.

is the very high cost to the enforcement agency of marshalling sufficient evidence to obtain a conviction, given existing principles of criminal procedure, including, notably, the burden of proof, restrictive rules of evidence and (in very serious cases) the requirement of a jury trial.[24] For example, in relation to an average consumer protection case involving the Trading Standards Service, one 'officer day' is typically spent on investigating a contravention, two days on issuing informal cautions, four days on issuing formal cautions and 10 days on preparing criminal prosecutions. And, for the last of these, there would in addition be five days of senior management time, as well as legal costs.[25]

If we inquire further why the safeguards apply to the criminal process, the conventional answer is that they protect the innocent from wrongful conviction[26] and thus, in terms of our economic framework, reduce C_e (error costs).[27] Nevertheless, the greater the precautions that are taken to reduce C_e, the greater the increases to C_a (administrative costs) and the more the deterrence system is undermined because of the reduction in p (probability of conviction).

Of course, it is very difficult to identify with any precision the optimal trade-off between the benefits of deterrence and administrative and error costs.[28] Using American empirical criminal justice data on some of the cost variables, Hylton and Khanna feel able to conclude that the higher standard of proof required in criminal cases (compared with civil cases) cannot be justified by the reduction in error costs rationale.[29] That may or may not be right insofar as it applies to mainstream criminal offences. Perhaps the traditional procedural safeguards associated with the criminal justice system approximate to the optimal level, once account is taken of the fact that criminal conviction for such offences often leads to imprisonment and generally a high level of social stigma. But intuition suggests that in a regulatory context, where the defendants are mostly firms, the costs of a wrongful conviction should not be exaggerated. Imprisonment is not in practice an option, and stigma may not be serious. If that intuition is correct, the reliance on criminal justice sanctions for ordinary regulatory contraventions is not optimal.[30] This observation ought to lead to

[24] *Ibid*, at 255–63.

[25] Private communication from the Local Authorities Coordinating Office on Regulatory Services.

[26] G Williams, *The Proof of Guilt: A Study of the English Criminal Trial*, 2nd edn. (London, Stevens & Sons, 1958) at 154–8.

[27] R A Posner, 'An Economic Approach to Legal Procedure and Judicial Administration' (1973) 2 *Journal of Legal Studies* 399.

[28] Cf L Kaplow, 'The Value of Accuracy in Adjudication: An Economic Analysis' (1994) 23 Journal of Legal Studies 307.

[29] KN Hylton and VS Khanna, 'Toward an Economic Theory of Criminal Procedure' (2007) 15 *Supreme Court Economic Review* (forthcoming).

[30] Posner, above n27, at 416, reaches the same conclusion. See also Garoupa and Gomez-Pomar, above n16.

consideration of other sanctions, notably administrative financial penalties which will be considered in the next section.

Note that this reasoning does not imply removal of criminal liability. For general deterrence purposes, it may be important that the criminal process is seen to be used on occasions. Putting the same point another way, if traders generally perceive the value of p to be significantly higher than in reality is the case, there is no reason to disturb this impression if it can contribute to a higher level of compliance.[31] Further, criminal justice prosecutions and sanctions may be necessary to induce compliance in the case of individual traders who repeatedly offend and where alternative systems provide inadequate deterrence. Finally, it must be recognised that the criminal justice system is concerned not only to deter and repress unlawful conduct, but also to reflect moral values within a given society regarding what is 'wrongful'. And criminal prosecutions may be appropriate for those whose conduct is regarded as so repugnant morally as to justify such proceedings being taken, irrespective of deterrence considerations.

D. ADMINISTRATIVE FINANCIAL PENALTIES

In his consultation document, Richard Macrory comes out strongly in favour of administrative financial penalties, which he says can:

> provide an intermediate step between the formal, costly and stigmatic action of criminal prosecution and the more informal means of advice and persuasion to get firms into compliance [and]...can also be flexible and take a more customized approach in dealing with regulatory non-compliance.[32]

In terms of the economic framework, it is not difficult to support these arguments.[33] If, as we can assume, administrative financial penalties can readily be imposed without a formal hearing and without satisfying the evidentiary threshold required in criminal justice cases, then p will be substantially increased. The consequences are striking. Suppose that on average p becomes 0.4 (I will explain below, in section 5, why it should not be much higher) and that D remains at £5,000. Even without significant informal costs (qE), the system will now deter unlawful activities generating profits up to £2,000. Moreover, this is done with a very considerable saving in administrative costs (C_a).

[31] The empirical work of Keith Hawkins (above n9) underscores the importance of this point.

[32] Macrory, above n13, at paras 3.9–3.10.

[33] See also RM Brown, 'Administrative and Criminal Penalties in the Enforcement of Occupational Health and Safety Legislation' (1992) 30 *Osgoode Hall Law Journal* 691, which uses data drawn from contrasting administrative and criminal justice regimes to reinforce the arguments.

Now, of course, it must be recognised that administrative financial penalties are likely to give rise to increased error costs (C_e) because, without the higher evidentiary thresholds required for liability in the criminal justice system, some administrative penalties will be wrongly imposed. But the problem should not be exaggerated: the adverse consequences of an inappropriately imposed administrative financial penalty are likely to be small relative to those which would be incurred when a trader is known to have been condemned in a court. In any event, as envisaged by Macrory, there would be a right of appeal against the imposition, perhaps to a newly created regulatory tribunal.[34]

To reduce administrative costs further, and indeed to eliminate the risk that the amount of the penalty would vary between local agencies, there could be a system of fixed penalties—these are already familiar to those who park their vehicles unlawfully.[35] This approach may be justified for very minor regulatory offences where there is pressure to reduce administrative costs, but otherwise deterrence considerations favour discretion, up to a maximum amount, because that enables the agencies to tailor the penalty to likely values of U.[36]

In considering the level at which that maximum will be set, account must also be taken of human rights considerations.[37] This is because Article 6(1) of the European Convention on Human Rights provides that 'in the determination ... of any criminal charge against him, everyone is entitled to a fair and public hearing within a reasonable time by an independent and impartial tribunal' and the fact that an administrative sanction does not use the language of the criminal law does not prevent the application of this provision.[38] In deciding whether an imposition constitutes a 'criminal charge', regard is had to whether it has 'a punitive character',[39] and clearly the severity of the sanction is relevant for this purpose.[40]

E. TARGETING ENFORCEMENT INTERVENTIONS

Some of the major criticisms by business of the present system have been that interaction between firms and regulators is too cumbersome and time-consuming and regulators do not give enough emphasis to providing advice

[34] Macrory, above n13, at paras. 3.48–3.51.
[35] Fixed Penalty Order 2000, SI 2000/2792.
[36] See also Macrory, above n13, at paras. 3.32–3.36.
[37] A Guinchard, 'Fixing the Boundaries of the Concept of Crime: The Challenge for Human Rights' (2005) 54 *International and Comparative Law Quarterly* 719.
[38] *Deweer v Belgium* (1980) 2 EHRR 439.
[39] *Öztürk v Germany* (1984) 6 EHRR 409.
[40] *Benham v United Kingdom* (1996) 22 EHRR 293, at 323.

in order to secure compliance. Hampton's response is to be found in his first three recommendations:

— entrenching the principle of risk assessment throughout the regulatory system, so that the burden of enforcement falls most on highest-risk businesses, and least on those with the best records of compliance;
— in particular, ensuring that inspection activity is better focused, reduced where possible but, if necessary, enhanced where there is good cause ...;
— making much more use of advice, again applying the principle of risk assessment.[41]

Cost-effectiveness provides a straightforward rationalisation of the use of risk assessment in relation to enforcement agency monitoring. Clearly, q (the likelihood of a contravention being detected) is increased if the monitoring strategy itself reflects the likelihood that a contravention will have occurred among the businesses being inspected. The risk assessment model is typically based on objective criteria such as a trader's record in relation to previous contraventions, complaints by third parties, geographic location, age of the trader's plant, and size.[42] But it might also involve variables requiring some subjective judgement by agency officials, for example, the experience and ability of the firm's staff and their attitude to compliance, and the inclusion of these variables in the model may add so significantly to the costs of monitoring as to be self-defeating.[43]

An equally important, but more complex, set of issues arises when a contravention has been detected by, or notified to, the agency. Normally the latter has a range of possible actions including: doing nothing except providing informal advice or warning to the trader; issuing a formal warning; and instituting proceedings for a formal sanction, typically a financial penalty. Now, as we have seen in section C, the variance in administrative costs (C_a) between these options is enormous and well-designed targeting, of the kind envisaged by Hampton, should ensure that the costly options are used only when the benefits to be derived justify the choice.

To explore this policy issue, take the distinction between a first offender and a trader who has committed a second or repeated contravention. Given that many, perhaps most, first offences are the result of inadvertence or an insufficient understanding of legal obligations, it is not likely that punishing the offender (or taking formal steps toward that end) will in fact ensure future compliance better than dismissing the case with advice and/or an informal warning. Note too that a heavy-handed approach, for little or no additional benefit, will not only generate increased administrative costs; it

[41] Hampton, above n11, at 8.
[42] OECD, above n10, at 38.
[43] OECD, above n10, at 41.

will also involve significant additional costs to traders. And these are likely to include 'indignation costs' which may motivate them to initiate appeals against decisions, leading to yet more administrative costs.[44]

The theoretical work of economists has underpinned the importance of the Hampton approach to exercising enforcement discretion. For example,[45] Harrington has modelled the relationship between an enforcement agency and firms as a game in which profit-maximising firms have to decide whether or not to comply with the law, and the agency, aiming to maximise compliance, has to decide whether or not to punish a firm which decides not to comply.[46] For the purposes of the game, the agency classifies all firms into two groups, G_1 and G_2: the first is monitored only rarely, while the second is monitored regularly and, if found to contravene, receives a substantial penalty. Initially the agency does not have sufficient information on which to classify firms. The first monitoring enables it to do so. If a firm is found to comply, it is classified as G_1.[47] If it is found to have committed a contravention, it is classified as G_2; it will not be punished, but it will know that another detected contravention will lead to the prescribed punishment and that the chance of the contravention being detected (q) is now relatively high, given that it will be subjected to regular monitoring. So it must be seen regularly to comply, thus enabling it to be reclassified as G_1. Institutional arrangements which facilitate the game being played to these outcomes should lead to the goals of firms and agencies being met at lowest cost.

There is one final observation to make in this section. An important implication of the above analysis is that, in general, traders should be allowed one contravention without significant adverse consequences. That policy will not be appropriate in relation to some, probably a small minority of, regulatory contraventions which can generate a large amount of harm. In relation to these the system should be designed to deter even first offences.

F. ALTERNATIVES AND COMPLEMENTS TO FINANCIAL PENALTIES

A financial penalty is the most frequently encountered sanction for regulatory contraventions and, for the purposes of deterrence, appropriately so. The principal advantage of this instrument is that the amount can be

44 E Bardach and RA Kagan, *Going by the Book: The Problem of Regulatory Unreasonableness* (Philadelphia, Penn, Temple University Press, 1982).

45 See also P Fenn and C Veljanovski, 'A Positive Economic Theory of Regulatory Enforcement' (1982) 98 *Economic Journal* 1055; and, for a different analysis of the same phenomenon, see Ayres and Braithwaite, above n9.

46 W Harrington, 'Enforcement Leverage When Penalties Are Restricted' (1988) 37 *Journal of Public Economics* 29.

47 The game can be played opportunistically by a firm, ensuring that it is seen to comply on the first inspection, and only then deciding to contravene. Hence the importance of some residual monitoring.

determined by reference to the deterrence goal, so that, when discounted by the probability of the sanction being imposed (p) and when added to qE, it exceeds the trader's likely profits (U) and should thus induce compliance. In fixing the amount for this purpose, courts can then take account not only of the likely level of profit to have been secured by the trader from the contravention but also of the likelihood of the contravention being detected and punished. Financial penalties should be a cost-effective means of inducing compliance, because, relative to most other sanctions, they are generally not expensive to administer.

If the maximum which the legislation allows by way of financial penalty is less than what is necessary for deterrence purposes, then there are other financial sanctions which may usefully complement it. For example, the trader may be required to reimburse the agency for some of the costs of prosecuting the case or may be required to pay compensation to those who suffered loss as a result of the illegal act. More problematic is the situation where the trader's wealth falls, or more particularly available assets fall, below the required amount. Criminal justice systems tend often to resort to imprisonment for offenders without the means to pay fines but in a regulatory context that is, except in cases of deliberate and morally repugnant conduct, an unsatisfactory solution, not least because of the huge costs that this sanction entails both for taxpayers and for convicted individuals.

In terms of alternatives to imprisonment, we should note, first, that the available assets of traders can effectively be increased by an order disgorging profits obtained by means of, or confiscating goods connected in some way with, the contravention.[48] Then account can be taken of commercial reputation, which plays a key role in certain markets, particularly if traders have an interest in maintaining an ongoing relationship with customers and thereby acquiring and retaining their goodwill. In consequence, the costs which publicity imposes may, in some contexts at least, be higher than those resulting from other sanctions.[49] Compared to financial penalties, it also has the advantage that payments do not have to be collected, and problems do not arise from the trader's limited wealth or its availability. The issuing of adverse publicity, or 'naming and shaming' as it is sometimes called, may therefore be highly effective in inducing compliance even when the costs are discounted to take account of a relatively low p and even in the absence of another penalty. Moreover, publicity does not normally give rise to significant additional administrative expenditure. This option therefore would seem to be particularly cost-effective. However error costs following a

[48] R Bowles, M Faure and N Garoupa, 'Forfeiture of Illegal Gain: An Economic Perspective' (2005) 25 *Oxford Journal of Legal Studies* 275.

[49] M Karpoff and J R Lott, 'The Reputational Penalty Firms Bear from Committing Criminal Fraud' (1993) 36 *Journal of Law and Economics* 757.

wrong condemnation can be particularly high and are not easily eliminated if, on appeal, the determination of guilt is found to have been improperly made. The trade-off between deterrence and error costs is therefore likely to be appropriate only if a court has determined guilt by reference to criminal procedures.

Some regulated activities must be operated in accordance with a licensing system and, if there are contraventions, it may be possible for a court to suspend or revoke the licence. This is a severe penalty, as potentially it deprives traders of their chosen livelihood and, for deterrence purposes, it is likely to be much more effective as an ultimate penalty than imprisonment. Although post-imposition monitoring is necessary to ensure that the trader does not continue the trading activity, it is certainly a less costly option than imprisonment. Moreover, to traders it may appear to be a more realistic possibility than imprisonment, since the reluctance of courts to imprison traders for relatively minor offences is well known. Of course, like imprisonment, a wrong decision can give rise to very large error costs; therefore a court decision justifying the suspension or revocation is essential.

In the absence of a licensing system, the equivalent outcome can be secured by what is sometimes called 'negative licensing',[50] a judicial order depriving the defendant of the right lawfully to practise a specific trade or profession. Although such a 'cease trading' order potentially may be as powerful a sanction as the suspension or revocation of an actual licence, there may be problems in defining the scope of the prohibition for it to be legally effective.[51]

Under most regulatory regimes, persistently defaulting traders can be subjected to an injunction or a 'cease offence' order, issued by a court. No financial sanction is involved, and in terms of deterrence it is not clear that this device is likely to be significantly more effective than a formal warning issued by an administrative agency, except to the extent that the court setting may have a psychological impact on the trader's propensity to comply. The argument for the civil justice order is therefore based primarily on a perceived need to prevent continuing unlawful activity in the individual case, rather than to deter more generally. The power of the court to uphold the order by means of further sanctions, such as imprisonment for contempt, is available for this purpose. The order may thus be effective to prevent serious harm which might otherwise arise from continuing or further contraventions. Even a harsh criminal justice regime may 'bite' too late to avoid these consequences.

[50] A Ogus, *Regulation: Legal Form and Economic Theory* (Oxford, Hart Publishing, 2004) at 222.

[51] Eg, under the Estate Agency Act 1979, s3(2)(a), an individual can be banned from 'doing any estate agency work', but it is far from clear what is covered by that phrase.

G. VICTIM AND THIRD PARTY INVOLVEMENT IN ENFORCEMENT

A disappointing feature of the Hampton and Macrory Reviews is their apparent failure to give serious consideration to the role of victims and third parties in the regulatory enforcement process.[52] There are two dimensions which warrant attention.

The first is the potential overlap between regulatory regimes and private law. Many public law regulatory contraventions, if they cause harm, also constitute infringements of some private law rights. If the private right is enforced, or traders perceive that such enforcement is plausible, this will enhance the inducement to compliance supplied by the public system, in that it will add significantly to qE and maybe also to pD. Notice, too, that there are advantages to private enforcement. In particular, the aggrieved individual/victim normally stands personally to benefit from a successful claim, and thus has a motivation for an efficient investment in enforcement which does not apply to a public official.[53]

Of course, the private right may not in practice be enforced for a variety of familiar reasons: the victim may not know of the facts which constitute the infringement, or that a private legal remedy is available; or the costs of obtaining adequate evidence of the infringement and of instituting remedial proceedings may be too high, especially relative to any compensation to which the infringement may give rise. There are many general ways of enhancing awareness of private rights and facilitating their enforcement. They include, for example: the provision of institutions such as small claims courts for the cheap adjudication of disputes; the facilitating of 'class' or 'group' legal actions; and the granting of 'punitive' or 'triple' damages as compensation for the infringement of certain private rights.

These topics relate to the civil justice system more generally and do not have particular relevance for regulatory enforcement. More germane are instruments for linking private law and regulatory enforcement. Two in particular call for closer scrutiny by policy-makers in pursuit of better regulation. The first is the action in tort for breach of statutory duty. Whether a regulatory contravention can itself give rise to a private right in tort appears in English law, unlike that of many other jurisdictions,[54] to be rather arbitrary. It depends on whether the legislation imposing the regulatory obligation can be interpreted as authorising such an action and judges have tended to assume that Parliament could not so have intended, although it

[52] Macrory (above n13, at para. 5.7) considers 'victims' restoration' and 'community participation' under the rubric of 'restorative justice', but these are dealt with as alternatives to the conventional sanctions regime and its enforcement.

[53] WM Landes and RA Posner, 'The Private Enforcement of Law' (1975) 4 Journal of Legal Studies 1; MA Cohen and PH Rubin, 'Private Enforcement of Public Policy' (1985) 3 *Yale Journal on Regulation* 167.

[54] JA Jolowicz, *International Encyclopedia of Common Law* (Tübingen, JCB Mohr, 1972), xi, ch 13, 4–15.

is difficult to discern general principles.[55] In appropriate cases (see further below) cost-effective enforcement of regulation would be assisted by a more generous approach.[56]

The second possibility is largely unknown in the common law world but is available in some European legal systems.[57] The private law claim might formally be joined as '*partie civile*' to criminal law enforcement proceedings, thus enabling the individual right-holder to rely on the evidence furnished for the public law action. This device has the advantage of increasing the value of both D (since damages are added to any penal sanction) and q (since private individuals are motivated to detect contraventions without having to fear an escalation of the costs of enforcement). In consequence deterrence should be strengthened with scale economies.

Independent of the enforcement of private rights is the linked, but more delicate, issue of the extent to which victims, competitor traders and other third parties may be permitted to contribute to public law enforcement by, for example, initiating an administrative or criminal action against the trader. English law has a long tradition of the private prosecution of criminal offences[58] but, notwithstanding a general legislative right for its continuance,[59] there are a large number of offences in relation to which the consent of the Director of Public Prosecutions or of the Attorney-General to the prosecution is first required.[60] In a study of this area by the Law Commission, the incidence of such consent was found to be 'haphazard' and lacking a 'unifying principle'.[61] The Commission's own view was that consent should be required only if there is a likelihood of the defendant invoking a human rights defence, there is a national security or international element, or the offence in question creates a 'high risk that the right of private prosecution will be abused and the institution of proceedings will cause the defendant irreparable harm'.[62]

The Law Commission's recommendation has not been implemented, and perhaps wisely so. Their report fails to take sufficient account of the complexity of the issue in relation to regulatory enforcement, as opposed to mainstream crime. Although, at first glance, there would appear to be the same strong cost-effective deterrence argument for prosecution that

[55] KM Stanton, 'New Forms of the Tort of Breach of Statutory Duty' (2004) 120 *LQR* 324.

[56] For arguments see M Stephenson, 'Public Regulation of Private Enforcement: The Case for Expanding the Role of Administrative Agencies' (2005) 91 *Virginia Law Review* 93.

[57] M Chiavario, 'Private Parties: The Rights of the Defendant and the Victim' in M Delmas-Marty et al. (eds), *European Criminal Procedures* (Cambridge, Cambridge University Press, 2005), ch. 10.

[58] See Sir JF Stephen, *History of the Criminal Law in England* (London, Macmillan, 1883) 493–503.

[59] Prosecution for Offences Act 1985, s6(1).

[60] See Law Commission Report No. 255, 'Consent to Prosecutions' (London, TSO, 1998).

[61] *Ibid*, at para. 4.17.

[62] *Ibid*, paras 1.24–1.25.

we have seen in relation to the enforcement of private rights, there is the problem that third party activism can defeat, or at least undermine, sensible enforcement policy, where this dictates that a given trader should not be the subject of formal enforcement procedures. We have already seen (in section E) that in some circumstances—notably in relation to first offenders committing minor contraventions—taking administrative, civil or criminal proceedings may not be cost-effective. Enforcement by the third party is unlikely to be motivated by deterrence. In the case of a victim it may be to exact vengeance, or at least to secure some compensation. In the case of another trader, it may simply be to impose costs on a competitor. These motivations are not always inappropriate and, particularly as regards victim compensation, they may be judged to override considerations purely of deterrence. Nevertheless on balance it may be preferable, in relation to many regulatory regimes, for the right of third parties to initiate formal proceedings for the imposition of sanctions to be subject to approval by a relevant public agency.

H. CONCLUSIONS

Devising 'better regulation' without sufficient attention to the enforcement dimension is unsatisfactory.[63] This chapter has explored the central dilemma encountered by enforcement agencies, that of ensuring adequate compliance without engaging in a heavy-handed approach. It has attempted to show how an economic framework can generate some valuable insights into how the dilemma ought to be addressed in a cost-effective manner.

The key feature of the analysis is the recognition that defaulting traders need to be faced with financial penalties without enforcement agencies having to resort to the criminal justice system. This idea, though familiar in many other jurisdictions, is still relatively novel in the United Kingdom. Even though it is enthusiastically recommended in the Macrory Review, that does not ensure that it will prove to be politically acceptable. One way of selling the idea to industry, which may be sceptical of allowing administrators powers of punishment, may be some explicit recognition that a single regulatory contravention, at least where it does not cause much harm, does not call for a robust response. Another possibility is to remove the language of the criminal law and punishment from the device, so that it is treated as a financial charge or tax. All of this is not to deny a role for the

[63] This is even more the case where the regulation is transnational, as with much European law, and requires enforcement by national enforcement agencies. See A Ogus, 'Enforcing Consumer Protection Regulation in a European Context' in HB Schäfer and HJ Lwowski (eds), *Konsequenzen wirtschaftsrechtlicher Normen: Festschrift für Claus Ott zum 65 Geburtstag* (Wiesbaden, Deutscher Universitäts-Verlag, 2002) 263–78. I have not addressed the issue in this ch.

criminal justice system within regulatory enforcement, but that role should be essentially residual, being invoked where other methods fail to deter or where conduct is morally repugnant.

Finally, there are issues regarding the involvement of victims and third parties in the enforcement process, whether in relation to an independent set of private rights or else as alternative enforcers of the public regime. These have been neglected, but require some careful consideration if they are usefully to complement the work of public agencies.

7

The Legislative and Regulatory Reform Bill 2006—A Legislative Trojan Horse?

SEAMUS BURNS*

THIS CHAPTER WILL examine the potentially seismic and far-reaching implications of the enactment of the Legislative and Regulatory Reform Bill 2006. Sections A and B will consider the background to the introduction of the Bill and the alleged reasons for its passage. Section C contains a detailed consideration and evaluation of the key clauses in the Bill along with an evaluation of some of the main potential risks associated with it. Section D provides an analysis of the wider constitutional consequences of the Bill and Section E draws together the final lessons to be learnt.

A. BACKGROUND TO THE INTRODUCTION OF THE BILL

The passage of the Legislative and Regulatory Reform Bill 2006 (the Bill) through Parliament was initially routine, low-key and inconspicuous but subsequently highly visible and controversial. It must be viewed in the context of the attempts of previous governments (both Labour and Conservative) to deregulate to help both the public and voluntary sectors of business, whilst also making it easier and quicker for governments to regulate generally. The two previous pieces of legislation addressing these twin policy objectives were the Deregulation and Contracting Out Act 1994, passed by a Conservative administration, and the Regulatory Reform Act 2001, enacted by the current Labour government. Thus the desire and impetus to facilitate the passage of quicker and more responsive regulation, and simultaneously to eliminate or at least reduce the regulatory shackles and bureaucracy on businesses (both large and small) and the public and voluntary sectors, is by no means new.

* LLB, MA, Pg Dip. F, H Ed, CPLS, Solicitor, Senior Lecturer in Law at Sheffield Hallam University.

In addition, the Bill must be assessed in the light of the present government's other attempts to cut red tape and bureaucracy. These were highlighted by the Chancellor of the Exchequer in his Budget of March 2005, where he mapped out a radical programme of regulatory reform involving the Government's full acceptance of and commitment to the recommendations of the Hampton Report[1] and also the recommendations of the Better Regulation Task Force report, 'Less is More'.[2] One of the key recommendations of the latter report was the recognition that the Regulatory Reform Act 2001 was not working as well as was originally envisaged. This recommendation formed part of the justification for the introduction of the Bill.

Furthermore, Jim Murphy, the Parliamentary Under-Secretary of State for the Cabinet Office, emphasised that the government was not just concerned about better new regulation, but was equally aware of the regulatory burdens of the stock of existing regulation. Thus, the government had in place two important initiatives to tackle the existing stock of regulation, namely the project to reduce administrative burdens and the imminent departmental simplification plans. Regarding the first of these, namely the project to reduce administrative burdens, Jim Murphy stated that the aim of this initiative was to:

> reduce the cost and burden to business of administering regulation by focussing regulatory resources on areas of greatest risk. Reducing the burden of complying with regulation for the vast majority of compliant business should result in one third fewer inspections and twenty-five per cent less form-filling.[3]

In other words, arguably correctly and fairly, the aim is to pursue a policy of lighter touch regulation involving less frequent and less thorough inspections, and less pointless bureaucracy generally, being imposed upon businesses/public sector bodies which comply with regulations. Secondly, Jim Murphy said:

> In addition, all Departments will have published simplification plans by the time of this year's pre-Budget report. As well as containing proposals to meet targets for the reduction in admin burdens, those plans will include wider simplification measures to deregulate, consolidate and rationalise regulation.[4]

Indeed, several governmental departments and bodies have already published their simplification plans, including the Department for Trade and Industry, the Department for Environment, Food and Rural Affairs, and the Health and Safety Executive.

[1] 'Reducing Administrative Burdens: Effective Inspection and Enforcement', Review of the Regulatory Reform Act 2001 (London, Cabinet Office, July 2005).

[2] Better Regulation Task Force, 'Less is More: Reducing Burdens, Improving Outcomes' (London, Better Regulation Task Force, Mar 2005).

[3] HC Debs, vol 987, col 1051, 9 Feb 2006.

[4] *Ibid.*

B. THE REASONS FOR PASSING THE LEGISLATIVE AND REGULATORY REFORM BILL

The reasons given by the government for pressing ahead with the Bill are many, and certainly on first impression powerful and compelling. How could anyone logically argue against the introduction of a measure which purportedly will result in better and more proportionate regulation, whilst at the same time maintaining and enhancing the UK's economic prosperity, and furthermore continuing to improve the citizen's public services? Jim Murphy states that the Bill is part of the Government's radical approach to better regulation and in fact 'central to delivering it'.[5] He also says that the Bill, as well as providing a more proportionate method of delivering better regulation reforms to legislation, will 'help to promote a real change in the culture of regulation and inspection'.[6]

The government make much of the argument that the UK is in 2006 one of the best places in the global economy to do business, what with allegedly one of the lowest levels of administrative burden of any of the key industrialised economies. Mr Murphy places reliance on a World Bank survey in September 2005 which, in addition to finding that the UK had the most straightforward employment law (not necessarily the best or fairest!) in the EU:

> ranked the UK second in the EU and ninth in the world for the best business conditions. However, there is no room to be complacent about our economic position. The global economy presents us with huge challenges, not least from the emerging major economies of India and China.[7]

The government's case, put simply, is that unless it can deliver better and less burdensome regulation and inspection to our captains of industry and also to would-be industrial/business investors who are contemplating locating in the UK, the UK will sacrifice its present economic attractiveness, with significant detrimental consequences. Support for this contention is found in the Better Regulation Task Force report,[8] which estimates that British national income could be boosted by as much as 1 per cent per year if the government delivered on its better regulation objectives.

Another major feature of the Bill is the implementation of non-contentious/controversial recommendations of the Law Commission, the Scottish Law Commission and the Northern Ireland Law Commission. This is being done by means of the alternative legislative method enshrined in the Bill in order to save scarce Parliamentary time by avoiding time-consuming primary legislation. Jim Murphy flags up the rather depressing and damning

5 Above n3 at 1048.
6 *Ibid*, at 1048.
7 *Ibid*, at 1049.
8 Above n2.

statistic concerning the inordinate delay between the making of recommendations in Law Commission Reports and their ultimate implementation by the government in legislation (where the reports are implemented at all):

> On average, they have waited about seven and a half years to be implemented. It cannot be right to allow them to gather dust on shelves.[9]

Rather worryingly, the Minister furthermore acknowledges the large number of Law Commission proposals that have not been implemented by the government and admits tacitly that in quite a few cases the government's failure to do so cannot be explained by their controversial nature:

> I believe that twenty-nine of the Law Commission's proposals have not yet been implemented, and that the Government consider about sixteen of them to be non-contentious, at least in part.[10]

A further compelling reason for the Bill is the inadequacy and ineffectiveness of the existing law in this area, in the form of the Regulatory Reform Act 2001 (the 2001 Act). This statute is described by Jim Murphy, in words reminiscent of those used by Home Secretary John Reid to describe the Home Office in May 2006, as 'not fit for purpose'.[11] Several serious flaws in the existing law, which arguably have contributed to fewer Regulatory Reform Orders (RROs; a form of secondary legislation) being passed, include, first, the concept of legal burdens. This concept is referred to in the 2001 Act, on which the regulatory reform power is based and, according to Jim Murphy, is 'narrow and technically complicated'.[12] The Minister continued:

> Secondly, technical restrictions such as the two-year rule, which prevents a regulation from being reformed until it has been in effect for two years, have blocked useful reform.[13]

The point here is that if a regulation is defective there can be no good reason to wait an arbitrary two years before remedying or jettisoning it. The third fundamental flaw with the existing RRO power is that:

> the technical nature of the Act has meant that the work involved in preparing orders is not proportionate to the effect of the orders; nor is that analysis focused on the merits of the proposal as it should be.[14]

Hence, until February 2006, only 27 RROs had been delivered, whereas the government had anticipated that at least 60 RROs would have been

[9] Above n3, at 1049.
[10] *Ibid*, at 1054.
[11] *Ibid*, at 1052.
[12] *Ibid*, at 1053.
[13] *Ibid*.
[14] *Ibid*.

passed within this timeframe. A rather glaring example of how slowly the alternative legislative process can work in practice is the Regulatory Reform (Sugar Beet Research and Education) Order 2003. This was referred to several times during the passage of the Bill through Parliament, and Alison Seabeck, a backbench Labour MP said of it that:

> The consultation-to-order-made process on the Regulatory Reform (Sugar Beet Research and Education) Order 2003 lasted one thousand nine hundred and twenty-four days, of which only one hundred and thirteen days were for parliamentary scrutiny.[15]

Jim Murphy contends that one of the major advantages of the Bill is that it 'removes technical limitations such as the legal burdens concept, and makes the RRO power simpler to use'[16] and that the exercise of this power will in turn lead to the achievement of better governmental regulation.

The government recognised that, given the potentially wide ambit of the Bill, considerable safeguards and restrictions concerning the exercise of the powers contained therein would have to be included. Jim Murphy conceded that the order-making power under the Bill (ie the RRO power) would enable the conferral of legislative functions on persons or bodies, and would also permit sub-delegation. Also, it would confer a new power on ministers to lay statutory instruments. However, that power would itself be subject to the negative or affirmative resolution procedure. Jim Murphy stated that the government believed that this was 'an important restriction, which will ensure proper parliamentary scrutiny of the exercise of that function by Ministers'.[17] In addition, a minister intending to make an order conferring legislative functions on a minister would have to lay an explanatory document before Parliament, giving reasons for the creation of a power to legislate and specifying the procedural safeguards attached to the power. This requirement to provide justification and reasons for wielding the power under the Bill theoretically prevents, or at least restricts, the ability of ministers to exercise the power in an arbitrary and indiscriminate fashion. If possible, the minister is expected to lay regulations in draft (not the actual RROs) before Parliament to demonstrate precisely how such powers will be exercised. It is to be hoped that this practice will again promote accountability and facilitate greater Parliamentary scrutiny and involvement.

To address the concerns of critics who fear that the government will misuse and abuse its powers to make RROs, the government also emphasised the further safeguard contained in the Bill, namely that before a minister can embark on the order-making process he or she must be satisfied that five preconditions have been met. These conditions are contained in clause

[15] HC Debs, vol 987, col 1081, 6 Feb 2006.
[16] Above n3, at 1053.
[17] *Ibid*, at 1054.

4 of the Bill. They are, first, that there must be no non-legislative alternatives to the order; secondly, that the effect of the proposal must be proportionate to its policy objectives; thirdly, that the proposal must strike a fair balance between the public interest in its implementation and the interests of any individuals who would be adversely affected by it; fourthly, that the order must not remove any necessary protections; and finally, that the order must not prevent any person from continuing to exercise any right or freedom which that person may reasonably expect to continue to exercise. If a minister is making an RRO which is intended merely to restate legislation or codify the common law then a further additional precondition must be satisfied, namely that the minister must be satisfied that the order will make the law more accessible or more easily understood.

Again, Jim Murphy was at pains to reassure Parliament that the government was not furnishing itself with a legislative blank cheque, and that the wide powers in the Bill would be used appropriately, when he stated that:

> An order cannot create or increase criminal penalties beyond a specified limit; it cannot create new powers for forcible entry, search or seizure; it cannot compel the giving of evidence; and it cannot impose or increase taxation.[18]

Also, an effective statutory consultation on the proposals must then be carried out before the order-making process can commence. As the Minister stated, 'it is envisaged that a Minister would have to undertake statutory public consultation during a twelve-week period'.[19] This presumably would allow relevant parties, stakeholders and members of the public to feed in their views on proposals for orders.

Yet a further safeguard mentioned by the government was the giving of a veto to the two relevant committees of Parliament (the Regulatory Reform Committee in the House of Commons and the Delegated Powers and Regulatory Reform Committee in the House of Lords), to veto inappropriate or unacceptable orders. The Minister gave an apparently categorical assurance of this in the House of Commons:

> I am giving a clear undertaking today that orders will not be used to implement highly controversial reforms, that they will not be forced through in the face of opposition from the Committees of this House and that the Committees' views on what is appropriate for delivery by order will be final.[20]

Thus:

> The Regulatory Reform Committee and its equivalent in another place will be central to the policing of the preconditions and safeguards on the face of the Bill

[18] *Ibid*, at 1055.
[19] *Ibid*, at 1057.
[20] *Ibid*, at 1058–9.

and to the scrutiny of proposals in general. Committees in both Houses will have the right to recommend amendments to draft orders or to veto them completely. Parliament's role remains paramount.[21]

The government's submission is that this is tangible evidence of its genuine commitment not to bypass Parliament or to regard it as some form of legislative rubber-stamp. Nevertheless, the Bill must be sufficiently flexible to fulfil the intention of all sides in Parliament to ease the burden of regulation on the public and voluntary sectors of business, and of course to reflect the government's democratic mandate to implement its policies.

C. THE KEY CLAUSES OF THE BILL

The Bill brought from the Commons on 17 May 2006 consists of four Parts and one Schedule. Part 1 relates to order-making powers (and comprises the majority of the content of the Bill). Part 2 concerns regulators. Part 3 pertains to legislation relating to the European Communities, etc. Finally, Part 4 concerns supplementary and general matters. The Schedule contains relevant sections in previous Acts that are repealed, including virtually all of the Regulatory Reform Act 2001.

Clause 1 of the Bill provides:

(1) A Minister of the Crown may by order under this section make any provision which he considers would serve the purpose in subsection (2).
(2) That purpose is removing or reducing any burden, or the overall burdens, resulting directly or indirectly for any person from any legislation.

Clause 1(3) then proceeds to elaborate and define what is meant by this term 'a burden' for the purposes of the legislation. According to clause 1(3), it means any of the following: a financial cost; an administrative inconvenience; an obstacle to efficiency, productivity or profitability; or a sanction, criminal or otherwise, for doing or not doing anything in the course of any activity. As if the width of this clause were not sufficiently huge, clause 1(4) provides that 'a body or person may bear a burden of financial cost or administrative inconvenience as a result of the form of any legislation…'. Presumably this includes any case where the legislation is hard to understand, although it is tempting to note that many pieces of legislation could be judged to be hard to understand and that no guidance is given on whose perspective should be adopted when making judgements of this kind.

[21] *Ibid.*

'Legislation' is specifically defined in clause 1(6) to include public general Acts and local Acts, 'whether passed before or after the commencement of this section', as well as Orders in Council, orders, rules, regulations, schemes, warrants, byelaws and other subordinate instruments, made at any time, under an Act. This definition effectively catches virtually all legislation, including primary legislation.

Clause 1(7), again, is extremely wide in scope, and gives a Minister power to pass:

(a) provision conferring functions on any person (including functions of legislating or functions relating to the charging of fees),
(b) provision modifying the functions conferred on any person by any enactment,
(c) provision transferring, or providing for the transfer or delegation of, the functions conferred on any person by any enactment,
(d) provision abolishing a body or office established by or under an enactment, and provision made by amending or repealing any enactment.

This clause gives a minister very extensive powers to make orders giving a person law-making capacity. It also provides the power to charge individuals fees. Presumably this could be used to create some sort of licensing body and give that body powers to pass laws concerning the area in question and to charge people licensing fees. The Minister is empowered, too, to change areas of competence or functions that have been conferred on an individual by statute, to transfer or delegate such functions to another person, or even to abolish a body or office set up under an Act.[22]

The seemingly innocuous (at least at first glance) clause 1(8) confers a power on the Minister to pass an order making such consequential, supplementary, incidental or transitional provision, as he, the Minister, considers appropriate. The subjective nature of this test gives cause for concern, given the overall width of the powers conferred on ministers by the Bill.

Under clause 2(1) of the Bill, a minister may make any provision by Order which he considers serves the purpose of ensuring that the exercise of regulatory functions complies with certain principles. These regulatory principles are set out in clause 2(3):

(a) regulatory activities should be carried out in a way which is transparent, accountable, proportionate and consistent;
(b) regulatory activities should be targeted only at cases in which action is needed.

[22] Such bodies might include the Unrelated Live Transplant Regulatory Authority (ULTRA), which was set up by the Human Organ Transplantation Act 1989 and regulates unrelated live transplants between unrelated live donors in organ transplant cases, and the Human Fertilisation and Embryology Authority, which was set up by the Human Fertilisation and Embryology Act 1990 and regulates the creation, storage and use of, and experimentation with, embryos outside the body.

The five regulatory principles contained in clause 2(3)(a)(b), which must be complied with by all persons and bodies exercising regulatory functions, are in keeping with the Better Regulation Commission's (formerly, until 1 January 2006, the Better Regulation Task Force's) Five Principles of Good Regulation.

The meaning of the expression 'regulatory function' is defined in clause 34(1) as:

> (a) a function under any enactment of imposing requirements, restrictions or conditions, or setting standards or giving guidance, in relation to any activity,
> (b) a function which relates to the securing of compliance with, or the enforcement of, requirements, restrictions, conditions, standards or guidance which under or by virtue of any enactment relate to any activity.

A regulatory function does not include any function of conducting criminal or civil proceedings, but does in general include functions 'exercisable by or on behalf of the Crown'.[23] Clause 34(2)(b) provides that reference to 'any activity' in clause 34 includes providing any goods or services, or employing or offering employment to any person.

The potential range of provisions that may be made by a minister under clause 2(4)(a)–(e) in order to secure that regulatory functions are exercised in accordance with the five regulatory principles is significant and extensive. It includes provisions: modifying the way in which a regulatory function is exercised by any person; amending the constitution of a body established by an enactment and exercising regulatory functions; transferring or delegating the regulatory functions conferred on any person; creating a new body or office holder who can exercise transferred or delegated powers and regulatory functions; and, ultimately, using the power to make orders amending or repealing any legislation to abolish a body or office established by an enactment. Oliver Heald, a backbench Conservative MP, articulates the concerns of a sizeable number of MPs over the sweeping powers given to government ministers in Part 1 of the Bill when he states that it:

> is of concern due to the breadth of the power taken by the Government to replace, amend or introduce legislation.[24]

Oliver Heald also points out that it is not mandatory that any provisions (RROs) passed have to have any deregulatory consequences at all. He says:

> The Bill extends the scope of powers available to Ministers while relaxing the constraints of parliamentary scrutiny. Ministers will be able to amend, repeal or

23 Legislative and Regulatory Reform Bill 2006, cl 34(2)(a).
24 HC Debs, vol 987, col 1064, 6 Feb 2006.

> pass primary legislation without going through the normal parliamentary procedures. There is no requirement that such measures should have a deregulatory effect, so the danger is that we shall have legislation, regulation and parliamentary corner-cutting with no deregulation at all.[25]

This note of scepticism is reiterated by a Liberal Democrat backbench MP, David Heath. He notes that the reduction of regulation and improvement of regulatory technique have been the clarion calls of successive governments, and that it tends to be assumed that:

> a Bill that declares itself to be a vehicle for regulatory reform is transparently a good thing. It is the parliamentary equivalent of motherhood and apple pie to say that we all want to reduce the burdens of regulation.[26]

However, one good end, namely deregulation/better regulation, does not necessarily justify dubious and potentially dangerous means to achieve that good end. It is also important to bear in mind that there may in fact be more than one end being pursued, and that these other ends may not be good at all. Mr Heath hence cautions against an over-zealous and enthusiastic welcome for the Bill:

> Any Bill, the prospectus of which is to reduce the regulatory burden, should be welcomed, but-and it is a big but-as the poet had it, 'timeo Danaos et dona ferentis [sic].' I fear a Greek bearing gifts or, to put it in modern form, if it sounds too good to be true, it probably is too good to be true. The Bill is a classic case of that.[27]

Clause 3 of the Bill outlines the power of a minister to make an order (RRO) to implement the recommendations of any of the United Kingdom Law Commissions. Orders that may be made include:

(a) provision amending or abolishing any rule of law,
(b) provision codifying rules of law,
(c) provision conferring functions on any person (including functions of legislating or functions relating to the charging of fees),
(d) provision modifying the functions conferred on any person by any enactment,
(e) provision transferring, or providing for the transfer or delegation of, the functions conferred on any person by any enactment,
(f) provision abolishing a body or office established by or under an enactment, and provision made by amending or repealing any enactment.

[25] *Ibid*, at 1063.
[26] HC Debs, vol 987, col 1069, 6 Feb 2006.
[27] *Ibid*.

The government argument in justification of clause 3 of the Bill is that it will be an effective mechanism for 'breaking the backlog of unimplemented reports'.[28] In 1993 the Hansard Society described Law Commission Bills as probably among the most carefully prepared of all Bills and, as Lord Bassam contended:

> these legislative cakes are properly baked. Conflicting views have usually been reconciled and objections overcome. Therefore, unless they arouse opposition on political, moral or social grounds, they should be ready for a simple passage into law.[29]

Mr Heald, in the House of Commons, however, makes the point that whilst Law Commission reports and recommendations are well considered, researched and drafted by non-partisan experts in the field, they may well deal with a very controversial issue, albeit agreed on by the Law Commission, but one nonetheless that ought to be considered, debated and agreed upon by Parliament. He says:

> The Law Commission is considering measures to introduce palimony-giving people who have lived together equal rights with those who divorce. It is also considering how to deal with tenant's rights and the termination of tenancies and with criminal law reform, including reform of the law of murder and the question of provocation in domestic violence.[30]

Mr Heald comments that, while he may well agree with the Law Commission recommendations on some or all of these issues, that is beside the point. The point is that these are issues which:

> honourable Members will want to discuss on the Floor of the House in the normal way because there are strong feelings about them in the House.[31]

Such discussion means that backbench MPs from all of the three major parties, as well as the various smaller parties, are provided with an opportunity, albeit limited, to influence the content of legislation. At the very least, they are afforded a chance to comment on, and debate the merits of, proposed legislation.

Alison Seabeck, a Labour MP, largely endorses the above criticisms of clause 3, flagging up her concerns as to what exactly constitutes an 'uncontroversial' Law Commission recommendation. She observes that 'the meaning of the word is not clear in the Bill'.[32] She notes that in the wrong hands

[28] Lord Bassam of Brighton, government minister promoting the Bill in the House of Lords. See HL Debs, vol 109, col 126, 13 June 2006.

[29] *Ibid*, at 125.

[30] Above n24, at 1064.

[31] *Ibid*.

[32] Above n15, at 1082.

the Bill 'could be used to implement decisions that had not been thoroughly reviewed by the House'.[33]

David Howarth, a Liberal Democrat backbench MP, reinforces the previous criticisms of the Bill by emphasising, 'that many Law Commission matters are controversial and political, not just technical'.[34] Hence, if some parts or indeed the whole of certain Law Commission reports/recommendations are controversial or political, then really they ought to be debated and discussed in front of the full House of Commons (and House of Lords), rather than be nodded through by a minister in the guise of an RRO. Mr Howarth speculates that one of the main contributing factors to Law Commission proposals gathering dust on the shelf and not being enacted by governments:

> is that the Government have been overactive in bringing forward their own Bills. More importantly, recent Parliaments have not had many fifth years.[35]

In the fifth year of a Parliament, Law Commission Bills were traditionally used to fill up the legislative programme, due to the government of the day having run out of legislative steam and ideas or, more cynically, in some instances having run out of ideas on how to repackage or spin old policies yet again. It is patently obvious that there is broad consensus, if not unanimity, in Parliament as to the desirability of creating a better method for passing many of the Law Commission recommendations. But, as Mr Howarth states, even though that is the case, nevertheless 'it is not necessary to combine that with a proposal in Part 1 of the Bill that is a constitutional danger'.[36] At first sight, clause 3 appears to be an example of government ministers bringing gifts, here providing for supposedly uncontroversial Law Commission Bills to be passed by a quicker alternative process for the benefit of Parliament and the public. Unfortunately, the gift (the Bill) has potentially much less palatable consequences, which may not manifest themselves until some time in the future.

Douglas Carswell, a Conservative MP, continues with this theme. He comments:

> Superficially the Bill makes a great deal of sense, but behind the headlines it is not all that it seems. If it did what it says on the tin, I would support it wholeheartedly, but it does not, so I will not.[37]

In fact, the Bill seems reminiscent of the Greeks graciously and generously leaving the Trojan horse behind on the beach following their apparent

[33] *Ibid*.
[34] HC Debs, vol 987, col 1094, 6 Feb 2006.
[35] *Ibid*, at 1095.
[36] *Ibid*.
[37] HC Debs, vol 987, col 1096, 6 Feb 2006.

departure, to be taken in by the unsuspecting Trojans with such terrible consequences for their city and citizens. Referring to clause 3, and in the context of criticising the import of Part 1 of the Bill generally, Mr Carswell states:

> Part 1 enables Ministers to reform legislation or implement recommendations of the Law Commission by order. Law would, in effect, be made without reference to democratically elected parliamentarians. There would be a further extension of the power of a remote Executive and unaccountable national regulators.[38]

Clauses 4–12 of the Bill include restrictions on the use of the order-making power given to ministers under the previous clauses. Clause 4 sets out a series of conditions that must be satisfied before orders can be made under clauses 1–3. Clause 4(1) states:

> A Minister may not make provision under section 1(1), 2(1) or 3(1) unless he considers that the conditions in subsection (2), where relevant, are satisfied in relation to that provision.

This would seem to lift the obligation to consider the conditions in subsection (2) before making orders in the event that they are not relevant. This again may tend to nullify, or at least dilute, some of the supposed protections or safeguards built into the Bill.

The conditions that must be satisfied before a minister can make provision under the three subsections are specified in clause 4(2). Under that provision, the minister must consider that:

(a) the policy objective intended to be secured by the provision could not be satisfactorily secured by non-legislative means;
(b) the effect of the provision is proportionate to the policy objective;
(c) the provision, taken as a whole, strikes a fair balance between the public interest and the interests of any person adversely affected by it;
(d) the provision does not remove any necessary protection;
(e) the provision does not prevent any person from continuing to exercise any right or freedom which that person might reasonably expect to continue to exercise.

Jim Murphy, commenting on these preconditions, which he believed were stronger than those in the Regulatory Reform Act 2001, said that '[a] Minister wishing to make an order under the new power must ensure that those stringent safeguards are observed'.[39] By contrast, David Howarth challenges the alleged effectiveness of the restrictions in the Bill:

[38] *Ibid*, at 1097.
[39] Above n3, at 1055.

> All the alleged restrictions are worded so subjectively that none of them, even the ones containing words such as 'reasonable', will turn out to be justiciable.[40]

However, it is worth noting that this is a view that has been challenged by Francis Bennion.[41]

Under clause 4(3), in relation to provisions that merely restate an enactment, or alternatively codify a rule of law, a minister does not have to be satisfied that the five conditions referred to in clause 4(2) are satisfied. On the issue of the construction to be given to the term 'restating' an enactment, Stephen Hammond, a Conservative backbench MP, was insistent that clause 4(3) ought to apply only where existing legislation is merely being clarified, as opposed to being replaced with something new. He said that '"[r]estate" implies powers to clarify legislation; it does not necessarily mean altering the substance'.[42]

Finally, under clause 4(4), a minister may not make a provision restating an enactment or codifying a rule of law under subsection 1(1), (2), or (3) unless he considers that the condition in subsection 4(5) is satisfied, namely that the provision would make the law more accessible or more easily understood.

Clause 5 creates further restrictions and imposes further conditions on the exercise of the order-making powers under the Bill, in that it stipulates that orders made under Part 1 may not make provision to confer a legislative function on a Minister of the Crown (alone or otherwise) unless two further conditions are complied with. These further conditions are specified in subsections (2) and (3):

> (2) The condition in this subsection is that the function is exercisable by statutory instrument.
> (3) The condition in this subsection is that such a statutory instrument—
> (a) is subject to annulment in pursuance of a resolution of either House of Parliament; or
> (b) is not to be made unless a draft of the statutory instrument has been laid before and approved by a resolution of each House of Parliament.

Thus, the first condition is that a Minister of the Crown must exercise the function of legislating that has been conferred on him by an RRO by making a statutory instrument. The second condition is that such a statutory instrument is subject to either the negative resolution procedure or the affirmative resolution procedure. There are certain other procedural

[40] Above n34, at 1055.
[41] See F Bennion in [2006] *NLJ*, 853, at 857.
[42] HC Debs, vol 987, col 1092, 6 Feb 2006.

requirements that must be adhered to. These are set out under clauses 13–15, which will be evaluated later in greater detail.

Jim Murphy, whilst accepting that the proposed regulatory reform power in the Bill does indeed herald significant changes to the way Parliament passes some legislation, counters this acknowledgement by arguing that in the final analysis Parliament actually accepted the need for an alternative legislative method five years earlier, when it passed the Regulatory Reform Act 2001. He contends that the 2006 Bill is an improved version of the earlier Act, and unequivocally reassures the House of Commons that:

> The Bill will not undermine the legislative rights of the House or its role in scrutinising Government proposals; on the contrary, the Government would like to see the House playing a much fuller role in pursuing the better regulation agenda and scrutinising more Government proposals to improve our regulatory landscape.[43]

The 'father of the House' (House of Commons), Alan Williams, a Labour backbench MP, does not have any quibbles or reservations about the intent of the Bill, or indeed the bona fides of the government, but does have worries about the Bill's potential impact and about its high constitutional significance. He draws attention to the dangers inherent in the high volume of legislation going through Parliament. In short, this results in members of both Houses being physically unable to devote sufficient time to adequately scrutinising legislation, and this in turn leads to this inadequately scrutinised legislation being inflicted on the general public. The Bill will not improve this regrettable situation, and may in fact make it worse, since it is likely to result in legislation being passed more quickly, with even less parliamentary scrutiny. Alan Williams said:

> We have inadequately monitored legislation and, under the Bill, Ministers will have the ability to amend primary legislation with a truncated order-making procedure. Inadequate primary legislation will therefore be subject to an inadequate procedure.[44]

Whilst recognising that copious ministerial assurances and undertakings have been supplied to MPs in relation to the government's intent to provide safeguards and protections to prevent abuses, Mr Williams nonetheless adds:

> The Bill is remarkably devoid of safeguards and guarantees. I welcome assurances, but in parliamentary terms, there is no assurance as good as an assurance written into a Bill.[45]

[43] Above n3, at 1052.
[44] HC Debs, vol 987, col 1068, 6 Feb 2006.
[45] *Ibid.*

It should be noted that the conditions in clause 5 of the Bill do not apply to an order conferring a function of legislating on someone other than a minister, eg where the function of making bye-laws is conferred on a local authority. Nor, under clause 5(4), do they apply to a provision which merely restates an enactment.

Clause 6 is one of the shortest clauses in the Bill, and provides that:

> (1) An order under this Part may not make provision to impose or increase taxation...

Clause 6(2) states that clause 6(1) 'does not apply to provisions which merely restate an enactment'. Again, Jim Murphy specifically refers to this RRO 'no go area', which he describes as an additional restriction which is essential to ensure that the order-making power 'is used appropriately'.[46] However, whilst this clause apparently prevents the imposing or increasing of taxation, it is silent on whether taxation can be reduced, or even in some cases scrapped. This was a point raised by Kenneth Clarke, the former Conservative Chancellor of the Exchequer, who again gave the government the benefit of the doubt concerning its good intentions and motives underpinning the Bill, but stated that 'its terms are still amazingly broad terms'[47] and that they 'could be used to abolish a tax, to relieve an interest group or trade from a burden of taxation'.[48] Government verbal assurances about such orders having first to be subject to consultation by interested groups and acceptable to various Select Committees do not provide a sufficiently robust safeguard, such as that which would exist if such orders were subject to full parliamentary debate. Mr Clarke emphasised this flaw in the Bill by giving the illustration that a future government might, for example, be inclined to repeal the climate change levy. Such a change would be entirely consistent with the terms of clause 6 and could be given effect to by statutory instrument, subject only to the notional safeguards being complied with, eg the appropriate consultation and approval being forthcoming. Mr Clarke stated:

> [I]t seems to me that that could be done by statutory instrument so long as the Government ensured that they had a majority on the relevant Select Committees.[49]

The point here is surely that lowering or scrapping taxes are matters of such great importance that they should not be decided upon by a minister (part of the Executive) and contained in a piece of secondary legislation, but rather ought to be considered in full by Parliament and enacted using

[46] Above n3, at 1055.
[47] HC Debs, vol 687, col 717, 15 May 2006.
[48] *Ibid*.
[49] *Ibid*, at 720.

primary legislation. This would reflect the major significance of this key function in running a state. Jim Murphy's replacement as the Parliamentary Secretary at the Cabinet Office, Pat McFadden, whilst stating that it would not be possible to use the powers in the Bill to create new taxes, and that in practice tax reforms would be dealt with in either the Finance Bill or a tax law rewriting project, nevertheless said that 'it will be possible to reduce a tax if it meets the procedures and safeguards'.[50] A Labour backbench MP, Mark Fisher, makes a telling dual criticism of clause 6, effectively supporting Mr Clarke. He says, first, that many companies would see the climate change levy as a 'barrier to productivity'[51] and arguably an issue ripe for deregulation under the terms of clause 1 of the Bill. Secondly, he notes that clause 6 is about precluding taxation:

> but it precludes only the ability to impose or increase taxes. Why does it not include the ability to reduce or delete taxes?[52]

Clause 7 relates to criminal offences and not surprisingly generated vociferous criticism in Parliament. It provides that:

> (1) An order under this Part may not make provision to create a new offence that is punishable, or increase the penalty for an existing offence so that it is punishable—
> (a) on indictment, with imprisonment for a term exceeding two years; or
> (b) on summary conviction, with—
> (i) imprisonment for a term exceeding the normal maximum term; or
> (ii) a fine exceeding level 5 on the standard scale.

Clause 7(2) defines the meaning of 'the normal maximum term' as being 51 weeks in the case of summary offences, 12 months in the case of offences triable either way in England and Wales, and six months in relation to offences triable either way in Scotland or Northern Ireland. Whilst this clause sets limits on the order-making powers under the Bill in relation to criminal offences, it nonetheless permits ministers to increase sanctions for breaking a range of criminal offences. This was a point strongly endorsed by Edward Garnier QC MP, who forcefully states that this clause cannot be regarded as some modest proposal addressing only minor and technical criminal offences, and therefore a matter that parliamentarians should not be getting over-anxious about:

[50] HC Debs, vol 687, col 720, 15 May 2006.
[51] HC Debs, vol 687, col 722, 15 May 2006.
[52] *Ibid.*

> However, it is quite clear that, under clause 6, the Minister is not prevented from adding to the criminal statute book offences that attract a penalty of up to two years. There are plenty of offences that the criminal courts deal with now that carry a maximum penalty of up to two years.[53]

This ties in with an example given by Rob Marris about a minister deciding to increase the penalty for using a hand-held mobile phone while driving from three points on a driver's licence to 18 months' imprisonment, and his observation that:

> Many members would regard increasing the current penalty for using a hand-held mobile phone while driving from three points on one's driving licence to eighteen months' imprisonment as rather more than a regulatory reform.[54]

Mr Heath reiterates these concerns when he rhetorically asks:

> When would it be appropriate for a Minister to increase the penalty for criminal offences without primary legislation and recourse to the House? It is an inappropriate power.[55]

Mr McFadden, by contrast, insists that all that the Bill is aiming to achieve with regard to criminal offences is to allow ministers to propose by order to decriminalise offences or to reduce or remove sanctions for regulatory offences. It is not giving ministers a blank cheque to create a raft of new criminal offences at a whim. Thus:

> [the] Government believe that it should be possible to decriminalise or reduce sanctions on people who have not complied with regulatory obligations in cases in which targeted sanctions are no longer considered appropriate.[56]

Kenneth Clarke is adamant that clause 7 and the order-making procedure in the Bill could even 'be used to end the illegality of fox hunting'[57] even though the House of Commons spent in excess of 700 hours debating the issue before passing primary legislation. Indeed, Mr Clarke goes further by suggesting that the order-making power could be used by the government to effect changes in areas traditionally viewed as conscience issues:

[53] HC Debs, vol 687, col 718, 15 May 2006.
[54] HC Debs, vol 987, col 1057, 6 Feb 2006.
[55] Above n26, at 1071.
[56] Above n50, at 723.
[57] Above n47, at 742.
[58] *Ibid*.

> I do not approve of euthanasia or assisted suicide, but the criminal penalty on that act could be lifted under the Bill, subject only to the safeguards on which the Minister relies.[58]

Clause 8 provides that:

> (1) An order under this Part may not make provision to—
> (a) authorise any forcible entry, search or seizure; or
> (b) compel the giving of evidence.

Further restrictions on the scope of the order-making powers under the Bill are contained in clause 9, which provides that orders cannot amend or repeal Part 1 of the Bill, nor, significantly, the Human Rights Act 1998. Implicit in this restriction is that the Human Rights Act 1998 is to be given partial entrenchment, in that a ministerial order under the Bill cannot repeal/amend provisions of the Act; only primary legislation can do so.

Clauses 10–12 of the Bill (which are subject to clauses 1(8) and 2(5) or 3(5)) state that orders cannot be made which affect areas within the legislative competence of the Scottish Parliament, or which amend or repeal Northern Irish legislation, or which confer, modify, remove or restate any provision which confers a function on the Welsh Assembly, except with the agreement of the Assembly. Again, this is clear recognition of the reality of devolution in the United Kingdom. Devolved powers, once given, cannot generally be removed or altered by mere secondary legislation under the Bill.

Further safeguards and protections are built into the Bill to prevent potential abuses of the order-making powers conferred under it, in clauses 13–19. Clause 13 provides:

> (1) An order under this Part must be made by statutory instrument.
> (2) A Minister may not make an order under this Part unless—
> (a) he has consulted in accordance with section 14;
> (b) following the consultation, he has laid a draft order and explanatory document before Parliament in accordance with section 15; and
> (c) the order is made, as determined under section 16, in accordance with-
> (i) the negative resolution procedure (see section 17);
> (ii) the affirmative resolution procedure (see section 18); or
> (iii) the super-affirmative resolution procedure (see section 19).

The requirement that there should be consultation before a draft order is laid before Parliament is outlined in clause 14. This specifies that the minister must consult such organisations as appear to him to be representative of interests substantially affected by the proposals, including bodies/holders of office under an Act, the Welsh Assembly if necessary, the various Law Commissions and such other persons as he considers appropriate.

Following the consultation process, the minister, if he wishes to make an order under the Bill, must under clause 15:

> lay before Parliament—
>
> (a) a draft of the order, together with
> (b) an explanatory document.

The explanatory document will, as its name suggests, explain under which power in the Bill the provision in the order is made, give reasons for the provision, explain why the minister believes the five conditions in clause 4 are satisfied, identify and give reasons for any functions of legislating conferred by the order, identify the procedural requirements attaching to the exercise of any such functions, and provide details of any consultation undertaken, any representations received as a result thereof and any changes made as a result thereof. Finally, where the order is based upon clause 1 (reducing burdens), the explanatory document will provide an assessment of the extent to which the provision made in the order will remove or reduce burdens. These requirements serve the purpose of upholding the accountability of the minister to Parliament.

Under clause 16, the minister must also recommend which one of the three procedures in clauses 17–19 are applicable before an order can be made, again with reasons for this ministerial recommendation.

As stated earlier, under clause 23 in Part 2 of the Bill, any person exercising a regulatory function must have regard to the principles outlined in clause 23(2), namely that:

> (a) regulatory activities should be carried out in a way which is transparent, accountable, proportionate and consistent;
> (b) regulatory activities should be targeted only at cases in which action is needed.

D. THE WIDER CONSTITUTIONAL CONSEQUENCES OF THE BILL

David Howarth, commenting on the nature and potential scope of the Bill, says:

[59] Above n34, at 1093.

> This seems to me to be extraordinary legislation. It proposes changes to the legislative process that in any other country in Europe, and perhaps in the world, would require a constitutional amendment.[59]

Of course, the snag in the United Kingdom is that, currently and for the foreseeable future, we do not possess a written constitution. Our constitution is unwritten. Hence, a simple Act of Parliament can make a radical change to the accepted way of doing things in our state and have huge constitutional implications, and yet the Act does not have to go through a special procedure to be passed, nor to be amended or repealed. Furthermore, even Acts of a fundamental or constituent nature (eg the Act of Union 1800, which abolished the Parliaments of the United Kingdom and of Ireland and created the Parliament of the United Kingdom and Ireland) are not entrenched and therefore do not enjoy special status, and can be repealed in the same way as any non-constitutional Act. Thus, Parliament (or, perhaps more realistically, the government) can legitimately, and more importantly legally and constitutionally, pass such legislation as the Regulatory and Legislative Reform Bill 2006. Oliver Heald describes the Bill as 'constitutionally novel'.[60] However, in fairness, it has to be admitted that the power of the government to change primary legislation by secondary legislation (so-called 'Henry the Eighth clauses') is not new—this is the method that can be used by ministers to make remedial orders under section 10 of the Human Rights Act 1998. This is also the way that ministers give effect to binding European Union laws. Under section 2(2) of the European Communities Act 1972, ministers are given power by Parliament to pass secondary legislation giving effect to binding EU law, without the necessity of having recourse to Parliament and engaging in the time-consuming activity of passing primary legislation in a body where time is a very scarce and precious commodity.

Under the traditional theory of the separation of powers, it is Parliament that makes and passes laws. It is, after all, the legislature. The Executive formulates policy, implements policy and governs the state. The Executive is not only comprised of the Prime Minister, ministers and the government generally, but also includes the civil service (both central and local government). Thus, the Executive, under the strict or pure theory of separation of powers, is not meant to pass laws. As Bradley and Ewing state:

> The executive function broadly comprises the whole corpus of authority to govern...The general direction of policy includes the initiation of legislation, the

[60] Above n24, at 1063.

[61] AW Bradley and KD Ewing, *Constitutional and Administrative Law*, 13th edn (Edinburgh, Longman, 2003) at 80.

> maintenance of order, the promotion of social and economic welfare, administration of public services and conduct of the external relations of the state.[61]

Underpinning the theory of the separation of powers in any state, whether it has a written or unwritten constitution, is the notion that an over-concentration of power in the hands of one person or body is potentially very dangerous to democracy, the rights and freedoms of the citizen, and to the general health and well-being of the state. If one individual or body becomes too powerful and is able to wield its powers more freely and with fewer restraints, the temptation to abuse those powers may well increase too. This concern, of course, was identified hundreds of years ago, and is not a recent phenomenon. Indeed, John Locke in 1690 stated:

> It may be too great a temptation to human frailty, apt to grasp at power, for the same persons who have the power of making laws, to have also in their hands the power to execute them, whereby they may exempt themselves from obedience to the laws they make, and suit the law, both in its making and execution, to their own private advantage.[62]

Hobbes pointed to the growth of the 'leviathan' state and, if he were alive today, he could be referring to the influence and power of the Executive in the state. The French jurist, Montesquieu, provided the classic formulation of the doctrine of separation of powers in the early eighteenth century. He argued that in a state power is divided into three distinct areas and exercised by three generally distinct bodies, namely the legislative, executive and the judicial, and that this separation of powers promotes liberty in the state. Hence, his famous proposition:

> When the legislative and executive powers are united in the same person, or in the same body of magistrates, there can be no liberty. Again, there is no liberty, if the judicial power be not separated from the legislative and executive...There would be an end to everything, were the same man, or the same body, whether of the nobles or of the people, to exercise those three powers, that of enacting laws, that of executing the public resolutions, and of trying the cause of individuals.[63]

Clearly, it would be impractical and unrealistic to insist on a pure application of the theory of the separation of powers in a state, as the three powers have a relationship with each other and interact with and influence each other. In the United Kingdom, there is no *clear* demarcation of powers in practice. Nonetheless, there is evidently a *broad* separation of powers, even if there are some overlaps of powers and personnel in each body.

[62] J Locke, *Second Treatise of Civil Government* (ed Laslett, 1690), ch 12, para 143.
[63] Baron de Montesquieu, *De l'Esprit des Lois (The Spirit of the Laws)* (eds Cohler, Miller and Stone, 1748), Bk 11, ch. 6.

Relating this theoretical exposition to the Bill, the argument would be that the Bill will inevitably result in more powers being given to an already over-powerful Executive. This concentration of powers is fraught with peril. Christopher Chope, a Conservative backbench MP, made the observation that:

> the Bill is in danger of being the sort of subtle sleight of hand of which a Member of the Magic Circle would be proud. It is calculated to give much more power to the Government and the Executive, at the expense of Parliament. One reading of the Bill leads one to the conclusion that its primary purpose is not to remove burdens from business or people, but to remove the burden of having to legislate from the Government...The Bill is the ultimate guillotine for debate and discussion.[64]

The 'burden of having to legislate' refers to the government being compelled to use primary legislation to give effect to controversial, embarrassing or difficult issues, rather than using the streamlined, quicker alternative legislative procedure in the Bill. If governments are forced to use primary legislation, they have to justify and give reasons for their policies and proposed legislation to both Houses of Parliament, and if the justifications and reasons offered are poor or inadequate they will be embarrassed and held to account. Further, they may be forced to climb down on some of the more controversial aspects of their Bills, or conceivably may even jettison Bills.

David Howarth MP makes the point that there must be some value in Parliament debating and discussing proposed legislation (which is very often government legislation). This is a vital function of Parliament. MPs, and indeed peers, should not just be engaged in a ritualised rubber-stamping exercise of legislative measures, and should not be viewed as lobby fodder to vote through or object impotently to legislation. David Howarth said:

> My reaction against this Bill was mainly prompted by thinking about what the Government really believe about the value of discussion. The Bill achieves a reduction in discussion from that for full primary legislation to one of the procedures used for secondary legislation. As a new Member, it struck me that our function is more than just voting. One of the functions is to deliberate and discuss, and to influence the Government's thinking.[65]

And, as Rob Marris MP said, the government's safeguards, assurances and restrictions may sound reassuring, but unlike primary legislation, which can be discussed and debated much more thoroughly in second reading, committee, report and third readings in both chambers, 'statutory instruments are not amendable under our current procedures'.[66]

[64] HC Debs, vol 987, col 1079, 6 Feb 2006.
[65] Above n34, at 1095.
[66] Above n49, at 1095.

Walter Bagehot once described the Crown as a dignified rather than an efficient part of our constitution, and it may be that it is becoming increasingly plausible to level the same accusation at Parliament. The increased law-making powers given to the Executive under the Bill seem to be strong evidence of this. Douglas Carswell put it this way:

> It was Walter Bagehot who said in the 19th century that the Crown had ceased to be part of what he called the efficient part of the constitution, and had become the dignified part. By that, he meant that it had the trappings of power, but not the reality. My fear is that although this democratically elected Parliament has the trappings of power here in our ornate Chamber, real power is increasingly moving elsewhere. This Bill will only exacerbate that process.[67]

There is certainly an observable movement of power away from Westminster and towards the government and, internationally, the European Union institutions.

Perhaps it is scarce wonder that when the Bill was at its second reading in the House of Commons, six Cambridge University professors were so incensed by the sheer scope of the Bill that they were prompted to write that the Bill was much more than a simple streamlining measure to help industry and to reduce red tape. They said that if it passed as it stood:

> the Bill would make it possible for the Government, by delegated legislation, to do (inter alia) the following:
>
> — create a new offence of incitement to religious hatred, punishable with two years' imprisonment;
> — curtail or abolish jury trial;
> — permit the Home Secretary to place citizens under house arrest;
> — allow the Prime Minister to sack judges;
> — rewrite the law on nationality and immigration;
> — 'reform' Magna Carta (or what remains of it).[68]

David Pannick QC was equally scathing in his condemnation of the wide reach of the Bill. He said:

> It will confer astonishingly broad powers on ministers to make the law of the land...It speaks volumes for the ever-increasing arrogance of this Government that it has introduced the Legislative and Regulatory Reform Bill and does not even understand the opposition to it.[69]

[67] Above n37, at 1098.
[68] Professor JR Spencer QC and others, letter to *The Times,* 16 Feb 2006.
[69] David Pannick QC, article in *The Times,* 28 Feb 2006.
[70] AV Dicey, *The Law of the Constitution* (London, Msacmillan, 1885) 39–40.

Advocates of the Bill would retort that it is Parliament that is being asked to confer these extensive law-making powers on ministers. On that basis, if the Bill passes it will reflect the will of Parliament, and of course parliamentary sovereignty is one of the central principles of the United Kingdom's unwritten constitution. Dicey famously stated in 1885 that:

> under the English Constitution, [Parliament has] the right to make or unmake any law whatever; and...no person or body is recognised by the law of England as having a right to override or set aside the legislation of Parliament.[70]

Following on from this, Burns states:

> Under the theory of parliamentary supremacy, once Parliament passes an Act, our courts are bound to give effect and recognise its legal validity. By the same token, the domestic courts would be bound to uphold the legal validity of [the Bill] if it became enacted—despite the width and unprecedented nature of the powers given to ministers to amend, repeal, or replace any legislation by means of merely passing statutory instruments.[71]

E. CONCLUSIONS

The controversy and heat generated by the passage of the Bill through Parliament will have served a highly useful purpose if it wakes up parliamentarians and the public to the fact that too much legislation (statutes, delegated legislation and EU law) generally is being passed. This would be problematical enough if it consisted mainly of good effective law, but of course this is not the case. Alarmingly, Oliver Heald MP has noted that the House of Commons library:

> has shown that there are three thousand eight hundred and eighty-seven regulations a year on average under this Government – fifteen every working day.[72]

This view is supported by Dr Tony Wright MP, who correctly states:

> The Bill is about legislation, and it reminds us that we are a legislative sausage machine here. Governments come along, they give us stuff, and they stuff it into the machine. We process it—more or less—and it comes out the other end.[73]

However, applying manufacturing and industrial jargon, there is too much disparate and unrefined sausage meat, and the sausage machine (Parliament) does not satisfy BS5750 Standard and is simply unable to cope satisfactorily with the sheer volume of legislation. Dr Wright adds:

[71] S Burns, 'Tipping the Balance' [2006] *NLJ* 787–8.
[72] Above n24, at 1063.
[73] HC Debs, vol 987, col 1073, 6 Feb 2006.
[74] *Ibid.*

> This Government and all Governments legislate too much. We legislate badly, we scrutinise legislation inadequately, and we do not revisit it when we have passed it-we simply go on to the next bit. We all suffer because of that.[74]

Governments of all persuasions feel compelled to legislate and regulate. It appears to be their *raison d'être*. If they are not passing laws, they perceive themselves to be failing as a government. Again, Dr Wright comments:

> The virility test for Ministers and for Departments is how much they can get in the legislative programme this year, not whether what they got in last year is working well and doing the things that they said it was going to do. At some point, we shall have to get hold of that huge issue, which goes against the culture of every Government and of the whole Government machine.[75]

The final lessons to be drawn from the passage of the Bill are that statutory provisions that authorise persons other than Parliament to make laws and change primary legislation should be rigorously examined by Parliament and used very sparingly by sensible governments. Parliament should robustly reassert its role of rigorously holding the Executive to account. As Christopher Chope MP said:

> It was Enoch Powell who once succinctly described to me the importance of the procedures of the House...He said that in the absence of a written constitution, the procedures of Parliament and of the Commons in particular are, effectively, our constitution: our protection of the people and their liberties against the Executive. That is why today's debate and this Bill are of such importance'.[76]

Parliament should curb the government's natural inclinations to legislate at every opportunity. It is also important that we recognise that many of Parliament's procedures for passing legislation, while they may have been effective in the nineteenth and possibly early and mid twentieth centuries, are not fit for purpose in the late twentieth century and early twenty-first century, and must be modernised now as a matter of urgency.

[75] *Ibid*, at 1075.
[76] Above n64, at 1078.

8

Better Regulation by Abdication?—Remarks on Parliamentary Democracy and Governmental Law-Making

MICHAEL BOHLANDER*

> No man can put a greater value than I hope I do, and shall do, upon the desires and advices of the Parliament.
>
> Oliver Cromwell, Speech to the House of Commons, 8 April 1657.

> That in all other particulars which concern the calling and holding of Parliaments, your Highness will be pleased that the laws and statutes of the land be observed and kept; and that no laws be altered, suspended, abrogated or repealed, or new law made, but by Act of Parliament.
>
> Humble Petition and Advice, 25 May 1657.

A. INTRODUCTION

BETTER REGULATION IS a good thing. We all want to be governed in an efficient and effective manner. We do not want the government to waste money, time or resources. We want to live our lives in peace and safety, while at the same time enjoying our full civil liberties. Governments usually want to fulfill these expectations. But we also want to have our say on what we perceive society's best interests to be. We want to participate and make sure the political class knows what its employer, the people, wants it to do. We usually do this by electing people from amongst

* Professor of Law at Durham University, Dr. iur., Richter am Landgericht a.D. This chapter is based on the author's article, 'A More Onerous Procedure?' [2006] *NLJ* 525.

our midst to decide by what laws we are to be governed, to represent our interests vis-à-vis the people in government, and to provide a certain control of their actions. This is usually called a parliament and is a basic tenet of democratic systems all over the world—or so we think. However, we also know that this approach would be too naïve: The delegates that are elected are almost without exception members of political parties, one of which usually is the ruling one. This means that our 'raw' interests undergo a first filtering process according to the agenda of the party in question, and a second filtering process according to the rules of political comity that exist and are followed by all members of the same party, and sometimes even across party lines. Having a permanent meeting of our representatives where the opposition parties are also present and possess some rights of control is probably still the best way to keep the executive in check. In addition to the above, however, certain pressures may come to bear on the parliament and the executive over which they have no control, such as, for example, international obligations or events and developments we would classify as coming near to the level of *force majeure*. Nothing new there, you will say.

Governments like *force majeure* arguments. They give them a reason to say that, while it is true that the people would rather enjoy their civil liberties, circumstances beyond their control force them to curtail them, as, for example, in the so-called 'war on terrorism'. Some of these arguments may be justifiable and genuine, but some of them are not and are merely a thinly veiled disguise for an ideologically motivated executive encroachment on the will of the people. The true reason for such an encroachment may be that the executive believes that it has better information and thus knows better what is best for us. The German word for such knowledge born out of superior insight and the ensuing patronising attitude is *Herrschaftswissen*. Neither is this a modern development, nor can we deny that in some scenarios the government may indeed have better information that for some reasons it might be difficult or even dangerous to share with the general population. However, that cannot be the rule—it must remain the exception.

Yet modern politics appears to have subscribed to a change in paradigm. The arguments set out above cause government politicians to try to avoid the cumbersome checks and balances of parliamentary discourse whenever possible, and make the law themselves. Because of the pressing need to be flexible and capable of adapting and responding to rapidly arising new situations and necessities, the understanding is that the parliamentary process is too slow and unwieldy for such flexibility. Government law-making can be done out of genuine persuasion that the parliamentary process is unsuitable, but it is equally open to abuse. This chapter will address a recent example in the UK.

B. THE LEGISLATIVE AND REGULATORY REFORM BILL 2006—OPENING PANDORA'S BOX?

Three hundred and forty-four years after the acceptance of the Humble Petition and Advice, the Regulatory Reform Act 2001 was introduced. This in essence dealt with regulating businesses and other administrative matters, and allowed Crown Ministers to amend primary legislation by statutory instrument. The amending order could, at the time, be made only with the approval of Parliament and was required to relate to legislation that had been in force for more than two years. During the first four years of the 2001 Act's operation the government monitored its application in practice and, based on a report by the Better Regulation Task Force in March 2005,[1] decided to revisit the ambit of the act. Not surprisingly, from the point of view of any executive branch of government anywhere, it was felt that the 2001 Act was much too restricted in its application. Enter the Legislative and Regulatory Reform Bill of 11 January 2006. Its proclaimed aim is to streamline the process of reforming legislation. Its ambit is much wider than the 2001 Act, in that it applies to any area of law. Based on well-known historical precedent, it has already been called a 'Henry VIII bill'.

The Legislative and Regulatory Reform Bill (LRRB) allows in its sections 1(1)(a), (3)(a), and 2(1) for a Minister of the Crown to reform, amend, repeal, restate or replace legislation or implement recommendations of any of the Law Commissions by statutory instrument (section 4(2)), even if this would mean amending an Act of Parliament, such as, for example, the Human Rights Act 1998 or the legislation on the remand in custody of terrorist suspects. 'Restate' would also encompass 'removing an ambiguity' (section 18), which can in practice mean a material change in the law depending on how an ambiguity is perceived and resolved. The Bill also allows for such an order to confer order-making powers on any person or to modify the functions conferred on any person by legislation, including the function of legislation (see section 2(2)(a)(b)). Section 3 makes the Minister's discretion as to when to use his order-making power dependent upon a cluster of legally vague concepts such as 'satisfactorily', 'proportionate', 'fair balance', 'necessary' or 'reasonably' (section 2(2)), even if these concepts may have achieved more specific legal meaning based on the development of the administrative case law.

Under section 6(1) the LRRB even authorises the Minister to enact criminal legislation in any field of law. This is subject to certain parameters, but is without any limit (under section 6(6)) if the Minister is implementing a recommendation of one of the Law Commissions. Even common law rules

[1] Better Regulation Task Force, 'Less is More', Reducing Burdens, Improving Outcomes (Mar 2005), available at www.brc.gov.uk/downloads/pdf/lessismore.pdf. (last accessed 21 Feb 2007).

may be amended in this way. Section 7(3)(b) allows the creation of new powers of forcible entry if this is supported by Law Commission recommendations. Against the background of section 11(2) and (3), the consultation process for such a Law Commission-based proposal can be seriously curtailed, because the consultation process before the Commission is taken into account.

In this way, for example, a Criminal Code based on a Law Commission recommendation could be introduced in the guise of replacing all existing criminal statutes and common law rules—all by secondary legislation. Whether that is a likely scenario is another matter, as is the problem of whether the amending law would retain its status as secondary legislation, or whether it would take on the status of the amended primary legislation. The latter might have a serious impact on the question of how far the courts could control the new legislation, for example, under the Human Rights Act 1998. The question of who appoints the Law Commissioners, and on which criteria, would achieve much greater significance under such a system.

There are, of course, safeguards of some sort: Sections 12–16 introduce a new regime for parliamentary participation in the decision-making process which allows, among other things, for a so-called 'negative resolution procedure' (section 14). This means, in effect, that if neither House of Parliament requests a 'more onerous procedure', as the Explanatory Notes term it, mere inactivity of either House will result in the order becoming law. The decision will, absent any provision to the contrary, have to be taken with a simple majority in each House, meaning that for the current government, for example, the House of Commons is not a real numerical hurdle. In theory, the order-making powers under the LRRB could be used to do away with these very safeguards as well.

One must confess as a German that when reading this Bill, one is involuntarily, but instantly, reminded of an infamous piece of legislation from the darkest period of one's own country. It was the so-called '*Ermächtigungsgesetz*' of 23 March 1933, the exact title in English being 'Law to Remedy the Distress of the People and the Reich'. This Act was very brief and its relevant provisions read as follows:

> Article 1:
>
> In addition to the procedure prescribed by the constitution, laws of the Reich may also be enacted by the government of the Reich...
>
> Article 2:
>
> Laws enacted by the government of the Reich may deviate from the constitution as long as they do not affect the institutions of the Reichstag and the Reichsrat. The rights of the President remain undisturbed...

Article 4:

> Reich treaties with foreign states which affect matters of Reich legislation shall not require the approval of the bodies concerned with legislation. The government of the Reich shall issue the regulations required for the execution of such treaties...

I am not for a moment insinuating that the British government can or should in any way be compared to the National-Socialist regime of 1933–45. The 1933 Act was much more far-reaching in its approach than the LRRB and an instrument of the premeditated take-over of the governmental and legislative power by the Nazis. What is worrying about the LRRB is the underlying negative and shortsighted attitude to the exigencies of a full and proper democratic and, above all, parliamentary discourse, and the unforeseeable consequences the Bill may have in the future, when governments of a different colour may use the legislation for their ends.

The checks and balances built into a parliamentary system tend to frustrate pro-active politicians who want to go ahead with projects they honestly feel are important and right for the well-being of the country, but which they know will encounter resistance from another sector of society. The government's recent defeats in Parliament, especially in the fields of human rights, national security, terrorism and police powers, are an excellent example for this. The statements made by some members of the government after they lost such votes betrayed a disturbing lack of respect for the legislature as the supreme law-making body in the UK. The wisdom and loyalty of individual MPs who had voted against the government was questioned and a lack of responsibility vis-à-vis the best interests of the country imputed to them.

The LRRB, against this background, leaves a lingering doubt about whether the government may not be hoping to obtain a means of circumventing such resistance whenever possible. Here the legislature is in effect being asked to abdicate part of its core function: the full control of the executive power and its general policies. Given the sometimes almost missionary fervour displayed by individual politicians in the debates, especially as far as the alleged demands of national security are concerned, such a development should make anyone wary. Calls for decisive action in moments of perceived public crisis are often not based on cool reasoning, yet in the heat of the political battle it is, in such times, all too easy to accuse those who voice words of warning and restraint of neglecting their duty towards their country. It is at the end of the day only the majorities in both Houses and the personal integrity of their delegates that will decide whether legislation such as the LRRB can be abused and to what extent. There may be legitimate reasons for delegating legislative powers to the executive, but these reasons should always be clearly defined and the delegation should be clearly confined to those reasons. Neither is the case as far as the LRRB is concerned.

C. CONCLUSION

On the international level, for example the EU, there have been longstanding complaints that there is too little direct democratic legitimation of those governing bodies that make the really important decisions which impact directly on the lives of many millions of citizens. Why against such a background one should opt for reducing the direct democratic substance of domestic systems is open to question. Parliamentary democracy with its checks and balances can be a cumbersome system and frustrate desires for progress. Yet that is hardly a good reason to exchange a system that can become bogged down by the struggle between the *agendae* of different political parties for a system where one party gets its way without any effective resistance. Maybe it is time to go back to the roots and listen again to Aristotle, who wrote in his *Politics*:

> If liberty and equality, as is thought by some are chiefly to be found in democracy, they will be best attained when all persons alike share in the government to the utmost.[2]

In this day and age, this should be a banal saying that in one form or another every pupil and student will have heard at least once during his or her education. It is a testimony to the worrying state of affairs in the *res publica* that one is required to repeat such platitudes on account of actual government activity.

[2] Politics, Book 4, IV.

9

Is Less More? Better Regulation and the Small Enterprise

JOHN KITCHING*

DELIVERING BETTER REGULATION for business is a key policy objective for the UK government.[1] Unnecessary or poorly drafted regulation, policy-makers argue, imposes costs that impede business start-up, development and growth. This ultimately weakens national economic performance from which, it is argued, businesses, employees and consumers all suffer.[2] One estimate, derived from government sources, suggests that implementing new legislation has cost UK businesses more than £55 billion since 1998.[3] Other sources, in contrast, note the 'business-friendliness' of the UK regulatory regime; the World Bank places the UK sixth out of 175 countries in terms of the ease of doing business[4] and the World Economic Forum ranks the UK's public institutions tenth out of 125 countries in their Global Competitiveness Index.[5] Notwithstanding these

* Senior Researcher at the Small Business Research Centre, Kingston University. The author is grateful to the Small Business Service for funding the study upon which this chapter is based, to all members of the research team (Mark Hart, Nick Wilson, Robert Blackburn, David Smallbone, Rosemary Athayde, Steve Fleetwood, Andy Pratt) and to Julia Rouse and Will Eadson for commenting on earlier drafts.

[1] HM Treasury, *Budget 2006: 'A Strong and Strengthening Economy: Investing in Britain's Future'* (London, HM Treasury, 2006).

[2] Better Regulation Executive, *A Bill for Better Regulation: Consultation Document* (London, Cabinet Office, 2005).

[3] British Chambers of Commerce, *Burdens Barometer 2007*, available at www.chamberonline.co.uk/policy/pdf/burdens_barometer_2007.pdf.

[4] World Bank, *Doing Business in 2007: How to Reform* (Washington, DC, World Bank, 2006). Assessments are made in terms of 10 'indicator sets' all of which have regulatory implications: starting a business; dealing with licences; employing workers; registering property; getting credit; protecting investors; paying taxes; trading across borders; enforcing contracts; and closing a business.

[5] World Economic Forum, *Global Competitiveness Report 2006/7* (Basingstoke, Palgrave Macmillan, 2006). Country rankings are based on judgements relating to 9 'pillars': institutions; infrastructure; macroeconomy; health and primary education; higher education and training; market efficiency; technological readiness; business sophistication; and innovation. Again, regulation is directly relevant to each of these issues.

contradictory signals, reducing 'regulatory burdens' constitutes a major component of the government's better regulation agenda.[6]

Small businesses are argued to suffer disproportionately from regulation.[7] Some suggest that compliance costs are 35 per cent higher for businesses with fewer than 20 employees than for those with more than 500 staff.[8] Small enterprises, defined as those with fewer than 50 workers, are major contributors to the UK business stock, employment and turnover, comprising 99 per cent of the UK's 4.3 million enterprises, employing 47 per cent of the business sector workforce and generating 36 per cent of business turnover in 2005.[9] Supporting small business has become a key pillar of public policy[10] and developing better regulation is one of the seven strategic themes around which small business policy is based.[11]

This chapter considers current UK regulatory initiatives in the light of new thinking and research concerning the impact of regulation on small business performance. Particular attention is paid to the proposals to measure the 'administrative burdens' of regulation and to set targets for their reduction that arise out of the Better Regulation Task Force report, *Regulation—Less is More: Reducing Burdens, Improving Outcomes*.[12] To begin, a reconceptualisation of the causal influence of regulation on business performance is proposed, before the evidence base on regulation and small business performance is reviewed. Next, the better regulation policy agenda is discussed, particularly as it concerns small enterprises, before empirical material from a new study is presented to highlight the value of the approach proposed. To conclude, the implications arising for policy-makers are discussed.

A. RETHINKING REGULATION

Three definitions of 'regulation' have been identified in the literature: a binding set of rules; all state action designed to influence behaviour; and all forms of social control or influence.[13] Our concern with government regulation

[6] HM Government, *Simplification Plans: A Summary* (2006), available at www.cabinetoffice.gov.uk/regulation/documents/simplification/summary.pdf.

[7] I Fletcher, 'A Small Business Perspective on Regulation in the UK' (2001) 21 *Economic Affairs* 17; Small Business Council, *Annual Report 2005*, available at www.sbs.gov.uk/SBS_Gov_files/sbc/SBCAnnualReport2005.pdf.

[8] F Chittenden, S Kauser and P Poutziouris, *Regulatory Burdens of Small Business: A Literature Review* (London, Small Business Service, 2002), available at www.sbs.gov.uk/content/analytical/research/Regulation-Report.pdf.

[9] See www.sbs.gov.uk/SBS_Gov_files/researchandstats/SMEstats2005pr.pdf.

[10] HM Treasury/Small Business Service, *Enterprise Britain: a Modern Approach to Meeting the Enterprise Challenge* (London, TSO, 2002).

[11] Small Business Service, *A Government Action Plan for Small Business* (London, Small Business Service, 2004).

[12] Better Regulation Task Force, *Regulation—Less is More: Reducing Burdens, Improving Outcomes* (London, Better Regulation Task Force, 2005).

[13] R Baldwin and M Cave, *Understanding Regulation* (Oxford, OUP, 1999).

centres on the first of these definitions. Regulation can be defined as the legal and administrative rules created, applied and enforced by state institutions—at local, national and transnational level—that both mandate and prohibit actions by individuals and organisations, with infringements subject to criminal, civil and administrative penalties. All sub-national, national and transnational bodies possessing powers to design, implement and enforce legal and administrative rules, including tax-raising and collecting powers, fall within the remit. This includes the 63 national regulators, 203 trading standards offices and 408 environmental health offices in the 486 UK local authorities covered by the Hampton Report,[14] as well as the European Union and World Trade Organisation, which both set regulations governing trade between member states.

Regulation causally influences small business performance by enabling, motivating and/or constraining small business owners' projects and those of other stakeholders whose actions causally affect them, including actual and potential competitors, customers, employees, suppliers, infrastructure providers and regulatory authorities. Regulatory *enablers* make certain actions possible; regulatory *motivators* provide an incentive to agents (small business owners and other stakeholders) to act in particular ways rather than others; and regulatory *constraints* limit the scope for agents to act. The conventional understanding offered in much previous research centres on the constraining tendencies of regulation, particularly the obligations placed upon small business owners; the role of enabling and motivating tendencies is usually ignored or understated, yet these are absolutely crucial to market exchange and the performance of businesses.

Regulation is a *necessary* condition of sustaining an advanced market economy such as exists in the UK. Without a regulatory framework, the market system could not function. There are no regulation-free spaces, though this does not explain the specific form regulations do, or should, take, nor guarantee that regulatory policy objectives will be achieved. Private property, contract and money are essential preconditions for the development of an advanced market economy;[15] all presuppose an active government role as regulator. Consider the difficult transition to a market economy in Russia since the early 1990s where the rule of law and private property rights have not been deeply institutionalised.[16] Government bodies regulate through the criminal and civil law codes to protect the person, private property and contract, and to provide infrastructure and public goods that enable and support market exchange. These regulations are enabling for

[14] P Hampton, *Reducing Administrative Burdens: Effective Inspection and Enforcement: Final Report* (London, HM Treasury, 2005).

[15] A Sayer, *Radical Political Economy: A Critique* (Oxford, Blackwell, 1995).

[16] M Safavian, D Graham and C Gonzalez-Vega, 'Corruption and Microenterprises in Russia' (2001) 29 *World Development* 1215.

individuals wishing to create businesses, acquire and deploy resources, and engage in trade.[17] Governments regulate to establish a financial system that enables the provision of credit to business investors; a welfare system that enables the supply of healthy, educated and 'disciplined' individuals to create and to staff businesses; a defence and national security system that enables trading activity to be free from external threats; a science base, and energy, transport and communications infrastructures that business owners can utilise in order to trade. Even where these activities are carried out by private sector organisations, the government's role in enabling them is necessary and could be provided by no other institution. Moreover, by contributing to the creation of behavioural norms, regulation can stabilise trading conditions that facilitate market exchange and long-term business investment.

The regulatory framework constitutes part of the broader context that shapes, but does not determine, business owners' resources, goals and performance. By mandating or prohibiting action by small business owners and other stakeholders whose actions causally affect them, regulation can influence start-up, resource acquisition and deployment, and the realisation of product sales. From the perspective of a particular business owner, such causal influences operate both directly and indirectly. By placing obligations upon owner-managers, regulation can constrain small business performance by requiring them to take action to comply. But by influencing their resources and reasoning,[18] regulation motivates product and process innovation in order to cut costs and/or increase trading revenues, although this may occur without business owners' conscious acknowledgement.

Regulation also impacts on business performance indirectly, via its influence on other stakeholders. Where competitors, customers, employees or investors adapt *their* behaviour to regulatory change, this necessarily causally influences, in however modest a way, the performance of those businesses with which they interact, or choose not to interact. For instance, regulation outlawing 'anti-competitive' practices is indirectly enabling for other business owners with the resources and motivations to exploit a more 'level playing field'.[19] The causal chains constituting the 'invisible hand' of regulation, connecting particular regulatory interventions to the performance of particular small businesses could therefore be long and complex. The vast majority of researchers have focused on the direct, constraining influences of regulation on small business performance, yet direct and indirect enabling and motivating influences may exert a more profound impact.

[17] To describe these as public goods does not mean that all are able to benefit equally from them in practice.

[18] R Pawson and N Tilley, *Realistic Evaluation* (London, Sage, 1997).

[19] An Office of Fair Trading telephone survey found that 22% of SME owners, employing between 10 and 250 staff, reported being victims of anti-competitive behaviour (Office of Fair Trading, 'OFT Urges SMEs to Report Anti-Competitive Practices', press release 21 July 2005, available at www.oft.gov.uk/News/Press+releases/2005/129-05.htm).

Regulation does not, therefore, generate uniform business performance effects. Outcomes depend not only on the properties of specific regulations in terms of the quantity and quality of demands made upon those to whom they are addressed, but also on *how* small business owners, and other stakeholders whose actions causally affect them, adapt to them. The existence of a regulation does not, of course, guarantee that those regulated will adapt in the manner desired by regulators, although non-compliance risks legal and economic sanctions. If no-one changes their behaviour as a consequence of regulatory change, whether intentionally or inadvertently, its impact on business performance is nil.

B. REGULATION AND SMALL BUSINESS PERFORMANCE: WHAT DOES THE EVIDENCE BASE TELL US?

A systematic search of data sources was undertaken to compile the evidence base on regulation and small business performance. A large number of studies were identified, and can be categorised in terms of the following types:

— business burden studies;
— compliance cost studies;
— business decision-making and competitiveness studies.[20]

Business burden studies typically present quantitative survey data on business owners' perceptions, or rankings, of regulation (or particular regulations) as a 'burden' (or other synonym) in relation to business 'performance' (or other outcome indicator).[21] One major official survey, incorporating 7,505

[20] For a more detailed discussion of the evidence base see J Kitching, 'A Burden on Business? Reviewing the Evidence Base on Regulation and Small Business Performance' (2006) 24 *Environment and Planning C: Government and Policy* 799.

[21] Eg, see A Cosh, A Hughes and E Wood, 'Innovation: Scale, Objectives and Constraints' in ESRC Centre for Business Research (ed), *The Changing State of British Enterprise* (Cambridge, ESRC Centre for Business Research, University of Cambridge, 1996); A Cosh and E Wood, 'Innovation: Scale, Objectives and Constraints' in A Cosh and A Hughes (eds), *Enterprise Britain* (Cambridge, ESRC Centre for Business Research, University of Cambridge, 1996); S Carter, S Tagg, S Ennis and J Webb, *Lifting the Barriers to Growth in UK Small Businesses* (London, Federation of Small Businesses, 2002); S Carter, C Mason and S Tagg, *Lifting the Barriers to Growth in UK Small Businesses* (London, Federation of Small Businesses, 2004); S Carter, C Mason and S Tagg, *Lifting the Barriers to Growth in UK Small Businesses* (London, Federation of Small Businesses, 2006); R Blackburn and M Hart, *Small Firms' Awareness and Knowledge of Individual Employment Rights* (London, DTI Employment Relations Research Series No 14, 2002); A Cosh and A Hughes, 'Innovation Activity: Outputs, Inputs, Intentions and Constraints', in A Cosh and A Hughes (eds), *Enterprise Challenged* (Cambridge, ESRC Centre for Business Research, University of Cambridge, 2003); J Atkinson and J Hurstfield, *Small Business Service Annual Survey of Small Businesses: UK 2003,* available at www.sbs.gov.uk/content/analytical/sbsannualsmesurvey2003.pdf; Rural Shops Alliance, *Legislation—Regulation: The Red Tape Burden on Rural Retailers* (Dorchester: RSA/Countryside Agency/MMBU, 2005); R Baldwin and R Anderson, *Inspector at the Door 2005: The Real Costs of Regulation* (London, Federation of Small Businesses, 2005).

firms employing up to 250 employees in a range of industries, found that 31 per cent of owners cited 'regulation' as an obstacle to business success (13 per cent cited it as the main obstacle) and 24 per cent cited 'taxation' (8 per cent main obstacle). 'Competition' and 'the economy' were, however, reported more frequently as obstacles to business success than regulation and taxation.[22]

Surveys of business owners' perceptions of regulation suffer from serious shortcomings. First, survey data offer little insight into the meaning of, and influences on, owners' perceptions of regulation and, therefore, little explanation is provided of the variation in reported perceptions, either within or across studies. Second, surveys are unable to provide robust data on respondents' awareness and understanding of their regulatory obligations,[23] or their attitudes to compliance, both of which mediate the influence of regulation on business performance. Distinct attitudes to compliance have been identified, from the 'unaware'[24] and the 'avoider'[25] through 'vulnerable compliance',[26] where business owners are uncertain whether they are in compliance, to 'proactive learners'[27] that treat regulatory interventions as opportunities for learning and improvement. Third, and crucially, many surveys explicitly or implicitly treat regulation one-sidedly as a cost or constraint, neglecting the ways in which regulation can enable and motivate action that generates higher levels of business performance. Fourth, and most importantly, survey data of owners' perceptions provide little insight into the causal processes through which regulations shape small business performance. Simply reporting owners' perceptions gives no indication of whether, and how, business owners—and other stakeholders whose actions causally affect them—adapt to regulation. Survey data rely too strongly on superficial 'sound-bite' responses which provide good headlines but, at best, tell us only what business owners *think* about regulation rather than what they *do* about it.

Compliance cost studies attempt to quantify the administrative costs—and very occasionally, the benefits—to business owners of regulatory compliance. Business owners, it is argued, face an opportunity cost in diverting scarce resources away from more productive, profit-generating activities

[22] Small Business Service, *Annual Survey of Small Businesses: UK 2004/5*, available at www.sbs.gov.uk/SBS_Gov_files/researchandstats/ASBS-Report.pdf.

[23] C Atkinson and S Curtis, 'The Impact of the Employment Regulation on the Employment Relationship in SMEs' (2004), 11 *Journal of Small Business and Enterprise Development* 486.

[24] L Harris, 'Small Firm Responses to Employment Regulation' (2002) 9 *Journal of Small Business and Enterprise Development* 296.

[25] I Vickers, P James, D Smallbone and R Baldock, 'Understanding Small Firm Responses to Regulation: the Case of Workplace Health and Safety' (2005) 26 *Policy Studies* 149.

[26] J Petts, A Herd, S Gerrard and C Horne, 'The Climate and Culture of Environmental Compliance Within SMEs' (1999) 8 *Business Strategy and the Environment* 14.

[27] Vickers *et al*, above n25.

in order to discover, interpret and comply with regulatory obligations.[28] Methods of calculating compliance costs vary but usually involve imputing monetary costs to labour time estimates associated with administering regulations, plus some monetary estimate for advisors' fees, and additional capital and operating costs incurred. Much of this cost is fixed and small businesses are said to be unable to spread these costs across large-scale operations due to their lack of internal resources (time, money, specialist expertise) with which to handle regulations and, because of their lower asset base, are less resilient to regulatory shocks.

Compliance cost studies, however, also have deficiencies. They tend to adopt a narrow and static focus on costs, often quantify phenomena that are best understood in qualitative terms, and conceptualise regulation in terms of the administrative activities surrounding compliance rather than as a dynamic force shaping business performance outcomes. Simply measuring compliance costs tells us very little about how or why regulation might cause small business owners to adapt to regulatory change in particular ways in particular settings—for instance, by encouraging product and process innovation—nor how these adaptations impact upon business performance. Headline-grabbing reports of 'regulation increases business costs by £55m'[29] or 'the cost of regulation to the UK economy is between ten and twelve per cent of GDP'[30] inevitably reinforce the assumption that regulation imposes only costs and constraints on business owners, yet inevitably they simplify and misrepresent complex social processes. Moreover, emphasis is placed on those costs that can be quantified easily or, alternatively, attempts are made to force qualitative phenomena into a quantitative cost-benefit framework. The psychological costs of discovering, interpreting and complying with regulation, for example, are no doubt important influences on owner-manager behaviour, both motivating and constraining, but because they are very difficult to quantify, it might be wiser not to treat them numerically.

[28] D Collard, S Green, M Godwin and L Maskell, *The Tax Compliance Costs for Employers of PAYE and National Insurance in 1995–96* (London, Inland Revenue Economics Papers No 3, 1998); Chittenden *et al*, above n8; F Chittenden, S Kauser and P Poutziouris, 'Tax Regulation and Small Business in the USA, UK, Australia and New Zealand' (2003) 21 *International Small Business Journal* 93; F Chittenden, P Poutziouris, S Kauser and M Shamutkova, 'Income Tax Self-Assessment Compliance Costs: Empirical Evidence from the UK' in C Gray and G Bannock (eds), *Government Regulation and the Small Firm* (Milton Keynes, ISBE/SERT, 2005); F Chittenden, S Kauser and P Poutziouris 'PAYE-NIC Compliance Costs: Empirical Evidence from the UK SME Economy' (2005) 23 *International Small Business Journal* 635; R Lancaster, R Ward, P Talbot and A Brazier, *Costs of Compliance with Health and Safety Regulations in SMEs* (Norwich, TSO, 2003); S Kauser, F Chittenden, P Poutziouris and B Sloan, 'Corporation Tax Self-Assessment Compliance Costs: Empirical Evidence from the UK' in Gray and Bannock (eds), above; KPMG, *Administrative Burdens —HMRC Measurement Project* (2006), available at www.hmrc.gov.uk/news/admin-burdens.pdf.

[29] British Chambers of Commerce, above n3.

[30] Better Regulation Task Force, above n12.

The third group of studies, those concerned with business competitiveness and decision-making, examine how and why small business owners adapt to regulation, and with what consequences for business start-up, performance and growth. Individuals' perceptions of business regulation often deter business start-up,[31] though other studies comparing actual and prospective owners' views suggest that those considering start-up and business growth tend to over-estimate regulation and tax as real burdens.[32] Neither of these two studies, however, considered whether regulation might *encourage* business formation by creating market opportunities, providing guidance on running a business, or by creating a 'level playing field' upon which small businesses are better able to compete. Differences between prospective and actual business owners' views might be explicable, in part at least, in terms of the power and pervasiveness of 'anti-regulation' discourses in society, which constrain business start-up among those lacking prior business experience.

Regulation also influences business development and growth. Most quantitative surveys report that regulation has impeded expansion, to widely varying degrees, rather than assisted it.[33] Qualitative studies offer deeper insights into the causal processes through which regulation generates change in business performance by demonstrating how it motivates business owners to modify business practices and/or products within particular social contexts that support or hinder these adaptations. For example, small employers have adapted to the National Minimum Wage (NMW) in a variety of ways with no single type of response dominant: absorption with no further adaptations to business practice; increased product prices; reductions in labour time; work intensification; cuts in training and non-pay benefits; product and process innovation; or by choosing not to comply.[34] Most small employers have adapted to the NMW with limited disruption to existing practice either because the costs imposed by regulation were

[31] NOP Social & Political, *Small Business Service Household Survey of Entrepreneurship 2003* (2004), available at www.sbs.gov.uk/content/analytical/household-survey-2003.doc.

[32] G Allinson, P Braidford, M Houston and I Stone, *Myths Surrounding Starting and Running a Business* (London, Small Business Service, 2005), available at www.sbs.gov.uk/SBS_Gov_files/researchandstats/MythsReport.pdf; G Allinson, P Braidford, M Houston and I Stone, *Myths Surrounding Growing a Business* (London, Small Business Service, 2006), available at http://www.sbs.gov.uk/SBS_Gov_files/researchandstats/MythsSurroundingGrowingABusiness2006.pdf.

[33] Eg, NatWest/SERT, 'Government Regulations and Paperwork' (2004) 20 *Quarterly Survey of Small Business* 3, available at www.serteam.co.uk/d-commerce/NatWest_SERTeam_Q3_2004_Government_Regulations_&_Paperwork_04q3_09.pdf; Chittenden *et al*, above n28; Small Business Service, above n22.

[34] Eg, J Arrowsmith, M Gilman, P Edwards and M Ram, 'The Impact of the National Minimum Wage in Small Firms' (2003) 41 *British Journal of Industrial Relations* 435; M Ram, M Gilman, J Arrowsmith and P Edwards, 'Once More into the Sunset? Asian Clothing Firms after the National Minimum Wage' (2003) 21 *Environment and Planning C: Government and Policy* 71; J Heyes and A Gray, 'Small Firms and the National Minimum Wage: Implications for Pay and Training Practices in the British Private Service Sector' (2004) 25 *Policy Studies* 209.

minimal, or because the firm's product market position and 'informal' workplace relationships enabled cost increases to be absorbed, or passed on to customers as higher prices, without serious problems.[35] Where product market competition was intense and businesses were struggling, however, regulatory change has been reported as aggravating an already precarious market position, forcing some businesses to the edge of legality or, in some cases, into closure.[36] In some cases, businesses have been 'shocked' into implementing product innovations; such innovations being contingent upon a wide range of influences, including the severity of the regulatory shock and the availability of financial and labour resources to adapt.[37]

Regulation does not produce uniform small business performance consequences; these depend on how owners, and others whose actions causally affect them, exercise their agency and adapt to regulation. These obvious points can be lost in aggregate quantitative data on business owners' perceptions of regulation and estimates of compliance costs. But by focusing on business owners' *conscious* adjustments to regulatory change, it is possible to neglect the unacknowledged 'invisible hand' of regulation, which enables, motivates and constrains small business performance without explicitly entering agents' reasoning. For example, property and contract rights enabling business owners to take ownership of and deploy resources, and to realise product sales, are essential for business owners to conduct trade, irrespective of whether these rights are recognised and reported as causally influential by business owners themselves.

C. THE BETTER REGULATION AGENDA: ORIGINS AND EVOLUTION

The origins of the current better regulation agenda lie in the *deregulation* initiatives implemented by the Thatcher and Major governments of the 1980s and early 1990s, aimed at reducing 'burdens on business', particularly for small firms.[38] A primary objective of both the current and earlier

[35] P Edwards, M Ram and J Black, *The Impact of Employment Legislation on Small Firms: a Case Study Analysis* (London, DTI Employment Relations Research Series No 20, 2003); P Edwards, M Ram and J Black, 'Why Does Employment Legislation Not Damage Small Firms?' (2004) 31 *Journal of Law and Society* 245.

[36] Ram *et al*, above n34.

[37] D Grimshaw and M Carroll, 'Adjusting the National Minimum Wage: Constraints and Incentives to Change in Six Low-Paying Sectors' (2006) 37 *Industrial Relations Journal* 22.

[38] Department of Trade and Industry, *Burdens on Business* (London, HMSO, 1985); Department of Employment, *Building Businesses...Not Barriers* (Cmnd 9794, London, HMSO, 1986); Department of Trade and Industry, *Releasing Enterprise* (Cm 512, London, HMSO, 1988); Department of Trade and Industry, *Deregulation: Cutting Red Tape* (London, HMSO, 1994). The *Lifting the Burden* White Paper (Minister without Portfolio 1985: Annex 1, Cmnd 9571) listed a number of measures undertaken from 1979–85 with regard to the environment, tax and social security, employment, trade and industry, transport, agriculture and home affairs.

initiatives has been to 'release enterprise',[39] to stimulate self-employment and business ownership, while accepting the importance of regulatory safeguards for consumers and the general public. Each new regulatory proposal was made subject to 'a systematic assessment of its impact on business enterprise'.[40] In practice, such assessments focused primarily on costs with little attention given to the benefits;[41] indeed, these subsequently became known as compliance cost assessments. A 'central task force' was established within the Department of Employment (named the Enterprise and Deregulation Unit, subsequently shortened to the Deregulation Unit) to scrutinise departmental assessments of regulatory proposals. The deregulation initiative was relaunched in the early 1990s with a published list of 3,500 regulations argued to be imposing costs on business and 600 proposals for reform.[42]

Since 1997, the Labour government has continued the policy focus on regulation, albeit one discursively constructed as *better* regulation,[43] as part of a broader programme of 'modernising Government'.[44] Substantively, the thrust of policy is very similar to that of earlier Conservative administrations: attempting to reduce the administrative costs of compliance for business owners while acknowledging the crucial role of regulatory safeguards.[45] Symptomatic of the new policy rhetoric, the Better Regulation Unit replaced the Deregulation Unit, was subsequently renamed the Regulatory Impact Unit at Cabinet Office and then, in 2005, became the Better Regulation Executive with responsibility for driving the agenda forward. The Better Regulation Task Force, a business-led body, was established in 1997 to provide independent advice to government on regulatory matters (renamed the Better Regulation Commission in 2006). A Ministerial Panel for Regulatory Accountability, now chaired by the Prime Minister, was set up in 1999 to scrutinise major regulatory plans.

In May 2005, the government launched the Better Regulation Action Plan.[46] Action Plan objectives include simplifying, consolidating and reducing

[39] Department of Trade and Industry, *Releasing Enterprise*, above n 38.

[40] Department of Trade and Industry, *Burdens on Business*, above n38, at 13.

[41] J Froud, R Boden, A Ogus and P Stubbs, 'Toeing the Line: Compliance Cost Assessment in Britain' (1994) 22 *Policy and Politics* 313; J Froud and A Ogus, '"Rational" Social Regulation and Compliance Cost Assessment' (1996) 74 *Public Administration* 221.

[42] Department of Trade and Industry, *Deregulation: Cutting Red Tape*, above n38.

[43] HM Treasury, *Pre-Budget Report 1997* (London, HM Treasury, 1997); HM Treasury, above n1.

[44] Cabinet Office, *Modernising Government* (Cm 4310, London, TSO, 1999).

[45] It is worth recalling that the term 'better regulation' appears in several of the 1980s policy statements (eg, Minister without Portfolio, *Lifting the Burden*, above n38; Department of Employment, *Building Businesses...Not Barriers*, above n38; Department of Trade and Industry, *Releasing Enterprise*, above n38).

[46] HM Treasury, 'Chancellor launches Better Regulation Action Plan' (2005), available at www.hm-treasury.gov.uk/newsroom_and_speeches/press/2005/press_50_05.cfm.

regulation, including that arising from the tax system; reducing the number of regulatory bodies;[47] applying a risk-based approach to inspection and enforcement; achieving consistency in enforcement practices across local authority areas; reforming penalty systems; encouraging EU regulatory reform;[48] and ensuring appropriate implementation of EU law. The Action Plan was strongly influenced by the *Less is More* report on the measurement and reduction of 'administrative burdens' and the Hampton Report on inspection and enforcement.[49] As a consequence, 19 government departments and agencies have submitted simplification plans setting out how they intend to reduce administrative burdens for businesses and the third sector.[50] The new Legislative and Regulatory Reform Act 2006, moreover, extends government powers to amend legislation by Regulatory Reform Order

Policy-makers have been particularly concerned with the impact of regulation on small businesses since the mid-1980s.[51] A 'Think Small First' principle was explicitly adopted in the 1990s[52] and continues to shape policy.[53] Government has already taken steps to improve small business owners' experience of using the tax system. Measures include cutting the tax return for half a million businesses from 16 pages to four, extending flexible tax payment schemes, requiring businesses to provide information only once, developing a single point of contact for all tax queries and setting targets for reducing the administration burden of dealing with tax returns, forms, audits and inspections.[54]

Delivering better regulation is one of the Small Business Service's four priority policy areas for 2006–7, along with building an enterprise culture, opening up public procurement and simplification of business support.[55]

[47] The Hampton report (2005), above n14, initially proposed consolidating 31 national regulators into 7 thematic bodies, but the process has already gone further than this. 19 national departments, regulators and agencies have been merged into 6 organisations, the Insolvency Service and the DTI Companies Investigation Branch have been merged, and a further 12 bodies are being considered for merger (HM Treasury/Better Regulation Executive/Cabinet Office, *Implementing Hampton: From Enforcement to Compliance* (2006), available at www.hm-treasury.gov.uk/media/2DA/8A/hampton_compliance281106.pdf.

[48] Regulatory reform programmes are an international phenomenon. Reform is underway in the European Union (European Commission, Action Plan: Simplifying and Improving the Regulatory Environment, COM(2002)278), with a similar emphasis on simplification (European Commission, Implementing the Community Lisbon Programme: A Strategy for the Simplification of the Regulatory Environment, Brussels, COM(2005)535).

[49] Better Regulation Task Force, *Regulation—Less is More*, above n12; Hampton, above n14.

[50] HM Government, Simplification Plans, above n6.

[51] Department of Trade and Industry, *Burdens on Business*, above n38.

[52] Department of Trade and Industry, *Deregulation: Cutting Red Tape*, above n38.

[53] Small Business Service, *Think Small First* (London, Small Business Service, 2001); Small Business Service, above n11.

[54] Her Majesty's Revenue and Customs, *Progress Towards a New Relationship* (2006), available at www.hmrc.gov.uk/budget2006/new-relationship.pdf.

[55] Small Business Service, *Business Plan 2006* (London, DTI, 2006).

Regulators are required to give specific consideration to the likely impact of regulatory proposals on small businesses. Exemptions and enforcement guidelines for small businesses play a part in policy, although the assumption is that the reduction of administrative burdens and simplification are likely to improve the regulatory context for *all* businesses.

For all major regulatory proposals, regulators are required to complete a Regulatory Impact Assessment (RIA), the successor to the compliance cost assessment and risk assessment procedures. From May 2007 a new Impact Assessment (IA) will replace the RIA, with the acts of providing a simpler, more transparent process that will be embedded in the earliest stage at play making. IAs require those proposing new regulation to:[56]

— define the purpose of the regulatory proposal;
— consider non-regulatory routes to achieving policy objectives
— consult with affected parties as early as possible;
— undertake a cost-benefit analysis of regulatory and non-regulatory options;[57] economic, social and environmental costs and benefits should be monetised wherever possible,
— conduct a Small Firms Impact Test[58] to examine the likely effects of proposals on small businesses; and
— conduct post-implementation reviews of regulations to determine whether they are having the intended effect and are achieving policy objectives.

The RIA process has been subject to strong criticism. The National Audit Office suggests that three types of RIA can be distinguished: those that have no impact on policy development and are produced simply to meet the formal requirement ('pro-forma RIAs'); those that have only a limited impact on policy, possibly because they are started too late ('informative RIAs'); and those that inform and genuinely challenge policy development ('integrated RIAs').[59] Many RIAs fall into the first two categories rather than being integrated, leading some to question whether RIAs are a 'false dawn'.[60] RIAs have been criticised for failing to: specify clearly the problem that the proposed regulation is intended to address; consider non-regulatory alternatives of achieving policy objectives; quantify all anticipated costs and benefits of

[56] RIA guidance is available at www.cabinetoffice.gov.uk/regulation/ria/ia_guidance/index.asp.

[57] Perhaps the major difference between the current better regulation agenda and the initiatives of the 1980s–90s is the more explicit consideration of benefits as well as costs in the assessment process.

[58] The test was made mandatory in 2003. A predecessor Small Firms Litmus Test was introduced to the compliance cost assessment procedure in 1994.

[59] National Audit Office, *Evaluation of Regulatory Impact Assessments Compendium Report 2004/5* (London, TSO, 2005).

[60] D Parker, 'Regulatory Impact Assessment—a False Dawn?', Centre for the Study of Regulated Industries, Occasional Lecture 15 (2006), available at www.bath.ac.uk/cri/pubpdf/Occasional%20Lectures/15.%20Parker.pdf.

regulatory and non-regulatory options;[61] assess likely compliance levels; specify how the impact of regulation would be monitored and evaluated; and conduct the Small Firms Impact Test.[62] Alternatively, RIAs have been criticised for estimating the costs and benefits of regulatory and non-regulatory options with a curious precision as single point estimates rather than as ranges, reflecting uncertainties regarding the assumptions and data from which they are derived.[63] Quantifying costs and benefits is, moreover, vulnerable to political considerations[64] and can be extremely difficult, particularly where costs and benefits are intangible or likely to accrue over a long period of time,[65] or where the impact of regulation depends on the exercise of delegated powers under primary legislation.[66] A recently commenced public consultation to improve RIAs proposes greater quantification of the costs and benefits of policy options and further consideration to be given to the removal, simplification and consolidation of existing regulation when a new regulation is proposed.[67]

There has been substantial policy activity with regard to regulatory issues in recent years, but what exactly is better regulation? The rhetorical switch to better regulation explicitly draws attention to the *quality* of regulation, although this only shifts the definitional problem: how is quality to be defined? Policy-makers emphasise process criteria in evaluating regulatory quality, rather than criteria concerning the consequences of regulation. The Better Regulation Task Force has elaborated five principles of good regulation (proportionality, accountability, consistency, transparency and targeting), all of which focus on the process of regulation.[68] The *Less is*

[61] Similar criticisms were made of compliance cost assessments (Froud and Ogus, above n41).

[62] T Ambler, F Chittenden and M Obodovski, *Are Regulators Raising Their Game? UK Regulatory Impact Assessments in 2002/3* (2004), available at www.chamberonline.co.uk/policy/issues/red_tape/redtape2004.pdf; T Ambler, F Chittenden and C Hwang, *Regulation: Another Form of Taxation?* (2005), available at www.chamberonline.co.uk/policy/pdf/ria_report_2005.pdf; T Ambler, F Chittenden and K Ahuja, *Regulators: Box Tickers or Burdens Busters?* (2006), available at www.chamberonline.co.uk/policy/pdf/RIA_2006.pdf; C Jacobs, *Improving the Quality of Regulatory Impact Assessments in the UK* (London, Centre on Regulation and Competition, Working Paper No 102, 2005); National Audit Office, *Evaluation of Regulatory Impact Assessments Compendium Report 2003–04* (London, TSO, 2004); National Audit Office, above n59; National Audit Office, *Evaluation of Regulatory Impact Assessments 2005–06* (London, TSO, 2006); National Audit Office, *Supporting Small Businesses* (London, TSO, 2006).

[63] National Audit Office, *Evaluation of Regulatory Impact Assessments Compendium Report 2003–04*, above n62; National Audit Office, *Evaluation of Regulatory Impact Assessments Compendium Report 2004/5*, above n59.

[64] F Vibert, 'The Limits of Regulatory Reform in the EU' (2006) 26 *Economic Affairs* 17.

[65] Kitching, above n20.

[66] R Baldwin, *Rules and Government* (Oxford, Clarendon Press, 1995).

[67] Better Regulation Executive, *The Tools to Deliver Better Regulation: Consultation Document* (London, Cabinet Office, 2006).

[68] Better Regulation Task Force, *Principles of Good Regulation* (London, Better Regulation Task Force, 2003).

More report and the Administrative Burdens Reduction and Simplification agendas derived from it adopt a quantitative approach to regulatory quality.[69] *Less is More* proposed a 'one in, one out' approach, whereby for each new regulation proposed an existing one is removed. Although perhaps not to be interpreted literally, such an approach erroneously assumes that fewer regulations are necessarily better for business; yet what matters is whether business owners and others (consumers, investors, employees) obtain the protection they require enabling them to engage in market exchange as buyers, sellers and investors. Nor can it be assumed that the Better Regulation Task Force's five principles can be achieved simultaneously, without trade-offs; for example, clarifying regulatory obligations and enforcement procedures to achieve transparency might, by being comprehensive, require disproportionate effort to understand them.[70]

Reductions in, and simplification of, the administrative requirements of regulation are not ends in themselves. Rather, they are means to achieving wider policy objectives, which include—but are not confined to—creating a better environment for business.[71] There is no necessary connection between reducing and simplifying regulation and improved business performance. The acid test of regulation, therefore, should be whether it enables and motivates business owners to adapt business practices and products in ways that contribute to enhanced business performance and, by extension, to improved national economic performance. It is this *dynamic* influence on business performance with which policy-makers should be concerned, and this depends on far more than the administrative burdens of regulatory compliance. By lowering compliance costs, reducing administrative burdens might, paradoxically, *weaken* business owners' motivation to innovate because they perceive no *additional* incentive to adapt business practices and products. Moreover, government must make trade-offs between conflicting policy objectives when developing regulation policy; reducing 'regulatory burdens' on small business owners may put at risk other valued objectives such as employee, consumer and environmental protection.[72]

D. IDENTIFYING THE DIVERSE EFFECTS OF REGULATION: DATA FROM A NEW STUDY

Studies of regulation and small business performance have focused primarily on a subset of regulatory tendencies—the direct, constraining tendencies

[69] Better Regulation Task Force, *Regulation—Less is More*, above n12.

[70] Better Regulation Task Force, *Enforcement* (London, Better Regulation Task Force, 1999).

[71] Better Regulation Executive, above n2.

[72] T May and J McHugh, 'Small Business Policy: A Political Consensus?' (2002) 73 *Political Quarterly* 76.

associated with placing obligations on small businesses that restrict the resources allocated to 'productive' business activities. These are important but must be situated in the broader context of the full range of regulatory tendencies that shape small business performance—including indirect, and enabling and motivating tendencies. To illustrate the range of tendencies, data from a recent study undertaken for the Small Business Service are presented.[73] Face-to-face interviews were carried out with 124 owners (or senior managers) in enterprises with fewer than 250 employees; 43 per cent of the sample were micro businesses (fewer than 10 employees) and a further 44 per cent employed between 10 and 49 staff. Respondents were asked about the influences on, and barriers to, business performance, before focusing explicitly on regulation. The cases presented here have been selected specifically to illustrate the wide range of regulatory tendencies, in contrast to the direct constraining tendencies upon which surveys of owner-managers' perceptions and compliance cost studies typically concentrate. It should be emphasised that these cases are chosen for illustrative purposes only; no claim is made that the performance outcomes and business contexts reported in these cases are typical of the wider small business population.

Case Business 1— E-procurement Services

The first case, a university spin-out company, had developed a new web-based e-procurement tool; its experience illustrates how regulation can be enabling for business performance by supporting new markets. The business was founded during the dotcom bubble burst of 2000 using £7 million equity funding from a venture capitalist and employed 10 employees at the time of interview. This leading-edge product provides access to a regularly updated database of life sciences suppliers' products and can be customised for each client. Benefits include substantial purchasing economies, a complete audit trail, and a high-quality after-sales service. At the time of the interview, sales turnover was growing rapidly but the company was not yet in profit. Very substantial investments were made in R&D/product development prior to start-up but, given the uncertain market conditions prevailing during 2000, the first sale took a year to secure.

The initial aim was to enable the university to buy reagents for scientific research from a multitude of suppliers; now the tool has been acquired by new clients in the Higher Education sector and covers 2,000 product lines (including computers and stationery). Finding clients has been difficult partly because of the external market environment, in particular, the need

[73] Small Business Research Centre, *The Impact of Regulation on Small Business Performance* (London, report for the Small Business Service, 2006).

to build credibility in a new product and long sales cycles (typically two years). There are only two direct competitors, but both are reported to lack a product of similar quality and familiarity with the HE sector.

The respondent reported that regulation was not an issue and that some business owners might use it as an excuse for poor performance. Regulation has exerted a number of specific enabling impacts upon the business. First, regulation has provided intellectual property protection in the software tool, prohibiting unauthorised use and imitation by others, and thereby encouraged investment in product development from which sales have begun to flow. Second, regulation has indirectly enabled business performance by discouraging 'cowboy operators' from entering or remaining in the market-place and conferring client and investor credibility on surviving providers, both of which enable enhanced competitiveness. Moreover, the shift towards e-procurement by UK local authorities means that suppliers need to develop their e-procurement capabilities if they are to win government contracts; this is likely to stimulate further demand for the company's product.

Case Business 2— Electrical Contractor

Case 2 is a good example of the indirect constraining influence of regulation on small business performance. It illustrates how regulatory change modifies the opportunity structure encountered by small business owners and other stakeholders with whom they causally interact—in this case, employees—with strong impacts on business performance. The business was bought from the founder in 1990 and employed 10 people at the time of interview, with the occasional use of subcontractors for work peaks. There had been a steady growth in sales turnover and profits prior to last year (£900,000 sales per annum), although the owner expected to break even this year.

The introduction of Part P regulations stipulating that residential electrical installations can be tested only by 'competent persons' had compelled the owner to provide new training to his employees. This in turn encouraged five qualified employees to leave the firm on the same day in order to set up their own businesses. This mass exodus had caused major business disruption and generated serious knock-on effects on business performance. To service existing contracts, the employer personally had to go 'back on the tools' and increase his use of labour subcontractors—a practice he had previously held doubts about on quality grounds. Moreover, the employer's focus on existing clients meant he had been unable to devote sufficient time to winning new business, with a consequent decline in new contracts and business sales.

By providing Part P training to employees, the employer inadvertently set in train a series of events that impacted adversely on business turnover and profitability and to which the business had to adapt. The example highlights the contingency of regulatory outcomes, and the crucial role of human agency in causing particular business performance effects. Had the employees chosen to act differently, or the employer taken pre-emptive action to forestall them leaving, business performance outcomes would have been different.

Case Business 3—Document Storage Services

Case 3 illustrates the multiple, diverse influences regulation exerts on small business performance. The business, founded in 1991, had expanded from two people to 160 staff in 11 major city locations and annual sales had increased dramatically from £180,000 to £6 million. Having exploited a 'prime mover' advantage by being the first supplier of document storage services in its home city, the business had enjoyed massive business growth, investment in new premises, responding to clients' requests for new services (electronic storage, scanning, destruction) being the key to expansion. Profitability had risen and fallen depending on the timing of investments in new premises. Price had increasingly become more important in clients' purchasing decisions as larger rivals entered the market and competition had intensified.

Regulation was not reported as an influence on business performance until prompted by the interviewer but, once the issue was raised, the owner complained that high business rates limited the finance available for business development; that the compliance cost of time, though unmeasured, was a 'pain in the arse' (tempered by the knowledge that other companies have to deal with the same regulations); and that he had experienced difficulties in being able to dismiss employees. Pressed on these issues, the owner reported that impacts were difficult to measure and were perhaps more of an irritant than a major impediment to performance. Regulation was also reported as generating less tangible outcomes such as eroding employees' personal responsibility as well as having direct effects on owners' decisions and actions.

Further questioning revealed the owner's ambivalent feelings towards regulation. These included acknowledging (if not applauding) the benefits of regulation, while also reporting little, if any, impact upon business decision-making! Although, initially unacknowledged, the owner accepted that regulation had created major market opportunities by placing a statutory obligation on certain businesses—for example, health and law businesses—to keep records for periods of time. For businesses occupying expensive high street locations, contracting out document storage and thereby using space more productively can achieve economies. Failure to report such benefits until prompted suggests that survey methods capturing initial 'knee-jerk' responses from business owners are likely to overstate the importance of the constraining tendencies of regulation. Without deeper probing, the enabling and motivating tendencies of regulation may go unreported and even unnoticed by business owners themselves.

These three examples demonstrate that a much broader conceptualisation of regulation and its impact on business performance is needed than the vast majority of small business researchers have adopted hitherto. Regulation generates multiple tendencies simultaneously—enabling, motivating and constraining—that exert a causal influence on small business performance. The cases demonstrate the importance of human agency in connecting regulation to business performance outcomes: regulation produces effects only through shaping the actions of small business owners and others with whom they interact. The data presented also highlight the benefits of not relying exclusively on business owners' discursive constructions of regulation and its causal influence on business performance, particularly initial and unexamined replies to survey questions. Indeed, considerable interviewer effort is often required to encourage respondents to consider the enabling and motivating tendencies of regulation. Even this might not suffice; regulation can contribute to performance outcomes without owners' conscious acknowledgement. This enhanced understanding of regulation and its causal impact on small business performance can inform policy development by encouraging policy-makers to consider the enabling and motivating influences of regulation *as well as* the costs and constraints it imposes, and to recognise the manifold paths through which regulation impacts directly and indirectly on small business performance.

E. CONCLUSION

Developing better regulation has been a key policy objective for UK governments since the 1980s. Small businesses have been one of the major intended beneficiaries of this policy agenda. The emphasis on *better* regulation by government since 1997 constitutes an important shift in rhetoric, rather than a major substantive change. The agenda has been defined primarily in terms of changes to regulatory processes which, it is assumed, if implemented will bring about improved business performance. There is, however, no necessary connection between changes in regulatory processes and business performance outcomes. The central issue for policy-makers should be whether, and how, small business owners are able to adapt practices and products as a consequence of regulation in ways that contribute to improved performance outcomes and, by extension, to national economic performance.

The evidence base on the effects of regulation on small business performance is partial and one-sided. Many studies fail to conceptualise regulation and its causal impact on business performance outcomes adequately, emphasising only the costs and constraining tendencies. More sophisticated approaches, using qualitative data, demonstrate that regulation generates enabling and motivating tendencies that can bring about improvements in business performance as well as imposing constraints. These influences operate directly and also indirectly by influencing the behaviour of those whose actions causally affect small business performance outcomes—actual and potential competitors, customers, employees, suppliers, infrastructure providers and regulatory authorities. These tendencies operate simultaneously and give rise to a *net* impact of regulation on each small enterprise. Which regulatory tendencies exert the most powerful influence on business performance in particular cases depends on the capacities and motivation of small business owners to adapt to regulatory change, and the wider contexts that enable or constrain those adaptations.

Unless policy-makers recognise the full range of regulatory tendencies, their impact on small business performance, and the conditions that support or hinder them, policy interventions are likely to produce unwanted consequences. Initiatives based on the assumption that 'less regulation is more' and on 'reducing administrative burdens' focus solely on regulations and their properties rather than on business owners' adaptive capabilities. Reducing administrative burdens might be much less important than other levers policy-makers might use to support small businesses—including interventions to develop owner-managers' capabilities, or to provide easier access to valuable resources (finance, skilled labour, information) and a stable framework of market competition that enables business start-up, development and access to product markets. Reducing administrative burdens may do nothing to motivate innovation or investment, or enable access to finance, skilled labour, advice and infrastructure. Indeed, by cutting the time and possibly other costs of compliance, it might reduce the incentive to develop new products and processes to maintain competitiveness; continuing along the current low-cost path might appear more attractive to some business owners because there is little incentive to change. Less regulation might not, therefore, be more, if it does not enable superior small business performance outcomes. Indeed, less regulation might well be substantially less if it does nothing to enable or motivate investment, innovation and competition, or to foster consumer, investor and trader confidence.

10

The Politics of EC Regulation

R DANIEL KELEMEN* AND ANAND MENON**

Martin Shapiro, in a discussion of legal scholarship on the European Union, refers witheringly to:

> constitutional law without politics...[which] presents the Community as a juristic idea; the written constitution as a sacred text; the professional community as a legal truth; the case law as the inevitable working out of the correct implications of the constitutional text; and the constitutional court as the disembodied voice of right reason and constitutional theology.[1]

Clearly, we are not here about to assert that such a judgement holds true of all legal scholarship, and certainly not of that to be found in the rest of this volume. Yet we do maintain that a purely legal perspective on European integration, and perhaps particularly on its regulatory role, will reveal only a partial, and potentially misleading, picture, redolent of the elephant famously painted by Donald Puchala's blind men.[2]

The purpose of this chapter is straightforward. We aim to provide a brief overview of the politics of EC regulation, and to do so in four stages. First, we consider where the need for regulation comes from. Secondly, we investigate the processes by which the EC goes about the business of regulation. Thirdly, we examine the changing nature of EC regulation. Fourthly, we consider some normative implications of the Union's regulatory role. A concluding section briefly reviews some of the broader political factors that may impact upon EC regulatory policy.

* Associate Professor of Political Science at Rutgers University.

** Professor of European Politics and Director of the European Research Institute, University of Birmingham.

[1] M Shapiro, 'Comparative Law and Comparative Politics' (1980) 53 *Southern Californian Law Review* 537.

[2] D Puchala, 'Of Blind Men, Elephants, and International Integration' (1972) 10 *Journal of Common Market Studies* 267.

A. THE DRIVERS OF EC REGULATION

Political scientists have advanced numerous explanations for EC regulation. In general terms, its desirability is seen to stem from the problem of 'negative externalities'—the undesirable impact of regulation (or the lack of regulation) in one country on another. Explanations for the scope of EC regulation range from the active role of the European Commission, to that of national or transnational interest groups.[3] Some have been moved to view the Union as a 'regulatory state', pointing to its lack of distributive or redistributive powers in order to explain its striking reliance on the regulatory mode of governance.[4]

More specifically, we can identify a number of factors that account for what has been a significant increase in the amount of EC regulation over the course of the last two decades. Most EC regulation adopted since the mid-1980s has been linked, either directly or indirectly, to the drive to 'complete' the Single Market. This may strike some as a paradox: the Single Market, after all, has been viewed by friends and foes alike as a neoliberal project aimed primarily at dismantling barriers to trade. However, from the outset, Delors' project of completing the Single Market involved far more than mere deregulation. Creating an open, and level, playing field for business involved replacing the patchwork of national regulations with harmonised measures at the EC level. This deregulation–reregulation dynamic was driven primarily by three sets of forces: political pressure from pro-regulation Member States, entrepreneurship of a European Commission eager to champion 'the people's Europe', and the functional demands of regulating a diverse and dynamic pan-European market.

For Member State governments whose voting publics demanded high regulatory standards in areas such as environmental or consumer protection, acquiescing in EC inspired deregulation was simply not acceptable. Such governments reacted to the downward pressure on their regulations—coming either from attacks on their legality (as non-tariff barriers) or simply from enhanced competitition from 'lax' states—by demanding the establishment of common regulatory standards at the EC level. In other words, they refused to engage in a regulatory 'race-to-the-bottom' and instead demanded that the EC engineer a pan-European 'race-to-the-top'. Such states, led by Germany, sought to use political influence and market power to reregulate Europe in their image.

Why, one might fairly ask, would laggard states acquiesce in this race-to-the-top, forcing them to raise production costs and surrender competitive advantages they had derived from their lower standards? The answer lies in

[3] M Thatcher, 'European Regulation' in J Richardson (ed), *European Union: Power and Policy-Making*. 2nd edn. (London, Routledge, 2001) at 303.

[4] G Majone, 'The Rise of the Regulatory State in Europe' (1994) 17(3) *West European Politics* 78; G Majone, *Regulating Europe* (London, Routledge, 1996).

what scholars of regulatory competition refer to as 'the California effect'.[5] The California effect can arise in the context of a common market, when an economically and politically powerful jurisdiction has a preference for high standards of regulatory protection in areas such as public health, consumer or environmental protection. In these circumstances, the 'California' (or in the EU's case Germany) can use its market power and political influence as a lever to force up the regulatory standards of laggard jurisdictions. In some cases, laggards are compelled to raise standards in order to gain access to valuable export markets in states with high standards. In other cases, powerful jurisdictions convince laggards to raise standards through mixtures of side-payments[6] and policy log-rolls, and—just perhaps—moral suasion. Finally, in some cases in the EU, laggards were simply outvoted under the Single European Act's qualified majority voting system.

The second key driver of EC level reregulation was the European Commission. Germany, the Netherlands, Denmark and other Member States that wanted to see the EC pressure regulatory laggards to raise their standards found an enthusiastic ally in the European Commission. In launching the Single Market, the Delors Commission was sensitive to criticisms from the Left that the EC in general and the Single Market project in particular were merely instruments of big business. Delors' own ideological predispositions made him uncomfortable with such an idea. Moreover, and with strong backing from the European Parliament, the Commission saw regulatory activity as a means of enhancing the EC's popular appeal by demonstrating its ability to address areas of great public concern, such as social, consumer and environmental regulation.

Thus, the dismantling of national regulatory barriers was coupled with 'flanking policies' in areas such as social, consumer and environmental regulation designed to ensure high levels of protection across the EC. Likewise, during moments of clear regulatory failure at the national level, such as the BSE crisis, when national governments could hardly claim that their regulatory regimes were successful, the Commission was more than willing to step in with proposals for enhancing the EC's role in protecting the public.

Finally, the very nature of the EC's Single Market influenced both the style and scope of EC regulation. When, in response to the political pressures mentioned above, EC policy-makers attempted to re-regulate at the European level, they confronted a number of functional pressures inherent

[5] D Vogel, *Trading Up: Consumer and Environmental Regulation in a Global Economy* (Cambridge, Mass, Harvard University Press, 1997).

[6] Revealingly, the SEA was followed by a massive increase in the funds provided for poorer EC regions; whilst never admitted officially by the EU, such payments represent a form of compensation for what poorer regions regard as potentially economically harmful EU initiatives: see D Allen, 'Cohesion and the Structural Funds: Competing Pressures for Reform?' in H Wallace, W Wallace and MA Pollack (eds), *Policy-Making in the European Union* (Oxford, OUP, 2003).

in regulating an open, dynamic market on a continental scale. The dynamic that emerged in the EC followed a familiar pattern that Steven Vogel identified in earlier studies of liberalisation in Japan and the UK; a dynamic in which 'freer markets' actually require 'more rules'.[7] EC policy-makers had to craft regulatory frameworks suited to markets with a great diversity of players (including foreign firms) and little trust between regulators and the regulated. They could not adopt the sorts of informal, flexible (and often opaque) approaches to regulation that many governments had relied on at the national level. To be effective and legitimate, EC regulation had to promote a level playing field across the Community and ensure equal treatment for new entrants and foreign firms. Thus, EC regulation often relied on a rather formal, legalistic approach to regulation. Ultimately, as national regulatory practices were dismantled, they were replaced with new EC level regulations that involved more red tape than the national systems they replaced.

Finally, it is worth noting that in a number of policy areas the politics of blame avoidance encouraged the growth of the EC's regulatory power. In other contexts, political scientists have explained the decision to delegate responsibilities to independent bodies such as the Commission as a function of a desire on the part of politicians to avoid blame. Delegation, according to this view, represents a means of shifting responsibility to other decision-makers. As Fiorina puts it, by delegating:

> legislators not only avoid the time and trouble of making specific decisions, they avoid or at best disguise their responsibility for the consequences of the decisions ultimately made.[8]

Elements of such thinking are clearly discernible behind the recent debate in the UK about the possibility of devolving operational matters pertaining to the National Health Service to an 'independent' body.[9] Appreciating this dynamic is of crucial importance for understanding the current state of the EC and its regulatory implications. To take but one example, the decision to share regulatory authority between national capitals and the EU post-BSE can be seen in this light.

Certainly, the motives for the delegation of powers by the Member States to the European Commission are far too varied and complex to be reduced to such a simple formula, yet, as we illustrate in subsequent sections, the blame shifting potential of delegation has not gone unnoticed by national politicians.

[7] S Vogel, *Freer Markets, More Rules* (Ithaca, NY, Cornell University Press, 1996).

[8] M Fiorina, 'Legislative Choice of Regulatory Forms: Legal Process or Administrative Process?' (1982) 39 *Public Choice* 33, at 47.

[9] Some might argue, of course, that politicians aspire to have their cake and eat it, by blaming a supposedly independent body whilst, at the same time, designing it in such a way as to be able to control it.

B. THE REGULATORY PROCESS

Many of those who argue in favour of EC regulation do so based on claims regarding the efficacy of the process of EC regulation. Thus, Majone famously argues that the Commission makes an ideal and highly credible regulator because it is less likely to be captured by an individual firm or industry than are national regulatory authorities, and hence more inclined to be tough and enforce sanctions than the latter.[10] Gatsios and Seabright give a practical example:

> Where pollution has international effects, and fines impose significant competitive disadvantages on firms that compete internationally, firms are likely to believe—correctly—that national regulators will be unwilling to investigate and fine them as rigorously if they determine the level of enforcement unilaterally as if they had done so by international agreement. And the less rigorously they believe that regulatory standards will be enforced, the weaker will be their attempts at compliance.[11]

This is all very well in principle. Yet many of the claims regarding the efficacy of the EC regulatory process are based on assumptions concerning the neutrality and political independence of the European Commission, on the claim that 'transfer of powers [to an international authority] makes it easier to avoid regulatory capture'.[12] Such assumptions are at best questionable. As in the case of the nation state itself, the Commission has discovered that:

> increasing intervention makes [the Commission] more clearly an arena of social conflict and makes its constituent parts more attractive for take-over. In other words, the contradictions of civil society become more embedded in [it] as [it] more deeply penetrates civil society, potentially undermining both its coherence as a corporate actor and its autonomy.[13]

Political and regulatory authorities, in other words, can become victims of their own success. The expanding EC regulatory agenda, which has come to encompass ever more politically salient aspects of socio-economic management, has increased the attractiveness of the Commission as a target for capture by those private interests it seeks to regulate. Witness, for

[10] G Majone, 'Europe's "Democratic Deficit": The Question of Standards' (1998) 4 *European Law Journal* 5 at 17–18.

[11] K Gatsios and P Seabright, 'Regulation in the European Community' (1989) 5(2) *Oxford Review of Economic Policy* 49.

[12] *Ibid*.

[13] D Rueschemeyer and PB Evans, 'The State and Economic Transformation: Towards an Analysis of the Conditions Underlying Effective Intervention' in PB Evans, D Rueschemeyer and AT Skocpol (eds), *Bringing the State Back In* (Cambridge, Cambridge University Press, 1985) at 69.

example, the influence exerted by the European advertising industry over early attempts on the part of the Community to carve out a role for itself in broadcasting policy (to the point of having advertising defined as a 'service' in a 1984 Green Paper).[14]

Moreover, capture is particularly problematic for an international institution such as the EC, in that the objects of its regulatory activity are sovereign states as well as private actors. The concern here is that states exercise significant control over the nature, resources and functioning of the Commission. Recent years have witnessed a marked trend on the part of national governments to try to limit the autonomy and influence of the Commission.

Partly, this is through the creation of policy processes that limit its role. The so-called Open Method of Cooperation (OMC), increasingly relied upon for aspects of social and particularly employment policy, represents a case in point, limiting the powers of the Commission in favour of a decentralised system of benchmarking and providing for no centralised enforcement mechanisms.

Perhaps more importantly, national governments are ultimately in charge of the staffing of the Commission. As the EC becomes a more important regulatory actor, national governments have become increasingly preoccupied with their ability to shape its actions from within. Interview evidence gleaned from discussions with numerous senior Commission officials between 1999 and 2006 reveals that capitals go to great lengths to 'place' nationals in strategically important posts within the Commission. The high profile wrangling between national governments over the trade off between the number of Commissioners and the voting weights in the Council in the context of debates about the Constitutional Treaty revealed all too clearly the degree to which the notion of an impartial and independent Commission has been eroded. Similarly, the recent proposal by EU finance ministers to cut the Commission's staff by approximately 8.5 per cent sends another clear signal, if any was needed, that the Member States ultimately determine the level of the Commission's administrative capacity.

Equally insidiously, governments have become adept at criticising the Commission for decisions that do not chime with their preferences. Several Spanish ministers have recently done so over Commission attempts to investigate the legislation brought in to allow the Spanish electricity and gas regulator to block foreign takeovers. Public political criticism of the Commission for implementing rules to which the Member States have themselves signed up is at best disingenuous and at worst potentially damaging. At a time when public support for the EC is fragile, the fear of

[14] M Fraser, 'Television' in H Kassim and A Menon (eds), *The European Union and National Industrial Policy* (London, Routledge, 1996) at 204–25.

provoking such reactions may, at the least, serve to render the Commission reluctant to wield its powers to the full in defence of the Treaty.

Challenges to the Commission do not emanate merely from the Member States. A variety of regulatory networks and comitology committees have long contributed to the regulatory process and, in the case of comitology committees, acted as overseers of policy implementation by the Commission. More recently, a number of EC level regulatory agencies have been created outside the Commission hierarchy, partly as a consequence of Member States' refusal to provide the Commission with the resources necessary to carry out the new regulatory tasks emerging from the single market programme.[15] After 1989, the Council, Commission and European Parliament struck a compromise in which new staff, resources and regulatory responsibilities would be delegated to decentralised, 'independent' European regulatory agencies, rather than to the European Commission itself.

The creation of agencies can be viewed as a sign of the erosion of the Commission's power, in that they perform some functions that the Commission might otherwise have performed, and are controlled by management boards dominated by national government representatives. Ultimately, however, the creation of agencies may best be viewed as a process linked to the increasing politicisation of the Commission. With more and more routine regulatory tasks being delegated to EC agencies, the Commission is increasingly left to focus on the altogether more political tasks of driving forward the policy agenda and enforcing EC regulation, sometimes in the face of stiff national resistance.

Negotiations between the Member States are also crucial in terms of shaping the Union's regulatory activity. That the EC now impinges on increasingly sensitive aspects of national economic management should come as no surprise. The Member States are, after all, currently haggling over those aspects of the Single Market that proved too contentious for agreement to be reached earlier in the process of market building. Such haggling becomes more difficult as the stakes increase. A recent example of this phenomenon and its possible consequences was provided by negotiations over the Takeover Directive. Agreement on this was finally reached in 2004—after 13 years during which the Commission had unsuccessfully proposed legislation. Yet this proved possible only on the basis that opt-outs be available to Member States on the need to consult shareholders on bids and on the legality of certain forms of takeover defences. Twenty-one Member States have decided to opt out of the provisions on the latter, while Germany, Denmark, Luxembourg, Poland and the Netherlands have opted out of the former. And all this without taking account of the fact that the Directive itself will doubtless be implemented in different ways

[15] D Kelemen, 'The Politics of "Eurocratic" Structure and the New European Agencies' (2002) 25(4) *West European Politics* 93. See also the contribution of Vibert to this book.

in the different Member States. Our point here is not that Member States are unable to legislate on issues concerning the Single Market—indeed the recent agreement on the Services Directive clearly shows that they can. The point rather is that Member States are doing their utmost to wriggle out of making firm commitments to market integration by exploiting opt-outs and derogations. With the proliferation of opt-outs, derogations and toothless policy instruments, compounded in their effects by increasing reliance on toothless procedures such as the OMC, the danger is that the supposedly Single Market may wither into little more than a loose patchwork of non-binding regulatory good intentions.

C. NEW DIRECTIONS IN EC REGULATION

While the Single Market initiative kick-started the process of re-regulation at the EU level in the late 1980s, major regulatory failures at the national level and growing public scepticism concerning both science and business propelled the process forward throughout the late 1990s and up to the present day. As David Vogel has pointed out, throughout much of the 1990s, the prevailing public sentiments in Europe concerning regulation resembled those in the US during the 1970s. Dramatic regulatory failures at the state level, coupled with (and contributing to) mounting public concern over the safety of new technologies and distrust of business, led to heightened demands for regulatory protection from the 'federal' level. In the EU, national regulatory failures in the 1990s including those concerning BSE, AIDS-tainted blood and dioxin in chicken feed contributed to a sense that national regulatory regimes were not up to the challenge of protecting consumers and public health.

More generally, mounting public concern over the safety of new technologies—above all genetically modified organisms (GMOs) in the food supply—led to increased public support for relying on 'the precautionary principle' as a basis for regulation. The resolution on the precautionary principle[16] adopted by national leaders at the Nice Summit in 2000 provided a firm basis for relying on the principle as a guideline in EU regulation. The precautionary principle, at least as applied by the EU after Nice, empowered regulators to act to address 'urgent' risks even in the absence of scientific data concerning risk levels. Moreover, regulators were called on to be open to public participation, to take a 'multi-disciplinary' approach and to consider the 'public acceptability' of their regulatory decisions. In short, regulators were given a green light to adopt regulations where there was considerable public perception of, and concern over, risk, even in the absence of conclusive evidence. This precautionary approach encouraged

[16] Nice European Council, Presidency Conclusions, Annex III, 7–9 Dec 2000.

EU regulation on issues such as GMOs and bovine growth hormone, which could not have been justified strictly on the basis of available scientific evidence.

Regulatory failures have not been confined to areas such as food safety; major corporate scandals also undermined confidence in the national regulation of business conduct and increased pressure for EU level controls. Following US accounting and securities scandals such as those involving Enron and Worldcom, similar malpractice came to light in Europe, involving notably Parmalat and Ahold. The failure of national regulators to control corporate malfeasance strengthened the arguments of those interest groups, governments and EU officials that hoped to see the EU play a greater role in protecting investors, for instance through its increasingly stringent regime for securities regulation.

As the volume of EC regulation has grown, so too has the number of initiatives launched by EC policy-makers promising to 'reduce' or 'improve' regulation. When confronted with particular policy challenges—removing sewage from drinking water, protecting consumers from dangerous foodstuffs, combating corporate fraud—voters, politicians and interest groups often fight for strict regulations. However, when confronted with the entire body of regulation and regulatory procedures that result from such worthy initiatives, many of the same voters and politicians decry the excessive regulation and red tape. EC red tape is a tempting target for EC and particularly national politicians anxious to find a scapegoat for economic underperformance.

At the EC level, at least since the Delors' Commission's *relance* of the Single Market, policy-makers have coupled their regulatory initiatives with ceremonial self-flagellation concerning the inflexibility of EC regulation and the need to 'simplify' and 'improve' it. The 'new approach' which underpinned the 1992 initiative promised to move away from 'total harmonisation' and make EC regulation more flexible so that it could better accommodate distinct national approaches. The Santer Commission launched its regulatory simplification initiative promising that the EC would 'do less in order to do it better'.[17] The Prodi Commission produced an action plan on better regulation, linked to the Lisbon Agenda.[18] The Barroso Commission raised the profile of such efforts with its 2005 'better regulation' initiative, which promised to improve the regulatory environment for business by simplifying EC regulation. Barroso's better regulation initiative also required that new and existing legislative proposals be subject to 'regulatory impact assessment' that takes into account the

[17] Commission Communication on 'Simpler Legislation for the Internal Market' (SLIM), COM(1996)204 final, 8 May 1996.

[18] Communication from the Commission: Action Plan 'Simplifying and Improving the Regulatory Environment', COM(2002)278 final, 5 May 2002.

Lisbon Strategy's objectives.[19] These attacks on old-fashioned, inflexible, top-down, command-and-control regulation have been linked to promises to promote new, more flexible modes of regulation, including the Open Method of Coordination (OMC) mentioned above.

Despite all the fanfare surrounding such initiatives, they are unlikely significantly to alter patterns of EC regulation. The Barroso Commission's Better Regulation initiative may lead to some consolidation and simplification of directives and regulations, and new modes of governance such as the OMC may become more prevalent in marginal areas of EC competence such as social policy. However, the drive for Better Regulation and efforts to promote new flexible modes of governance will be limited by many of the same forces that have stymied such initiatives in the past. The tendency to produce detailed, inflexible regulations is deeply rooted in the EC's political system. With its extreme fragmentation of political power and the distrust between EC policy-makers and the Member State administrations that implement most EC policy, the EC is simply not a polity structured to produce simple, flexible and informal regulation. For one thing, a structure containing a number of very different Member States is almost inevitably going to incorporate elements of the regulatory traditions of each. Each new wave of enlargement has seen new regulatory priorities adopted that reflect the traditions of the accession states (witness Portugal's insistence on the need to define carrots as fruit as a function of that country's curious jam-making proclivities). Over-regulation in this instance is a function of the weakness and permeability of Brussels to Member States' demands, rather than of an overweening excessively regulatory Commission.

Moreover, satisfying the increasing democratic demands for openness, transparency and legal certainty in the EC's regulatory processes, not least demands emanating from the European Parliament, will require further formalisation of EC regulations and regulatory procedures. In short, more red tape.

D. NORMATIVE QUESTIONS

Particularly since the inception of the Single Market, there has been a marked increase in the regulatory activity of the EU/EC, all of which poses a normative question regarding the legitimacy of the Union as a regulatory body. Exponents of the so-called democratic deficit are often acerbic in their critiques of the legitimacy of the EC system. Most recently, Follesdal and Hix have argued that the crucial weakness of the EC system in

[19] Communication from the Commission to the Council and the European Parliament: 'Better Regulation for Growth and Jobs in the European Union', COM(2005)97 final, 16 Mar 2005.

normative terms stems from the lack of political contestation within it, a situation which they argue could be remedied via measures such as allowing the direct election of the Commission President.[20]

There are several possible responses to such critiques. Andrew Moravcsik, for instance, argues that a crucial feature distinguishing the EC from traditional federal states is its relative lack of competence over core areas of public policy (and of interest to electorates). In the crucial areas of education, culture, infrastructure, redistribution and defence, Moravcsik emphasises, the Union enjoys little, if any, real capacity for effective action.[21] In short, the EC's rather limited degree of democratic legitimation is perfectly adequate for the rather limited role it plays.

For Majone, regulation is about Pareto efficiency and can be distinguished, in both substantive and legitimacy terms, from redistributive policies:

> Efficiency-oriented policies attempt to increase the aggregate welfare of society, while redistributive policies are designed to improve the welfare of one particular group in society at the expense of other groups. In a nutshell: redistributive policies can be legitimated only by majoritarian means and thus cannot be delegated to institutions independent of the political process; efficiency-oriented policies, on the other hand, are basically legitimated by results, and hence may be delegated to such institutions, provided an adequate system of accountability is in place.[22]

Consequently, it is wholly appropriate that the Union, with its largely regulatory role, relies largely on output legitimation. The unelected nature of the Commission and Court serves to ensure the Pareto optimality of the EU's regulatory decisions, which would be compromised by resort to processes of input legitimation.[23]

Delegation in these areas, both in Member States and in the EC, often occurs precisely in order to shelter agencies from the vicissitudes of democratic politics. Delegated institutions are necessary to provide credible commitments and overcome problems of time inconsistencies inherent in the actions of politicians with an eye perpetually on the next election. The key distinction here is between what Fritz Scharpf has labelled 'input legitimacy'—suggesting a chain of accountability linking those governing to those governed—and 'output legitimacy'—conferred when those exercising

[20] A Follesdal and S Hix, 'Why There is a Democratic Deficit in the EC: A Response to Majone and Moravscik' (2006) 44 *Journal of Common Market Studies* 533.

[21] Interestingly, what this means is that EC activity is largely confined to areas where delegation to non-majoritarian institutions is the norm in the Member States themselves: see A Moravcsik, 'Federalism in the European Union: Rhetoric and Reality' in K Nicolaidis and R Howse (eds), *The Federal Vision: Legitimacy and Levels of Governance in the United States and the European Union* (Oxford, OUP, 2001) at 161–87.

[22] Majone, above n10, at 26.

[23] *Ibid*; G Majone, 'The European Commission: The Limits of Centralization and the Perils of Parliamentarization' (2002) 15(3) *Governance* 375.

political power are able to meet the expectations of the governed.[24] The economic benefits generated by the Single Market, commonly portrayed as evidence of the efficiency gains to be garnered via transnational regulation, are often held up as examples of the ability of the Community to generate legitimacy via efficiency.[25]

The legitimising potential of the Union, moreover, extends further than simply the justification of its own existence via its efficiency. The basis of the legitimacy of the nation state itself has changed over time. Once purely procedural, it too is now increasingly performance related.[26] However, states acting individually are no longer capable of performing adequately. Whether or not one buys into the extreme view of globalisation, according to which it is eroding the 'the authority, legitimacy, policy- making capacity and policy-implementing effectiveness of the state',[27] increasing interstate trade and consequent interdependence has reduced the ability of individual governments to deliver to their electorates. Institutions such as the EC provide a means of reinforcing this ability, through both addressing the problem of negative externalities of the actions of other governments and allowing these states more effectively to shape the global economy.[28] In this context, it is important to grasp that the Union not only secures output legitimacy of its own, but also serves to address problems of output legitimacy at the national level.[29]

Whatever the limits of the EC's legitimacy as a regulator, it is important to recognise that many Member States' governments are themselves far from paragons in this regard. Many critiques of EC regulation emphasise the lack of openness and transparency in EC regulatory procedures. However, these critiques hold up the EC against a non-existent ideal-type and do not withstand comparison with existing democracies. Indeed, in his comparative study, Zweifel found that the EC's policy-making processes were as open and transparent as those in Switzerland and the US.[30] More generally, in terms of openness, transparency and accountability of regulators, the EC compares favourably with the governments of most EC Member States. The traditional national regulatory systems in the EC Member States had

[24] FW Scharpf, *Governing in Europe: Effective and Democratic?* (Oxford, OUP, 1999).

[25] A Menon and S Weatherill, 'Democratic Politics in a globalising World: The European Rescue of National Democracy', unpublished paper.

[26] S Bartolini, 'Old and New Peripheries in the Processes of European Territorial Integration' in CK Ansell and G di Palma (eds), *Restructuring Territoriality: Europe and the US Compared* (Cambridge, Cambridge University Press, 2004) at 25–6.

[27] PG Cerny, 'Globalization and the Changing Logic of Collective Action' (1995) 49(4) *International Organization* 595, at 621.

[28] A Hurrell and A Menon, 'Institutions, International Relations and the State in Western Europe' in J Hayward and A Menon (eds), *Governing Europe* (Oxford, OUP, 2003).

[29] Menon and Weatherill, above n25.

[30] T Zweifel, *Democratic Deficit? Institutions and Regulation in the European Union, Switzerland, and the United States* (Boulder, Colo, Rowman and Littlefield, 2002).

many virtues, but transparency and accountability were not among them.[31] The EC may fall short of role models of transparent government, such as Finland and Sweden, but it surely presents an improvement on national regulatory systems long characterised by opacity and corruption, such as those in Greece, Italy and, perhaps, France. The EC's relative transparency and accountability are reflected in public opinion. Eurobarometer surveys routinely find that more European citizens trust EU institutions than trust their national political institutions (with 41 per cent responding that they 'tend to trust' the EU, while only 30 per cent 'tend to trust' national institutions).[32] Many Europeans may distrust faceless Brussels bureaucrats. But even more of them distrust their national politicians.

As Member States' administrations are increasingly occupied with the implementation of EC policies, they are finding themselves pressured to abandon their traditional administrative practices and comply with the EC's more strictly codified procedures.[33] For countries that have long been laggards in terms of regulatory transparency and accountability, EC requirements are forcing them to enhance opportunities for participation and for holding regulators accountable for their decisions. For instance, one effective way of enhancing transparency is to require regulators to provide reasons for their decisions. As Shapiro says:

> [giving] reasons is a device for enhancing democratic influences on administration by making government more transparent. The reasons giving administrator is likely to make more reasonable decisions than he or she otherwise might and is more subject to general public surveillance.[34]

Article 253 of the Treaty of Rome requires that '[r]egulations, directives and decisions of the Council and of the Commission shall state the reasons on which they are based'. This EC-mandated Giving Reasons Requirement stands in stark contrast to traditional procedural requirements in most Member States, which included no requirement for regulators to give reasons. Thus the spread of the EC's Giving Reasons Requirement, like the spread of many other EC requirements concerning legal certainty and transparency, has substantially 'democratised' the regulatory process at the national level.

[31] RD Kelemen, 'Federalism and Democratization: The US and EU in Comparative Perspective' in A Menon and M Schain (eds), *Comparative Federalism: The European Union and the United States* (Oxford, OUP, 2007).

[32] European Commission, *Eurobarometer No. 61: Public Opinion in the EU 15—First Results* (May 2004) 5.

[33] J Schwarze, *Administrative Law under European Influence: On the convergence of the Administrative Laws of the EC Member States* (Baden Baden, Nomos Verlagsgesellschaft, 1996).

[34] M Shapiro, 'The Giving-reasons Requirement' [1992] *The University of Chicago Legal Forum* 180, at 183.

A final possible defence against so-called 'democratic' critiques of the Union requires a (grudging) acceptance of the need for political scientists to pay more attention to the workings and impact of the law. For all its shortcomings in this regard (see above), delegation has long been recognised by political scientists as providing a barrier to regulatory capture. In the case of the EU, prevention of capture is supplemented by another highly political rationale. Simply put, national political processes are not attuned to the transnational realities of market integration in Europe. Specifically, they tend to exclude or fail adequately to represent not only diffuse domestic interests, but also those extra-national actors profoundly affected by national regulations. The application of EC rules serves to correct such malfunctions. This, it has been argued, is notably the case with free movement cases such as *Cassis de Dijon,*[35] and with applications of Treaty rules on state aids and public monopolies.[36] EU law provides a mechanism for out-of-state interests, unrepresented in purely national political processes, to seek redress against national regulatory activity incompatible with the Treaty. Seen in this light, the Union is capable not merely of legitimising both itself and the Member States via its ability to enhance economic efficiency, but also of modernising national democratic systems increasingly out of step with the realities of a transnational market-place.[37]

E. CONCLUSIONS

A new series of challenges has emerged to confront the European Union as it strives to carry out its new regulatory functions. New regulatory challenges often require complex solutions, rendered all the more difficult because of the need to reach agreement between 27 Member States. At the same time, political pressures within the Member States mitigate against what some characterise as 'excessive' regulation. Perhaps more worryingly, politics is increasingly coming to shape the mechanisms by which EC regulations are promulgated, threatening not only the ability of the European Commission to play its role in an impartial manner but also the quality and effectiveness of those regulations finally issued. And, at the same time, voices are raised to criticise the legitimacy of EC activity in this realm.

If there is a general lesson to be gleaned from the above, it is that the nature of EC regulatory activity is shaped by a myriad of—not least political—forces. However rational the economic and legal cases for regulation beyond the nation state may be, political incentives and loyalties often

[35] Case 120/78 *Rewe-Zentral AG vBundesmonopolverwaltung für Branntwein* [1979] ECR 649.

[36] Menon and Weatherill, above n25.

[37] D Chalmers, 'The Reconstitution of European Public Spheres' (2003) 9 *European Law Journal* 127, especially at 184–5.

function on the basis of a different logic: the 'functional need for human cooperation rarely coincides with the territorial scope of community'.[38]

Above and beyond specific incentives that influence the politics of EC regulation—such as the incentives that encourage national politicians to blame the Union for their woes and claim credit for its successes—the prevailing political atmosphere can impact upon EC regulatory activity. As we have argued at greater length elsewhere,[39] the EC remains remarkably stable and robust despite recent spats between the Member States and much political rhetoric suggesting it has entered a period of profound crisis. Yet the potential implications of the prevailing political mood following budgetary squabbles, the demise of the constitutional treaty and profound soul searching over enlargement are serious.

For one thing, the proclivity on the part of national political leaders, as the Union becomes more politically salient at home, to attempt to control all of its workings at the expense of the autonomy of the Commission augurs ill for the effective regulation of the market. Of equal concern is the danger that, confronted with a series of high profile problems on the European Council agenda, national political leaders forget about the apparently more mundane yet practically tremendously important undertaking of completing the Single Market. Political will is required in order to tackle head-on many of the problems confronting the Union acting in its regulatory capacity. Political posturing combining theological debates on institutions with a proclivity to attack the EC at every opportunity will only exacerbate what to us appears to be a serious threat to the Union's core function of economic management.

[38] L Hooghe and G Marks, 'Europe's Blues: Theoretical Soul-Searching after the Rejection of the European Constitution', *PS: Political Science and Politics* (Apr 2006) 247.

[39] D Kelemen and A Menon, 'Crisis? What Crisis?' (2006) 13 *Public Policy Research* 71.

11

The EU Better Regulation Agenda

ELISABETTA OLIVI*

TODAY WE ARE all more conscious about the need for better law-making, better regulation, than we were in the past. Rightly so, not least since better regulation has become a major political issue that goes far beyond the question of how we can create more favourable framework conditions for competitiveness, growth and jobs.

The evident crisis of legitimacy for European integration in some Member States is partly linked to the public perception of the EU as a bureaucratic monster, a monster whose tentacles leave no village untouched and with nothing better to do than chop off every difference and blend it into the European sauce. Nobody should underestimate the strength of such perceptions.

Indeed we are facing a twofold challenge—we must counter these misperceptions more energetically than before and we must deliver policy results that visibly demonstrate that European integration is beneficial for European citizens. In concrete terms we need to make sure that the European legal system is fully adapted to the needs and opportunities of today and tomorrow while reflecting the best principles of law-making.

Such principles should in the view of the Commission include the requirement to regulate at EU level only when there is a real need and where it is clear that the objective cannot be reached as effectively by national measures. This principle of subsidiarity has been with us for many years but needs continuously to be followed up.

We should strive for the lightest and most cost-efficient form of legislation. If voluntary agreements or self-regulation are possible we should aim to use them. But we must also appreciate that for many areas there is a need for more legislation: take for example the fight against terrorism.

* Senior Policy Adviser at the London Representation of the European Commission. This chapter is based on her speech to the Clifford Chance conference on 17 March 2006 and has not been updated to take account of more recent commission policy.

If it has been decided to legislate, it should be done in a transparent way. To set up an efficient process for stakeholder consultations and to provide clarity over who stands for what has not proved to be that easy. Differences in traditions, cultures and languages influence the process and provide fertile ground for misinterpretations.

And, finally, we must recognise that better regulation in the EU can only be achieved in true partnership between all involved.

In this context I welcome the strong political tone set by the UK Presidency. Better regulation is not just a question of bureaucracy. Better regulation is a central political project that we can accomplish only together. The UK is also a good example of how to put better regulation at the top of the political agenda and how to translate policy goals into actions. The impressive work by the Better Regulation Taskforce under the skilful leadership of Sir David Arculus is particularly inspiring. The report, *Get Connected—Effective Engagement in the EU,* which was published in September 2005 is a good example.[1] I welcome its analyses and its concrete recommendations, which will provide useful input for further improvement of the Commission's approach to consultations.

We need also to appreciate fully why we have European legislation. Imagine if we had gathered here together 20 years ago. I am sure that the subject of our conference would not have been Better Regulation. Instead it is likely that we would have complained about the national fragmentation of our markets and the lack of a legal area that could provide for the free movement of persons, goods, services and capital. We would have asked for EU action. Back in those days the Single Market was just a dream in the minds of idealists. Technical and other barriers to trade were the rule of the day. Today, the Single Market is for the most part a reality. Although sometimes complicated and complex it is a remarkable improvement compared with the fragmented reality it replaced. It provides an important contribution to our increasing prosperity.

Let me now turn to the need for making fast and visible progress. We need to be sure that what we decide to do is well grounded and will be the right response to the problem with which we are faced. And we have to do so in full transparency. This is why the Commission in March 2005 launched a new and comprehensive approach to better regulation. This new approach is based on three pillars.

The first pillar concerns *pending legislation*. The Commission has recently screened all proposals that have been pending in the Council and Parliament for a significant time. In total we are talking about 183 such proposals. In September 2005, the Commission announced its intention to withdraw 68

[1] Better Regulation Task Force, Get Connected—Effective Engagement in the EU (London, Better Regulation Task Force, Sept 2005), available at www.brc.gov.uk/publications/getconnectedentry.asp.

pending proposals as a result of this extended screening. It is the first time that any Commission has embarked on such an extensive exercise and decided to withdraw more than one third of the tabled proposals. Since we are discussing draft legislation, the withdrawal will not change the regulatory reality, either for citizens or for the functioning of the internal market. However the exercise has made several things crystal clear. First, the total number of pending pieces of legislation was not as high as I had imagined. Secondly, we found strong reasons in two thirds of the cases for keeping them in the legislative process. And, finally, the remaining one third no longer meets our criteria for better regulation. This exercise is therefore the first test case as regards the credibility of our policy for better regulation.

The second pillar entails a substantial *simplification exercise*. The objective is to screen all existing legislation with a view to its modernisation. The EU has simplified legislation before. However this time we intend to go further than just a technical exercise. On 25 October 2005 the Commission tabled a three-year action programme. It will put substantially more emphasis on the economic consequences of legislation. The approach will be competitiveness-driven and should lead to a more user-friendly legal system. We will seriously analyse whether any adverse impacts on competitiveness are proportionate to the policy aims of the relevant piece of legislation. At this stage, we are concentrating on three priority areas for further simplification measures—the automotive, construction and waste sectors. These sectors have been selected, respectively, because of the large accumulation of EU legislation, because of the considerable importance of the sector to overall economic competitiveness and because of the number of complaints received from industry. Other sectors will follow. To this end the Commission has started a broad public consultation. The Member States, major European associations and the broader public have been invited to provide us with their input on how to improve the overall EU regulatory environment. We have already received more than 600 reactions on our website and 300 concrete suggestions for simplifications from Member States and representatives of industry. These contributions will be important for our work and I can assure you that we will look into each suggestion.

Simplification should not however be seen as a Trojan horse for reducing essential regulatory protection in relation to, for instance, consumer protection or the protection of the environment. The real question in each case is whether the approach originally chosen is the most effective for achieving the objectives set. Simplification can therefore mean everything from a simple codification to a modification of the regulatory approach chosen. It could also in some cases mean repealing existing legislation.

The third pillar concerns new legislative proposals, to which from this year the Commission applies a stringent principle. We will put forward only proposals that have undergone an *impact assessment*. This approach should guarantee that we know the full costs and benefits of future legislation.

We are also working on a common EU method to assess administrative costs, which is particularly important for SMEs and public administrations. Furthermore, we will table new initiatives for legislation only if it has been shown that other methods such as voluntary agreements will not sufficiently address the problems and will therefore be insufficient to meet the agreed objectives. Such in-depth impact assessment will serve as a useful tool in the process of decision-making as to whether or not to launch a new legislative proposal. But we have to keep in mind the whole legislative process. I believe that it would be desirable that the in-depth impact assessment should also be applied if, for instance, the European Parliament decides on substantial changes to the initial proposal.

Let me stress that the regulatory environment can be improved only if the initiatives that we take at EU level are matched by equally ambitious programmes in the Member States. We must always remember that the regulatory environment for businesses is to a very large extent made up of national regulations that do not originate from the EU. The so-called 'gold plating' of European legislation in the process of its transposition into national legislation is a worrying development in this context. According to a recent Dutch study, more than half of the obstacles which were associated with European legislation resulted from additional national requirements.[2] If we are going for a lighter Community regulatory environment it should not be immediately filled up with new national rules or new technical barriers at national level. If we manage to create more freedom wherever possible we should allow the actors freely to play their game.

I do not underestimate the challenge before us. We will have to work hard to achieve our ambitious goals. Each existing or future law was or will be influenced by countless people in various functions, such as experts, Parliamentary rapporteurs, representatives of Member States, and lobbyists. All of these will defend 'their babies'. However, despite all the anticipated difficulties, I am convinced that, with a collective commitment to sustainable regulatory reform, we can achieve positive results soon.

We need such results urgently as a better and more efficient regulatory environment is crucial for Europe's competitiveness and its ability to achieve growth and jobs.

[2] Dutch EU Assessment Group, 'The Relative Impacts of EU and National Legislation' (Netherlands National Press Office, May 2006).

12

Regulating Working Time—Beyond Subordination?

JEFF KENNER*

OWING ITS ORIGINS to the Factories Acts of the 1800s,[1] which gradually regulated working hours in the emerging industrial society of northern England,[2] the EU's Working Time Directive[3] seeks to redress the inherent inequality of bargaining power in the employment relationship[4] by setting 'minimum requirements' for, inter alia, paid holidays, working hours and rest periods.[5] It places limits on both the *personal* and *economic* subordination of the worker. The exercise of the employer's personal managerial prerogative is made subject to an overriding obligation to ensure the protection of the safety and health of every worker.[6] The universal principle that 'labour is not a commodity'[7] resonates in the

* Professor of European Law, University of Nottingham.

[1] 8 Factories Acts were introduced in the UK between 1802 and 1878. This legislation influenced the process of regulation of working conditions in industrialised Europe in the 19th century. See further B Leigh Hutchins and A Harrison, *A History of Factory Legislation* (London, Frank Cass, 1966).

[2] See generally E Hobsbawm, *Industry and Empire* (Harmondsworth, Pelican, 1969).

[3] Dir 2003/88/EC of the European Parliament and Council of 4 Nov 2003 concerning certain aspects of the organisation of working time [2003] OJ L299/9. The consolidated text replaces Dir 93/104/EC [1993] OJ L307/18, as amended by Dir 2000/34/EC [2000] OJ L195/41. All references in this ch are to the provisions of Dir 2003/88 unless otherwise indicated.

[4] On the theory of subordination see P Davies and M Freedland, *Kahn-Freund's Labour and the Law*, 3rd edn (London, Stevens, 1983).

[5] The term 'minimum requirements' in Art 137(2) EC 'does not limit Community action to the lowest common denominator, or even to the lowest level of protection established by the various Member States, but means that Member States are free to provide a level of protection more stringent than that resulting from Community law, high as it may be': Case C–84/94 *UK v Council (Working Time Directive)* [1996] ECR I–5755, para 56.

[6] See Cases C–397–C–403/01 *Pfeiffer and Others* [2004] ECR I–8835, para 100, referring to the wording of the Dir and its purpose and scheme.

[7] 'The Declaration of Philadelphia' (1944), Constitution of the International Labour Organisation, available at www.ilo.org. See P O'Higgins, 'Labour is not a Commodity—an Irish Contribution to International Labour Law (1997) 26 *Industrial Law Journal* 225.

declaration that the improvement of workers' safety, hygiene and health at work is 'an objective which should not be subordinated to purely economic considerations'.[8] The sheer ambition of the Directive to protect workers' health and safety is, however, tempered by a desire for greater flexibility in the organisation of work and the distribution of working time.[9] It is this inner tension that explains the Directive's complexity, the regularity of litigation and the constant pressure for revision over the last 10 years. It also helps us to understand its bi-dimensional structure. First, in order to meet the requirement of protection, the Directive's point of reference is the continuum of time in the life of every worker, which has to be categorised and objectified according to a strict bipolarity between subordinate working time and independent free time.[10] Secondly, the requirement of flexibility leads to differentiated solutions allowing for substantial derogations from several of the core provisions, variation by collective agreements and phased implementation. Such differentiation is a hallmark not just of political division and compromise but also of a desire to maintain market freedoms and diversity within national social systems.[11]

Balancing each of these elements is an intricate problem for regulators, both EU and national, and the courts. This chapter will examine the rationale for regulation in this area, the structure of the Directive and its overall coherence. The first part places the legal framework of regulation of working time in context. In the second part the main features of bipolarity are explored by reference to the regulation of free time and working time. Finally, the third part identifies and evaluates specific examples of flexibility within the Directive.

A. THE LEGAL FRAMEWORK OF REGULATION OF WORKING TIME IN THE EU

Regulation of working time and paid holidays at the national level was a concern for the Community from its earliest days,[12] but proposals for harmonisation in this area did not emerge until the 1980s. During the

[8] Recital 4 of the preamble.

[9] See European Commission, 'Growth Competitiveness, Employment: The Challenges and Ways Forward into the 21st Century', Bull EC Supp 6/93, at 124. See also recital 15 of the preamble.

[10] See especially A Supiot, *Beyond Employment: Changes in Work and the Future of Labour Law in Europe* (Oxford, OUP, 2001), ch 3.

[11] For an explanation of the EU's approach to social regulation see the Council Res of 6 Dec 1994 on Certain Aspects for a European Union Social Policy: a Contribution to Economic and Social Convergence in the Union [1994] OJ C368/3.

[12] See Art 142 EC on the requirement to maintain the existing equivalence between paid holiday schemes in the Member States, and Council Rec 75/457/EEC on the principles of the 40-hour week and four weeks' annual paid holiday [1975] OJ L199/32.

Delors Presidency of the European Commission two distinctive strands of social policy were advanced that combined to act as catalysts for regulatory action.[13]

The first strand, the 'social dimension' of the internal market, arose out of a desire for economic and social balance in the integration process. In parallel with developments in consumer, public health and environmental law, regulation of social policy has been advanced on the basis of risk assessment, taking account of scientific developments and objective general interests, including high standards of health and safety in product design and manufacture. The Framework Safety and Health Directive is best understood as a proportionate response aimed at the 'elimination of risk and accident factors' in the standard workplace.[14] Consistent with the approach in policy areas referred to in Article 95(3) EC, minimum harmonisation is regarded as a necessary antidote to actual or perceived risks arising from any negative side effects of the market liberalisation process. Advocates of the social dimension suggested that fair competition would be possible in the internal market only if there was a level playing field of employment laws across the Member States to prevent undercutting of labour standards or 'social dumping'.[15] For example, Directive 89/686 on the harmonisation of laws concerning personal protective equipment seeks, as its fundamental objective, to remove barriers to trade in the production and manufacture of such equipment while, at the same time, ensuring that workers using the equipment are protected by a high level of safety standards in its specifications.[16]

Logically, the rationale for such measures would apply more generally to internal market proposals directly concerning workers' health and safety where it could be verified that harmonisation would be necessary to eliminate appreciable distortions of competition.[17] In practice, however, prospects for a coherent social dimension were foreclosed by the exclusion of measures concerning 'the rights and interests of employed persons' from the scope of Article 95 EC.[18] Recourse to alternative legal bases, either Article 94 or 308 EC, even if justified under the subsidiarity principle, required unanimity in the Council during a period when the United Kingdom was prepared

[13] See further J Kenner, *EU Employment Law* (Oxford, Hart Publishing, 2003), chs 4 and 5.

[14] Art 1 of Dir 89/391/EEC [1989] OJ L183/1.

[15] For a recent revival of these arguments see the furore over the Commission's proposal for a dir on services in the internal market: http://ec.europa.eu/internal_market/services/services-dir/proposal_en.htm.

[16] Dir 89/686/EEC [1989] OJ L399/18. See also the Machinery Dir, 89/392/EEC [1989] OJ L183/9. Adoption of these dirs on the basis of Art 95(1) EC was expressly approved by Léger AG in *UK v. Council*, above n5, para 73.

[17] See Case C–376/98 *Germany v European Parliament and Council (Tobacco Advertising)* [2000] ECR I–8419, para 106.

[18] Art 95(2) EC.

to veto Community social legislation.[19] Instead, a separate pathway was created via Article 118a (now 137) EC, for directives concerning improvements, especially in the working environment, to protect workers' health and safety. This somewhat artificial distinction between discrete internal market objectives and social policy objectives was confirmed by the Court of Justice when upholding the legality of the original version of the Working Time Directive on the basis of a strict delimitation between Articles 95 and 137 EC.[20]

The second strand of policy can be traced to a nascent 'social citizenship' model of integration. Under the first strand, EU social policies have been developed as a by-product of the economic integration process rather than as an independent aspiration. By contrast, the second strand, in its most advanced form, would recognise the entitlement of all workers to minimum standards of employment protection without any linkage with the process of economic integration. On this basis an autonomous rationale for the integration of social laws of the Member States has been advanced utilising the language of fundamental rights. First, through a process of iteration, the Court has elevated the 'social aim' of Article 141 EC on equal pay between men and women to the status of a fundamental human right that is overarching and takes precedence over its 'economic aim' of eliminating distortions of competition between undertakings in different Member States.[21] Secondly, the Community's declaration of a Social Charter[22] has provided a soft legal foundation for recognising workers as 'social citizens'[23] entitled to a menu of 'fundamental social rights', a status formally recognised in the Treaty of Amsterdam[24] and linked to international legal obligations of the Member States.[25]

[19] See B Hepple, 'Social Rights in the European Economic Community: A British Perspective' (1990) 11 *Comparative Labour Law Journal* 425.

[20] *UK v. Council*, above n5, paras 12 and 21. The Court ruled that the insertion of Art 137(2) EC conferred upon the Community internal competence in the area of social policy, and it therefore constitutes a more specific rule than Art 94 or 95 EC where the principal aim of the measure in question is the protection of the health and safety of workers: see J Kenner, 'A Distinctive Legal Base for Social Policy?—The Court of Justice Answers a "Delicate Question"' (1997) 22 *European Law Review* 579.

[21] See Case C–50/96 *Deutsche Telekom AG v Schröder* [2000] ECR I–743, para 57.

[22] Adopted as a 'solemn declaration' by 11 of the 12 Heads of State or Government of the Member States of the European Community meeting at Strasbourg on 9 Dec 1989. The UK rejected the Charter. For the text see *Social Europe* 6/90 (Brussels, European Commission, 1990).

[23] Although the language of citizenship was excised from the final draft, the Charter was to provide a springboard for later developments. See especially the *Comité des Sages* report, *For a Europe of Civic and Social Rights* (Luxembourg, European Communities, 1996) and The Charter of Fundamental Rights of the European Union [2000] OJ C364/1.

[24] Direct reference to the Social Charter as a source of fundamental social rights can be found in Art 136 (ex Art 117) EC.

[25] Art 136 EC refers directly to the Council of Europe's European Social Charter of 1961. The Charter of Fundamental Rights of the European Union [2000] OJ C364/1, draws from the Revised European Social Charter of 1996.

Both strands of policy can be found in the Working Time Directive. The first strand can be detected in the original preamble, which describes it as a 'practical contribution' towards the creation of the internal market.[26] As with all social policy directives, it must take account of 'the need to maintain the competitiveness of the Community economy'.[27] The Treaty requirement to avoid imposing constraints that would 'hold back' the creation and development of small and medium-sized undertakings[28] is reflected in flexibility provisions in the Directive,[29] such as variable reference periods for calculating average weekly working time.[30] By contrast, the option for Member States to allow individual workers voluntarily to opt out from maximum weekly working time[31] was born out of political necessity and is liable to create further distortions in competition.[32]

The second strand is identifiable in provisions sourced directly from the Social Charter.[33] In particular, point 8 proclaims the right of every worker to a weekly rest period and to annual paid leave as set out, respectively, in Articles 5 and 7 of the Directive.[34] On this basis, and with specific reference to the Social Charter, the Court has repeatedly held that the 'entitlement' of every worker to a minimum of four weeks' paid annual leave must be regarded as 'a particularly important principle of Community social law' from which there can be no derogations and the implementation of which must be confined within the limits expressly laid down by the Directive itself.[35] It follows that the Directive is intended to enable the worker *actually to take* the leave to which he is entitled.[36] Equally the worker must be entitled to 'actual rest' with a view to ensuring effective protection of his safety and health.[37] When non-binding guidelines were issued by the UK to employers, advising them that they must 'make sure that workers *can*

[26] Recital 6 of Dir 93/104/EC.

[27] Art 136 EC.

[28] Art 137(2)(b) EC.

[29] See the finding of the Court in *UK v Council*, above n5, and Cases C–184/02 and C–223/02 *Spain and Finland v European Parliament and Council* [2004] ECR I–7789, para 74.

[30] Arts 16(b), 17(3), 18 and 19.

[31] Art 22(1). The maximum weekly working time provisions are contained in Art 6.

[32] See the Commission's proposals to revise the Dir, COM(2004)607 and COM(2005)246. See further J Kenner, 'Working Time, Jaeger and the Seven-Year Itch' (2004–5) 11 *Columbia Journal of European Law* 53.

[33] Also in the original version of the text: recital 4 of the preamble to Dir 93/104.

[34] See also Art 31 of the Charter of Fundamental Rights, above n23. Recital 6 of the preamble to the Dir also refers to the need to take account of the principles of the International Labour Organisation with regard to the organisation of working time, including those relating to night work.

[35] See Case C–173/99 *BECTU* [2001] ECR I–4881, para 43; Case C–342/01 *Merino Gómez* [2004] ECR I–2605, para 29; Case C–124/05 *FNV v The Netherlands* [2006] ECR I–3423, para 28, and Cases C–131/04 and C–257/04 *Robinson-Steele and Others* [2006] ECR I–2531, para 48.

[36] *Ibid*, at para 49.

[37] *Merino Gómez*, above n35, at para 30; *FNV*, above n35, at para 29.

take their rest but are not required to make sure they *do* take their rest',[38] the Commission successfully contended that such guidelines would endorse and encourage a practice of non-compliance on the part of employers.[39] The Court held that Member States are under an obligation to guarantee that workers 'must actually benefit' from the daily and weekly rest periods provided for by the Directive.[40] The guidelines were clearly liable to render the rights enshrined in those provisions 'meaningless' and were incompatible with the objective of the Directive.[41]

Equally significant is the above-mentioned requirement that improvement of workers' safety, hygiene and health, 'should not be subordinated to purely economic considerations'.[42] Despite its rhetorical nature, this rule has been applied directly by the Court in *Jaeger*[43] when addressing concerns raised by Germany about the economic consequences of a finding that 'on-call time' worked by hospital doctors should be counted in its entirety as 'working time' for the purposes of the Directive. Germany had contended that such a ruling might lead to an increase in staffing requirements of 24 per cent at an estimated cost of €1.75 billion.[44] In previous cases concerning sex discrimination, economic factors had led the Court not to apply its rulings to claims prior to the date of judgment,[45] or even to accept arguments based on economic considerations as objective justification for such discrimination.[46] In respect of the provisions granting entitlements under the Working Time Directive, however, the Court held that no such limitations or exceptions based on 'economic and organisational consequences' were permitted.[47]

The Framework Safety and Health Directive, with its emphasis on risk assessment and preventing accidents and illnesses at work, is an important point of reference,[48] but the concepts of 'safety', 'health' and the 'working environment' in Article 137 EC also reinforce social citizenship and address the personal subordination of the worker in the employment relationship.

[38] Department of Trade and Industry, *Your Guide to the Working Time Regulations* (July 2003), available at www.dti.gov.uk/employment/employment-legislation/employment-guidance/ (italics in the original).

[39] Case C–484/04 *Commission v UK (Working Time Directive)*, judgment of 7 Sept 2006 (not yet reported).

[40] *Ibid*, at paras 39 and 40.

[41] *Ibid*, at para 44.

[42] Recital 4 of the preamble.

[43] Case C–151/02 *Landeshauptstadt Kiel v Jaeger* [2003] ECR I–8389.

[44] *Ibid.* See para 44 of the AG's opinion.

[45] Case 43/75 *Defrenne v Sabena* [1976] ECR 455 and Case C–262/88 *Barber v GRE* [1990] ECR I–1889.

[46] Case 170/84 *Bilka Kaufhaus v Weber* [1986] ECR 1607, discussed by S Fredman, 'European Community Discrimination Law: A Critique' (1992) 21 *Industrial Law Journal* 119.

[47] *Jaeger*, above n43, paras 66 and 67.

[48] Recital 3 of the preamble.

In *UK v Council* the Court ruled that these terms should be interpreted broadly to embrace 'all factors, physical or otherwise, capable of affecting the health and safety of the worker *in his working environment*'.[49] The Court derived support from the World Health Organisation's definition of 'health' as a state of 'complete physical, mental and social well-being'.[50] In highlighting the link between the worker and 'his working environment', the Court may have been influenced by ergonomic theories that elevate the importance of the physiological and physical capabilities of the individual citizen/worker in the immediate environment of his workplace and beyond.[51] From this standpoint, regulation of certain aspects of working time contributes to the health and contentment of citizens throughout their working life. Most significantly, it offers an alternative approach to the employment relationship that subverts the convention of subordination. Such an approach is exemplified by Article 13 of the Directive, which refers, somewhat tantalisingly, to an obligation on Member States to ensure that employers alleviate patterned or monotonous work by taking account of the 'general principle of adapting work to the worker'. This provision lacks substance, referring only to 'breaks during working time' as part of the solution, but it recognises that the worker is not an automaton and, therefore, the requirements of the enterprise have to be attuned to the needs of the individual worker as an autonomous human being.

B. FREE TIME AND WORKING TIME—INTRINSICALLY BIPOLAR CONCEPTS?

Each of these policy strands informs us about the dynamic evolution of the Directive and its underlying values. The shape of the core provisions broadly resembles the systematised approach of national laws in this area.[52] If we unpack these provisions we can identify two distinct features, both of which relate to the regulation of time in the life of the individual worker:

1. The entitlement of every worker to *free time* or *rest periods* without loss of pay.
2. Measurement and limitation of the length of *working time*. This includes rules governing the *organisation of working time* and the health and safety protection afforded to workers carrying out night work and shifts.

[49] *UK v Council*, above n5, para 15, emphasis added.

[50] *Ibid.*

[51] For elaboration see 'The Salisch Report' of the European Parliament, 'The Concept of the Working Environment and the Scope of Art 118a of the EEC Treaty', PE DOC A 2-226/88, 21 Oct 1988.

[52] See Supiot, above n10, at 59.

Under the scheme of the Directive these two parts are mutually exclusive. Article 2 defines 'working time' as:

> any period during which the worker is working, at the employer's disposal and carrying out his activity or duties, in accordance with national laws and/or practice.

Conversely a 'rest period' is 'any period *which is not working time*'.[53] Thus the law is based on a strict division of working life and family life. As Supiot has observed, the designation of 'working time' is a measure of subordination that, on the one hand, 'limits the employer's hold on the worker's life' and, on the other, 'allows the employer to evaluate his services'.[54] Working time bookends the worker's obligations and standardises the periods of the employer's control. Within a standard homogenous employment relationship the bifurcation of a worker's time is a useful organisational tool for scheduling working hours, overtime, annual leave, shifts and rest periods. Consistently with the dominant post-war Fordist model of industrial relations, it provides a normative framework of working weeks, days and hours for collective bargaining.[55]

Although the standard employment relationship is now outmoded, the Directive fits within this long-established model by providing measurable periods for minimum requirements or entitlements. Minimum periods of daily and weekly rest are laid down.[56] Within 'working time' there is an entitlement to rest breaks during each six-hour period.[57] The length of night work is restricted to an average of eight hours in any 24-hour period.[58] Maximum weekly working time is based on an average of 48 hours for each seven-day period, including overtime.[59] Each of these provisions is subject to a degree of flexibility. Examples of permitted differentiation will be discussed in the next part, but for now the immediate question is: what are the regulatory consequences of this bipolar approach to working time and free time?

[53] Emphasis added.

[54] See Supiot, above n10, at 60.

[55] *Ibid*, at 61. Supiot, at 1, describes the Fordist model as 'a large industrial business engaged in mass production based on a narrow specialization of jobs and competencies and pyramidal management (hierarchical structure of labour, separation between product design and manufacture)'.

[56] Art 3 contains an entitlement for every worker to a minimum daily rest period of 11 consecutive hours per 24-hour period. Under Art 5 there must be an additional minimum uninterrupted rest period of 24 hours per each seven-day period normally calculated, under Art 16(a), over a reference period not exceeding 14 days.

[57] Art 4. The duration and terms of rest breaks are to be laid down in collective agreements or, failing that, by national legislation.

[58] Art 8.

[59] Art 6. Under Art 16(b) the reference period for this calculation is normally a period not exceeding four months.

The first issue to consider is the guarantee of free time. The Directive provides for a quantifiable amount of autonomous free time for every worker that is an absolute limit on the period of subordination. For this part of the work/rest equation, bipolarity ensures clear and simplified regulation in Article 7. Every worker is entitled to at least four weeks' paid annual leave. Paid leave cannot be replaced by an allowance in lieu, except where the employment relationship is terminated. Member States shall ensure this entitlement in accordance with 'the conditions...laid down by national legislation and/or practice'. The reference to national rules allows for flexibility in form but not effect. Normative mechanisms may vary according to the diversity of national systems but the ultimate obligation remains with the state. The 'state guarantee' must provide an effective right protecting all individuals intended to be covered by the Directive and capable of enforcement by them before national courts.[60] Thus, in *BECTU*, a condition imposed by the UK, under which entitlement to leave was not available until a worker had accrued 13 weeks' service, was held to fall outside the margin of discretion afforded to Member States because it had the effect of preventing certain workers from enjoying any entitlement to paid annual leave and, therefore, was contrary to its objective as it negated an individual right expressly granted in the Directive and sourced from the Social Charter.[61] There was no escape clause for the Member State as, in the absence of any possible derogation, and confined within the limits laid down in the Directive, it was not able unilaterally to restrict a directly effective entitlement that was conferred on all workers.[62] It followed that when, in *FNV*[63] and *Robinson-Steele*,[64] workers were offered financial compensation in lieu of annual leave, or 'rolled-up' holiday pay as part of their hourly or daily remuneration, the employers' schemes were found to be outside the limits laid down in the Directive. The possibility of financial compensation, such as payment in lieu, would create an incentive, incompatible with the objectives of the Directive, not to take leave or encourage employees not to do so.[65] It might be possible for an employer to pay sums additional to remuneration for work actually done and already paid for, to be set off against specific leave, but only if this was transparent and comprehensible.[66]

[60] For judicial recognition of the 'state guarantee' in social policy dirs see Case 143/83 *Commission v Denmark* [1985] ECR 427, at 434–5. The state guarantee has been reinforced by Art 137(3) EC, discussed below.

[61] *BECTU*, above n35, at para 48.

[62] *Ibid*, at para 50.

[63] Above n35.

[64] Above n35.

[65] *FNV*, above n35, at para 32.

[66] *Robinson-Steele*, above n35, at para 66. The burden of proof is on the employer.

In the Court's rulings in these cases the linkage between the mandatory entitlement to annual leave and the obligation of payment during leave was decisive because, as 'two aspects of a single right', the purpose of the requirement of payment is to put the worker on leave in a position that is, as regards remuneration, 'comparable to periods of work'.[67] On this basis, even though Article 137(5) EC excludes 'pay' from the legislative scope of social policy directives, it allows for a requirement of paid annual leave in this context because it is inextricably linked to fulfilling the primary health and safety objective and it does not regulate the actual amount of remuneration paid by the employer.[68] Moreover, the prohibition on payment in lieu is intended to ensure that a worker is normally entitled to 'actual rest'.[69] Payment for annual leave is a safeguard, therefore, not only for the guarantee in Article 7, but also of the entitlement of the worker actually to take his or her daily and weekly 'rest', under Articles 3 and 5, as reinforced in *Commission v UK*.[70]

The second feature of the Directive, the regulation of measured working time, has been brought to the fore in three cases referred from national courts concerning the length of working time of 'on-call' workers in the health and residential care sectors.[71] Typically, as in *SIMAP*,[72] *Jaeger*[73] and *Dellas*,[74] workers would be required, during periods of inactivity, to be on call at the employer's premises and ready to return to active duties. The employer would provide facilities for workers to wait, rest or even sleep during lengthy periods of inactivity. The Court had to decide whether inactive time on-call should be counted in its entirety as 'working time' or, alternatively, whether it fell into an intermediate or grey category— neither working time nor a rest period.

In each case the Court chose the former on the basis of a broad cumulative interpretation of the three criteria in the definition of 'working time'. Under that definition, 'working time' is to *include* 'any period' when the worker is (1) 'working', (2) 'at the employer's disposal' and (3) 'carrying out his *activity or duties*'.[75] In *SIMAP* the fact that the doctors in question were obliged to be present and available at the health centre with a view to providing their professional services meant that they were carrying out their duties in that instance.[76] Only by counting this entire period as

[67] *Ibid*, at para 58.

[68] Case C–14/04 *Dellas v Secrétariat général du gouvernement* [2005] ECR I–10253, at para 38.

[69] *BECTU*, above n35, at para 44, *Merino Gómez*, above n35, at para 30.

[70] Case C–484/04, above n39.

[71] See further Kenner, above n32.

[72] Case C–303/98 *SIMAP v Conselleria de Sanidad y Consumo de la Generalidad Valenciana* [2000] ECR I–7963.

[73] Above n43.

[74] Above n68.

[75] Art 2(1).

[76] *SIMAP*, above n72, at para 48.

working time was it possible to protect their health and safety by ensuring that they would have minimum periods of rest and adequate breaks.[77] An intermediate category of inactive working time simply did not fit with the bipolar scheme of the Directive. In *Dellas* the Court ruled that, as working time and rest periods are mutually exclusive, the intensity of the work done by the employee and his output are not among the characteristic elements of the concept of 'working time'.[78] For example, even though the doctors in *Jaeger* were inactive for, on average, 49 per cent of their time at the hospital this did not alter the fact that they could be directed by the employer to provide their services for as often and as long as necessary, and without any limitation, during this period.[79]

One advantage of a rigid dichotomy between working time and other time is the certainty that it provides as a measure precisely to calculate subordinate time, to limit its length and determine the periods of actual rest to be taken. In turn, this facilitates the operation of related provisions, such as the special protection afforded to night workers and those working shifts.[80] Minimum requirements, once measured and applied, are deemed proportionate to the health and safety objectives. Legal certainty was undoubtedly a factor in the judicial assessment, but the underlying logic lies with the Court's recognition of the power relationship between the employer and the individual worker during the period of control. As Advocate General Saggio noted in *SIMAP*, whenever the worker is required to be at the employer's premises and at his disposal he is 'separated from his family, and cannot pursue his own interests'.[81] The Directive necessarily distinguishes between working time and family life because, as the Court observed in *Jaeger*, during on-call time the worker is denied autonomy, as he is at a place determined by the employer for the whole duration where he 'is subject to appreciably greater restraints since he has to remain apart from his family and social environment'.[82]

For the Member States involved, or affected by these rulings, the stakes were high, not only financially but also because of the regulatory consequences. At the time of these cases the individual opt-out from the average 48-hour maximum working week in Article 6(b) was available generally only in the UK.[83] The Court has confirmed in *Pfeiffer* that Article 6(b) imposes on Member States, in unequivocal terms, a precise obligation as to

[77] *Ibid*, at paras 48–49.
[78] *Dellas*, above n68, at paras 42–43.
[79] *Jaeger*, above n43, at para 57.
[80] See especially Arts 9–13.
[81] *SIMAP*, above n72, at para 37.
[82] *Jaeger*, above n43, at para 65.
[83] Art 22(1) (ex Art 18(1)(b)). See COM(2003)843, at para 2.2.1.1. For analysis see C Barnard, S Deakin and R Hobbs, 'Opting out of the 48-Hour Week: Employer Necessity or Individual Choice? An Empirical Study of the Operation of Art 18(1)(b) of the Working Time Directive in the UK' (2003) 32 *Industrial Law Journal* 223.

the result to be achieved irrespective of variables in the reference periods and, notwithstanding the derogations, because it is possible to determine the minimum protection that must be provided in any event.[84] Moreover, Member States cannot unilaterally determine the scope of 'working time' or a 'rest period' because these constitute concepts of Community law that must be given an 'autonomous interpretation" in accordance with objective characteristics by reference to the scheme and purpose of the Directive.[85] In *Dellas*, France had introduced a maximum 35-hour working week as a 'more favourable provision' to protect workers' health and safety, permitted by the Directive.[86] However, the effect of calculating the entirety of the worker's on-call time as working time was to increase his average working week to 60 hours in violation of the minimum requirements. In *Jaeger* the Court ruled that allowance must be made for rest periods and breaks during on-call time, or immediately afterwards, to prevent the worker from experiencing a state of fatigue or overload, and because the worker would not be able to remove himself from the working environment after a period of work, and any later rest period would not afford the necessary protection.[87] Other derogations in Article 17(3) did not apply to the definition of 'working time' or the basic entitlement to maximum weekly working time.[88]

The fall-out from this trilogy of rulings has had two immediate consequences. First, it has led to a shift in the attitude of both the Commission and several Member States towards the individual opt-out from the 48-hour working week. Several Member States have introduced the opt-out in the health sector.[89] Luxembourg has extended it to the hotel and catering sectors. Following their accession, Cyprus and Malta have followed the UK by making it generally available.[90] The Commission, having originally sought to abolish the opt-out at the review stage, has now proposed a temporary, but possibly indefinite, reprieve.[91] We will return to this issue, and particularly the question of individual consent to opting out, in the next part.

Secondly, in its attempts to revise the Directive, and following pressure from Member States, the Commission has proposed that on-call time[92] should be sub-divided into its active and inactive parts. In the latest version of the proposals, the active part of on-call time, the period

[84] *Pfeiffer*, above n6, at paras 103–105.
[85] *Jaeger*, above n43, at para 58, and *Dellas*, above n68, at paras 44–45.
[86] Art 15.
[87] *Jaeger*, above n43, at paras 94–96.
[88] *Ibid*, at paras 80–88.
[89] France, Germany, the Netherlands, Spain, and, from the 2004 accession, Estonia, Hungary, Latvia, Lithuania and Slovenia, have introduced or proposed legislation: see COM(2003)843, at para 2.2.2.
[90] *Ibid*.
[91] See the amended draft of Art 22 proposed in COM(2005)246.
[92] In the draft of Art 2, *ibid*, the Commission propose the following definition of 'on-call time' in para 1a: '[a] period during which the worker has the obligation to be available.

during which 'the worker effectively carries out his activity or duties', shall always be regarded as working time. The inactive part, when the worker 'is not required by his employer to effectively carry out his activity or duties', shall not be regarded as working time unless decided otherwise by national law.[93] It would also not be taken into account in calculating the rest periods.[94]

The Commission's proposal to move the goalposts by creating a new binary divide within on-call time would reverse the approach taken by the Court on this narrow issue. It would also offer an alternative for Member States which have reasoned that the strict distinction between working time and rest periods forces them to introduce or extend the opt-out to sectors where on-call working is common practice, without any certainty that the option will be widely taken up by the workers concerned. The changes proposed would not alter the bipolar structure of the Directive. Rather, they would introduce a refinement, for a specific group of workers, of the measurement of working time and rest periods. Nevertheless, by shifting the definition of subordinate time to exclude periods where the on-call worker is inactive but 'at the employer's disposal', regarded as meaning within the ambit of the performance of the worker's duties,[95] they would restrict the worker's period of autonomous time and run counter to the ethos of the Directive.

C. EVALUATING FLEXIBILITY IN THE WORKING TIME DIRECTIVE

Employment law tends towards differentiation at all levels and a degree of flexibility is inevitable, indeed desirable, within a decentralised system designed to 'support and complement' the activities of the Member States.[96] Social policy occupies an ambiguous space close to the periphery of the European integration process. Within this space diverse approaches to employment law have been encouraged so long as the general direction has been towards a 'gradual convergence',[97] allowing for more stringent protective measures.[98] Not surprisingly, therefore, social policy has provided

[93] *Ibid*. This would include the possibility of a collective agreement or agreement between the social partners permitted by national law.

[94] *Ibid*.

[95] *Dellas*, above n68, at para 48, *SIMAP*, above n72, at para 48, and *Jaeger*, above n43, at paras 49 and 63.

[96] Art 137(1) EC. See further C Barnard, 'Flexibility and Social Policy' in G de Búrca and J Scott (eds), *Constitutional Change in the EU: From Uniformity to Flexibility?* (Oxford, Hart Publishing, 2000) 197; and F Tuytschaever, *Differentiation in European Union Law* (Oxford, Hart Publishing, 1999).

[97] Resolution on Social Policy, above n11.

[98] Art 137(4) EC.

a laboratory in which a variety of flexible experiments, both procedural and substantive, have been tested. Examples of flexibility in employment directives include: specific derogations, variations by collective bargaining, optional provisions, restrictions of scope, gradual implementation and, exceptionally, opt-out clauses. Four specific examples of flexibility in the Working Time Directive are evaluated in this part of the chapter, taking into account, in particular, their conformity with health and safety objectives, their effect on the coherence of the legislation, and the wider policy aim of economic and social balance.

The first type of flexibility is found in several provisions that allow for gradual implementation over a transitional period beyond the formal deadline for transposition. Article 137(2)(b) EC specifies that social policy directives are a 'means' for the adoption of 'minimum requirements for gradual implementation having regard to the conditions and technical rules obtaining in each of the Member States'. Where there is a straightforward transitional provision the impact at national levels can be staggered over a period of time, but the ultimate result is eventually guaranteed. For example, Article 22(2) permits Member States to introduce or maintain a minimum requirement of three weeks' paid annual leave for three years after the implementation date. The four-week minimum had to be applied thereafter.[99] Article 17(5), concerning trainee doctors, introduced on amendment, provides for a five-year phased reduction of maximum weekly working hours from 1 August 2004. This provision is slightly more complex, in allowing for a two-year extension if Member States have difficulty complying due to their responsibilities for the 'delivery of health services and medical care', and an additional year for 'special difficulties'. Although a 12-year period for full transposition is exceptional, it takes account of the organisational demands, costs, and the need to balance the protection of workers with the requirements of delivering a public service.

In each case where a transitional provision is applied, there is a reporting obligation to the Commission which, in respect of trainee doctors, includes notification and justification of the reasons for extending beyond five years. In *Mangold*[100] the precise scope of similar transitional provisions on combating age discrimination[101] have been tested. The Court held that such provisions imply that the Member State which 'exceptionally enjoys' the extended period is 'progressively to take concrete measures for the purpose of there and then approximating its legislation to the result prescribed by that directive'.[102] Moreover, the conforming obligation remains with the

[99] From 23 Nov 1999.

[100] Case C–144/04 *Mangold v Helm* [2005] ECR I–9981.

[101] Dir 2000/78/EC of 27 Nov 2000 establishing a general framework for equal treatment in employment and occupation [2000] OJ L303/16.

[102] *Mangold*, above n101, at paras 71–72.

state throughout the implementation stage including any extended period. In particular, during these periods, the state 'must refrain' from taking any measure liable seriously to compromise the attainment of the prescribed result.[103] This would include introducing domestic laws concerned with implementation if they were in conflict with the directive in question. Ultimately, the national court must set aside any conflicting rule even where the period for transposition has not yet expired.[104]

As discussed earlier, the Court has recognised the particular importance of the right to annual leave, to enjoy rest periods and, more generally, the obligation to guarantee that each of the minimum requirements is observed for the actual benefit of every worker.[105] The status of these provisions is analogous with the principle of non-discrimination applied in *Mangold*. Moreover, under Article 23, flexibility afforded to Member States is subject to compliance with the minimum requirements, and implementation 'shall not constitute valid grounds for reducing the general level of protection afforded to workers'. In sum, as a means to a prescribed end, the latitude offered to Member States is circumscribed by a requirement of full compliance on expiry and non-retrogression throughout the period of implementation.

Reference periods for the calculation of weekly rest, maximum weekly working time and night work form a second category of flexible provisions.[106] The core reference periods, like the transitional periods, are not derogations but, rather, are designed to enable the Directive to be adapted to conditions at national or industry level, post-implementation, for reasons directly connected with the organisation of work without compromising health and safety objectives. For example, maximum weekly working time may be calculated over a reference period not exceeding four months, a period that allows for ebb and flow in orders, production and the activity of workers, factors that are especially important for small and medium-sized businesses. Consistent with the subsidiarity principle, reference periods facilitate choice over the intensity of regulation within the overall framework of the Directive.

The standard reference periods in Article 16 are expressly worded, coherent and strike a balance between flexibility for business and protection for workers. However, the reference periods are inextricably linked with a third example of flexibility, in the form of specified derogations in Articles 17–19.

In its 'state of implementation' report the Commission observed, with understatement, that the derogations in Article 17 'may cause difficulties in understanding' in what is a 'relatively complex piece of law'.[107] Article 17

[103] *Ibid*, at para 68. Applying Case C–129/96 *Inter-Environnement Wallonie* [1997] ECR I–7411, at para 45.
[104] *Ibid*, at paras 77–78.
[105] See *Commission v UK*, above n39, at paras 38–41.
[106] Art 16.
[107] COM(2000)787, at 3.

permits Member States to derogate from certain of the minimum requirements both in substance, to meet the needs of specific types or conditions of work or activity, and in procedure, allowing limited scope for variation by means of collective agreements. Unlike the individual opt-out in Article 22, these derogations are not general exceptions, but they do allow for flexibility of application providing that the basic principles of the Directive are retained.[108]

Article 17 contains three groups of derogations. The widest category is Article 17(1), which permits derogations from all minimum requirements except paid annual leave. It can only be applied, however, on account of the specific characteristics of the activity concerned, where the duration of working time is 'not measured and/or predetermined or can be determined by the workers themselves'. In particular, Article 17(1) may apply in the case of managing executives or other persons 'with autonomous decision-taking powers', family workers, or workers officiating at religious ceremonies. In *Commission v UK* the Court ruled that Article 17(1) applies only to workers 'whose working time *as a whole*' is not measured or predetermined or self-determined.[109] Such workers would be wholly autonomous, in choosing when to work or rest, effectively excluding from the derogation any worker who is personally subordinate to the employer in respect of those choices. Thus, Article 17(1) was not applicable to the doctors in *Jaeger*, as their activities did not have these special characteristics.[110] This derogation allows for flexibility in the absence of direct personal control by the employer over day-to-day activity, such as in the case of unsupervised home workers, but the retention of the general principle of health and safety protection for these workers is consistent with a degree of economic subordination in such working relationships. These workers are still entitled to 'actual rest' and the distinction between working time and free time applies to them,[111] but it is very difficult, in practice, to envisage how employers can be expected to enforce any cut-off point between periods of working time and rest in the absence of personal control.

The second type of derogation, in Article 17(2), allows for flexibility in the application of the provisions on rest breaks, rest periods, the length of night work and reference periods.[112] This derogation is of general application irrespective of the activities of workers affected, but can be brought into operation only by *specific means*, either through national law or by collective or industry-wide agreements. In each case the measures applied must ensure that the workers concerned are afforded 'equivalent periods of

[108] *Ibid.*
[109] *Commission v UK*, above n39, at para 20 (emphasis added).
[110] *Jaeger*, above n43, at para 83.
[111] *Ibid*, at para 91.
[112] Arts 3,4,5,8 and 16.

compensatory rest' or in 'exceptional cases', in which it is not possible 'for objective reasons' to grant such rest, they must be afforded 'appropriate protection'. It follows that, as every worker must benefit from effective rest,[113] during such 'compensatory rest' periods the worker must not be subject to any obligation vis-à-vis his employer that may prevent him from pursuing freely and without interruption his own interests in order to neutralise the effects of work on his safety or health.[114] This derogation presents an opportunity for diverse means to be applied to vary the provisions concerning 'rest' but, save in exceptional cases, the periods of working time and rest must be measured, and the minimum requirements remain the point of reference. In order to strengthen protection in this area the Commission initially proposed that 'compensatory rest' should be made available within 72 hours of the working time in question,[115] but the latest version of the draft revised Directive would merely provide that such rest must be afforded 'within a reasonable period to be determined by national legislation or collective agreement'.[116]

Finally, Article 17(3) allows for flexibility in the application of the same set of minimum requirements as in the preceding paragraph, and also allows for collective agreements, in the case of workers who are:

(a) at distant places of work;[117]
(b) involved in security and surveillance activities;[118]
(c) carrying out activities involving the need for continuity of service or production;[119]
(d) in agriculture, tourism and postal services, where there is a foreseeable surge of activity; or
(e) in rail transport.[120]

In *Jaeger* the Court noted that these derogations have been 'exhaustively enumerated' and do not allow for any variation to maximum weekly working time except in relation to the length of the reference period.[121] More generally, the derogations in Article 17 must be interpreted in such a way that 'their scope is limited to what is strictly necessary in order to safeguard

113 *Commission v UK*, above n39, at para 40.
114 *Jaeger*, above n43, at para 94.
115 COM(2004)607.
116 COM(2005)246.
117 Either: 'where the worker's place of work and his place of residence are distant from one another, including offshore work'; or 'where the worker's different places of work are distant from one another'.
118 Requiring 'a permanent presence in order to protect property and persons'.
119 Examples listed include, inter alia, hospital staff, dock or airport workers, media staff or people working in the emergency services, utilities, agriculture and urban transport.
120 This applies, inter alia, where workers' activities are intermittent, or on board trains, or linked to transport timetables.
121 *Jaeger*, above n43, at paras 80–83.

the interests which those derogations enable to be protected'.[122] It is significant to note that the broader purpose of the derogations is being recognised here, not just to allow for the diversity of national systems of social law, but also to pursue objectives related to meeting demand and continuity of production in important economic sectors and public services. It is submitted that a proportionality test is, however, of limited use in determining the scope of the protection of such vague 'interests'.

Each of these derogations allows for variation of the reference periods in Article 16, but the first paragraph of Article 19 provides that the period for calculating the 48-hour week should not exceed six months. However, this period may, exceptionally, be extended to 12 months, but *only* by means of a collective agreement or an agreement by the two sides of industry. Such extensions must be concluded 'for objective or technical reasons concerning the organisation of work' subject to 'compliance' with the general principles relating to the safety and health of workers. The Commission's implementation report found that the 12-month option was available in the majority of Member States.[123] This may explain why, in a significant shift towards greater flexibility, the Commission's revised proposal to amend the Directive would, if adopted, delete the present four-month reference period and allow for working hours to be calculated over a period not exceeding 12 months either by collective agreement or by national law. If this option is chosen, further complexity will be added by requirements for the employer, first, to inform and consult workers and/or their representatives 'in good time' concerning the introduction of such a reference period. This is based on the employee involvement procedure in the Collective Redundancies Directive[124] and similar legislation, and is wholly inappropriate for a directive providing for minimum requirements for individual workers. Moreover, if information and consultation are to be introduced into the Directive they ought to be applied more generally to other flexible provisions and not just to this specific reference period. Secondly, the employer must take 'the measures necessary' to avoid or overcome any risk relating to health and safety 'that could arise' from the introduction of such a reference period. This would place a rather imprecise obligation on the employer to carry out a highly speculative risk assessment that, once again, would apply only to this particular derogation.

One common feature of the derogations in Article 17 is the role of the two sides of industry, or the 'social partners', in the process of determining the scope of national or sectoral variations of the specified minimum requirements. Article 18 supplements this by providing a general clause for the use of collective agreements to make derogations from the provisions

[122] *Ibid*, at para 89.
[123] COM(2000)787, at 14–17.
[124] Dir 98/59/EC [1998] OJ L225/16.

on rest breaks and rest periods, the length of night work and the reference periods.[125] Utilisation of this form of horizontal transposition was novel when the Directive was adopted in 1993, but is now common practice in Member States where such agreements are legally binding.[126] It can now be found in Article 137(3) EC, allowing for implementation of directives by management and labour, so long as the state guarantees the result that they impose. In *Pfeiffer* the Court ruled that the conforming result imposed by the Directive is a guarantee of a better level of protection of workers' health and safety and, therefore, the duty of the national court is to have regard to the 'whole body of rules of national law' to ensure that it is fully effective.[127] These rules would include collective agreements whenever they replaced or supplemented legislative provisions.

Each of these types of flexibility can be categorised as a 'weak' form of differentiation, in the sense that they can be accommodated within the broad scope of EU law on the safety and health of workers and the policy framework of Articles 136–137 EC. The place of such provisions in the Directive can be explained by the need to take account of diversity in the organisation of work, the variety of business and public service activities, and procedural differences in Member States, especially over the role of collective bargaining.

By contrast, the fourth example of flexibility, the individual opt-out or exclusion from the 48-hour week, is a 'strong' instance of differentiation because, even though it requires respect for the 'general principles' of the safety and health of workers, it nonetheless permits Member States to introduce an exception that falls outside the framework of commonality in the Directive and is, at least potentially, at odds with Treaty objectives. Under Article 22(1) Member States have the option '*not to apply* Article 6',[128] the limit on maximum working time and related reference periods, subject to a series of conditions. In particular, Member States must ensure that no employer requires a worker to work more than the average 48 hours per week over the reference period unless he has first obtained the worker's agreement to perform such work. Any worker refusing to give his agreement must not be subjected to a detriment. Employers are obliged to keep up-to-date records of workers carrying out such work to be placed at the disposal of the competent authorities. The authorities may request information about individual cases. Re-examination of the opt-out was to be carried out within seven years of implementation.

[125] Collective agreements may also be used to facilitate provisions more favourable to the protection of workers' health and safety, Art 15; and to create detailed arrangements for trainee doctors, Art 17(5); mobile and offshore workers, Art 20; and workers on board seagoing vessels, Art 21.

[126] This is not the case in the Republic of Ireland and the UK.

[127] *Pfeiffer*, above n6, at paras 91 and 118.

[128] Emphasis added.

Much of the debate surrounding the opt-out has focused on its general application only in the UK in the immediate post-implementation period. This was important because, if widely taken up by employers and workers, it would create a significant divergence in the laws of the Member States. According to research conducted in the UK in 2003 approximately four million people, or 16 per cent of the workforce, were working more than 48 hours per week on average, 38 per cent of whom worked over 55 hours.[129] A separate survey found that 33 per cent of workers in the UK had signed an opt-out agreement.[130] Moreover, as part of a 'light touch' approach to regulation, the UK weakened the record-keeping requirements when it amended its regulations in 1999.[131] Empirical research by Barnard *et al* has concluded that the opt-out is regarded 'as the most convenient and effective mechanism for avoiding the forty-eight-hour limit on weekly working time'.[132]

One finding from the research is of particular importance. In the UK individually agreed contracts are the normal method of establishing and maintaining employment relationships. This has led to widespread use of the opt-out as a standard term at the inception of the employment relationship.[133] New employees are placed under considerable pressure at the most unequal stage of the employment relationship. According to the Commission 'freedom of choice is compromised at that moment'.[134]

The issue of worker consent to the opt-out is central to the problem of subordination in the employment relationship that the Directive was supposed to address, specifically with regard to limits on working hours. The question of consent was raised by a German court in *Pfeiffer*,[135] a case involving ambulance crews which were working more than 48 hours per week without their individual agreement.[136] In his opinion Advocate General Ruiz-Jarabo Colomer referred to the conditions in Article 22(1) as 'guarantees' attached to the worker's consent, as the 'most vulnerable party', to prevent an employer from obtaining from the worker, 'through subterfuge or intimidation', a waiver of his rights to the 48-hour weekly limit.[137] The Court was just as forthright, finding that:[138]

> Any derogation from those minimum requirements must therefore be accompanied by all the safeguards necessary to ensure that, if the worker concerned

[129] COM(2003)843, at 10–11.
[130] *Ibid*, at 13.
[131] Barnard *et al*, above n83, at 224. Employers are required to record only the names of the workers concerned and not the number of hours actually worked.
[132] *Ibid*.
[133] *Ibid*, at 245–6.
[134] COM(2003)843, at 9.
[135] Above n6.
[136] The Court rejected the notion that a collective agreement could substitute for individual consent: *ibid*, at para 81.
[137] Ibid, at paras 47–49.
[138] Ibid, at para 82 (emphasis added).

> is encouraged to relinquish a social right which has been directly conferred on him by the directive, he must do so freely and with full knowledge of all the facts. Those requirements are all the more important given that *the worker must be regarded as the weaker party to the employment contract* and it is therefore necessary to prevent the employer being in a position to disregard the intentions of the other party to the contract or to impose on that party a restriction of his rights without him having expressly given his consent in that regard.

The combined effect of the research from the UK and the dicta in *Pfeiffer* has propelled the Commission to propose several amendments to the opt-out. It is a moot point whether, but for the 'on-call' cases, its abolition would have been proposed. Instead the Commission proposes to phase it out subject to an escape clause. In the revised draft[139] the opt-out will end after three years but a Member State may ask the Commission for a further extension beyond that date 'for reasons relating to their labour market arrangements'.[140] Once again there would be an evaluation report after three years.

One suggested provision is somewhat incongruous. The Commission now propose a maximum working week of 55 hours in any week, reduced from 65 hours in the original, for workers exercising the opt-out, unless a collective agreement allows otherwise. Oddly, there is no such limitation in the reference periods in Article 16 or the related derogations. Indeed the proposed standard reference period of 12 months would almost inevitably comprise certain weeks where more than 55 hours per week are worked in many instances, especially as overtime has to be included as part of the calculation. This idea is also problematic because it indicates that a 55-hour *average* working week would satisfy the health and safety requirements of workers who have consented to longer hours, almost certainly the most vulnerable, but for all others the minimum requirement for their protection would be an average of 48 hours.

These proposals raise the distant prospect of convergence on the horizon, but there is little likelihood of agreement being reached on the Commission's terms. Suggested amendments to the requirements for workers to consent to opting out are of greater interest. The Commission propose that a worker's agreement 'given at the time of the signature' of the employment contract or during any probation period 'shall be null and void'. Any agreement shall be valid for a period not exceeding one year, renewable.[141] Such changes would help to prevent 'intimidation' at the very outset of the employment contract, but it is far from clear how soon pressure may be brought to bear,

[139] COM(2005)246: amendments to Art 22.
[140] The Commission 'shall decide' on the response, giving reasons for its decision.
[141] Existing agreements in place before the revision would remain valid for a period not exceeding one year from that date.

especially if there is no probation period. In the UK, employees are not entitled to claim 'unfair dismissal' until after one year of continuous employment.[142] During this period the worker concerned would be especially vulnerable to coercion, and the prospect of refusing to renew may offer little succour. Alternatively, a proposal not to allow such agreements to take effect for at least 18 months after the formation of the contract would provide greater certainty and more effective protection. Strengthening of the position of new employees may, however, discourage employers from taking on new staff and may create inequalities in workplaces where the opt-out is standard.

D. CONCLUSION

This chapter has explored three underlying features of the regulation of working time in the EU. In each case, analysis has revealed inner tensions and polarities within the policy framework and structure of regulation that have influenced the content and interpretation of this complex measure and contributed to the present impasse over its revision and future direction.

Social market and social citizenship rationales formed the backdrop to the adoption of the Working Time Directive. In those parts where the social citizenship strand has been in the ascendancy, as in the case of the entitlement to four weeks' paid annual leave, it has afforded, sometimes for the first time, an exercisable right to genuine family time for workers in an employment relationship. The fact that this right is separate from the organisation of working time in the scheme of the Directive facilitates the simplicity of regulation in this instance. More generally, however, the notion that a worker is a social citizen entitled actually to enjoy the full benefits of the 'minimum requirements' is double-edged. The imperatives of the social market tend towards flexibility and, at best, gradual convergence. The combination of flexibility and subsidiarity in the social policy context is consistent with the pluralistic nature of the employment relationship but, paradoxically, with the exception of the opt-out from the 48-hour week, the key players are not the parties to the employment relationship but the 'social partners', who may have no direct mandate from the citizen/worker.

The bipolar nature of working time and free time is important not just conceptually, but also as a pivot for the functioning of the minimum requirements, specifically the measurement and limitation of that part of a worker's time that is deemed to be subordinate. Bipolarity provides a degree of certainty, but it is a complete misfit with the rapidly changing world of work. It has been tailored to a 'standard' homogeneous employment relationship where

[142] Employment Rights Act 1996, s108.

a worker, usually male, typically works full-time on a permanent basis for the same employer for his whole career without a break, carrying out similar tasks with limited decision-making powers.[143] Increasingly, 'non-standard' heterogeneous employment has become the norm. These workers are often female and working on part-time, fixed-term and/or temporary contracts. They are likely to be mobile, willing to change jobs—often out of necessity—and able to be more autonomous in determining their working and family time within 'flexible firms'.[144] The axis of subordination has changed. In a shift of emphasis the Advocate General in *Dellas* observed that a 'bipolar relationship...precludes new concepts and does not take account of the latest developments in industrial relations'.[145]

The Working Time Directive stands out as perhaps the most far-reaching example of flexibility in the field of EU employment law. Flexible provisions play a complex and, necessarily, ambivalent role that is not necessarily inimical to its basic health and safety objectives. Variations in reference periods and provisions allowing for gradual implementation may be regarded as broadly integrative in character. By contrast, the individualised opt-out from the 48-hour week is, at best, disintegrative in the short term, and the longer it is maintained the greater is the likelihood of retrogression. Among the suggested alternatives, the proposed standardisation of the 12-month reference period for calculating working time, or an expansion of the categories of workers deemed to be 'autonomous'[146] might offer more flexibility for employers and workers alike without the need to have recourse to a divisive opt-out.

Regulation of working time is, of necessity, complex because the problem of subordination of labour in the employment relationship requires attenuated solutions both in the conventional sense, to countervail the power of the market, and also, beyond subordination, to provide more opportunities for workers to exercise choice over the balance of their working and family time.

[143] See U Mückenberger, 'Non-standard Forms of Work and the Role of Changes in Labour and Social Security Regulation' (1989) 17 *International Journal of the Sociology of Law* 381.

[144] This strand of policy development can be traced back to a Commission Green Paper, 'Partnership for a New Organisation of Work', Bull EU Supp 4/97.

[145] *Dellas*, above n68, at para 67.

[146] Under Art 17(1).

13

Legal Options: Towards Better EC Company Law Regulation

GÉRARD HERTIG* AND JOSEPH A McCAHERY**

SINCE THE 1980S, legal options have been the subject of heated debate in the United States, and such debate has already led to a number of important reforms. Default rules and a variety of option techniques now feature in a wide range of contexts. In particular, they have been employed to accommodate the diversity in organisation, capital structure and lines of business. Increasingly, options have begun to play an important role in shaping the EU company and securities law rules that we observe today. Similarly, law-makers at the Member State level are injecting elements of optional law into the current round of reforms on economic policy and company law.

These debates about options have largely focused on the economic impact of switching a particular default rule. Options are often heralded by proponents as providing firms, where contracts are silent or incomplete, with an array of contractual terms on particular subjects, such as capital contributions, dividend rate, management remuneration and tenure, which encourage efficient contracting. A basic insight into this line of research is that default rules can create beneficial effects where standardisation *ex ante* is not yet feasible, and in that sense the defaults create a system of rights that parties are free to contract around. With legal options, parties are permitted to opt out of default terms and can select a particular rule that suits their needs. This approach, as proponents argue, is necessary as it allows business parties to reduce information problems and lower the cost of contracting that they otherwise would incur.

* Professor of Law, Swiss Federal Institute of Technology (ETH Zurich).

** Professor of Corporate Governance and Innovation, University of Amsterdam Faculty of Economics and Econometrics and Professor of Financial Market Regulation, Tilburg University Faculty of Law. This chapter is an updated version of G Hertig and JA McCahery, 'A Legal Options Approach to EC Company Law' in G Ferrarini and E Wymeersch (eds), *Investor Protection in Europe* (Oxford, Oxford University Press, 2006).

On the other hand, opponents argue that, despite the positive features of options, there are a number of situations where a mandatory rule would certainly benefit shareholders against the self-interested conduct of insiders. There are, it is argued, strong reasons to believe that under some circumstances a mandatory rule may be desirable to protect third parties. Moreover, the use of a mandatory rule may be justified where the law or regulation in question is uncertain or unclear. Proponents of this approach argue that if a switch to an enabling regime imposes excessive costs for firms, then it may not be justified to have firms choose legal terms, in particular, if the choice is suboptimal for the firm.

A significant part of the modern debate on options has involved the balancing of potential benefits and costs in comparison to mandatory rules. Many legal scholars have approached their analysis of options by pointing to the important ways in which options are likely to influence the productivity of firms. According to this view, options can ensure that companies are able to select arrangements that may cause fewer difficulties, allow for the possibility of efficiency-enhancing measures that can be expected to reduce transaction costs, and promote the institutional environment that could facilitate choice between regulatory regimes. In particular, a strain of the finance literature that has been influential in corporate legal scholarship has argued that facilitating choice is likely to enhance individual options pricing and may well, in certain circumstances, give rise to welfare effects. For some proponents, such a regime is also likely to have a significant effect on the preferences and behaviour of individuals. However, regardless of the extent to which default rules may inflict damage on some parties or may be more costly than the benefits created, there is sufficient evidence suggesting that the value of options is considerable and that expanded choice over corporate law rules is desirable, given the high costs of mandates that govern the affairs of companies in the EU and make it difficult for company participants to adopt cost-saving rules that benefit shareholders and control managerial opportunism.

The debate over legal options has also involved the cross-country comparison of their use, revealing some interesting results about the effect of default rules on firm performance. The enabling structure of US state law, for example, supplies firms with few mandates and offers a menu of default rules that allow firms to economise on transaction costs such as drafting, information and enforcement costs, and to limit opportunism and fill in gap-ridden contracts. If *ex ante* constraints are desired, the burden is on the equity holder or creditor to constrain the management with explicit contract terms. The US approach, which leaves central matters unconstrained, encourages firms to take an active role in defining the relationships between the participants inside the firm and the representation of the firm in its dealings with outside participants, particularly creditors. For proponents of this approach, firms have different sets of choices available to solve problems that can inhibit innovation and reduce productive efficiency.

A familiar complaint in the EU is that firms enjoy too few opportunities to select freely between legal rules and jurisdictions when structuring their relationships. Some scholars argue that the absence of state competition in the EU is the main reason law-makers, on both the EU and national levels, have brought about a burdensome and undesirable system of regulation that provides few incentives and choices for firms to become more efficient. To the extent that firms have continued to face considerable regulatory barriers to opting into a different corporate law regime, then the law-maker would face few pressures from organised interest groups to provide default rules that would maximise social welfare. In this respect, the regulatory competition model suggests providing much-needed incentives for governments to give credible assurance to firms that law-makers can be relied on to supply optimal legal rules which are attractive to many different types of firms.

A central issue in the debate has been whether the EC's reliance on a narrow range of legal mechanisms is the main factor constraining the move toward choice. This is important because existing theory and practice suggest that the process of providing for more flexible law, such as those provisions introduced by best practice recommendations, fails to control for the distinctively mandatory characteristics of 'comply and explain' measures, which are often linked to a country's corporation law and can be interpreted by the courts. In this context, the EC has sought to introduce a widespread set of initiatives in the areas of accounting, auditing, corporate governance and company law based on the need to establish better and more flexible regulatory mechanisms. In order to achieve these aims, the Commission articulated its views on the measures required to improve EU legislation in its Communication on Modernising Company Law and Enhancing Corporate Governance in the EU—A Plan to Move Forward ('Action Plan'). As for the Action Plan, the policy decisions taken by the Commission were shaped by the need to align principal–agent interests in the wake of the Enron and Parmalat scandals by providing more shareholder-oriented rules, including offering more shareholder rights, improving transparency and strengthening the position of non-executive directors.

To this end, the EU legislative agenda has been designed to deal with cross-border mobility, board structure, financial and non-financial disclosure, director and management remuneration, appointment of auditors, managers' and directors' conflicts of interests and shareholder voting rights. The prevailing EU regulatory strategy in corporate governance and company law relies on a combination of directives, recommendations and self-regulation to accommodate these wide-ranging regulatory reforms. The conventional wisdom is that the EC Action Plan will succeed in creating the type of legal framework needed to enable firms to compete more effectively in a dynamic and changing business environment. While few question the potential benefits of the Commission's reforms, several scholars have asked whether there might be better, lower-cost legal strategies that could be used to deliver more effective results for the benefit of investors.[1] Some authors are less than sanguine about whether the EC will be able to determine which menu of rules will have the greatest beneficial effect on shareholders.

This chapter argues that an options system is preferable to a mandatory regime since it favours shareholder welfare as the basis for assessing the proposed regulatory reforms. Regulatory intervention through legal options, moreover, is a more effective policy instrument because it allows firms to pursue cost-saving arrangements that better match their needs. This chapter will explain the beneficial aspects of an EC company law reform policy that makes use of opt-in and opt-out default rules to improve flexibility and firm performance. A limited menu of default rules will be proposed in order to avoid legislative paralysis, and as a means for allowing regulators to assess the effect of options on firm behavior. It can be expected that the proposed opt-ins and opt-outs will improve firm quality by providing firms with an enhanced set of rules allowing them to respond better to market needs and other risks.

There could potentially be concerns that optional arrangements may be subject to behavioural shortcomings. Some studies suggest that default rules can induce cognitive distortions that can have significant effects when people treat them like endowments. This occurs particularly when an entitlement is embedded in a contract. On this view, even if a default rule is biased in favour of a group of individuals, it will have no positive impact on these people. Moreover, there is also evidence that points to the stickiness of default rules making it more difficult for firms to opt out of legal provisions. Even if this point has some validity, many commentators have observed that these results are at odds with the widely accepted intuition that default rules may have little impact on distribution. Moreover, even if cognitive defects are sometimes difficult to overcome, it is argued that a switch in the default rule may have desirable effects by improving welfare.[2] Finally, since it seems likely that the possible cognitive problems associated with defaults rules are not substantial, it makes great sense to provide for options so as to achieve the benefits that cannot be accomplished by harmonised directives in the field of company law.

That said, there are good reasons for recommending a cautious, piecemeal approach to the introduction of options into the law-making process at this stage. First, putting too many reform items on the agenda may create the very same implementation delay and complexity issues that afflict the mandatory

[1] P Davies, 'Enron and Corporate Governance Reforms in the UK and European Community' in J Armour and JA McCahery (eds), *After Enron: Improving Corporate Law and Modernising Securities Regulation in Europe and the US* (Oxford, Hart Publishing, 2006).

[2] See CR Sunstein, 'Switching the Default Rule' (2002) 77 *New York University Law Review* 106.

harmonisation approach. Secondly, it is always preferable to adopt a step-by-step approach when introducing new regulatory mechanisms, especially when there is a risk of legal diversity becoming excessive.

The regulation of EC company law through a system of legal options has several advantages over the present regime. First, the use of options would permit the EC and Member States to limit the risk of further intrusions by the European Court of Justice (ECJ) in the company law-making process. Secondly, to the extent that the options approach is preferred by interest groups and companies, they will have strong incentives to support the approach through increased demand for the use of options in most corporate law areas.

This chapter will proceed as follows. Part A lays out the structure of the regulatory competition argument and considers how the structure of EC company law has become more responsive to the market-place as a consequence of decisions by the ECJ and the corporate law-making process in the EU. Part B assesses the advantages of the pro-choice approach over the mandatory EC company law regime. Part C applies the legal options model in developing menus of default rules to regulate transparency, accounts and director liability. This chapter argues that a step-by-step approach implementing options is likely to yield higher benefits than mandatory corporate law provisions. Part D recommends a limited number of opt-in and opt-out provisions that would reduce conflict and perhaps be socially optimal. Part E concludes.

A. ON REGULATORY ARBITRAGE AND COMPETITION

This section considers the workings of regulatory competition in the EU, questioning whether corporate law in the EU can be considered the product of competitive market forces. Some commentators contend that questions of regulatory competition are closely related to the questions of mandatory versus enabling rules, and the level of firm choice generally.

While the EU does not have competition between Member States to create the law that governs public corporations, there is evidence that some forms of competition may be emerging. First, the evidence suggests that, while regulatory competition remains close to non-existent within the EU, the appearance of new judgments from the ECJ supports the inference that regulatory arbitrage is an imminent possibility. Secondly, the threat of state competition, which is less attractive to weakly responsive states, such as France and Germany, can remarkably give rise to a mechanism, such as a system of legal options, for establishing freedom of choice without firms having to move anywhere.

Accordingly, one of the most important debates in European company law is whether a 'market for corporate law' will ultimately emerge within the European Union and, if so, whether it will be based on a Delaware-like model in which companies can freely select their country of incorporation. This is, of course, a politically charged question and therefore a somewhat undifferentiated debate. In particular, commentators often fail to distinguish between corporate finance, company formation and restructuring issues.[3] Conversely, competition between states in the US is generally assumed to be very active, whereas recent research shows that the reality is subtler. However, there is evidence that domicile choices by US corporations can affect their value and/or provide significant benefits for their managers and controlling shareholders.[4] The absence in Europe of anything resembling American charter competition must therefore mean that there are substantive regulatory barriers to jurisdictional competition.[5]

To start, EU company law can be viewed largely as an incomplete and rather ineffective set of provisions. The reasons: Member States have been repeatedly unable to agree on important substantive issues, there has been a pro-decentralisation presumption resulting from the EU subsidiarity principle, and we have witnessed a lack of implementation of EU directives by Member States. This has allowed for continuing diversity in Member State corporate law. At the same time, the rather strong divergence about the 'optimal' corporate regime has had the effect of sustaining significant opposition to regulatory arbitrage and competition.

Nevertheless, US commentators in particular have argued that change is imminent. Cross-border acquisitions by firms that have cheaper access to external capital because of higher investor protection levels should bring corporate governance amendments.[6] The replacement of banks by institutional shareholders as the main corporate governance actor, should have a similar effect. In other words, transformations occurring in the market place will result in increased convergence of rules.

In contrast, many European scholars are not as optimistic about the prospects for market-induced reform, given the existence of a strong coalition of interest groups and other path-dependent forces. In particular, the repeated failures, until recently, to pass a Directive on Takeovers show the power of those who benefit from the status quo to block transformational measures.

[3] S Grundmann, 'Regulatory Competition in European Company Law—Some Different Gains?' in G Ferrarini, KJ Hopt and E Wymeersch (eds), *Capital Markets in the Age of the EURO* (The Hague, Kluwer, 2002).

[4] M Kahan and E Kamar, 'The Myth of State Competition in Corporate Law' (2002) 55 *Stanford Law Review* 679; LA Bebchuk and A Hamdani, 'Optimal Defaults for Corporate Law Evolution' (2002) 96 *Northwestern University Law Review* 489.

[5] S Deakin, 'Regulatory Competition versus Harmonization in European Company Law' in D Esty and D Geradin (eds), *Regulatory Competition and Economic Integration* (Oxford, OUP, 2001); J McCahery and EPM Vermeulen, 'The Evolution of Closely Held Business Forms in Europe' (2001) 26 *Journal of Corporation Law* 857.

[6] R Gilson, 'Globalizing Corporate Governance' (2001) 49 *American Journal of Comparative Law* 329.

Of course, institutional barriers at the EU level are not the sole or even main reason for past regulatory and judicial conservatism. Under the *siège réel* (real seat) doctrine, which is followed by the majority of EU Member States, a corporation must be incorporated in the Member State where it has its central administration. As a result, opting into another Member State's corporate law is often unattractive because of significant tax implications, especially for corporations that have used conservative accounting to build up hidden reserves. This barrier to regulatory arbitrage and competition is compounded by employee participation structures, German co-determination being the best known but not the only example. Indeed, by reducing the ability of legislators to respond to managerial or shareholder preferences, employee participation favours regulatory conservatism. Judicial conservatism, for its part, has at least as much to do with Member States' reluctance to facilitate or even permit shareholder litigation as it does with EU law deficiencies.

1. The Evolution of EC Company Law

The EC has built a record of company law reform that enjoys a mixed reputation. Early legislation has been praised for quickly developing a company law infrastructure that was in some important respects similar to the corporate law structures in most Member States. Secondly, the Commission was successful in implementing laws that facilitated cross-border trading by minimising the risk of companies or their transactions being considered void in other Member States. Thirdly, the EU, having adopted accounting and capital maintenance rules aimed at protecting minority shareholders and creditors, was able to secure some enthusiasm for Commission efforts in devising mechanisms dealing with financial assistance and disclosure.

In the past two decades, however, the situation has changed. A series of high profile legislative efforts by the European Commission, ranging from the regulation of takeover bids to establishing new business entities, ran into conflict with the European Parliament. What explains the shift in legislative policy-making authority encountered by the EC? Influential theories of EU law-making emphasise that policy-making space became very limited due to the mixed motives of Member States.[7] The presumption that Member States should want to weaken, not strengthen, the Commission's company law agenda has led some scholars to entertain the possibility that major company law reforms are not considered important enough for member governments to mobilise resources to achieve legislative compromises.[8]

[7] M Pollack, *The Engines of European Integration, Delegation, Agency, and Agenda Setting in the EU* (Oxford, OUP, 2003).

[8] J Wouters, 'European Company Law: Quo Vadis' (2000) 37 *Common Market Law Review* 257.

In order to regain significant agenda-setting powers and the ability to conclude agreements, the Commission eventually reversed its legislative strategy in this area. No single explanation can be offered for the strategy eventually embraced by the Commission. Standard public choice theory would explain the shift in terms of organised special interest groups persuading Commission policy-makers that the group's preferences would serve the policy-makers' own political interests and would become useful in putting together a winning coalition.[9] Naturally there are numerous other explanations to consider. It is surely no coincidence that the Commission sought to counter the moves of Member State governments that sought to block reforms by placing the Lisbon Council's objectives as a top priority, so as to strengthen their policy goals.[10] Similarly, policy-makers may have had an incentive to take an early position on the US corporate scandals in order to shift the expectations of domestic voters, which could be expected to have guided Member State governments' subsequent behaviour. This is clearly represented by the efforts of the Market Commissioner to have the High Level Group of Company Law Experts reach beyond their original mandate to recommend certain audit and accounting and rules regarding publication of annual accounts.[11]

Perhaps more fundamentally, the EC has responded to the direct political influence of the European Court of Justice's decisions on freedom of establishment.[12] These ECJ decisions have challenged the core elements of the *siège réel* (real seat) doctrine, challenging some of the main principles enshrined in the company law frameworks in the majority of Member States. A growing number of studies have demonstrated the direct effect of the ECJ's judgments on the cross-border mobility of start-up companies.[13] With regard to established companies, the impact of the ECJ case law is subject to debate, as it remains costly for them to switch from one Member State's regime to another. Nonetheless, the ECJ decisions have increased the attractiveness of regulatory arbitrage, which may make it easier for corporations to select among legal rules from diverse company law codes.

Even though these disruptive features have induced the EC policy-makers to adopt a less constraining legislative approach, the existing means of opting

[9] AK Dixit and J Londegan, 'Ideology, Tactics, and Efficiency in Redistributive Politics' (1998) 113 *Quarterly Journal of Economics* 497.

[10] See Presidency Conclusions, Lisbon European Council of 23–24 June 2000, available at http://ue.eu.int/en/Info/eurocouncil/index.htm. See also http://europa.eu.int/comm/internmarket/en/company/company/news/01-1237.htm.

[11] Communication from the commission to the Council and European Parliament, *Modernising Company Law and Enhancing Corporate Governance in the European Union—A plan to move forward* Com (2003) 284 final 21 May 2003.

[12] Case C–212/97 *Centros Ltd v Erthvers- og Selskabbsstyrelsen* [1999] ECR I–1459, [1999] 2 CMLR 551 (*Centros*); Case C–208/00 *Überseering BV v Nordic Construction Company Baumanagement GmbH* [2002] ECR I–9919 (*Überseering*); and Case C–167/01, *Kamer van Koophandel en Fabrieken voor Amsterdam v Inspire Art Ltd* [2003] ECR I–10155 (*Inspire Art*). These judgments are available at http://europa.eu.int/cj/en/content/juris/index.htm.

[13] M Becht, C Mayer and H Wagner, 'Corporate Mobility and the Cost of Regulation', ECGI Law Working Paper N. 70/2006, available at www.ssrn.com.

out of EC law are in practice quite limited. For example, the Commission proposed, in a radical departure from its previous policy, that Member States and firms be allowed to opt out of Articles 9 (board neutrality) and 11 (break-through rule) of the Takeover Directive.[14] The provision of the opt-out was received favourably by Member States, ending a regulatory deadlock that had lasted for more than a decade.

That said, the Commission has subsequently created a large and growing number of soft law initiatives that link together national governments' substantive policy concerns with EU level policy-makers' concerns to succeed in transforming their relationship with Member States in terms of agenda setting and the implementation of corporate law rules. The provision of flexible corporate law rules has many advantages. From an efficiency standpoint, non-mandatory soft law measures can provide a range of value-maximising procedures to firms. Correspondingly, the greater range of choice in the selection of policy-making instruments makes it easier to avoid the costs of relying on rigid instruments alone to implement new measures. The Commission can choose to:

1) Enact mandatory EU provisions (as was generally done in the past);
2) Offer Member States a choice among a finite number of EU-defined options (an approach originally adopted in the Accounting Directives);
3) Enact harmonised provisions, but empower Member States to opt out of them (an approach adopted by the Takeover Directive);
4) Enable firms to opt out of applicable Member State provisions by providing substitutable EU provisions (as was also done in the Takeover Directive);
5) Adopt an EU regime that firms can opt out of (which has not been tried yet, but is in line with the flexible approach adopted by the Takeover Directive); or
6) Abstain from legislating.[15]

2. Impact on Regulatory Arbitrage and Competition

Overall, it is also intuitive that while many of the policy changes discussed above can have some impact on regulatory arbitrage, the practical effect of these changes across the board on cross-border mobility, charter competition

[14] Dir 2004/25/EC [2004] OJ L142/12.

[15] Furthermore, reformers can combine approaches. Eg, the Takeover Bids Dir allows Member States to opt out of its board neutrality and prohibition of defensive measures provisions, while enabling firms incorporated in Member States that do so to opt into the EU regime. Or, to take another example, firms could be allowed to opt out of their domestic regime not only to escape mandatory provision, but also when EU law has a standardisation advantage over Member States' default provisions.

and freedom of choice is so far quite limited. Exit taxes or workers' protection and other social constraints are more important to increasing choice than the effect of the Commission's new soft law approach to company law-making.

It is well known that tax constraints are a significant barrier to midstream reincorporations. The ECJ's ruling in the *Daily Mail* case shows clearly that a midstream reincorporation will trigger exit taxes on hidden reserves, effectively restricting the demand for chartering.[16] Conversely, there is evidence that corporate law does not significantly constrain tax-driven firm mobility.[17] The same is true for social constraints. The attractiveness of incorporation or reincorporation is often seriously reduced by such steps having no effect on the applicable labour law—a situation that is likely to persist in the longer run, given unwavering opposition to the adoption of EU corporate governance provisions that would affect the scope of German co-determination requirements. Note also that corporate law considerations are unlikely significantly to affect labour-driven firm mobility.

On the other hand, the ECJ's recent rulings on freedom of establishment can and do challenge the existing EC tax landscape. Since 2000, the ECJ has repeatedly ruled that tax provisions are precluded by the freedom of establishment principle if they discriminate between domestic and foreign subsidiaries, and more generally between domestic and international groups. More importantly, Member States have generally proven unsuccessful in trying to justify such discrimination by arguing that it is necessary to ensure the coherence of the national tax system or to preserve the tax base.[18] This is both in sharp contrast with the ECJ's earlier reluctance to interfere with tax barriers to cross-border activities (as exemplified by *Daily Mail* and *Bachmann*[19]) and in line with the ECJ's recent pro-freedom of incorporation and reincorporation cases.

As a consequence of these tax cases and the implementation of the Merger Directive,[20] commentators are confident that the current tax barriers to cross-border reincorporation will be removed shortly by the ECJ.[21]

[16] Case 81/1987 *Regina v HM. Treasury and Comm'rs of Inland Revenue, ex parte Daily Mail and General Trust Plc* [1988] ECR 5483.

[17] See GR Simpson, 'EU's tax changes scatter corporations', *The Wall Street Journal* (European edn), 9 Oct 2003, at A6.

[18] See eg Case C–324/00 *Lankhorst-Hohorst GmbH v Finanzamt Steinfurt* [2002] ECR I–1179—a German tax case; Case C–168/01 *Bosal Holding BV v Staatssecretaris van Financiën* [2003] ECR I–9409—a Dutch tax case; Case C–446/03 *Marks & Spencer plc v David Hasley (HM Inspector of Taxes)*, not yet reported—a UK tax case. These judgments are available at http://europa.eu.int/cj/en/content/juris/index.htm.

[19] Case C–204/90 *Bachmann* [1992] ECR I–249.

[20] See Council Dir 90/434/EEC [1990] OJ L225/00 on the common system of taxation applicable to mergers, divisions, transfer of assets and exchanges of shares concerning companies of different Member States.

[21] W Schön, 'EC Company Statute and Taxation: Tax Issues and Constraints to Reorganizations and Reincorporations in the EU', Working Paper, Max Planck Institute (Munich, 2003).

Such optimism finds support in the *de Lasteyrie du Saillant* judgment.[22] The ECJ ruled in favour of an individual who moved to France from Belgium and objected to having to provide a guarantee in respect of a tax bill on the future sale of a shareholding. The Court indicated that the principle of freedom of establishment precludes a Member State keen to prevent a risk of tax avoidance from taxing latent increases in value when a taxpayer transfers his residence outside that state.

While the pattern in ECJ case law suggests that the Court is likely to rule in favour of restricting Member States from levying corporate exit taxes on foregone claims and hidden reserves, this is by no mean certain. Should the ECJ eventually do so, larger established companies would be the main beneficiaries. However, this class of companies may be made worse off by changes to the *status quo*, as the EC reforms are likely to trigger tax measures at the domestic and international level that could prove more costly than the gains from greater freedom of movement.[23] In this case, there is some evidence that Member States, in particular the UK, systematically adjust their tax laws to minimise the impact of ECJ judgments and that freedom of establishment case law is driven by smaller rather than larger firms—an indication that the latter do not expect to gain significantly from it.

This does not mean that only those firms that can afford reincorporation will benefit from regulatory arbitrage and regulatory competition in the corporate law area. The trend set in train by the *Centros, Überseering* and *Inspire Art* judgments has directly influenced the policy space of the European Commission and led to greater policy-making uncertainty with respect to its reform agenda. Hence, the introduction of the new Directive on cross-border mergers, and the announcement of plans for a directive on the cross-border transfer of the administrative offices of firms can be considered as initiatives that evidence the shift toward a mobility-oriented law-making agenda. In addition, various Member States have responded to the demands of domestic firms for innovative company law terms. An ever-wider array of Member States, such as Ireland, the UK, Luxembourg and the Netherlands, have prioritised the creation of corporate law rules that directly benefit footloose foreign companies operating in other jurisdictions.

But others, France and Germany in particular, have responded by attempting to make reincorporation in the UK less economically attractive.[24] Despite these efforts, nearly 30,000 German entrepreneurs have since 2002

[22] Case C–9/02 *Hughes de Lasteyrie du Saillant v Ministère de l'Economie, des Finances et de l'Industrie* [2004] ECR I–2409.

[23] G Hertig, 'Efficient Fostering of EU Regulatory Competition' (2004) 76 *Swiss Review of Business Law* 360.

[24] See K Heine, 'Regulatory Competition Between Company Laws in the European Union: the Überseering Case' (2003) 38 *Intereconomics* 102; EPM Vermeulen, *The Evolution of Legal Business Forms in Europe and the United States* (The Hague, Kluwer Law International, 2003).

registered their companies as UK limited companies as it is cheaper and less burdensome than registering as a GmbH. While Germany's reputation as a business-friendly environment for start-ups is now under strain, pressures have not built up sufficiently to force through German legislative measures that would involve substantial costs to incumbent groups. At the legislative level, major reforms that would involve deviations from the current rules on the preservation of share capital and the notarial deed requirement for the transfer of shares are unlikely to find political support in the near future. Accordingly, German law-makers have recently proposed measures designed to create a modernised GmbH that would make it easier and quicker to incorporate a GmbH, offer a transparent shareholder structure and protect creditors against exploitative and dilutive strategies on the part of the owners of a GmbH.[25]

This analysis offers a positive understanding of the state of regulatory competition in the EU. Naturally, it is quite different from that of the American states in the late nineteenth century. There charter competition was new and unexpected. Competitive response was slow because the home states were mesmerised by antitrust policy concerns. In today's EU, the Member States know all about the possibility of competition as they play their indefinitely repeated game. They have moved to forestall competition in the past, and can be expected to update their strategies to account for ECJ developments. The upshot is that there is little potential for competitive-based law-making to facilitate policy innovation in the short-term. It is in this regard that legal options may be a solution to the absence of a feedback mechanism that induces law-makers to respond to investor preferences.

B. THE BENEFITS OF A PRO-CHOICE APPROACH

That said, there is an important role for legal options in the EU and Member State law-making processes. Legal options refer to the *ex ante* and *ex post* choices that are created by law. Commentators in Europe have emphasised that law-makers have tended to introduce choice-enhancing provisions when they have found it difficult and costly to resolve a legislative conflict. This explains why the European Commission, for example, chose to resolve an interest group-induced deadlock over the Takeover Directive by creating legal provisions that allow Member States the option whether to implement the board neutrality and the breakthrough provisions. Even though it is debatable whether the new legislation will have dramatic efficiency or

[25] See JA McCahery, EPM Vermeulen, M Hisatake and J Saito, 'The New Company Law: What Matters in an Innovative Economy?' [2007] *European Business Organization Law Review* (forthcoming).

distributional effects, the decision to provide Member States and firms with freedom of choice when no intermediate solutions existed can be considered a credible approach to law reform. Suffice it to say that there is some evidence that allowing Member States to opt out of certain provisions in a piece of proposed legislation may sometimes be the only practical way to ensure that the rules in question, which might be capable of benefiting a large number of firms, become law.

1. Economic Theory of Incomplete Contracts and Default Rules

This section sets out to analyse the main features of the pro-choice approach as applied to corporate law. As many corporate contracts are incomplete, the section will focus on the standard gap-filling approaches that provide definitive default terms for completing contracts. In practice, of course, these approaches are not always suitable for gap-filling because they do not rely on the priority of the bargain. By contrast, we focus on how opt-in and opt-out rules are likely to be a step in the right direction for EC company law.

The economic theory of incomplete contracts is an important foundation for the financial structure of the firm and can play an important role in deciding how to resolve conflicts when there is a missing term or a contract is opaque.[26] A contract is complete only if all relevant contingencies and corresponding control rights are specified unambiguously. It is worth bearing in mind that parties may deliberately choose a non-contingent contract or be unable to design a contract that deals with all contingencies *ex ante*.[27]

The literature predicts that particular types of agreement may be incomplete due to informational asymmetries and the fact that the inherent limitations of contractual language make it impossible to contract for all future contingencies. The intuition behind this approach is that the parties could perhaps write a complete contract if they could focus on a breach and through backward induction develop a full set of optional terms to govern the contract. For many, there is some question whether parties, despite economic theory's rationality assumptions, can depend on backward induction to deal with their long-term contracting problems.[28]

[26] WW Bratton, M Hviid and JA McCahery, 'Repeated Games, Social Norms and Incomplete Contracts' in C Willett (ed), *Aspects of Fairness in Contract* (London, Blackstone Press, 1996).

[27] O Hart and J Moore, 'Cooperatives vs. Outside Ownership', NBER Working Paper No 6421, (London, National Bureau of Economic Research, 1998).

[28] E Posner, 'Economic Analysis of Contract Law after Three Decades: Success or Failure' (2003) 112 *Yale Law Journal* 829.

At the same time, the theory of incomplete contracts has proceeded on the assumption that actions are non-contractable *ex ante* but contractable *ex post*. Since symmetrically informed business parties write contract terms *ex ante* based on their own needs, they expect courts to enforce them even if fundamental terms are left undefined. On this view, courts should not intervene *ex post* since it may leave the parties worse off. In recent years, however, there has been a shift toward a more liberal gap-filling approach which diagnoses the different sources of incompleteness and provides the appropriate gap-filling term.[29]

The theory of law and economics has produced an impressive variety of gap-filling alternatives. Prominent scholars have argued that corporate law should provide a set of gap-filling rules that hypothetical parties would have bargained for.[30] The adoption of an efficient set of default rules provides firms with opportunities and solutions that otherwise would not be available and reduces the transaction costs of opting into specific terms. Naturally, business parties who find the default rule undesirable would remain free to opt out and contract into a term they prefer.

Over the years, scholars have challenged whether market-mimicking rules encourage efficiency, positing that under other circumstances the majoritarian default rule does not have any efficient effects at all, and that courts presumably will find it more complex to apply such defaults to all types of firms.[31] A contrasting approach is offered by scholars who endorse the penalty default doctrine, which recommends forcing parties, in some situations, to share information as they bargain around default rules. For example, to the extent that the enforcement of a liquidated damages clause can limit externalities to third parties, this 'penalty' default may create an important efficiency effect.[32] Even if penalty defaults could limit negative externalities, it is not clear at all whether the doctrine could become effective generally, as it does not deal directly with the specific contractual variables discussed in the literature, nor does it necessarily take up the preferred set of damages to impose on the breaching party.[33]

Putting aside this debate, it is suggested that European countries can benefit greatly by adopting reforms that may allow corporations to select from a menu of default arrangements. This chapter will deal with how a corporate law regime using both opt-in and opt-out rules can yield benefits for business parties and shareholders.

[29] O Ben-Shahar, 'Agreeing to Disagree: Filling Gaps in Deliberately Incomplete Contracts' [2004] *Wisconsin Law Review* 389.

[30] F Easterbrook and DR Fischel, *The Economic Structure of Corporate Law* (Cambridge, Mass, Harvard University Press, 1991).

[31] Posner, above n28; Ben-Shahar, above n29.

[32] I Ayres, *Optional Law: Real Options in the Structure of Legal Entitlements* (Chicago, Ill, University of Chicago Press, 2005).

[33] Posner, above n28.

2. Opt-in and Opt-out Rules in EC Company Law

It follows from the above discussion that, if the European Commission were to introduce reforms designed to provide a menu of optional rules, the benefits of this legislation could result in increased incentives to improve productivity, thereby increasing shareholder value. Yet, given the ever-changing nature of the business environment in which firms compete, an effective enabling approach ideally should include both opt-in and opt-out procedures.[34] To illustrate this point, law-makers could draft an opt-in provision that allows shareholders a choice in favour of a provision giving firm investors the right to sue directors (a procedural option) or a regime which allows them to benefit from appraisal rights (a substantive option) in case of a squeeze-out.

Naturally, the shift toward an opt-in/opt-out approach that could diminish member governments' conflicts and regulatory deadlocks will increase the value of the EC company law regime. The beneficial effects are likely to include the development of a richer regulatory menu, allowing for alternative contractual arrangements when abstaining from law-making is not an alternative. In the past, such situations may have led, to the extent that some member governments could constrain the Commission's initiatives, to the adoption of mandatory corporate law arrangements where there was a significant risk that the rules would be biased in favour of one set of contracting parties or another.[35] Still, such arrangements may not cause economic actors difficulties in achieving an efficient bargaining outcome if they are free to substitute an alternative to the mandatory rule. Thus, by giving business parties the opportunity to opt in and opt out of biased and costly rules, their interests can be protected against regulatory interventions that they deem costly and ineffective. Moreover, another potential benefit of this approach is that firms can benefit directly from the choice of *à-la-carte* legal rules without having to reincorporate into a more friendly Member State company law regime.

Conversely, the uncertainty surrounding a policy that permits business parties to decide among optional default rules may create some scepticism about the wealth effects of this approach. There are a number of reasons. First, allowing shareholders to opt into or out of EU law or any Member State's rules could undermine, given the heterogeneous preferences of Member States, the incentives bearing on the Commission to propose

[34] C Jolls and CR Sunstein, 'Debiasing Through Law' (2005) (Working Paper, available at http://ssrn.com).

[35] EA O'Hara, 'Opting Out of Regulation: A Public Choice Analysis of Contractual Choice of Law' (2000) 53 *Vanderbilt Law Review* 1551; J Rachlinski and CR Farina, 'Cognitive Psychology and Optimal Government Design' (2002) 87 *Cornell Law Review* 549; R Korobkin, 'The Endowment Effect and Legal Analysis' (2003) 97 *Northwestern Law Review* 1227.

and implement legislation. In particular, moving from a mandatory harmonisation regime or an 'abstain or comply' approach to a clear choice rule with multiple alternatives may increase (albeit probably only slightly) the chances of deadlock by preventing the emergence of clear majorities. Secondly, the process of introducing enhanced contractual choice could significantly increase the number of legal options available, thereby making it more difficult and costly for business parties to ascertain and select the most appropriate default rule.

Finally, while the presumption is that parties tend toward efficient outcomes, it may be necessary for regulators—who care about efficiency—to introduce the conditions which enable the parties to achieve that result. In some cases, this will require the creation of stringent mandatory provisions, rather than defaults, in order to constrain opportunistic behaviour. Economic theory indicates that costly opportunism typically occurs at the entry or exit stages. Under this approach, minority investors would be better off with a mandatory provision, such as a fair value squeeze-out rule, that protects them from opportunism by controlling shareholders and managers. Some commentators argue, moreover, that stringent mandatory rules can protect entrepreneurs from early stage hold-up problems, which is likely to promote social welfare by facilitating the absolute number of start-ups.[36] What emerges from these arguments is the observation that policy-makers must, when designing mandatory and default rules, find the proper balance between the different interests to constrain opportunism and to ensure that parties reach efficient agreements.

3. Endowment Effects and Legal Options

As discussed earlier, studies of legal options and default rules show that alternative rules can have an impact on distributive consequences. It is well know that cognitive distortions such as the endowment effect can explain why economic actors do not always reach efficient outcomes. The endowment effect, which is reflected in people's preferences for the status quo, can be observed in laboratory experiments. Still, the cost of the endowment effect for markets remains uncertain.[37] Naturally, while there is no denying that the investors may not exhibit significant or systematic cognitive biases,[38]

[36] A Hyytinen and T Takalo, 'Corporate Law and Small Business Finance: Mandatory v. Enabling Rules' (2005) 6 *European Business Organisation Law Review* 449.

[37] EL Glaeser, 'Psychology and the Market' (2004) 94 *American Economic Review* 408; CR Plott and K Zeiler, 'The Willingness to Pay—Willingness to Accept Gap, the "Endowment Effect," Subject Misconceptions, and Experimental Procedures for Eliciting Valuations' (2005) 95 *American Economic Review* 530.

[38] See also J Arlen, M Spitzer and E Talley, 'Endowment Effects Within Corporate Agency Relationships' (2002) 31 *Journal of Legal Studies* 1.

the regulatory implications are not yet well understood.[39] Yet the behavioural analysis of legal options is a robust literature that takes seriously the implications of cognitive biases for legal rules and economic welfare.[40]

Default rules are a potentially attractive option for law reformers. There are two possible arguments supporting the switch to defaults. First, law-makers could reduce the cost of contracting by providing off-the-shelf provisions that are efficient without being sticky. Default rules avoid the costs of negotiating and drafting a customised term, and most economic actors can benefit from a rule that encourages cost savings for business parties. At the same time, offering a firm a set of opt-in provisions that depart from Member States' corporate governance codes may also have the beneficial effect of allowing firms to exit inefficient one-size-fits-all rules while reducing the transaction and reputation costs of justifying to investors why they are not in compliance with a code of good practice recommendation.

Again, it can be argued that default rules can deter the opportunistic conduct of majority shareholders and managers more effectively than the current mandatory regime. For example, flipping over a current default rule, such as the limited liability default rule, to the presumption of unlimited liability for corporate tortfeasors under some conditions, could have an important deterrent effect, as the redistributive consequences for contract creditors who would capture larger gains would be significant.[41] To be sure, flipping over the default rule may not—for reasons discussed earlier—serve to benefit the intended group.[42] Secondly, investors may resist opting into a more favourable EU regime because a status quo bias makes them prefer the existing national corporate law regime or because they do not want the firm to adopt an approach that deviates from the mean.[43] Thus, ignoring stickiness may result in EU law-makers adopting an opt-in instead of an opt-out or mandatory rule in the mistaken belief that this less interventionist step will suffice to remedy inefficiencies at the Member State level.

Here again, it is difficult to compare these advantages and disadvantages in the abstract, even more so considering that cognitive biases are context specific. On the other hand, it appears that there is no indication that legal options should be avoided provided some attention is given to their efficiency in terms of status quo bias or excessive optimism of confidence. Overall, this chapter argues that adopting pro-choice provisions will prove advantageous to the interests of firms and investors. The opportunity for firms

[39] Korokbin, above n35.

[40] See O Bar-Gill, 'Pricing Legal Options: A Behavioral Perspective' (2005), New York University Law and Economics Working paper, no 04–05; Jolls and Sunstein, above n34.

[41] H Hansmann and R Kraakman, 'Toward Unlimited Shareholder Liability for Corporate Torts' (1991) 100 *Yale Law Journal* 1879.

[42] Sunstein, above n2.

[43] *Ibid.*

to select rules that they prefer without having to reincorporate in another Member State is likely to lead to significant cost savings. Three possible drawbacks—capture by select groups or interests, excessive diversity and cognitive uncertainties—can be easily addressed by the following proposals. First, adopting entry/exit voting rules should prevent one constituency (managers, controlling shareholders, minorities) from acting opportunistically. Secondly, any increase in legal diversity should benefit most European firms as their needs tend to differ across classes. While some firms may suffer higher costs because of reduced standardisation, this should not prove sufficient to outweigh the benefits for other firms.[44] Thirdly, adopting a step-by-step approach, under which a limited number of legal options are tested during an introductory phase, should limit the risk of regulatory inefficiencies or distortions.

C. STEP-BY-STEP REFORM RECOMMENDATIONS

In this section, a set of reform suggestions based on the above investigation into opt-in and opt-out default provisions is developed. It is crucial to note that when developing a law reform proposal based on the model of regulatory choice, the process may be complex and place a burden on policymakers and regulators. Most studies suggest that the introduction of an effective new regulatory mechanism cannot be expected to be incorporated within the existing framework without proper consideration and assessment regarding the impact of the instrument on other rules and regulations, as well as the effect of such an approach for investors, creditors and other stakeholders. Therefore, any new shift in regulatory approach will necessarily require proponents to show how the proposed instrument or measure will significantly reduce costs and protect the interests of stakeholders.

That said, any attempt to propose a new EC company law reform based on a default rule analysis will be likely to create significant market and regulatory uncertainties. In this respect, it is proposed that the introduction of the options approach should occur initially in only a handful of areas. By adopting a simpler, unbundled approach it may be possible to pay closer inspection to the respective merits of the default measures and whether they are likely to be effective in practice. In the next sections, the company law and governance law that are best suited to mandates and the areas that would benefit, in principle, from legal options will be examined. This will permit us to propose a step-by-step approach allowing for early adoption of a limited number of legal options. A trial introductory phase would permit benchmarking and testing of their use and potential impact.

[44] E Berglöf and M Burkart, 'European Takeover Regulation', *Economic Policy* (April 2003), 171.

1. Mandatory Requirements

As noted above, the introduction of legal options does not eliminate the need for mandatory requirements to address the contracting problems of firms. A good example is corporate disclosure, an area in which regulatory mandates have significant coordination and standardisation advantages. It is worth noting also that legal options may have to be complemented by mandatory procedural rules.[45] In the next section, for example, we will show that EU opt-in or opt-out provisions would make little sense as a governance mechanism in a controlling shareholders environment unless reinforced by approval requirements such as minority shareholder or judicial ratification.

In recent years, the EU has adopted a fair number of transparency requirements. Despite the demand for more disclosure and the importance of such information for asset allocations, scholars have questioned the effectiveness of these reforms without the creation of an agency, such as a European SEC, to create credible incentives to induce firms to make reliable and accurate disclosure of financial and non-financial information.[46] Since none of the crucial enforcement mechanisms or institutions are likely to be introduced in the short term, it may not make much sense to propose new corporate disclosure requirements that will end up increasing cost to firms and provide little additional information to investors. Still, it appears that the mechanism of disclosure is particularly crucial for investors, especially in light of the recent sequence of increasingly blatant instances of misinformation by public companies (culminating with the Parmalat scandal). Hence, the emphasis given to it by policy-makers, despite the absence of effective enforcement bodies, is understandable.

The EU has recently adopted new auditing standards as well as requirements to rotate auditors on a regular basis and to designate a single, fully responsible auditor for groups of companies. However, some commentators question the efficiency of some of these new reforms for protecting the interests of investors. For example, even though Italy has been the first (and only) Member State to introduce auditor rotation requirements, it seems that this measure did little to prevent the Parmalat scandal—and may even have contributed to it. On the other hand, imposing some level of gatekeeper supervision could reinforce investors' confidence[47] and prevent

[45] G Hertig and JA McCahery, 'An Agenda for Reform: Company and Takeover Law in Europe' in G Ferrarini, K Hopt, J Winter and E Wymeersch (eds), *Modern Company and Takeover Law in Europe* (Oxford, OUP, 2004).

[46] G Hertig and R Lee, 'Four Predictions about the Future of Securities Regulation' (2003) 3 *Journal of Corporate Law Studies* 359.

[47] P Jain, J Kim and Z Rezaee, 'The Sarbanes-Oxley Act of 2002 and Market Liquidity' (2003), Working Paper, available at http://at ssrn.com.

auditors' liability from becoming prohibitive.[48] A case can thus be made for new auditing regulation that addresses some of the perceived technical shortcomings and the conflicts of interest problems that have contributed to costly governance failures.

Several comparative studies have shown that another, related, technique to reinforce investor confidence would be for the EU to liberalise the barriers to private enforcement.[49] Given the importance of ensuring effective financial reporting and limiting opportunism, law-makers could simply recognise all shareholders of firms incorporated in the EU as having the right to sue for breaches of shareholder voting rules and for violations of managerial or controlling shareholder fiduciary duties. At the same time, Member States could also be required to establish courts specialising in shareholder litigation, with the French Tribunal de Commerce, the German Handelsgericht or the Delaware Chancery Court as a possible model. Finally, the EU could further introduce reforms leading to the adoption of pre-trial discovery procedures and mass litigation devices such as class actions and contingent fees. Such a shift would build on mechanisms that already exist (in law or in fact) in several Member States, and would therefore appear to reinforce and extend the institutions that exist in these countries.

Yet there are a number of objections that could be advanced against such proposals. First, there is the view that EU policy-makers should address only substantive law issues, leaving the enforcement of company law and securities regulation to member governments. While the case can be made for such a view, it is not very persuasive, particularly in light of the level of harmful activity and the complexity of the regulatory task. In any event, EU policy-makers and the Commission naturally assume that the need for effective enforcement is a high priority of the EU and, given the large number of Member States' enforcement systems that clash with the fundamental objective of providing equivalent levels of substantive protection across the internal market, the EU has a role that would favour its intervention.[50]

Another, more fundamental, objection is that facilitating private litigation is not necessarily an effective or efficient means of curbing internal governance abuses. This is a difficult topic to tackle, not least because the evidence is murky. For example, US class actions were much criticised in the early 1990s as the source of abusive legal actions against auditors, and civil procedure reforms were passed to curtail their effectiveness. Today, these types of reforms are listed among the top reasons why auditors undertook

[48] JC Coffee, *Gatekeepers* (New York, OUP, 2006).

[49] G Hertig and JA McCahery, 'Company and Takeover Law Reforms in Europe: Misguided Harmonization Efforts or Regulatory Competition' (2003) 4 *European Business Organisation Law Review* 179.

[50] See Dir 2004/48/EC on the enforcement of intellectual property rights [2004] OJ L195/16; Market Abuse Dir 2003/6/EC [2003] OJ L96/16.

the more risky and conflicting activities that facilitated the occurrence of corporate scandals in recent years.[51] Or, to take another example, the jury system is often considered a crucial reason why damages awards are larger (and the level of litigation higher) in the US than in Europe. The empirical evidence, however, is mixed.[52] The effect of fees reforms on enforcement levels is yet another area where there is no clear direction which could give guidance in the debate. For many years, the law and economics literature has suggested that contingent fees are the fuel that has powered US-type litigation. Conversely, an apparently innocuous reduction of filing fees was apparently sufficient by itself to cause an impressive increase in shareholder litigation in Japan.[53]

It would seem that these studies make it difficult summarily to dismiss the efficiency of an EU-imposed reduction in enforcement barriers. On the other hand, it cannot be disputed that such a reform presupposes a sophisticated economic analysis of the costs and benefits of the proposed measures and their effect on other rules and procedures as well. More importantly, mandatory enforcement reforms would face fierce opposition by Member States, which challenge the facilitation of litigation on political, cultural or even protectionist grounds. In other words, any attempt to impose a reduction in enforcement barriers is likely to face considerable delay or even defeat. In short, it would make little sense to introduce mandatory requirements in this area. On the other hand, the ease with which the UK has sought to introduce new regulation on auditing and shareholder litigation suggests that some countries would certainly benefit from enhanced enforcement through private litigation and mandatory disclosure in order to shore up weak institutions.

2. Adopting EU Legal Options

In this section, it is proposed that the EU should adopt a regime that gives firms the freedom to choose among a menu of legal rules. A first step in this direction would be the adoption of a select number of opt-in provisions.

This menu approach, which was previously adopted by the EC in the case of the accounting directives, permits Member States to choose among more or less conservative standards as well as to exempt small to medium-sized firms (SMEs) from specific requirements deemed to be too costly. It is suggested

[51] Coffee, above n48.

[52] See T Eisenberg *et al.*, 'Juries, Judges, and Punitive Damages: An Empirical Study' (2002) 87 *Cornell Law Review* 743; and cf J Hersch and W Kip Viscusi, 'Punitive Damages: How Judges and Juries Perform' (2004) 33 *Journal of Legal Studies* 1.

[53] MD West, 'Why Shareholder Sue: The Evidence from Japan' (2002) 30 *Journal of Legal Studies* 351.

that this approach has important beneficial effects. It makes it easier for firms to identify variations in the Member States' rules. There is some evidence, moreover, that enhanced choice will lead Member States to switch to a less demanding regime for SMEs, and hence reduce the regulatory burden for this class of firms.

It is worth pointing out, however, that the Commission's experience with the accounting directives has been far from successful. To be sure, whilst there are a number of factors responsible, it seems likely that the problems may be primarily due to the options being designed to deal with regulatory concerns other than efficiency. More generally, the experience tends to confirm that it is generally a mistake to impose a fixed menu of options from the top. On the one hand, standardisation benefits are significantly reduced by such an approach, as there is no single set of EU provisions that firms and investors can rely upon. On the other hand, harmonisation costs are likely to increase. An additional key point is that adopting a finite menu of EU options will reduce Member States' willingness to compromise, as they have good reason to hope that a hard stance will ensure the adoption of an option that is close to their own preferences. Unfortunately, the likely result will be an inefficient set of options which has few benefits and thus is all the more difficult to justify. Secondly, the existence of multiple options should increase the petrifaction effect, as amendments would have to be coordinated and should thus be more difficult to pass than when there is only one mandate or one legal option. The potential weaknesses of the 'menu of legal options' approach suggest that it is not ideally suited to the current institutional and political environment, and hence should not be considered as an appropriate mechanism for the on-going company law reforms.

D. OPTING OUT OF EU PROVISIONS

It was argued earlier that an opting out approach is more efficient than a mandates approach, particularly where there are significant variations in corporate governance systems and company law regimes across the EU. In such a situation, a single mandatory set of EU provisions would have a different impact in each Member State, with many firms incurring costs far in excess of standardisation and other benefits. For example, differences in the use of the open corporate form by smaller firms and shareholder structures (dispersed or concentrated) can considerably affect the efficiency of director independence mandates.

By contrast, permitting Member States or firms to opt out of EU provisions should eliminate most of the costs due to legal diversity. Unsurprisingly this is particularly relevant in light of the debate on one-share-one-vote. The EC has recently announced plans to introduce legislation that would mandate one-share-one-vote. Most studies indicated that, within the EU, there are voting systems in which block-holders enjoy all or most of the private benefits. This appears to be a consequence of the use in many systems of dual class stock, non-voting ownership certificates, trust companies and other cash-flow rights. To be sure, there are instances of legal systems in which the 'one-share-one-vote' rule is central to the control of the company. Moreover, while many European firms commonly use dual class shares, there are significant differences in their impact across EU Member States.[54]

Given this diversity, the question is whether shareholders would support an EU proposal where there is some uncertainty about its potential outcome. Indeed, there are complex economic arguments in respect of the efficiency of the one-share-one-vote rule. On the one hand, deviations from the one-share-one-vote rule may decrease controlling shareholders' cost of capital[55] and possibly increase takeover efficiency.[56] On the other hand, the issue of dual class voting shares may facilitate the transfer of resources from the company to a large shareholder and lead to the oppression of minority shareholders. Thus shareholders, in balancing these considerations, will have to take account of a large number of factors in determining what capital structure can be expected to produce the highest value. This is a complex firm-specific undertaking, and shareholders may prefer having a one-share-one-vote regime that they can opt out of rather than having it imposed upon them.

This one-share-one-vote example is not meant to imply that opt-outs are costless. First, stickiness may prevent firms from opting out of all but the most costly EU provisions. Stickiness costs may, however, be reduced by adopting EU provisions that are tilted in favour of shareholders,[57] Secondly, allowing Member States to opt out of legal rules reduces the standardisation advantage of EU law-making, especially when corporate law regimes vary significantly. This is, however, precisely the situation where Member States are likely to oppose or delay mandatory harmonisation, but agree on opt-out provisions. Indeed, member governments' opposition to EU law-making should remain relatively light when they themselves are allowed to opt out. Naturally, opposition could be more significant when firms also have the right to opt out, but this can be mitigated by combining Member State opt-out powers and the firm's right to opt back into EU law.

[54] Deminor Ratings Service for Investors, 'Application of the One-Share-One-Vote Principle in Europe' (Mar 2005).

[55] O Hart and J Moore, 'Cooperatives vs. Outside Ownership' (1998), NBER Working Paper No 6421.

[56] But see JC Coates, 'Explaining Variations in Takeover Defenses: Blame the Lawyers' (2001) 89 *California Law Review* 1301; JA McCahery *et al.*, *The Economics of the Proposed Takeover Bids Directive* (Brussels, Centre for European Policy Studies, 2003).

[57] LA Bebchuk and A Hamdani, 'Optimal Defaults for Corporate Law Evolution' (2002) 96 *Northwestern University Law Review* 489.

That said, most studies indicate that it would be more efficient for the EU to adopt legal provisions with opting-out possibilities in many areas of company law and corporate governance. Such a proposal would have a number of advantages. First, it could enable Member States to opt out of the equitable price, squeeze-out and sell-out provisions in the Takeover Directive. Secondly, new firms would be subject to one-share-one-vote, no staggered boards, no voting caps, no pyramid structures requirements, but allowed to opt out in favour of the regime of the Member State in which they are incorporated—the latter limitation aiming at ensuring some degree of uniformity and transparency. Thirdly, shareholders of both new firms and firms established in new Member States could be given standing to sue for breaches of shareholder voting rules and violations of fiduciary duties, but be allowed to opt out in favour of the regime of the Member State in which they are incorporated. (By contrast, established firms in pre-2004 Member States could be permitted to opt into such a regime.)

At this stage, however, there are several cautions against the adoption of opt-out provisions in these areas of corporate law. In practice, such a reform could place too many items on the reform agenda, thereby creating the very same delay in implementation that has arisen under the Commission's mandatory company law harmonisation programme. At the same time, public choice theory predicts that it is always preferable to adopt a step-by-step approach when introducing new regulatory mechanisms. Finally, the shift to opt-out provisions must remain limited to avoid excessive legal diversity.

1. Opting into EU Law

Opting in to EU law is a key issue which is considered in this section. As argued above, it is submitted that EU intervention could increase firms' choice while avoiding reincorporation issues by supplying firms with selective opt-in provisions that allow them to opt out of *specific* Member State-level company law arrangements—as opposed to the full opt-out brought by reincorporation.

The opt-in approach may be cost-effective since it provides firms with a small menu of provisions, lowering transaction costs and increasing the degree of legal certainty. Firms may also be better served by opt-ins that credibly signal a commitment to comply with state-of-the-art regulation. Another important factor is that opt-in provisions can be useful for companies that must address legal difficulties, such as workers' participation requirements.

The opt-in approach, however, may also be compelled by political expediency. Subjecting an EU opt-in proposal on related party transactions, for instance, to a shareholder vote would have an impact in terms of constraining controlling shareholder opportunism—but still looks better than forgoing any intervention. Member States may also favour opt-in provisions to prevent the adoption of more efficient opting-out provisions. A potential example is a proposal on dividend rights for minority shareholders. Likewise, Member States could support opt-in provisions because they are likely to increase legal diversity and either make it more difficult for investors to ascertain the costs of their domestic regime or increase their own corporate law's stickiness.

Thus, the adoption of opt-in provisions, under certain conditions, could prove to be less cost-effective than expected. In such circumstances, caution is welcome when choosing opt-ins for existing companies, particularly when there are hard choices. Overall, it seems likely that the benefits of an opt-in approach will generally exceed its costs in areas where Member States have adopted costly mandatory provisions that cannot be dismantled through mandatory or opt-out EU intervention. In addition, the opt-in approach should be an appropriate one in areas where Member State law is diverse, but standardisation or 'best practice' signalling is important for investors or stakeholders.

Opt-ins seem particularly suited to dealing with Member States' mandatory provisions on employee participation structures, multiple voting and dividend rights, as well as on various takeover issues (board neutrality, mandatory bid thresholds and exit prices). However, EU mandatory requirements might, in some cases, be required to complement such opt-in arrangements, both to prevent Member States from opposing their adoption and to minimise managerial and shareholder opportunism. Thus, opting into EU employee participation provisions could, for instance, be made subject to third party approval by court ratification. Similarly, opting into EU multiple voting and dividend rights provisions or into EU mandatory bid thresholds and exit prices might be made subject to qualified majority or minority shareholder approval.

As far as standardisation and signalisation are concerned, new firms or firms incorporated in new Member States should benefit from opt-in provisions that establish simple and transparent procedures for the disclosure and approval of related party transactions (be it self-dealing, compensation agreements or the appropriation of corporate opportunities).

Finally, the opt-in approach could serve a pro-enforcement function. Under this approach, existing firms in 'old' Member States would be encouraged to choose this arrangement. To be sure, managers or controlling shareholders may resist such a move, fearing a reduction of their private benefits due to minority shareholder litigation. However, it may not even be necessary to give the majority of minority shareholders power to exercise the opt-in option for it to be effective. As recent events have shown, managers or controlling shareholders may endorse an opt-in measure, to the extent that it provides a civil enforcement alternative to criminal investigations and sanctions.

E. CONCLUSION: THE FUTURE OF THE PRO-CHOICE APPROACH

The review presented above suggests that it may be feasible in the near term for the EU to adopt the options approach. However, the EU's experience with options could prove short-lived if it cannot quickly develop a feasible role for them. Should options not play the role promised, the Commission could easily slip back into anti-choice mode if it perceived that there were better ways to maximise its role in the legislative process. In this respect, the Commission could be expected to revert to a mandatory approach should this secure the support of a law-making majority comprising Member States and members of the European Parliament opposed to regulatory arbitrage and competition.

However, it may be difficult for policy-makers to limit the momentum of the pro-freedom movement that has been opened up by the ECJ's freedom of establishment judgments. It is well established that legislative attempts to counter major case law developments are usually unsuccessful.[58] It is not unusual to see diverging positions gradually eroding toward a common middle ground, but this process is time-consuming and firms are unlikely to remain idle throughout the convergence process. Secondly, access to the pro-freedom path is now substantially controlled by the judiciary and pro-choice Member States, and is therefore largely outside the reach of a political alliance comprising the European Commission and anti-choice constituencies.

Moreover, it seems likely that Member States and interest groups opposed to regulatory arbitrage and competition may find it preferable to 'guide' firms' legal regime strategies through pro-choice EU legislation rather than engage in less effective mandatory harmonisation exercises. Indeed, given the mentioned history of slow reaction to major case law developments and continued diversity of national governance regimes, one should expect years of intergovernmental negotiations on the possible terms of the new mandatory measures. While generally accepted by parties in the past, this cumbersome process is unlikely to prove sustainable in the face of continuing regulatory arbitrage and competition.

On the other hand, a pro-choice approach could serve significantly ro accelerate the law-making process. More importantly, the approach is likely to permit EU law-makers to set the framework within which regulatory arbitrage and competition take place. Indeed, EU legal options have two major advantages. First, their standardisation value automatically extends to the EU as a whole. Secondly, they allow for selective choices. Firms will

[58] RD Cooter and T Ginsburg, 'Comparative Judicial Discretion' (1996) 16 *International Review of Law and Economics* 295.

be able to opt into those EU provisions they prefer, whereas Member States can offer only full opt-ins (incorporation or reincorporation results in the applicability of the corporate law regime as a whole).

Should the Commission be unable to obtain the required majority of Member States to endorse a reform programme based on options, it could revert to its earlier pro-mandatory harmonisation approach bias. More significantly, as demonstrated by the Takeover Bids Directive experience, such a reversal may even further tilt the balance in favour of pro-choice regulation by prompting reactions that will force the Commission to replace mandatory proposals with optional ones.

While it is difficult to predict with certainty, it is foreseeable that the Commission will move toward the adoption of a pro-choice approach, as such an approach provides the best mechanism to maximise the potential for successfully adopting and implementing 'essential' legislation. This assumption is reinforced by a variety of other considerations. Moreover, a review of the legislative history of the Takeover Bids Directive suggests that the key institutional actors within the EU have already recognised that there is no longer one single approach to regulatory design in corporate law provisions. Pro-choice arrangements are seen as a favoured mechanism to secure benefits in unrelated areas (eg trading takeover provisions against temporary workers legislation), to target regulatory beneficiaries (eg by allowing sophisticated capital market players to opt out of investor protection provisions) or to facilitate the EU enlargement process (eg by permitting firms in new Member States to signal their commitment to 'best practice' by opting into EU corporate law provisions). Thus, while options do not in themselves create efficiency, they are crucial for parties to bargain to such conclusions. A review of the evidence above suggests that EU company law may be in deficit and that options can play an important role in promoting the goals of economic integration.

14

Latest Developments in European Corporate Governance in Light of Better Regulation Efforts

DANIELA WEBER-REY*

STRENGTHENING SHAREHOLDER RIGHTS, reinforcing protection for employees and creditors and increasing the efficiency and competitiveness of business are the main aims of the Action Plan on 'Modernising Company Law and Enhancing Corporate Governance in the European Union—A Plan to Move Forward'[1] (CGAP) submitted by the Commission in 2003.

Whilst the CGAP sets forth a benchmark for improving the convergence of the European regulations in the fields of company law and corporate governance, it was not developed as a static instrument. Having been built under a Better Regulation approach—as becomes clear through the guiding political criteria[2]—its aims are to be developed and adapted to the constantly changing European environment.

The purpose of this chapter is to provide an overview of the efforts pursued during recent years at a European level in the field of corporate governance, in particular those having the CGAP (and its development) as a main driver. The chapter will also take into consideration the challenging endeavour to achieve Better Regulation.

* LLM, Attorney-at-law and partner, Clifford Chance, Frankfurt am Main; Member of the Advisory Group on Company Law Corporate Governance of the European Commission. I wish to thank Ana Paula Tavares, Transaction Lawyer at Clifford Chance, Frankfurt office, for her valuable assistance in the preparation of this chapter. Developments until 30 Sept 2006 have been taken into account.

[1] Communication from the Commission to the Council and to the European Parliament, Brussels, COM(2003)284 of 21 May 2003 (CGAP).

[2] *Ibid*, at 4–5.

A. THE CGAP OF THE EUROPEAN COMMISSION

1. Roots, Aims and Development

The CGAP goes back to the final report, 'Corporate Governance in the EU and the Modernisation of European Community Law', which was submitted by the High Level Group of Company Law Experts (chaired by Professor Jaap Winter) on 4 November 2002.[3] The High Level Group of Company Law Experts in its report invited the Commission to develop an Action Plan for Company Law and the European Council of 20 and 21 March 2003 confirmed the need for the adoption of an Action Plan by the Commission. The CGAP tackles, in essence, the recommendations of the High Level Group of Company Law Experts and is substantiated by the acknowledgement by the Commission that the framework of conditions for regulatory activities in the fields of company law and corporate governance in Europe urgently need modernisation and that this aim could be achieved either by adjusting existing corporate law instruments of the EU or by supplementing these with the aid of a limited number of new, tailor-made instruments.[4] The main areas to be covered are corporate governance, capital maintenance, corporate groups and pyramids, corporate restructuring, European Private Company, European Cooperatives and other forms of enterprises (see Figure 14.1).

In line with that, the CGAP sets out a comprehensive set of prioritised measures for adoption in the short (2003–5), medium (2006–8) and long term. The initiatives on corporate governance issues—intended to boost confidence in the capital markets—have all been classified as having short or medium term priority, and all short-term measures have already been adopted or, at least, been tabled (see Figure 14.2).[5]

Contents of the Corporate Governance Action Plan
Corporate Governance
Capital maintenance and alteration
Corporate restructuring and mobility
Groups of companies and pyramids
The European Private Company, European Co-operative Society and other EU legal forms of enterprise
Enhancing the transparency of national legal forms of enterprise

Figure 14.1—Contents of the Corporate Governance Action Plan.

[3] Available at http://ec.europa.eu/internal_market/company/docs/modern/report_en.pdf.

[4] Above n1, at 7.

[5] Directorate General Internal Market and Services, 'Consultation on Future Priorities for the Action Plan on Modernising Company Law and Enhancing Corporate Governance in the European Union', 20 Dec 2005, available at http://ec.europa.eu/internal_market/company/docs/consultation/final_report_en.pdf, at 2.

Short term measures 2003-2005	CONSULTATION	Medium term measures 2006-2008	Long term measures 2009 onwards
Corporate Governance European legal forms Capital maintenance Restructuring Groups of companies		Corporate Governance European legal forms Capital maintenance Restructuring Groups of companies Pyramids Transparency of national legal forms	Capital maintenance

Figure 14.2—Status of the Corporate Governance Action Plan.

In the meantime, much has changed in the European political and economic environment, and in particular a new awareness has surged that Europe needs an improved regulatory environment. This led the Commission to initiate a consultation procedure on the future priorities of the CGAP[6] so as to shed more light on its overall objectives, the context in which future priorities are to be implemented and the relevance of medium and long term measures, all of which have to be seen against the background of the Lisbon Strategy for growth and jobs,[7] as well as the objective of modernising and simplifying corporate law, in particular, to achieve 'Better Regulation'.[8] The issue of Better Regulation was also tackled by a consultation on the future Single Market policy launched by the Commission in April 2006.[9] The report on the public consultation[10] evidences that respondents applaud the Commission's efforts under the Better Regulation agenda, in particular the increasing use of consultations. There is broad agreement that Better Regulation efforts should be undertaken at both the EU and national levels. Support is also provided for the idea of

[6] Directorate General Internal Market and Services, 'Consultation and Hearing on Future Priorities for the Action Plan on Modernizing Company Law and Enhancing Corporate Governance in the European Union—Summary Report' (July 2006).

[7] The Lisbon Summit of Mar 2000 had set out a plan to reinvigorate Europe's economy and boost employment. This plan was re-launched by the European Commission in 2005. The 'renewed' efforts aim to revitalise the Lisbon Strategy—the EU's economic reform agenda from 2000. The EU Commission perceives that there is a need for action, as 5 years after its launch, the Lisbon Strategy was by a long way not on track to deliver the expected results: see Communication to the Spring European Council, 'Working Together for Growth and Jobs, a New Start for the Lisbon Strategy', COM(2005)24, at 2 and 19 ff; and Communication from the Commission to the Council and the European Parliament, 'Common Actions for Growth and Employment: The Community Lisbon Programme', COM(2005)330 of 20 July 2005, at 2.

[8] Above n6, at 2, 7, 24, 30 and 35.

[9] Available at http://ec.europa.eu/internal_market/strategy/docs/consultation_en.pdf.

[10] 'Public Consultation on a Future Single Market policy: Summary of Responses', SEC(2006)1215, 20 Sept 2006, available at http://ec.europa.eu/internal_market/strategy/docs/report-from-consultation_en.pdf.

screening national rules. Nevertheless, respondents request better feedback showing how stakeholders' views were taken into account and suggest practical improvements to impact on assessments and evaluations.[11]

2. The Better Regulation Approach to Corporate Governance

The measures proposed by the Commission in the CGAP are not intended to be developed arbitrarily by the Commission. The Commission has long recognised that EU-wide regulation can achieve the goals striven for within the EU only if the differences in the legal systems of the Member States and the appropriate economic considerations are taken into account.[12] The aim of Better Regulation can be achieved only in that way.

But what exactly does Better Regulation mean? Basically, Better Regulation means ensuring that the regulatory environment is simple and of high quality, that regulation is used only when necessary and that the burdens it imposes are proportionate to its aim. Its tools are an integrated impact assessment system, characterised by an analysis of the economic, social and environmental impacts of a legislative proposal, clear, consistent and transparent consultation rules and a simplification programme establishing criteria for a systematic assessment of existing legislation and preventing it from becoming obsolete.[13]

Consulting experts in the relevant fields when devising EU initiatives in the areas of company law and corporate governance will ensure that the results of the regulatory efforts make economic sense and will ultimately also be accepted by Member States. This is of considerable importance, particularly in the area of corporate governance and in the light of the urgent need to boost confidence in the capital markets. A good regulatory approach to corporate governance issues is a *conditio sine qua non* for the markets to function smoothly. Corporate governance legislation must therefore create adequate transparency standards, but must not overburden the companies.

It is important to understand this concept of Better Regulation as being the way to attain a lean regulatory environment which aims at imposing only as much of a burden as is necessary to reach the intended aims. This partially explains why the principles-based approach, built on the idea of 'substance over form', is gaining terrain in the European corporate

[11] Above n10, at 19–21.

[12] Eg L Goldschmidt and M Becht, 'Corporate Governance Principles and Recommendations', report for the European Association of Securities Dealers (May 2000) at 3; and European Corporate Governance Forum, Minutes of the Meeting of 20 Jan 2005, at 1.

[13] European Policy Forum, 'Evaluating Better Regulation: Building the System' (London, City Research Series no 9, 2006) at 4.

governance arena at the expense of the rules-based approach, which has attracted too much criticism in the United States in the last couple of years.

B. DIFFERING REGULATORY APPROACHES IN THE UNITED STATES AND THE EUROPEAN UNION

1. USA: Sarbanes–Oxley Act

The Sarbanes–Oxley Act (SOX),[14] named after its authors, Paul S Sarbanes, the chairman of the Senate Banking Committee, and Representative Michael G Oxley, was the reaction of the United States to various financial scandals (Enron and WorldCom, amongst others) and a general downturn in the global economy. Besides a reform of management responsibilities and an increase in the liability of auditors, requirements regarding the correctness of financial reporting were reinforced considerably. Self-regulation came to an end for the auditing profession and a new supervisory committee was established, namely the Public Company Oversight Accounting Board, to oversee the auditors of public companies.

The SOX has, in the meantime, drawn criticism. The tighter regulation of accounting and internal control structures is proving to be not only expensive but also largely ineffective.[15] From the American perspective, the high consequential costs of US-American capital markets legislation is also cause for concern. In the case of several non-US companies, those costs led to attempts to withdraw from the US capital market, or have decreased willingness to strive to list a company on the US stock exchange.[16] Even an extension of the deadline for foreign and smaller companies to fulfil the particularly contentious section 404 of the SOX, which was passed on 9 August 2006, does not really help under the circumstances, especially as a general revision of the SOX may not occur in the short term.[17]

The supervision of auditors and advisors being one of the key objectives of the SOX, it is odd to see that the same auditors and the same groups of advisors, as well as software firms, are in large part the ones whuch have ultimately benefited from the regulations.[18] Most notably the auditing

[14] The SOX entered into force on 30 June 2002.

[15] D Fockenbrock, 'Sarbanes–Oxley-Act—Außer Spesen nichts gewesen', *Handelsblatt*, 14 Mar 2006, at 16.

[16] A study conducted by Price Waterhouse Coopers and the BDI on 'Corporate Governance in Deutschland' (London, Price Waterhouse Coopers/EDI, Nov 2005) reached the same conclusion, as did a study recently conducted by the City of London and the London Stock Exchange entitled 'The Cost of Capital: An International Comparison' (June 2006), available at http://oxera.com.

[17] Oxford Analytica, 'SEC Tweaks Sarbanes-Oxley Rules', *Forbes Magazine*, 16 Aug 2006, available at http://forbes.com.

[18] 'Sarbanes-Oxley Act—A Price Worth Paying?', *The Economist*, 19 May 2006, available at http://economist.com.

firms are currently experiencing a boom due to an increase in the need for advice resulting from the implementation of and compliance with the statutory regulations. The misconduct of individual auditors which triggered the over-regulation through the SOX is now resulting in a considerably increased volume of work for the entire profession.

Most recently, US Treasury Secretary Henry Paulson suggested that some measures imposed by the SOX may need readjustment.[19] The onerous frame for listings in the US led to nine out of the 10 major IPOs carried out worldwide excluding a listing at a US exchange. Shortly after Paulson's statement, SEC Chairman Christopher Cox expressed the SEC's intention:

> to be sensitive and responsive to the particular needs of smaller public companies and foreign private issuers, and to minimize the burdens that Section 404 may impose on them.[20]

This approach may be regarded as the first step away from the strict rules of the SOX. A commission in charge of reviewing certain legislation with impact on US capital markets and in particular the SOX has meanwhile been set up and its recommendations are expected by the end of November 2006.[21] However, the market does not expect true changes. In connection therewith, the question arises whether the so-called 'rules-based' approach conceived in accordance with the US model is also suitable for Europe.

2. European Union: Corporate Governance Action Plan

Similarly to the SOX, the Corporate Governance Action Plan (CGAP) was passed under the influence of several financial scandals in the United States and Europe (eg the Ahold scandal[22]), with the principal objective being to reinforce confidence in the financial markets. The aim of the CGAP is neither to harmonise corporate governance standards which have developed in the individual Member States over the last few years and decades, nor to introduce a mandatory corporate governance regime in the EU. On the

[19] S Taub, 'Paulson: Regs Went Too Far', *CFO*, 1 Aug 2006, available at http://cfo.com.

[20] 'SEC Proposes Rules to Ease Sarbanes-Oxley Requirements for Smaller Public Companies, Foreign Private Issuers', *Roundtable Weekly*, available at www.rer.org/roundtable/previousissues/Roundtable_Weekly_Aug11_2006.cfm; SEC Release No 33-8730A; SEC Release No 33-8731 and summary at www.sec.gov/news/press/2006/2006-136.htm (9 Aug 2006).

[21] 'Weniger Marktregulierung in Amerika geplant—Ausschluß von Wirtschaftsvertretern erarbeitet Vorschläge für eine Reform von Sarbanes-Oxley', *Frankfurter Allgemeine Zeitung*, 13 Sept 2006, at 13.

[22] The former European Commissioner for the Internal Market Frits Bolkestein described the Enron, WorldCom, Ahold and (following the launch of the Action Plan) Parmalat financial scandals as being part of a 'hall of shame', SPEECH/04/331 of 24 June 2004.

contrary, the Action Plan is expressly not meant to constitute a European Corporate Governance Code.[23] Rather, a corporate governance regime harmonising a number of key areas is meant to be created through the harmonisation of some key provisions in conjunction with close coordination of national legislation in accordance with the principles prescribed by the Action Plan.[24] Convergence of corporate governance should evolve in a natural way rather than being enforced. This principle-based approach, which is the mandatory consequence of the EU's subsidiarity system,[25] permits the flexible use of a variety of regulatory instruments which are available to the European legislator (see Figure 14.3).

USA	EU
Sarbanes-Oxley Act (SOX) (2002) • Protect investors by improving the accuracy and reliability of corporate disclosure. • Far-reaching rules on accounting oversight, auditor independence, corporate responsibility, enhanced financial disclosure and corporate and criminal fraud accountability. • Establishing a far-reaching enforcement and punishment regime.	**Corporate Governance Action Plan (2003)** • No "one-size-fits-all" approach given the many different national Corporate Governance models. • Combination of harmonising a few essential rules with closer co-ordination between national codes. • No European Corporate Governance Code.
⇩	⇩
Rules-based approach	Principle-based approach
⇩	⇩
• SOX is criticized as exemplifying "low-quality legislative decision-making in the context of a crisis" with high administrative costs. • Many European companies are keen to withdraw their US listing to escape Sarbanes-Oxley.	• The revised Lisbon Agenda of 2005 aims at focusing the EU's effort on two principle tasks: accelerate growth and generate more employment and better jobs. • One of the eight key actions of the Lisbon Agenda is to improve and simplify the regulatory framework in which business operates.

Figure 14.3—Different Approaches in the EU and in the USA.

[23] Above n1, at 13; this position was also expressly supported by the European Corporate Governance Forum in its opinion on the 'comply or explain' principle of 22 Feb 2006, available at http://ec.europa.eu/internal_market/company/docs/ecgforum/ecgf-comply-explain_en.pdf.

[24] MEMO/03/112 dated 21 Mar 2003.

[25] Art 5 EC The subsidiarity principle is one of the policy guidelines of the CGAP, cf above n1, at 5, and was also referred to as one of the key guidelines by participants in the consultation on the other priorities of the Action Plan: cf above n6.

3. Rules-based v. Principles-based

The EU approach is substantially different from the one followed in the United States. The SOX is based on a strict set of rules (rules-based), whereas in the EU the more flexible principles-based regulation applies. In other words, in contrast to the United States where the top priority is the highest possible degree of legal certainty achieved by the application of strict rules which prescribe detailed procedures intended to cover any potential scenario, in Europe the aim is to implement fundamental standards and principles granting flexibility while following a minimum harmonisation approach.

Several measures developed as a consequence of the CGAP do not provide for any binding regulation. Rather, they are intended to exert pressure, in the form of recommendations, on both European companies to improve their corporate governance and on the Member States and regulatory authorities for an improved implementation of those improvements,[26] ultimately resulting in convergence[27] in the EU and achieving the objectives of the revised Lisbon Strategy.[28]

In the United States, the rules-based approach is frequently blamed as being a potential contributory cause of the US corporate and accounting scandals, as detailed regulations also show how to develop measures which can be used to circumvent such regulations.[29] Principles, on the other hand, can by virtue of the variability of their implementation, be achieved with less cost and greater flexibility.

Whilst some authors express the view that non-binding principles of a non-obligatory nature are of little value,[30] other commentators are now increasingly holding the view that good corporate governance can be achieved—or can be achieved only—through the flexibility which is an inherent feature of the principles-based approach. Steps should be taken to promote appropriate values and ethical behaviour which ensure compliance: in other words, a commitment to the principles.[31] The desire to earn the reputation of being reliable in the market is ultimately also an incentive to comply with directives.

On the strength of past experience with the SOX, Europe stands to learn from the mistakes of others and has the chance to develop different

[26] Above n24.

[27] Being the mildest method besides harmonisation or simplification at the EU level.

[28] Above n7.

[29] Cf P Leibfried and P Meixner, 'Konvergenz der Rechnungslegung, Bestandsaufnahme und Versuch einer Prognose' (2006) 4 *Der Schweizer Treuhänder* 211.

[30] PA Gourevitch and J Shinn, *Political Power and Corporate Control: The New Global Politics of Corporate Governance* (Princeton, NJ, Princeton University Press, 2005), cited by LH Teslik, 'Governing Corporations in a Shrinking World' (22 Feb 2006), available at www.cfr.org/publication.

[31] DL Seidman, 'The New "How" Of Effective Board Governance' (12 July 2005), available at http://forbes.com.

approaches. There is no single universal solution and no 'one-size-fits-all' approach to good corporate governance. There are various models available which are, however, all largely based on generally applicable principles.[32] In any event, Europe has set itself the challenge of modernising its company law and corporate governance framework under the underlying principle of Better Regulation.

C. STRIVING TO ACHIEVE BETTER REGULATION

1. The Need for Change

One of the basic characteristics of Better Regulation is to leave what is good as it is, abolish what is not needed and change what is obsolete.[33] The revision of the CGAP must thus be seen in this context. Due to the general improvement in the overall economic situation over the last few years in conjunction with a restoration of confidence in financial markets, some of the original objectives of both the SOX and the CGAP have over the years become outdated and must be revised. Whilst criticism of the SOX in its current form grows in the United States,[34] the European Commission has reacted by putting any medium and long-term measures of the CGAP, which had not been implemented, on the agenda for consultation.[35] This consultation[36] was intended to examine any CGAP measures yet to be taken in the light of both the revised Lisbon Strategy for economic growth and jobs[37] and the Better Regulation principles so as to determine the further course of action.

2. Better Regulation Initiative

The issue of Better Regulation was first taken up at the European level at the Edinburgh European summit of December 1992.[38] European heads of state decided to make the task of simplifying and improving the EU

[32] OECD Principles of Corporate Governance (Paris, OECD, 2004), available at http://www.oecd.org/dataoecd/32/18/31557724.pdf, at 13.

[33] Communication from the Commission, 'Action Plan "Simplifying and improving the regulatory environment"', COM(2002)278.

[34] Above nn18, 31 and R Romano, 'Quack Corporate Governance' (Winter 2005–6) *Regulation* 36.

[35] Cf.sect D.

[36] Above n5.

[37] Above n7.

[38] Better Regulation initiatives have already been pursued in several EU Member States for several years. In the late 1990s, the Netherlands had already introduced its Standard Costs Model (cf, eg, www.actal.nl) and also the UK promoted a simplification and improvement of legislation as early as 1997 through the launch of the Better Regulation Task Force (in the meantime superseded by the Better Regulation Commission): see www.brc.gov.uk/.

regulatory environment one of the Community's main priorities. In 1996, the so-called SLIM Initiative (Simpler Legislation for the Internal Market) was introduced.[39] In the years that followed, the results were limited, though mainly due to the complexity of the task and the lack of real political support. By 2001, the SLIM Initiative had reviewed 17 legislative areas[40] during five consecutive phases and undertook simplification and streamlining.

In July 2001, the Commission published a White Paper on the issue of 'European Governance'[41] which, amongst other things, provided for the improvement of the quality and effectiveness of legislative procedures. Following the White Paper, in 2003 the Commission published three consecutive statements on (a) simplification and improvement of the surrounding regulatory environment,[42] (b) impact assessments,[43] and (c) increased consultation of interested parties.[44] These statements are intended to contribute to the improvement of the quality and transparency of the Commission's work. In 2003 the Commission published a statement entitled 'Updating and Simplifying the Community *Acquis*'[45] which intends to show how company law can be made clearer, more understandable and more concise.

In order to ensure that the legal framework of the EU meets the requirements of the twenty-first century, a new initiative was launched by the Commission in 2005 building on previous initiatives for Better Regulation,[46] which is aimed at simplifying the existing and future *acquis communautaire*.[47] The special relevance of this initiative is most notably recognisable by the fact that the Commission identified Better Regulation as constituting one of the key measures in pursuing the objectives of the

[39] Above n33; further information on SLIM initiatives is available at http://europa.eu.int/comm/internal_market/simplification/index_de.htm.

[40] The reviewed areas included the First and Second Company Law Dirs as well as eg insurance law.

[41] 'European Governance—a white paper', COM(2001)428, of 25 July 2001.

[42] Above n33.

[43] 'Communication from the Commission on impact assessment', COM(2002)276, of 5 June 2002.

[44] Consultation document, 'Towards a reinforced culture of consultation and dialogue—Proposal for general principles and minimum standards for consultation of interested parties by the Commission', COM(2002)277, of 5 June 2002.

[45] Communication from the Commission to the Council, the European Parliament, the European Economic and Social Committee and the Committee of the Regions, 'Updating and simplifying the Community acquis', COM(2003)71, of 11 Feb 2003; cf below n47.

[46] Communication from the Commission to the Council and the European Parliament, 'Better Regulation for Growth and Jobs in the European Union', COM(2005)97, of 16 Mar 2005.

[47] The *acquis communautaire* includes all legislation which is binding on all the EU Member States, as well as primary legislation (Treaties of the European Union) and secondary legislation (regs, dirs, recs, etc).

renewed Lisbon Strategy focusing on delivering stronger growth and creating more jobs.[48] In the Commission communication 'Better Regulation for Growth and Jobs in the European Union'[49] the concept for the Better Regulation initiative was proposed, building on previous initiatives. Political objectives are addressed within this framework: (i) Better Regulation, (ii) better design of regulations so as to increase the benefits for citizens, (iii) reinforcement of the respect for and the effectiveness of the rules, and (iv) minimisation of the cost burden of those required to abide by the new rules, all of which are in line with the principles of reasonableness and subsidiarity.[50]

To achieve these objectives, the Commission has a number of tools and processes at its disposal, and it is now making more use of them than it did in the past. Such tools and processes include: (i) withdrawal or modification of pending legislative proposals, (ii) measures to simplify existing legislation, and (iii) improved impact assessments and increased use of public consultation.[51]

(a) Withdrawal or Modification of Pending Legislative Proposals

In this context,[52] 183 legislative proposals[53] pending before the European Parliament and Council were screened prior to 27 September 2005. On 17 March 2006, the Commission withdrew 67 new legislative proposals as an outcome of the screening process. The pending legislative proposals were scrutinised according to whether the respective proposals (i) were consistent with the new Lisbon strategy for growth and jobs, and thus able to contribute to competitiveness, (ii) met the Better Regulation standards, (iii) would have a realistic chance of being adopted if they were left on the table, or (iv) had, in the meantime, become obsolete. Among the legislative proposals that were screened and ultimately withdrawn were the Statute of the European Association and the Statute of the European Mutual Society, two projects which were among the medium-term measures of the CGAP. [54]

[48] Communication from the Commission to the Council and the European Parliament, 'Common Actions for Growth and Employment: The Community Lisbon Programme', COM(2005)330, of 20 July 2005, at 4.

[49] Above n46.

[50] Above n49, at 2.

[51] Further information is available at http://ec.europa.eu/enterprise/regulation/better_regulation/index_de.htm#with.

[52] Communication from the Commission to the Council and the European Parliament, 'Outcome of the screening of legislative proposals pending before the legislator', COM(2005)462, of 27 Sept 2005.

[53] All pending proposals dated before 1 Jan 2004.

[54] See sect C.3 below regarding the position of the European Parliament as to the withdrawal of proposals.

(b) Measures to Simplify Existing Legislation

The main aim of the Better Regulation Initiative is to simplify the existing *acquis communautaire* which at the end of 2005 consisted of 80,000 pages.[55] Using various measures available to it, the Commission plans to simplify 222 basic items of legislation consisting of, all in all, over 1,400 related legal acts between 2005 and 2008.[56] It remains unclear to what extent the Commission's objectives can be fulfilled within the proposed timeframe. Of the 54 simplification proposals which were planned for 2006, only five had been completed by mid-year.[57]

(i) Repealing EU legislation Acts which have become irrelevant or obsolete due to technical or technological progress or the evolution of policies pursued by the European Union shall, in future, be reviewed and formally repealed. A key problem in this respect is that it can be argued that the repeal of an EU act should be followed by the repeal of the corresponding national implementing legislation.

To ensure that future acts meet Better Regulations requirements, review clauses or sunset clauses[58] have been introduced into Commission legislative proposals to compel the legislator to check regularly the relevance, effectiveness and proportionality of the regulations in force and to facilitate any repeal of acts in future. Irrespective thereof, a review of existing EU legislation every couple of years has become standard practice in many areas of EU law.

(ii) Codification The Commission has set itself the goal of codifying all Community secondary legislation by 2007 to provide more readable and legally secure texts. Such codification is a noble aim, but pure codification without further adjustments seems hardly feasible. The recasting of legislation takes a long time, needs a large number of resources and may not bring the expected simplification. To take the example of the United Kingdom, where company law has been undergoing recasting for 10 years, the new Company Law Act will be over 50 per cent longer than the original legislation and case law it is codifying. This codification programme thus runs the risk of 'opening Pandora's box'.

[55] Communication of the Commission to the European Parliament, the Council, the European Economic and Social Committee and the Committee of the Regions, 'Implementing the Community Lisbon programme: A strategy for the simplification of the regulatory environment', COM(2005)535 of 25 Oct 2005.

[56] IP/05/1343 of 25 Oct 2005.

[57] W Proissl, 'Barrosos Agenda gerät ins Stocken', 13 July 2006, available at www.ftd.de.

[58] Whilst a sunset clause results in the withdrawal of the relevant legislation containing such clause after a certain period of time, a review clause means that the legislator is compelled to check the further relevance and reasonableness of the relevant legislation in force after a certain period of time: cf above n55, at 7.

(iii) Recasting to clarify and improve consistency Recasting simultaneously amends and codifies the legal acts in question. Priority will be given to the merging of legal acts to maximise synergies and minimise overlaps and redundancies. An example of this is the simplification of the Second Company Law Directive which established a system giving minimum guarantees to shareholders and creditors where public limited companies are set up or alter their share capital.[59] This system was found to be too inflexible and costly[60] and, therefore, agreement was reached on a proposal containing numerous modifications, which has been available since 13 July 2006.[61] As in the case of pure codification, simultaneous amendment and codification likewise entail a risk of overreaching by unnecessarily modifying provisions which have proven to be beneficial and sensible, at great expense and for minimal benefit.

(iv) More co-regulation and self-regulation 'Soft' legal instruments such as co-regulation and self-regulation are alternative ways of implementing certain policy objectives. They are considered to be far more cost-efficient and expedient methods than the classical legislative tools. Standardisation by independent bodies is an example of a well recognised 'co-regulation' instrument.[62]

The principle of 'comply or explain' is also part of the category of self-regulatory measures. According to EU Commissioner Charlie McCreevy, the principle of 'comply or explain' is a central element of European corporate governance.[63] It provides for more flexible and market-led regulation.[64] However, in Europe there is an awareness that the principle of 'comply or explain' can work only if its surrounding regulatory framework ensures that companies comply with corporate governance rules or provide proper justification for any deviation from them.[65] The requirements imposed on companies to issue a public statement confirming their compliance with

[59] 2nd Council Dir 77/91/EEC of 13 Dec 1976 on the co-ordination of safeguards which, for the protection of the interests of shareholders and others, are imposed by Member States on companies in accordance with the 2nd para of Art 58 of the Treaty, in respect of the formation of public limited liability companies and the maintenance and alteration of their capital, with a view to making such safeguards equivalent 1977 OJ L26/1; the provisional text for an amendment of the 2nd Company Dir has been available since 13 July 2006: see PE-CONS 3608/06.

[60] In 1999 by the SLIM Group (SLIM—Simpler Legislation for the Internal Market) and in 2002 once again by the High Level Group of Company Law Experts.

[61] PE-CONS 3608/06 of 13 July 2006 and IP/06/312 of 14 Mar 2006.

[62] Eg, the CE marking of products indicates that the relevant product is safe, was approved and registered and may be marketed throughout the EU: cf MEMO/05/394 of 25 Oct 2005, at 5.

[63] See IP/06/269 of 6 Mar 2006.

[64] Declaration by the European Corporate Governance Forum on the principle of 'comply-or-explain' of 22 Feb 2006, available at http://europa.eu.int/comm/internal_market/company/docs/ecgforum/ecgf-comply-explain_en.pdf.

[65] IP/06/269 of 6 Mar 2006.

the corporate governance rules will increasingly lead to companies complying with the relevant principles of corporate governance, the motivation of companies for this being to enhance their credibility and to boost the confidence of investors. This is definitely a step towards reaching the aim of self-regulation.

The principle of 'comply or explain' was introduced with legally binding effect for the first time by Directive 2006/46/EC of 16 August 2006,[66] which provides for an obligation to publish a Corporate Governance Statement. This must be transposed into national law by Member States by 5 September 2008.[67] Pursuant thereto,[68] all companies whose securities are admitted to trading on a regulated market and which have their corporate seats situated within the Community are in the future to provide a statement in their business reports confirming their compliance with corporate governance standards.[69] This also means that companies without listed shares but having other financial instruments listed on a regulated market have in the future to issue a correspondent statement.

The minimum requirements that should be met by such statements include, amongst other things, (i) a reference to the corporate governance code to which the company is subject and/or to which the company voluntarily committed, and (ii) a declaration of deviations from the code in compliance with national law or, as the case may be, a justification of the

[66] Dir 2006/46/EC of the European Parliament and of the Council of 14 June 2006, amending Council Dirs 78/660/EEC on the annual accounts of certain types of companies, 83/349/EEC on consolidated accounts, 86/635/EEC on the annual accounts and consolidated accounts of banks and other financial institutions, and 91/674/EEC on the annual accounts and consolidated accounts of insurance undertakings 2006 OJ L224/49.

[67] In Germany for instance, an instrument referred to as based on a 'comply or explain' principle was introduced on 25 July 2002 in the form of the declaration of compliance provided for in s161 of the German Stock Corporation Act (Aktiengesetz, AktG). Although this instrument is considered to embody a 'comply or explain' principle, it is in fact more a principle of 'comply or state non-compliance', without any information on why any corporate governance rules are not being complied with. In accordance with s161 of the German Act on Public Limited Companies, the executive board and supervisory board of a publicly listed stock corporation are required to issue an annual declaration that the company has complied and is complying with the recommendations of the Government Commission on the German Corporate Governance Code and to declare which recommendations have not been or are not being applied: See J Semler, in B Kropff and J Semler (eds), *Münchener Kommentar* (2003), margin n 11, on s161 of the German Act on Public Limited Companies; and T Baums *et.al.*, *Bericht der Regierungskommission Corporate Governance* (Cologne, 10 July 2001), margin n 8 ff.

[68] Art 46a of Dir 78/660/EEC 1978 OJ L222/11.

[69] Even companies that have not issued shares traded on a regulated market, but have issued other securities traded on such a market must issue such a declaration. According to the German Securities Trading Act (Wertpapierhandelgesetz, WpHG) the obligation is thus also directed not only at companies having issued shares but also at companies having issued certificates representing shares, bonds, profit-participation certificates, warrants and other securities which are comparable to shares (eg interim certificates) or bonds (eg those containing a contractual right to recover a debt or performance undertakings) and investment fund units which are issued by a German or by a foreign investment company.

non-application of the entire code or individual provisions thereof in compliance with the principle of 'comply or explain'. This will reach beyond the obligation pursuant to section 161 of the German Stock Corporation Act,[70] as upon implementation of the Directive the relevant companies not accepting the code or parts thereof will not only have to declare their non-acceptance but will also have to explain why they do not accept. The extent of the underlying explanation is, however, not prescribed in the Directive. A general explanation, even solely subjective in nature, may well suffice.

(v) The use of regulations as a simplification tool Unlike co-regulation and self-regulation, using 'strict' legal instruments can under certain circumstances be conducive to simplification. Unlike directives, regulations are not only directly applicable but they can also be amended relatively easily. The use of regulations instead of directives can help to avoid the trap of diverging interpretations in the implementation phase in the Member States, and will simplify handling pressing matters, thus guaranteeing that all Member States are subject to the same rules at the same time. In addition, this procedure has the advantage that attention is focused on practical enforcement of, and compliance with, the relevant EU rules/requirements. In particular, the practice of gold-plating, whereby national bodies exceed the terms of European directives when implementing them into national law, should thus be avoided. By substituting directives with regulations, the lengthy implementation procedure imposed on each Member State by directives and the repetition of this each time there are technical amendments can be avoided.

(c) Improved Impact Assessment and Increased Use of Public Consultation Procedures

Regulatory Impact Assessments (RIA) are of paramount importance for Better Regulation. Although they are not binding, they do help the decision process[71] and serve to evaluate the likely economic, social and environmental impacts of legislative measures, to improve the quality of proposals and to assess different options. In future years, all key initiatives undertaken by the Commission will be subject to a comprehensive impact assessment.

The involvement of affected or interested parties in the legislative process is to be reinforced by increased consultation procedures involving these groups, primarily with regard to impact assessments, to ensure better quality of the legislative measures and to increase transparency.

An example of public consultation and extensive impact assessments is the proposal for a directive on facilitating the exercise of shareholder

[70] Above n67.
[71] European Policy Forum, above n5, at 4.

rights. After holding two public consultations, the Commission submitted a proposal for a directive[72] on 5 January 2006, which, among other things, is intended to facilitate the timely access to complete information by shareholders in respect of shareholders' meetings and the exercising of voting rights by postal vote.[73] Once the proposal for a directive had been published, the Commission submitted a comprehensive impact assessment of the Directive.[74] Despite these precautionary measures, the submission of the proposal for a directive sparked an intense discussion amongst experts on individual issues. It is obvious that an impact assessment does not mean that all issues in connection with the Directive can be dealt with exhaustively and satisfactorily.[75] Nevertheless, Impact Assessments provide the chance to address the opinions and concerns of those companies affected by a proposed measure and to avoid any unnecessary or unnecessarily burdensome regulations.[76]

3. Revised Approach to Better Regulation

The Commission's approach to Better Regulation as described above may be about to undergo a review, resulting from the most recent motion of the European Parliament.[77] In its Motion for a European Parliament Resolution,[78] the European Parliament highlights the importance of Better Regulation and accepts that simplification of the *acquis* can be an efficient tool to enhance the coherence of Community legislation, in particular in the field of company law. However, the European Parliament highlights at the same time that simplification does not mean deregulation, and that withdrawals of proposals previously submitted by the Commission cannot be justified by reference to Better Regulation. This goes against one of the main approaches of the Commission in the field of Better Regulation, which is the withdrawal or modification of pending legislative proposals[79] and seems to question the essence of Better Regulation.

[72] COM(2005)685 of 5 Jan 2006.

[73] IP/06/10 of 10 Jan 2006.

[74] Commission staff working document, 'Annex to the Proposal for a Directive of the European Parliament and of the Council on the exercise of voting rights by shareholders of companies having their registered office in a Member State and whose shares are admitted to trading on a regulated market and amending Dir 2004/109/EC—impact assessment', SEC(2006)181 of 17 Feb 2006.

[75] For criticism of Impact Assessments see 'Was soll der Quatsch?', *Frankfurter Allgemeine Zeitung*, 22 Aug 2006, at 15.

[76] *Ibid.*

[77] 'Report of the European Parliament on recent developments and prospects in relation to company law' (2006/2051 (INI)), 4 July 2006.

[78] Part of *ibid*, in the version submitted by the Committee on Legal Affairs, 26 June 2006.

[79] See sect C.2.I above.

Considering the current review of the European comitology procedure which will lead to a new 'regulatory procedure with scrutiny',[80] giving the Parliament enlarged powers and in particular the competence to scrutinise the adoption of 'quasi-legislative'[81] measures by the Commission and to block implementing decisions taken by the Commission, it becomes clear that the Parliament wishes to regain a stronger control over European law-making, even if that be to the detriment of Better Regulation (see Figure 14.4).

Whether the current approach to Better Regulation will only slightly change or whether it will be thoroughly reviewed—leading to the substitution of Better Regulation by a 'quasi-Better Regulation', remains to be seen. It is clear, however, that the Commission wants to pursue compliance with its Better Regulation principles.[82]

D. FUTURE PRIORITIES OF THE CGAP

1. Background for the Review of the CGAP

Independently of the most recent changes to the comitology procedure and approach to Better Regulation,[83] the development of the CGAP is to be seen in light of the efforts to achieve Better Regulation, as it has been understood hitherto. Consequently, complying with the premise that legislation and recommendations must not be static but rather flexible enough to adapt to economical and political changes, the Commission conducted a consultation to examine the extent to which the medium and long-term measures under the CGAP of 2003 and the Lisbon Strategy need to be modified. The goal was furthermore to determine whether, on the basis of the Commission's efforts to achieve Better Regulation, simplification of European legislation in the field of company law is feasible and/or necessary.[84]

As a result of changes to the economic and regulatory environment, today's framework conditions differ from those at the time of the adoption of the original Action Plan. It has to be ensured that the Action Plan—as

[80] Report of the European Parliament on the conclusion of an interinstitutional agreement taking a form of a joint statement concerning the draft for a Council Decision amending Dec 1999/468/EC laying down the procedures for the exercise of implementing powers conferred on the Commission (new regulatory procedure with scrutiny) (10126/1/2006-C6-0208/2006-2006/2152(ACI)), including accompanying statements, 3 July 2006.

[81] Statement to be adopted at a forthcoming trialogue between the European Parliament, the Council and the Commission, Annex 1 to *ibid*.

[82] Below n86.

[83] See sect A.2.

[84] In detail, the consultation consisted of questions which were aimed at clarifying and evaluating the following issues: the overall aim and context for future priorities; the relevance of medium and long-term measures in light of the Lisbon Agenda; and the benefit of modernising and simplifying company law, with particular regard to the Better Regulation efforts.

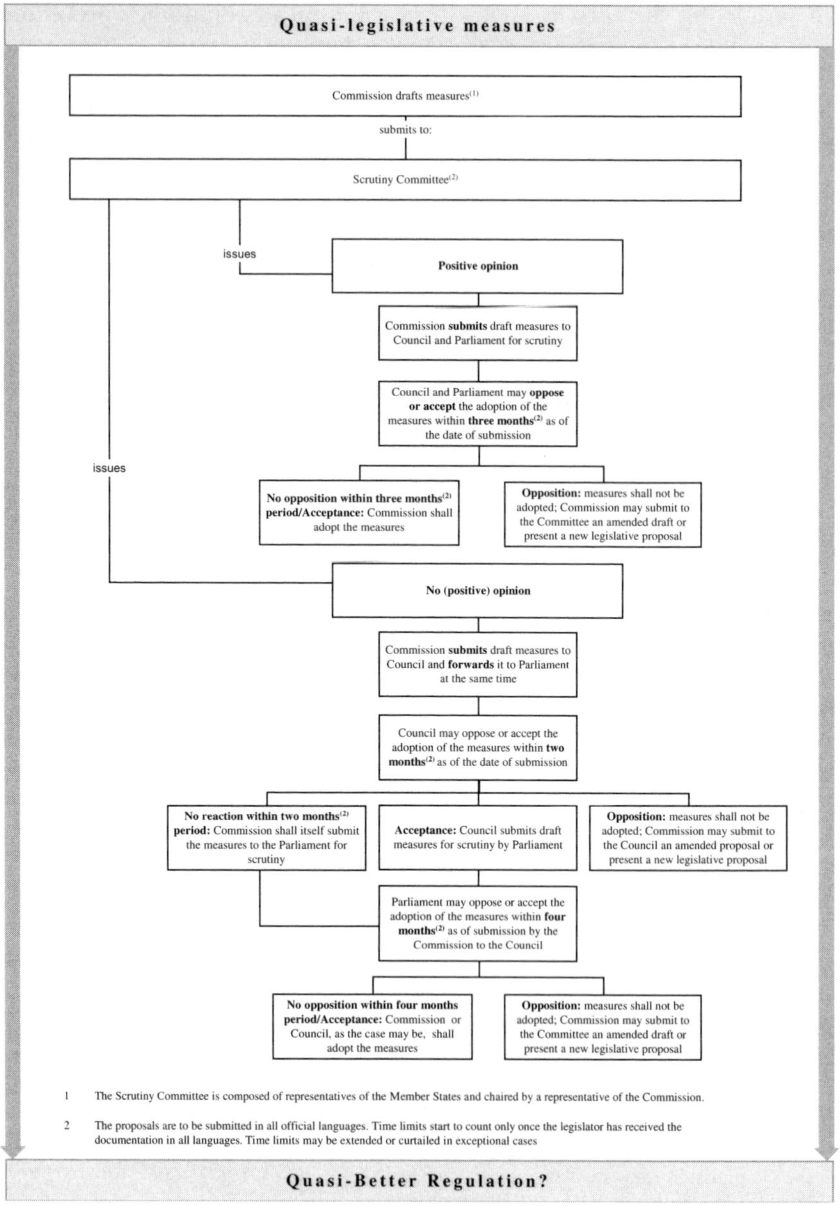

Figure 14.4—The New Comitology Procedure with Scrutiny.

adapted or refocused—continues to meet the requirements of the market and seeks to ensure its effectiveness and efficiency.

2. Public Consultation

The consultation which was concluded on 31 March 2006 was attended by 266 interest groups in total, from both Member States of the European Union and third countries.[85]

(a) Support for the Application of Better Regulation Principles

A large number of participants supported increasingly using consultation in the future as a way for them to be better involved in the legislative process. In particular, the Better Regulation principles[86] presented in the consultation were greatly appreciated and a large majority of the participants were in favour of a stricter application of the principles of subsidiarity and proportionality and a simplification and improvement of legislation. A certain 'regulatory fatigue' is evident, however, and, on the one hand, having completed the measures under the Financial Services Action Plan (FSAP)[87] and, on the other hand, pronounced themselves in favour of the short-term priorities for the CGAP, several participants long for a stabilisation phase. However, it is not their wish that the regulatory process be halted entirely, in particular in the areas in which measures at the EU level are essential.[88]

(b) Disclosure of Institutional Investors' Voting Policies

In the area of Corporate Governance, the consultation raises the question to what extent increased disclosure of investment policies and policies with respect to the exercise of voting rights of institutional investors should be regulated.[89] This question evoked various responses. On the one hand, it was claimed that further regulatory measures in this area could create

[85] Above n6, at 2.

[86] The Better Regulation principles presented included the following: (i) increased consultations of the affected parties, (ii) greater focus of legislative initiatives on measures which are (a) indispensable and (b) keep any burden on companies to a minimum, and (iii) carrying out impact assessments on a regular basis: above n5, at 5.

[87] Communication of the Commission, 'Implementing the framework for financial markets: action plan', COM(1999)232, at 22 ff.

[88] In particular, the drafts of the Dir on the Transfer of the Registered Office and the Reg on a European Company were referred to in this respect.

[89] Directorate General for Internal Market and Services, 'Consultation on Future Priorities for the Action Plan on Modernising Company Law And Enhancing Corporate Governance in the European Union', available at http://ec.europa.eu/internal_market/company/docs/consultation/consultation_en.pdf, at 7. See also Summary Report, above n6, at 12 ff.

administrative impediments, and many participants are in favour of such matters being dealt with on a contractual level. On the other hand, several participants emphasised that a solution under European law is desirable in order to create a level playing field in all Member States.

(c) Board Structure

The push for a uniform Europe-wide solution in respect of the choice between a one-tier board structure (with executive and non-executive directors) and a two-tier board structure (with managing directors and supervisory directors) was deemed by the majority of the consultation participants not to require regulatory action.[90] Should a regulation nevertheless be introduced at European level, the consultation participants would prefer a general principle-based approach, if possible. [91]

(d) Proportionality of Capital and Control

The consultation likewise addressed the issue of how shareholder rights can be further strengthened. Whilst several participants would prefer this matter to be dealt with at EU level, others, by contrast, are of the view that shareholders' interests are already adequately protected. The proposal that received most support was that of introducing an EU-wide right of shareholders to demand a special audit, whereas only a minority of consultation participants supported other proposals such as the possibility to appoint and remove members of the management or administrative corporate bodies and to facilitate communications between shareholders.

Whether shareholders' rights should be extended and whether further rules and regulations are in accordance with Better Regulation principles is at least worthy of discussion. Better Regulation—in connection with the principles of subsidiarity and proportionality—implies that the mildest and least onerous method should be chosen.[92] The regulations currently under discussion, including the introduction of a mandatory right for shareholders to demand a special audit or, as the case may be, an extension of the existing regulations in that respect, may result in an abuse of shareholders' rights—a challenge Germany is still trying to tackle. The current proposal for a directive on shareholders' rights[93] and the other regulations discussed in the consultation, on the one hand, afford shareholders additional rights, but on the other hand place severe burdens on companies. For the purpose of creating a level playing field between shareholders, finding more of a balance between the rights granted

[90] *Ibid*, n6, at 32.
[91] Above n 6, at 19.
[92] Above n72.
[93] Above n6, at 13.

and the duties imposed—to prevent abuse—should at least be taken into consideration.

The 'one share, one vote' principle is also being discussed and the proposal to carry out a study of the pros and cons of this principle meets with great approval. However, opinion is divided on what further action should be taken in this regard.

(e) Management Responsibility

In respect of reinforcing the responsibility of members of management or administrative corporate bodies,[94] a majority of the consultation participants pronounced themselves against intervention at the EU level due to the existence of major differences between the national legal systems and given that there were no material cross-border impediments to be remedied in that respect.

3. Public Hearing

The Directorate General for Internal Market and Services organised a public hearing on future priorities for the Action Plan on the Modernisation of Company Law and Corporate Governance on 3 May 2006 in Brussels. More than 300 people took part in what was a very comprehensive exchange of views.

The views expressed in the consultation were largely affirmed. In particular, it was advocated that future EU initiatives should aim to (i) abolish impediments to freedom of movement of capital and to freedom of establishment, and (ii) afford flexibility to companies.

During the hearing, four panels examined the issues of (i) shareholders' rights and obligations, (ii) modernisation and simplification of European company law, (iii) responsibility of directors/internal control, and (iv) corporate mobility and restructuring.[95]

(a) Panel on Shareholders' Rights and Obligations

The panel found that priority should be given to the proposal for a directive on the exercise of shareholders' rights, including the issues of 'one share, one vote', and the mandatory disclosure of voting policies of institutional investors. The issue of shareholder democracy, and in particular 'one share, one vote', gave rise to different opinions, with some participants supporting an action at EU level and others strongly opposing any EU initiative on shareholder democracy.

[94] *Ibid*, at 3.
[95] Above n89, at 29 ff.

It was also highlighted that shareholders' rights are connected with shareholders' obligations. Transparency should be the overriding principle and Better Regulation would have to be about achieving transparency and creating a level playing field with minimal interference.

(b) Modernisation and Simplification of European Company Law

The main issues addressed focused on codification and the potential risk of recasting on the one hand and on the necessity to pay more attention to the needs of SMEs on the other hand.

The panel considered that simplification might provide an appropriate remedy to face the regulatory fatigue caused by the different layers of regulation. Codification would improve the readability and clarity of terms and definitions. However, recasting the legislation would risk opening Pandora's box and needs thus to be approached carefully.

Simplification and modernisation should be the drivers of all reform. Therefore, a functional approach is needed. The level of detail of rules imposed on companies should be adequate in relation to the structures of companies. Rules applying to SMEs should be less burdensome than those applied to listed companies. However, it should also be taken into account that the increasing regulatory burden on listed companies creates a tendency to avoid the burden of the capital markets and to delist.

(c) Responsibility of Directors/Internal Control

The panel took the view that the primary responsibility of directors vis-à-vis shareholders but also all other stakeholders is to ensure the long-term existence of the company through the choice of a proper company strategy. As far as the responsibilities of directors are concerned, the panel agreed that much had been covered by the short-term measures set out by the CGAP.

The panel was not persuaded by the need for the Commission to introduce an option for companies regarding board structures (one-tier board v two-tier board) and considered that a recommendation would be the farthest the Commission should go in this area.

(d) Corporate Mobility and Restructuring

Main discussion issues were the transfer of a company's corporate seat, European Private Company Statute and the European Foundation. There was general agreement among the panel members that there is a need for a directive on cross-border transfer of the registered office.

As regards the European Private Company (EPC), opposing views were expressed regarding its necessity and characteristics, with more interventions in favour of such a new legal form. Panel members intervening in favour of an EPC Statute pointed out that legal costs incurred by setting up different companies in different Member States can be so high for SMEs that it discourages them from operating across borders.

The European Foundation was seen as being a long-term measure. It should first be ascertained whether a European Foundation model would be necessary at all. The results of the public consultation and hearing are being examined by the European Commission and a further course of action in respect of the CGAP will be determined on the basis of those results.

E. SUMMARY

Meanwhile, Better Regulation has solid roots. The concept is built upon previous endeavours pursued by institutions to make Community rules more efficient. The revised comitology procedure and the demand of the European Parliament for a deeper involvement in the law-making practice seem to set a framework for a new development of the Better Regulation concept. Hopefully, the Commission will nonetheless be able to pursue its path of Better Regulation.

Better Regulation is important and necessary to avoid red tape and to maintain confidence in capital markets. If the burdens on companies are too cumbersome, this will lead to too many companies being taken private. Such a situation is unhealthy for capital markets and makes it necessary for us to sit down and think how we can make life easier for companies. The issue of Better Regulation is thus relevant not only for SMEs but for all players in the European economy.

Notwithstanding the recent discussions on the Better Regulation concept, the objective of the CGAP is—within the framework of the revised Lisbon Strategy—to ensure stronger growth and more jobs. It is therefore of paramount importance that the implementation of the second and third phases will be as successful as that of the first phase which has already been completed.

Irrespective of what will be the further developments in the fields of corporate governance, it is clear that further action should be taken at national and at EU level (in compliance with the principles of the Commission's Initiative on Better Regulations) further to ensure that companies have the required flexibility and capacity to act. At the same time, it is important that legislators manage to achieve convergence, hopefully even harmonisation, in terms of corporate governance and regulatory standards. This must be achieved without the imposition of unacceptable burdens on companies so as not to provide further obstacles to the implementation of the revised Lisbon Strategy instead of promoting it. The difficulties of implementing the Lisbon Agreement are challenging enough as it stands.[96]

[96] Cf T Benner and JM Witte, 'Ein Forum der Beliebigkeit', *Handelsblatt*, 19 Aug 2006, at 8.

15

Impact Assessment in the EU

FRANCIS CHITTENDEN,* TIM AMBLER**
AND DEMING XIAO***

POLICIES ADDRESSING THE regulatory agenda have been gaining momentum in developed nations for around 30 years. For example, in the USA Congress embarked on regulatory reform by passing the Regulatory Flexibility Act of 1980. In the EU early notions of regulatory reform were articulated at the 1992 Edinburgh Council.[1] At the time, the issue of improving regulations was closely linked to three main drivers of EU regulatory concerns: competitiveness, good governance and sustainable development. Subsequently, at the 2000 Lisbon European Council, competitiveness came to the fore of European thinking.[2] But that does not necessarily mean that the primary driver for Impact Assessment is the desire to ensure that proposed regulations enhance, or are at least consistent with, the Lisbon concordat. It could be argued that issues associated with governance and sustainable development remain more central.[3]

This chapter examines the first three years of Impact Assessment (IA) within the EU and seeks to draw conclusions about the underlying motivations for the current IA process. The text is divided into six sections. We begin with a review of the literature relating to regulation and Impact Assessment, identifying competing theories that seek to explain the role of regulation in the socio-political landscape. Section B then considers the stated objectives of the EU Impact Assessment initiative. Section C reviews the EU work programme that drives the IA process. Section D considers the various actors in the IA process and the inter-linkages between

* ACCA Professor of Small Business Finance, Manchester Business School.
** Senior Fellow, London Business School.
*** MBA Course Participant, Manchester Business School.

[1] RE Lofstedt, 'The Swing of the Regulatory Pendulum in Europe: From Precautionary Principle to Regulatory Impact Analysis' (2004) 28 *Journal of Risk and Uncertainty* 237.

[2] F Vibert, 'The Limits of Regulatory Reform in EU' (2006) 26 *Journal of Institute of Economic Affairs* 3, at 17–21.

[3] N Lee and C Kirkpatrick, 'Evidence-based Policy-making in Europe: An Evaluation of European Commission Integrated Impact Assessments' (2006) 24 *Impact Assessment and Project Appraisal* 1, at 23–33.

them. Section E considers the output from the first three years of Impact Assessment within the EU and what this tells us about the underlying objectives, whether articulated or not. The final section discusses the findings and considers the implications for the future of the IA system.

A. REVIEW OF THE LITERATURE

The following review seeks to define regulation, to explore the need for regulation in modern economies and, in this context, to consider the role of impact assessment.

In terms of defining regulation, there seems to be no widely accepted definition, although regulations are generally perceived as rules that constrain the behaviour of individuals or businesses. The US Office of Management and Budget (OMB) defines regulation as a statement by an agency to implement, interpret or prescribe law or policy or to describe the procedure or practice of an agency.[4] In addition, the Organisation for Economic Co-operation and Development (OECD) recognises regulation as one of a range of policy instruments that can be used by governments to achieve their policy objectives.[5] In common parlance the other main 'levers of government' are taxation and spending. In this vein Guash and Hahn observe that a possible reason for the recent increase in regulations related to health, safety and the environment is that the political need to limit tax increases is creating incentives to use regulation: when legislators are constrained by existing spending and tax levels, regulations provide another tool for achieving political outcomes.[6]

According to OMB,[7] the three main areas of government policy where regulation plays a significant role are social, process and economic regulations. Social regulations address benefits to society such as health and safety, transport, employment, environmental and other similar benefits. Process regulations address the mechanics of governments, such as administration and paperwork, government forms for taxation, immigration and procurement and the collection of statistics. Economic regulations seek to alter the commercial and financial frameworks and markets. They are usually intended to promote fair competition, for example by imposing restrictions on prices or on firms entering or exiting lines of business in a way that

[4] Office of Management and Budget, 'Report to Congress on the Costs and Benefits of Federal Regulations' (Washington, DC, The White House, 1997).

[5] OECD, *Regulatory Policies in OECD Countries: From Interventionism to Regulatory Governance* (Paris, OECD, 2002).

[6] JL Guash and RW Hahn, 'The Costs and Benefits of Regulation: Implications for Developing Countries' (1999) 14 *The World Bank Research Observer* 1.

[7] Above n4.

might cause harm to the economic interest of other businesses or consumers. Unsurprisingly, perhaps, these three main areas of regulatory activity are remarkably similar to the sources of concern identified by the 1992 Edinburgh Council,[8] and we return to this later in the chapter.

An important theme in the literature seeks to answer the question, why regulate? In this regard, there are three strands to economic thinking: the public interest theory of regulation associated with Arthur Pigou, the contracting theory associated with Ronald Coase, and the capture theory of George Stigler. A number of papers explore these three theories and present evidence on the relevance of each.[9]

There are three main criticisms of these related theories. The first is that the public interest theory exaggerates the extent of market failure and does not recognise the ability of competition to address many of the alleged problems. The second critique, raised by contracting theory, holds that where competition and private orderings do not address market failures, courts can do so. With well-functioning courts enforcing property rights and contracts, the scope for desirable regulations is reduced. The World Bank's data support this: countries with more efficient courts tend to regulate more lightly.[10] Thirdly, capture theory criticises the assumption that a government is benevolent and competent. Incumbent business interests typically capture the process of regulation. Regulation not only fails to counter monopoly pricing but may even sustain it. In addition, even where regulators try to promote social welfare, they may lack the capacity to do so, and regulation can make things worse. On the one hand, research provides empirical evidence to support this conclusion. On the other hand, consumers are generally happy with many of the regulations that protect them.

Djankov *et al* showed the influence of established legal systems on the propensity to regulate and the form of regulation adopted, with common law systems leaning towards more liberal market structures having recourse to the courts and civil law countries tending towards state regulation. They identified five legal systems currently operating in the EU, including English (common law); French (civil law); German; Scandinavian and Socialist (associated with the USSR) systems. In labour laws, these established legal traditions were found to influence the nature of the regulatory regime adopted.[11]

[8] RE Lofstedt 'The Swing of the Regulatory Pendulum in Europe: From Precautionary Principle to Regulatory Impact Analysis',(2004) 28 *Journal of Risk and Uncertainty* 237.

[9] See eg: World Bank, *Doing in Business 2004: Understanding Regulations* (Washington, DC, World Bank, 2003); and S Djankov, E Glaeser, R La Porta, F Lopez-de-Silanes, and A Shleifer, 'The New Comparative Economics' (2003) XXXI *Journal of Comparative Economics* 595.

[10] World Bank, above n9.

[11] Djankov *et al*, above n9.

The World Bank study develops another theory, called 'the enforcement theory', which recognises the benefits of public sector involvement in at least some activities. It argues that there is a basic trade-off between two social costs: the cost of private injury and the cost of state intervention. Private injury refers to the ability of private agents to harm others, and state intervention refers to the ability of government officials to expropriate from agents through bureaucratic hassle or the confiscation of property.[12] The enforcement theory implies that there is a need for appropriate choices to be made about the nature and form of government intervention according to the type of activity and administrative capacity available. It may be said that the enforcement theory attempts to place the relevance of each of the alternative theories in a contextual framework.

A further important issue to consider is the role of Impact Assessment. The aims of Impact Assessments are 'to enhance the empirical basis of political decisions and to make the regulatory process more transparent and accountable'.[13] Impact Assessment may also be seen as a means of ensuring that proposed regulation complies with a set of predetermined principles, such as those suggested in the UK by the Better Regulation Task Force.[14] The process of Impact Assessment may be seen by liberals as the centrepiece of regulatory reform that places constraints on arbitrary political decision-making.[15] However, Vibert raises a number of reservations about the extent to which IAs can fulfil their objectives:[16]

— Technical reservations. These relate to the method adopted by IAs to quantify the costs and benefits of proposed regulations, especially benefits, notably in areas such as social and environmental regulations. Since the Commission has given social and environmental aspects particular weight in the overall calculations, cost-benefit analysis is vulnerable to the suspicion of potential manipulation and bias. Similarly, consultation, an integral element of IA preparation, is subject to the charge that the process may be structured so as to gain support for a proposal rather than to focus on collecting evidence about its desirability or otherwise.

— Concerns about institutional behaviour. Liberals centre their scepticism on the incentives created by the Commission's 'right of initiative'. The IA guidelines announced by the Commission in 2005 clearly indicate that the Commission will not let IAs hamper its ability to act and

[12] World Bank, above n9.

[13] CM Radaelli, 'The Diffusion of Regulatory Impact Analysis—Best Practice or Lesson-drawing' (2004) 43 *European Journal of Political Research* 723.

[14] BRTF, *Principles of Better Regulation* (London, Cabinet Office, 2005).

[15] F Vibert, 'The Limits of Regulatory Reform in EU' (2006) 26 *Journal of Institute of Economic Affairs* 2, at 17–21.

[16] *Ibid.*

would not willingly embrace IAs if these were seen as a device to clip the wings of bureaucrats. The guidance states, '[t]he adoption of a policy proposal is a political decision that belongs solely to the College (of Commissioners), not to officials or technical experts'.[17] In a similar vein it could be argued that the mindset and procedures of the Council have just not caught up with the discipline of IAs, and it is believed that IAs will not alter the basic temptation of Member States with heavy regulation to use their voting power in Council to add to the costs of jurisdictions with a tradition of light touch regulation. Further, Vibert postulates that the EU Parliament has difficulty in adapting its culture to evidence-based approaches to legislation. Parliament lacks capacity to carry out Impact Assessment on its own amendments, and its legislative procedures fail to mesh with the Commission's IA procedures. Vibert suggests that the net result of policy-making in the Parliament and Council of Ministers, combined with a politicised Commission, is that the institutional setting is not one within which IAs are likely to be effective in stemming the flow of regulation that may have the potential to damage market competitiveness.[18]

— The rule-making environment. Some believe an important purpose of EU legislation is to open up the Single Market. However, others insist that EU conventions carry social benefits that outweigh any countervailing economic costs. Consequently, there is no settled view of what market order the EU should aspire to achieve. Meanwhile, rather than allowing different preferences and approaches to be tested in different jurisdictions to prove their worth, the Single Market initiative has tended to create a legislative regime centralised in Brussels that reduces lesson-learning from different approaches and protects clumsy regulation from exposure to less heavy-handed approaches.

Whilst the process of IA preparation within the EU is still in the early stages of development and many questions remain unanswered, a normative analysis of the IA system might conclude that Impact Assessment has three main objectives:[19]

1. To challenge the need for new regulation.
2. To improve the new regulation to make it less burdensome and/or more effective.
3. To create the mechanism for review and revision of, or rescission of, the regulation at a later date.

[17] European Commission Impact Assessment Guidelines, SEC(2005)791, available at http://europa.eu.int/comm/secretariat_general/impact/practice_en.htm.

[18] Above n15, at 17–21.

[19] T Ambler, F Chittenden and C Hwang, *Regulation: Another Form of Taxation?* (London, British Chambers of Commerce, 2005).

In spite of its potential weaknesses, there seems to be a consensus that Impact Assessment is a mechanism to increase transparency and accountability in the regulatory process. Impact Assessment in the EU might, therefore, be most widely used where there was the intention that rule-makers should comply with some over-riding goals that the political process was seeking to adhere to, although in the EU the substance of these overriding goals is far from clear.

The three types of regulation identified by the OMB, namely social, process and economic, suggest these research questions:

1. To what extent does Impact Assessment support 'sustainable development' through changing environment, health, security and international relations?
2. To what extent does Impact Assessment reduce government process, ie reduce the administrative burdens imposed by government and clarify or simplify legal codes?
3. To what extent does Impact Assessment support a single competitive but fair EU market, eg by removing protectionist legislation that adds to consumer costs?

In seeking to draw conclusions about the role of Impact Assessment in the EU, we first examine the stated objectives and current features of this initiative.

B. IMPACT ASSESSMENT IN THE EU

According to the Impact Assessment guidelines,[20] IAs provide *ex ante* analyses of social, economic and environmental impacts for a variety of purposes including coordination within the Commission, openness to external stakeholders and transparency in decision-making. In addition the IA guidance states that the process contributes to both the Lisbon competitiveness commitments and sustainable development strategies by improving the quality of policy proposals, and keeping EU intervention as simple as possible. Finally, IAs explain why action is necessary and the regulatory response is appropriate, or alternatively why no action should be taken.

It can be seen from the above that, perhaps unsurprisingly, the IA guidance claims that these (in principle) quite simple documents can fulfil a multiplicity of roles. Thus the guidance is framed in a way that could appeal to enthusiasts of all three of the main agendas cited above, ie competitiveness, sustainable development and good governance, even though it must be recognised that there will be tensions between these competing objectives.

[20] European Commission Impact Assessment Guidelines, above n17.

This attempt to widen the appeal of IAs is perhaps one of the reasons the guidance appears to be growing in complexity. For example the 2005 guidance is 47 pages in length and replaced the 2002 version[21] that was almost one third shorter at 33 pages. The latest version[22] is 49 pages long.

According to the current guidelines, IAs are triggered by all regulatory proposals, White Papers, expenditure programmes and negotiating guidelines for international agreements (with an economic, social or environmental impact) that appear on the Commission Work Programme.[23] Some flexibility to bypass the IA process is allowed (eg for urgent matters of security). The availability of some sensitive IAs is restricted, for example where the content might influence the outcome of negotiations with parties outside the EU. Green Papers and proposals for consultation with Social Partners are exempted from the IA process.

There are two stages in the assessment process. The first is the preparation of an initial review or road map and, where subsequently deemed appropriate, the second is the preparation of the full IA. The full Impact Assessment process includes six steps and also provides for stakeholder consultation and the collection of expertise as an integral part of the process:

1. Identify the problem.
2. Define the objectives.
3. Develop main policy options.
4. Analyse their impacts.
5. Compare the options.
6. Outline policy monitoring and evaluation.[24]

C. THE EU WORK PROGRAMME

The EU work programme is typically constructed around a number of key themes. The 2006 work programme identified the following items which are broadly similar to those expressed in the 2005 programme:[25]

> *Prosperity:* An essential function of public policy is to ensure that the conditions to support prosperity are in place to the benefit of citizens and businesses alike. This means stable regulatory systems, appropriate economic policies, the provision of economic opportunity, and investing in a skilled and entrepreneurial population. It means all relevant aspects of the EU's own work must be subject to the highest standards of better regulation. More work to develop the conditions to stimulate

[21] European Commission Communication on Impact Assessment, COM(2002)76.

[22] European Commission Impact Assessment Guidelines, above n17.

[23] 'Unlocking Europe's Full Potential', Commission Legislative and Work Programme 2006, COM(2005)531 final, available at http://ec.europa.eu/governance/impact/docs/ia_2006/com_2005_0531_en.pdf.

[24] Source: IA Guidelines, SEC(2005)791 final, 15 June 2005.

[25] COM(2005)531 final, above n23.

growth and create more and better jobs remains central to the Commission's tasks in 2006.

Solidarity: Solidarity and social justice are critical to the way the EU works. This is about building the society we want for ourselves and for future generations. It is about fostering quality of life and recognising shared responsibilities such as protecting the environment. It is about promoting a healthy society with citizens who remain confident in the face of change, as a foundation stone for prosperity and security.

Security: Scarcely a day passes without a reminder of the threats to citizens' security. Recent events have again brought this sharply into focus. The Madrid and London bombings, natural disasters at home and worldwide, the threat of avian flu and a possible human influenza pandemic, energy and transport crises: these are just the most obvious examples where daily life has been turned upside-down or where risk has moved from the possible to the probable.

External: To reach its strategic objectives, Europe cannot work alone. The recent textile negotiations with China, the latest famine in Niger, the security situation in Iraq, the Middle East Peace Process: external events constantly remind us that prosperity, solidarity and security might be European objectives but cannot depend only on what we achieve at home. Europe must do more than simply react to the external world: it must also contribute more proactively to shaping it.

Underpinning these four areas of Commission initiative is a fifth area relating to the processes by which such actions will be implemented:[26]

Delivery and Better Regulation: Effective policy delivery is central to the credibility and legitimacy of the European Union. But it is not only about what policies are chosen: how policies are developed and how they are implemented is equally important. In 2005, the Commission stepped up its existing work on better regulation to ensure that the regulatory framework in the EU meets today's requirements. This aims to reinforce the contribution from better regulation to growth and jobs while continuing to take into account the social and environmental objectives and good governance.

D. THE ACTORS AND THEIR ROLES

In order to support the Delivery and Better Regulation objectives a number of initiatives are taking place. The Personnel and Administration Directorate-General (DG Admin) and the Secretariat General run training sessions on IA for Commission staff. In addition, some directorates-general (DGs) offer specialised training relevant to their responsibilities and there is the opportunity for sharing knowledge through, for example, DG Budget's IntraComm site. Furthermore, because there is methodological overlap between IA and

[26] *Ibid.*

ex ante evaluation, the Commission website indicates that some established evaluation training modules are also relevant to Impact Assessment.

Commission guidelines for collecting and using expertise are useful where external assistance is brought to bear, and within the Commission this practice is common. Since 2005 the Scientific INformAtion for Policy Support in Europe (SINAPSE) database has also been available. Further, an Inter-Service Steering Group (ISSG) is compulsory for all items of a cross-cutting nature, and the IA guidelines state that when no ISSG is envisaged justification for this decision must be provided.[27]

Proposals undergoing Impact Assessment are subject to formal Inter-Service Consultation (ISC), and this process covers the IA Report and annexes, as well as the Explanatory Memorandum accompanying the draft proposal. There is an element of quality control attached to this process because where the ISC considers that the IA report does not reach a satisfactory standard an unfavourable opinion may be issued.

The final IA report has the status of a Commission Staff Working Document and is used to support arguments for the merits of the Commission's proposal in the Council and/or European Parliament.

Figure 15.1, below, presents a diagram showing the actors in the IA process.[28]

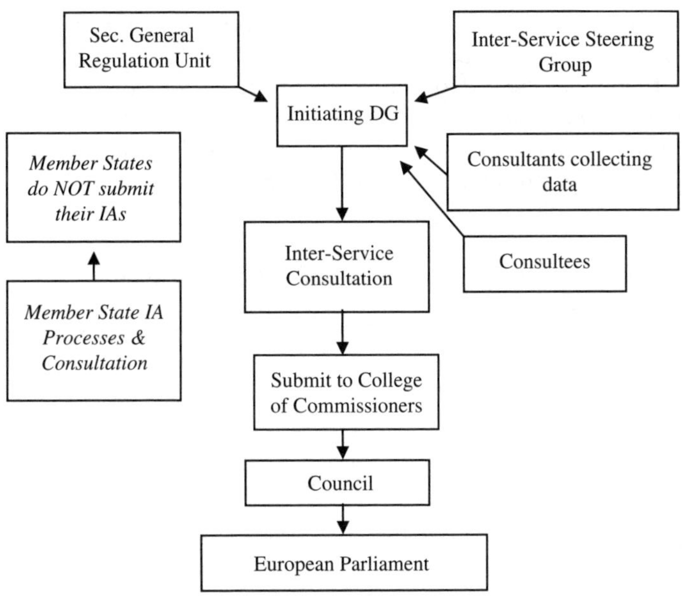

Figure 15.1—The Actors in the IA Process.

[27] European Commission Impact Assessment Guidelines, above n17.
[28] Source: prepared by the authors.

It might have been expected that Member States would submit the relevant national IA, or partial IA drawn up to inform negotiations with Commission officials, so that the EU IA is informed by national analysis of the impact of proposed regulations. However, based upon analysis conducted in the UK it appears that this does not happen in practice, and discussion with EU officials has confirmed that there is no formal link between national IAs and the Commission's IA document.[29] Interestingly the Commission's own flow chart of the IA process shows that information and opinions from Member States are obtained as part of the 'data collection' process, described as 'Member State IA Consultation', but it is difficult to gauge the extent to which this happens in practice. What can be said with certainty is that the Commission prepares its EU-wide IA without the benefit of engaging with IA processes at national level, unless Member States are pro-active at drawing attention to the potentially diverse national impacts that may result. To some extent this 'missing link' may make proposed regulations more vulnerable to alteration by the Parliament, although freedom from such a link must provide greater flexibility for the Commission to prepare IAs without having to wait for Member States to undertake their national analysis.

E. ROAD MAPS AND IMPACT ASSESSMENTS PRODUCED

In order to gather evidence on the focus of the EU's regulatory programme in practice we set out below (Table 15.1) an analysis of the road maps and Impact Assessments produced in recent years, based on the four key themes in the EU work programme, as identified above.

Table 15.1: Number and Subject of Road Maps 2005 and 2006[30]

Subject	**Number**	**Percentage of Total**
Prosperity	59	29
Solidarity	59	29
Security	54	26
External Responsibility	32	16
Total	**204**	**100**

[29] T Ambler, F Chittenden and C Hwang, *Regulation: Another Form of Taxation?* (London, British Chambers of Commerce, 2005).

[30] Source: based upon http://europa.eu.int/comm/secretariat_general/impact/practice_en.htm.

Road maps can also be described as 'initial impact screening documents',[31] and it can be seen from Table 15.1 that 204 road maps were produced in respect of the 2005 and 2006 work programmes. In number these are approximately evenly divided between Prosperity, Solidarity and Security, with External Affairs receiving less attention.

The production of road maps can be compared with the distribution of Impact Assessments subsequently prepared. Because the assembly of IAs can take a considerable period of time, for this analysis we examine all IAs produced since the initiative was introduced, effectively in 2003. The number of IAs completed has been building up gradually, as may be seen from Table 15.2:

Table 15.2: Numbers of IAs Produced by Year

Year	**2003**	**2004**	**2005**
Number of IAs	21	30	76

The number of IAs needs to be compared with the rate of production of legislation by the EU, which is as follows:

Table 15.3: EU Legislation Published 2003 to 2005

Year	**2003**	**2004**	**2005**
Directives	153	177	133
Regulations	2461	2462	2331
Decisions	804	1095	849

From Table 15.3 it may be seen that IAs are produced for a small proportion of legislation introduced by the EU, about 2.3 per cent in 2005.

Table 15.4: How Many IAs have been Produced and What were they About?[32]

Subject	**Number of IAs**	**Percentage of Total**
Prosperity Index	49	39
Solidarity	31	24
Security	16	13
External	31	24
Total	**127**	**100**

[31] Above n23.
[32] Source: based upon http://ec.europa.eu/governance/impact/practice_en.htm.

Table 15.4 shows that the largest proportion of IAs produced in the period 2003–5 related to the Prosperity Index (39 per cent), with Solidarity and External Affairs being of roughly equal proportions at 24 per cent. Prima facie, this analysis is interesting, as it shows that the road map (or initial Impact Assessment process) appears to reduce the number of Impact Assessments conducted for Commission actions under the heading of Security. Indeed the importance attached to conducting IAs to consider the impact and to seek to maximise the effectiveness of proposals relating to Prosperity is apparent. However some care is needed as the time periods of these samples of road maps and IAs do not exactly match.

Whilst potentially interesting, this analysis has not assisted our objective of gaining insights into the underlying motivations for the promotion of Impact Assessment by actors within the EU, other than to confirm the attention given to measures relating to Prosperity. To gain a better understanding we need to explore the purpose of each regulation that has been subject to IA scrutiny. An initial clue may be found by examining the directorates-general responsible for the initiatives. Twenty-one DGs (of 37) have conducted an IA and Table 15.5 lists the 12 DGs that have produced more than four such documents.

Table 15.5: DGs Producing More than Four IAs 2003–5[33]

Directorate-General	Number of IAs	Percentage of Total
Environment	18	14
Transportation & Energy	16	13
Justice etc.	13	10
Enterprise	8	6
Market	8	6
Development	8	6
Information Society	8	6
Education	7	6
Employment	7	6
Agriculture	5	4
Fish	5	4
Health	5	4
Sub-total	108	85
Other DGs	19	15
Total	127	100

[33] Source: based upon http://europa.eu.int/comm/secretariat_general/impact/practice_en.htm.

In Table 15.5 the balance appears to shift, with the Sustainability issues associated with environmental regulations, including those related to Transport and Energy, being central to the remits of two of the top three DGs engaging with the early years of the IA process. Of course it must be acknowledged that secure energy supplies and efficient transport infrastructure are also essential for underpinning economic growth. An alternative perspective would be that the combination of the business interests in Energy and Transport, plus DGs Enterprise, Markets and Employment, together accounted for 40 IAs, almost one third of the total. However, in the EU some employment issues such as equal opportunities relate more to the theme of Solidarity than to Prosperity.[34]

For a more rigorous investigation it may be useful to examine the stated objectives of the Community Actions identified in the IAs themselves. A classification of these documents, based on reading the 'Problem Definition' section of the IAs that are summarised in Table 15.5 above is enlightening. For the purposes of presentation we classify the IAs scrutinised under the headings identified by the Edinburgh Council, as noted by Lofstedt.[35]

Table 15.6: Stated Objectives of the Proposed Actions subject to IAs 2003–5

Objective	**Competitiveness**	**Sustainability**	**Governance**
Number of IAs	47	85	35

The results in Table 15.6 lead to the conclusion that actions associated with Sustainability are the principal subject of IAs. However, reading the IAs showed that many examine proposed Community Actions that influence more than one area of activity. Thirty-seven of the IAs considered issues that had consequences for Sustainability as well as either Competitiveness or Economic Governance objectives, and some of these IAs had consequences for all three. This is important. Whilst Sustainability issues represent the largest single group of IAs, almost half of these also relate to issues of either Competitiveness or Economic Governance. If the 37 with multiple objectives are deducted from the total of 85 Sustainability IAs this provides a net total of 48, roughly equivalent to the number of IAs for Competitiveness and slightly larger that those relating to Economic Governance.

F. DISCUSSION

In this chapter we have sought to address a number of questions. We began by noting that 'Better Regulation' has been pursued in the USA for some

[34] Above n23.
[35] Above n1.

30 years and has been on the EU agenda for about half this time. However, formal IAs have been conducted by the Commission only since the start of 2003, although a more limited forerunner of the system existed in the form of '*fiche d'impact*'. We then described the current IA system in the EU, identifying the actors involved. It appears that even though Member States are invited to submit national IAs to the Commission in order to inform preparation of the EU-wide Impact Assessment, this happens rarely. However, Member States' views are sought as part of the IA 'data collection' process.

Indeed in many countries empirical evidence of the influence of IA is limited, partly because systems must necessarily have been in place for some time before appropriate evaluations can be made. In Europe, in contrast to the USA, the discipline of formal *ex ante* assessment of the impact of regulations is relatively novel. In Member States where evidence does exist, it is not particularly encouraging. For example, the National Audit Office in the UK has concluded that a majority of UK Regulatory Impact Assessments (RIAs) are prepared in a pro forma way and consequently have relatively little impact on the manner in which regulations are introduced.[36] These findings are consistent with other evidence based on successive annual reviews of the UK IA system.[37]

A comparative study of the impact of IAs on EU regulation in Member States has produced some potentially more encouraging results. In a study for DG Enterprise, Ramboll Management concluded that where EU regulations had been subject to Impact Assessment within Member States the resulting compliance costs were lower than in countries where no *ex ante* assessment of the impacts was made.[38] On a slightly less encouraging note, Vibert analysed the output of the first two years of the IA system and concluded that, although it was functioning, a number of recommendations for improvement could be made, including remodelling consultations to guard against confirmatory bias, strengthening the evidence base in IAs, introducing independent reviews of the evidence and wider consideration of non-legislative approaches.[39] Since these studies examined the first two years of

[36] NAO, 'Evaluation of Regulatory Impact Assessments 2005–06', Report by the Comptroller and Auditor General (HC 1305 Session 2005–06).

[37] T Ambler, F Chittenden and K Ahuja, *Regulators: Box Tickers or Burdens Busters?* (London, British Chambers of Commerce, 2006); T Ambler, F Chittenden and C Hwang, *Regulation: Another Form of Taxation* (London, British Chambers of Commerce, 2005); T Ambler, F Chittenden and M Obodovski, *Are Regulators Raising Their Game? UK Regulatory Impact Assessments in 2002/3* (London, British Chambers of Commerce, 2004); T Ambler, F Chittenden and M Shamutkova, *Do Regulators Play By the Rules? An Audit of UK Regulatory Impact Assessments* (London, British Chambers of Commerce, 2003).

[38] Ramboll Management, 'Ex-Post Evaluation of EC Legislation And its Burden on Business', Final Report (Brussels, EC, 2005).

[39] F Vibert, *The EU's New System of Regulatory Impact Assessment—A Scorecard* (London, European Policy Forum, 2004); F Vibert, *The Itch to Regulate: Confirmation Bias and the EC's New System of Impact Assessment* (London, European Policy Forum, 2005).

the IA system, it is unsurprising that there was scope for improvement and the system will probably take some time to become more effective. Vibert also notes some grounds for concern about whether the IA system as currently operating will be respected as an effective technique.[40] For example the IA system is open to criticisms that cost-benefit analysis may not be fully objective and that the consultation process is subject to confirmatory bias. An important issue here is the degree of fit with the current institutional structures in the EU, especially the roles of the Council and Parliament.

In addition we noted that the IA guidance has been framed in such a way that it may appeal to a broad spectrum of constituents, including those concerned about environmental issues and social objectives as well as the competitiveness agenda. Consequently, although it is claimed that the Lisbon Concordat presents the guiding framework by which new legislation should be judged, it is far from clear that this is where the centre of gravity of the IA process lies. In order better to judge the underlying motives for conducting IAs we presented an analysis of the output from the system to date.

We noted that IAs consider a very small number of proposed regulations, ie 76 in 2005 compared with the 133 directives published in that year, together with over 2,000 regulations, although in this latter case it has been shown that the vast majority will be of minor import, relating for example to routinely establishing the price of certain foodstuffs.[41] Clearly a balance is needed here, and road maps are intended to identify those items in the Commission work plan worthy of further attention.

It was noted that the largest proportion of IAs are classified by the Commission as relating to the Prosperity Index, although Sustainability issues also feature strongly. In an attempt to gain deeper insights we then analysed IAs by examining their 'Problem Definition' sections and allocating them across the three headings identified by the Edinburgh Council. Regulations that focus particularly upon the administrative and legal processes with which citizens and businesses must comply were allocated to the Competitiveness heading; regulations relating to the environment, social issues, security and international relations were allocated to the Sustainability heading; and, finally, regulations relating to economic governance, such as those that deal with the ability of actors to engage in rent-seeking, were allocated to the Governance heading.

The outcome of this analysis showed that Sustainability issues featured most strongly in the proposals subject to IA. However, in almost half of these cases the proposed measures also had consequences relating to one or both of the Competitiveness or Governance categories. This is encouraging, for there is an undeniable logic in carefully examining proposed regulations

[40] F Vibert, *supra*, n. 2.

[41] T Ambler, F Chittenden and M Obodovski, *How Much Regulation is Gold Plate? A Study of UK Elaboration of EU Directives* (London, British Chambers of Commerce, 2004).

that seek to achieve objectives in one area, but that inevitably introduce costs in another.

In such situations the objective of better regulation is to pursue the desired goal if, and some would argue only if, this can be done in such a way that other interests are not unduly harmed. Recognising that the role for IAs is to resolve, as far as possible, these very real tensions, the diligence with which IAs are prepared and the efficacy of the consultation and negotiation processes must be managed with a high degree of skill.

Based upon more then seven years of experience in the UK, in which the IA process has been found lacking,[42] not in principle but rather in practical application, this is a formidable goal. In a theoretical context it appears that the role of IA is to determine, so far as is possible, the appropriate balance between the risks identified by the 'Enforcement Theory of Regulation'.[43] However, the Legal Theory of Regulation raises doubts about whether it is possible for IAs prepared in Brussels to be properly informed, without the benefit of first completing regulatory appraisals and detailed cost-benefit analyses in countries operating under the several different types of legal system that exist in the EU.

[42] NAO, above n36.
[43] World Bank, above n9.

16

Inter-institutionalising EU Impact Assessment

ANNE CM MEUWESE*

NORMS OF VARIOUS origins and legal status govern the European legislative process. Next to provisions found in the EC Treaty and in secondary legislation,[1] legislative practices, joint declarations and constraints imposed by national constitutional norms[2] are relevant, and also norms of a more internal or bureaucratic nature. The latest addition to this latter set of norms is the requirement to perform Impact Assessment (IA) of major legislative and policy proposals. As the showpiece of the 'Better Regulation' programme IA is meant to address both problems of competitiveness[3] and constitutional legitimacy.[4] In 2002 the Impact Assessment procedure was introduced by the European Commission following recommendations from the Mandelkern group on better regulation[5] as a 'general purpose impact analysis tool' meant to 'integrate, reinforce, streamline and replace' all existing practices in the field of *ex ante* evaluation.[6]

* Research fellow in politics at the University of Exeter and visiting fellow and PhD candidate in law at Leiden University.

1 Eg the Comitology Dec. See EU Council Dec 1999/468/EC of 28 June 1999 on procedures for the exercise of implementing powers conferred on the Commission [1999] OJ L184/23.

2 Eg the Danish procedure which fetters the actions of a minister in the Council to a parliamentary mandate.

3 European Commission Communication, 'Better Regulation for Growth and Jobs in the European Union', COM(2005)97, 16 Mar 2005.

4 To give just one example of a policy document making the link between better regulation and legitimacy: see European Commission, Staff Working Document on EU Common Methodology for assessing administrative costs, SEC(2005)1329 at 24: '[b]etter regulation principles provide that it is important to assess the impact of proposed measures and review existing regulation from the point of view of those affected'.

5 The Mandelkern Group was composed of Member States' experts on better regulation and chaired by Dieudonné Mandelkern, a French government official. It was set up by Ministers of Public Administration in Nov 2000 to provide recommendations for a strategy to improve the European regulatory environment. The Mandelkern report was presented to the Laeken European Council in Nov 2001.

6 European Commission, Communication on Better Lawmaking, COM(2002)275 final, 5 June 2002.

The European Commission's Impact Assessment procedure[7] consists of a series of key analyses to be conducted at the bureaucratic level. They are: problem identification, definition of the objectives, development of the main policy options, impact analysis, comparison of the options in the light of their impact, and an outline for policy monitoring and evaluation.[8] These analyses should be started as early on in the policy process as possible, which means before the proposal is published or even decided upon. Stakeholder consultation and the gathering of experts' opinions are integrated into the IA process in the sense that they should inform the assessment. An IA report,[9] published together with the proposal, serves to summarise the results, highlighting the trade-offs between the impacts associated with the policy options. During 2003 this project functioned as a pilot; from 2004 onwards it matured gradually; and in 2005 it became fully operational, covering all proposals in the Commission's Legislative and Work Programme.[10]

Initially this procedure did not raise the interest of many stakeholders and commentators, which is rather surprising, given the fact that the American equivalent—regulatory impact analysis—has always given rise to much controversy.[11] But this has changed now that the IA procedure has grown out of its pilot phase and is taken to the next level of institutionalisation, as evidenced by the presentation of new Impact Assessment Guidelines[12] by the European Commission in June 2005 and the adoption of an Inter-institutional Common Approach to Impact Assessment by the three Institutions in November 2005.[13] This latter document contains a further elaboration of the pre-existing idea[14] that the European Parliament and the Council should not only use Commission IAs but also produce their own.

[7] In this ch 'Impact Assessment at the EU level' will be referred to as 'EU IA'. Although it is true that the procedure was initiated and developed by the European Commission, there has been a rapid expansion of the procedure to the European Parliament and the Council, and there is at least a formal agreement between the 3 Institutions that their use of IA is based on the same principles and ground rules.

[8] European Commission, Impact Assessment Guidelines, SEC(2005)791, 15 June 2006, with an update on 15 Mar 2006.

[9] Often simply referred to as the 'Impact Assessment', even if in fact the term 'Impact Assessment' covers the whole process and not just the report.

[10] Above n3.

[11] Eg A Sen, 'The Discipline of Cost-Benefit Analysis' (2000) 29 *Journal of Legal Studies* 931. For a summary of the debate in the US see also A Renda, *Impact Assessment in the EU: The State of the Art and the Art of the State* (Brussels, Centre for European Policy Studies, 2006) at 18 and 85.

[12] Above n8.

[13] European Parliament, Council and Commission, *Common Approach to Impact Assessment* (Nov 2005), available at http://ec.europa.eu/governance/impact/docs/key_docs/ii_common_approach_to_ia_en.pdf

[14] European Parliament, Council and Commission, *Inter-Institutional Agreement on Better Lawmaking*, [2003] OJ C321/1.

These days there is a heated debate and a fast-growing body of literature, mostly addressing the performance of EU IA.[15] A problematic aspect of this approach to the topic is that it presupposes a consensus on the goals of EU IA from which benchmarks can then be derived. However, in spite of the ongoing institutionalisation of the procedure, fundamental confusion and disagreement among the stakeholders of IA persists. This lack of consensus most visibly concerns the substantive goals of IA. The fact that different players in the debate quote different goals ranging from 'deregulation' and 'achieving the greatest net benefits for society' to 'ensuring the sustainability of policies' need not be a problem however. The Commission has explicitly stated that IA should serve as 'an aid to decision-making, not a substitute for political judgement'.[16] This implies that EU IA is not meant to foster one particular flavour of regulatory reform. Nor is it part of a system of regulatory review in the thick sense as it is practised in the United States, where the Office of Management and Budget can veto an agency rule on the basis of the IA. This certainly leaves room for debate on the question whether the perceived shift of EU better regulation policy was legitimate,[17] but this chapter focuses on what it claims to be a disagreement of a more fundamental type: disagreement regarding the role and status of Impact Assessment in the European legislative process. The lack of clarity on this issue is already apparent in the Commission's statement quoted above: if IA is to function as 'an aid to decision-making, not a substitute for political judgement', which concepts of 'decision-making' and 'political judgement' did the Commission have in mind and what is the relationship between the two? In view of the emphasis placed in policy documents on better regulation being a 'joint responsibility',[18] it is not just the Commission's vision that is relevant, but also those of the European Parliament, the Council of Ministers, individual Member States and other stakeholders. In the context of 'inter-institutionalisation' of the IA procedure the phrase 'aid not substitute' should be taken to refer to the whole chain of political decision-making leading to the adoption of legislation, rather than just to the political decision-making within the College of

[15] Eg Renda, above n11; F Vibert, *The EU's New System of Regulatory Impact Assessment—a Scorecard* (London, EPF, 2004); F Vibert, *The Itch to Regulate: Confirmation Bias and the European Commission's New System of Impact Assessment* (London, EPF, 2005); D Wilkinson *et al*, *For Better or for Worse? The EU's 'Better Regulation' Agenda and the Environment* (London, IEEP, 2005).

[16] European Commission, Communication from the Commission on Impact Assessment, COM(2002)276 final, at 3.

[17] CM Radaelli, 'Whither Better Regulation for the Lisbon Agenda?' (2007) 14 *Journal of European Public Policy* 190.

[18] Press release 9501/05 of the Competitiveness Council meeting, Luxembourg, 6 and 7 June 2005.

Commissioners.[19] It seems, then, that EU IA is developing in the direction of an information tool for the EU legislator as a whole rather than as a decision tool for only a part of it. At the same time IA is supposed to contribute to the formulation of a concrete proposal by the European Commission. The instrument has also been charged with many sub-goals, such as improving and simplifying the regulatory environment, ensuring consistency between Community policies, enhancing communication with the citizen and changing the legislative culture within the European Commission.

The question arises what it means to 'inform the EU legislator' through the use of Impact Assessment. This chapter explores this question against the background of the gradual expansion of the IA procedure into the European Parliament and the Council. The hypothesis is that different actors use the IA procedure with different models in the back of their minds, linked to their preferences on certain constitutional issues. Finally it will be argued that if the function of IA in the legislative process is not clarified the capacity of IA to contribute to constitutional legitimacy in the EU is compromised.

A. REGULATING THE EU LEGISLATOR?

The first problem when thinking of Impact Assessment as an information tool for the legislator is that there is no such clearly demarcated entity in the EU. Compared to national constitutional systems, regulatory authority at the EU level is particularly scattered, layered, constrained and fragile. The European legislator consists potentially of many co-actors[20] and the exact composition depends on the area that is being regulated and the instrument and procedure that the Treaty prescribes accordingly. Even if many Commission documents refer to 'the legislator' or the 'legislative authority'[21] implying that it does not see itself as part of this body, the role of the Commission is so central that it is fair to say that the European Commission, the European Parliament and the Council of Ministers are the three co-legislators. Furthermore, checks and balances in the EU legislative process are somewhat of an oddity from the point of view of

[19] This is confirmed by the wording—eg 'a global strategy for better lawmaking throughout the entire EU legislative process'—in European Commission, 'Better Regulation for Growth and Jobs in the European Union', Communication from the Commission to the Council and the European Parliament, SEC(2005)175, at 4.

[20] The term comes from EMH Hirsch Ballin and LAJ Senden, *Co-actorship in the Development of European Law-making* (The Hague, TMC Asser Press, 2005).

[21] Sometimes even with a capital 'L': see eg COM(2005)462 final.

comparative public law. The complex structure of the institutional balance between the three Institutions involved in law-making culminates in the peculiar role of the Commission. As an independent Institution, the Commission has the sole right of initiative in order to counterbalance the risks that majority voting in the European Parliament and Council poses for the smaller countries.[22]

Now where does IA come in? By most standards the legitimacy of EC legislation is intimately linked to the Community method and to the institutional balance that makes this method possible. However, it is also a fact that many of the problems of legislative quality arise from the fact that legislative texts have to be negotiated between three legislative Institutions. To quote the Commission, '[i]deally, agreements on new legislation should not be achieved at the cost of unduly complex solutions that lower the legislative quality'.[23] Clearly one of the more implicit goals of IA is to temper the negotiation culture among the co-legislators. The introduction of IA as a tool that precedes the proposals and then travels with them through the legislative process could influence the conditions within which the institutional balance had been functioning until then. It would be a mistake to ignore what Radaelli has described as the:

> pivotal position of [IA] [which] stems from the fact that it provides standards for the whole process of policy formulation, by showing how consultation, the socio-economic costs and benefits, and the major trade-offs in policy choice have been taken into account in the assessment of regulatory proposals.[24]

Normative discourse on regulatory legitimacy always refers to 'the same evaluative criteria: expertise, proceduralization, subsidiarity'.[25] An Impact Assessment system is one of the mechanisms through which the relative importance of these criteria in legislative decision-making is determined. And through the concrete process of carrying out an IA these criteria are operationalised. Even though IA obviously cannot be equated with the decision-making itself, the procedure sheds light on the motives and arguments of the respective actors through their engagement with IA. Examples of how this might work are given later on in this chapter.

[22] J Temple Lang, 'Checks and Balances in the European Union: The Institutional Structure and the Community Method' (2006) 12 *European Public Law* 127.

[23] European Commission, Report from the Commission, 'Better Lawmaking 2003' (11th Report), COM(2003)770 final, at 4.

[24] CM Radaelli, 'Diffusion without Convergence: How Political Context Shapes the Adoption of Regulatory Impact Assessment' (2005) 12 *Journal of European Public Policy* 924.

[25] G Majone, 'Regulatory Legitimacy in the United States and the European Union' in R Howse and K Nicolaidis (eds), *The Federal Vision: Legitimacy and Levels of Governance in the United States and the European Union* (Oxford, OUP 2001), at 252—75.

B. INTER-INSTITUTIONALISING IA

Whether or not IA will come to function as an important source and force in the legislative process will at least in part depend on the status of the IA reports in that process. This section takes a look at the rules which stipulate how IA should be handled among the Institutions and who is responsible and accountable for which elements of the procedure.

The Inter-institutional Agreement on Better Lawmaking of 2003 already contained the possibility for the European Parliament and the Council to carry out IA, but the wording was still non-committal:

> [w]here the codecision procedure applies, the European Parliament and Council may, on the basis of jointly defined criteria and procedures, have impact assessments carried out prior to the adoption of any substantive amendment, either at first reading or at the conciliation stage.[26]

The agreement then goes on to state that as soon as possible, and after an assessment of their respective experiences by the Institutions, the establishment of a common methodology is to be considered. In November 2005 the Common Approach to Impact Assessment was agreed by the Commission, Council and Parliament, after preparations by the 'correspondents group', a sub-group of the High-Level Technical Group for Inter-institutional Cooperation.[27] This document amounts to a renewal by the European Parliament and the Council of their commitment to carry out IAs on substantive amendments and to use Commission IAs in their legislative deliberations. It does not contain a substantive common methodology, however, but instead sets out some traffic rules and some principles of EU IA. These include:

- — Integrated and balanced coverage of potential impacts (social, economic and environmental);
- — Coverage of short and long term costs and benefits (where possible);
- — Integration of subsidiarity and proportionality;
- — Attention to monitoring and evaluation in the IA;
- — Rigorous and comprehensive assessment based on accurate, objective and complete information;

[26] Above n14.

[27] The UK presidency had prepared a compromise text after a meeting of the Working Party on Competitiveness and Growth on 21 Sept 2005, which was subsequently updated after COREPER had examined it. The correspondents of the European Parliament and of the Commission agreed to a new compromise text. The Conference of Presidents formally adopted the Common Approach on 6 July 2006 after a plenary debate on Better Regulation was held on 4 Apr 2006 and four parliamentary reports on better law-making were adopted on 16 May 2006.

— Principle of proportionate analysis ('[t]he impact assessment's depth and scope will be determined by the likely impacts of the proposed action'[28]);
— Consideration of a range of legislative and non-legislative options (applies to the Commission only);
— Transparency (all IAs are to be published on websites);
— Consultation for IAs ('where reasonably possible and without causing undue delay in the legislative process');
— Cooperation (the Institutions will inform each other of current IA work).

These principles are hardly contentious. The same goes for the methodology to be used, despite the absence of a common methodology in the Common Approach. The European Commission's flexible approach to the choice of economic tools to use in an IA (quantification and even monetisation are desirable, but only where suitable[29]) has gained rather wide acceptance, except among the dedicated fans of American-style IA. Its very flexibility makes it difficult to disagree with this approach.

The real problematic issues are questions such as 'should Council and Parliament be allowed to ask the Commission to revisit its IA?', 'what is to be done when an important proposal does not have an IA accompanying it?' or 'how are we to make sure the IA has an impact but does not fetter the discretionary powers of the respective co-legislators too much?' These questions are addressed in the Common Approach, but not answered unambiguously. The obligation for the European Parliament and the Council to carry out IAs became subject to the qualification, 'when they consider this to be appropriate and necessary for the legislative process'.[30] Besides, the decision on what constitutes a 'substantive' amendment[31] remains for each respective Institution to determine as long as '[t]his decision ... reflect[s] the shared and balanced commitment to impact assessment and to Better Lawmaking in general'.[32] Because the practice of EU IA outside the Commission is limited—until recently there was only one much advertised experiment with IA in Council[33] and some exercises in the Parliament which, until recently, did not explicitly go under the label of IA—there is not much material to draw from when interpreting the ground rules on inter-institutional use of IA. A rough picture of the approaches by the two main legislative Institutions can be drawn though.

[28] Above n8, at 8.
[29] *Ibid*, at 37—8.
[30] Common Approach, above n13, pt 14.
[31] See n26 above and the corresponding text.
[32] *Ibid*, at pt 3.

1. IA in the European Parliament

The European Parliament has always approached issues of regulatory reform from the perspective of its preoccupation with preserving its own legislative powers. In 2001 it asked the Commission not to finalise the Action Plan on Better Regulation until the end of the consultation period for the White Paper on Governance (March 2002), because the choices that were to be made also touched upon the prerogatives of the Parliament.[34] Although the European Parliament was very critical of the Action Plan on Better Regulation, some MEPs have come to discover that parts of the better regulation strategy, and especially Impact Assessment, may have something to offer. The idea that 'effective democratic accountability is only possible if Parliament has sufficient information on the consequences of legislation on social, economic and environmental aspects' is expressed in the 'Doorn report', which is an own-initiative report from the Parliament on the subject of Impact Assessment.[35] The report defines Impact Assessment as a:

> straightforward mapping out of the consequences on social, economic and environmental aspects, and also a mapping out of the policy alternatives that are available to the legislator in that scenario.[36]

The Parliament cannot formally require the Commission to explain more clearly the reasons behind legislative proposals, let alone force the Commission to exercise its right of initiative, but IA could bring about a silent erosion of the Commission's 'hidden veto power'[37] by opening up the early phases of the policy-making and agenda-setting processes. A slightly ambivalent attitude—should IA be seen as a threat to democracy, or rather as an extra means of control over the pre-legislative stage?—is typical for the current thinking about IA within the European Parliament.

As for the practice of IA in the Parliament, Impact Assessments have been said to be 'completely invisible' within the political process.[38] However

[33] The Dutch Presidency chose the Commission's proposal for a dir on batteries and accumulators for a pilot project on IA of substantive amendments.

[34] The written version of this request is laid down in the Kaufmann report on the White Paper on Governance (Brussels, European Parliament, 15 Nov 2001) at pt 31, which contains some firm wording.

[35] European Parliament, 'Report on Assessment of the Impact of Community Legislation and the Consultation Procedures' (Doorn Report) (Brussels, European Parliament, 24 Mar 2004) at 5.

[36] *Ibid*, at 6.

[37] T Burns, 'Better Lawmaking? An Evaluation of Lawmaking in the European Community' in PP Craig and C Harlow (eds), *Lawmaking in the European Union* (London, Kluwer International, 1998).

[38] Mr John Cridland was quoted as saying, 'I also think that within the political process that then ensues impact assessments are completely invisible and both the Parliament and the Council need to get on board with this'. See House of Lords, 'Ensuring Effective Regulation in the EU. Report with Evidence', 9th Report of Session 2005—06, at 7 of the Minutes of Evidence.

there are signs of a change of mood, as illustrated by a comment in the report of the Environment Committee on the period 1999—2004 by then chairman Caroline Jackson:

> Another very topical issue has been that of impact assessments and whether more use needs to be made of them, and subject to which underlying criteria and practical conditions.[39]

In fact the Environment Committee has been something of a pioneer when it comes to producing its own Impact Assessments of substantive amendments[40] as well as scrutinising Commission IAs[41] (the two modes of use of IA in Parliament). The committee concluded a framework contract with the Institute for European Environmental Policy (IEEP) on regulatory policy assessments in the environmental area, with a view to improving legislative assistance to members of the ENVI Committee.[42] As early as 2004 it commissioned a study on the potential impacts of amendments tabled by one of its rapporteurs on the Fourth Daughter Directive on Air Quality. Unfortunately the IA study came too late for it to play a role in the debate, given the constraints imposed by the agenda of the European Parliament plenary session.[43] Misfit with parliamentary procedures is often cited as the main reason for slow progress in implementing IA by the Parliament.[44]

Under the same framework contract,[45] a small series of reviews of Commission IAs have been produced, under the label of briefing notes, which mainly serve as countercheck in legislative deliberations.[46] Furthermore

[39] Activity Report of the 1999—2004 Committee on Environment, Public Health and Consumer Policy.

[40] Art 30 of the 2003 Inter-Institutional Agreement on Better Lawmaking, above n14, which states that the European Parliament may, where the co-decision procedure applies, 'have impact assessments carried out prior to the adoption of any substantive amendment, either at first reading or at the conciliation stage': see above n14.

[41] Common Approach, above n13, pt 12. At the Conference on Impact Assessment organised by the European Commission on 20 Mar 2006 in Brussels, the speaker from the European Parliament named pesticides regulation and the thematic strategy on marine environment as dossiers in which a request may be made to the Commission to complement its IAs.

[42] See www.europarl.eu.int/comparl/envi/externalexpertise/default_en.htm (last accessed 27 Mar 2006).

[43] Interview with MEP Dorette Corbey.

[44] G Mather and F Vibert, *Evaluating Better Regulation: Building the System* (London, European Policy Forum, City Research Series, 2006) at 20.

[45] Framework contract seem to be the route of choice: the European Parliament has recently published two calls for tender for new framework contracts on Impact Assessment studies, one specifically for the Committee on Legal Affairs, the other of a more general nature.

[46] Eg IEEP, *Proposed air quality Directive: Assessment of the Environmental impact of Parliament's amended proposal, Policy Brief for the EP Environment Committee* , IP/A/ENVI/FWC/2005-35 (Brussels, IEEP, 2006); IEEP, *Proposed Directive on the Protection of Groundwater Against Pollution, Policy Brief for the EP Environment Committee*, EP/IV/A/2003/09/01 (Brussels, IEEP, 2003).

the IMCO Committee commissioned an IA on the proposal for a directive on pre-packed products—perhaps the first parliamentary IA presented under that label—in an attempt to show that the Commission had consulted selectively and that its proposal was too 'deregulatory'.[47]

2. IA in the Council of Ministers

Rather than the institutional effects of better regulation and Impact Assessment, the substantive goals of these policies, most notably enhancing the competitiveness of European businesses and strengthening sustainable development, have been the main interest for the Council in the past. But after taking the obligation to use IA upon itself so unequivocally in the Common Approach, the Council had to refocus its thinking towards the implementation of IA into its decision-making procedures. IA as a phenomenon is particularly alien to the highly politicised decision-making in Council, where '[c]ompromises will not be put at risk by evidence'.[48] However, in the Conclusions of the November 2005 Competitiveness Council, the Common Approach was welcomed and the Council committed itself to undertaking to 'embed it into Council work on Impact Assessment'. It also reaffirmed:

> its intention to carry out impact assessments on substantive Council amendments, to be determined by the appropriate Council preparatory bodies, to legislative proposals, with a view to developing best practice, in line with the commitment in the Inter-institutional Agreement on Better law-making, without prejudice to the legislator's capacity to propose amendments.[49]

This commitment has materialised in the production by the Austrian presidency of internal guidance for working party chairs on how to deal with IA.[50] This document contains some traffic rules both on the use of Commission IAs and on the production of IAs on substantive amendments. At present, similar rules do not exist for the Parliament. The document recommends to chairs of working parties that they pose the following key

[47] European Parliament, Impact Assessment. Parliament's Amendments to a Commission Proposal on Nominal Quantities for Pre-Packed Products (Brussels, European Parliament, 2005).

[48] G Mather and F Vibert, *Evaluating Better Regulation: Building the System* (London, City Research Series, 2006), 21.

[49] Press release, Council of Ministers, 'Conclusions of the Competitiveness Council of 28—29 November 2005', at 17 and 18.

[50] Council of Ministers, 'Handling IAs in Council: Indicative guidance for Working Party Chairs' (Brussels, Council of Ministers, 15 May 2006).

question as the basis for the scrutiny of a Commission IA: does the IA 'provide sufficient information to inform positions and for well-informed debate on the proposal?'.[51] But to the inevitable follow-up question of what should be done when the answer is 'no' the document does not provide any real answer; the guidance offered on this issue comes down to engaging in informal negotiations with the Commission on whether further IA work could be done.

It is not only in the existence of explicit guidance, but also in practice that the implementation of the IA procedure in the Council differs from that in the Parliament. The experiment initiated by the Dutch presidency to produce an IA on substantive amendments to the Directive on Batteries and Accumulators has been highly publicised, but became stranded in the COREPER phase. A paper from the UK presidency on progress on Impact Assessment reports two more low-profile Council experiments, namely on the Potato Cyst Nematode Directive and the Forest Law Enforcement, Governance and Trade Regulation, as well as 12 instances of Commission IAs that have been put on the agenda of working parties. Scrutinising Commission IAs as part of the preparation of political decision-making, is the easy part, for the Council and the Secretariat has already developed some sort of routine for supporting working parties in this scrutiny process.[52] It is the routine production of the Council's own IAs that is most eagerly awaited, because this could involve an important shift in the way the Council operates. In the Commission's words:

> [w]hile Parliament usually provided a justification for its amendments, anecdotal evidence suggests that this was rarely the case for Council's amendments.[53]

It is not surprising, then, that the Commission would welcome an obligation to conduct IAs of Third Pillar initiatives, where 'compliance with the principles of subsidiarity and proportionality was more often stated than demonstrated'.[54] A review clause of the Common Approach suggests that in the context of the review of the document in two years' time, 'as appropriate, Council Impact Assessment on specific initiatives presented by one or more Member States concerning their economic, environmental and social aspects' could be considered.[55]

[51] *Ibid*, pt 14.
[52] Interview with a Council Secretariat official.
[53] European Commission, Report from the Commission, 'Better Lawmaking 2004' (12th Report), COM(2005)98 final, at 6.
[54] *Ibid.*
[55] Common Approach, above n13, pt 19.

C. INFORMING, GUIDING, JUSTIFYING...

The word 'informing' in the phrase 'informing the legislator' implies a very humble and neutral role. This is at odds with the roots of IA, which can be found in the United States, where this type of *ex ante* evaluation can even be crucial for the legality of a regulatory decision. But in the EU context the phrase is also problematic, as becomes apparent from a closer analysis of a statement from the first Commission Communication on IA, which speaks of using IA to 'guide and justify the choice of the right instrument at the appropriate level of intensity of European action'.[56] The same document then goes on to state that IA will also:

> provide the legislator with more accurate and better structured information on the positive and negative impacts, having regard to economic, social and environmental aspects. Thirdly, it will constitute a means of selecting, during the work programming phase, *those initiatives which are really necessary*.[57]

It is submitted that these functions are contradictory and illustrate well the tension inherent in the use of IA as an 'information tool'. According to the 2002 Communication on Better Lawmaking, EU IA needs 'to guide', 'to justify', 'to inform' and 'to select'. Below a typology of IA is presented which uses these four verbs as starting points and shows that they correspond to fundamentally different possible functions of IA which cannot easily be reconciled. More importantly, which of these functions one attributes—explicitly or implicitly—to EU IA depends on one's conception of EU lawmaking and the appropriate constitutional roles of each of the actors in it.

1. Speaking Truth to Power

A possible function of IA in the legislative process is to deliver a more objective analysis, which can 'speak truth to power'.[58] Guidance provided to the legislator is of a strong kind and could even amount to dictating the content of decisions. For what is a legislator to do when faced with 'the truth'? An

[56] European Commission, 'European Governance: Better Lawmaking', Communication from the Commission, COM(2002)275 final, at 3.

[57] *Ibid*, at 3—4 (emphasis in the original).

[58] The famous catchphrase 'speaking truth to power' is the title of a book on policy analysis written by Aaron Wildavsky in 1979. The book describes the state of the art of the field of policy analysis in its early days and proposes how to establish policy analysis as a discipline in its own right. This should not be taken to mean that Wildavsky believes policy analysis amounts to 'speaking truth to power'. After mentioning the phrase for the first time in the introduction (at 1) he even adds between brackets the exclamation 'if only we had either!'. Indeed, he insists (at 17) that policy analysis is about 'relationships between people' : see A Wildavsky, *Speaking Truth to Power: The Art and Craft of Policy Analysis* (Boston, Mass, Little Brown & Co, 1979).

IA model built around this function is the closest to the intellectual roots of IA as a means of controlling rule-making power delegated to agencies.[59] However, it is not an obvious choice for the EU IA system which is designed for use in the 'primary' legislative process, and therefore needs to avoid substituting political decision-making. For when an IA is perceived as containing the objective truth, the only way it can justify a regulatory decision is when this decision follows the recommendations that the IA report inevitably contains, turning IA effectively into a decision-making tool. And yet 'speaking truth to power' seems to be the function meant when IA is presented as 'a means of selecting, during the work programming phase, *those initiatives which are really necessary*'.[60] Obviously the qualification 'during the work programming phase; has been added, but it is hard to see how IA can play fundamentally different roles in different stages of the legislative procedure. A document which purports to have looked at all regulatory and non-regulatory options and to have selected the optimal one will be hard to adapt in the face of amendments.

2. Reason-giving for Legislative Decisions

At the other side of the spectrum, IA can help politicians to convince stakeholders and citizens of the virtues of the legislation or policy at hand. If one equates 'political decision-making' with 'power' this will be the most appropriate goal for EU IA. In this approach IA serves most and for all to justify legislative and policy decisions. and the extent to which the analysis has influenced or guided the decision is not clear. A document like that is not necessarily without value; Article 253 of the EC Treaty even contains an explicit requirement to give reasons for legislative decisions.[61] The question remains, however, whether IA is the appropriate instrument for this, especially when the Explanatory Memorandum already has a justificatory function. Because of the higher level of ambition normally associated with IA, there is the risk that IAs aimed at mere 'justifying' could come to serve as:

> shields to allow decisions to be routinized, reasons for any findings to be produced with ease, and decision-makers to be both insulated from political pressures and lent authority for any particular exercise of power.[62]

[59] EA Posner, 'Controlling Agencies with Cost-Benefit Analysis: A Positive Political Theory Perspective', John M Olin Law & Economics Working Papers, 2nd series, no 119 (Chicago, Ill, University of Chicago, 2001).

[60] Above n55, at 4.

[61] Art 253 EC states: '[r]egulations, directives and decisions adopted jointly by the European Parliament and the Council, and such acts adopted by the Council or the Commission, shall state the reasons on which they are based and shall refer to any proposals or opinions which were required to be obtained pursuant to this Treaty.'

[62] R Baldwin, *Rules and Government* (Oxford, Clarendon Press, 1995).

In more neutral words: using EU IA for 'reason-giving' could reduce it from an 'information tool' to a 'communication tool'. It is thus for good reasons that the Common Approach states that:

> [t]he rigour, objectivity and comprehensive nature of the analysis should mean that the impact assessment is not a simple justification of the initiative or the substantive amendment. [63]

However, since the EU IA system contains many contradictory intentions and incentives we need to retain 'reason-giving for legislative decisions' in this typology.

3. Providing a Forum for Stakeholder Input

Thirdly, IA can provide a forum for stakeholder input. Here being an 'aid to political decision-making' means helping stakeholders to express their preferences in the legislative process. The IA report then runs the risk of being reduced to a document summarising the consultation, whereas the very idea behind IA is to go beyond that by providing at least some degree of objective, reproduceable analysis. It is evident that an IA of this type cannot live up to the ambition of 'informing the legislator' in any sense that goes beyond the policy-making instruments that were already in place before the launch of the IA procedure. Yet, like the previous function discussed, IA as 'consultation plus' cannot be excluded in advance as a possible function for EU IA. This is because (a) it is sometimes proposed as an ideal function and (b) it can certainly be witnessed in practice now and then (see the example of the REACH IA below).

There are two further possible functions that IA can have in the legislative process, which are more convincing because they are more comprehensive and more refined. They are not necessarily contradictory, but emphasise different elements in the IA procedure and—if really implemented—require different institutional designs.

4. Highlighting Trade-offs

Perhaps the best hope for EU IA to 'inform' political decision-making in such a way that 'power' can process the information on offer is for the IA report to focus on highlighting trade-offs. This is indeed the very function emphasised in numerous Commission policy documents on IA, but it has

[63] Common Approach, above n13, pt 5.

turned out rather tricky to implement in practice. The first characteristic of this approach is that, instead of claiming that the IA report contains 'the truth', several policy options and their impacts are ranked according to several decision-making criteria (multi-criteria analysis). It is then up to the decision-maker to decide which criterion he wants to use in order to select one option. Stakeholders will then at the very least be able to hold the decision-maker accountable for this decision and challenge both the arguments and the evidence on the basis of the IA. Not every decision would be directly justified by an IA, but on a macro level legitimacy would be enhanced by the presence of the IA regime. This approach comes closest to the direction the Institutions apparently want for EU IA when they declare in the Common Approach that:

> [c]areful consideration of the evidence presented in the impact assessment should allow the relevant institution to decide on whether to proceed with the proposal or amendment and/or to shape the proposal or amendment in the light of its potential impacts.[64]

But then again quasi-legal provisions of this kind determine only a small part of the practical functioning of EU IA. Besides, other provisions in the same document, notably the 'escape clause' that IA must not 'prejudice the legislator's capacity to propose amendments' send a rather different message.

This approach suffers from two problems. The first is peculiar to the way IA is set in the EU legislative process: what happens when the European Parliament or the Council wants to use a different decision-making criterion from the Commission? The second problem is universal. This approach comes down to a compromise between the 'truth to power' approach and the 'reason-giving' approach, thereby running the risk of slipping into either. Can transparency ever be so strong that stakeholders will be able to distinguish between IAs that 'select', those that merely 'justify' and those that really 'inform', especially when it is—in the absence of any enforcement mechanisms—very easy to claim one thing and do the other?

5. Structuring the Discourse

The last option is possibly even trickier but also more promising. EU IA could also guide the legislative process in a procedural way, by structuring the legislative discourse. The obligation to take into account the information from IAs could be construed in such a way as to provide incentives for non-strategic arguing, thereby contributing to a proceduralisation of the

[64] Common Approach, above n13, at pt 6.

lawmaking process. This approach is of course vulnerable to all the familiar criticisms of the literature on deliberative democracy. However, if IA has one inherent strength it is that it is non-hierarchical by its very nature. An advantage for EU IA could be that this function is less static by virtue of being less dependent on one excellent original Impact Assessment. To illustrate, it has emerged from interviews with national civil servants who go to Council working parties that they are mainly interested in carrying out IA because it provides arguments. Without getting into the question whether deliberation is a viable decision-making mode for the Council, it is worthwhile to point out that in order to keep all parties on board the IA ship it may be necessary to ensure that EU IA is centrally about arguing, whilst heavy procedural rules—which admittedly are currently non-existent—would have to ensure a non-hierarchical structure.

D. ILLUSTRATING THE FUNCTIONS OF IA IN INTER-INSTITUTIONAL PRACTICE

Below three concrete institutional issues connected to the EU IA procedure are discussed through the lens of the five different functions presented above.

1. The Debate on External Review

From time to time the question whether Commission IAs should be subject to external review by independent (economics) experts returns to the debate on the future development of the EU IA system.[65] Lobby groups are usually in favour on the ground that such a review could be 'an alternative way of getting market expertise into the analysis'.[66] The European Parliament has also repeatedly expressed a preference for some kind of independent review on a structural basis. In the explanatory statement to his report, Doorn argues in favour of an independent institution that can monitor 'the implementation of an impact assessment', which would allegedly prevent Impact Assessment from being 'turned into an instrument for opposing undesired legislation in an undemocratic manner'.[67] The idea that the IA

[65] The debate even goes back to the early days. See the joint statement by the 4 consecutive EU Presidencies (Ireland, Netherlands, Luxembourg and the UK) of 26 Jan 2001 in which the presidencies asked that Commission IAs undergo a more formal quality control before adoption of the proposal.

[66] European Policy Forum, *Reducing the Regulatory Burden: The Arrival of Meaningful Regulatory Impact Analysis* (London, City Research Series, 2004) at 27.

[67] European Parliament, 'Doorn report', above n34.

procedure should undergo a mandatory peer review process is repeated in the McCarthy report, a recent report on better regulation focussing on internal market legislation.[68] The argument can be summarised as follows: the Commission is a stakeholder in the process, and therefore by definition cannot be trusted to provide an objective analysis. Possible counter-arguments are that:

> the Commission will already have much of the data and subject expertise needed for impact assessment, setting up an external body to do the analysis is likely to be more costly than the present system and to introduce delays in the legislative programme which the present system, when running well, should be able to avoid.[69]

The Commission has so far resisted systematic external review of individual IAs, although Vice-President Verheugen has expressed sympathy for the idea of 'an independent Task Force running the shop as far as better regulation is concerned'[70] and an independent review of the IA *system* is underway. Recently, plans to set up a special board composed of high-level Commission officials in a personal capacity who would review the Commission IAs and report directly to the President have been revealed.[71] Indeed, when discussing whether independent review should be part of the institutional design of the EU it is important to remember that such review could take many forms.[72] Which form is the most appropriate depends partly on the preferred function of IA.

In any case the example of the REACH IA shows how lack of agreement on who should review (and produce) Impact Assessments can reduce IA to a 'forum for stakeholder input'. The original IA on REACH, a major proposal for a regulation on the registration of chemicals, as produced by the Commission was accepted by almost none of the stakeholders.[73] Several of them, including a number of Member States, then went on to produce their

[68] European Parliament, 'Report on the Implementation, Consequences and Impact of the Internal Market Legislation in Force (McCarthy Report) (Brussels, European Parliament, 23 Mar 2006).

[69] M Courtney, 'Contribution from the Regulatory Impact Unit, Cabinet Office, UK, to accompany presentation by Dr. Mark Courtney at the Public Hearing on Impact Assessment of Community Legislation, Committee on Legal Affairs and Internal Market, European Parliament' (Brussels, European Parliament, 22 Jan 2004).

[70] G Verheugen, speech delivered at UK Presidency Better Regulation Conference, Edinburgh, 23 Sept 2005.

[71] European Commission, Communication, 'A Strategic Review of Better Regulation in the European Union', COM(2006) 689 final, 14 Nov 2006, at 8.

[72] The options proposed in Mather and Vibert, above n43, are the following: strengthen oversight capacity of Secretariat-General, a new unit reporting to Commission President, the Court of Auditors, a new independent agency and private informal review.

[73] As became clear during the workshop on IA of REACH which the Commission organised on 21 Nov 2003.

own assessments, the total number exceeding 40. The Dutch presidency made an attempt to mediate between different assessments when it organised a workshop on the REACH Impact Assessments on 25—27 October 2004 for Council experts in order to 'bring together the results of the studies already available and to consider the lessons to be drawn from them'.[74] In the meantime stakeholders, in particular industry lobby groups, had started negotiations with DG Environment and DG Enterprise to review the initial Impact Assessment. The result of this was a Memorandum of Understanding between CEFIC, UNICE, DG Environment and DG Enterprise containing the commitment to 'provide a framework for the efficient undertaking of further investigations on business impacts of REACH'. To the REACH Working Group entitled 'Further Work on Impact Assessment' that was subsequently established to oversee the further IA work for which KPMG was contracted, a broader group of stakeholders was invited (industry, trade unions, environmental and consumer NGOs). Some stakeholders felt that despite these efforts the process lacked legitimacy, and some environmental NGOs even decided to withdraw their cooperation, citing 'major deficiencies in both the methodology and transparency of the process'[75] as their reasons.

In the 'truth to power' approach such a negotiated revision of the Commission IA is problematic and possibly could have been prevented by external review of the original IA by independent scientists and economists. In the 'structuring the discourse' approach it need not be problematic, and may even be desirable, when stakeholders start a debate on the basis of IA and then review their preferences. However due to lack of procedural rules ('what counts as an IA?', 'who has access to which information?'), the REACH IA process did little more than help stakeholders to express their political preferences (effectively the 'forum for stakeholder input' model). If it is true that the REACH case is when EU IA matured,[76] then it has an uncertain future ahead of it.

2. The Right of Initiative

The policy roots of EU IA lie in the White Paper on Governance, which was aimed at fostering institutional change without amending the Treaties and

[74] Netherlands Presidency of the EU, Conclusions and Recommendations of Workshop on REACH Impact Assessments, held on 25—27 Oct 2004 in The Hague, The Netherlands.

[75] Statement from WWF and the European Environmental Bureau (EEB), 16 July 2004.

[76] John Cridland said at a hearing, 'I think impact assessments came of age with the REACH proposals on chemicals but, my word, it was a painful process': see House of Lords, 'Ensuring Effective Regulation in the EU. Report with Evidence', 9th Report of Session 2005—06 (London, House of Lords, 2005), at 7 of the Minutes of Evidence.

within the framework of the Community method.[77] The Commission has insisted that IA 'should help the Commission to exercise its right of initiative and to promote the Community method by means of fully informed political decisions'.[78] The IA procedure has been designed accordingly: it is the Commission's prerogative to draw up the IA report and postpone its publication until the proposal is ready. However, the insistence that Commission IAs first and foremost serve to facilitate internal policy preparation is fundamentally at odds with the notion of Commission IAs as starting points for legislative debates within and between all three Institutions. The idea that more than one option is analysed in the IA process and that the results are published in the IA report is an interesting element of the procedure in this respect. Another possible challenge for an undisturbed exercise of the right of initiative is the decision to publish road maps giving a first indication of the main areas to be assessed and the planning of IA together with the Work Programme as of 2005.[79]

The implications that IA can have for the exercise of the right of initiative are illustrated by the case of the Air Quality Thematic Strategy (CAFE). On the basis of one of the most comprehensive IAs ever produced by the Commission,[80] a proposal was selected which ranked in the comparison only second in terms of expected net benefits to society (mainly environmental). Consequently several MEPs and stakeholders argued that the Commission was not taking into account the results of IA.[81] Clearly, but probably unconsciously, they had a 'truth to power' function for IA in mind; a type of IA that points to the optimal policy, which is defined as the policy delivering the highest net benefits to society. However, in a 'highlighting trade-offs' model, preferring a policy representing only the second highest level of ambition for political reasons is perfectly acceptable and corresponds to a political exercise of the right of initiative. But in that case it would have helped convince the co-legislators and stakeholders that its use of IA was legitimate if the Commission had indicated why it chose this specific policy (which was, after all, ranked second according to the prevailing IA criterion). The same goes for the 'structuring the discourse' function, for which however the CAFE IA case can tentatively be seen as a silent

[77] European Commission, White Paper on Governance, COM(2001)428 final.

[78] European Commission, 'Impact Assessment: Next Steps. In Support of Competitiveness and Sustainable Development', Commission Staff Working Paper, SEC(2004)1377, at 3.

[79] *Ibid*, at 5.

[80] European Commission, Impact Assessment of the Communication on Thematic Strategy on Air Pollution and the Directive on Ambient Air Quality and Cleaner Air for Europe, Commission staff Working Paper, SEC(2005)1133.

[81] European Parliament, 'Report on the Thematic Strategy on Air Pollution, Committee on the Environment, Public Health and Food Safety', Rapporteur: Dorette Corbey (Brussels, European Parliament, 30 June 2006).

victory. There is evidence that IA was used as the starting point for legislative discussions in each of the Institutions.[82] And the contention over the legitimate use of IA in this case has at least forced some actors to go beyond repeating their arguments and to articulate the presuppositions behind their preferences. Above all this case illustrates how the actors involved in the EU IA system are not ready to embrace one of the functions set out above as the core function of IA in the legislative process and develop the procedure accordingly.

3. The Evidence Base of EU Legislation

Finally—as already suggested above—a link can be established between the policy preference to shift towards evidence-based decision-making and the legal obligation to *prove* that the EU is competent (principle of attributed powers, Article 5(1) EC Treaty) and—in the case of shared competences—can do *better* (principle of subsidiarity, Article 5(2) EC Treaty). Because the subsidiarity principle is often interpreted as hinging essentially on the criterion of comparative efficiency, and because of the centrality of the internal market in many Treaty provisions, it was always the case that the determination of competence in the EC context could depend on the outcome of economic analysis. However, now with the increasing institutionalisation of IA, we have a concrete tool to implement this further.[83] Although the Court of Justice has tied its marginal review of compliance with the subsidiarity requirement to the duty to motivate,[84] it has so far never mentioned Impact Assessment. On 16 March 2006 Advocate-General Sharpston in her opinion

[82] ENVI news, 'Newsletter from the European Parliament's Environment, Public Health and Food Safety Committee', Feb 2006, confirms this for the European Parliament; a document from the UK presidency reports that in the Council working party on 24 Oct the CAFE IA was discussed; and at a seminar on EU Better Regulation entitled 'Assessing Impact' at the University of Manchester School of Law in Jan 2006, a Commission official stated that the IA has been used as the basis for discussion in the Competitiveness group of Commissioners.

[83] Arguably Art 5 EC and the Protocol on the application of the principles of subsidiarity and proportionality which the Treaty of Amsterdam added to the EC Treaty in 1997 together provide the constitutional basis for the IA procedure. In support of this argument it is worth noting that the reports delivering on the obligation for the Commission to report annually on the application of the principles of subsidiarity and proportionality to the European Council and the European Parliament in recent years have been published under the label of 'better lawmaking'. The reason given was that these issues are 'intimately linked as the measures introduced to improve regulation should make for better compliance with the principles of subsidiarity and proportionality, and vice versa': European Commission, Report from the Commission, 'Better Lawmaking 2003' (11th Report), COM(2003)770 final, at 3.

[84] The ECJ decided that Art 190 (now 253) EC did not require an explicit reference to the subsidiarity principle as long as the reasons EC action was necessary were stated in the recitals: Case C—233/94 *Germany v European Parliament and Council* [1997] ECR I—2405.

in *Spain v Council*[85] mentioned Impact Assessment '[i]n the absence of any impact study, certain choices made by the Commission and the Council appear arbitrary'. The Court in its judgment, whilst annulling part of Council Regulation 864/2004[86] which put in place a new Community support system for cotton because it breached the principle of proportionality for failure by the Council and Commission to take into account certain relevant costs, did not attach similar importance to the absence of an official IA as such.[87] Nor has the Court ever interpreted the reason-giving requirement of Article 253 in such a way as to oblige the Commission to enter into a dialogue with stakeholders, to consider the full costs and benefits of proposal or to engage in any other activity which is now incorporated in the IA procedure. It is still early days for EU IA, but at least the hypothesis seems warranted that IA can help strengthen the link between competence and evidence by moving the justification of a Commission proposal away from a narrow focus on finding a legal basis in the treaties.[88]

A next question is whether we can take the argument one step further by submitting that in the future a regulation or directive without IA will be deemed to lack legal basis. There is no concrete evidence that the triangle 'evidence base, legal base, Impact Assessment' is becoming this strong, but there are some indications that thinking within the Institutions and among stakeholders may develop in this direction. In fact the idea that a shift towards evidence-based decision-making should have consequences for the decision whether a proposal can become law goes back as far as the White Paper on Governance. It proposes that the Commission should 'withdraw proposals where inter-institutional bargaining undermines the Treaty principles of subsidiarity and proportionality or the proposal's objectives'.[89] A recent and firmer statement on the extent to which the Commission plans to tie the use of IA to the basis for legislation in the future was made by Commissioner McCreevy, who said that his Internal Market directorate-general would put forward proposals only 'if there is an economic case for legislative action'.[90] Commissioner Verheugen, at his examination by

[85] Case C—310/04 *Spain v Council,* judgment of 7 Sept 2006 (not yet reported).

[86] [2004] OJ L161/48.

[87] Yet it is interesting to note that in the European Parliament the conclusion of the AG has been taken to 'demonstrate and confirm the Court of Justice's increasing interest in this issue': Remarks by MEP Lehne during the plenary debate on better regulation on 4 Apr 2006.

[88] European Policy Forum, *Reducing the Regulatory Burden: The Arrival of Meaningful Regulatory Impact Analysis* (London, City Research Series, 2004).

[89] European Commission, White Paper on Governance, COM(2001)428 final, 25 July 2001.

[90] Speech by Charlie McCreevy on 'Better Regulation and the Financial Services Sector', delivered at a Seminar on 'Better Regulation: A European and Irish Perspective', Institute of European Affairs, Dublin, 21 June 2005.

the European Union Committee of the House of Lords on 4 July 2005, extended this principle to the other Institutions:

> If in the co-decision process Parliament and/or Council produce amendments, changes which are not only just minor but real changes, then there should be an Impact Assessment. If it is not there the Commission will make it very clear that the Commission does not feel that there is a sound basis for a proper decision.[91]

This is firm language indeed. If the Commission acted up to this statement by Verheugen, this could mean the introduction of IA to the ECJ. However, putting the faith of an IA into judicial hands would sit uneasily with the idea that IA should serve as an 'aid not substitute to political-decision making'. Indeed 'judicialising' IA fits best with the type of IA that aims to 'speak truth to power', a type that the Commission does not object to when it comes to keeping the Council and Parliament from over-regulating but is less keen on for internal decision-making purposes. Also, an IA drawn up with the possibility of review by a court in the back of the mind of the author is more likely to be aimed at 'justifying' rather than 'guiding'. And this brings us back to the hypothesis that lack of clarity on the role of IA in the legislative process is caused by implicit ambiguity regarding its core function.

The practice of EU IA hitherto offers no direct evidence that IA is acquiring strong legal relevance as yet, but the discourse is already shifting towards considering an IA as a prerequisite for legislative action. When the Commission announced (on 28 March 2006) a proposal for a regulation aimed at bringing down the costs of using mobile telephones abroad (roaming), lobby groups were quick to point out the absence of an IA:

> If the Commission continues to pursue the idea of legislation, it should first carry out a full impact assessment. This kind of analysis is a requirement of the Commission's own internal process guidelines.[92]

An Impact Assessment was produced by the Commission afterwards.[93] Now this course of action can still produce valuable results, but it can also—especially if it happens on a regular basis—give stakeholders a reason to be sceptical about the extent to which IA can ever 'guide' decision-making.

[91] House of Lords, 'Ensuring Effective Regulation in the EU. Report with Evidence', 9th Report of Session 2005—06 (London, House of Lords, 2005), at 25 of the Minutes of Evidence.

[92] GSM Association Press Release 2006, 'Further Roaming Regulation is Unnecessary and Potentially Damaging: GSMA Calls for a Full Impact Assessment of Any EU-wide Roaming Legislation', available at www.gsmworld.com/news/press_2006/press06_22.shtml.

[93] European Commission, 'Impact Assessment of Policy Options in Relation to a Commission Proposal for a Regulation of the European Parliament and of the Council on Roaming on Public Mobile Networks Within the Community', Commission Staff Working Paper, SEC(2006)925 (12 July 2006).

E. CONCLUSION

The purpose of this chapter is emphatically not to propose alternative benchmarks for evaluating EU IA. Its aim is to illustrate *potential* functions of IA as an instrument to inform the legislator. The chapter goes one step further by showing how these functions are linked to the development of certain institutional issues. The battle over IA mirrors competing views on EU law-making and governance and could explain many of the difficulties surrounding the implementation of IA in the EU policy process. Because the EU IA system emphasises evidence-based decision-making on the one hand and the primacy of the political level on the other, it has created an inherent tension which is bound to come out at some point in the actual law-making process, as is shown by some of the illustrations presented. Arguments about political choices associated with legislative proposals can easily become intertwined with arguments about the legitimacy of the Impact Assessment, because there is so much confusion over what can be expected from the procedure. On a more fundamental level it is submitted that failure to recognise the constitutional significance of EU IA causes the debate to be conducted in misleading terms. Thus, arguments which are really about the constitutional roles of different legislative actors can be disguised as arguments about the design of IA. Similarly, views on constitutional issues should be explicitly echoed in the debate on how to develop EU IA into a tool that can meaningfully inform the legislator.

17

Better Law-making

JANE WELCH*

THE EUROPEAN COMMISSION set out its policy priorities for financial services for the following five years in its White Paper on Financial Services Policy 2005–10.[1] The policy objectives included the following:

> [T]o implement, enforce and continuously evaluate the existing legislation and to apply rigorously the better regulation agenda to future initiatives.

The ultimate objective was to:

> consolidate dynamically towards an integrated, open, inclusive, competitive and economically efficient EU financial market.

These are laudable objectives but the emphasis on future 'initiatives' illustrates the limits to the Commission's power to deliver its policy agenda. The adoption of better EU financial services law requires the cooperation of the other institutional players in the EU law-making process—the European Parliament and the Council. Even if the Commission faithfully observes its commitment to:

> deploy the most open, transparent, evidence-based policy-making based on a dual commitment to open consultation and impact assessments, so as to ensure that sound rules are drawn up, adding value to the EU's financial services sector and consumers,[2]

there is nothing to stop either the Parliament or the Council introducing major changes to a Commission proposal during the EU legislative process, the effect of which can be to destroy the original Commission proposals.

* Director, European Financial and Corporate Law Centre, British Institute of International and Comparative Law.

[1] COM(2005)629.

[2] Commission White Paper on Financial Services Policy 2005–10, above n1.

The current preoccupation with 'better regulation' tends to focus almost exclusively on the process of implementation of EU legislation in the Member States[3] and on supervisory convergence in monitoring and enforcement of compliance with Community obligations. But the process of ensuring effective and consistent implementation of EU legislation is made much more difficult if the text adopted by the Council and Parliament is badly drafted, ambiguous or otherwise unclear. There is a limit to what the Commission can achieve by way of Interpretative Communications, if Member States choose not to follow the Commission's interpretation of particular provisions, and no evidence is as yet available as to how successful the process of supervisory convergence and agreed interpretation is proving. Ultimately, the Commission is left with the unenviable choice between accepting divergent implementation across the EU or taking a Member State to the European Court of Justice for failure to implement a directive correctly, in the hope that the Court will endorse the Commission's reading of the directive.

It is tempting to assume that, with the adoption of the measures set out in the Financial Services Action Plan and the Commission's self-denying ordinance on future financial services proposals, badly drafted legislation is no longer an issue and that attention would be better directed to implementation. But it is clear from the Commission's White Paper that new legislation is still contemplated in several areas. Initiatives may be proposed as a result of evaluation of the measures adopted under the Financial Services Action Plan, or as part of the process of simplification, codification and clarification of existing legislation, or where necessary to complete the Single Market in financial services.

It remains crucially important therefore to analyse the reasons EU financial services legislation so often fails to deliver the full benefits promised and to assess the solutions which have been put forward to see whether the future looks more promising. What follows concentrates on the roles of the Commission, Council and European Parliament in relation to Level One directives under the Lamfalussy process. The comments about policy formation and drafting competence apply equally, however, to Level Two measures.[4]

A. DRAFTING OF EU PROPOSALS

It has become a cliché to urge that EU law should be based on clear policy and backed up by a risk-based assessment that a legislative response to the

[3] See eg the Davidson Review in the UK: Better Regulation Executive, *Davidson Review of the Implementation of EU Legislation* (London, Cabinet Office, 28 Nov 2006).

[4] For an explanation of Level One and Level Two measures see Committee of Wise Men, 'The Regulation of European Securities Markets: Final Report' (Feb 2001)(the Lamfalussy Report.

problems identified is the most effective way of achieving the desired objective. The draft legislation should be proportionate, clear, unambiguous and as concise as possible. It is often assumed that legislation is invariably complex and detailed.[5] However, complexity and detail are largely a question of drafting style, and in the EU, as in the UK, it is often the case that obscure and tortuous drafting is an attempt to cover up disagreement or uncertainty about the policy objectives underpinning the particular measure. Detail does not necessarily provide clarity, but general principles can be equally vague or imprecise.

For this reason the arguments adduced in favour of 'soft law' or guidance—that it is more flexible, quicker to implement, and is clear and concise—seem misconceived. There are plenty of examples of clear concise legislative drafting, and equally many examples of soft law which go into interminable detail, prescribing every aspect of behaviour in every conceivable situation.[6] Each has a part to play, but in an internal market designed to give effect to the four freedoms under the Treaty and based on mutual recognition of harmonised standards, those standards need to be enshrined in legally binding instruments. The financial services directives impose obligations ultimately on financial institutions, but they also confer rights—rights which have to be legally protected if they are to be enforceable. The most common complaint heard from financial institutions is not that EU legislation takes too long to be adopted or that it is too detailed. It is rather that it is unclear, inappropriate or irrelevant,[7] and that in many cases it erects fresh barriers to freedom of establishment and freedom to provide services in place of those it purports to dismantle.

B. THE VALUE OF CONSULTATION

The consultation procedures established as a result of the Lamfalussy process[8] should ensure that, by the time a Commission proposal is put forward, it is on the basis of a sound, agreed policy. After a few early hiccups, the Commission is now fully committed to consultation. The first draft of the Market Abuse Directive was rushed out after minimal consultation after the 11 September tragedy on the ground that the Directive was needed urgently as part of the fight against terrorism.[9] Similarly, the Commission

5 This was certainly one of the complaints made by the Lamfalussy Report.

6 See, eg, national codes of conduct for particular trades or professions.

7 See, eg, the reaction in the UK to the Prospectus Dir [2003] OJ L345/64. The International Primary Markets Association (now part of the International Capital Markets Association 'ICMA')was particularly critical, arguing that the draft dir , as orginally proposed, would drive wholesale business, and particularly the international debt market, out of the EU.

8 For detailed examination see the chapter in this book by Niamh Moloney.

9 See the Explanatory Memorandum to COM(2001)281.

adopted the draft proposal on prospectuses without going through the full Lamfalussy consultation process.[10] The draft of the Markets in Financial Instruments Directive was amended at the last minute before adoption by the Commission, after a lengthy consultation period and a full impact assessment, to include controversial provisions on pre-trade transparency.[11]

C. THE IMPORTANCE OF DRAFTING

Much of the criticism directed at EU financial services legislation is aimed as much at the drafting as at the substance of the provisions. A Commission proposal is generally drafted by an official within the relevant Directorate-General (DG) which has competence in the subject matter. When a directive falls within the competence of two Directorates–General, for example DG Internal Market and DG SANCO, as was the case with the Distance Marketing Directive,[12] one DG will be in the lead.

Although the draftsman may be a lawyer, he will not have any training in legislative drafting. His principal concern is to get the policy agreed, internally within the Commission and externally with interested parties, and then to follow the draft through the EU legislative machinery. Often the official concerned will be a national 'expert' seconded to the Commission by a Member State to provide specialised policy input. But the draftsman is unlikely to be an expert on EU legislative drafting. Nor can he or she be expected to be familiar with the Community *acquis*, even in the financial services area. He or she may therefore be unable to identify and assess properly the implications of his or her proposal for other EU measures in order to determine whether they need to be amended or revoked. All too often, these problems emerge only in the course of negotiations in the Council working party, usually when a problem has been brought to the attention of a Member State. But by this time, the political pressure may be building to reach a compromise on the proposal as a whole and there may be insufficient time to resolve the issue, particularly if amendments are needed to a directive in another field of competence. When this happens, it is often left to Member States to make the best of a bad job in implementation. They may choose to ignore conflicting EU provisions or they may try to reconcile them as best they can.[13] In a perfect world, the consequential amendments

[10] See COM(2001)280.

[11] See COM(2002)625.

[12] Dir 2002/65/EC on the distance marketing of consumer financial services [2002] OJ L271/16.

[13] An example is the conflict between the right of the data subject to obtain information under the Data Protection Dir [1995] OJ L281/31, and the prohibition on 'tipping off', ie giving information to a customer that a suspicious transaction report has been made under the Money Laundering Dirs, Dir 2001/7/EC [2001] OJ L344/76, amending Dir 91/308/EEC [1991] OJ L166/77.

needed would be identified at the drafting stage wherever possible, so that they can be dealt with in the Commission proposal.

The Commission Legal Service could play more of a role in this respect, but is under-resourced and cannot allocate a lawyer full-time to help prepare a Commission proposal, even if the relevant DG were prepared to contemplate such a close working relationship. Although the Legal Service will give an opinion on the text of a Commission draft, its opinion can be overruled by a majority of the College of Commissioners which is responsible for adopting the draft. Moreover, the members of the Legal Service are not specialised draftsmen and cannot take responsibility for the drafting of a Commission proposal, and, once the proposal leaves the Commission, their role, such as it is, is over.

The importance of drafting has been recognised for some time. In 1998, the European Parliament, Council and Commission signed an Agreement on the quality of drafting of Community legislation.[14] The general principles listed could not be faulted, eg 'Community legislative acts shall be drafted clearly, simply and precisely'. Or:

> The purpose of the recitals is to set out concise reasons for the chief provisions of the enacting terms, without reproducing or paraphrasing them. They shall not contain normative provisions or political exhortations.

And again:

> The enacting terms of a binding act shall not include provisions of a non-normative nature, such as wishes or political declarations, or those which repeat or paraphrase passages or articles from the Treaties or those which restate legal provisions already in force.

Unfortunately, the Inter-Institutional Agreement is more honoured in the breach than in the observance. The e-Commerce Directive of 2000[15] is a classic example of a directive breaching each of the principles set out above. Controversy still rages about the meaning and scope of the so-called 'internal market' clause in Article 3, which is pivotal to interpreting the Directive and which can hardly be said to be 'drafted clearly, precisely and simply'. One of the recitals[16] contains a normative provision determining the place of establishment from which an electronic service is provided, for purposes of application of the Directive. Article 16 of the Directive contains an exhortatory provision urging Member States and the Commission to

[14] Interinstitutional Agreement of 22 Dec 1998 on Common Guidelines for the Quality of Drafting of Community Legislation [1999] OJ C73/1.

[15] Dir 2000/31/EC of 8 June 2000 on electronic commerce [2000] OJ L178/1.

[16] Recital 19.

encourage the drawing up of codes of conduct and the voluntary transmission of draft codes of conduct to the Commission.

It is not surprising that in September 2003 the European Parliament, Council and Commission came together again to sign another Interinstitutional Agreement on Better Law-making.[17] The emphasis this time was more on coordination between the three institutions of their legislative activity and, in particular, on the improvement of the coordination of their preparatory and legislative work in the context of the co-decision procedure. The Commission agreed to set out in the explanatory memorandum accompanying any proposal a statement of the legal arrangements already existing at Community level in the area affected by the proposal. The Commission would also give an account of the scope and the results of the prior consultation and impact assessments that it had undertaken.

D. IMPACT ASSESSMENTS

The three institutions nevertheless restated their commitment to the full application of the 1998 Agreement and concluded that more frequent use of impact assessments (both *ex ante* and *ex post*) would help to achieve better quality law. However, the agreement does not in fact commit either the Council or the European Parliament to carry out impact assessments before the adoption of any 'substantive amendment' to a Commission proposal. It merely states:

> Where the codecision procedure applies, the European Parliament and Council may, on the basis of jointly defined criteria and procedures, have impact assessments carried out prior to the adoption of any substantive amendment, either at first reading or at the conciliation stage.

Better quality law requires sound proportionate policy proposals, as well as competent drafting. By the time the Commission White Paper on Financial Services Policy was published, nearly 80 Impact Assessments had been carried out by the Commission, though not all were in the financial services area. In contrast, the European Parliament and Council had carried out only one. Impact Assessments estimate the costs and benefits of a proposed measure, taking into account the economic, social and environmental aspects where relevant, and, where appropriate, the impact on financial stability, proper functioning of markets and consumer protection. Commission Impact Assessments can be a useful tool in producing better law, but their usefulness is limited by the fact they cover only the initial Commission

[17] Parliament, Council and Commission, Interinstitutional Agreement on Better Law-Making [2003] OJ C321/1.

proposal and, as will be seen below, that proposal may well change significantly as a result of amendments introduced during negotiations in the Council working party or by the European Parliament.

E. NEGOTIATIONS IN THE COUNCIL WORKING PARTY

However perfect a draft may be when it emerges from the Commission as a formal proposal, the text can be changed out of all recognition during the first and second readings in the Council working party. This is a political negotiating process, with each Member State concerned to protect its own markets, institutions and consumers. Member States will assess the implications of the proposed measure for their domestic legislation and, as amendments are introduced, officials from each Member State need to keep the implications constantly under review. This can be difficult, particularly in relation to so-called 'horizontal' consumer protection measures, which can apply very widely to areas outside the competence of the leading government Department negotiating the directive. Much therefore depends on the willingness of the leading Department to consult other government departments and the public at large on current negotiations. The financial services industry has highly developed procedures for monitoring EU legislation, both on a national basis and through European-wide trade associations, and these associations are frequently able to alert their members to the implications of a new proposal early in the process. Members can then take the matter up with their national governments. Where a Member State is unwilling to pursue a particular issue or amendment, because it has other political priorities or is concerned not to use up its 'negotiating capital', the relevant interest group may have more success through a European association taking the matter up with the Commission, with other friendly Member States, or with the European Parliament.

The quality of the proposal emerging from the Council also depends on the competence of the negotiating officials. The contrast between the way in which the UK handles the negotiation of an EU directive and the preparation of a Parliamentary Bill was described in the Report prepared by Robin Bellis on implementation of EU Legislation.[18] He expressed surprise at the not uncommon practice of sending a relatively junior civil servant with no legal training or experience to attend meetings in Brussels, often without legal support. He contrasted this with the procedure adopted in the UK for a major Bill, where a Bill team would be set up, headed by a senior administrator, with lawyers involved from the outset.

[18] R Bellis, 'Implementation of EU Legislation', an independent study for the Foreign and Commonwealth Office ('The Bellis Report') (London, Foreign and Commonwealth Office, Nov 2003).

Given that EU directives can have a far greater impact on national law than a domestic Bill, this unbalanced allocation of resources seems to indicate a strange set of priorities and makes the oft- repeated commitments of the UK government to achieving better EU law sound somewhat hollow. One other major difference between the two legislative processes is that, in the case of a domestic Bill, a Bill team's policy proposals have to be conveyed to Parliamentary Counsel, whose task it is to convert the policy into the language of a Bill, and who remains responsible for ensuring the integrity of the text from the start to the finish of the Parliamentary process. The introduction of a similar institution at EU level—an independent Legislative Drafting Office—has been identified as a possible solution to the problem of 'sloppy and internally inconsistent' drafting.[19]

Such a body could do much to resolve the problems mentioned above, such as misuse of recitals and misuse of normative provisions. Member States frequently try to insert provisions into the recitals which are generally finalised after the substantive articles. In some cases these are provisions which they have been unable to get into the text of a directive and the result may be to obscure the legal effect of the directive; in other cases, it may be a attempt to fill a gap in a directive which was picked up too late to be included in the articles.[20] Unfortunately, such attempts to alter the effect of directives by tinkering with the recitals are likely to prove futile as far as the UK is concerned, since directives are normally implemented by means of regulations under section 2(2) of the European Communities Act 1972, which can only be used to implement 'any Community obligation of the United Kingdom, or [to enable] any such obligation to be implemented...'. Recitals do not impose Community obligations, and hence cannot be used as the basis for changing UK law.[21]

In other cases, recitals may conflict with the purpose and wording of a directive. One such recital was inserted in the Second Banking Directive, then verbatim into the Investment Services Directive, and finally into the Markets in Financial Instruments Directive (MiFID).[22] It reads:

> Whereas the principles of mutual recognition and of home Member State Control require the competent authorities of each Member State not to grant authorization or withdraw it where factors such as the activities programme, the geographical distribution or the activities actually carried on make it quite clear

[19] See R Wainright, 'Technique of Drafting European Community Legislation: Problems of Interpretation' [1996] *Statute Law Review* 7; 'The Bellis Report', above n18.

[20] One example is the recital in the 2nd Banking Dir [1989] OJ L386/1, stating that 'the Member State must require that the head office be situated in the same Member State as the registered office'.

[21] The UK was unable to rely on the recital cited in *ibid* to change domestic law in relation to head offices and had to wait for Art 3(2) of Dir 95/26/EC reinforcing prudential supervision [1995] OJ L168/7, before it could impose the necessary changes.

[22] [2004] OJ L145/1.

> that a credit institution has opted for the legal system of one Member State for the purpose of evading the stricter standards in force in another Member State in which it intends to carry on or carries on the greater part of its activities...

It is difficult to reconcile this recital with Community law, even as it stood in 1989. By 2004, when MiFID was adopted, it was clearly inconsistent with the basic principles underpinning the development of the Single Market in financial services and with the established case law of the European Court of Justice. Yet it appears as a normative provision in a directive recital. It is little comfort to dismiss such aberrations as merely the 'political letting off of steam of no legal significance'.[23] Without an independent guardian to watch over the wording of EU legislative instruments, such statements will continue to creep in, serving only to bring EU law into disrepute.

Not all deficiencies in directives can be blamed on drafting. Often there is a failure to work though the policy, the most common example being the lack of adequate transitional provisions in many directives. Again these tend to be left until the end of the negotiations in the Council working party, occasionally for the very good reason that there is no point in discussing transitional arrangements until the entire package has been decided and Member States are in a position to work out how to get from the pre-directive stage to the post implementation stage. But officials are by this time likely to be exhausted by the negotiating process and reluctant to spend yet more time on the arcane technical details of transitionals, however important these may prove to be in practice. The exhaustion factor may also be one of the reasons the Council has failed to produce an impact assessment in cases where it has substantially amended a Commission proposal, though to be of real value these should be produced by an independent body.

F. THE ROLE OF THE EUROPEAN PARLIAMENT IN THE LEGISLATIVE PROCESS

The European Parliament normally represents the last opportunity to secure changes to an EU proposal. The influence of the Parliament can be beneficial or destructive, depending on the political priorities of the day. An example of undisguised national protectionism can be found in the rejection of the proposed Takeover Directive in 2001 by MEPs driven by a coalition of German industry and trade unions. But on the other hand, the European Parliament has contributed to the improvement of several financial services directives, including the Prospectus Directive and the Markets in Financial Instruments Directive. It has the advantage of being able to tap directly into

[23] As in the Bellis Report, above n18, at 13.

the private sector through advisory panels of experts, and it is open to representations from industry, consumer groups and any other interested party.

Like the Council, the Parliament has, however, proved reluctant to produce impact assessments where it has introduced major changes to a draft directive, despite the commitments entered into in the 2003 Interinstitutional Agreement on Better Law-making.[24]

As far as drafting is concerned, the Parliament suffers from the same lack of drafting competence as the other two EU institutions. By the time a Commission proposal is finally adopted by the Council and the European Parliament, it may have gone through a first reading in the Council and separately in the European Parliament, followed by a second reading in both Council and Parliament, with amendments introduced at each stage. The task of producing, at the end of this process, a coherent text, which is compatible with Community law, is internally consistent and which still meets the original objectives is daunting in the extreme. It would, however, be easier to achieve if all three Community institutions could rely on the services of independent legislative drafting experts who would be responsible for ensuring the integrity of a legislative text from start to finish. Decisions on policy would remain with the institutions. Articulation of the policy should be in the hands of drafting experts.[25]

[24] Above n17.

[25] See the recommendations in the Bellis Report, above n18, at 25.

18

Law-making Risks in EC Financial Market Regulation after the Financial Services Action Plan

NIAMH MOLONEY*

ALTHOUGH THE FINANCIAL Services Action Plan (FSAP) period is most closely associated with massive regulatory change, it has also seen a dramatic evolution in the financial market law-making and policy formation process. This chapter examines the post-FSAP law-making and policy formation environment and finds that the FSAP will be reviewed and new rules will emerge through an institutionally complex, multi-actor, multi-dimensional law-making and policy formation process. Accountability and effectiveness risks are considerable. The Committee of European Securities Regulators (CESR) now plays a central role in the law-making and policy formation process, but it is a troublesome actor given the reach of its influence and the limitations on its accountability. The post-FSAP risk profile therefore not only includes the larger uncertainties as to the transformative effects of regulation on markets and the impact of the dilution of regulatory competition. It also includes considerable risks from the law-making and policy formation process which must be identified and mitigated if the larger uncertainties of the post-FSAP period are to be contained.

But it is also clear that the financial market law-making and policy formation process post-FSAP is a dynamic one. Mechanisms are being developed, albeit on an ad hoc basis, to counter the many risks attendant on the EC as the monopoly supplier of financial market regulation. The main players in the game appear to have emerged from the FSAP period with an enhanced understanding of the financial market law-making process, even if considerable weaknesses still remain. The development and review of the

* Professor of Capital Markets Law, University of Nottingham. I am very grateful to participants in the Oxford conference for their contributions and insights, particularly Sir Adam Ridley, and to Professor Eilís Ferran and Dr Jennifer Payne for their valuable comments on an earlier draft.

MiFID regime will provide an important test case as to whether law-making and policy formation risks can be managed in this uncertain but dynamic regulatory, institutional and market environment.

A. INTRODUCTION

The 1999 Financial Services Action Plan had two objectives.[1] It was designed to support the liberalisation and integration of EC financial markets through the harmonisation of national rules to support mutual recognition of national regulatory systems and pan-EC activity. It was also designed to provide the integrated pan-EC market-place with an upgraded regulatory framework for the new risk environment. Over the last seven years it has generated far-reaching change to the regulation, supervision and governance of the EC financial markets. Following the completion of the FSAP in 2005, the EC is now the primary regulator for the EC's financial markets.[2] A juggernaut of EC regulation is bearing down on the financial markets.[3] Institutional and governance reform has been dramatic. The EC's reach over the financial markets reflects the coincidence of legislative reform under the FSAP with the development of the Lamfalussy institutional process for financial market law-making.[4] Under the Lamfalussy process, the Commission adopts 'Level Two' detailed rules in the financial market sphere based on mandates in the related 'Level One' directive or regulation (adopted under normal inter-institutional procedures), advised by the Committee of European Securities Regulators (CESR, composed of national regulators), and supervised by the European Securities Committee (ESC, composed of Member State representatives). Level Three of the Lamfalussy process concerns convergence and consistency in the implementation and application of level one and level two rules. Level Four concerns enforcement.

[1] Implementing the Framework for Financial Markets: Action Plan, COM(1999)232.

[2] The EC's pre-eminent position is now widely accepted by the markets: '[i]t will not be many years before the FSA is no more than an agent of Brussels': O Lodge and H Flight, 'Latest MiFID offering tries to clear the fog', *Financial Times,* Fund Management Supp, 21 Aug 2006, at 8.

[3] Chief among the FSAP reforms were the financial market measures which addressed capital-raising and issuers, stock exchanges, market infrastructure (clearing and settlement), investment firms and investors. For a recent review of the FSAP's coverage see Commission, 'FSAP Evaluation, Part I: Process and Implementation' (Brussels, European Commission, Nov 2005) (the FSAP Implementation Report).

[4] Proposed in the Final Report of the Committee of Wise Men on the 'Regulation of European Securities Markets' (Brussels, European Commission, Feb 2001) (the Lamfalussy Report).

The reach of the FSAP is reflected in its cornerstone measure, the 2004 Markets in Financial Instruments Directive (MiFID) which regulates investment firms, investment services and securities trading.[5] A comparison with its precursor, the 1993 Investment Services Directive,[6] (ISD) is revealing. The ISD had 32 Articles, a number of which, most notoriously Article 11 on conduct of business regulation, did not achieve harmonisation. MiFID has 73 Articles, most of which are detailed and 21 of which are subject to the level two process. It has been implemented at level two by a directive of 55 Articles and a regulation of 41 Articles and two detailed annexes.[7] Although this chapter considers the FSAP generally, it uses MiFID as a microcosm of the FSAP process and the risks it has generated.

The FSAP period has produced a rich data-set on the evolution of regulatory design for the EC financial markets. But very considerable evidence is also now available as to its implications for the financial market law-making process.[8] The financial market law-making and policy formation process is also currently undergoing radical strategic change. The post-FSAP strategy for 2005–10 is set out in the Commission's important December 2005 White Paper. It does not present an extensive regulatory agenda.[9] It focuses instead on broad policy orientations and 'dynamic consolidation'.[10] There are four strands to the new agenda: (i) dynamic consolidation towards an integrated, open and efficient financial market; (ii) removal of the remaining economically significant barriers; (iii) implementation, enforcement and evaluation of existing legislation and rigorous application of the EC's 2002 Better Regulation agenda to new initiatives; and (iv) enhancement of supervisory cooperation and convergence and a strengthening of European

[5] Dir 2004/39/EC [2004] OJ L145/1. It has been described as a 'sprawling directive with far-reaching implications for any firm involved in buying and selling securities in Europe': Editorial, *Financial Times*, 23 Aug 2005, at 14.

[6] Dir 93/22/EC [1993] OJ L141/27.

[7] Commission Dir 2006/73/EC [2006] OJ L241/26 and Commission Reg (EC) No 1287/2006 [2006] OJ L241/7.

[8] Major assessments include: the Securities, Banking, Insurance, and Asset Management Expert Group Reports on the FSAP (May 2004), available at http://europa.eu.int/comm/internal_market/finances/actionplan; the Commission's June 2004 conference on 'European Financial Integration: Progress and Prospects', speeches available at http://europa.eu.int/comm/internal_market/speeches; the Commission's Autumn 2004 Consultation on the Expert Group Reports, responses available at http://forum.europa.eu.int/Public; the Assmussen Financial Services Committee Report on Financial Integration (FSC 4156/04); the European Parliament, 'Van den Burg Report on Current State of Integration of EU Financial Markets' (April 2005) A6-0087/2005; and the FSAP Implementation Report, above n3. Recent reports focusing on the Lamfalussy process include: Inter Institutional Monitoring Group, 'Third Report Monitoring the Lamfalussy Process' (Nov 2004); Commission, 'Working Document on Application of the Lamfalussy Process to EU Securities Market Legislation' (Nov 2004); and Inter Institutional Monitoring Group, 'First Interim Report Monitoring the Lamfalussy Process' (Mar 2006) ('first' as the initial Monitoring Group mandate had expired).

[9] Commission, White Paper on Financial Services Policy 2005–2010, COM(2005)629.

[10] *Ibid*, at 3.

influence in the global market-place. There is much that is good in this new agenda. A more sophisticated approach to regulatory design, for example, is clearly evident.[11] Post-FSAP, the Commission has emerged as considerably more confident and experienced in regulatory design, using a much larger toolbox which includes market discipline, codes of conduct, international standards, investor education and the threat of regulation in addition to traditional harmonisation.[12] This chapter, however, is concerned with the other major feature of the post-FSAP period—the concern to improve the effectiveness of law-making and the policy formation process.

This chapter argues that, given this new emphasis on process based on the evidence now emerging from the FSAP period, and in a reflection of the current government, regulatory and market preoccupation with more effective regulation,[13] close attention must be given to the EC's law-making and policy formation process for financial markets in the post-FSAP environment and to how the risks of this process can be contained.

[11] Perhaps the best example of the more nuanced approach concerns the development of clearing and settlement policy. Early indications suggested that a traditional dir might be employed to liberalise clearing and settlement. But a market-based strategy based on the adoption by the industry of a code of conduct was announced in July 2006. Unusually, the Commission has specified the particular results to be delivered by the code and set out a timetable for liberalisation, suggesting that this policy response was developed in close partnership with the industry. Commissioner McCreevy announced the new strategy in forceful terms: 'I expect full co-operation from the industry on this and a clear timetable. I recognise that this code of practice is not without risks. But then, financial markets are all about risks...It presents a challenge to the industry...if they fail regulators always have the range of measures at their disposal to force changes through': Commissioner McCreevy, Speech on 'Clearing and Settlement: The Way Forward', Economic and Monetary Affairs Committee of the European Parliament (11 July 2006) SPEECH/06/450, available at http://europa.eu/rapid/pressReleases. A Code of Conduct has since been adopted.

[12] The movement from harmonisation to more nuanced governance methods can be seen across EC policy. In the health care sector see T Hervey, 'The European Union and the Governance of Health Care' in G de Búrca and J Scott (eds), *Law and New Constitutionalism in the EU and the US* (Oxford, Hart Publishing, 2006).

[13] In the UK, the FSA has adopted an action plan on better regulation (FSA, Better Regulation. Action Plan (London, FSA, 2005)), while internationally the IOSCO (the International Organisation of Securities Commissions) Principles and Objectives of Securities Regulation (2003) address (at 8) rule-making in addition to substantive concerns. New structures are also being developed to consider law-making risks for particular financial market sectors. The Financial Markets Law Committee (an independent committee of the Bank of England) considers issues of legal uncertainty or misunderstandings which give rise to material risks within the framework of the wholesale financial markets.

On the markets, major actors domestically include trade associations such as the London Investment Banking Association (LIBA), an influential City trade association which has recently addressed effective policy formation and regulatory impact analysis (LIBA, *Annual Report* (London, LIBA, 2005), at 20–1 and 22–3) and the Corporation of London, which frequently speaks on City concerns and has produced a report on 'Reducing the Regulatory Burden: the Arrival of Meaningful Regulatory Impact Analysis' (July 2004). Internationally, the International Council of Securities Associations (ICSA), which represents a wide range of financial market self-regulatory and trade associations, regularly addresses the effectiveness of the regulatory process. Recent initiatives include the ICSA Statement on Regulatory and Self Regulatory Consultation Practices (Oct 2004), available at www.icsa-int.com and the current development of ICSA Principles for Better Regulation.

B. THE UNCERTAIN POST-FSAP ENVIRONMENT

Rule-making for the financial markets is in principle a complex[14] and risk-laden process[15] which reflects an intricate interplay of public, private, international and domestic interests and influences. But the post-FSAP regulatory environment is beset by particular risks and uncertainties. The chief risk for the FSAP is that it produces costly and complex legal and institutional change but does not have positive transformative effects on the markets.[16] Whether or not the FSAP is ultimately trivial,[17] save with respect to its costs, depends on a complex series of variables. These include the effectiveness of implementation and enforcement,[18] and, institutionally, the effectiveness of CESR in supporting supervisory convergence at level three. The post-FSAP agenda is at least closely focused on these risks[19] and has

[14] On the multiplicity of interactions between public and private actors in the financial market sphere see J Black, 'Decentring Regulation: Understanding the Role of Regulation and Self Regulation in a "Post Regulatory World"' (2001) 54 *Current Legal Problems* 103 and 'Mapping the Contours of Contemporary Financial Services Regulation' [2002] *Journal of Corporate Law Studies* 253 which uses an 'enrolment' analysis to map and critique the regulatory environment.

[15] See generally L Zingales, 'The Costs and Benefits of Financial Market Regulation', European Corporate Governance Institute, Law Working Paper No 21/2004 (2004), available at http://ssrn.com/abstract=536682. In addition to the two major drivers of cost (regulatory agencies and market compliance, including deterrence effects), these include: prejudicing market mechanisms and self-regulation (A Ogus, *Legal Form and Economic Theory* (Oxford, Hart Publishing, 1994) at 107–11); over-reaction (L Ribstein, 'Bubble Laws' (2003) 40 *Houston Law Review* 77); and public choice risks (J Coates, 'Private v Political Choice in Securities Regulation: A Political Cost-Benefit Analysis' (2001) 41 *Virginia Journal of International Law* 531). Recent scholarship also suggests that financial regulators are handicapped by systematic biases: S Choi and A Pritchard, 'Behavioural Economics and the SEC', available at http://ssrn.com/abstract=389560.

[16] The Commission has admitted that, contrary to the FSAP's 'distinct institutional and legislative legacy', it was difficult to assess whether it was improving cross-border opportunities for investors and investment firms. See Commission, *10th FSAP Report* (Brussels, European Commission, 0000) at 14.

[17] For a powerful analysis of EC company law as 'trivial' (the term builds on the analysis by Bernard Black of trivial rules as rules which are optional, market-mimicking, changeable or unimportant): see B Black, 'Is Corporate Law Trivial? A Political and Economic Analysis' (1990) 84 *North Western University Law Review* 542) given its limited influence on the governance and management of EC companies: see L Enriques, 'EC Company Law Directives and Regulations: How Trivial Are They' (2006) 27 *University of Pennsylvania Journal of International Economic Law* 1.

[18] The optimal model for enforcement remains opaque, not least due to a paucity of empirical data and analysis. For a major cross-jurisdictional assessment which examines the limited empirical evidence and the difficulties in assessing the optimal level of intervention see H Jackson, 'Variations in the Intensity of Financial Regulation: Preliminary Evidence and Potential Implications', Discussion Paper 521, 08/2005 (2005), John M Olin Center for Law, Economics and Business, Harvard University, available at www.harvard.edu/programs/olin_center.

[19] White Paper, above n9, at 5–7. The implementation process is currently unfolding and will largely depend on the success of CESR in encouraging convergence (see sect F, below). An early indication of the tougher approach to enforcement came in Aug 2006 when the Commission moved against 16 Member States for failure to implement the Market Abuse Dir (Dir 2003/6/EC [2003] OJ L96/16) and its level two implementing measures. See Commission Press Release IP/05/1035, 3 Aug 2006.

widespread institutional and market support in this regard.[20] But it also depends on more elusive factors, chief among them whether the FSAP has correctly judged the costs and benefits of the new regime (in terms of direct costs to market participants and the risks of harmonisation over regulatory competition) and whether the FSAP can have transformative effects on market behaviour.

The uncertain relationship between law and financial market characteristics and development is the subject of a recent but well-established and lively scholarship.[21] So too is the relationship between the financial markets and wider economic growth.[22] The Commission's commitment to the financial markets as agents of economic growth and to law as a means of driving market integration appears unshakeable,[23] even if it is more a matter of hope than experience[24] and, less benignly, potentially a reflection of public choice pressures. But one of the most striking aspects of the post-FSAP policy debate is the extent to which it reveals more widespread

[20] See, eg, Van den Burg Report, above n8, at A.1–4; ESC Minutes, 14 Dec 2004 (ESC 43/2004); and Mar 2006 Inter Institutional Monitoring Group, above n8, at 16. On the market's support see, eg, the Securities Expert Group Report, above n8, at 16–17; the Response of the British Banking Association to the Expert Group Reports, 26 July 2004, and the Response of the Financial Services Consumer Panel to the Expert Group Reports, 21 Sept 2004, both at Responses to the Commission's Nov 2004 Consultation on the Expert Group Reports, above n8.

[21] This scholarship is spearheaded by the influential and controversial work of economists La Porta, Lopez de Silanes, Shleifer, and Vishny (LLSV): see R La Porta, F Lopez de Silanes, A Shleifer and R Vishny, 'Investor Protection and Corporate Governance' (2000) 58 *Journal of Finance* 3. For a recent application in the insider dealing sphere see L Beny, 'Do Insider Trading Laws Matter? Some Preliminary Comparative Evidence' (2005) 7 *American Law and Economics Review* 144. Major critiques include: J Coffee, 'The Rise of Dispersed Ownership: the Roles of Law and the State in the Separation of Ownership and Control' (2001) 111 *Yale Law Journal* 1; and J Franks, C Mayer and S Rossi, 'The Origination and Evolution of Ownership and Control', European Corporate Governance Institute, Finance Working Paper No 09/2003 (2003), available at www.ssrn.com/abstractid=354381.

[22] See, eg, R King and R Levine, 'Finance and Growth: Schumpeter Might Be Right' (1993) 108 *Quarterly Journal of Economics* 681; R Rajan and L Zingales, 'Financial Dependence and Growth' (1998) 88 *American Economic Review* 559; R Levine, 'Law, Finance and Economic Growth' (1999) 8 *Journal of Financial Intermediation* 8; and M Khan and A Senhadji, 'Financial Development and Economic Growth: An Overview', IMF Working Paper/00/209 (2000), available at www.imf.org/external/pubs.

[23] White Paper, above n9, Annex II (Impact Assessment), at 3–7 and 10. It rehearses the traditional arguments in support of the financial markets as a driver of EC economic growth. These include the 2002 London Economics Report (London Economics, 'Quantification of the Macro-Economic Impact of Integration of EU Financial Markets, Final Report to the European Commission' (London, London Economics, Nov 2002)) and the 2002 CEPR Report (M Giannetti, L Guiso, T Japelli, M Padula, and M Pagano, 'Financial Market Integration, Corporate Financing and Growth', European Economy: Economic Papers no 179 (Brussels, European Commission, 2002)).

[24] The Commission is rather evasive on the evidence supporting a more direct connection between EC policy intervention and positive market outcomes, simply stating that 'past actions have been proven to have a positive impact [on weaknesses in financial market integration]': White Paper, above n9, at 10.

institutional and market nervousness as to the limits of harmonisation and of regulation. Uncertainty as to the ability of the FSAP to drive market change dominates the 2004 Expert Groups.[25] CESR, which might have been expected to take a sympathetic view of the link between EC regulation and market integration to support its institutional and market position, recently noted in its 2005 *Annual Report* that the extent to which investors, issuers, intermediaries and market infrastructure providers will use the new regulatory framework remains to be seen.[26]

More specific uncertainties abound across the FSAP. The MiFID regime is particularly problematic. One of the biggest open questions it raises is whether investment firms which execute client trading orders internally against their own trading books (rather than directing them to a trading market) will change their business models and take the form of 'systematic internalisers'. MiFID requires investment firms which internalise trades on a regular basis to be regulated as 'systematic internalisers' and to become subject to costly and controversial transparency rules which may threaten their trading positions. Investment firms may, given the risks and costs of the new regime, reduce their internalisation activities, potentially decreasing market liquidity, increasing the costs of trading, and defeating one of MiFID's major objectives.[27] The impact of MiFID's new order execution model, which is based on competition between regulated markets, multilateral trading systems and systematic internalisers, on price formation, execution quality and liquidity more generally, and on the robustness of the trade transparency regime, is also uncertain.[28] The projected upfront costs of MiFID in terms of Information Technology, compliance and risk management systems are immense.[29] The success of the extensive new conduct of business regime in promoting investor protection under a

[25] See, eg, the Securities Expert Group Report, above n8, at 9–10; and the British Banking Association response to the Commission's Autumn 2004 Consultation on the Expert Group Reports, above n8, which noted (at 2) that there are 'significant question marks over the value of attempting such an integration exercise except on a limited and targeted basis'.

[26] CESR, *Annual Report* (2005), Foreword by the Chairman, at 5.

[27] B Riley, 'Goodbye to the Club', *Financial World*, June 2006, at 22. Investment firms are being advised to consider carefully the business case for the systematic internaliser model, particularly with respect to IT costs related to transparency requirements: see J Neasham, 'Eyes on the IT horizon', *The Banker*, Supplement on Countdown to MiFID, May 2006, 50 at 50–1. One senior City figure has suggested that the additional regulatory burden means that only the largest institutions will exploit the strategic opportunities represented by the MiFID regime: A Belchambers, 'No time like the present in, *ibid*, 54 at 55.

[28] See, eg, CESR's Call for Evidence on Consolidation of Market Data (Mar 2006), CESR 06-134 and the 24 Apr 2006 response (available at www.isda.org/speeches) by a group of 12 trade associations which argues that any fragmentation in market transparency data (pricing information) would not lead to a reduction in execution quality but could be controlled by market forces.

[29] Some estimates place the cost of MiFID implementation across the EC at over £8 billion: see B Jopson, 'Regulatory overhaul brings rising hopes', *Financial Times*, 16 Feb 2006, at 3.

maximum harmonisation regime also remains unclear,[30] although its costs are undisputed.[31]

The FSAP in combination with the Lamfalussy process has also severely diluted regulatory competition in the production of laws as a potential driver of optimal regulation and market integration.[32] The appropriate level of harmonisation for the financial markets continues to generate political debate,[33] although all the indications suggest that any new policy initiatives will be based on a more nuanced mix of mechanisms. But harmonisation trumps regulatory competition in the FSAP regime. FSAP measures harmonise at a very high level of detail, and in some cases adopt express maximum harmonisation mechanisms.[34] The level two process leaves very little room for Member State discretion and frequently produces rules which amount to de facto maximum harmonisation. The 2006 MiFID Level Two Directive, for example, is highly detailed, although it is stated to be flexible and adapted to the diversity of investment firms.[35] The Commission has

[30] L Enriques, 'Conflicts of Interest in Investment Services: The Price and Uncertain Impact of MiFID's Regulatory Framework' in G Ferrarini and E Wymeersch (eds), *Investor Protection in Europe. Corporate Law Making, the MiFID and Beyond* (Oxford, OUP, 2006) at 321 and N Moloney, 'Effective Policy Design for the Retail Investment Services Market' in *ibid*, at 382.

[31] One survey has reported that for one investment firm (with a client base of 80–100,000 investors), the cost of MiFID implementation could be in excess of £15 million. See APCIMS Response to Commission Working Document on Conduct of Business Rules, Best Execution, Client Order Handling Rules, Eligible Counterparties, Clarification of the Definition and Investment Advice, and Financial Instruments (July 2005), available at http://ec.europa.eu/internal_market/securities/isd/consultation/replies.

[32] The relationship between harmonisation and regulatory competition is a much-debated and unresolved question in EC financial market regulation and company law: see eg, J Armour, 'Who Should Make Corporate Law? EC Legislation versus Regulatory Competition' (2005) 58 *Current Legal Problems* 369 (in the context of company law); E Ferran, *Building an EU Securities Market* (Cambridge, CUP, 2004) at 50–7 (in the context of the primary markets and capital-raising); CEPS, *EU Financial Regulation and Supervision Beyond 2005* (Brussels, CEPS Task Force Report no 54, 2005) at 9–10 and 13–25 (from the FSAP perspective generally); and S Deakin, 'Legal Diversity and Regulatory Competition: Which Model for Europe?', Centre for Business Research, University of Cambridge, Working Paper No 323 (Mar 2006) (considering the US and EC experience in the labour and corporate spheres). A massive US literature considers the impact of regulatory competition on securities markets and international capital-raising. For contrasting perspectives see R Romano, 'Empowering Investors: A Market Approach to Securities Regulation' (1996) 107 *Yale Law Journal* 2359 and M Fox, 'Retaining Mandatory Issuer Disclosure: Why Issuer Choice is Not Investor Empowerment' (1999) 85 *Virginia Law Review* 1335.

[33] See, eg, the ESC '*tour de table*' at the opening of negotiations on the MiFID level two regime which revealed considerable differences: ESC Minutes, 25 Feb 2005 (ESC 13/2005).

[34] This is the case with the Prospectus Dir 2003/71/EC [2003] OJ L345/64.

[35] Recital 11 states that a 'regulatory regime should be adapted to [investment firm] diversity while imposing certain fundamental requirements which are appropriate for all firms'. The evolution in EC financial market regulation is well reflected by this characterisation of the detailed MiFID Level Two Dir, above n7. While it contains specific measures designed to support flexibility (under Art. 6 whether an independent compliance officer is required depends on the nature, scale and complexity of its business) and general calibration measures (whether a firm deals with retail or professional investors tailors the range of obligations applicable across the Dir), overall it introduces an unprecedented degree of prescription on the regulation of investment firms. The Commission's Background Note to the first draft of the MiFID Level Two Dir (Brussels, DRAFT 6 Feb 2006), by contrast, describes the Dir (at 7) as 'establish[ing] a highly harmonised legal regime' and amounting to 'exhaustive harmonisation'.

also indicated that it may issue interpretative Communications on the Level Two Directive,[36] while the MiFID level three process (section F.5, below) looks set to produce detailed guidelines. Indeed, the Commission's notable unwillingness to pursue a '26th regime' for financial services and products[37] suggests a reluctance to introduce optionality and choice into financial regulation in the absence of very clear demand from the markets.

In addition, the ability of Member States to 'gold-plate' legislation by adding additional obligations on implementation has been severely circumscribed. The MiFID implementation process has been accompanied by significant concerns, particularly in the UK, that the MiFID Level One and Two regime would be gold-plated, increasing its cost and complexity for the industry.[38] Article 4 of the MiFID Level Two Directive, an 'infamous' provision which was very heavily negotiated in the ESC,[39] restricts the extent to which Member States can impose additional obligations. Member States may do so only where the rules in question are objectively justified and proportionate and address specific risks to investor protection or market integrity not adequately addressed by the Directive.[40] Article 4 is designed to promote the Commission's post-FSAP Better Regulation agenda by limiting the addition of costly national requirements.[41] But it reinforces the extent to which EC financial market regulation is now the product of EC processes. In the UK, powerful market interests, supported by high-level political backing, are now demanding that MiFID implementation be based on a 'copy-over' of EC rules on to the national/FSA rulebook.[42] Given the often trenchant City opposition to EC market rules,

[36] MiFID Level Two Dir, above n7, recital 12.

[37] Speech by Commissioner McCreevy on 'Improving Decision-Making and Completing the Single Financial Market', EUROFI Conference, Brussels, 7 June 2006; White Paper, above n9, at 13.

[38] See, eg, Editorial, 'London's financiers are miffed by MiFID', *Financial Times*, 17 Aug 2006, at 12; and B Jopson, 'Financial Services Directive is Latest Focus of City Concern about FSA Restrictions', *Financial Times*, 17 Aug 2006, at 2, noting that the FSA is seen as an 'occasionally overzealous implementer of European law'.

[39] Lodge and Flight, above n2, describing Art 4 as requiring 'regulators to go cap in hand to Brussels to seek leave to apply an existing rule or two'. Divisions on Art 4 are clearly apparent in the ESC minutes between Member States seeking flexibility in implementation and those demanding strict harmonisation: see ESC Minutes, 22–23 Feb 2006 (ESC/12/2006), 29–30 Mar 2006 (ESC/15/2006) and 26–27 Apr 2006 (ESC/28/2006). Discussions appear to have continued until just before the final vote in June 2006.

[40] The specific risks addressed must be of particular importance given the Member State's market structure or the measure must address risks that emerge or become evident after MiFID comes into force and are not otherwise regulated by other Community measures. Reporting obligations to the Commission are also imposed.

[41] HM Treasury and FSA, *Joint Implementation Plan for MiFID* (London, HM Treasury/FSA, May 2006), at 4.

[42] MiFID Connect, a powerful group of the 11 major trade associations active in the UK market has called for a copy-out approach: see P Davies and B Jopson, 'Fears over EU rules unite City groups', *Financial Times*, 16 Aug 2006, at 1. City Minister Ed Balls has recognised the need to ensure that MiFID 'is not implemented with unnecessary and burdensome gold-plating': See Jopson, above n38.

this is a graphic illustration of the extent of the EC's reach over the financial markets. Although determined national regulatory interests can often find a way to introduce gold-plating rules in the face of maximum harmonisation requirements,[43] it appears that national market interests and, accordingly, national drivers for regulatory competition, are increasingly reflecting EC priorities.[44]

This chapter does not seek to address these very large questions whether, and the extent to which, the FSAP integration project will be successful, its risks and the role of law in this regard, and whether the dilution of regulatory competition will have prejudicial effects. But it can be argued that the outcomes of the FSAP are highly uncertain given these two variables. This fundamental uncertainty calls for a close focus on any additional risks generated by the law-making and policy formation process in the post-FSAP period if optimal results are to be achieved or, at least, prejudice to the market-place avoided.[45]

Financial market policy has also entered an unstable phase post-FSAP. By comparison with the FSAP, the current agenda is limited in terms of specific initiatives but ambitious in terms of its attempts to secure optimal policy-making, implementation and enforcement. It does not possess the political attractiveness of the FSAP's specific agenda of 42 measures.[46] It may not attract the acute political and market attention of the FSAP given its focus on less glamorous priorities. But, as discussed in the following sections, much of the success of the FSAP will depend on whether the post-FSAP

[43] Ferran highlights the possibility that maximum harmonisation under the Prospectus Dir's prospectus disclosure regime could be subverted by the adoption of disclosure rules as admission to trading requirements for regulated markets: see above n32, at 145.

[44] The UK FSA has committed to taking the Art 4 responsibility seriously and mirroring EC wording where possible: see above n41, at 5. In October 2006, the FSA produced its important consultation on the implementation of the MiFID Level Two conduct of business regime. In a groundbreaking approach, implementation is based on 'intelligent copy-over' of the EC regime: FSA, Consultation Paper 06/19 on Reforming Conduct of Business Regulation and Consultation Paper 06/20 on Financial Promotion and other Communications.

[45] Ferran has persuasively argued that 'the lack of guidance on how law matters to the development of securities markets suggests that there could be dangerous uncertainty in the regulatory process...if there are effective safeguards built into the process...the fact that we do not have a clear starting point in the form of a comprehensive blue print of all the laws that are conducive to securities market growth, becomes a much less troubling exercise than it might be otherwise': see above n32, at 58.

[46] The Commission has reported that consultations on what would become its White Paper agenda generated 'respect for choosing a difficult and politically less "appealing" avenue'.: see White Paper, above n9, Annex III, Resumé of Contributions Received from Market Participants on the Green Paper on Financial Services Policy 2005–2010, at 5. Others are more uncertain. CESR'S Market Participants Consultative Group found that the Commission's Green Paper on Financial Services 2005–10 (COM(2005)177), which is not fundamentally different in orientation from the final White Paper, did not contain a clear message. See CESR, *Annual Report* (2005) at 7.

period will contain law-making and policy formation risks and provide for effective review and revision of the FSAP, and thereby mitigate its larger uncertainty risks.

More generally, the EC has now become the monopoly supplier of financial market regulation[47] at a time of uncertainty. While a range of risks attach to this development,[48] this chapter argues that the post-FSAP environment has generated specific risks to financial market law-making and policy formation which must be identified and managed.

C. RISKS TO THE EFFECTIVENESS OF LAW-MAKING AND POLICY FORMATION

1. The Effectiveness of the Law-making and Policy Formation Process

Given that the outcomes of the FSAP are uncertain and costly, and given the limited potential for corrective action from regulatory competition, the recent strategy shift in EC financial market policy towards ensuring the effectiveness of the law-making and policy formation process is welcome. Whether this shift will generate positive results is, however, uncertain, although some trends in the post-FSAP agenda bode well.

2. Macro Policy Design

One of the best examples of the increased sophistication of the EC financial market policy-making process came in the 2005 White Paper. It sets out in detail the process the Commission intends to follow in deciding whether and how to intervene in the financial markets in the future and explains how the post-FSAP 2005–10 agenda was established. In principle, and the quality of the analysis aside, this is a watershed.

[47] The rules and norms which direct financial market behaviour extend far beyond legislation to include a range of other measures including international codes of conduct, trade association codes and standard form contracts, all of which lead ultimately towards the 'decentred' regulation of financial markets: see Black, above n14. This ch is concerned with the EC rules which govern financial markets and addresses decentred rules only where they form a major part of EC financial market policy.

[48] Regulators and the quality of regulation are, of course, subject to a range of risks, including the risks attendant on a dilution of regulatory competition and which arise from the fundamental monopoly risk which 'immuni[zes] them from the stringent constraints of the market': see Choi and Pritchard, above n15, at 5. These are exaggerated in the EC context when regulatory power moves from the 25 Member States centrally. On the monopoly costs of EC harmonisation see, eg, L Enriques, 'Company Law Harmonization Reconsidered: What Role for the EC', European Corporate Governance Institute Working Paper No 53/2005 (2005) at 16–18, available at http://ssrn.com/abstract=850005.

The construction of the post-FSAP agenda stands in stark contrast to the genesis of the massive FSAP regulatory regime. It remains difficult to discern any considered basis for the FSAP. It was essentially reactive, based on weaknesses in the existing regulatory regime in delivering integration in the financial market sector and on concerns that the potential benefits of monetary union were not being realised.[49] The Plan as a whole and its discrete measures were for the most part adopted without evidence or regulatory impact analysis.[50] It was a creature of an unusual combination of the attractiveness of the Commission's use of a regulatory 'package',[51] exuberant stock market conditions in the shape of the dotcom boom, strong market support, given the initial focus of the FSAP on wholesale market integration, and political support[52] linked to the high profile Lisbon economic agenda.[53] The most extensive examination of financial market integration to date, the 2002 London Economics study,[54] was not commissioned, and did not report until after the FSAP was well underway. The FSAP itself was cast in rather loose terms as an 'aspirational programme for rapid progress towards a single financial market' and as an 'illustrative plan'.[55] The 2005 FSAP Implementation Report makes clear how the FSAP developed its own internal momentum, free of any internal controls on the development of the FSAP agenda. New legislative measures were introduced where the FSAP originally called for political agreement on earlier measures or for revisions to existing legislation, while the scope of other measures went far beyond the scope envisaged by the FSAP.[56]

[49] On the genesis of the FSAP see N Moloney, *EC Securities Regulation* (Oxford, OUP, 2002) at 25–32 and Ferran, above n32, at 4–5.

[50] On the weaknesses in the analysis supporting adoption of the 2004 Transparency Dir 2004/109/EC [2004] OJ L390/38 see, eg, CEPS, above n32, at 10–11. The most infamous example continues to be the 2003 Prospectus Dir, the initial version of which threatened to disrupt the wholesale debt market. The Commission has acknowledged that the original proposal, which reflected neither cost-benefit analysis nor public consultation, involved a 'serious error' and that the ensuing 'fracas reflected badly on the new [Lamfalussy] legislative process': FSAP Implementation Report, above n3, at 14.

[51] The Commission has described the FSAP as notable 'in that it was announced as a package' and suggested that individual initiatives would not have had the same momentum: *ibid*, at 5–6.

[52] 21 of the FSAP's measures were adopted by the European Parliament and Council in under 22 months: see *ibid*, at 6.

[53] The Lisbon agenda was designed to make the EU 'the most competitive and dynamic knowledge-based economy in the world, capable of sustainable economic growth with more and better jobs and greater social cohesion': See Lisbon Council Conclusions, 23–24 Mar 2000. The Commission has suggested that the Lisbon agenda 'was one that the world's press, public leaders and private individuals all came to know' and that the linkage between the FSAP, which was endorsed by the Lisbon European Council, and this agenda gave impetus to the FSAP: see FSAP Implementation Report, above n3, at 6.

[54] London Economics Report, above n23.

[55] FSAP, above n1, at 2.

[56] FSAP Implementation Report, above n3, at 26. The intervening Enron/dotcom collapse had very considerable impact on the developing company law and corporate governance programme (see, eg, G Hertig, 'On-going Board Reforms: One-Size-Fits-All and Regulatory Capture', European Corporate Governance Institute Law Working Paper No 25/2005 (2005), available at http://papers.ssrn.com.abstract=676417), but had less influence on the financial market aspects of the FSAP.

The 2005–10 agenda, by contrast, has emerged following the general post-FSAP review,[57] consultations on the precursor May 2005 Green Paper[58] and a review of the major policy options set out in the White Paper.[59] The Commission's stated objective for the 2005–10 agenda was to reach 'an optimal mix of policy options with a general trend'. It identified five generic policy options (take no further action; repeal existing legislation or proposals; ensure follow-up of past policy action; dynamic consolidation of the FSAP framework based on extensive follow-up; and new initiatives). These were examined with respect to their potential qualitative impact on the main strategic directions of the new agenda, namely integration, market functioning (competition, stability, integrity and consumer protection), the administrative burdens on companies, and global effectiveness, and on a sliding scale from 'very positive' to 'potentially substantial negative impact'. It is heartening that the analysis did not shirk negative assessments of EC intervention (such as with respect to unintended regulatory spillover and prejudice to international relations) although, inevitably, overall the tendency was to assign positive values to intervention.[60] Dynamic consolidation was identified as the optimal overall policy choice. The White Paper also applied this five option analysis to the limited number of specific interventions proposed[61] and committed to detailed and quantitative impact assessment of any precise policy actions adopted under the new agenda. Although the assessment is limited, and short on quantitative analysis, it represents an important step towards a more effective policy formation process.

The Commission has also put in place the architecture to assess the FSAP's impact on market integration. The annual Financial Integration Monitor, first published in 2004,[62] quantitatively assesses progress towards financial market integration and represents the first sustained attempt by the Commission to track the progress of integration.

The Lamfalussy process is regularly described as a 'learning by doing' process for all involved.[63] Similarly, the FSAP period can be regarded as a master-class for the Commission in financial market law-making and the policy formation process. The Commission is only (and belatedly) beginning to address the intricacies of effective policy formation for the financial markets

[57] FSAP Implementation Report, above n3.

[58] COM(2005)177. Responses are collated in the White Paper, above n9, Annex III, Resume of Contributions received from Market Participants on the Green Paper on Financial Services Policy. A public hearing took place in Brussels in July 2005.

[59] White Paper, above n9, Annex II, Impact Assessment.

[60] The impact of new initiatives on progress towards integration was assigned the highest positive impact rating on the questionable ground that 'the FSAP experience has shown that legislative initiatives can have a decisive impact on progress towards integration': *ibid*, at 14.

[61] Including with respect to: retail financial services; clearing and settlement; asset management; financial analysts and rating agencies.

[62] Available at http://europa.eu.int/comm/internal_market.finances/cross-sector/index_en.htm#monitor.

[63] See, eg, Mar 2006 Inter Institutional Monitoring Group, above n8, at 5.

as it switches from FSAP fire-fighting, as the policy shift from integration to regulation is embedded, and as the sharpest political and institutional tensions of the FSAP period recede. Nonetheless, the comparison between the construction of the FSAP and the 2005–10 agenda suggests some degree of institutional learning and, at the very least, a dynamism to the Commission's approach to post-FSAP policy formation that bodes well for the future.

3. Micro Policy Design and Cost-Benefit Analysis

Under the new approach to policy-making, any new measures will be subject to *ex ante* cost-benefit analysis. *Ex post* analysis of the impact of FSAP measures is to occur by 2009.[64] *Ex post* cost-benefit analysis is the more critical given the scale of the FSAP regime and the lighter intervention expected under the 2005–10 agenda. But it carries the risk of being of limited value because benchmarks to assess the effectiveness of particular FSAP measures were not established at the time of their adoption. A larger question arises. Very considerable difficulties attach to assessing the success of financial market regulation.[65] These include the complexities which arise in assessing the success of measures in terms of the classic but difficult to quantify objectives of market regulation, such as delivering investor confidence and investor protection.[66] These difficulties are compounded in the EC. How can the success of particular FSAP measures be assessed when there is no agreement as to the overarching objectives of EC financial market regulation (see section D, below)? Any assessment of the benefits of FSAP measures might be expected to include traditional objectives (such as investor protection, market stability, market efficiency) as well as EC-specific objectives with respect to integration—not least given the decided shift under the FSAP towards market regulation. But there is no agreement as to these objectives and how they should be articulated and assessed.[67]

[64] White Paper, above n9, at 6.

[65] See generally C Goodhart, 'Regulating the Regulator—An Economist's Perspective on Accountability and Control' in E Ferran and C Goodhart (eds), *Regulating Financial Services and Markets in the 21st* Century (Oxford, Hart Publishing, 2001) at 151.

[66] Difficulties include how the hypothetical contracts that investors would choose given conditions of perfect information and rationality can be replicated, and the identification of the investor or investor group(s) which would act as a proxy(ies) to assess investor protection: 'cost benefit analysis is difficult, perhaps even intractable, particularly on the benefit side': Jackson, above n18, at 4–11. For an analysis of the market impact of regulation in terms of 'market confidence', based on a share price proxy, see J Lawrence, 'The Economics of Market Confidence: (Ac)Costing Securities Market Regulation', available at www.ssrn.com/abstract=2046432.

[67] Zingales, who has argued in principle for financial market regulation to be assessed by a government agency on the lines of the US Office for Management and Budget, has suggested that, in support of effective cost-benefit analysis, regulation should contain a clear statement of goals and the means through which goals should be achieved: see above n15, at 36. The

There is also a very considerable risk of market fatigue limiting the effectiveness of any related consultations, as the market is now struggling to implement the vast FSAP programme, which involves detailed domestic consultations on Level One and Level Two implementation.[68] This follows the relentless wave of consultations on all aspects of the FSAP, but particularly on CESR's Level Two advice.

Cost-benefit analysis was particularly problematic in CESR during the MiFID Level Two process. Although CESR has declared itself committed to cost-benefit analysis,[69] it operates under considerable resource constraints[70] and there is little evidence of cost-benefit analysis during the formation of its MiFID Level Two advice. This emerged as a matter of considerable concern during CESR consultations,[71] in the Commission's White Paper[72] and in subsequent discussions in the ESC.[73] Institutional and resource support has now been given to CESR in the form of ECONET. ECONET was established in August 2006 as part of the wider reforms to CESR's operation (see section F.6 below) and is designed to enhance CESR's ability at Level Three to report on financial market developments and to anticipate market change. It is also to evaluate, develop and maintain CESR's approach to impact analysis, in line with CESR's commitment to more extensive use of economic analysis and evidence-based methodologies.[74] Although risks attach to in-house cost-benefit analysis, a combination of in-house and industry analysis should reduce these risks.

A combined approach which includes effective and objective cost-benefit analysis by the EC institutions is all the more important given the growing influence of the market's trade associations which wield large resources and can engage in sophisticated analysis.[75] The challenge for effective

FSAP regime is highly problematic in this regard. Eg, although the EC's approach to investor protection is evolving, it is not yet clear, even within discrete measures such as MiFID, whether a paternalistic or choice-based model is developing. See further N Moloney, 'Building a Retail Investment Culture through Law: the 2004 Markets in Financial Instruments Directive' (2005) 6 *European Business Organisation Law Review* 341.

[68] See, eg, the UK's extensive implementation programme for MiFID, spearheaded by the FSA, which has generated a series of lengthy consultation papers (the framework agenda is set out in the Joint Implementation Plan: see above n41).

[69] CESR's 'Technical Advice on Level Two Implementing Measures on the First Set of Mandates, Markets in Financial Instruments Directive', Feedback Statement (Jan 2005) CESR/05-025 (the January Feedback Statement), at 4.

[70] The 2005 *Annual Report* describes (at 78) a staff of 23.

[71] Jan Feedback Statement, above n69, at 4.

[72] White Paper, above n9, in which the Commission in a rather careful statement recognised (at 9) the 'good work carried out by the level three committees' but suggested that their advice would 'benefit if screened additionally in terms of impact and proportionality by a panel of expert economists'.

[73] ESC Minutes, 23 Feb 2005 (ESC/13/2005).

[74] CESR, *Annual Report* (2005), Foreword by the Chairman, at 5.

[75] This may be linked to their recognition of the power of economic arguments in legitimising interest group positions: see Zingales, above n15, at 3. For a recent example see the 2005 report by a powerful coalition of US and UK market associations calling for greater

law-making and policy formation is to harness this market expertise appropriately.[76] There are some signs of cost-benefit analysis being outsourced to the market. One of the most controversial provisions in MiFID is the obligation placed on the Commission under Article 65 to report on whether MiFID's already highly controversial transparency regime for equity markets should be extended to other markets. A group of influential UK and European trade associations has combined to commission research into the European bond market to inform the industry's contribution to the Commission's review,[77] which has been welcomed by the Commission[78] although it has pledged to keep an 'open mind'.[79] In a positive indication of how the Commission intends to approach new policy areas post-FSAP, the Commission published a Call for Evidence on extending the transparency regime in June 2006 which makes clear that public consultations will be undertaken, expert advice will be sought from CESR, and the new European Securities Market Expert Group (see section E.1 below) will be consulted.[80] Strong market input should therefore be counterbalanced and distilled into the final policy response. The Call for Evidence also sets out the Commission's methodology, how impact assessments will be used, the proposed scope of the Commission's analysis, and the possible rationales for intervention.[81] As an example of how to build a response to a sensitive and complex area where market interests are likely to be organised, vocal and expert, the Commission's approach augurs well for interventions in controversial areas currently on the agenda, including private equity and hedge funds.

convergence in EC and US regulation to support cross-border wholesale dealings in equities and equity derivatives, which chimes with the political high profile of EC/US financial market regulatory dialogue. The extensive report (in 2 vols) is designed to capture the costs of regulatory compliance in the transatlantic trading market and make the business case for a more coherent framework of regulation: see EU–US Coalition on Financial Regulation, *The Transatlantic Dialogue in Financial Services: The Case for Regulatory Simplification and Trading Efficiency* (2005).

[76] See C Scott, 'Analysing Regulatory Space: Fragmented Resources and Institutional Design' [2001] *Public Law* 329.

[77] The London Investment Banking Association, the Association of British Insurers, the Investment Management Association, the European High Yield Association and the European Primary Dealers' Association (LIBA *Annual Report* (2005), Chairman's Statement, at 3). The extensive report was published in May 2006 (entitled *European Corporate Bond Markets: Transparency, Liquidity, and Efficiency*').

[78] As noted in *ibid*, Chairman's Statement, at 3.

[79] ESC Minutes, 8–9 June 2006 (ESC/32/2006).

[80] Commission, Call for Evidence, Pre- and Post-Trade Transparency Provisions of the Markets in Financial Instruments Dir in Relation to Transactions in Classes of Financial Instruments Other Than Shares, 12 June 2006.

[81] Unusually, the Call for Evidence refers (at 7) to a review of the relevant academic and institutional literature.

4. Evidence-gathering and the Policy Formation Process

But the effectiveness of the financial market policy formation process depends on more than cost-benefit analysis of particular measures. A more sophisticated evidence-based assessment is needed of the conceptual basis of EC financial market policy. EC financial market policy is now making important choices for the financial markets concerning, for example, the role of disclosure, investor competence, and the importance of collective investment, and making key decisions on difficult questions of regulatory design concerning, for example, hedge funds, credit rating agencies and market transparency, with which regulators internationally are grappling. In order to increase the likelihood of specific measures minimising the risks of intervention, large-scale studies on investor behaviour and market risks are needed to inform policy-making as the market develops.[82]

There is some evidence of this type of analysis,[83] but it is very limited.[84] In particular, after the FSAP a massive disclosure system is now in place for the retail investment markets covering public offerings, investment advice, collective investment and the marketing of financial services.[85] But evidence which can inform the subsequent review of these measures, new policy initiatives and the development of convergence at Level Three is needed on how investors behave across the EC, how they make decisions, key cognitive weaknesses, common errors in investment, and which disclosure formats are most effective.[86] Supporting institutional structures are in place, in that CESR could provide a mechanism through which the institutional experience of EC supervisors in gathering and interpreting market data could be transmitted.

[82] On the need for greater evidence on investor decision-making patterns to inform regulation see, eg, H Jackson, 'To What Extent Should Individual Investors Rely on the Mechanisms of Market Efficiency: A Preliminary Investigation of Dispersion in Investor Returns' (2003) 28 *Journal of Corporation Law* 671; and A Jackson, 'The Aggregate Behaviour of Individual Investors' (2003), available at www. ssrn.com/abstract=536942.

[83] See, eg, Commission Rec 384/2004/EC on Dir 85/611/EEC on the simplified prospectus [2004] OJ L144/42 on the disclosure required by the EC's UCITS (mutual fund) product. The Rec noted that progress was needed on investors' disclosure needs with respect to cross-border comparability and recommended that Member States test the UCITS Rec in practice and report to the Commission. See recital 11.

[84] FIN-USE, eg, has called for studies into how retail investors react to disclosure, specifically UCITS summary prospectus disclosure, particularly as 'no market testing was carried out with consumers'.: FIN-USE, *Financial Services, Consumers and Small Businesses: A User Perspective on the Reports on Banking, Asset Management, Securities and Insurance of the Post FSAP Stocktaking Groups* (Oct 2004) at 25.

[85] 1985 UCITS Dir (Dir 85/611/EC [1985] OJ L375/3), 2002 Distance Marketing of Financial Services Dir (Dir 2002/65/EC [2002] OJ L271/16), 2003 Prospectus Dir, above n34, 2004 Transparency Dir, above n50, and MiFID.

[86] Calls from the market and regulators for research into pan-EC investor behaviour include the Consumer Association's Response to the Commission's 'Autumn 2004 Consultation on the Expert Group Reports, above n8, at 10, and J Tiner (chief executive FSA), Speech on 'European Financial Integration: Progress and Prospects', Commission Conference (22 June 2004), available at www.fsa.gov.uk.pubs/speeches.

5. Ongoing Review to Manage Law-making Risks

One of the distinctive features of FSAP legislation is the extent to which it includes formal review and reporting clauses. These are particularly important in the financial market sphere. While financial markets are dynamic, rules are static and can have unintended consequences.[87] This is particularly the case across different market sectors (such as the small and medium-sized enterprise sector).[88] Increased risks also arise where the drafting of rules reflects difficult political compromises, as was the case with the MiFID transparency regime for systematic internalisers, which has resulted in a highly complex regime demanding further amplification at Levels Two and Three.[89] The widely acknowledged prevalence of petrification risks in EC financial market regulation[90] can be seen in the attempts to revisit company and financial market regulation through the SLIM initiative for company law[91] and the 2005 White Paper, which seeks to simplify, codify and clarify financial services and markets regulation.[92] These risks are heightened in the Lamfalussy-designed, highly-detailed post-FSAP regulatory environment, given that detailed legislation can require market participants to shoe-horn new techniques and products into obsolete and inflexible regulatory frameworks.[93]

Where resource constraints exist post-FSAP, and where difficult political issues may be re-opened at a time of heightened political tensions if markets continue to integrate and as the full reach of the Lamfalussy structure

[87] This concern is frequently raised by the markets internationally and in the context of the FSAP: see, eg, the ICSA Statement on Consultation Practices (2004), above n13, and Letter from Lord Woolf, Chairman of the Financial Markets Law Committee to the European Commission (15 June 2006), available at www/fmlc.org/papers/Ltr2FreissEC, which called on the Commission to develop mechanisms, including effective cost-benefit analysis, to reduce the risks of static regulation.

[88] The MiFID regime, eg, potentially prejudices the efficient supply of private equity funding to SMEs by bringing private equity firms into the regulatory net as 'investment advisers' and imposing best execution publication requirements: see Report of the Alternative Investment Expert Group, 'Developing European Private Equity' (July 2006), at 24.

[89] Internationally, the difficult negotiations between the EC and the IASB on financial reporting standard IAS 39 on the reporting of derivative instruments and hedging techniques, and the subsequent 'carve-out' of the standard for the EC's financial reporting regime, have led to market uncertainty and the 'longest, most complex and most muddled set of rules in the book': B Jopson, 'A challenge taken on but not surmounted', *Financial Times*, International Accountancy Supp, 8 Sept 2005, at 2.

[90] Identified as a risk of harmonisation in one of the first major assessments of EC company and financial services regulation: R Buxbaum and K Hopt, *Legal Harmonisation and the Business Enterprise* (Berlin, de Gruyter, 1988).

[91] Recommendations by the Company Law SLIM Working Group on the Simplification of the First and Second Company Law Directives (Sept 1999).

[92] Above n9, at 6.

[93] The inflexibility of static but highly detailed rules has recently been raised as a particular source of risk to the wholesale markets post-FSAP by the Financial Markets Law Committee: see Lord Woolf Letter, above n87.

emerges, review clauses that impose formal reporting obligations on the Commission provide an important review mechanism for flawed legislation which may otherwise fall victim to institutional inertia.[94]

The prevalence of these clauses partly reflects the comitology process and the uneasy settlement between the Parliament, the Commission and the Council concerning the Parliament's callback rights under comitology procedures[95] following the collapse of the Constitutional Treaty.[96] In the financial markets sphere, this has resulted in the insertion of 'sunset clauses' in FSAP measures which grant Level Two law-making powers to the Commission. These clauses suspend the operation of Lamfalussy powers after defined timeframes.[97] They also provide an opportunity for assessing the effectiveness of the particular delegation and the appropriateness of its scope.

Substantive review obligations are also built into the FSAP measures. Article 31 of the 2003 Prospectus Directive subjects the entire Directive to a Commission assessment of its application, while Article 6(3) of the 2004 Transparency Directive requires the Commission to report on the transparency of quarterly reporting by issuers under the Directive's attenuated quarterly regime. MiFID's review obligations are extensive. Article 65 imposes a series of reporting and review obligations on the Commission with respect to a number of the Directive's more sensitive provisions, including the transparency regime which applies to systematic internalisers and which almost drove MiFID to deadlock following very difficult political negotiations.[98] Reporting obligations have also been built into the level two MiFID measures. The controversial MiFID Level Two Directive Article 4 prohibition on gold-plating has been subject to a reporting requirement on its application.[99] The initial signs are that these reporting obligations will be taken seriously and may represent an important safety valve for the

[94] Choi and Pritchard note that 'the market corrects its mistakes; regulators frequently resist doing so': above n15, at 6.

[95] Set out in a letter from Commissioner Bolkestein to the Chairman of the Parliament's Economic and Monetary Affairs Committee (Oct 2001) (available at http://europa.eu.int/rapid/pressRelease) and in the 2002 Prodi Declaration to the European Parliament (available at http://europa.eu.int/comm/internal_market/securities/docs/lamfalussy). Agreement was reached on a new comitology settlement in summer 2006.

[96] The governance risks of the comitology process have been subject to extensive review: see, eg, C Harlow, *Accountability in the European Union* (Oxford, OUP, 2002) at 67–71.

[97] MiFID Art 64(3), eg, suspends the Dir's level two delegations on 1 Apr 2008. The European Parliament and Council may renew the level two powers (acting on a Commission proposal) but must review the exercise of the Level Two delegation prior to the suspension date. These clauses are under review following the comitology settlement.

[98] Art 65(2) requires the Commission to report to the European Parliament and Council by 20 Apr 2008.

[99] Art 4(4) requires the Commission to report to the European Parliament and Council on the application of A4 by 31 Dec 2009.

MiFID regime as it develops. CESR's level three MiFID agenda[100] focuses in particular on the Commission's reporting obligations and prioritises the preparatory reviews which, it now appears, the Commission will require CESR to undertake. ECONET is designed in part to support effective information-gathering by CESR in advising the Commission on its reporting obligations.

But review clauses also carry risks, in that they may inappropriately dictate the shape of future policy. MiFID's transparency regime for securities trading, which is designed to support efficient price formation, proved to be the most controversial aspect of MiFID. It is, however, restricted to the equity markets. Debt markets operate under very different transparency and price formation mechanisms, being less liquid than the equity markets, dominated by institutional and block traders, and more affected by macro economic conditions, such as interest rate movements, than by trading and pricing information. The risk always existed that the ever-present danger of regulatory creep in EC financial market policy would pull debt and other markets into the transparency regime.[101] This risk was averted during the MiFID negotiations. But Article 65(1) is something of a hostage to fortune, in that it requires the Commission, on the basis of public consultations and following discussion with competent authorities, to report to the European Parliament and the Council on the possible extension of the regime to non-equity markets. Although, as outlined in section C.3 above, the Commission appears to be adopting a cautious approach to this question, clauses of this nature run the risk that politically controversial questions are disposed of by review clauses that may result in institutional momentum and public choice pressures building up behind inappropriate measures. All the indications are that very considerable resources and political time are being devoted to the Article 65 transparency report, even before the impact of the new transparency regime on equity market liquidity becomes clear. Once a regulatory question is placed on the policy agenda, it becomes very difficult to remove it. Clearing and settlement remain the notable exceptions to the rule that once EC resources are galvanised behind an issue some degree of intervention follows. This is now all the more the case with the momentum generated by the Lamfalussy process and the risks of CESR's involvement (see section F below). The effectiveness of the review process is therefore dependent on the management of the risks posed by the law-making and policy formation environment generally.

[100] CESR, Work Programme on MiFID Level Three Work (July 2006) CESR/06-413. The initial Level Three Work Programme for 2006–7 was published in Oct 2006 (CESR/550b).

[101] The Prospectus Dir's extensive disclosure regime for public offers can be analysed as an example of retail disclosure standards leaking across to the sophisticated wholesale markets. As a result, the exemption regime from the Dir for debt offerings, private placements and offers to sophisticated investors was fiercely negotiated.

D. STATEMENT OF OBJECTIVES AND PRINCIPLES OF FINANCIAL MARKET REGULATION

There are, therefore, indications of growing sophistication in the policy formation and law-making process, although risks remain. The risks of the law-making and policy formation process could be further contained by a benchmark agreement as to the objectives of financial market regulation against which current measures could be reviewed and new initiatives tested. Whether these objectives are implicit in the current regime and what the elements of any such agreement should be are questions for another day. But in principle an agreed statement of the objectives of EC financial market regulation could mitigate the law-making and process risks which exacerbate the wider uncertainty risks of the FSAP. It could carry benefits across a number of dimensions, including cost-benefit analysis, accountability and regulatory consistency.

Notwithstanding the scale of the FSAP and the growing sophistication of the policy formation process, there is still little evidence of a considered institutional position on the purposes of market intervention beyond free movement, even as the regime has moved far beyond free movement imperatives in its regulatory design.

A statement of objectives could, however, provide an important benchmark for assessing new measures and increasing the likelihood of effective cost-benefit analysis (section C.3 above).

It could also manage the risks which national interests pose to the FSAP review process, law-making post-FSAP, and the implementation process. CESR Chairman van Leeuwen has recently pointed to the 'serious tensions' which could arise as markets integrate, the pace of consolidation increases, and legitimate national interests are affected, and called for a balance to be found between 'market forces and political factors'.[102] An agreed Level One regulation setting out the purposes of financial market regulation could focus political attention on the purposes of regulation in the new market-place and temper the potentially destructive effects of national interests as the regime is implemented. It could also support the emergence of the much sought-after 'European reflex' in CESR and the ESC and support CESR's legitimacy (see section F.2 below). It might also increase the likelihood of future Level One measures being limited to principles. Although the Lamfalussy model is based on the adoption of principles-based Level One measures, this has not been the experience under the FSAP, which has produced highly detailed Level One measures. While this is partly a reflection of political realities and a reluctance to devolve rules to the developing Level Two and Level Three processes,

[102] Reported in ESC Minutes, 26 June 2006 (ESC/35/2006).

particularly where policy controversies arise,[103] an agreed statement of regulatory objectives might build greater trust at Level One.

Greater clarity as to the purposes of the new regulatory regime might also control inconsistencies across the regime.[104] For example, the 2005 White Paper calls for a cross-sector consistency check across the financial market directives, particularly with respect to the profile of disclosure which is now provided to investors across a range of directives.[105] But if this is to be effective, it cannot occur in a conceptual vacuum and should be based on an evidence-based model of investor competence and reflect clear regulatory objectives with respect to the execution of disclosure policy. A closer institutional focus on investor protection, risk tolerance and investor competence might also have prevented the current serious inconsistency in the UCITS mutual fund regime. The 'UCITS III' revisions to the UCITS investment limit rules,[106] which have led to the retail-focused, 'gold standard' UCITS mutual fund product becoming a potentially high risk product, capable of adopting hedge-fund-like strategies, were not reflected in MiFID's distribution, disclosure and advice regime for investment products and services, including UCITS. Under MiFID, UCITS is still a 'non-complex' product and is available for advice-free, execution-only services (trade execution services provided without advice), notwithstanding the change to its risk profile.

The 2001 Lamfalussy Report called for a conceptual framework of over-arching principles, enacted by the Parliament and Council or adopted through a Treaty revision.[107] But no formal progress has been made in this direction. This reflects in part the shallow roots of the FSAP. By contrast, the 2003 Company Law Action Plan,[108] which has introduced far-reaching regulatory reforms to EC company law, was based in a report by a group of academic and policy experts.[109] The High Level Group Report placed its reforms in the context of a conceptual discussion

[103] Ferrarini has identified the Level One/Two decision as 'more political than doctrinal': G Ferrarini, 'Contract Standards and the Markets in Financial Instruments Directive: An Assessment of the Lamfalussy Regulatory Architecture' (2005) 1 *European Review of Contract Law* 19, at 29

[104] The inconsistencies across EC financial market law are a particular concern of the Financial Markets Law Committee: see generally Financial Markets Law Committee, Paper 119, 'Conflicts between FSAP Directives' (Dec 2005) and Lord Woolf Letter, above n87.

[105] Above n9, at 6–7.

[106] Dir 2001/108/EC [2002] OJ L41/35 and Rec 2004/383 EC on the Use by UCITS of Financial Derivatives [2004] OJ L144/33.

[107] Above n 4, at 22.

[108] Commission, 'Modernising Company Law and Enhancing Corporate Governance in the European Union—A Plan to Move Forward', COM(2003)284.

[109] High Level Group of Company Law Experts, *A Modern Regulatory Framework for Company Law in Europe* (2002).

on key company law and policy questions such as the nature of disclosure and the impact of the EC's dispersed and block-holding share ownership divide on policy formation.[110] No such discussion as to the purpose of regulation in the risk environment of an integrated market informed the FSAP's construction.

That difficult questions arise as to which principles should govern financial market regulation is an understatement.[111] Traditional regulatory objectives could be balanced with EC market integration objectives and policy-making requirements.[112] A more ambitious, and EC-sensitive list could include more nuanced objectives such as building financial capability and the promotion of effective diversification for investors.[113] The immediate political and institutional pressure to deliver the FSAP has now lifted. At the same time, the institutions have amassed considerable institutional experience in dealing with complex regulatory questions. While considerable divergences remain across the Member States with respect to the purposes of regulation,[114] evidence is emerging of a more considered approach to EC regulation in the areas currently under discussion, from which a statement of principles could be drawn.[115] The Commission is

[110] See, eg its discussion of disclosure as a regulatory tool at 33–4.

[111] For an analysis of the underlying goals of financial services regulation in the highly sophisticated US regime see H Jackson, 'Regulation of a Multisectored Financial Services Industry: An Exploratory Essay' (1999) 77 *Washington University Law Quarterly* 319. In the UK context see C Mayer, 'Regulatory Principles and the Financial Services and Markets Act 2000' in Ferran and Goodhart, above n65, at 25.

[112] The Lamfalussy principles cover: maintaining confidence in European securities markets; maintaining high levels of prudential supervision; contributing to the efforts of prudential supervisors to ensure systemic stability; ensuring appropriate levels of consumer protection are proportionate to risk; respecting subsidiarity and proportionality; promoting competition; ensuring regulation is efficient and encourages innovation; and taking account of the European and international dimension of securities markets.

[113] On diversification as a key objective of modern investor protection see Jackson, above n82, and C Camerer, 'Regulation for Conservatives: Behavioural Economics and the Case for "Asymmetric Paternalism"' (2003) 151 *University of Pennsylvania Law Review* 1211, at 1236.

[114] CESR has pointed to pan-EC divergences in regulatory objectives and priorities as a key risk to the effectiveness of networked, pan-EC supervision: CESR, Preliminary Progress Report, 'Which Supervisory Tools for the EU Securities Market? An Analytical Paper by CESR' (Oct 2004) (the Himalaya Report) (CESR 04-333f), at 12.

[115] The emerging approach to investment fund reform, eg, has seen the Commission and the ESC considering retail investor competence, the relevance of risk-based regulation for the EC market, the link between distribution and product regulation, and the connection between product disclosure and investment advice: see Commission, Green Paper on the Enhancement of the EU Framework for Investment Funds (July 2005), COM(2005)314, and ESC Minutes, 3 Mar 2005 (ESC 12/2005). The Commission's Background Note on the first draft of the MiFID Level Two Dir, above n35, at 6–7, attempts to justify the need for intervention in terms of investor confidence as a public good and the risks of informational asymmetries, but the analysis is very limited. Signs of a more considered approach have also emerged in the 2006 Call for Evidence on non-equity market transparency, above n79.

also slowly moving in this direction at a macro level: the cost-benefit analysis in the 2005 White Paper assesses the 2005–10 agenda against 'market functioning' criteria which include competition and investor protection. The ideological obstacles may not therefore be insuperable and there is evidence of institutional and market support.[116] Whether the political will exists is uncertain.

E. THE INSTITUTIONAL ENVIRONMENT

1. Institutional Fragmentation and Co-ordination Risks

As the EC moves to being the monopoly supplier of complex and politically sensitive financial market regulation, the governance risks of EC policy-making sharply increase. But in sharp contrast to the earlier FSAP phase, EC financial market policy is now developed in a considerably more complex institutional environment, exacerbating these risks.

A rapid growth has occurred in the number of bodies inhabiting the financial market policy landscape. In the early FSAP phase, policy was developed under usual inter-institutional processes with limited input from specialised policy actors.[117] Policy development and law-making are now fractured across a range of actors, potentially generating co-ordination, consistency and accountability risks.[118] Institutional co-ordination is all the more important as EC financial market policy has traditionally been dealt with in a segmented rather than a risk-based fashion, with discrete measures addressing issuers and prospectuses, investment funds, and investment firms and trading markets, and given the underlying conceptual untidiness in EC financial market regulation.

[116] The Van den Burg Report argued that financial market law and policy 'should be based on key principles of the type recommended by the Lamfalussy Report': see above n8, at A.9. The Securities Expert Group also recommended that the Lamfalussy principles be 'properly written' into EC law. The potential difficulties in agreeing on a list can, however, be seen in the Group's recommendation of an additional 4 principles, including that EC policy promote a reduction in the cost of capital for issuers and increased real returns for investors: see above n8, at 9.

[117] Pre-proposal consultations were usually limited to 'hand picked industry representatives' and the now largely defunct Contact Committees (without comitology powers) established under the original, pre-FSAP series of financial market dirs. These included the European Securities Committee and the UCITS Contact Committee. Membership of these committees tended to be composed of high level officials. Specific advisory bodies were typically not used. See, eg, the consideration of early FSAP policy-making in the FSAP Implementation Report, above n3, at 14–15.

[118] On institutional coordination and consistency risks in US financial market policy see R Petschnigg, 'The Institutional Framework for Financial Market Policy in the USA Seen From an EU Perspective', European Central Bank Occasional Paper Series No 35 (2005), available at http://ssrn.com/abstract=752095.

Under the Lamfalussy structures, the Commission, the ESC, and CESR appear to be working effectively.[119] Financial market questions are also considered, however, by the Committee of European Banking Supervisors and the European Central Bank, particularly with respect to prudential and market stability risks. This generates coordination risks, as became clear when diverging positions emerged between the Commission and the European Central Bank on the treatment of hedge funds in 2006.[120] Although the EC's response to hedge funds is awaited, a coordinated response to this complex question is essential if the multiple risks raised by hedge funds across a multi-actor risk chain are to be appropriately monitored and contained.[121] Financial reporting issues, which are central to financial market regulation, are also fractured between the different accounting committees which advise on the Commission's adoption and endorsement of International Accounting Standards and International Financial Reporting Standards (IAS/IFRS) (namely, the Accounting Regulatory Committee (ARC)), the European Financial Reporting Advisory Group (EFRAG), and the Standards Advice Review Group) and CESR which addresses the enforcement and implementation of IAS/IFRS through its CESR-FIN group.

There is evidence of greater coordination and communication between the Lamfalussy committees in particular. CESR, the Committee of European Banking Supervisors (CEBS), and the Committee of European Insurance and Occupational Pensions Supervisors (CEIOPS) have developed a cross-sector work agenda and now operate under a 2005 Joint Protocol which coordinates their activities, although it remains to be seen whether resource strains will prejudice its effectiveness. The policy shift away from new legislative measures and towards effective implementation, review and enforcement may also mitigate some of the strains which institutional coordination in this new environment are likely to place on law-making.

Policy coordination risks are, of course, weaker where the bodies in question are simply consultative and review bodies. But the sheer volume of bodies now advising the Commission on financial market policy raises questions about the ability of the market to sustain this level of consultation at a time of post-FSAP strain and about the legitimacy and effectiveness of the

[119] See sect F below. For an extended analysis of inter-institutional dynamics under the Lamfalussy process in the context of the Prospectus Dir and the Market Abuse Dir see Ferran, above n32, at 67–82.

[120] In June 2006 the ECB published a graphic warning of the major risks posed by hedge funds to global market stability: see ECB, *Financial Stability Review* (June 2006). By contrast, the Commission's approach has been more relaxed and directed towards facilitating hedge funds as a key source of market liquidity and an important risk transfer mechanism: see, eg, Commissioner McCreevy, Speech to Commission Hearing on Investment Funds, 13 Oct 2005, available at http://europa.eu.int/rapid/pressReleases; ESC Minutes, 3 Mar 2005 (ESC 12/2005); and the Investment Funds Green Paper, above n115, at 9.

[121] N Moloney, 'The EC and the Hedge Fund Challenge: A Test Case for EC Securities Policy After the Financial Services Action Plan' [2006] *Journal of Corporate Law Studies* 1.

consultation process as a result. This is all the more the case as consultations are rarely co-ordinated across CESR, the Commission and other bodies mandated to carry out consultations.[122] As part of its policy of enhanced consultation, the Commission has constituted a new series of industry committees including the Expert Groups on Alternative Investment Funds and on Market Efficiency to advise on the direction of EC funds policy after the 2005 Investment Funds Green Paper, and the European Securities Market Expert Group that will advise on securities policy generally.[123] Although an additional risk potentially arises that self-interest and prestige incentives will provoke these bodies to support costly and unnecessary new legislation,[124] FSAP advisory bodies have tended to call for restraint and limited intervention.[125]

The multiplicity of advisory bodies may also mask the risks that consultation and policy formation may be unbalanced in the post-FSAP period and that capture risks may be aggravated. Consultation exercises are almost entirely dominated by industry and wholesale market interests. The statistics are stark. Across all the consultations held by CESR from October 2002 until June 2005 on various FSAP measures, including the MiFID conduct of business regime, there were 1,680 responses, of which only 13 represented consumer groups.[126] More specifically, of the 77 responses to CESR's First Draft Level Two Advice on the MiFID regime[127] (which included advice on the disclosure provided by investment firms to investors), only one (the Danish Shareholders' Association) formally represented the interests of private investors.[128] Of the 78 to the Second Draft Level Two Advice,[129] which addressed advice and suitability assessments, a matter of particular concern for retail investors, only four (the Danish Shareholders Association, the Swedish Shareholders Association, the Federation of German Consumer Organisations, and the UK Financial Services Consumer Panel) represented

[122] The Mar 2006 Inter Institutional Monitoring Group noted market concern that consultations on the same subject had been carried out by different institutions and at different times: see above n8, at 12.

[123] ESC Minutes, 26 June 2006 (ESC/35/2006).

[124] Enriques, above n48, at 55–65.

[125] The 2004 Securities Expert Group, eg, called for greater use of market-based non-legislative solutions to new problems: see above n8, at 11. Similarly, the Investment Fund Expert Group on Private Equity (above n88) called for a facilitative rather than a regulatory approach to the development of private equity funds (which are essential to the funding of smaller companies), including a common but 'non-legislative' approach to the definition of private placement which would support pan-EC market access by private equity funds.

[126] H McKeen-Edwards and I Roberge, 'Efficiency Over Democracy? The Case of Monetary and Financial Services Sector Integration in Europe', available at http://web.uvic.ca/europe/pdf/hmckeen-iroberge.

[127] CESR, 'Advice on Possible Implementing Measures of the Directive 2004/39/EC on Markets in Financial Instruments—Consultation Paper' (June 2004) CESR/04-261b.

[128] Responses available at www.cesr.eu.org/index,php?page=responses&id=37.

[129] CESR, 'Draft Technical Advice on Possible Implementing Measures of the Directive 2004/39/EC on Markets in Financial Instruments—Second Set of Mandates—Consultation Paper' (Oct 2004) CESR/04-562.

retail interests.[130] Market interests are also becoming increasingly sophisticated in developing policy positions and building pan-EC and cross-sector lobbying networks.[131] This is not least because the monopoly position of the EC provides a clear focus for lobbying activities. They are also calling for greater contact with policy-makers and are unapologetic as to the need for expert market advice to inform policy-making.[132] Perhaps in a reflection of this mood, and in order to support its institutional position, the new range of bodies advising the Commission represents, almost entirely, market interests. But this also reflects the difficulties involved in organising the diffuse, typically nationally-based, and poorly resourced consumer and retail investor constituency. The public choice risks of the EC's position as monopoly supplier of financial market regulation are already aggravated by this intense concentration of highly resourced and expert market interests.[133] The new and complex institutional environment may only deepen this risk. This matters with respect to substantive issues of regulatory design.[134]

[130] Responses available at www.cesr.eu.org/index,php?page=responses&id=44.

[131] The London Investment Banking Association has emerged as one of the leading lobbyists on EC financial market policy, building pan-EC positions among the European investment banking industry through its links with the Association Française des Entreprises d'Investissement (AEFI), the Italian Association of Financial Intermediaries (ASSOSIM) and the Swedish Securities Dealers' Association, and developing alliances with major trade associations (such as the International Capital Market Association) as appropriate. See, eg, the detailed coverage of EC policy in its 2004 and 2005 Annual Reports.

Summer 2006 saw a 'highly unusual cooperative effort' between the major trade associations active in the UK markets (LIBA, the Association of British Insurers, the Investment Management Association and the British Banking Association) to address the costs of MiFID implementation: P Davis and B Jopson, 'Fears over EU rules unite City groups', *Financial Times*, 16 Aug 2006, 1.

Other FSAP- and MiFID-driven alliances include the MiFID Joint Working Group (the JWG), which is a pan-EC alliance of financial services IT associations. It successfully lobbied on the systems implications of the MiFID Level Two rules: see M Imeson, 'Time to Replace Talk with Action', *The Banker*, Supplement on Countdown to MiFID, May 2006, 48.

[132] See, eg, Securities Expert Group, above n8, at 14–15. The Financial Markets Law Committee has pointed to the benefits to the Commission in terms of its 'leverage[ing] its own limited resources': Lord Woolf Letter, above n87.

[133] Enriques, above n48, at 16.

[134] See, eg, the evolution of the MiFID conflict of interest regime during which market interests successfully lobbied against an abstention rule in the Dir where a firm could not organise itself so as to avoid a risk of prejudice to client interests through conflicts of interests: J Herbst, 'Revision of the ISD' (2003) 11 *Journal of Financial Regulation and Compliance* 211, at 215–16. At Level Two, CESR has displayed some willingness to face down market interests, albeit in a somewhat counter-intuitive fashion. Although it bowed to market pressure in removing a requirement that Chinese walls be used to establish independence from conflicts of interest through a separation of activities in particular circumstances, replacing it with a requirement that they be established where relevant, it refused to weaken its stance on conflict of interest protection for sophisticated counterparties in the face of strong market criticism: Jan Feedback Statement, above n69, at 23 and 25. Other notable changes in CESR's position in the face of fierce market opposition include the removal of generic investment advice from MiFID's investment advice regime and the scope of its suitability obligations. CESR has proved itself more robust in other traditional battle grounds for investor protection: see sect F below.

It also matters with respect to the general direction and mechanisms of policy-making.[135] Capture risks across the Lamfalussy process are also likely to reduce with more effective consumer involvement. Particular policy questions, notably with respect to the wholesale markets, demand, of course, expert market advice which can reduce the severe information asymmetries that the EC institutions can suffer from in financial market policy design.[136] But regulation is not composed of water-tight compartments and issues of concern to the wholesale sector can leak across eventually to the retail markets.

After a long period in obscurity and rather late in the day, weaknesses in consumer and retail governance have now been recognised by the EC institutions.[137] In a conscious attempt to build consumer governance capacity, the Commission, which has become increasingly concerned about retail governance,[138] constituted FIN-USE in July 2003 as an Expert Forum to examine financial services policies from the user/demand side perspective.[139] FIN-USE has become a robust and vocal policy actor and is increasingly appearing in EC consultations where previously there was little or no retail input.[140] Following a White Paper commitment to promoting retail governance,[141] in May 2006 the Commission also established the Financial Services Consumer Group (FSCG)[142] to build financial expertise in the retail sector and provide more effective consumer input. In establishing FIN-USE and the FSCG the Commission's approach to advisory bodies has taken on a new dimension. It has constituted these bodies in a deliberate attempt to build greater capacity, given the lack of expertise suffered by retail

[135] See, eg, the UK Financial Services Consumer Panel which takes a more sceptical approach to the current support for cost-benefit analysis, noting that cost-benefit analysis can be a crude tool in practice and calling for more attention to be paid to the promotion of consumer confidence: see Responses to the Commission's Autumn 2004 Consultation on the Expert Group Reports, above n8, at 3. More generally, FIN-USE has queried the extent to which integrated financial markets support consumer choice and lower prices: FIN USE, above n84, at 4.

[136] Ferran, above n32, 90–1.

[137] The Council has urged more effective retail participation (2587th Meeting of the Council Press Release, Council Conclusions (Economic and Monetary Affairs) (2 June 2004) at 12), as has the European Parliament in the Van den Burg Report, above n8, at A.8. On weaknesses in retail governance see further Moloney, above n30, at 416–21.

[138] Retail governance has emerged as a major theme of the Commission's post-FSAP agenda. In its Report on FSAP Implementation, eg, it acknowledged the criticism of poor retail and consumer involvement in financial services policy-making and the need for concrete measures: see above n3, at 17.

[139] Commission Press Release IP/03/1119, 25 July 2003.

[140] It participated, eg, in the consultations on the Mar 2006 Inter Institutional Group Report on the Lamfalussy process. By contrast, the earlier Dec 2003 Report (Inter-Institutional Monitoring Group 'Second Interim Report Monitoring the Lamfalussy Process' (Dec 2003)) referred (at 29) to a 'considerable problem' relating to the representation of retail investors.

[141] White Paper, above n9, at 7–9.

[142] Commission Press Release IP/06/806, 20 June 2006.

investor interests in assessing complex financial regulation, and to support the formation of a retail lobby in the EC which will ultimately influence policy formation. As such, it reflects the emergence of a more imaginative and capacity-building approach to the law-making process which may dilute the wider risks of the FSAP period.

2. Accountability Risks and International Standards

A focus on governance and accountability is all the more important given that EC financial market regulation is increasingly importing international standards that are adopted by international standard-setting bodies with insecure governance and accountability foundations. Probably the most high profile example concerns the EC's new financial reporting and auditing regime for corporate disclosure. The International Accounting Standards Board (IASB) is an international, private standard-setting body which adopts the International Accounting Standards and International Financial Reporting Standards (IAS/IFRS) which, following the 2002 IAS Regulation,[143] must now be followed by publicly-listed companies in the EC for their consolidated accounts. IFRS are, however, endorsed by the Commission, advised and supervised under comitology procedures by the network of accounting committees. The Commission has also been a robust critic of IASB governance and called for greater EC representation on its board—to some effect.[144] A similar comitology model will apply to the importation of International Standards on Auditing (ISA) adopted by the International Auditing and Assurance Standards Board (IAASB) under the 2006 Eighth Directive on the Statutory Auditor.[145] While the endorsement mechanism supports the legitimacy of IAS/IFRS and ISA in the EC, risks remain. It is politically difficult for the EC to adjust international standards internally under comitology procedures where specific concerns arise, given the prejudicial consequences for international convergence. This was graphically illustrated by the international furore following the 'carve-out' by the Commission of IAS 39 on the reporting of financial derivatives and hedging techniques given EC market and regulatory concerns.[146]

[143] Reg (EC) 1606/2002 [2002] OJ L243/1.

[144] P Walton, 'The EU and the IASB', Feb 2005 IFRS Direct, available at www.accaglobal.com/ifrs/directarticles; IASC, Changes to the IASCF Constitution (Report of the IASC Foundation Trustees, July 2005).

[145] Dir 2006/43/EC [2006] OJ L157/87.

[146] The acknowledgment in the IASC Annual Report that it 'has, of course, been disappointing that the European Union has carved out of our main financial instruments standards' (International Accounting Standards Committee Foundation, *Annual Report* (2004), 12) hid a frequently ill-tempered debate.

The Commission was clearly uncomfortable with this action and stressed that the carve-out was 'exceptional and temporary' and 'not the preferred solution...the Commission prefers full endorsement of any international accounting standard'. [147]

While the IASB's indirect influence generates most controversy, international standards are now emerging across EC financial market policy and without the comitology review applied to IAS/IFRS. This is particularly the case with the non-binding standards produced by the International Organisation of Securities Commissions (IOSCO). One of the more controversial questions faced by the Commission in the current phase of policy formation concerns the risks posed by credit rating agencies, as gatekeepers to the markets, given the conflict of interest risks to which they are subject and the recent high profile failures by credit rating agencies to assess risk to bondholders in cases such as *Parmalat*.[148] Following CESR's advice,[149] the Commission decided against imposing EC regulation but called on the credit rating industry to adopt voluntarily the 2004 IOSCO Standards.[150] Although the Standards have not been formally endorsed by the EC or given any binding effect, they have effectively become a quasi-mandatory code for the EC credit rating agency industry and compliance is reviewed by CESR. This development is positive, in that it reflects the Commission's increasing use of a wide range of regulatory tools beyond binding legislation. But the Standards have been imported from IOSCO, an international body without formal accountability links, with limited transparency as to its activities and decision-making procedures, and which has been criticised as forming a 'closed policy network'.[151] The dynamics of IOSCO's operation are not clear and the nature of the influence exercised by key market actors and powerful regulators is opaque. CESR has been the main filter on the appropriateness of the Standards and, ultimately, the source of their legitimacy as the notional EC standard. But CESR's accountability and legitimacy is insecure (see section F.2 below). IOSCO's 2003 Standards for Investment Analysts[152] have also been used by CESR in developing its controversial Level Two

[147] Commission, 'IAS 39 Financial Instruments: Recognition and Measurement—Frequently Asked Questions' (19 Nov 2004) MEMO/04/265.

[148] See generally G Ferrarini and P Giudici, 'Financial Scandals and the Role of Private Enforcement: The Parmalat Case', European Corporate Governance Institute, Law Working Paper No 40/2005 (2005), available at www.ecgi.org/wp and on http://ssrn.com/abstract=730403.

[149] CESR, 'Technical Advice to the European Commission Concerning Credit Rating Agencies' (2005).

[150] IOSCO, Code of Conduct for Rating Agencies (2004).

[151] G Underhill and X Zhang, 'Global Structures and Political Imperatives: In Search of Normative Underpinnings for International Financial Order' in G Underhill and X Zhang (eds), *International Financial Governance Under Stress: Global Structures Versus National Imperatives* (Cambridge, Cambridge University Press, 2003), at 77.

[152] IOSCO, *Report on Analyst Conflict of Interest* (2003) and IOSCO, *Statement of Principles for Addressing Sell-Side Securities Analysts' Conflicts of Interests* (2003).

advice for the conflict of interest rules applicable to investment research under MiFID,[153] while the Commission has suggested that IOSCO standards could be used by national authorities in implementing and applying MiFID, as long as these standards do not conflict with MiFID.[154]

As the Commission appears increasingly willing to rely on soft law techniques and self-regulation in financial market policy,[155] the influence of codes of conduct produced by international bodies is likely only to increase. The EC institutions appear to be alert to this emerging risk. In its 2005 Green Paper the Commission noted that the governance and accountability risks of global standard-setters was becoming of 'growing political importance' and called for a strengthening of public oversight in order to ensure 'appropriate reflection of stakeholders, satisfactory transparency, due process and sustainable financing'.[156] The European Parliament has also expressed similar concerns in the 2005 Van Den Burg Report.[157] The growing accountability risk may be somewhat mitigated by the Commission's recent tentative suggestions that a coordinated position be taken by the EC, where Member States participate in international standard-setting bodies such as IOSCO, the IAASB and the IASB,[158] but considerably greater attention needs to be given to the process whereby these standards are imported and to the governance structures of these bodies.

F. CESR AND ACCOUNTABILITY RISKS

1. Wide-ranging Influence

The most significant institutional risk to accountability and legitimacy in the post-FSAP law-making and policy formation environment comes from CESR, which is emerging as the most influential actor in EC financial market policy. The sheer scale of CESR's influence over EC financial market regulation is only now becoming apparent.[159]

[153] CESR, 'Technical Advice on Possible Implementing Measures of the Directive 2004/39/EC' (Apr 2005) CESR/05-290b, at 20.

[154] MiFID Background Document, above n35, at 7.

[155] See generally L Senden, *Soft Law in European Community Law* (Oxford, Hart Publishing, 2004).

[156] Above n46, at 7.

[157] It was 'concerned to ensure political and democratic accountability' where international standard-setters 'touch on major policy principles that should be decided at the political level': above n8, at B.21

[158] White Paper, above n9, at 15.

[159] For earlier analyses of how CESR's role and influence would develop see G Hertig and R Lee, 'Four Predictions on the Future of EU Securities Regulation' [2003] *Journal of Corporate Law Studies* 359 and M McKee, 'The Unpredictable Future of European Securities Regulation' (2003) 18 *Journal of International Banking Law and Regulation* 277.

It is clear from the CESR/Commission/ESC dynamic that CESR's advice is heavily influential on the shape of Level Two measures (see section F.4 below). Beyond Level Two, and arguably more importantly, CESR is increasingly exercising direct influence over the financial markets, without the filter of the ESC/Commission/Parliament oversight over the Level Two process, with its non-binding Level Three activities. Level Three is designed to support convergence and consistency in the implementation and application of Level One and Level Two rules. It has been developed by CESR to involve: co-ordinated implementation of EC law; regulatory convergence and supervisory convergence.[160] Its range of activities at Level Three is becoming formidable. This is made abundantly clear by CESR's 2005 Annual Report, which notes that 2006 would:

> witness CESR's metamorphosis from being primarily a regulatory advisory body to becoming a body which is well on its way to becoming an operational network of supervisors...[161]

On the Level Three policy dimension, for example, CESR is developing a specific policy towards the retail investor, including outreach activities to encourage investor involvement in governance and investor education. This development shows CESR acting independently as policy-maker, building a model for a coherent EC retail investor policy, which is currently lacking in Level One measures. Given the increasing political profile of retail investor policy, this activity takes CESR into potentially choppy waters and into the classic domain of the traditional regulator—retail investor protection. Through its Level Three monitoring activities, it is reviewing compliance by credit rating agencies with the IOSCO Code of Conduct for Rating Agencies. Its activities in reviewing rating agencies and reporting to the Commission, while based on a voluntary agreement with the sector and following a request from the Commission,[162] give CESR the colour of a European regulatory agency. Its other Level Three activities currently include institutional, enforcement and regulatory measures such as: the development of a mediation mechanism to support supervisory convergence and resolve supervisory disputes; co-ordinating the implementation and enforcement of the new IAS/IFRS reporting regime through its CESR-Fin operational group; and the development of non-binding standards and recommendations concerning the application of the Level Two Prospectus Regulation[163] and the cross-border notification of passporting

[160] CESR, 'The Role of CESR at "Level 3" Under the Lamfalussy Process' (Apr 2004), CESR/04-104b.

[161] CESR, above n26, Foreword by the Chairman.

[162] Speech by Commissioner McCreevy, Federation of European Securities Exchanges, Brussels, 26 May 2005.

[163] Commission Reg 809/2004/EC [2004] OJ L149/1.

UCITS funds. CESR will also play a central role in the preparation of the Commission's reviews and reports of controversial MiFID provisions under MiFID Article 65 and, as with its Level Two advice, may steer the direction of the final policy response, although specific Commission mandates will be required.[164]

It remains to be seen whether these non-binding activities will generate supervisory convergence, but their potential to dictate supervisory and regulatory practices is considerable. Level Three is expressly designed to promote convergence through techniques such as guidance, peer pressure and information exchange.[165] But the lack of transparency in CESR decision-making makes it impossible to assess the degree of consensus behind each measure.

CESR's influence is likely only to increase as cross-sector links strengthen and new advisory bodies are developed. The CESR will, for example, have observer status on the new European Securities Markets Expert Group. It has formal links with CEBS and CEIOPS through the Joint Protocol and Joint Work Programme. Given its greater experience, higher profile and the more extensive mandates it has enjoyed under the financial market directives, it seems likely that CESR will exert considerable influence across these committees. This is also true of its relationship with the accounting committees. Although the ARC, EFRAG and the Standards Advice Review Group oversee the adoption of IAS/IFRS reporting standards by the Commission, CESR remains influential through its CESR-Fin committee and has observer status on ARC and EFRAG. CESR is also developing considerable political influence. It increasingly acts as a high-level adviser to the Council by reporting to the Financial Services Committee of the Council on supervisory convergence and to the Financial Stability Table of the Council's Economic and Financial Committee on issues related to the overall stability of the EU financial system.[166] CESR therefore sits at the centre of the inter-institutional web and the burgeoning network of Lamfalussy committees and advisory bodies. It looks set to have a unique institutional perspective and influence on policy formation.

CESR's growing stature and influence also reflect deepening transatlantic links and the developing dialogue between the EC and US on upstream regulatory developments (particularly with respect to hedge fund risk and credit rating agencies) and downstream problems (chief among them the now-resolved dispute concerning the difficulties European issuers face in de-listing from US exchanges and avoiding US Sarbanes–Oxley requirements,

[164] CESR, MiFID Level Three Agenda, above n100, at 1–2.

[165] See generally CESR Level Three Report, above n160.

[166] See, eg, CESR's report to the FSC on supervisory convergence (CESR/05-202). CESR's FST reports include a review of offshore centres (with CEBS and CEIOPS) and a review of market conditions in the primary and secondary markets and the main risks to current economic developments: see CESR, above n26, at 72.

and the IFRS/US GAAP convergence debate on financial reporting). High level and increasingly successful political contacts between the Commission and the SEC continue through the US–EU Financial Markets Dialogue.[167] However CESR is emerging as the main point of contact for regular SEC negotiations and has entered into an agreement with the SEC on cooperation and collaboration on market risks and regulatory policy.[168] It has also entered into a formal agreement with the SEC on the enforcement of IFRS application, which places it at the centre of the highly sensitive EU/US negotiations on IFRS/GAAP convergence.[169] CESR also has a formal working relationship with the US Commodity Futures Trading Commission.[170] These links reinforce its institutional position as the pre-eminent policy actor in the financial markets area.

All this has developed from the original 2001 Commission Decision establishing CESR[171] as part of the Lamfalussy process and as an 'independent advisory group on securities within the Community' to advise the Commission, either on the Commission's initiative or on its own initiative, in particular with respect to Level Two implementing measures (Article 2). The original Lamfalussy Report, which was endorsed by the European Council,[172] recommended that Level Three produce guidelines on implementation develop recommendations and standards on issues not covered by EC law, and define best practice. CESR has formally deepened and widened the Level Three strategy through its 2004 reports on Level Three and on supervisory convergence,[173] and by its recent practice. Although both reports were, for the most part, accepted by the institutions,[174] CESR's influence now has a dynamic character.

2. Accountability Risks

Yet CESR's accountability is minimal. Given the reach of CESR's activities, considerable compliance and convergence risks may arise if its activities are not seen as legitimate. CESR is not formally accountable to the Member States or the EC institutions and sits somewhat adrift in the institutional

[167] For a review of its current activities see Commission Staff Working Document, 'Single Market in Financial Services Progress Report 2004–2005' (Jan 2006), SEC(2006)177, at 14–15.

[168] CESR, above n26, at 70.

[169] Press Release IP/06/1085, 3 Aug 2006.

[170] CESR Annual Report (2004), at 58.

[171] Commission Dec 2001/527/EC [2001] OJ L191/43.

[172] Res of the European Council on more effective securities market regulation in the European Union, Stockholm, 23 Mar 2001.

[173] CESR Level Three Report, above n160; Himalaya Report, above n113.

[174] See, eg, Commission, 'The Application of the Lamfalussy Process to EU Securities Market Legislation' (Brussels, European Commission, Nov 2004), at 10; the European Parliament Van den Burg Report, above n8, at B.13; and ESC Minutes, 15 Dec 2004 (ESC 1/2005), albeit that all expressed reservations about accountability.

structure. It declares itself to be independent.[175] The foundation Decision establishing CESR simply requires CESR to present an annual report to the Commission (Article 6) and to maintain close operational links with the Commission and the ESC (Article 4). Very little is known about how CESR makes decisions. CESR's original Charter provided only that in its Level Two advice CESR should identify and elaborate any dissenting opinions and that otherwise it would work by consensus of its members.[176] It is not clear whether in practice CESR votes or operates by consensus, although consensus appears to dominate. The extensive Level Two advice on the MiFID conduct of business, best execution and order handling regime, which provoked numerous points of controversy during the consultation process, does not, for example, contain any dissenting opinions.[177] But it is not clear how consensus is achieved, which Member States and regulatory traditions are influential, or whether national interests or prestige dynamics trump objective regulatory positions.[178] Very little is known about CESR's working and regulatory culture and how this influences its approach to market regulation.[179] Are its staff sourced from regulators, lawyers or market participants? Despite its influence, CESR has operated largely in secret.

Although it engages in extensive consultations, not only is the consultation process one-sided in that consumer interests are barely represented, but during the MiFID Level Two process CESR based its advice on previous work in its earlier incarnation as the informal standard-setting and dialogue body FESCO (the Forum of European Securities Commission),[180] which pre-set the agenda. There are also concerns that, with a membership base of 27 Member States, CESR does not take argued, conceptual positions on regulation in its Level Two advice or in its Level Three measures, but operates by consensus, layering different domestic approaches to form the final advice.[181] It is difficult to assess whether this is the case from the

[175] The CESR Annual Report, above n170, describes CESR (at 66) as 'an independent Committee of European Securities Regulators'.

[176] CESR Charter CESR/01-002, Art 5(5) and (6).

[177] CESR, 'Technical Advice on Possible Implementing Measures of Directive 2004/39/EC on Markets in Financial Instruments—First Set of Mandates' (Jan 2005), CESR/05-024c, at 45–70; and CESR, 'Technical Advice on Possible Implementing Measures of Directive 2004/39/EC on Markets in Financial Instruments—First Set of Mandates (Best Execution) and Second Set of Mandates' (Apr 2005), CESR/05-290b, at 25–45.

[178] One commentator has described CESR's members as 'strong minded, bathed in prestige and conditioned by national laws, politics and traditions': B Jopson, 'European regulators learn to sing in harmony', *Financial Times*, 17 Nov 2005, 14.

[179] Institutional culture can be a powerful force in shaping regulatory strategy. Donald Langevoort has examined the US SEC's culture in terms of its adherence to a 'creation story' of investor protection to which all its regulators subscribe: D Langevoort, 'Re-reading Cady, Roberts: The Ideology and Practice of Insider Trading Regulation' (1999) 99 *Columbia Law Review* 1319.

[180] Jan Feedback Statement, above n69, at 4.

different Level Two consultation documents through which CESR develops its advice. But it is certainly a challenge to draw out an articulated CESR position on market regulation.

Notwithstanding the repeated references to a 'European reflex' across EC policy rhetoric,[182] it is, for example, difficult to see a distinctly 'European' approach to regulation emerging across CESR's advice. There was little attempt in the Level Two MiFID advice on the disclosure which investment firms must provide to investors to address the specific risks faced by investors in pan-EC investing through imposing comparability and format requirements.[183] This may develop in time.[184] CESR's instincts also appear to be traditional in that it emerges as generally in favour of extensive disclosure and is robust in protecting investor interests in the face of market concerns about cost,[185] but there is limited discussion of its approach to regulation.

While this opacity as to its regulatory philosophy is arguably a reflection of the Commission mandates within which it operates, CESR's advice would be more securely buttressed against lack of accountability charges if it was placed within a politically agreed level one statement of regulatory objectives. This could be on the lines of section 2(2) of the UK Financial Services and Markets Act 2000, which requires the FSA to follow the regulatory objectives of market confidence, consumer protection, consumer awareness and the prevention of financial crime in its activities. As discussed in section D above, such a statement would also carry benefits for EC financial market law-making and policy formation generally. In this regard, CESR's recommendation in its 2004 Himalaya Report that it adopt a Mission Statement for EC securities regulators which would define the objectives of regulators concerning investor protection, market integration,

[181] The Mar 2006 Inter-institutional Monitoring Group saw a 'potential danger in the fact that the results...may be more "consensus" than "best practice" driven': see above n8, at 14. Concerns have also been raised by the Commission about the feasibility of CESR's consensual approach at level two: see Commission Report on the Lamfalussy Process, above n8, at 9.

[182] See, eg, Mar 2006 Inter-institutional Monitoring Group Report, above n8; Commission White Paper, above n9, Annex III, Resumé of Contributions Received from Market Participants on the Green Paper, at 10–11; and Speech by Commissioner McCreevy on 'Regulatory and Supervisory Challenges of Financial Integration', London, 27 June 2005, available at http://europa.eu.int/rapid/pressReleases.

[183] CESR Jan 2005 Advice on MiFID Level Two, above n177, at 45–72.

[184] CEPS has predicted that the Lamfalussy process should have a positive effect on the quality of market regulation by increasing contact between regulators: see above n32, at 6.

[185] See, eg, its insistence on imposing rigorous disclosure requirements on retail marketing communications which were criticised by the market as jeopardising general 'high level' marketing by investment firms. CESR responded that later disclosure 'may be insufficient to counteract the initial message portrayed in a marketing communication and on which the investment decision will often be based...CESR does not believe the proposed level of detail to be unduly onerous....or that a less detailed approach would not achieve the desired level of investor protection': Jan Feedback Statement, above n69, at 31.

market transparency and market integrity, and which could ultimately lead to overarching EC principles of securities regulation,[186] could support CESR's legitimacy and accountability.

3. An Evolving Accountability Model

As the initial frantic pace of FSAP Level One law-making has slowed, so too have the institutions appeared to become more alert to the growing influence of CESR. Most concern surrounds Level Three and the danger of CESR initiatives and guidance existing in a 'grey zone where political accountability is unclear'.[187] The 2004 Inter-Institutional Monitoring Group also raised concerns about Level Two, calling for CESR to disclose whenever a serious division in opinion arose in connection with its advice.[188] In its 2004 Report on the Lamfalussy Process, the Commission expressly addressed Level Three accountability risks and called for a clearer articulation of the role of Level Three, particularly with respect to protecting the institutional prerogatives of the Council, Parliament and Commission.[189] Ever conscious of its weak institutional position under Lamfalussy decision-making, and in line with its increased insistence on 'sunset clauses' to suspend Lamfalussy law-making powers in Level One measures,[190] the European Parliament has been the most vocal in the calls for greater accountability by CESR. In the 2005 Van den Burg Report, in order 'to guarantee democratic accountability' it specifically called for CESR (and CEBS and CEIOPS) to report semi-annually to the Parliament.[191] More aggressively, Parliament noted 'gaps in the political accountability of the supervisory system [and] gaps in parliamentary scrutiny and democratic control particularly with respect to work undertaken at level three'. It urged all Level Three committees 'to pay the utmost attention to providing a sound legal basis for their actions, avoiding dealing with political questions and preventing prejudice to upcoming Community law'.[192] CESR, which tellingly has shown itself

[186] Above n114, at 15.

[187] As described by certain (unidentified) ESC delegations: ESC Minutes, 15 Dec 2004 (ESC 1/2005).

[188] Inter-Institutional Monitoring Group, above n140, at 46.

[189] Commission, above n8, at 14. The 2005 Green Paper more mutedly referred to the need to improve the accountability and transparency of the 'whole process' and noted the status of the committees of supervisors as advisory bodies to the Commission: above n46, at 9.

[190] For a recent example see the 2006 MiFID Revision Dir which extends the MiFID implementation date. Art 1(2) suspends level two Lamfalussy powers under MiFID from 1 Apr 2008: Dir 2006/31/EC [2006] OJ L114/60. ESC Minutes reveal that Commissioner McCreevy 'had not been keen' on the comitology amendments but had accepted them in a spirit of compromise: see ESC Minutes, 19 Dec 2005 (ESC/01/2006).

[191] Above n8, at B.15. A similar call was made in the Parliament's Kauppi Report on Clearing and Settlement, A6-0180/2005.

very sensitive to accountability charges and, so far, politically adept in defusing tensions, has responded by 'establish[ing] clearer accountability links with Council Committees and with the European Parliament' during 2005. A new accountability framework to the Parliament was formalised in September 2005. It requires CESR, in effect, to communicate closely with the Parliament, particularly on any issues likely to have a legislative impact. CESR has also downplayed its regulatory convergence ambitions at Level Three[193] (which would involve CESR intervening in areas not covered by EC law and adopting 'autonomous standards as a common EC-wide regulatory approach to securities business which feeds into the regulatory process at EC level'[194]) following considerable institutional and market unease.[195] Initial moves towards the endorsement of supervisory convergence (non-binding CESR guidance on the application of Level One and Two rules at Level Three) have also been sidelined.[196] However, the line between Level Three supervisory convergence through 'guidance' and regulatory convergence seems a thin one.

More generally, recent evidence from the Commission's approach to the development of policy in new areas such as bond market transparency, hedge funds and private equity sees the Commission drawing on a wide range of market and institutional opinion and reducing the risks of over-reliance on CESR. The Commission's somewhat benign public statements on CESR's problematic accountability model (certainly by comparison with the Parliament's trenchant views) appear to be counter-balanced by an institutional determination in practice not to yield too much power to CESR.

CESR's accountability model is clearly evolving (see section F.6 below). Nonetheless, there is little to prevent CESR from increasing its powers over the markets at Level Three, as long as individual CESR members support its initiatives. Given that the net result is likely to be an increase in the prestige, power and resources of CESR members and heavier bargaining tools domestically, this seems unlikely. CESR's powers also depend on whether the accountability structures within which individual CESR members operate, internally and externally, are either supportive of CESR or ineffective in controlling what is an increasingly powerful, politically astute and

192 Van den Burg Report, above n8, at B.20.

193 CESR Chairman van Leeuwen reported to the ESC in Dec 2004 that the Himalaya Report was concerned with supervisory convergence and that regulatory convergence was not a priority: ESC Minutes (ESC1/2005), 15 Dec 2004, at 3.

194 CESR Level Three Report, above n160, at 8.

195 The Third Inter-Institutional Monitoring Group on the Lamfalussy Process (Nov 2004) expressed (at 47) considerable concern at Level Three regulatory convergence.

196 ESC Minutes, 15 Dec 2004 (ESC 1/2005). The Nov 2004 Inter-Institutional Monitoring Group noted that there was some scepticism from market participants to the principle of and need for official endorsement and a strong preference for non-binding co-ordination within CESR: see above n8, at 31 and 33.

market-networked body. The most severe accountability risk remains that Level Three activities could pre-empt formal legislative initiatives at Levels One and Two, although the current tenor of policy development appears to be towards convergence and market-led initiatives rather than formal legislation.

4. Accountability Risks and the MiFID Level Two Process

Level Two rules have already been adopted under the Prospectus and Market Abuse Directives.[197] The MiFID Level Two process, which concluded in September 2006, is, however, potentially the most revealing as to the dynamics of the Lamfalussy process and the accountability risks posed by CESR, given the greater experience of the committees, the controversies surrounding the MiFID regime, the massive scale of the Level Two delegations, the extensive market consultations, the wide-ranging reforms demanded by the new rules, and the potential costs of the regime. Given the scale of the MiFID Level Two regime, this discussion focuses on the new conduct of business regime, contained in Articles 26–50 of the MiFID Level Two Directive, which will demand major system and operational changes for investment firms in providing services to investors, domestically or on a pan-EC basis.

The accountability risks are reduced somewhat by the very high levels of consultation and transparency on the conduct of business regime. CESR issued a series of consultation papers on the conduct of business regime,[198] and two feedback papers[199] explaining its position, before presenting its final advice in January and April 2005.[200] The Commission then published two working drafts of the conduct of business rules[201] which were considered by the ESC and subjected to public consultation, prior to presenting a formal directive to the ESC in February 2006,[202] a revised version of which was approved by the ESC in June 2006.[203]

Although CESR's decision-making processes on MiFID are not formally transparent, the extensive consultation process on the conduct of business

[197] See, eg, the Prospectus Reg 809/2004/EC [2004] OJ L149/1 and Commission Dir 2003/125/EC [2003] OJ L339/73 on investment recommendations and disclosure of conflicts of interest.

[198] CESR/04-261b; CESR-04-562; CESR/04-603b; CESR/05-164.

[199] Above n69; and CESR's 'Technical Advice on Level Two Implementing Measures on the first set of Mandates, Markets in Financial Instruments Directive', Feedback Statement (Apr 2005). CESR/05-291b.

[200] Above n177.

[201] Working Document ESC 23/2005, rev 1 and rev 2.

[202] Draft Commission Dir, Brussels, DRAFT 6.02.2006.

[203] Draft Commission Dir, Brussels, DRAFT 30.06.2006.

regime, the final feedback document and the minuted discussions in the ESC all provide some insights into how CESR operates and its approach to regulation, which in turn provide some degree of transparency and, accordingly, accountability.[204]

As might be expected, the picture that emerges is mixed. CESR emerges as alive to the risks of over-regulation and sympathetic to market concerns, but robust in protecting investor interests.[205] It also appears that CESR's approach to the charged debate on harmonisation is pragmatic rather than ideological. While it noted the split in its consultations between those calling for detailed harmonisation to minimise divergences and those demanding flexibility, its declared approach was to adopt a principles-based approach which would not introduce maximum harmonisation[206] and to assess the level of detail on a case by case basis, depending on the issue in question.[207] Although initial discussions in the ESC on CESR's advice suggested concern about the level of detail in the advice,[208] in some respects CESR's approach is more flexible than the final rules. In its advice on the MiFID Article 19(2) marketing disclosure regime, for example, CESR suggested that Member States should not be prevented from adopting additional measures.[209] Article 4 of the MiFID Level Two Directive, however, imposes considerable restrictions on Member States before they can 'gold-plate' the Directive's requirements.

CESR is also clearly sensitive to the political and constitutional risks of the Level Two process. In a number of instances it noted legitimate market concerns but declined to respond, given the limitations of the MiFID mandate. There was a strong demand, for example, from the market that simple derivatives be included among the 'non-complex' instruments available for execution-only services. While CESR noted that derivatives could be straightforward instruments and was sympathetic to the genuine market concern on this point, it emphasised the political decision at Level One in the MiFID Directive to exclude derivatives from execution-only.[210] Similarly, while a number of consultees called for CESR to explain the Level Two 'know your client'/suitability regime (which differs in intensity according to whether full-scale advice or asset management services, more limited advice services or execution-only services are provided) on a general

[204] On market support of the connection between procedural transparency and accountability see the ICSA Consultation Principles, above n13.

[205] See sects E.1 and F.2 above, and this sect, below, on the ESC and CESR discussions.

[206] CESR Annual Report, above n26, at 17.

[207] Jan Feedback Document, above n69, at 4.

[208] ESC Minutes, 25 Feb (ESC 13/2005).

[209] Jan Feedback Document, above n69, at 30.

[210] *Ibid*, at 25.

conceptual basis, it declined, noting that its mandate did not allow it to provide general advice on the regime.[211]

The CESR accountability risks are also mitigated somewhat by what has emerged as an extensive review in the ESC and by the Commission of CESR advice.[212] Although the final conduct of business rules reflect CESR's advice to a very considerable degree, there are a number of important points of difference. Overall, the final conduct of business rules are less detailed, probably less subtle, clearer and more cost effective, and they provide less insurance for investment firms.[213] It is difficult to discern a conceptual or regulatory theme to the ESC revisions, which are most likely a reflection of political compromises—although the minutes suggest that the ESC operates largely by consensus (the rules were finally adopted by a unanimous vote),[214] with typically only one or two delegations raising concerns on particular issues. Disclosure requirements, for example, have been reduced. There was considerable market resistance to CESR's Level Two advice that disclosure on dispute resolution and redress systems be made to investors. This requirement was removed in the Commission and ESC discussions. CESR initially prohibited the use of simulated projections in marketing communications, and then, following strong market objections, forbade its use unless stringent requirements were followed. Following ESC/Commission discussions, simulated projections are now allowed, subject to compliance with less stringent criteria. CESR also required that competent authorities be empowered to require investment firms to furnish evidence of the accuracy of factual claims in marketing communications, generating strong objections from the market that this removed the usual burden of proof. This requirement was removed in the ESC/Commission discussions.

It also appears that the ESC/Commission discussions were particularly alert to the constitutional limitations of the Level Two process and to national sensitivities. A major point of difference between the CESR advice and the Level Two Directive concerns the retail investor/investment firm contract. In its advice, CESR required that a written contract be signed or consented to by the retail investor and imposed a number of minimum requirements on the contract.[215] This requirement was subject to very considerable resistance from the market on the grounds of, inter alia, lack

[211] *Ibid*, at 26.

[212] As Ferran has observed, although this slows down the legislative process and raises the risk of last minute mistakes based on subtle drafting changes, 'it ensures that the process of writing implementing measures is a genuine exercise...and not merely a rubber stamp': see above n32, at 89. The extensive final consultation which the Commission engages in on its level two working drafts also reduces accountability risks.

[213] Eg, following market requests for this clarification, CESR stated in its advice on how responsibility for a marketing communication was to be allocated where a number of investment firms were involved in its preparation. This has been dropped from the Dir.

[214] ESC Minutes, 26 June 2006 (ESC/35/2006).

[215] Jan Advice, above n177, at 59–64.

of competence by CESR as contract requirements interfered with national civil and contract law systems, and the very substantial costs involved in 're-papering' contracts. Although CESR in response sought 'to minimize conflict with national legal systems' and removed certain requirements, such as risk warnings (which market participants argued had no place in a contract), it retained the contract requirements in principle, noting that imposing minimum contract requirements would necessarily have an impact on national practices.[216] The Directive is sharply different. Article 39, which was heavily negotiated in the ESC, simply requires that an investment firm which provides advice other than investment advice to a new retail client must enter into a 'written basic agreement', on paper or in another durable medium, which sets out the essential rights and obligations of the firm and the client. In an attempt to reduce costs, this requirement applies only to investment services provided to a new client for the first time after the date of application of the Directive. Contract term requirements are not imposed, although certain of CESR's contract term requirements are re-cast as disclosure requirements. Chief among these is the controversial requirement, heavily resisted by the market during the consultation process, that investment firms providing portfolio management services establish an appropriate method of evaluation and comparison, such as a meaningful benchmark, to enable the client to assess the firm's performance (Article 30(3)). Nonetheless, it is clear from the ESC minutes that there was considerable unease up to the final vote, even about this attenuated requirement. The final version is clearly a compromise designed to allay concerns about potential interference with national rules.[217]

This concern to avoid competence risks was not always present during ESC discussions. The Commission has emerged as a key arbiter in ensuring that the limits of Level Two are respected. The inclusion of derivatives in 'non-complex' instruments arose repeatedly in the ESC notwithstanding their exclusion by CESR, as outlined above. In the last ESC meeting at which discussion on this issue was minuted, the Commission appears driven to some exasperation, noting that the agreement to exclude derivatives was a Level One decision and that Member States would find their inclusion at Level Two unacceptable.[218]

Gaps in accountability at Level Two remain. What, for example, is the status of CESR's Level Two advice which has not been incorporated into the Level Two Directive? The final advice contains detailed guidance on, for example, the types of activities which do not constitute 'investment

[216] Jan Feedback Document, above n69, at 37.

[217] See, in particular, ESC Minutes, 29–30 Mar 2006 (ESC/15/2006) and 26–27 Apr 2006 (ESC/28/2006).

[218] *Ibid.*

advice' and as such fall outside many of MiFID's requirements. It also sets out in detail examples of particular situations where risk warnings may be required. Although this guidance is not binding, it is likely to be influential on how national supervisors apply the new rules.

5. Accountability Risks and the MiFID Level Three Process

Although the parameters of the Level Three process are emerging, its shape is still largely unclear, as is reflected in the general institutional and market nervousness about the Level Three process.[219] In July 2006, however, CESR presented its MiFID Level Three agenda for consultation, following ESC agreement on the Level Two rules. The initial Work Programme for 2006–7 was published in October 2006.[220]

The Level Three process emerges as largely driven by the Commission and by 'cascades' from Level One and Level Two, rather than by CESR-driven initiatives. The risk of the MiFID Level Three agenda existing in a twilight zone where accountability is unclear is therefore considerably mitigated. A significant proportion of the Level Three agenda concerns CESR's preparatory work on the extensive reporting and review obligations required of the Commission under MiFID Article 65 and under the Level Two regime. While this activity seems benign, a number of these reports concern potentially explosive areas, particularly in the controversial and heavily negotiated transparency regime, as outlined in section C.5 above, and afford CESR the opportunity to influence the development of a highly sensitive aspect of EC financial market policy. Specific CESR guidance will also be adopted in a number of areas. But the emphasis is on practical and operational convergence and achieving a 'common understanding' (with respect to the operation of the MiFID passport, for example) and 'the development of convergent views' (with respect to the best execution regime for non-equity markets, for example). Of particular note here is that the Commission has driven certain of these areas from Level Two to Level Three. The MiFID Level Three agenda also includes cross-sector convergence and a number of initiatives of common concern to the banking, pension, insurance and securities sectors, including with respect to outsourcing. Overall, the Commission's imprints are evident on the Level Three agenda, which is heavily based on the Level One and Level Two regime, with limited evidence of CESR promoting its own regulatory agenda.

[219] See, eg, Mar 2006 Inter Institutional Monitoring Group Report, above n8, at 14.
[220] Above n100.

There are also signs more generally that CESR will adopt a restrained approach to Level Three. During the Level Two ESC/Commission discussions on the MiFID rules it frequently cautioned against moving measures from Level Two to Level Three—albeit that Level Three gives more freedom to CESR. It was particularly concerned that Level Three should not be used to escape from political decisions at Levels One and Two and, in a clear concern to avoid legitimacy risks, that any transfer from Level Two to Level Three be made explicit in the Level Two measure 'in order to have the political backing of the three EU institutions'.[221] It has also established criteria for choosing Level Three priorities based on whether a significant market failure exists, whether there is an EC-wide impact, and whether CESR can influence or create change.[222]

6. The New CESR Charter

July 2006 saw CESR make the first changes to its Charter since its inception, and a major change to CESR's decision-making structure.[223] The reforms are designed to respond to the decisive shift to Level Three operational activities. The most important reforms concern CESR decision-making. Article 5 of the CESR Charter[224] now provides for voting. While consensus remains the main mechanism for decision-making,[225] Level Two advice may be subject to a qualifying majority vote (following the rules applicable to the Council under the Treaty) where either the chair considers that there is a split of views or more than one member asks for a vote.[226] The Charter continues to specify that, irrespective of the decision-making procedure, dissenting opinions should be identified and elaborated in the final advice, but only where those members so wish. It also now requires that the advice should include the outcome of any vote. In a clear acknowledgement of the sensitivities of the Level Three process, the Charter now provides that Level Three work which is expressly requested by Community legislation, or directly related to Community legislation, must be subject to a unanimous vote where one or more members so requests. Where unanimity cannot be reached, the Commission must be informed.[227] The unanimity requirement

[221] ESC Minutes, 23 Feb 2005 (ESC 13/2005).
[222] CESR Annual Report, above n26, Foreword by the Chairman, at 5.
[223] CESR Press Release, 2 Aug 2006, CESR/06-303.
[224] Charter of the Committee of European Securities Regulators, CESR/06-289c.
[225] *Ibid*, Art 5(5).
[226] *Ibid*, Art 5(6).
[227] *Ibid*, Art 5(7).

is likely to provide an early test of the extent to which CESR can build a European approach to regulation, although it may also result in a lowest common denominator approach to Level Three.

This is a major change to CESR's decision-making. Transparency and accountability gaps remain in that it is unclear whether voting records will identify CESR members (and thereby regulatory traditions and potential political interests). Neither is it clear how CESR will decide on its highly controversial regulatory convergence activities, which are not directly related to Levels Two and Three, in the event that the regulatory convergence element of Level Three is resurrected. But these reforms suggest that CESR is sensitive to the accountability and legitimacy risks to its work. They are also a testament to the influence of the ESC and the Commission on CESR's development. In its 2004 Report on the Lamfalussy Process, the Commission had raised the possibility of voting in rather veiled terms, arguing that transparency and democratic accountability could be increased were CESR to adopt a 'more transparent set of procedures for adopting their advice and opinions'.[228] CESR proved resistant to this initially, arguing that there would not be any benefit in moving to majority voting, particularly at Level Three where standards were not binding.[229] Later discussions in the ESC raised the possibility of an accountability board to support CESR's accountability.[230] This form of direct accountability (popular in the US where it has been a feature of the post-Enron market reforms, including the establishment of the Public Companies Accounting Oversight Board which, inter alia, oversees accounting standard-setting by the FASB (a private standard-setter)) may have proved even more unpalatable to CESR. The ESC also seems to have supported changes to CESR's decision-making, particularly with respect to the transparency of voting.[231]

CESR's accountability model is evolving and looks set to develop as a hybrid model, based for the most part on indirect accountability links. The current dynamic period may well see the emergence of an optimal model which reflects the particular functions CESR exercises and the particular accountability risks it poses.[232] So far, the trend is towards promoting

[228] Above n8, at 9. The Commission's campaign was consistent, if low-key. In 2005, Internal Director General Schaub had also referred publicly to the difficulties in achieving consensus with potentially 27 CESR members and called for more transparent and accountable procedures for decision-making: see A Schaub, 'The Lamfalussy Process Four Years On' (2005) 13 *Journal of Financial Regulation and Compliance* 110, at 115.

[229] ESC Minutes, 18 Nov 2004 (ESC 43/2004).

[230] ESC Minutes, 15 Dec 2004 (ESC 1/2005).

[231] ESC Minutes, 18 Nov 2004 (ESC 43/2004).

[232] See Black, above n14 on the need for accountability models in financial market regulation to reflect the different functions of actors in the fragmented, decentred regulatory universe and for different combinations of accountability structures.

accountability through institutional change, in the form of greater transparency in decision-making, and through soft mechanisms, such as enhanced dialogue and communication with the EC institutions, rather than through the establishment of direct accountability links. Accountability is also enhanced through CESR's consultation processes. It has established tested and highly effective communication lines to the markets but it has also driven market interests to adopt more sophisticated and networked lobbying models[233] that should ensure that genuine European market expertise and legitimate concerns are reflected in regulation—as long as CESR remains uncaptured by market interests. The recent strengthening of its resources and capacity for cost-benefit analysis should act as a counter-balance.

The accountability of CESR is a difficult problem. It reflects the wider complexity of the dynamic process whereby the disciplines of the financial markets are established by a range of state and private actors and, in particular, powerful and expert market actors, albeit through the lens of the particular constitutional, institutional and political difficulties posed by the regulation of the EC's integrating financial markets. The risks posed by CESR must, however, be placed in the context of CESR's unique role in building a pan-EC and ultimately 'European' supervisory and regulatory capacity, without opening the Pandora's Box of the fully fledged federal regulator. At the very least, the dynamism of its accountability model since 2004 augurs well for the ability of the new policy formation and law-making environment to respond.

G. CONCLUSION

Although the FSAP period is most closely associated with massive regulatory change, it has also seen a dramatic evolution in financial market law-making and the policy formation process. This chapter sought to illustrate how financial market rules now emerge through an unwieldy, multi-actor, multi-dimensional process, laden with accountability and effectiveness risks, in which CESR plays a central, if somewhat troublesome, role. It also examined how the post-FSAP risk profile therefore includes considerable risks from the law-making and policy formation process which must be identified and mitigated if the larger uncertainties of the post-FSAP period are to be contained.

[233] See, eg, LIBA's building of networks with other trade associations in order to engage more effectively with the CESR MiFID consultations: LIBA, *Annual Report* (2005), Chairman's Statement.

It is clear that financial market law-making post-FSAP is dynamic and that mechanisms are being developed, albeit on an ad hoc basis, to counter the many risks attendant on the EC as monopoly supplier of financial market regulation. The players in the game appear to have emerged from the FSAP process with an enhanced understanding of the financial market law-making process, even if considerable weaknesses still remain. The development and review of the MiFID regime will provide an important test-case on whether law-making and policy formation risks can be managed in this uncertain but dynamic regulatory, institutional and market environment.

19

The Way Forward in European Securities Regulation: Regulatory Competition or Mandatory Regulation?

JENNIFER PAYNE*

THE DEVELOPMENT OF a single or integrated market in financial services in the EU has been on the agenda for almost 50 years,[1] and was given new impetus by the Lamfalussy report in 2001.[2] The EU has overwhelmingly adopted a regulatory competition rather than a mandatory regulation approach to achieve this goal to date. The purpose of this chapter is to consider whether the continuing reliance on this regulatory competition model is possible and desirable. In Section A the regulatory competition approach is analysed. In particular its core features, its strengths and its weaknesses are discussed. By contrast, in Section B the mandatory regulatory approach is considered, with emphasis on the possibility of a single pan-European securities regulator, a European Securities Commission, emerging onto the European scene. In Section C, the possible function and powers of any future European Securities Commission are considered. Section D concludes.

A. THE REGULATORY COMPETITION APPROACH

Traditionally, for the regulatory competition model to succeed three elements are necessary: a diversity of eligible regimes, the ability of entities to move between eligible regimes without excessive cost or inconvenience,

* Travers Smith Lecturer in Corporate Finance Law in the University of Oxford and Fellow of Merton College, Oxford.

[1] The Treaty of Rome (1957) envisaged a market in which there would be free movement of capital and services.

[2] 'The Regulation of European Securities Markets: Final Report' (Brussels, 15 Feb 2001).

and the propensity of governments to change their legal rules in response to the choices entities make in selecting among eligible regimes. Within the EU, regulatory competition has been implemented primarily through the Financial Services Action Plan (FSAP) and the Lamfalussy process.

The FSAP was a five year plan, launched by the European Commission in 2000, which aimed to integrate Europe's financial markets.[3] A substantial number of the 42 measures outlined in the Action Plan have been introduced within the five year timeframe,[4] thanks in large part to the adoption of the Lamfalussy approach, which was implemented on the recommendation of the Committee of 'Wise Men'. This Committee's remit was to conduct an examination of the mechanisms for regulating and supervising EU securities markets. The Committee's Reports[5] were very critical of the slow, rigid and complex regulatory process which was then in place and suggested a new approach involving a four level structure. This approach has been adopted. Level One essentially consists of primary legislation decided upon by the Council and Parliament in accordance with established law-making procedures. At Level Two the Commission, together with the European Securities Commission (ESC) and the Committee of European Securities Regulators (CESR), defines, proposes and decides on the technical implementing measures for Level One directives and regulations. The purpose of Level Three is to ensure consistent, timely and uniform implementation of Level One and Level Two legislation in Member States. Level Four is concerned to strengthen the enforcement of Community rules. The Lamfalussy process has made the law-making process in this area more streamlined, more flexible and faster.[6] This has led to a slew of recent directives which seek to advance the concept of a single market in financial services within the EU. Examples include the Market Abuse Directive,[7] the Transparency Directive,[8] the Prospectus Directive,[9] the Takeover Directive[10] and the Markets in Financial Instruments Directive (MiFID).[11]

[3] The Commission's FSAP proposal was contained in European Commission, 'Financial Services: Implementing the Framework for Financial Markets: Action Plan', COM(1999)232.

[4] Now that the 5-year period of the Financial Services Action Plan has come to an end, the European Commission has launched a consultation process to consider the effectiveness of the FSAP process, of the Lamfalussy process and on lessons learned from the FSAP generally: see www.europa.eu.int.

[5] The initial report of this Committee ('The Regulation of European Securities Markets: Initial Report' (Brussels, 9 Nov 2000)) appears as Annex 5 to the 'Final Report', above n2. Calls for a faster and more flexible law-making process were not new: see N Moloney, *EC Securities Regulation* (Oxford, OUP, 2002) 854–6.

[6] For a detailed account of the implementation and effect of the Lamfalussy proposals see N Moloney, *EC Securities Regulation* (Oxford, OUP, 2002), ch 3.

[7] Dir 2003/6/EC [2003] OJ L96/16.

[8] Dir 2004/109/EC [2004] OJ L390/38.

[9] Dir 2003/71/EC [2003] OJ L345/64.

[10] Dir 2004/25/EC [2004] OJ L142/12. The Takeover Directive was not dealt with under the Lamfalussy process.

[11] Dir 2004/39/EC [2004] OJ L145/1.

Two important aspects of these developments need to be noted. First, the Lamfalussy process is geared towards the mutual recognition of national securities markets. The aim is harmonisation and cooperation between Member States and not the imposition of some centralised regulator. In other words, 'supervisory convergence' rather than 'supervisory centralisation' is the goal. Secondly, the vast majority of the directives introduced by way of the FSAP have been minimum harmonisation measures, which has meant that, in theory at least, individual Member States have been able to add whatever regulatory structures they have deemed appropriate above and beyond the minimum levels that have been harmonised. This is an important condition for regulatory competition to exist. However, some recent developments have cast doubt on the ability of Member States to differentiate themselves in this way in practice.

First, not all directives introduced under the FSAP have been minimum harmonisation measures. The Prospectus Directive,[12] for example, is a maximum harmonisation directive. This is not to suggest that the Prospectus Directive allows no room for Member State flexibility in its implementation. Although it is not possible for Member States to impose additional requirements as to the contents of the prospectuses, it is still possible for them to impose additional requirements at a national level on those seeking a listing on an official list. This is what has happened in the UK, with super-equivalent listing requirements being imposed.[13] Therefore even though the Prospectus Directive is a maximum harmonisation directive, variation between Member States will still exist. It should be noted however that progressive and excessive use of maximum harmonisation could undermine the possibility of regulatory competition.[14]

More interestingly, even where directives are in fact introduced as minimum harmonisation measures, the rules applied by the different national regulators are increasingly being applied in a uniform manner across the EU. The primary reason for this trend is almost certainly the Lamfalussy process itself, and in particular the weight of rules emerging at Level Two to determine the technical implementing measures to the directives introduced under the FSAP.[15] This indirect form of maximum harmonisation does require us to consider whether sufficient latitude for national differentiation still exists in order to allow regulatory competition to succeed. It is suggested here that sufficient national differentiation is still possible. The directives do

[12] Dir 2003/71/EC, above n9.

[13] Eg, the Listing Principles set out in the revised Listing Rules: FSA, Listing Rules, ch 7.

[14] This applies to both direct and indirect forms of maximum harmonisation: see n15 below and its associated text as regards the development of indirect maximum harmonisation.

[15] Eg, the Prospective Directive is supplemented by EC Prospectus Reg 809/2004 [2004] OJ L149/1 (Level Two legislation) which contains the content requirements for prospectuses. This EC Regulation is directly effective in Member States and is a key element of the new Prospectus regime.

still allow Member States latitude to differentiate themselves in terms of the regulatory measures which they implement, even once the Level Two guidelines are applied. A good example of this relates to the Prospectus Directive. Although this is a maximum harmonisation directive, as discussed above, not only can super-equivalent listing requirements be imposed by Member States, allowing for differentiation,[16] but Member States continue to enjoy substantial scope to organise their own corporate governance disclosure obligations.[17] In addition, differentiation between Member States is still possible in relation to how effective the national regulator is in applying the rules, dealing with market participants, approving prospectuses, etc as compared to other Member State regulators. There is some evidence that 'supervisory competition' of this kind does exist. The Prospectus Directive provides for permanent home state control[18] as its basic position,[19] so that for the most part national regulators are shielded from competition by their monopoly with respect to their home issuers.[20] However, these rules are modified for debt securities with a minimum denomination of €1,000. In relation to these debt securities the rule is broadly one of issuer choice as between the Member State where the issuer has its registered office and the Member State where the securities are offered to the public or admitted to trading on a regulated market.[21] In practice the principal centres for bond issuing activity within the EU are London and Luxembourg and this modification of the rules in relation to debt securities means that these two centres can continue to dominate, and that supervisory competition operates to the advantage of these two centres in a very real way.

As a result, despite the direct and indirect forms of 'maximum harmonisation' described here, it is nevertheless suggested that the FSAP and the Lamfalussy process do provide the first and the third of the necessary elements for regulatory competition, namely a diversity of eligible regimes and the

[16] See above n13 and associated text.

[17] Corporate governance disclosures have been made the subject of separate initiatives in corporate, rather than securities, law. Although corporate governance merited only a brief mention in the original FSAP (COM(1999)232, 247, mentioned above in n3), following the Enron scandal the European Commission asked an experts' group to examine this issue, and this led to an Action Plan for Company Law (European Commission, 'Modernising Company Law and Enhancing Corporate Governance in the European Union—A Plan to Move Forward', COM(2003)284). Flesh has been put on the bones of these initial proposals in subsequent papers. The proposals in this area have demonstrated a lighter-touch approach to the organisation of institutional oversight than is in evidence in relation to core securities law disclosures.

[18] Ie, the Member State where EU-incorporated issuers have their registered office.

[19] Prospectus Dir (2003/71/EC), above n9, Art 2.1(m)(i). For non-EU issuers there is, broadly, a one-off opportunity to choose their EU home state, but then they are tied permanently and irrevocably to that chosen state: *ibid*, Art 2.1(m)(iii).

[20] The rigidity of these rules regarding the determination of home states has been criticised: see, eg, E Ferran, *Building an EU Securities Market* (Cambridge, Cambridge University Press, 2004) at 150–6.

[21] Prospectus Dir (2003/71/EC), above n9, Art 2.1(m)(ii).

propensity of governments to change their legal rules in response to the choices entities make in selecting among eligible regimes. The second element, the ability of entities to move between jurisdictions, is potentially more problematic as a result of the situs doctrine which severely constrains entity mobility. However, the recent ECJ decisions of *Centros*,[22] *Überseering*[23] and *Inspire Art*[24] suggest a change of direction on this issue.[25] It is notable, though, that in the context of securities regulation this issue has not been particularly problematic. In particular the concept of the European 'passport' allows providers of financial services to offer cross-border services or to open a branch in a Member State other than the home Member State without any need for additional authorisation.[26] The latest example of this passporting process is found within the Prospectus Directive, which allows prospectuses which are produced within one Member State to be passported into other Member States.[27] Effectively this means that if a host Member State has a more stringent set of requirements than an issuer's home state, the issuer can select and rely on the more lenient requirements of the home state to gain access to the host state's market.[28] Alternatively, the issuer, if it concludes that it is in its best interests to do so, can choose to comply with the tougher disclosure requirements of the host Member State.[29] In reality it

[22] Case C–212/97 [1999] 2 CMLR 551. For discussion see E Wymeersch, '*Centros*: A Landmark Decision in European Company Law', University of Ghent Financial Law Institute Working Paper 1999-15, Oct 1999, available at http://papers.ssrn.com; A Looijestijn-Clearie, '*Centros Ltd*—A Complete U-Turn in the Right of Establishment for Companies?' (2000) 49 *International and Comparative Law Quarterly* 621.

[23] Case C–208/00 [2002] ECR I–9919.

[24] Case C–167/01 [2003] ECR I–10155.

[25] See M Becht, C Mayer and H Wagner, 'Where Do Firms Incorporate?' (Sept 2006), ECGI Working Paper Series on Law, Working Paper No 70/2006, available at http://ssrn.com/author=906066.

[26] The European passport was substantially introduced via the Investment Services Dir (ISD), Dir 93/22/EEC [1993] OJ L141/27, but is improved by MiFID. Firms will be able to establish branches in other Member States and offer cross-border services in a wider range of cases, following the introduction of MiFID. Where a firm establishes a branch in another Member State, the host country is responsible for ensuring compliance with conduct of business requirements where services are provided within its territory.

[27] Dir 2003/71/EC, above n19, Arts 17–18.

[28] *Ibid*: a prospectus approved by the regulatory authority of one EEA state can be passported, enabling the issuer to make retail offers throughout the EEA without requiring further approvals from local regulatory authorities.

[29] This form of entity mobility is less than the sort of entity mobility some US academics propose because, subject to the decisions in *Centros, Überseering and Inspire Art* (above nn22–24), issuers are not generally free to choose the legal regime of a second, non-home Member State and then use that legal regime to raise funds in a third Member State or to raise capital within their home jurisdiction: see, eg, R Romano, 'Empowering Investors: A Market Approach to Securities Regulation' (1998) 107 *Yale Law Journal* 2359; SJ Choi and AT Guzman, 'Portable Reciprocity: Rethinking the International Reach of Securities Regulation' (1998) 71 *Southern California Law Review* 903. As a result, it can be argued that the current system within the EU does not quite achieve 'perfect' regulatory competition. For that, regulated entities—issuers and investors—would be able to choose the Member States' regulations with which they wish to comply without passporting and without listing in that other Member State.

is this latter route which has proved most popular, with exchanges competing to attract entities to them for their first, and generally only, listing.

Accordingly, the EU has all of the necessary elements in place for the regulatory competition model to succeed,[30] and indeed the strategy within the EU for achieving a single market for financial services to date has been based on the notion of regulatory arbitrage, rather than mandatory regulation such as that adopted by the US SEC. The extent of Europe's mandatory regulation has been to seek to make securities regulation uniform across Member States through its harmonisation programme. The approach has not been to adopt a single pan-European market but to allow national equity markets to persist, albeit with an increase in harmonisation and cooperation between them: 'supervisory convergence' rather than 'supervisory centralisation', as noted above. The reasons for this are difficult to pin down but are likely to include a number of elements.[31] The first is the lack of a common legal framework encouraging an equity culture across Europe, with UK corporate finance being predominantly equity based and continental Europe depending to a much greater extent on internally generated funds and bank loans. This contrasts very markedly with the US, where there is much greater homogeneity amongst the legal systems falling under the remit of the US SEC. One of the great political challenges facing the introduction of any European Securities Commission would be to find a way to unite the very disparate national regimes under a single harmonised regulatory regime to protect investors. Different Member States currently have different conceptions of the level of protection (above the minimum level prescribed by the directives) appropriate for investors, together with a diversity of conceptions about the role and powers of their own national regulators. Agreement about what a single European securities regulator should do would be difficult to achieve. The second possible reason for the EU's adoption of the regulatory arbitrage approach is the competition and political rivalry which has historically existed, and continues to exist, among national stock exchanges.[32] Despite the mergers which have taken place between some national stock exchanges, European national stock

[30] See, eg, D Charny, 'Competition Among Jurisdictions in Formulating Corporate Law Rules: An American Perspective on the "Race to the Bottom" in the European Communities' (1991) 32 *Harvard International Law Journal* 423. See also JM Sun and J Pelkmans, 'Regulatory Competition in the Single Market' (1995) 33 *Journal of Common Market Studies* 67; G Hertig, 'Regulatory Competition for EU Financial Services' (2000) 3 *Journal of International Economic Law* 349; HE Jackson and EJ Pan, 'Regulatory Competition in International Securities Markets: Evidence from Europe in 1999' (2001) 56 *Business Lawyer* 653.

[31] RS Karmel, 'The Case for a European Securities Commission' (1999) 38 *Columbia Journal of Transnational Law* 9.

[32] See M Onando, 'Competition among Exchanges or Financial Systems?' in G Ferrarini (ed), *European Securities Markets: The Investment Services Directive and Beyond* (London, Kluwer Law International, 1998).

exchanges are fundamentally in competition with one another with regard to liquidity, transparency and costs. The third possible factor is the culture of self-regulation that has traditionally existed in Europe and which militates against the centralisation and prescription which will follow from a single regulator. Finally, perhaps as a result of these first three factors, to date the political will to create a single pan-European market has been lacking.

However, according to the theory of regulatory competition, offering market participants a choice of legal regimes results in optimal regulation.[33] Regulatory competition promotes diversity and experimentation in the search for effective laws. Once offered a choice, market participants select the legal regime that best fits their needs. This approach therefore allows the content of the rules to be matched more effectively to the preferences of the consumers. Mandatory regulation does not provide this choice, ensuring that some market participants may be forced to comply with a legal regime that will produce sub-optimal benefits. Opponents of a European single regulator argue that private market incentives will find and maintain an optimal level of investor protection.[34] At the same time, legal regimes 'compete' for constituencies. Regulators who impose burdensome regulatory requirements will lose those constituents who are unwilling to comply with their regulations, while regulators with more beneficial regulatory requirements should become more popular. From a market efficiency perspective, regulatory competition should lead to superior regulation because regulators should modify their regulations to match the interests of those that bear the cost and incur the benefit of regulation as optimally as possible. This is the 'race to the top' hypothesis which is put forward by some commentators,[35] and indeed there is some evidence that this is taking place within the EU.[36] Another major advantage of regulatory competition is that

[33] For a discussion of the advantages of a regulatory competition approach see R Romano, 'Empowering Investors: A Market Approach to Securities Regulation' (1998) 107 *Yale Law Journal* 2359; SJ Choi and AT Guzman, 'Portable Reciprocity: Rethinking the International Reach of Securities Regulation' (1998) 71 *Southern California Law Review* 903, further developed in S Choi, 'Regulating Investors not Issuers: A Market-Based Proposal' (2000) 88 *California Law Review* 279, and AT Guzman, 'Capital Market Regulation in Developing Countries: A Proposal' (1999) 39 *Virginia Journal of International Law* 607; MB Fox, 'Retaining Mandatory Securities Disclosure: Why Issuer Choice is Not Investor Empowerment' (1999) 85 *Virginia Law Review* 1335.

[34] Eg, B Steil, 'The ISD and the Regulation of the European Market Structure' in B Steil (ed), *The European Equity Markets: The State of the Union and an Agenda for the Millenium* (London, The Royal Institute of International Affairs, 1996); A Whittaker, 'A European Law for Regulated Markets? Some Personal Views' in G Ferrarini (ed), *European Securities Markets: The Investment Services Directive and Beyond* (London, Kluwer Law International, 1998).

[35] Eg, JC Coffee, 'Racing towards the Top? The Impact of Cross-listings and Stock Market Competition on International Corporate Governance' (2002) 102 *Columbia Law Review* 1757.

[36] HE Jackson and EJ Pan, 'Regulatory Competition in International Securities Markets: Evidence from Europe in 1999' (2001) 56 *Business Lawyer* 653.

it permits the creation of a single market without requiring Member States to forfeit their regulatory power. This advantage is particularly important in the European context where Member States so far have proven very reluctant to give up control over their securities markets.

Of course there are criticisms that can be made of this approach. The first is that unfettered regulatory competition will lead to a 'race to the bottom' where regulators, competing for constituents, minimise their regulations to such a degree that their regulations provide less than adequate regulatory protection. Voluminous literature has been written on this point in the context of the Delaware effect in the US. The state of Delaware is the principal site for the incorporation of over 40 per cent of companies listed on the New York Stock Exchange and over 50 per cent of the top Fortune 500 companies. Some view this effect as being the result of a dilution in the standards of shareholder protection,[37] and the creation of pro-management rules which attract managers,[38] to whom decisions relating to the company's legal domicile typically fall. Others maintain that Delaware's success is as a result of the successful solutions it offers to the agency problems arising between shareholders and managers.[39] Yet others doubt that Delaware law is optimally efficient at all.[40] It is unlikely that this debate will ever be resolved. In the European context there has been no convergence to parallel the Delaware effect in the US. This could be because of the shorter time period within which convergence could have taken place. More plausibly, it could result from the variety of legal systems, common law and civil law (French, German, Scandinavian), present in the EU in contrast to the overwhelmingly common law origin of the legal systems in the US.[41] In the context of the competition between national stock

[37] W Cary, 'Federalism and Corporate law: Reflections upon Delaware' (1974) 83 *Yale Law Journal* 663.

[38] Eg, allowing potential takeover targets to put defensive mechanisms in place against the threat of a hostile takeover: see L Bebchuk and A Ferrell, 'Federalism and Takeover Law: The Race to Protect Managers from Takeovers' (1999) 99 *Columbia Law Review* 1168.

[39] R Winter, 'State Law, Shareholder Protection and the Theory of the Corporation' (1977) 6 *Journal of Legal Studies* 251; D Fischel, 'The "Race to the Bottom" Revisited: Reflections on Recent Developments in Delaware's Corporation Law' (1982) 76 *Northwestern University Law Review* 913; F Easterbrook, 'The Economics of Federalism' (1983) 26 *Journal of Law and Economics* 23; F Easterbrook and D Fischel, 'Voting in Corporate Law' (1983) 26 *Journal of Law and Economics* 395; R Romano, 'Law as a Product: Some Pieces of the Incorporation Puzzle' (1985) 1 *Journal of Law, Economics and Organization* 225; F Easterbrook and D Fischel, *The Economic Structure of Corporate Law* (Cambridge, Mass, Harvard University Press, 1991) ch 10.

[40] L Bebchuk, A Cohen and A Ferrell, 'Does the Evidence Favour State Competition in Corporate Law?' (2002) 90 *California Law Review* 1175.

[41] See E Glaeser and A Shleifer, 'Legal Origins' (2002) 117 *Quarterly Journal of Economics* 1193; S Deakin, 'Legal Diversity and Regulatory Competition: Which Model for Europe?', Centre for Business Research, University of Cambridge Working Paper No 323, Mar 2006, available at www.cbr.cam.ac.uk/pdf/WP323.pdf (accessed Feb 2007).

exchanges, stronger evidence of a Delaware effect can be seen, with the UK being a dominant player. However, there is little evidence of any race to the bottom between European stock exchanges. In a recent survey, Jackson and Pan reported:

> Issuers from less well-regulated European jurisdictions do not seem to be taking advantage of the issuer choice provisions of the E.U. law. Moreover, on numerous dimensions-involving both the form of securities disclosure and the intensity of due diligence efforts-market forces seem to require European issuers of common stock to disclose more information and prepare disclosure documents more carefully than legal rules formally require. At least in 1999, the race in the quality of securities regulation seems to be headed upwards and not downwards.[42]

Other criticisms of the system of regulatory arbitrage in place within Europe come from the Member States themselves. As Lee rightly points out, the primary ground upon which the Member States tend to judge the issue of whether regulatory competition or a single pan-European regulator is preferable is political. This is because 'there is no definitive and widely accepted answer from the economic and legal points of view as to whether there should be a [European SEC]'.[43] The principle of subsidiarity would militate in favour of the establishment of a single regulator if the objectives of securities regulation, ie the protection of investors, ensuring fair, efficient and transparent markets and the reduction of systemic risk,[44] cannot be sufficiently achieved at national level. However, it is not at all clear that these objectives *cannot* be achieved at national level, and if the question becomes whether these objectives are *better* achieved by central regulation rather than through competition between the national regulators then it is difficult to see how these questions can be answered.[45] As a result, it is not surprising that the main arguments in favour of and against a single regulator tend to be political.

Member States have a number of concerns. The first concern is a fear that their own national institutions might lose out in an internationally competitive environment, as indeed some are bound to do.[46] In particular Member States may wish to constrain the success of the UK as the dominant provider

[42] HE Jackson and EJ Pan, 'Regulatory Competition in International Securities Markets: Evidence from Europe in 1999' (2001) 56 *Business Lawyer* 653, at 657.

[43] See R Lee, 'Politics and the Creation of a European SEC: The Optimal UK Strategy—Constructive Inconsistency', Special paper No 161, LSE Financial Markets Group (Sept 2005), 22, available at http://ssrn.com/abstract=759449.

[44] These objectives are taken from International Organisation of Securities Commissions (IOSCO), *Objectives and Principles of Securities Regulation* (Feb 2002), available at www.iosco.org/library/pubdocs/pdf/IOSCOPD125.pdf (accessed Feb 2007).

[45] See Lee, above n43, at 22.

[46] G Hertig, 'Regulatory Competition for EU Financial Services' in DC Esty and D Geradin (eds), *Regulatory Competition and Economic Integration* (Oxford, OUP, 2001).

of financial services in the EU. One way to achieve this would be to create a centralised regulator able to constrain competition between markets, thereby ensuring a future for their national financial centres. A protectionist attitude may therefore favour the creation of a single regulator. There is also an allied political fear that in reality regulatory competition will result in Anglo-American practices and cultures being effectively forced onto the continental European world. Secondly, there is the opposite fear, not that the regulators in other Member States may be too dominant in the competitive environment, but rather that the regulators in some Member States may not be capable enough. This fear often focuses on the regulators of some of those states currently seeking accession to the EU. A single regulator could also address this concern, but would put pressure on the concept of home country control.

The official UK position has traditionally been in favour of regulatory competition.[47] To a large extent this reflects the general commitment of UK institutions to the idea of regulatory competition which is currently being promoted through the FSAP. At a more fundamental level however, the UK's support in this area reflects the expectation that the UK will benefit from regulatory competition. If it is accepted that the outcome of regulatory competition is a migration of companies from some states to others in search of the most attractive securities regime, and that there will therefore be winners and losers in this process, the UK generally regards itself as one of the likely winners. This is based on the current success of the UK in this arena. Any model which reduced competition or issuer choice could potentially threaten the UK's strong position. There is general contentment with the FSAP, which on the whole entailed changes of detail rather than substance with the way in which UK securities markets operate, and with the concept of mutual recognition. The approach of the UK has been to focus on delivering the FSAP and to support the Lamfalussy process,[48] and not to investigate the possibility of a single European regulator in this area.[49]

[47] See R Lee, 'Politics and the Creation of A European SEC: The Optimal UK Strategy—Constructive Inconsistency', Special paper No 161, LSE Financial Markets Group (Sept 2005), available at http://ssrn.com/abstract=759449. As Lee rightly argues, although it is possible to determine an official UK perspective on this issue, it can be difficult to determine a single view amongst participants in the financial markets, so that a single private sector position does not currently exist.

[48] See, eg, HM Treasury, Financial Services Authority and Bank of England, 'After the EU Financial Services Action Plan: A New Strategic Approach' (May 2004), available at www.hm-treasury.gov.uk/media/1B4/D3/1B4D3E5A-BCDC-D4B3-14E1EB2D499571C2.pdf (accessed Feb 2007); HM Treasury, Financial Services Authority and Bank of England, 'Supervising Financial Services in an Integrated European Single Market: A Discussion Paper' (Jan 2005), available at www.fsa.gov.uk/pubs/other/tripartite_dp.pdf (accessed Feb 2007).

[49] See House of Lords, Select Committee on the European Union, Forty-Fifth Report (18 Nov 2003) ('there is no case for a European Regulator for as far forward as we can realistically see' (Ch 4, para 91)), available at www.publications.parliament.uk/pa/ld200203/ldselect/ldeucom/192/19201.htm (accessed Feb 2007).

However, there are others within the EU who are increasingly interested in promoting the idea of a single European regulator, and indeed some who suggest that a pan-European securities regulator is unavoidable if Europe is serious about having a single financial market.[50]

B. A EUROPEAN SECURITIES COMMISSION

The idea of a European Securities Commission is not new.[51] It was considered, and rejected, by the Committee of Wise Men:

> First, the basic harmonised rules necessary for the appropriate functioning of an integrated market are not yet in place. Second, speedy action is needed to correct the identified shortcomings of the present regulatory framework; and speed requires reforms carried out within the confines of the present Treaty. Third, some time will be needed to ascertain whether any such reforms deliver, or fail to deliver, results.[52]

However the Committee did acknowledge that a pan-European securities regulator might have to be established if the structure it recommended, the Lamfalussy process, failed to achieve the desired results.[53] In its Himalaya report of 2004,[54] CESR raised the possibility of a single EU regulator once again, as part of its remit to identify and analyse the supervisory tools necessary to implement the FSAP. CESR did not recommend the establishment of a single European regulator, yet at the same time it recognised that the need to consider 'supervisory tools carrying a trans-national dimension' was closer in 2004 than it had been when the Lamfalussy Committee was established.[55] It is interesting to note that, while CESR stressed that only if the current legal framework fails should alternative models such as a

[50] N Walter, *The Banking Supervision Issue in Europe, A Briefing Paper for the Committee on Economic and Monetary affairs of the European Parliament* (2001), available at www.europarl.europa.eu/comparl/econ/pdf/emu/speeches/20010528/20010528_walters.pdf (accessed Feb 2007).

[51] See, eg, KJ Hopt, 'The Necessity of Co-ordinating or Approximating Economic Legislation, or of Supplementing or Replacing it by Community Law—A Report' (1976) 13 *Common Market Law Review* 245.

[52] The Committee of Wise Men, 'The Regulation of European Securities Markets: Initial Report' (Brussels, 9 Nov 2000) at 29. This Initial Report appears as Annex 5 to the 'The Regulation of European Securities Markets: Final Report' (Brussels, 15 Feb 2001).

[53] The Committee of Wise Men, above n2, at 95.

[54] CESR, 'Which Supervisory Tools for the EU Securities Market? A Preliminary Report' (Oct 2004), available at www.cesr-eu.org/index.php?page=consultation_details&id=48 (accessed Feb 2007).

[55] *Ibid*, at 3.

single European regulator be considered, CESR did then go on to consider what those other legal and supervisory tools might look like *if* they were called for.

So, one possible scenario leading to the introduction of a single European regulator in this area is the failure of the Lamfalussy process. Certainly some commentators have argued that it will fail to deliver the desired economic results.[56] However, most agree that it is still too soon to judge the success or failure of the system. The signs are encouraging though, at least when the Lamfalussy process is judged against the problems which the Wise Men initially set out to solve. The EU legislative process has been speeded up, and the FSAP programme can be regarded as a success to the extent that 39 of the suggested 42 legislative measures were introduced within the five year timetable. There is much greater consultation and transparency than previously. The creation of CESR has addressed many of the deficiencies regarding regulatory obligations to cooperate. On these criteria the Lamfalussy process can be judged a success so far[57] and it is unlikely that a consensus on the failure of the Lamfalussy process will be reached in the near future.

However, despite the words of the Wise Men back in 2000, this is not the only scenario in which a single European regulator may emerge. A second possibility is suggested by the Himalaya Report. While CESR stressed the fact that mutual recognition underlies the FSAP, and no change to this approach is suggested, CESR recognised that securities regulators across the EU have a diversity of powers in terms of their scope and rule-making, their supervisory and investigative means, the resources devoted to supervision and the manner in which these resources are deployed:

> The FSAP directives impose on the securities regulators additional heavy obligation [sic] to cooperate. It is CESR's view that these new legal obligations require all European securities regulators to have the same capacity to act. Any credible Home/Host relationship or Network arrangement cannot work if the relevant authorities do not have equivalent and rigorous powers to supervise, investigate, sanction and exchange information regarding investment services, issuers, auditors, regulated markets and UCITS.[58]

CESR noted that there is substantial diversity both as to the powers to supervise held by European regulators and the intensity with which those powers are exercised. CESR recommended a 'convergence of approaches

[56] G Hertig and R Lee, 'Four Predictions about the future of EU Securities Regulation' [2003] *Journal of Corporate Law Studies* 359.

[57] Of course if it is judged by other criteria, such as whether it has actually improved cross-border opportunities within the EU, it may not fare so well, although such an assessment would be very difficult to make.

[58] CESR, 'Which Supervisory Tools for the EU Securities Market? A Preliminary Report', above n54, at 2.

and decisions within the Network of securities regulators'.[59] CESR therefore suggests that a strengthening of the existing notion of supervisory convergence should take place. This envisages that the current elements of a single European securities market would remain in place, namely a commitment to Lamfalussy and the FSAP, but anticipates a political shift in favour of increased convergence between national regulators.[60] There has been a substantial degree of support within the EU for this idea.[61] The difficult issue is whether the degree of supervisory convergence envisaged can really be attained without 'supervisory tools carrying a trans-national dimension' being given to some form of pan-European organisation and without some measure of centralisation also being included in the mix. Two issues that have already been discussed in this chapter might encourage the movement towards increased centralisation. The first is the potential drift towards maximum, rather than minimum, harmonisation measures.[62] The second is the fact of European enlargement and the fear that regulators in other Member States, particularly the regulators of some of those states currently seeking accession to the EU, may not be capable enough. A single regulator could address this concern. Either development could reduce regulatory competition and increase the possibility of a more centralised system.

Although the first of these scenarios envisages some form of failure of the Lamfalussy process, the second does not necessarily require failure of that kind. It is therefore important to realise that even if the Lamfalussy process is judged to be an unmitigated success and is recognised as such within the EU, this does not mean that there will not be, or could not be, a single European regulator in the future. Indeed if the Lamfalussy process is judged to have been a success, this is likely to mean more cross-border trading which would potentially lead to a greater enthusiasm for centralisation and a pan–European strategy on securities regulation.[63]

This suggests that, as CESR has done, it is worth considering what the 'supervisory tools carrying a trans-national dimension' may look like *if* they are called for. It is clear that the introduction of any future single European regulator could be implemented in a wide variety of ways depending, in particular, on what role it is assigned and what powers it is given.

[59] *Ibid*, at 2–3.

[60] To some extent this convergence is already beginning to occur: see above nn54–55 and associated text.

[61] See Securities Expert Group, 'Financial Services Action Plan: Progress and Prospects' (May 2004), available at www.europeansecuritisation.com/pubs/FSAP_Stocktaking_Report.pdf (accessed Feb 2007); European Parliament,'Report on the current state of integration of EU financial markets' (2005/2026(INI)) (The Van den Burg Report) (Apr 2005); European Commission, White Paper or Financial Services 2005–2010 (Dec 2005), available at http://europa.eu/documents/comm/white_papers/index_en.htm#2005 (accessed Feb 2007).

[62] See above nn12–21 and associated text.

[63] See R Lee, 'Politics and the creation of A European SEC: The Optimal UK Strategy—Constructive Inconsistency', Special paper No 161, LSE Financial Markets Group (Sept 2005), available at http://ssrn.com/abstract=759449.

C. WHAT MIGHT A SINGLE EUROPEAN REGULATOR LOOK LIKE?

In terms of how a European Securities Commission might arise, the most likely development is via an expansion in the powers of one or other of the two new agencies created by the Lamfalussy process, namely the ESC or CESR. At the present time both the ESC and CESR have a role in this area, but arguably neither has sufficient power or, more importantly, sufficient autonomy to be regarded as a credible European regulator. Of course their powers and autonomy could be developed. Of the two organisations CESR is the preferable candidate. Perhaps the most important quality which must be present for a successful European Securities Commission to exist is an ability for the single regulator to take decisions independently of both Member States' regulators and the EU institutions. The members of CESR are independent of Member States, in the sense that the representatives are mostly not members of their respective governments, and they have expertise in regulating securities markets. By contrast the members of the ESC are generally highly placed bureaucrats in Member States' ministries.

The more difficult issue to determine is exactly what functions and powers any new European Securities Commission would be given. Such an organisation could have a wide variety of structural models, ranging from a small body with a limited range of activities acting alongside existing national regulators at one end, to a powerful body acting as a replacement for all national regulators at the other. However some informed guesses can be made about its likely form and role.

To start with, it is possible to define with some certainty some of the things that a European single regulator will *not* be. First, any European single regulator will not simply be an SEC along US lines. The US SEC, with its broad rule-making and enforcement powers, is a frequently cited model for a single European securities regulator. The appeal of the SEC is that it has been historically a successful and effective securities regulator, overseeing and nurturing the development of the largest, most sophisticated securities market in the world. However, there are a number of practical reasons why any European Securities Commission is unlikely to follow this model. One factor is that setting up such a body will require broad political support and it will be necessary to follow the path of least resistance. It is therefore unlikely that anything like the US SEC, with its wide remit and broad range of investigative and enforcement powers, will be established in a European context, given the current political climate. It would also be difficult to establish a European Securities Commission in the mold of the US SEC because of the vast political, economic and regulatory differences between the EU and the United States. When it was created in 1934, the SEC enjoyed the backing of a strong federal government and supremacy over states' securities regulation. At the same time, the United States was a unified country, with a strong core political and economic ideology. Most importantly, the United States already enjoyed a fully functioning single market. A European Securities Commission today would have of these advantages. A single European securities regulator would be even more challenged in exerting its authority over the European securities market than the SEC over the US securities market because it would have to compete against the SEC: a powerful, off-shore regulator that wields tremendous influence over the European securities market.

Secondly, it is unlikely that a European single regulator would have a say in prudential matters, ie action to prevent the insolvency of one financial intermediary firm spreading to others in a spillover effect.[64] It is extremely unlikely that political agreement could be reached in terms of giving a European Securities Commission a say in this area. Substantial powers, financial control and resources would be needed for a European single regulator to be able to act effectively in this area, by injecting liquidity into financial markets to prevent any threatened systemic collapse. This would be politically unpalatable to the Member States, to the current prudential supervisors within Member States, who might view this as a threat to their survival, and to the European Central Bank. While some degree of functional regulation of banks by a European Securities Commission may be desirable, for instance in relation to manipulative trading and consumer protection, it is extremely unlikely that such a Commission would assume responsibility for bank safety or capital adequacy regulation. Likewise, it is unlikely that a European Securities Commission would regulate insurance companies, except for some oversight of the barriers to cross-border investment and of mergers by insurance companies.

Thirdly, not only will any European Securities Commission not look like a US SEC, neither will it be the equivalent of a national regulator, such as the UK's Financial Services Authority. National market regulators and supervisors are likely to oppose strongly any transfer of market regulation or supervision to such a body because this would be a major threat to their own survival. In addition there seems to be little political will within the EU at present to wrest these powers from the national regulators.

Instead, the most likely role for a European Securities Commission, at least initially, would be to focus on corporate disclosure, setting and monitoring mandatory disclosure rules and transparency provisions.[65] Investors need consistency and comparability in financial statement presentations and timely disclosure of material corporate events, and it is increasingly

[64] G Hertig and R Lee, 'Four Predictions about the Future of EU Securities Regulation' [2003] *Journal of Corporate Law Studies* 359, at 374.

[65] *Ibid*, at 374–5. Another possible role which a European Securities Commission could take on is the role of policing financial intermediaries for manipulative and anti-competitive practices.

recognised that one of the ways to provide this is through centralised disclosure requirements.[66] As discussed above, the maximum harmonisation Prospectus Directive goes a long way in achieving this goal, although it still leaves open the possibility of additional requirements at national level being imposed, as in the UK, upon those seeking a listing on the official list, so that variations in relation to disclosure will still exist. In addition, as CESR's Himalaya Report[67] makes clear, it is not enough for harmonisation of the standards of disclosure to be set down if there is substantial disparity between national regulators regarding the power to supervise these issues and the intensity with which such powers are exercised. The increasing trend towards supervisory convergence therefore seems the most obvious route by which a pan-European regulator will arise, although the initial remit and role of such a body are likely to be narrow. One crucial issue will be the extent to which this body is given enforcement powers. In order to operate with any efficiency a single regulator will need to be given enforcement powers of some kind. This is likely to be controversial as the Member States will want to retain significant enforcement powers for themselves. Hertig and Lee have predicted that a 'European SEC' would get soft enforcement powers, ie the power to investigate breaches and to make its findings public, rather than any sanctioning powers, in order to solve this difficulty.[68] However, soft enforcement powers of this kind would not address the concerns raised by CESR in its Himalaya Report, and so there might be pressure for such a body to move into a more outright supervision and enforcement role.[69]

It is clear that a European Securities Commission of the type envisaged here would operate alongside existing national regulators, which would continue to regulate the banking and insurance sectors within their own jurisdictions, would continue to have considerable substantive powers in relation to the securities trading markets within their own jurisdiction and would continue to have a major enforcement role, at least initially. It is also probable that a European Securities Commission would be founded on the notion of supervisory convergence rather than supervisory centralisation. It would therefore grow from the Lamfalussy process rather than being

[66] See R Kraakman *et al*, *The Anatomy of Corporate Law* (Oxford, OUP, 2004) ch 8; R Romano, *The Advantage of Competitive Federalism for Securities Regulation* (Washington, DC, AEI press, 2002); MB Fox, 'The Issuer Choice Debate' (2001) 2 *Theoretical Inquiries in Law* 563.

[67] Above n54.

[68] Above n65, at 375–7.

[69] If the single regulator, most likely CESR, did move into an outright supervision and enforcement role, rather than merely supporting the process of supervisory convergence, this would raise a raft of difficult issues regarding CESR's enhanced powers, not least where these powers will come from, and some difficult constitutional (and political) questions regarding the likelihood of achieving this goal.

an alternative to that process. However, it is possible that, once a limited European Securities Commission of this kind were established, some 'creep' would occur, whereby a gradual increase in enforcement powers, possibly to address the concerns raised in the Himalaya Report, might be observed.

A factor which might encourage this 'creep' is a possible role for any European Securities Commission as a focus for increased levels of investor protection. A pan-European regulator might be able to improve investor protection by providing an efficient and effective forum for civil redress.[70] Although following the US down the route of civil litigation as a means of protecting investors may not be desirable, due to the expense and uncertainty of this option and the abuses to which it can give rise,[71] some form of pan-European arbitration system, akin to that operated by the securities industry in the US,[72] might be desirable. A centralised body of this kind could have an important role in setting standards for investor protection, including devising possible best practice models for a system of securities arbitration to be operated on a national level with a view to protecting investors. The FSAP recognised the need to develop efficient and effective judicial and extra-judicial dispute settlement mechanisms in the context of securities regulation, but went only so far as to recommend an EU-wide complaints network.[73] However, such a complaints network needs to be supplemented by an effective enforcement mechanism for investor complaints. There is now a network for dispute resolution in place (FIN-NET) but there are doubts whether it is effective in providing sufficient investor protection.[74] A pan-European securities regulator could potentially provide a more effective enforcement mechanism for investor complaints than exists at present, although, as discussed, it is unlikely that the Member States will be comfortable with handing over power and control of this kind, at least initially.

D. CONCLUSION

Equity markets now rival debt markets as a source of capital for European companies, particularly high-growth companies. As a result, investors and issuers demand larger, more liquid and more efficient equity markets. It

[70] Eg RS Karmel, 'The Case for a European Securities Commission' (1999) 38 *Columbia Journal of Transnational Law* 9, at 38.

[71] *Ibid*, at 38 and n128.

[72] See MI Steinberg, 'Securities Arbitration: Better for Investors than the Courts?' (1996) 62 *Brook Law Review* 1503.

[73] European Commission, 'Financial Services: Implementing the Framework for Financial Markets: Action Plan', COM(1999)232, 10.

[74] See N Maloney, 'Effective Policy Design for the Retail Investment Services Market: Challenges and Choices Post FSAP' in G Ferrarini and E Wymeersch (eds), *Investor Protection in Europe* (Oxford, OUP, 2006).

is therefore crucial that European securities regulation develops in a way which allows for the continuation of the tremendous growth in equity markets which has been observable over the last 20 years. Some argue that the present strategy of regulatory competition based on the FSAP and Lamfalussy is the correct approach, and this was certainly the view of the Committee of Wise Men when it considered this issue in 2000. As a result, the approach that has been adopted to develop the European single market for capital has been to recognise the jurisdiction of national exchanges while encouraging harmonisation of standards, and some level of cooperation between national stock exchanges. Others suggest that Europe needs a single securities market permitting pan-European offerings and that some form of centralised pan-European securities regulator, a European Securities Commission, is necessary to facilitate this development.

This chapter agrees with those who suggest that, while a single European regulator of some kind is not inevitable, it is certainly very likely, and that this is the case whether or not the Lamfalussy process is ultimately judged to have been a success. In fact, the Lamfalussy process is not likely to be acknowledged to have been a failure at any time in the near future and it is suggested here that a single regulator is most likely to grow from the Lamfalussy process itself, in particular from the concept of supervisory convergence, rather than being an alternative to that process. As a result the new regulator, mostly likely CESR, is likely to have a role in coordinating this process of supervisory convergence, although its initial remit and powers would almost certainly be narrow, focussing primarily on issues of corporate disclosure. This is a very different, and diminished, form of regulator than the one that the term 'pan-European securities regulator' might initially conjure up. It would not be akin in powers or scope to the US SEC or indeed to existing national regulators. It would grow from the existing regulatory competition approach rather than being in direct opposition to that model, and would therefore not be a triumph for mandatory regulation, at least initially. Of course, the further the idea of convergence is taken, the more pressure must inevitably be placed upon the regulatory competition model. It is possible that the impetus towards convergence, plus a possible drive towards making such an organisation a focus for increased investor protection, might well lead to increases in the remit and enforcement powers of such an organisation thereafter. The two interesting questions are then likely to be the extent of the 'supervisory tools carrying a trans-national dimension'[75] granted to the regulator to carry out its role, and whether the degree of supervisory convergence envisaged can be achieved without a measure of centralisation also being included in the mix.

[75] See above n55.

20

Better Regulation and the Role of EU Agencies

FRANK VIBERT*

THE EFFORT OF the EU to improve the quality of EU regulation rests on three elements. The first is the endorsement by the main institutions of the 'Integrated Impact Assessment' as an analytic tool for bringing together the empirical evidence behind an initiative. The second involves the formation and use of networks of national officials and regulators as a means to supplement the expertise and staff resources available within the Commission for sector regulation in the EU. The third component is the establishment of EU agencies. This chapter focuses on this third element.

Although for the purposes of this chapter agency creation is treated on its own, the common thread that links the three elements to better regulation is the effort being made by EU institutions to improve the quality of information and empirical evidence that enters into EU policy making. However, they address different aspects. Networks and agencies aim to achieve a better mobilisation of information across the EU, while impact assessment is about better analysis of the information gathered.

When the new wave of agency creation began in the EU, the initial reaction of academic observers was to stress the limits of their terms of reference. It seemed unlikely that they could play the kind of expansive role now played by independent bodies with regulatory powers in Member States.[1] This chapter argues that, despite terms of reference that set what appear to be tight limits on their powers and responsibilities, the new agencies can find 'opportunity points' in EU processes that will enable them to exert increasing influence on the content of EU legislation. On balance, this could help improve the quality of regulation in the EU.

* Director, European Policy Forum.

[1] See G Majone, 'The New European Agencies: Regulation by Information' (1997) 4(2) *Journal of European Public Policy* 262.

A. THE MOVE TO CREATE AGENCIES

1. The New Wave

In recent years there has been a spate of agency creation within the EU. The definitions of an 'agency' are somewhat arbitrary. Those agencies considered in this chapter have been created by a regulation,[2] have their own legal personality, are governed by European public law and have been created in the framework of the Union's first pillar covering the single market (the most relevant to the better regulation context).[3] This definition excludes those agencies created in the context of the Home Affairs and Common Foreign and Security Policy pillars. It also excludes those bodies that have the status of a Community Institution and the role of which is set out in the Treaty—such as the Court of Auditors, EIB and ECB. Currently, there are around 30 EU agencies on a broad definition of 'agency', and 22 that fall within the more limited definition used in this chapter. Most have been created since 1990, as shown below.

Table 20.1: Dates of Agency Creation

Prior to 1990	1990–2000	2001–present
2	10	10

2. Categorising

Trying to place the agencies within categories that describe their activities is somewhat arbitrary. The Commission paper setting out its view of their operational framework distinguished between two types of agency—those with executive profiles and those with regulatory ones.[4] 'Executive' agencies were defined as those with purely managerial functions; 'regulatory' agencies were defined as bodies helping the Commission to make decisions in order to regulate a specific sector.

This distinction between agencies with a 'managerial' role and those with a regulatory role in specific sectors is not entirely helpful because

[2] Initially agencies were set up under Art 308 EC, but since 2000 agency-establishing regs have been based on the provision of the Treaty constituting the legal basis for the policy field in which the particular agency operates (which may include Art 308). References to specific Arts in this ch are to the Arts in the founding reg of the agency concerned.

[3] EUMC/EFRA (for meanings of abbreviations see Annex 1) mainly focuses on first pillar matters, but also has responsibilities under the third pillar relating to police and judicial cooperation in criminal matters.

[4] Communication from the Commission, 'The Operating Framework for the European Regulatory Agencies', COM(2002)718 final of 11 Dec 2002.

'management'may typically be understood to include a regulatory function and a 'regulatory' role typically may be understood to include a decision-taking function. Neither assumption would be correct in the EU case. Moreover, in practice, while several agencies have responsibilities for specific sectors (such as fisheries or aviation) most have cross-sectoral reach (for example in relation to the environment or disease control or racism). Therefore, this chapter uses a different set of distinctions. It categorises EU agencies according to whether their main role is in assessing and evaluating a situation in the EU where policy action may be required, or whether their main role relates to compliance with and enforcement of EU policies, or whether they have been set up mainly in order to provide a service.

A representative example in the first category is provided by the European Centre for Disease Prevention and Control (ECDC) which assesses emerging threats to human health from communicable diseases. An example in the second category is the European Aviation Safety Agency (EASA) which ensures common aviation safety standards at the European level. Finally, an example in the third category is the Community Plant Variety Office (CPVO) which grants intellectual property rights for plant varieties in the EU. The categories into which the agencies fall are shown in the table below.

These categories are not ironclad. For example the responsibilities of EASA include contributing to environmental rule-making in aviation (noise and emissions), in addition to its main task of promoting safety standards through certification and inspections. It is agencies in the first two categories that are particularly relevant to the Better Regulation agenda.

Table 20.2: Categories of Agency[5]

Assessment and Evaluation	Compliance and Enforcement	Service Providers
ECDC	CFCA	CdT
EEA	EASA	Cedefop
EFSA	ECHA	CPVO
EMCDDA	EFRA/EUMC	EAR
EMEA	EMSA	EGSA
EOSHA	ERA	ENISA
EUROFOUND	FRONTEX	ETF
		OHIM

[5] Full titles and date of establishment are given in the Annex to this ch.

B. THE MOTIVATION

The wave of agency creation described above has paralleled the turn towards agency creation in national contexts. There, agency creation was very much associated with the so-called 'new public management' that began to exert influence in the 1980s. What characterised the new public administration was a desire to distinguish policy management from service delivery, a desire to move away from reliance on central government departments, a need for more flexible recruitment and career structures, and the introduction of practices from the private sector.[6]

These same factors are relevant in the EU context. As discussed further below, agencies have been seen as ways to improve the application, as opposed to initiation, of rules and policy in the EU. Decentralisation has also been viewed as a means of avoiding overburdening Commission staff in areas where specialised skills and expertise are needed. In addition, the agency structure may provide greater flexibility in employment, for example in relation to the secondment of staff or in the hiring of experts.[7] The language of the market can also be seen—for example in the use by EU agencies of the jargon of 'mission statements' for describing their terms of reference.

At the same time there are three particular drivers behind the formation of EU agencies that are special to policy-making in the EU context. The first is the need to correct for the asymmetry of information that exists in the EU between the information available in individual Member States and the information available in the central institutions. In a diversified Union of 27 Member States it is unlikely that the Commission can be in command of the precise conditions prevailing in each Member State in each policy area. An agency can provide for detailed focus on its particular field and aim to become authoritative in making EU-wide assessments.

The second, related driver has been the EU's need to tap into national sources of specialised and expert knowledge on a sustained and regular basis. Agencies organise and convene networks of national experts from the central departments of Member States' administrations, from national agencies in the same subject area and from other sources such as academia. For example, the EMEA brings together a network of 42 national competent authorities and 3,500 experts for underpinning its scientific work. While the Commission can also mobilise networks, an agency provides a venue for continuity of attention on a specific subject matter and for continuity in relationships, while the policy priorities of the Commission will fluctuate.

[6] For an overview see C Pollitt and G Bouckaert, *Public Management Reform: A Comparative Analysis*, 2nd edn (Oxford, OUP, 2004).

[7] Conditions of employment are generally those applying to all officials and servants of the European Communities.

The third driver has been the need to separate evidence drawn from Member State sources from the policy stance adopted by a Member State's government. Although the working groups of the Council are important sources of information on how a legislative proposal impacts on a particular Member State and the Commission also makes extensive use of ad hoc consultation mechanisms, it is not always easy to separate the views of national experts on the evidence from the policy stance of their member government. The Council represents above all a bargaining culture where evidence is tailored to support a case. The Commission may also be viewed as having an agenda that may lead it to be selective in its approach to evidence. Agencies have management boards and advisory committees that include government officials and national agency representatives as well as Commission appointees. However, they are intended to be independent so that they can operate in a less politicised setting and potentially can concentrate on the evidence.

Thus, in addition to the general influence of the new public management, the more particular drivers behind EU agency creation concern the EU's need to mobilise more reliable EU-wide sources of information and analysis for evidence-based policy-making. Many of the agencies emphasise their statutory duties as convenors of networks for this purpose, as shown in the box on their networking duties.

Box 20.1: Networking Duties

This Regulation establishes the European Environment Agency and aims at the setting up of a European environment information and observation network. EEA, Art1(1).

The Commission, the Agency, and the national aviation authorities shall exchange any information available to them in the context of the application of this Regulation. EASA, Art11(1).

The Centre shall have at its disposal the European Information Network on Drugs and Drug Addiction... EMCDDA, Art 5.

The Centre shall......coordinate the European networking of bodies operating in the fields within the centre's mission'. ECDC, Art3(2)(d).

The tasks of the Authority shall be......to establish a system of networks of organisations operating in the fields within its mission and be responsible for their operation. EFSA, Art 23(g).

In order to promote the establishment of a European railway area without borders......the Agency should....form an essential tool of dialogue, consultation and exchange between all the actors in the railway sector...ERA, Preamble, recital. 7.

The Agency will comprise.....a Forum for the exchange of information on enforcement activities. This forum implements the White Paper proposal to create a network of enforcement authorities. ECA Proposal, COM(2003)644/15, at 18.

C. TERMS OF REFERENCE AND THE COMPARISON WITH NATIONAL AGENCIES

1. The Restrictions on EU Agencies

What is unusual about the terms of reference of EU agencies is that, unlike agencies in national settings that have decision-making powers, EU agencies are generally restricted to the evidence-gathering role, to the giving of advice and the delivery of opinions.[8] The regulation establishing the ECDC is explicit: '[t]his regulation does not confer any regulatory powers on the Centre'.[9] Similarly, the regulation founding the EMCDDA states, '[t]he Centre may not take any measure which in any way goes beyond the sphere of information and the processing thereof'.[10] Formal decision power thus remains with the Commission, and the role of the agencies is to prepare the information and analysis for the Commission. For example the tasks of the EEA involve collecting and analysing data, providing the Community with information, monitoring, advising on systems for monitoring, assessing data on the state of the environment, ensuring the comparability of data, publishing reports, developing forecasting techniques and methods of assessing the costs of environmental damage, disseminating information to the general public and diffusing research information.[11] These terms of reference make clear that the Agency is to be an information provider but not a decision-taker. Similar provisions limiting the Authority to the provision of information, advice, technical and scientific support and to the communication of opinions apply in the case of EFSA.

The line between the assessment or evaluation role of agencies, their giving advice and opinions, and the actual rule-making role in terms of formal decisions and authorisations by the Commission is probably not quite as clear in practice as statutory terms of reference would seem to indicate. For reasons discussed later, if for example the EASA assesses what is or is not safe in aircraft or the EMEA evaluates what can or cannot be brought safely to market under accelerated procedures for new medicines, it is most unlikely that formal rules will not follow on an automatic basis.

A similar caution applies in the area of EU chemicals legislation. On paper, for example, the ECHA manages the registration procedures for dangerous chemicals, makes recommendations and issues opinions, but the

[8] Dehousse emphasises their information role in the absence of discretionary power: see R Dehousse, 'Regulation by Networks in the European Community: The Role of European Agencies' (1997) 4 *Journal of European Public Policy* 246.

[9] Council Reg.(EC) 851/2004 [2004] OJ L142/1, preamble, para 6.

[10] Reg (EEC) 302/1993 [1993] OJ L036/4, Art 1(2), and recast Reg.(EC) 1920/2006 [2006] OJ L376/3, Art.1(4).

[11] Council Reg (EEC) 1210/90 [1990] OJ L120/3, Art 2.

Commission retains the power of authorisation. The reality again is less clear-cut. For example, in the context of risk assessment the Commission noted:

> The Commission shall weigh the evidence and make a proposal. The Commission may *exceptionally* come forward with a proposal that is not in accord with the opinion of either Committee [of the agency].[12]

The implication of this language is that while the Commission reserves its decision-making powers, in practice it is unlikely that the Commission would challenge an agency opinion.

It is in this context that the discipline of the Integrated Impact Assessment adopted by the Commission may be relevant. In weighing the economic, social and environmental impact of a proposed measure, the Commission will wish to reserve its right to make a fully rounded judgement and may take a wider view of issues such as competitiveness that a specialised agency may not have assessed or may not be qualified to make a judgement on. For example, although EFSA is charged in its founding regulation with duties to carry out risk assessment, to mobilise scientific information and to pursue a high level of consumer protection, it is not under any statutory duty to carry out cost-benefit or cost effectiveness analysis of the opinions it delivers.

2. The Reasons for Restrictions

The main reason for the formal restrictions in the terms of reference of EU agencies is that, viewed from a principal/agent perspective, both the Commission and the Council have been concerned, as dual principals, about the potential threat to their own decision-making role. The Commission is concerned above all to protect its exclusive right of initiative and to make the normative judgements that enter into policy formation. The contrast with national settings is thus mainly accounted for by the way that the Commission has insisted on retaining its own powers. The functions entrusted to agencies in a national setting are to be found in the EU setting in the decision-making powers of the Commission itself. The decision-making powers retained by the Commission have the effect of removing EU agencies from the front line of decision-taking. They operate through the Commission, which in turn may need to win backing from the Council and Parliament. National agencies are front-line decision-takers; EU agencies by contrast stand one or two steps back from the front line.

12 COM(2003)644/15, at 38 (emphasis added).

The Council has also been keen to protect its own role in policy-making. Where, however, the Commission and the Council may have differed in their perspectives is that the Commission sometimes appears to have seen EU agency creation as a way to bring functions otherwise performed by agencies within Member States under an EU umbrella. In areas of the Treaty (such as the Single Market) where responsibilities are shared between the EU and Member States, agencies may provide a way for the Commission to get a grip on competences that would otherwise be exercised by the Member States and gradually to extend these competences. For example, recent EU legislation gives EMEA full responsibility for evaluating medicines intended for the treatment of HIV/AIDS, cancer, diabetes and neurological disorders, which now must be authorised through the EU centralised procedure.[13] Similarly EMSA has acquired operational tasks in oil pollution preparedness and response and EUMC has been converted from an agency concerned with racism and xenophobia into a Human Rights Agency covering all aspects of the EU's Charter of Fundamental Rights.

A related aspect of the Commission perspective is that the use of a regulation to create agencies helps bring the field of responsibility under directly applicable Community law rather than under directives that depend on Member States for their application. The Commission noted, for example, in the creation of ECHA that the use of a regulation would replace some 40 existing directives.[14]

From its perspective, the Council may have seen tight terms of reference as the means by which they could control any transfer of shared powers, or compensate for any loss of powers hitherto exercised by their national agencies, or for any loss of flexibility in the way Community law is applied. The way in which the Member States' appointees dominate management boards and advisory councils also seems to reflect this concern.

What this means is that agency creation has reflected contrasting objectives between the two principals. One—the Commission—has seen agencies as a way to get around obstacles created by Member States. The other—the Council representing those Member States—has seen agencies as a way of moderating the influence of the Commission.

It is these different and sometimes conflicting perspectives of the two principals on the role of the agent that accounts for the contrast between the currently restricted terms of reference of EU agencies and the more expansive terms of reference of agencies operating in national settings. The contrast is striking. In the context of individual Member States, independent agencies set at arm's length from central government departments can take an enormous variety of decisions. Independent economic regulators can decide on the market rules in their sectors of responsibility and decide

[13] EMEA/MB/378522/2005, at 3.
[14] COM(2003)644/15, at 12.

on the actions required if market failures are diagnosed that call for regulatory intervention. Economic regulators can also take action on social or environmental grounds, for example to maintain a universal service, or to protect low income groups or the elderly, or to enforce water quality standards. While some regulatory bodies are active in traditional and long-standing areas of social concern, such as health and safety, others have been set up in new areas of social concern such as privacy or racial discrimination or genetic engineering. In such settings they make value judgements and decisions on what is socially acceptable or not in highly sensitive areas. In national settings, independent agencies can investigate, prosecute, adjudicate on and levy and enforce penalties. They commonly provide extra-judicial means for citizens and citizens' groups for settling disputes or for obtaining redress. It is the sweep of functions, decision-making powers and enforcement authority belonging to national regulatory bodies that makes EU agencies seem powerless by comparison.

It is this contrast that has caused outside observers to stress the limitations of the role of EU agencies. The lack of discretionary powers vested in EU agencies seems to confine their potential role in contributing to the Better Regulation agenda in the EU to one of helping institutions such as the Commission to avoid mistakes.[15] This is an important but restricted back-up role. However, this diagnosis underestimates their potential.

D. OPPORTUNITY POINTS

EU agencies, despite their limited terms of reference and their limited powers compared with their counterparts within EU Member States, can exert influence in three main ways. They possess the influence inherent in epistemic communities; they can exploit institutional openings among the three main EU institutions; and they can exploit openings in EU processes.

1. Inherent Epistemic Power

EU agencies bring together like-minded professionals from the Member States and conjoin them with their own expertise. This gives them two sorts of power and influence. The first is the influence of 'epistemic communities' that comes from being able to forge alliances with national bodies in

[15] Majone views them as devices that reduce the risks of the traditional Community integration method: see G Majone, *Dilemmas of Integration* (Oxford, OUP, 2005).

the same field based on common beliefs, common methodologies, common assessments and common approaches to risk management and problem solving. The second source of influence derives from the risks facing those who challenge their expert analysis. Blame avoidance theory suggests that bodies charged with policy decisions will hesitate to challenge expert bodies because of their fear of being blamed for mistakes.

The power and influence of such epistemic communities are a matter of debate. Some accounts make them the prime movers in transmitting knowledge across boundaries and bringing about policy change.[16] Others are more sceptical.[17] The debate partly revolves around the place of 'consensus' in policy-making and partly around the value judgements employed. A consensus about the scientific evidence among the experts networked from Member States and the agency is likely to be a powerful persuader. Faced with a consensus in the scientific community, the Commission, as mentioned above, is most unlikely to issue a challenge on the evidence. Consensus is a powerful persuader not because it provides a test of whether a view is correct or not (which it does not) but because evidence is rarely unequivocal and inferences from data to conclusions rarely without challenge. The emergence of a consensus suggests that a path has been found by the specialists amidst the uncertainties. (Article 30 of the EFSA Founding Regulation deals specifically with its obligations when there are diverging scientific opinions.[18])

However policy is not just about evidence. It is also about the standards to apply to the evidence, where the burden of proof should lie and other value judgements about what makes a policy 'acceptable' or not. This is where the influence of epistemic communities may be contested. Experts and specialists are not necessarily well equipped to make these normative judgements. Moreover, on normative questions there may be different opinions and different Member States' traditions within the network and between the agency and the network. In addition, both the Commission and the Council may feel that it is in making normative judgements that they have a better grip on what may be acceptable to a broader public opinion than any agency. Thus, where normative differences are important the influence of an epistemic community and an assessment made by an agency may be more open to challenge. The complexity of the value judgements to be made is illustrated by Article14 of the Regulation governing EFSA, which in the space of one Article offers two different ways of defining the burden of proof in food safety (to show risk or to prove safety) and two different

[16] PM Haas, 'When Does Power Listen to Truth? A Constructivist Approach to the Policy Process' (2004) 11 *Journal of European Public Policy* 569.

[17] For an overview see PM Haas, 'Reconstructing Epistemic Communities' (2006), Paper presented at the Center for Global Change and Governance, Rutgers University.

[18] Reg (EC) 178/2002 [2002] OJ L31/16, art. 30.

standards of what is acceptable (Community standards and Member States' standards).[19]

2. Blame Avoidance

However, even if theories of pure epistemic power need to be treated with caution, blame avoidance provides a supplementary line of reasoning why agencies are likely to wield greater influence than might appear at first sight. Blame avoidance theory derives from electoral studies that emphasise the motivation of electorates to vote against those that they wish to punish for policy missteps.[20] It provides a reason why elected politicians might wish to defer to independent agencies rather than risk being blamed for gaps in knowledge, awkward facts or the politically inconvenient policy implications of empirical evidence.

In the case of EU institutions the application of blame theory is apparently diluted because electoral sanctions are weak. The electoral connection with the Parliament is weak for a number of well known reasons, such as low electoral turn-out and the importance of the patronage of party leaders for the positioning of candidates on party lists. By contrast, Member States' governments in the Council of Ministers are indeed concerned about their re-election, but majority voting and the role of the other institutions in decision-making provides them with many opportunities for blame shifting to others. The Commission is unelected and thus immune from direct electoral pressures entirely.

Nevertheless, despite weak electoral sanction in the EU, blame avoidance still operates. The Commission needs to be concerned about its standing with the Council and the Parliament—otherwise its right of initiative will lose its potency. As far as the Council is concerned, blame shifting is a game that the other institutions can play as well and blame can return to it.[21] Even if the impact of electorates on the Parliament lacks immediacy, what the Parliament cannot avoid is the myriad of special interests from business and civil society that swarm around regulatory issues. Moreover, in sensitive cases such as on environmental or health and safety issues such groups will be likely to convey strong feelings. The Parliament does not want to be targeted by a hostile advocacy group. Each institution therefore has its own set of reasons for not wanting to be blamed for a policy misstep.

[19] *Ibid*, Art 14.

[20] For the pathologies of blame avoidance see KR Weaver 'The Politics of Blame Avoidance' (1996) 6 *Journal of Public Policy* 371.

[21] For the distinction between blame shifting and blame reversion see C Hood, 'The Risk Game and the Blame Game' (2002) 37 *Government and Opposition* 15.

Because blame shifting is integral to the way the Brussels and Strasbourg institutions work, the implication is that if the agency and its associated groups of experts are united in their assessment of a complex situation or a sensitive problem it seems most unlikely that either the Commission or Council of Ministers or Parliament would want to challenge their technical assessments. The risks in doing so would be too high. Intuitively it might be argued that agencies are less likely to have influence where public opinion or sections of it hold strong views on the policy in question to which the other institutions feel they must respond. Blame avoidance theory, however, suggests otherwise. If politicians are concerned about avoiding blames for their actions they are even more likely to shift responsibilities in the direction of an agency on controversial issues. Diving for cover will seem the better option.

Just how much influence these two aspects of inherent epistemic power will provide is debatable. It may depend on the complexity of the technical background and it may depend on the familiarity of the politicians with the subject matter. Nevertheless, to deny that EU agencies can wield significant influence in decision-making and policy formation in their own field would seem unwarranted.

3. Institutional Openings

A second reason the influence of the agencies should not be underestimated is that they can exploit institutional openings. As described above, the main reason for the limits set in their terms of reference has been the desire on the part of the Commission and the Council to protect their own prerogatives. However this may turn agencies towards a different institutional player—the European Parliament.

The relationship of an agency to the European Parliament has two aspects. It can be modelled in terms of a principal–agent relationship where the Parliament is the principal. This seems appropriate when one considers the Parliament's scrutiny role in respect of agencies, where the relevant Parliamentary committee can summon the head of the agency to a hearing, or call for a report, or examine its activities in the process of giving a budget discharge.[22]

The other aspect of the relationship is that the Parliament is also a client of the agencies—a client for their output of analysis and information. For example, the Parliament may formally request an opinion from EFSA.[23] This puts the relationship on a different footing. The Parliament becomes

[22] The normal budget discharge procedure for agencies involves the Court of Auditors and the Parliament. Only the Court of Auditors (and its own Administrative Council) is involved in the case of an agency such as the CPVO that derives its budget wholly from fees.

[23] See above n18, Art 29(1)(b).

a body that is in need of what the agencies can provide—information of a cross-EU comparative nature, technical analysis about how to interpret the evidence and views about what policy interpretation to place on the analysis. Moreover, agencies are one of the few resources that the Parliament can turn to in order to challenge the views of the Commission or the Council. The right to amend proposals from the Commission and Council is what gives the European Parliament its power and agencies can provide the Parliament with reasons to exercise this power.

The dynamic behind this client relationship is that the Parliament has limited internal expertise of its own. Moreover, expert staff on its Secretariat are very conscious of the need not to cross over from a technical support role to a political role—a factor that can be inhibiting to the advice they provide. The Parliament can and does 'contract out' for expertise from academic and private sources, but contracting out has its own difficulties. The Parliament can also turn to interest groups and to NGOs for information. But these will often be seen to be tainted or self-serving. Agencies provide them with the least bad alternative as a source of information and analysis. The net result is that in important respects agencies and the European Parliament may find themselves as allies and partners. Thus agencies seem to be developing a close relationship with the specialised committees in the Parliament that cover the same field (such as the relationship between the EEA and the Parliament's environment committee).

4. Openings in EU Processes

EU processes also provide the agencies with potential openings. The Commission, the Council and the Parliament are each overwhelmingly focussed on the future regulatory and legislative agenda. Their reward and incentive system is geared to new measures. This has led to a well known neglect of implementation and compliance. It has also led to an almost complete neglect of lesson-learning from past regulation—the attempt to assess to what extent EU measures have fulfilled the objectives intended. Monitoring the effect of EU legislation, however, is an area where agencies have a natural role to play and where their information-gathering role becomes hugely important. In so far as lessons learnt from past measures should be incorporated in the preparation of new or recast measures then agencies will correspondingly become shapers also of the new.

The agency that appears to have led the way in pioneering this role is the EEA. Its 2001 report confirmed a widespread lack of knowledge in the EU at that time about the effectiveness of past environmental measures.[24]

[24] EEA, 'Reporting on Environmental Measures: Are We Being Effective?', Environmental Issue Report No 25 (2001).

It has followed up with two pilot studies on urban waste water treatment and packaging waste.[25] EEA strategy has now made *ex post* policy effectiveness analysis a priority area for its activities and is conducting further studies. Similarly, in its 2006 work programme the EMEA states that '[e]mphasis will be placed on full implementation of the Community legislation and on the monitoring of this implementation'.[26]

E. ACCOUNTABILITY

For the reasons discussed above it can be expected that over time EU agencies will take advantage of the opportunity structures offered by EU institutions and procedures to wield increasing influence over regulatory policy-making. The question then arises whether this influence is likely to improve the quality of regulation in the EU or not. The assets that agencies bring to the table, namely better quality EU-wide information, networked analysis and an advantage in pan-European lesson-learning, all point in the direction of a positive contribution to better regulation. The pointer in the other direction concerns accountability.

1. The Need

A system of accountability for the new agencies is important in the context of better regulation for two main reasons. First, public choice theory suggests that unaccountable bodies are likely to pursue their own agendas. In cases where the bodies have regulatory settings their own agendas may be expressed in terms of a desire to promote and create new and expanding areas for regulation rather than starting by considering what the market will or will not do or by taking proper account of the risks of regulatory failure. Such tendencies may be partly counteracted among economic regulators by a well-established theory of regulatory 'exit' when a fully competitive market-place has been achieved. Other regulators, for example in the fields of health, safety, social protection or the environment, have no analogous discipline provided by any corresponding theory of regulatory exit.

Secondly, unwatched bodies insulated from outside scrutiny can develop in-house biases or modes of thought. This can bias the selection of data and evidence, bias the interpretation of the evidence and lead to unrecognised and unacknowledged value judgements in drawing conclusions from the evidence. All lead to poor quality regulation.

[25] EEA. Policy Effectiveness Reports Nos 2 and 3, 'The Effectiveness of Urban Wastewater Treatment and Packaging Waste Management Systems' (2005).

[26] EMEA/MB/378522/2005, at 12.

The other side of the coin is the danger of political interference with agency independence. While unaccountable agencies are unlikely to be a force for better regulation, the issue for the EU is, as it is for the Member States, to devise a system of accountability that does not compromise agency independence. In the case of EU agencies their siting has reflected political bargaining in the Council at its worst. The new agencies are scattered throughout the EU from Heraklion to Helsinki. This diffusion coupled with the growing number of agencies makes questions of accountability more urgent to resolve. Their number is not as large as in some Member States (the UK has about 250 independent bodies with executive or regulatory functions) but the other EU institutions screen them from public view.

2. Channels of Accountability

In the case of agencies within national systems of parliamentary democracy, accountability is both to politicians and to courts. Accountability to the courts involves the threat of judicial review if agencies miss out on vital procedural steps or omit or misinterpret material facts. Political accountability runs to ministers and to parliaments.

In the case of the EU the same approach applies on paper. Judicial review of agency actions is possible through the Court of First Instance and the European Court of Justice. In respect of political accountability the other institutions also do not lack instruments for control of agencies. Agency terms of reference can be changed by amendments to their founding Regulation if they overstep their bounds, the agencies often depend on the EU budget for their financial resources and, as mentioned above, they are subject to regular scrutiny by the Parliament. Their executive heads are appointed through a partly political process and can be changed.[27] Nevertheless, how exactly to express this dual relationship to the law and to politics is more difficult than would seem to be the case.

From a theoretical perspective it is common to model the relationship with politicians in terms of a principal–agent model (ministers or parliaments standing as the principal). But the application of such models runs into difficulties when there are multiple principals and chains of agency relationships. Moreover, in democracies it is citizens who are the ultimate principal and there are difficulties in modelling ministers and parliaments as both agents and principals. In the case of the EU, multiple principals

[27] In the case of EFSA the Executive Director is appointed by the Management Board on a proposal by the Commission after open competition. The Management Board is appointed by the Council in consultation with the Parliament from a list drawn up by the Commission: see above n18, Art 25(1) and Art 26(1).

are the norm. The Council, Commission and Parliament each regard themselves in some way as the relevant principal—the Commission and Council because they do not want the agencies to overstep the line on policy (as noted above) and the Parliament because agencies fit within its general conception of its oversight role in respect of EU bodies. These different constituencies are reflected in the composition of managing boards. When agencies operate under multiple principals with possibly different objectives, the agent is more likely to be able to pursue its own agenda and accountability becomes more questionable. Moreover the chain of agency is also long. As mentioned above, in the EU the citizen is weakly connected with the main EU institutions, and even further removed from agencies.

As a practical matter further questions also arise. Judicial review of agencies in the EU is still largely uncharted waters.[28] The experience of other jurisdictions both in the US and the EU is that there are disputes over where precisely to draw the line between what merits review and what constitutes judicial interference. In respect of political accountability to ministers or to parliaments the same practical issue arises about how to distinguish between a merited review function and unmerited political interference. In some EU Member States the power of appointment or dismissal is used as a means to bring political influence to bear on the agency. In the case of the EU, experience with appointments to the ECB suggests similar dangers. EU agencies are exposed to these dangers because they have politically appointed boards and advisory councils. In a worst case scenario the EU could reap the worst of all possible worlds—agencies that are sufficiently out of sight to act according to their own agendas but not so far out of sight as to be immune from the risks of political and judicial interference.

What this means is that the EU lacks a settled theoretical and practical framework for agency accountability. This unsettled framework is not unique to the EU. It is the situation that prevails in the Member States and in other democracies around the world that have increasingly turned to independent unelected bodies for expertise in fact gathering and practical problem solving and struggle to reconcile the independence of such bodies with a framework for political and judicial control.[29] Nevertheless, if agencies such as those established in the EU are to operate to their full potential as sources of better regulation a clearer framework for accountability will need to be found.

[28] See D Curtin, 'Delegation to EU Non-Majoritarian Institutions' in D Gerardin, R Munoz, and N Petit (eds), *Regulation Through Agencies in the EU.* (Cheltenham, Edward Elgar, 2005) at 87–117.

[29] F Vibert, *The Rise of the Unelected: Democracy and the New Separation of Powers* (Cambridge, Cambridge University Press, forthcoming 2007).

F. CONCLUSIONS: BETTER REGULATION?

On balance it seems that critics that have emphasised the differences in the power and influence of agencies in the EU compared with their counterparts in Member States may have underestimated the opportunity structure for EU agencies. They have an advantage over their national counterparts in gathering EU-wide information and analysis, and an advantage over other institutions in the EU in their specialist roles and capabilities. Notwithstanding their limited terms of reference they are likely to acquire epistemic influence as authoritative sources of EU-wide information and opinions and as network managers. In addition, EU institutions and procedures offer them opportunity points to exert this influence, particularly in respect of a potential alliance with the European Parliament and in respect of lesson-learning from past EU measures. Their superior ability to gather policy-relevant information on an EU-wide basis and to draw lessons from past EU measures makes it likely that they can help improve the quality of future EU regulation. The risk on the other side is that the arrangements for agency accountability may make them vulnerable to political pressures.

There are further reasons to examine the future potential of such agencies in the context of better regulation. They occupy a middle ground between institutionalised networks of national regulators, such as those used in the financial sector under the Lamfalussy process, and a fully fledged EU regulatory agency with its own formal decision-taking powers. One question is whether this is a model that could be usefully extended into other sectors such as financial markets. A further related question is whether this 'middle ground', as currently defined in agency-founding regulations, is sustainable or not. The analysis suggests that under their current terms of reference there is a danger that agencies will gradually develop decision-making powers in practice, but in a way that is disguised from public view, is far from transparent about who is responsible for what kind of decision and where it will be unclear whether agencies are making political or empirical judgements. Thus, in order to make greater use of the potential of agencies for better regulation, a more general review of their terms of reference may be needed in order to look again at their relationship with the other institutions, to ensure that they subject their opinions and advice to Impact Analysis and to highlight where they offer a comparative advantage, for example in monitoring the effectiveness of past EU measures.

ANNEX: EU AGENCIES WITH SINGLE MARKET RESPONSIBILITIES

Dates are dates of establishment.

Those mainly with responsibility for assessment and evaluation:

European Centre for Disease Prevention and Control (ECDC). 2004.

European Environment Agency. (EEA). 1990.
European Food Safety Authority. (EFSA). 2002.
European Foundation for the Improvement of Living & Working Conditions. (EUROFOUND). 1975.
European Medicines Agency (EMEA). 1993.
European Monitoring Centre for Drugs and Drug Addiction. (EMCDDA). 1993.
European Agency for Safety and Health at Work. (EOSHA). 1994.
Those mainly with responsibility for compliance and enforcement:
Community Fisheries Control Agency. (CFCA). 2005.
European Aviation Safety Agency. (EASA). 2002.
European Chemicals Agency. (ECHA). 2003.
European Fundamental Rights Agency. (EFSA). 2006. (Including European Monitoring Centre on Racism and Zenophobia. (EUMC). 1997).
European Maritime Safety Agency. (EMSA). 2002.
European Railway Agency. (ERA). 2004.
European Agency for the Management of Operational Cooperation at the External borders. (FRONTEX). 2004.

Service providers:
European Centre for the Development of Vocational Training. (CEDEFOP). 1975.
Community Plant Variety Office. (CPVO). 1994.
Translation Centre for Bodies of the European Union. (CdT). 1994.
European Agency for Reconstruction. (EAR). 1999.
European GNSS Supervisory Authority. (EGSA). 2004.
European Network and Information Security Agency (ENISA). 2004
European Training Foundation. (ETF). 1990.
Office for Harmonisation in the Internal Market. (OHIM). 1993.

Annex

06 JUNE 2006

PRESS STATEMENT

BUSINESSES 'NOT HEARD' ON EU LEGISLATION

New research from Clifford Chance reveals views of European businesses on EU law-making

European businesses have delivered an unflattering assessment of the degree to which EU law-makers take their views into account when drafting new legislation. Fewer than one in three firms are satisfied the EU is listening to them; and 30 per cent simply do not know if their views are taken into account at all.

The research builds on a similar exercise carried out by Clifford Chance last year, which concentrated on the desirability and viability of a single contract law. In this study over 60 per cent of respondents say that EU law-making meets their commercial aspirations to make good use of the single market, and recognised strengths such as consistency and successful harmonisation. However there is widespread dissatisfaction with how the process works in practice.

Clifford Chance's research shows that the EU is performing worst on those factors that businesses consider 'most important' in getting their voice heard, notably concise information about the impact on, and understanding of, the commercial implications of law-making; the implementation process between national governments and the EU; and effective lobbying from trade/professional bodies.

A majority, 58 per cent of companies, is placing EU legislation as a high priority at board level and 75 per cent of firms reported that they expect an increase in the time they devote to EU law in the coming years. Against this background only 25 per cent of firms devote specialist resources to information gathering or presenting their views.

Stuart Popham, Clifford Chance's Senior Partner, said, 'We are seeing a clear trend of businesses feeling out of step with EU legislators as new regulations come out of Brussels. Smaller firms in particular cannot afford to keep tabs on new developments, and larger businesses appear to engage too little and too late. EU law-makers don't seem to appreciate commercial realities at the drafting stage so two things must happen: the EU has to communicate its intentions far more effectively, and to show that it is listening to businesses; and businesses must get involved much earlier in the legislative process.'

Helping more businesses to have a voice in EU law-making represents an opportunity for the EU to create real commercial advantage. Two-thirds of those who say their voice is heard favour EU law-making over that of the US; this compares with only one-third of those who do not feel listened to.

Mr. Popham concluded, 'When businesses feel their views have been taken into account, 75 per cent of them feel confident about EU law-making. If businesses and regulators can communicate effectively, it will be greatly to Europe's competitive advantage; get it wrong and businesses will become disengaged from the process of EU law-making, ultimately to the detriment of the European market as a whole.'

– ENDS –

For further information about this press release call: Anna Ward, Public Relations Manager, London on +44 (0) 207 006 2988 or Sarah Mandeno on +44 (0) 207 006 4112.

For further information about **Clifford Chance see www.cliffordchance.com.**

Notes to Editors:

The Clifford Chance research was conducted by Gracechurch Consulting, a London-based research consultancy, between 27 February and 8 March 2006. The quantitative survey was conducted by means of a telephone semi-structured survey. Each interview lasted around 30 minutes. The sample comprises 166 senior decision-makers in large and medium companies based in UK, France, Germany, Netherlands, Spain, Italy, Poland and Hungary. The sample comprises: multinationals (42%), international companies (37%), national companies (22%) All respondents had been directly involved in dealing with EU regulations in the past 12 months.

Highlights:

- On average, legal departments spend around 20 per cent of their time on EU law-making. 75 per cent says this is increasing
- 25 per cent claim to have EU legal specialists. But 40 per cent consider they would be more effective with more specialist resource

— 59 per cent say it is not easy to give feedback on EU regulations
— 32 per cent are satisfied that their voices are heard in EU law-making. 38 per cent say not very/at all satisfied and 30 per cent do not know
— 57 per cent are aware of the Commission's aim to make EU and national regulations less burdensome for business. However 63 per cent are not confident that the EU will produce legislation that is less burdensome. Also 56 per cent are not confident that the EU will produce legislation that is easier to apply or more effective
— 62 per cent consider, however, that EU law-making does meet their aspirations to make good use of the single market

Clifford Chance Limited Liability Partnership is the first fully integrated global law firm, with 28 offices in 19 countries. The firm aims to provide seamless global services to the world's leading financial institutions and multinational businesses.

Unrivalled in its international resources, Clifford Chance has over 3,300 legal advisers and is organised around six global practice areas: capital markets; corporate (including M&A); finance; litigation and dispute resolution; real estate; and tax, pensions and employment law.

CLIFFORD CHANCE

The Clifford Chance Survey
Business and EU Regulation

contents

If you would like to know more about the subjects covered in this publication or our services, please contact:

Stuart Popham +44 20 7006 2033
Michael Smyth +44 20 7006 8421
Kaarli H Eichhorn +32 2 533 5960

To email one of the above, please use
firstname.surname@cliffordchance.com

Clifford Chance LLP, 10 Upper Bank Street,
Canary Wharf, London E14 5JJ

www.cliffordchance.com

Foreword by Stuart Popham

Senior Partner, Clifford Chance

Welcome to Clifford Chance's annual business survey which this year focuses on "Business and EU Regulation".

European businesses have delivered an unflattering assessment of the degree to which EU law-makers take their views into account when drafting new legislation. Fewer than one in three firms are satisfied the EU is listening to them; and 30 per cent simply do not know if their views are taken into account at all.

Over 60 per cent of respondents say that EU law-making meets their commercial aspirations to make good use of the single market, and recognised strengths such as consistency and successful harmonisation. However, there is widespread dissatisfaction with how the process works in practice.

Clifford Chance's research shows that the EU is performing worst on those factors that businesses consider 'most important' in getting their voice heard, notably concise information about the impact on, and understanding of, the commercial implications of law-making.

A majority, 58 per cent of companies, gives EU legislation a high priority at board level and 75 per cent of firms reported that they expect an increase in the time they devote to EU law in the coming years. Against this background only 25 per cent of firms devote specialist resources to information gathering or presenting their views.

We are seeing a clear trend of businesses feeling out of step with EU legislators as new regulations come out of Brussels. Smaller firms in particular cannot afford to keep tabs on new developments, and larger businesses appear to engage too little and too late. EU law-makers don't seem to appreciate commercial realities at the drafting stage so two things must happen: the EU has to communicate its intentions far more effectively, and businesses must get involved much earlier in the legislative process.

Helping more businesses to have a voice in EU law-making represents an opportunity for the EU to create real commercial advantage.

If businesses and regulators can communicate effectively, it will be greatly to Europe's competitive advantage; get it wrong and businesses will become disengaged from the process of EU law-making, ultimately to their detriment.

Stuart Popham

2006 Survey Objectives

To understand European businesses' experience of EU law-making

How effective is the process of consultation and implementation?
- **What works well and what does not?**

The extent to which European businesses believe that
- **they have effective channels to give feedback**
- **they understand the impact of regulation**
- **information is comprehensible**
- **their views are taken into account**
- **the implementation of policy is effective**

Sample and Methodology

Company Size

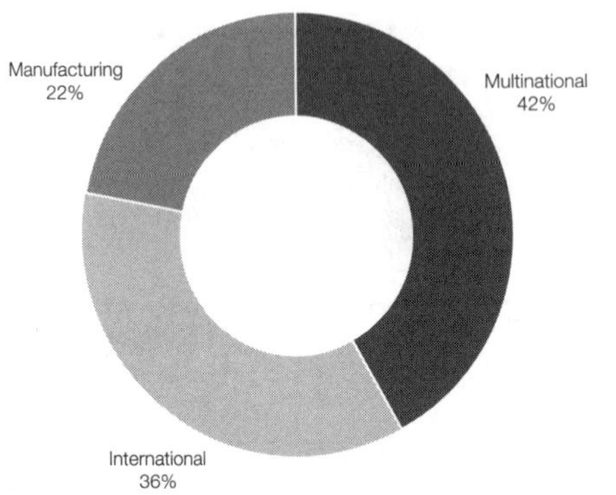

Sector

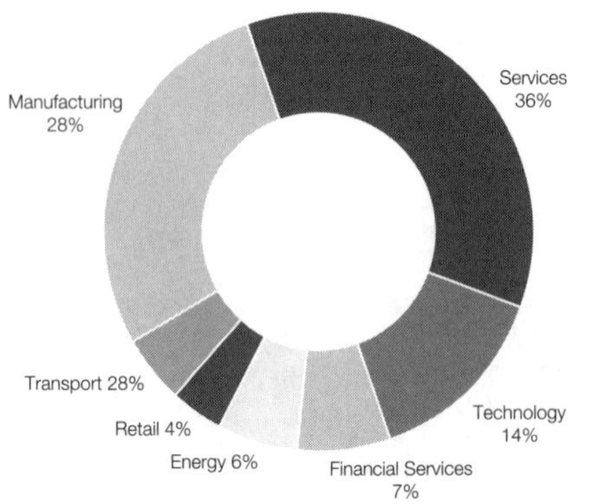

Qualitative stage

- 11 in-depth interviews
- Lasting 1 hour

Quantitative stage

- 166 semi-structured interviews
- 30-minute telephone interview
- A range of senior legal decision-makers
- All had dealt with EU law in the last 12 months
- Fieldwork 27th Feb – 8th March 2006

Countries covered

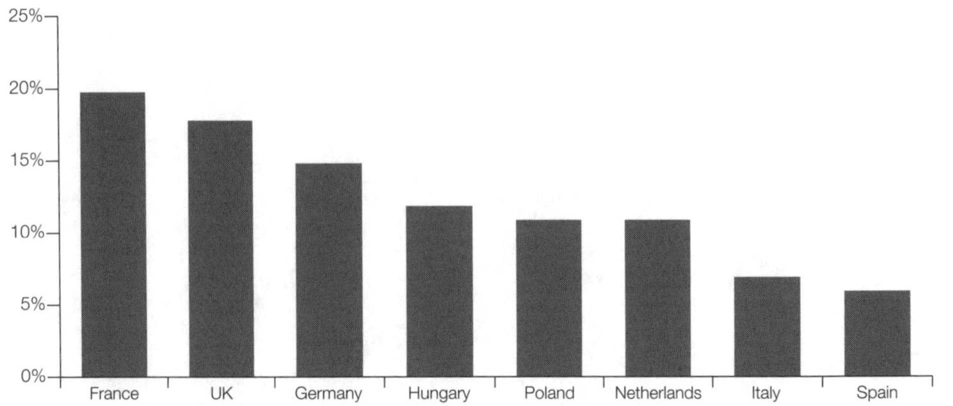

What does business think of EU law-making?

EU legislation a high priority and business is pro-EU goals

The business community is aware of the great importance that EU policies and regulation have and the profound impact they have on business. European businesses generally believe that the EU is better placed to tackle the questions that will improve their possibilities of doing business. They need Europe. EU legislation is a high priority and business broadly supports the EU's aims.

At a time when a number of EU Member States have been accused of protectionism and with Member States less enthusiastic about opening up their markets to their European neighbours, businesses today appear to see the European Commission and the EU as guarantors of efficient European governance, in contrast to the much despised Brussels bureaucracy of old.

It is true that the Commission is not standing idly by when Member States frustrate the EU's internal market rules and the beginning of 2006 has seen legal proceedings initiated against Member States in a large number of cases.

European businesses' views on whether EU legislation is high, medium, or low priority in comparison with national legislation

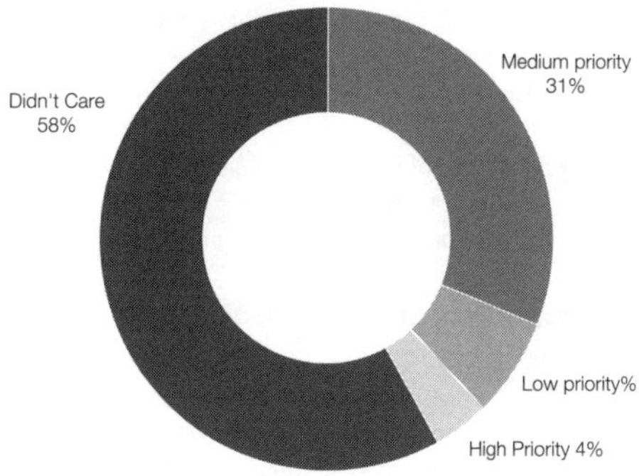

Where does business see problems?

Widespread dissatisfaction with practice

Identification and management of EU regulation is a key element of success for any company active in Europe. But businesses are frustrated that they cannot keep track of upcoming laws and this is something that particularly concerns SMEs that are not active in cross-border activities in the EU.

There are a number of improvements that can be made by businesses to connect better with EU law-making and thereby maximise business potential.

Dissatisfaction around process and implementation

The key concerns for any business is whether a legislator fully understands the commerical implications of an upcoming law and provides information on the impact that this law will have. Respondents believe that the EU is performing poorly in this respect.

European businesses believe that the EU's bureaucratic process is too complex and too long. This is their key concern. With the EU's constitutional treaty having failed to receive the backing of a majority of French and Dutch voters, its aim of boosting the effectiveness of the EU decision-making process has failed. While parliaments in a number of other Member States have ratified the treaty, its future appears bleak with EU leaders extending their "period of reflection" on how to proceed. With the addition of Bulgaria and Romania to the EU's ranks next year, decision-making in Brussels and Strasbourg will not be made any easier.

Businesses also indicate that they are unhappy with the way that EU legislation is implemented at Member State level. Companies regard a clear and and consistent legal framework as essential to enable them to run their operations smoothly. The use of directives (which means that the precise form of implementation is left up to Member States) in contrast to regulations (which are binding and directly applicable across the EU) allows Member States flexibility to find the best way of balancing existing national laws with new EU legislation. A failure to implement or inadequate implementation is, however, the rule rather than the exception and businesses will often encounter a patchwork of differing legal standards across the EU.

The Commission's Better Regulation strategy has acknowledged that this is a problem and the Commission has set out, as one of its action items, to replace directives with regulations to avoid Member States taking different approaches to implementation and, in particular, to eradicate so-called gold-plating.

Businesses lack specialist resources and appear to engage relatively late in the process

- **EU not exposed to market/commercial interests at drafting stage**
- **Resource question: only a quarter of European businesses employ EU specialists**
- **So, business tends to be reactive:**
  - **Fire-fighting with EU and National Governments when White/Green Papers issued**
  - **Difficulty in interpreting draft laws**

How effectively are EU specialist resources applied in the process?

- **EU laws perceived as high board priority**
  - **But companies not engaging early in the process when they could influence the overall direction**
- **Trade and professional bodies do not appear to engage early either**
  - **Trade press is main source of information on important upcoming laws, even for multinationals**

Bureaucratic process complex and too long

Key concerns with EU law-making	
Bureaucratic process/complex/too long	17%
Inconsistent national level implementation	14%
Poor communication/voice not heard	8%
Law impractical for business	6%
Law not clear/vague	5%
Clash/confusion with existing laws	5%
Too costly to impliment	3%

Do the Member States perform better than the EU?

Brussels – a handy scapegoat for poorly performing Member States?

The EU has failed to engage European citizens. After the failed referendums in France and the Netherlands on the EU constitutional treaty, a reflection period was announced in June last year. Commission Vice-President Margot Wallström has also launched a so-called "Plan D" to promote more public discussion about the EU between citizens and decision-makers.

But is it the EU European citizens have in mind when criticism is voiced against the EU's performance ?

Companies are dissatisfied with implementation. But national politicians throughout the EU still tend to use the EU as a scapegoat for unpopular decisions, and pretend that Brussels is an aggressive outside force that hinders national priority-setting.

If implementation is what respondents are unhappy with, it appears as though any criticism against Brussels should instead be directed against the Member States' capitals - after all it is the Member States who are in charge of implementation.

It is common to poke fun at the Lisbon agenda, the EU's strategy for making the EU the most dynamic and competitive economy in the world by 2010 (as adopted by the European Council in 2000). The EU can set the agenda, but radical reforms, ambition and commitments are required from the Member States to reach the goals encapsulated in the Lisbon agenda.

The chief responsibility for the success or failure of EU regulation also lies with the Member States. It is up to each and every national government to comply with the rules they have themselves adopted in Brussels and to take implementation seriously.

Q. Do you think that you have more of an opportunity to get your voice heard in national law-making compared to EU law-making?

	Yes	No	Don't know
UK	43%	27%	30%
France	60%	34%	6%
Germany	54%	38%	8%
Netherlands	56%	33%	11%
Italy	67%	25%	8%
Spain	60%	30%	10%
Hungary	47%	37%	16%
Poland	28%	33%	39%

The majority of businesses believe it is easier to make their voices heard at the Member State level

Q. Generally speaking, how do you think EU law-making compares with your national government's law-making in terms of effectiveness?

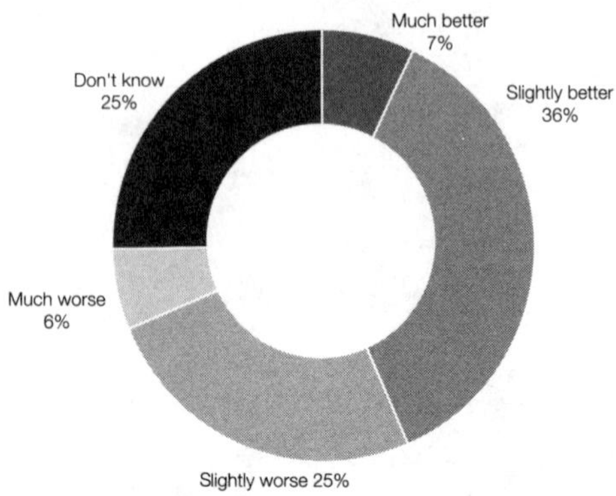

But 45% of businesses think EU law is "much" or "slightly better" than national laws

"40% of business are confident that the effect of EU law on their business will be generally positive in the future"

The Single Market benefits business

The EU's Single Market has been put in place to benefit the economies of each of the 25 Member States. The move towards a uniform set of rules and the ongoing removal of trade barriers has undoubtedly led to a reduction in business costs as well as increasing competition and stimulating efficiency, thereby benefiting consumers and encouraging the creation of jobs and growth. Business understands this and is keen to reap the benefits of the the Single Market.

Since the creation of the Single Market, work to improve its operation and effectiveness has been ongoing. The Commission has prioritised efforts to improve implementation and enforcement of Single Market rules; lightening the burden of regulation on businesses; and liberalisation in areas such as utilities, services and public procurement.

The survey also shows that businesses are more positive regarding EU law-making when linked to the Single Market.

Q. How well does EU law-making meet your commercial aspirations to make good use of the single market i.e. striking a practical balance between being well regulated while still allowing businesses to grow?

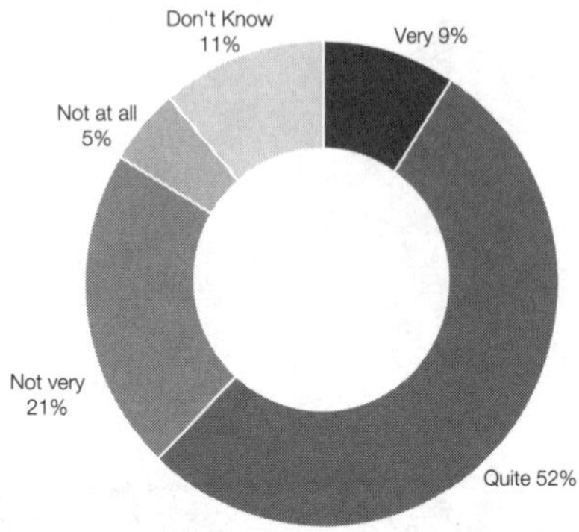

What about the future?

The Commission is committed to its better regulation agenda, realising its potential for generating more growth and employment in Europe.

In 2005, the Commission presented a three-year programme to simplify existing EU legislation to honour its commitment to cut unnecessary red tape and end-over-regulation. The Commission has proposed to repeal, codify, recast or modify more than 200 basic pieces of legislation and over 1,400 related legal instruments in the next three years.

Early in 2006, the Commission established a new group of national regulatory experts who will advise the Commission on its strategy to simplify and improve EU legislation and to facilitate the development of better regulation measures at both EU and national level.

From now on tougher impact assessment guidelines will mean that all important EU legislative proposals will be screened for potentially significant negative impacts on competitiveness.

European businesses have confidence in these developments and companies appear to believe that the effect on their operations will be generally positive, with only a few expressing reservations. Surveys in the past have shown that European companies estimate that if legislation were to be improved, they could cut down significantly on compliance, thereby saving billions of euros.

But the Commission has an uphill struggle in maintaining this process of simplification and steering it through the European Parliament and the Council. Again, the responsibility of implementation will lie with the Member States after adoption has taken place at EU level, and a good end result will only be achieved when Member States sign up to the better regulation agenda themselves.

Q. Thinking about the next two years, do you consider the overall effect of EU law-making on your business will be:

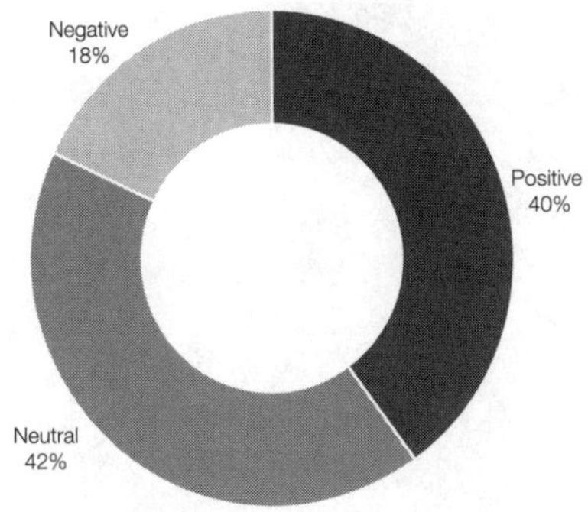

"More systematic consultation and proactive cooperation with all stakeholders to involve these in the policy-making process at an early stage is needed"

Imperatives for change

What EU policy-makers could do

1 European businesses retain confidence in the future of EU law-making, but they view the lack of access to information as a key concern. 40% of respondents consider the EU to be "worse" than national lawmakers in this regard and only a third of companies are satisfied that their voice is listened to by the EU. The Commission must therefore increase its efforts to shorten the distance between Brussels and stakeholders who wish to have a say when key laws are being adopted in the EU.

2 While businesses are unhappy with the consultation process, there is a difference between larger companies and SMEs. 53% of larger companies believe it is "not very easy/not at all easy" to give feedback on EU legislation. This rises to 67% in the case of SMEs, who may lack the resources to make their voice heard at EU level. More systematic consultation and co-operation with all stakeholders in the policy-making process at an early stage is needed. The Commission's new policy for SMEs, adopted in November 2005 is therefore a welcome development.

3 The Commission must make good its promise to reinforce a constructive dialogue not only with regulators at the EU and national levels but also with stakeholders. Poor implementation of EU law is still a key concern for businesses.

4 The Commission needs to do more to encourage businesses to engage better and earlier in the process so that their commercial interests are taken into account. The Commission should not expect stakeholders to come to them at all times - Brussels must be more proactive in seeking businesses' views. There is a window of opportunity for getting business more involved. Otherwise the risk is that business becomes disconnected and disillusioned.

Imperatives for change

What business could do

1 Businesses need actively to raise their awareness of EU policies. While company boards perceive EU laws as a key priority, companies also need to grasp what tools they can to engage early in the legislative process.

2 Utilising specialist resources has a positive impact. On average, around 20% of the time is spent dealing with EU laws. Three quarters of respondents said that EU law work is increasing. This underlines that there is a need for EU legal and policy expertise and that this need is growing. Moreover, only 25% of respondents indicated that they currently employ EU specialists. The majority of companies who do employ EU specialists currently say they are listened to (of those who do not, only a quarter believe that they have a say). This shows that the addition of specialist EU capabilities has a significant impact on knowledge and involvement in key EU regulatory developments.

3 To whom do businesses turn today to receive information about upcoming EU legislation? Respondents believe that the three top resources are the professional sector press, industry associations and law firms. Legal providers are therefore one of the key actors in helping businesses to identify legal issues at EU level.

4 Trade associations are currently the most popular route for businesses to give feedback to Brussels. Almost 40% of respondents use this as their main channel of feedback. However, only 13% of businesses believe that lobbying works well through trade associations.

An increasing role for law firms

The results of this survey show that, despite the significant efforts the Commission is devoting to better regulation, many companies do not feel their voice is listened to at EU level. This is particularly the case with SMEs. Businesses are keen to keep better track of developments in Brussels and to be consulted at an early stage.

Respondents believe that their legal advisers are well placed to advise on EU legal developments and assist them in reaching the proper people in Brussels when they have an important message to convey.

That should not come as a surprise. Increasingly lawyers are required not only to tell their commercial clients the shape of the law as it currently is but also the shape it may assume in future. That does not require lawyers to become lobbyists, but it does require attorneys proactively to engage with legislators and regulators on a proactive and dynamic basis. This is increasingly the job of the public policy specialists at Clifford Chance.

Michael Smyth
Head of Public Policy

About us

Clifford Chance is a truly integrated global law firm.

We advise governments, financial institutions, commercial enterprises, and regulatory bodies.

With 28 offices in 19 countries throughout the Americas, Asia, Europe and the Middle East, we offer in-depth local knowledge and a uniquely global perspective.

Clifford Chance lawyers advise internationally and domestically, under common law and civil law systems, in local and cross-border transactions; on day-to-day operations and the most challenging deals.

Need to contact us...

Brussels
Clifford Chance
Avenue Louise 65
Box 2
1050 Brussels
Belgium

Switchboard: +32 2 533 5911
Fax: +32 2 533 5959

London
Clifford Chance
10 Upper Bank Street
London
E14 5JJ
England

Switchboard: +44 20 7006 1000
Fax: +44 20 7006 5555

Index